W9-BSA-617

Encyclopedia of Marriage and the Family

Editorial Board

Encyclopedia of Marriage and the Family

VOLUME 2

DAVID LEVINSON
Editor in Chief

MACMILLAN LIBRARY REFERENCE USA
SIMON & SCHUSTER MACMILLAN
New York

SIMON & SCHUSTER AND PRENTICE HALL INTERNATIONAL
London Mexico City New Delhi Singapore Sydney Toronto

Simon & Schuster Macmillan
866 Third Avenue, New York, NY 10022

PRINTED IN THE UNITED STATES OF AMERICA

printing number
1 2 3 4 5 6 7 8 9 10

LIBRARY OF CONGRESS CATALOGING-IN-PUBLICATION DATA

Encyclopedia of marriage and the family / David Levinson, editor in chief.
p. cm.
Includes bibliographical references and index.
ISBN 0-02-897235-X (set)
1. Marriage—Encyclopedias. 2. Family—Encyclopedias.
I. Levinson, David, 1947–
HQ9.E52 1995
306.8′03—dc20 95-18682
CIP

The paper used in this publication meets the requirements of ANSI/NISO Z39.48-1992.

I

INCEST

Incest is defined as sexual exploitation of a person who is legally unable to give informed consent due to age or intellectual and/or physical impairment by an older person having a close family blood tie (e.g., parent, aunt, uncle, sibling) or a substitute for such a blood tie (e.g., stepparent, stepbrother, stepsister). In short, incest can be defined as the sexual exploitation of a child by a relative with more power.

Sexual exploitation includes sexual intercourse, but it also may include exhibitionism, masturbation, anal intercourse, exposure to sexually oriented media, or any acts that have a sexually stimulating component for either the victim or the perpetrator (Renvoize 1993).

The number of children who experience some form of sexual abuse is estimated to be one-third of all girls and one-fifth of all boys (Renvoize 1993). Estimates have risen steadily since the late 1960s as knowledge of child sexual abuse and incest has increased. The often painful and shameful aspects of sexual abuse within the family make the collection of data very difficult. The criminal nature of incestuous behavior and a tendency as a society to blame the victim help to keep families where incest occurs both isolated and secretive.

Based on adult reports of incest experiences as child victims, there is increasing evidence that child sexual abuse has been and continues to be a significant life event for many children. Incest is a chronic and painful childhood experience with long-term debilitating effects. As human services professionals and as society at large become more aware of the prevalence of incest, more skills are being developed in the art of healing this injury.

There is some controversy over the validity of the statistics that report the frequency of incest. It is generally thought by professionals that the underreporting of incest is prevalent due to the secrecy, shame, and criminal ramifications surrounding the event. However, two factors that may actually inflate the statistics on incest frequency should also be considered. False reports by children of non-offending parents, especially in divorce-custody situations, may account for an increase in reported incidents. Additionally, there has been criticism that therapists may "encourage" reports through a process of recovering memories "forgotten" by the patient. Patients often recall past forgotten events through the association of other memories, especially in treatment focusing on childhood experiences, but this therapeutic process can also lead to the patient unconsciously "inventing" events to accommodate the treatment. Even considering false reporting and misuse of recovering memories, it is still very likely that the number of incest cases is underreported.

Sibling incest is often thought to be the least harmful form. While one of the key aspects of incest is the difference in power between the perpetrator and the victim, sexual behavior between two siblings of equal power, where touching, looking, and exploring are mutual decisions, can still pose problems for the participants and/or parents. Clinical experience indicates that mutually agreed-upon sexual exploration by two siblings within a family does exist, but these instances are short-lived and isolated, with minimal physical contact. Most cases of sibling sexual behavior that continue for more than a few events seem to produce confusion and emotional distress for at least one of the participants. It appears that some form of coercion is needed very quickly to continue the sexual behavior.

What Diana Russell (1986) calls the "myth of mutuality" in relation to sibling incest may put the victim in a psychologically and physically vulnerable position. In her research with adult women, she found that 78 percent of her subjects who had had childhood sexual experiences reported that their sexual behavior with brothers was abusive. When the reported sexual behavior was with a sister, 50 percent of the subjects experienced the behavior as abusive. Approximately half reported sibling incest as extremely upsetting, and another quarter as somewhat upsetting. The degree of coercion and the emotional harm in sibling incest may be more underestimated than incest in general.

Forms of Coercion

Coercion can take a variety of forms. Physical force can be used to coerce desired behavior. Coercion can also take the form of threats of physical harm to the victim or threats to others that the victim cares about. Withdrawal of love and affection can be used to coerce a victim. Some victims are manipulated by rewards of money, objects, and/or time with the perpetrator. It is not uncommon for men to claim that they never "forced" a daughter to do anything she did not want to do. Incest perpetrators often use elaborate methods of persuasion to manipulate victims. The public stereotype of the incest perpetrator is often that of a father or father figure who uses force and physical power to gain compliance. While this certainly does occur, a more likely occurrence is that of a perpetrator who uses a variety of manipulative techniques.

Commonly, an incestuous parent will manipulate children by telling them that they are special and that their sexual activity is a form of special love and attention. Extra privileges and extra attention are often showered on the victim. The victim often has adult status over his or her siblings. The relationship between the perpetrator and the victim may gradually become more sexualized. The child is conditioned, often over years, to accept the sexual behavior desired by the perpetrator. Many incest offenders never have penetration with their victims and therefore rationalize their behaviors as nonsexual. It is important in the understanding of incest to be aware of how the victim is often slowly and methodically brought into the incestuous relationship as a willing and active partner. Most incest victims experience confusion about their own reactions to the incest experience. It is this betrayal of innocence and resultant confusion, along with the loss of control and power over one's own behavior, that lead to the emotional and psychological impact on the victim. Victims often experience, both at the time of the incestuous act and later as adults, a sense of shame, a feeling of powerlessness, and a loss of their childhood.

Effects on Victims

The effects of sexual abuse on children and their later development into adulthood depend on at least five important factors: the age of the child, the duration of the abuse, the type of the abuse, the manner in which the child frames the abuse, and the ability of the child to heal.

The age of the child when molestation occurs and its relationship to the degree of psychological injury is not clearly agreed upon by clinicians (Gomes-Schwartz, Horowitz, and Cardarelli 1990). Some believe that because children of a very young age are less able to comprehend the abusive relationship, they are less harmed by it. Others contend that the system may simply be less able to recognize and measure the effects on a very young child. The question of the age of the victim is probably most important in the choice of his or her treatment and the healing process. The younger the child, the more important becomes the reactions of those around the child. With all children and especially with younger children, there is a tendency for them to assume blame for any anger, fear, or disruption that occurs in their environment. Treatment often emphasizes adults assuring children that they are not responsible for family disruption. It is normal for an incestuous father to be removed from the home after incest is discovered. The victim normally assumes responsibility for the disruption and resultant emotional pain suffered by other family members, with fantasies of "If only I had been good" or "If I hadn't told anyone, then Mother would still be happy and Daddy would be home" and "It's my fault Daddy left." Especially young children are generally egocentric. Part of the normal development of a child is to change from a self-centered, poor observer of others' behavior to an individual capable of empathy and seeing his or her own behavior objectively. Molestation by a trusted parent can arrest this normal development.

The duration of abuse is also not clearly linked to the degree of injury. The assumption that "the longer the abuse goes on, the more severe the effect" is neither refuted nor strongly supported by research (Gomes-Schwartz, Horowitz, and Cardarelli 1990).

The data on the relationship between the type of sexual behavior and the impact on the child suggest two important considerations (Gomes-Schwartz, Horowitz, and Cardarelli 1990). First, the greater the degree of nonsexual violence, the greater the harm.

Second, genital contact of the victim by the perpetrator appears to have greater harm than nongenital sexual abuse. Both variables—nonsexual violence and direct genital manipulation—serve to increase the victim's general sense of helplessness and confusion.

How the victim frames the incest experience also makes a difference in the effect of the abuse. It is likely that there are important gender differences in how girls and boys make sense out of incest experiences. Girls tend to view the incest experience within the larger context of the child–adult relationship. A female child is likely to be more concerned with the perpetrator's feelings and with family stability. A boy may focus more on his own sexual experience. Adult women molested by a parent have indicated a genuine concern, even as very young girls, for the happiness and stability of the perpetrator and other family members. Adult males who have been molested by fathers appear to be concerned about issues related to homosexual feelings and control of their own impulses. All children, whether male or female, attempt to make sense of or to create an explanation for the incestuous relationship. This need to understand is part of the healing process.

The ability of people to heal from a damaging experience is related to their ability to confront their own feelings of fear, terror, anger, rage, confusion, helplessness, and vulnerability. Children, like adults, vary in their ability to acknowledge their feelings. When faced with strong feelings they will not or cannot deal with, people deny their existence. A child whose father repeatedly manipulates him or her to perform oral sex may rationalize it as "He's my father and would never hurt me"; "He's upset because he and Mom fight"; "I deserve this because I'm bad"; or "I deserve this because I'm special." Whatever the rationalization, this denial of the child's feelings of confusion and betrayal helps the child survive the incest. However, denial and rationalization have an emotional cost. A common report of adult victims of childhood incest is a clear sense of removing oneself from the event. A sense that it was being done to someone else and/or a sense of leaving the body during the sexual contact are common reports. Denial allows individuals to experience the event and continue to function when they have no alternatives. The danger is that denial becomes the "preferred" or most common behavior to deal with stress. Moving beyond denial to healing requires that the incest victims allow themselves to experience the feelings of confusion, rage, and helplessness.

To manipulate the victim, most incest perpetrators foster in the child a set of behaviors that help the child maintain the denial and self-deception needed to survive an ongoing incestuous relationship. The effects of this on the victim can be manifested in a number of ways, including fear of violence, sex, intimacy, and people of the same sex as the perpetrator. Confusion of gender identity, as well as uncontrolled sexual activity, may also result. There is often a need to care for and control others, at home, school, and work. Feelings of isolation, shame, and guilt, often not associated with any specific activity, help to foster a poor self-image, which may lead to suicidal behavior. There is also a tendency for victims of incest to suffer from other disorders, such as sleep disturbances, nightmares, depression, and eating disorders. Incestuous relationships are at a minimum a contributing factor to the above effects, and for countless victims, they are the primary contributor.

Victims also will often present the following questions. These usually occur in treatment as the victim begins the healing process:

- What if I enjoyed the abuse?
- Why didn't anybody stop it?
- Why did he (she) do it?
- Why me? What did I do to deserve this?
- Can I get better, heal, become a whole person?
- Why did I allow the abuse?

This last question often indicates that the victim is struggling with the concept of who is actually responsible for the molestation. The placing of blame on oneself helps the victim deny that at times he or she is helpless. Placing blame on the perpetrator may offer relief from responsibility, but it puts the victim in the position of being powerless. The victim needs to struggle with the concept of responsibility and the ability to respond. As a child, there are certainly times of complete helplessness, but also there are often options. Part of the process of healing is the victim's awareness of the context within which he or she made choices. Often, in treatment, victims gain a sense of empowerment when they can begin to trace the development of the incestuous relationship over time. Typically, victims can account for a gradual increase in their ability to make choices and implement them. Victims have often stated that at a certain time they were able to stop the incest perpetrator's manipulations with the threat of breaking secrecy. One victim reported a great sense of empowerment when she was able to acknowledge her behavior to her two younger sisters and to a therapist; she told of first using the threat of disclosure to stop her stepfather's assaults on her, and then she used the threat to protect her sisters. She reported that she was able to accomplish this at age twelve, after three years of incest, and without damaging the marital relationship. Both sisters report to her no history of incest. "Why did I allow the incest?" becomes more clear when the relationship is seen as a series of events where the victim as a child had limited options.

Profile of Offenders

Incest perpetrators are not a homogeneous group of men. Indeed, incest perpetrators are not limited only to fathers. Mothers are also capable of sexual assault against their children. Most of the research and clinical experience with incest perpetrators has been with male perpetrators. Knowledge of female incest offenders is limited by lack of experience with this population. In addition, fewer female offenders are willing to admit to committing acts of sexual abuse against children (Allen 1991).

It is often assumed that women are less motivated by sexual behavior and more likely to empathize with the victim's experience. Additionally, society may consider women to be sexually harmless: "What damage can be done without a penis and without penetration?" These assumptions illustrate a conception of incest and sexual abuse that focuses on the act of intercourse only. Victims, students, the general public, and professionals all share the assumption that if penetration has not occurred, then there has not been an assault. However, people are beginning to appreciate and understand that incest is a sexual assault that takes place in the context of a relationship. The child is often "groomed" and "sexually trained" to become an active participant in the abuse. The child's trust is violated by the parent because the child is sexualized and manipulated to participate. This betrayal by a parent need not and often does not include penetration. However, there continues to be a greater reluctance to admit that mothers or other females commit incest than to admit that fathers or other males commit incest.

Much incest treatment is based on an understanding of male and female gender roles. This theoretical bias toward men posing a greater threat may also interfere with the ability to acknowledge the existence of female perpetrators. Male gender role theory through male dominance and socialization emphasizing sexual exploitation may help to explain the higher rate of father incest. However, incestuous behavior cannot be explained *only* through male sexual aggression. The reasons why women commit incest may be different. Gender expectations and socializations may be different for males and for female perpetrators, but this does not mean that one form of incest is less harmful to the victim than the other.

In a cooperative study of seventy-five male sexual abusers and sixty-five female perpetrators (Allen 1991), the following similarities were found for male and female abusers. Both offenders have no difference in educational levels. Both offenders are more likely to report their marriages as less stable than those of their parents. Both offenders report that their need for emotional fulfillment is greater than their need for sexual fulfillment. Both offenders are most likely to commit offenses within the immediate and extended family. Both offenders are more likely to assault a member of the other gender. Both offenders report the least intrusive form of offending (exhibitionism, voyeurism, touching) to be more frequent than oral, vaginal, or anal intercourse. Both offenders are optimistic that child sexual abusers can change their behaviors.

The following differences were found when female offenders were compared to male offenders (Allen 1991). Women offenders are less likely to report committing sexual activities with children. Women offenders are more likely to report their own experience as victims of sexual abuse. Women offenders report lower marital satisfaction. Women offenders report greater satisfaction with the relationship with their children. Women offenders report more sexual satisfaction with their spouses/partners. Women offenders report having more sexual partners. Women offenders report significantly higher *need* for both emotional and sexual fulfillment. Women offenders report more physical abuse, as victims, by their spouses/partners. Women offenders are more likely to report their own acts of physical abuse. Women offenders are much less likely to acknowledge guilt. Women offenders are more likely to report physical abuse in their family of origin.

What may be most important in understanding female incest offenders may be that like male offenders, they are not necessarily mentally ill, retarded, or obviously different in a clearly discernible way. Incest, whether perpetrated by a male or a female, needs secrecy to maintain the betrayal. The harm that incest does to the victim is magnified by the secrecy and by the shame associated with incest. Incest committed by women needs to be acknowledged and examined, as has been done and continues to be done with men.

Men as incest perpetrators are not a homogeneous group. As part of a grant from the National Center on Child Abuse and Neglect, L. J. Williams and David Finkelhor (1992) identified five distinct types of incestuous fathers: sexually preoccupied, adolescent regressive, instrumental sexual gratifiers, emotionally dependent offenders, and angry retaliators. This typology helps to foster better understanding of the motivations for abuse and may enable better treatment for incest perpetrators. It should be kept in mind that an offender may not "fit" perfectly into one type; most offenders are a combination of one or more types.

Sexually preoccupied offenders are characterized by a sexual interest in their victim, usually from an early age. This offender usually begins molesting the child before age six and continues the molestation past puberty. Penetration of the victim is common, with many molestations occurring. The offender is highly sexualized and may have an extensive history of abuse in childhood.

Adolescent regressive offenders have a conscious sexual interest in their victims but usually do not begin molesting until the victims approach or reach puberty. These offenders generally report their molestations in a manner in which they sound like adolescents themselves.

Instrumental sexual gratifiers use the victim as a vehicle for sexual fantasy. These offenders are more sporadic in their offending, and they often associate the action with remorse.

Emotionally dependent offenders are often lonely and depressed. Sex is not a primary motivator; rather, these offenders often romanticize their need for closeness and intimacy.

Angry retaliators demonstrate low sexual arousal toward their victims but instead use the sexual assault to focus their anger. Often, the assault on the victim is in retaliation for a real or imagined infidelity or abandonment by a spouse.

Incest perpetrators commit incest for a variety of reasons. A useful distinction for treatment of male incest offenders is to conceptualize them as having poor skills in dealing with their emotions. Many offenders demonstrate poor empathy skills and a marked inability to observe the behavior of others effectively. These men are often emotionally in a developmental stage equivalent to that of the child they are assaulting. This lack of emotional development provides a clue to use in treatment.

Treatment of Offenders

The characteristics of a healing environment are openness, honesty, support, and worthiness. Incest families are characterized by secrecy, deception, isolation, and worthlessness. Early in treatment, offenders will commonly protest society's and the criminal justice system's "overreaction" to their behavior.

Offenders will often protest that the child liked the behavior, never objected, and was already sexually active and therefore not harmed by it. As the perpetrator begins to understand the effects on the victim of the secrecy and deception the incestuous relationship requires, he or she begins to break through the denial and rationalizations.

The first treatment goal for offenders is the complete admission of their crime, the total acceptance of their responsibility, and appropriate remorse for their actions. This requires the offender to abandon the need for secrets and deception and to begin the process of healing. Most treatment of offenders also includes an attempt to increase the offender's empathy for the victim. The hope is that by increasing the perpetrator's understanding of the pain and harm victims experience, the offender will be more motivated to control personal behavior.

Conclusion

Incest is becoming better understood, and society's ability to treat this form of sexual assault is improving. The need to reduce the harm done by incest can best be served by the reduction in secrecy in incest families. This can be accomplished by victims, perpetrators, and other family members not permitting the secrets to exist from generation to generation.

(*See also:* Child Abuse and Neglect: Sociological Aspects; Child Abuse and Neglect: Emotional and Psychological Aspects; Incest Taboo; Personality Development; Sexuality in the Life Cycle)

BIBLIOGRAPHY

Allen, C. M. (1991). *Women and Men Who Sexually Abuse Children.* Orwell, VT: Safer Society Press.

Bass, E., and Davis, L. (1988). *The Courage to Heal.* New York: Harper & Row.

Beitchman, J. H.; Zucker, K. J.; Hood, J. E.; DaCosta, G. A.; Akman, D.; and Cassavia, E. (1992). "A Review of the Long-Term Effects of Child Sexual Abuse." *Child Abuse and Neglect: The International Journal* 16:101–118.

Gil, E., and Johnson, T. C. (1993). *Sexualized Children.* Rockville, MD: Launch Press.

Gomes-Schwartz, B.; Horowitz, J.; and Cardarelli, A. (1990). *Child Sexual Abuse.* Newbury Park, CA: Sage Publications.

Lew, M. (1988). *Victims No Longer.* New York: Nevraumont.

Madanes, C. (1990). *Sex, Love, and Violence.* New York: W. W. Norton.

National Center on Child Abuse and Neglect (NCCAN). (1981). *Study Findings: National Study of Incidence and Severity of Child Abuse and Neglect.* Washington, DC: U.S. Department of Health, Education, and Welfare.

Parker, H., and Parker, S. (1986). "Father–Daughter Sexual Abuse: An Emerging Perspective." *American Journal of Orthopsychiatry* 56:531–549.

Renvoize, J. (1993). *Innocents Betrayed.* London: Routledge.

Russell, D. E. H. (1986). *The Secret Trauma: Incest in the Lives of Girls and Women.* New York: Basic Books.

Straus, M. A. (1990). "Measuring Intrafamily Conflict and Violence: The Conflict Tactics (CT) Scale." In *Physical Violence in American Families: Risk Factors and Adaptations to Violence in 8,145 Families*, ed. M. A. Straus and R. J. Gelles. New Brunswick, NJ: Transaction.

Williams, L. J., and Finkelhor, D. (1990). "The Characteristics of Incestuous Fathers: A Review of Recent Studies." In *The Handbook of Sexual Assault: Issues, Theories, and Treatment of the Offender*, ed. W. Marshall, D. Laws, and H. Barbaree. New York: Plenum.

Williams, L. J., and Finkelhor, D. (1992). *The Characteristics of Incestuous Fathers.* Report in partial fulfillment of a grant from the National Center on Child Abuse and Neglect, Washington, DC.

Stanley Parker

INCEST TABOO

The incest taboo is one of the oldest and most perplexing enigmas encountered by students of society and culture. Long proposed as a "cultural universal," Western scholars have historically believed that the taboo was a key to important insights into the human condition. For these reasons, research and theorizing on the incest taboo have a long and replete history.

Although the incest taboo varies in meaning across societies, it is generally presented as a consequential rule of prohibition, frequently encompassing religious sanctions and forbidding sexual contact (and, by extension, marriage) between certain categories of relatives and family members. Recurrently incorporated in this taboo are the nuclear (parents and children) and immediate (e.g., grandparents, aunts and uncles, nieces and nephews, first cousins) families. In societies with descent group structures (e.g., lineages, clans), the incest rule often extends to include all or most of one's kinship group, reaching to very distantly related kin (Murdock 1949).

A thorough understanding of the incest taboo necessarily recognizes this rule as a significant part of a larger system of sexual regulations. In turn, these sexual regulations are an important component of the extensive normative structure regulating family, marriage, and kinship systems. In many instances, scholars have focused on the incest taboo as if it were independent of the more enveloping social structure and culture. Knowing how this prohibition relates to other aspects and changes in the society is fundamental for a thorough comprehension of the taboo's existence and operation.

Cross-cultural variations in the incest taboo embody numerous facets. While it appears that most societies have some sort of incest rule, the rule is not universal. Whereas many societies deem the incest taboo to be extremely serious, there are others who view the taboo more casually. Sanctions for violating the taboo reflect a similar continuum. Individuals in some societies simply express disapproval or distaste when incest occurs, as one might in the presence of very bad manners. In other communities, the act of incest is portrayed as "horrifying" or "unthinkable" and transgressors may be put to death or cast out of the society.

In many instances, the incest taboo is intricately entwined with religious canon and, thus, proscribes supernatural sanctions against violators, or even against the society as a whole (Leavitt 1989). In modern societies, scientific justifications have replaced religious ones and religious sanctions have been replaced with notions of biological harm.

Historical Sketch

One of the earliest recorded Western scholars concerned with the incest taboo was Plutarch (A.D. 46–120?), a Greek philosopher and priest. His writings anticipated two modern theories; the first is referred to as "alliance theory," and the second focuses on familial conflict avoidance. Alliance theory concludes that the incest taboo exists to create an outward reaching network of cooperative kin, a primary social structure essential for human survival. In the second instance, it has been argued that the incest restriction exists to prevent fatally destructive conflicts within the family. Similar to Plutarch, the Roman historian Tacitus (A.D. 56–120) also offered a theoretical framework suggesting alliance networks as the reason for the incest prohibition in Roman society (Honigmann 1976).

In addition to alliances, Augustine (A.D. 354–430) proposed a natural aversion to incest and an "inherent sense of decency" preventing incestuous relationships. Thomas Aquinas (A.D. 1225–1274) also subscribed to alliance theory and added the assertion that incest hindered child development. Aquinas believed that close kin marriages encouraged lust and ended in disruptive role conflicts that could destroy the family (Honigmann 1976).

With the formal development of the social sciences in the nineteenth and twentieth centuries, there was a continuation of these same historical themes. For instance, George Murdock (1949) and Yehudi Cohen (1978) carried on the alliance theory hypotheses, while Sigmund Freud (1950) and Talcott Parsons (1954) continued the argument that incestuous relations are destructive to the family.

Charles Darwin, in *The Descent of Man* (1871), accepted the family conflict model but gave it an evolutionary foundation by speculating that those families allowing incest would be destroyed by sexual jealousy. As a consequence, Darwin proposed that inherited traits allowing incest would be selected against in the evolutionary process. Darwin's proposal that certain behaviors are genetically based and inheritable was not new. It was Darwin's mechanism of change (natural selection) that was innovative.

Edward Westermarck, in *The History of Human Marriage* (1891), employed Darwin's evolutionary mechanism but speculated that incest avoidance emerged as an instinct to prevent the harm produced by inbreeding. Westermarck hypothesized that this instinct was activated when people were raised in close proximity, as in families. While he believed that this aversion would be manifested most commonly between siblings, he also hypothesized that repugnance would develop when unrelated children were reared together. This same thesis is currently argued by sociobiologists whose ideas originated on the supposition that the social behavior in all animal species is grounded in a genetic inheritance shaped by natural selection.

Explanations outside of the historical stream have also occurred. One of the most notable, "demographic theory," was first offered by Mariam Slater (1959) and expounded further by Charles Case (1969). It was their contention that demographic characteristics of breeding populations (e.g., life expectancy, birth order, and the distribution of sex among siblings) would make incestuous activity in the immediate family unlikely and short-lived.

Parsons (1954) offered a "socialization theory" asserting that the incest taboo is part of a normative structure employing eroticism (in the broadest sense) and its withdrawal as a system of positive and negative sanctions in the socialization of children. The physical affection offered by parents and other adults (often relatives) acts as a powerful reward for "proper" behavior in children just as its withdrawal acts as a forceful punishment.

Parsons claimed that this is an affective process because of the deeply social nature of the human species. For Parsons, the incest taboo is part of the system of sexual regulations. Drawing a boundary beyond which the family may not wander in imparting erotic rewards forces the adolescent child to participate in the larger society in order to find greater sexual fulfillment. In doing so, the child ties the society together with marriage and kin relationships—affiliations that carry the strongest socioeconomic obligations.

Nature Versus Nurture

This historical sketch discloses explanations of the incest taboo that are quite diverse. In the incest taboo polemic, the most pronounced historical contention reproduces the age-old "mind/body" split deeply engraved in Western thought. Those prescribing biologically inherited traits and those postulating that behavior is acquired through experience and learning continue to dominate the discussion of this subject.

With Edward O. Wilson's *Sociobiology* (1975), the extension of Darwin's natural selection theory to social behavior experienced a zealous revival. Although sociobiology has been represented as a "new science" (Radner and Radner 1982, p. 92), the notion that social behavior evolves, even in humans, is at least as old as Darwin's theory.

Sociobiologists who study human behavior (human sociobiologists) have supported their theory of incest/inbreeding avoidance by employing four expansive empirical areas (the universal nature of and compliance with incest rules, the evidence of inbreeding harm, ethnological and animal research on inbreeding avoidance, and the kibbutzim), along with Arthur Wolf's studies of marriage practices between children raised together (Leavitt 1990; Ruse 1981–1982; Wolf 1966, 1968, 1970; Wolf and Huang 1980). A critical look at this data has raised significant questions regarding their support for human sociobiological hypotheses. Specifically, the deleterious hypothesis associated with inbreeding that underlies this evolutionary thesis has been called into serious question (Livingstone 1969; Shields 1982).

Sociobiologists have challenged environmental learning theories by arguing that the incest taboo, especially as it applies to the nuclear family, is too uniform to be accounted for by cultural phenomenon. As Joseph Shepher (1983, p. 9) argues, "If we find uniformity of behavior throughout an entire species, we can hardly ascribe this uniformity to culture, for *culture is variability par excellence; it cannot cause universals*. Universals exist *in spite of culture* [emphasis in original]."

This view oversimplifies the issue by omitting the fact that human behavior is molded by a general environmental circumstance, not by culture per se. Moreover, the term "universal" has a different meaning in biology than in social science. In social science, this concept is a matter of the degree of generalization and social creation, that is, whether one wants to look for particulars and uniqueness or for generalities and uniformity.

Scientific method (Occam's razor) indicates that an environment/learning explanation is superior to a biogenetic explanation because the former is less complex and requires fewer ontological assumptions. Learning/environment theory simply assumes that human beings are able to modify their behavior as a result of their environmental experience, an assumption human sociobiologists do not deny. It is not difficult to imagine that all human groups, as part of the same species, must deal with similar problems and situations that might well produce analogous responses like incest rules. The fact that sociobiologists find learning theory inadequate to explain complex human behavior likely stems from an incomplete comprehension of the potency of the learning process in environments.

Sibling Marriage and Human Isolates

There are several instances of sociocultural communities where incest and/or close inbreeding have occurred on a regular and even systematic basis. One of the more conspicuous examples is the Roman Egyptians of the first three centuries A.D. A plethora of documentary evidence has been unearthed concerning Egyptian commoners who practiced brother–sister marriage (Hopkins 1980). Russell Middleton (1962) argues that there is little ambiguity in these documents; it is clear from recovered Egyptian census records that sibling marriages accounted for 15 to 21 percent of all unions.

Even more abundant is the evidence provided by human isolates; small isolated communities where the degree of inbreeding is determined by the size, extent, and length of isolation (Leavitt 1990). These communities have been common and represent the rule for preagricultural paleolithic societies.

A well-documented example of a human isolate is the Samaritan community of the Middle East. From about 200 B.C., when the Samaritans broke completely from Jewish society, until the twentieth century, the Samaritan population declined dramatically due largely to persecution by more powerful neighbors. At the end of World War II, the Samaritan population numbered 146 individuals, a population that had remained relatively stable for 100 years. By the 1980s, however, the population had increased and the Samaritans consisted of two communities, each of about 250 individuals (Bonne-Tamir 1980; Jamieson 1982; Talmon 1977).

Inbreeding in the Samaritan communities has been intensified by three established customs. First, Samaritan religion prohibits marriage with individuals outside of their faith. Second, the Samaritans limit their marriages to extended family lineages. Third, they prefer cousin marriage. Batsheva Bonne-Tamir (1980) has observed that nearly 85 percent of all Samaritan marriages are between first or second cousins. However, over a long period of time, the Samaritans have revealed no higher rate of genetic disease than other populations.

This data strongly suggest that the incest taboo exists for reasons other than the prevention of close inbreeding. Moreover, such examples convincingly demonstrate that the incest prohibition is not a product of natural selection.

Sociocultural Evolutionary History

An understanding of the incest taboo is enhanced when examined in the context of a sociocultural evolutionary history (Leavitt 1989). To give clarity to this history, it is important to first understand the general organizational framework of human kinship groups (or descent systems) that comprise a fundamental component of human communities.

In the broadest outline, descent systems are either bilateral or unilineal. Bilateral systems, like the one found in American society, are rather diffuse and equally include the relatives of both an individual's parents. In this system, a person is not usually acquainted with relatives beyond first or second cousins, and ritual or formal activities beyond the most immediate family are typically absent.

In a unilineal kinship system, all members of the kinship group trace their ancestry to a common progenitor (either mythical or actual). If this founder was male, descent is traced through the male line (patrilineal); if the founder was female, ancestry is traced through the female line (matrilineal). In a few rare instances, there are societies of double or dual descent in which each individual inherits two descent group memberships. Because membership in unilineal descent groups is determined by an individual's descendancy from a single ancestor, only some of a person's relatives will belong to their kinship group.

Societies with unilineal descent systems are commonly organized around lineages or clans, kinship organizations including hundreds of people recognized as blood relatives. These groups are the organizational backbone of the society and orchestrate most societal activities, including political, economic, military, religious, and educational functions.

The earliest and technostructurally simplest societies (hunting and gathering or foraging societies) typically consisted of a tribe incorporating a number of small nomadic bands organized through bilateral descent. To ensure that the bands remained unified, even though they ranged far apart and saw each other occasionally, band exogamy was practiced. This simply meant that a person had to marry and have sex with a partner outside of the immediate family and group. In this way, the bands were tied together by blood and marriage, ensuring the survival of the tribe (Johnson and Earle 1987).

At the end of the last Ice Age (10,000 B.C.), the earth's climate and megafauna changed sufficiently to begin moving human communities toward agriculture (Harris 1977). With this change came a need for more sophisticated social structures, especially for politico-military and economic activities. These structural and institutional changes encouraged the appearance of unilineal descent groups. As life became increasingly sedentary and communities grew in size, access to resources became increasingly crucial as did the need to defend fertile farmland.

By extending the incest taboo to encompass lineage or clan members, the kinship group forced its children into marriages of alliance with other descent groups. Such marriages carried reciprocal obligations for economic and military assistance essential for survival. So important were these marriage bonds that parents and other kin commonly determined who their young would marry (arranged marriage). Frequently, an exchange of gifts between family groups (bride price, dowry, groom wealth) and encouragement of the couple to have many children made the kin group association strong and stable (Johnson and Earle 1987).

As human societies continued to grow and evolve technologically and structurally (including larger settlements), the incest taboo began to contract, encompassing fewer and fewer relatives. New organizational structures not based on kinship ties or descent became increasingly common and were more efficient for operating larger, more complex societies. These new institutions were part of the development of the state, which through its own bureaucratic agencies ensured political and economic alliances.

With the appearance of modern industrial societies, the incest taboo was reduced to the nuclear family and a few other immediate relatives (Cohen 1978). Punishments for the violation of the incest taboo have followed a similar evolutionary pathway. Where the incest taboo was extended, its violation has generally been punished more severely. As this prohibition contracted to include fewer categories of relatives, sanctions for violations of the incest proscription have tended to become less severe (Leavitt 1989).

(*See also:* Extended Family; Fictive Kinship; Incest; Kinship; Nuclear Family)

BIBLIOGRAPHY

Bonne-Tamir, B. (1980). "The Samaritans: A Living Ancient Isolate." In *Population Structure and Genetic Disorders*, ed. A. W. Eriksson, H. R. Forsius, H. R. Nevanlinna, P. L. Workman, and R. K. Norio. London: Academic Press.

Case, C. C. (1969). "Comments." *Current Anthropology* 10:50–51.

Cohen, Y. (1978). "Disappearance of the Incest Taboo." *Human Nature* 1:72–78.

Darwin, C. (1871). *The Descent of Man.* London: John Murray.

Freud, S. (1950). *Totem and Taboo.* London: Routledge & Kegan Paul.

Harris, M. (1977). *Cannibals and Kings. The Origins of Cultures.* New York: Random House.

Honigmann, J. J. (1976). *The Development of Anthropological Ideas.* Homewood, IL: Dorsey Press.

Hopkins, K. (1980). "Brother–Sister Marriage in Roman Egypt." *Comparative Studies in Society and History* 22:303–354.

Jamieson, J. W. (1982). "The Samaritans." *Mankind Quarterly* 23:141–148.

Johnson, A. W., and Earle, T. (1987). *The Evolution of Human Societies: From Foraging Group to Agrarian State.* Stanford, CA: Stanford University Press.

Leavitt, G. C. (1989). "Disappearance of the Incest Taboo: A Cross-Cultural Test of General Evolutionary Hypotheses." *American Anthropologist* 91:116–131.

Leavitt, G. C. (1990). "Sociobiological Explanations of Incest Avoidance: A Critical Review of Evidential Claims." *American Anthropologist* 92:971–993.

Livingstone, F. B. (1969). "Genetics, Ecology, and the Origins of Incest and Exogamy." *Current Anthropology* 10:45–61.

Middleton, R. (1962). "Brother–Sister and Father–Daughter Marriage in Ancient Egypt." *American Sociological Review* 27:603–611.

Murdock, G. P. (1949). *Social Structure.* New York: Free Press.

Parsons, T. (1954). "The Incest Taboo in Relation to Social Structure and the Socialization of the Child." *British Journal of Sociology* 5:101–117.

Radner, D., and Radner, M. (1982). *Science and Unreason.* Belmont, CA: Wadsworth.

Ruse, M. (1981–1982). "Is Human Sociobiology a New Paradigm?" *Philosophical Forum* 13:119–143.

Shepher, J. (1983). *Incest: A Biosocial View.* New York: Academic Press.

Shields, W. M. (1982). *Philosophy, Inbreeding, and the Evolution of Sex.* Albany: State University of New York Press.

Slater, M. K. (1959). "Ecological Factors in the Origin of Incest." *American Anthropologist* 61:1042–1059.

Talmon, S. (1977). "The Samaritans." *Scientific American* 236:100–108.

Westermarck, E. A. (1891). *The History of Human Marriage.* London: Macmillan.

Wilson, E. O. (1975). *Sociobiology: The New Synthesis.* Cambridge, MA: Belknap Press.

Wolf, A. P. (1966). "Childhood Association, Sexual Attraction, and the Incest Taboo: A Chinese Case." *American Anthropologist* 68:883–898.

Wolf, A. P. (1968). "Adopt a Daughter-in-Law, Marry a Sister: A Chinese Solution to the Problem of the Incest Taboo." *American Anthropologist* 70:864–874.

Wolf, A. P. (1970). "Childhood Association and Sexual Attraction: A Further Test of the Westermarck Hypothesis." *American Anthropologist* 72:503–515.

Wolf, A. P., and Huang, C. (1980). *Marriage and Adoption in China, 1845–1945.* Stanford, CA: Stanford University Press.

Gregory C. Leavitt

INFANTICIDE

Infanticide is the deliberate killing of infants under the age of one year. This restricted definition conceptualizes infanticide as a postnatal abortion procedure rather than as a type of child abuse. Infanticide and abortion are often used as family planning mechanisms, carried out to protect the health of unweaned children, the family economy, or the mother's social standing. Information on the killing of children older than one year is given in this entry only when it pertains to other issues being discussed or when the ages of the victims seem to include infants less than a year old.

In modern societies, where infants are born in hospitals, their birth certificates confer citizenship. However, throughout most of human history, babies were born at home and infanticide was a private action done by family members. For this reason, reports about infanticide are often absent or inaccurate, particularly in places having laws against the act.

A number of authors infer infanticide from family size and female infanticide from sex ratios. These indirect measures have been criticized because small family size may result from long postpartum sex taboos, high child mortality, selling unwanted children, or giving them up for adoption. Skewed sex ratios may result from neglect of daughters or underreporting females to census takers.

Prevalence

Marvin Harris (1977) calls infanticide the most widely used method of population control during much of human history. Infanticide, like abortion, seems to occur in virtually all contemporary tribal societies, although the frequency of infanticide varies considerably. The practice has been described in hunter-gatherer, horticulturist, and agrarian societies (Dickemann 1975), as well as among Australian Aborigines (Cowlishaw 1978) and Eskimos (Chapman 1980). It is relatively infrequent in Africa, probably because of the value of large families to agricultural and pastoral people and the high infant mortality rates (Williamson 1978).

Infanticide has been documented in the ancient civilizations of Greece, Rome, Egypt, Israel, China, and Western Europe. Infanticide, particularly female infanticide, was common among the classical Greeks and Romans. Spartans exposed unfit infants of both sexes. Infanticide was so common in Greece and Rome that the average family was small and seldom had more than one daughter (Boswell 1988).

Infanticide and infant abandonment occurred throughout Europe, despite Christian prohibitions against it. Its frequency increased during the Black Death plague in the fourteenth century and became a widespread problem in the eighteenth century, an age of rapid population growth. In the eighteenth and nineteenth centuries, servants were not permitted to marry or have children, forcing many servant girls to kill or abandon their infants, who were often fathered by their masters. In nineteenth-century Europe and in other technologically advanced nations, the introduction of the condom and increased public concern for children began to decrease infanticide rates (Boswell 1988; Langer 1974).

In most twentieth-century nations, the increase of adoption; the spread of contraception; and the legalization of abortion, allowing for safe abortions under medical supervision, increasingly have made infanticide an unnecessary and outdated method of birth control.

Time of Occurrence

Infanticide is usually carried out at birth or in the first month, before the performance of the infant's birth ceremony. These ceremonies, which incorporate the infants into their kin groups and give them identity and legal status, often take place between the second and fourth weeks and may be delayed if the infant is sickly. In some societies, infants are not considered human or members of the family and community until after their birth ceremonies. The performance of infanticide *before* the birth ceremony indicates that it is conceptualized as a postnatal abortion (Daly and Wilson 1984; Minturn 1989a, 1989b).

In the sample studied by Leigh Minturn and Jerry Stashak (1982), infanticide was performed by mothers or midwives in 79 percent of societies and by fathers or other men in only 15 percent. Birth ceremonies, on the other hand, were performed by fathers and other men in 69 percent and by women only in 22 percent of the societies, with adults of both sexes participating in the ceremony for the remaining societies. These results suggest that unwanted newborns are killed by women before they are presented to the lawgiving men for the birth ceremonies.

Methods

Infanticide is sometimes done quickly by strangling, crushing the skull, smothering, or poisoning. Other common methods of infanticide include exposure, abandonment, and overlaying.

Exposure. Exposure relieves parents and midwives of the responsibility of actually killing infants. The exposed infant is placed somewhere away from the community where the elements or animals will kill it. The prevalence of legends about the survival and subsequent good fortune of exposed infants (Moses, Oedipus, Romulus and Remus, Tom Jones) suggests that this method reduced the guilt of child killing. A singular modern exception to distant exposure occurs in modern hospitals, where legal constraints prohibit any method of killing a seriously handicapped infant except via the withholding of food and water, which amounts to exposing the infant in the presence of his or her caregivers (Lund 1985).

Urban exposure. Urban exposure of infants was common throughout Europe until the nineteenth century. In medieval Europe, infants were left in the streets, on trash heaps, and at church steps. European urban exposure became most frequent during the eighteenth century, when numerous poor women abandoned infants in streets or foundling homes and Parisian garbage collectors picked up abandoned infants on their rounds. However, urban exposure was not confined to Europe. During the seventeenth century, Jesuit missionaries to China found that several thousand babies were thrown into the streets and collected with the trash (Boswell 1988; Langer 1974).

Foundling homes. Public outrage over urban exposure of infants led to the establishment of foundling homes in Europe. The mortality rates of infants in these homes was as high as 90 percent. Wet nurses employed in foundling homes neglected infants and sometimes killed them so frequently that they were called "killer nurses" or "angel makers." In effect, consigning infants to these homes amounted to institutionalized urban exposure. Foundling homes allowed parents to abandon unwanted infants without fear of prosecution. As this practice became openly acceptable in the eighteenth century, attitudes toward outright infanticide became more lenient (Boswell 1988; Breiner 1990; Langer 1974). Foundling homes proved to be so ineffectual that, in the late nineteenth century, France and Britain passed laws requiring them to be licensed. Government support for unwed mothers began to replace foundling homes and orphanages in a number of countries (Langer 1974).

Overlaying. Infant death by overlaying—the accidental smothering of a baby by rolling over on it in bed—was common in Europe from the early Middle Ages through the nineteenth century. It is not always clear from the records whether overlaying occurred before or after birth ceremonies, but most overlay victims seem to have been less than one year old. Overlaying was recognized in law and religion. Sleeping with infants was discouraged and sometimes illegal (Kellum 1974). It has been suggested that some overlaying deaths in nineteenth-century England were due to Sudden Infant Death Syndrome (SIDS), which is related to nutritional tetany, and that the upper classes blamed such deaths on overlaying to disassociate themselves from the poor (Hansen 1979). Ethnographies report numerous societies where mothers or both parents routinely sleep with infants, often with older children in the bed, but do not report overlaying. It seems that this belief was, in large part, a legal fiction that allowed infanticide deaths to be declared accidental.

Victims of Infanticide

Two studies of folk and tribal societies drawn from the Human Relations Area Files (HRAF) at Yale University report similar results to each other (Daly and Wilson 1984; Minturn and Stashak 1982). The most frequently killed infants are illegitimate (57%, 53%); weak or deformed (60%, 53%); twins and triplets (40%,

40%); or excess because of family size or circumstances of birth spacing (31%, 23%). Minturn and Stashak (1982) also found infants are killed because they are the results of abnormal births (20%); unwanted, usually because the mothers are too old or too young to raise children (27%); or females (17%).

Comparison of these results with those of a study done by George Devereux (1976) of abortion in tribal societies indicates that the victims of abortion and infanticide are the same types of infants, not surprising since the motive in both is the elimination of unwanted infants.

Infrequently, ethnographers report infanticide because of incest, kinship considerations, quarrels between parents, sacrifice, or war (Daly and Wilson 1984; Williamson 1978).

Female Infanticide

Female infanticide is the only type of infanticide still widely practiced. Female infanticide at birth and indirect female infanticide through neglect are still widespread in Third World countries.

Ethnographic reports of female infanticide, however, are relatively rare. Minturn and Stashak (1982) report it in 17 percent of their societies, Martin King Whyte (1978) in only 6 percent. Female infanticide has also been estimated from sex ratios, with a note that some societies reporting the absence of this custom have suspiciously skewed sex ratios favoring boys (Divale and Harris 1976). When reporting twin infanticides, ethnographers often note that if only one twin of a dual-sex pair is kept, it is usually the boy (Granzberg 1973).

In India and China, this custom of female infanticide dates back centuries. Female infanticide in India is most common in the northwestern states (Miller 1981; Minturn 1993), but it has also been reported for groups in the south. The poverty of China's peasants and its frequent famines are two reasons for female infanticide. In both India and China, female infanticide is increasingly being replaced by female feticide after amniocentesis to determine fetal sex. The one-child policy of Communist China and the two-child policy of India have increased the prevalence of sons (Jefferey, Jefferey, and Lyon 1984).

Theories

Sarah B. Hrdy and Glenn Hausfater (1984) cite five functional categories of reasons for infanticide in animals in general: (1) exploitation of the infant as a resource, usually cannibalism; (2) competition for resources; (3) sexual selection; (4) parental increase of their own lifetime reproductive success by eliminating particular offspring; and (5) social pathology. Human infanticide includes examples of all of these functions (Daly and Wilson 1984; Dickemann 1984; Hrdy and Hausfater 1984; Scrimshaw 1984).

Resource competition is a popular theory of human infanticide. The threat of famine has been cited as the explanation for infanticide among Eskimos, Australian Aborigines, and Yanomamö. In Imperial China, Japan, and Europe, infanticide was used to control population and avoid starvation and social disruption. This was especially true for female infanticide, since eliminating females is a much more efficient form of population control than eliminating males.

Other theories of reasons for female infanticide include hypergymous marriage and large dowries (Dickemann 1979); differential values of children for their potential contributions to the parental kin groups (Hughes 1981); and high mortality rate of men in hunting (Riches 1974). The theory that female infanticide is a form of population control in warrior societies (Divale and Harris 1976) has been challenged by several authors who note many flaws in the original study (Fjellman 1979; Hirschfeld, Howe, and Levin 1978; Kang, Horan, and Reis 1979).

Acceptability and Legality

It has been suggested that infanticide and abortion may be underreported in tribal societies because of the presence of missionaries and colonial governments who deem these practices to be illegal (Divale and Harris 1976). Reports of infanticide prosecution by colonial governments are virtually absent in HRAF records. When babies are born at home, infanticide laws are seldom enforceable.

Ethnographic reports of abortion and infanticide are considerably more frequent than reports of punishments for either action, suggesting that tribal law was frequently permissive about both practices. A study of seventy-eight societies found no information on punishment of abortion for sixty-seven of them, and information on punishment of infanticide was so rare that it could not be coded. The absence of punishment may be viewed as recognition of parental rights to dispose of unwanted infants. Some tribal societies explicitly recognize this right until the cord is cut, until after the birth ceremony, or in a few societies, until the infant is weaned (Minturn 1989a).

Although infanticide was a capital offense in many countries for centuries, there is evidence that courts frequently took measures to avoid or mitigate punishment and that a variety of beliefs supported acquittals. In many courts, infanticidal mothers might successfully plead insanity. Eighteenth-century courts greatly extended the scope of the insanity plea by citing, as reason for dismissal of infanticide cases, the belief that pregnancy itself may make women deranged (Boswell 1988). As infanticide became more frequent, courts became more lenient, particularly when defendants were poor, unwed mothers.

Penalties also varied according to the method of killing. In the early Middle Ages, infanticide by exposure, a widespread practice of poor parents, was not a criminal offense. Overlaying was punished by one year on bread and water and two more years without wine or meat. This three-year penance, which became the standard punishment for overlaying, was shorter than the penalty for the accidental killing of adults (Kellum 1974).

Conclusion

There are four ways to avoid conceiving or to eliminate unwanted children: abstinence, contraception, abortion, and infanticide. Although abstinence was and is practiced in some societies by customs of late marriage, postpartum sex taboos, and customary periods of celibacy, it has never prevented all unwanted pregnancies. When these occurred in the past, infanticide was the safest method for disposing of the unwanted children. As medical advancements have been made, however, contraception and abortion have become more widely used and have replaced abstinence and infanticide as forms of birth control.

(*See also:* Abortion: Medical and Social Aspects; Birth Control: Contraceptive Methods; Birth Control: Sociocultural and Historical Aspects; Family Planning)

BIBLIOGRAPHY

Birdsell, J. B. (1968). "Some Predictions for the Pleistocene Based on Equilibrium Systems Among Recent Hunter-Gatherers." In *Man the Hunter,* ed. R. B. Lee and I. DeVore. Chicago: Aldine.

Boswell, J. (1988). *The Kindness of Strangers: The Abandonment of Children in Western Europe from Late Antiquity to the Renaissance.* New York: Pantheon.

Breiner, S. J. (1990). *Slaughter of the Innocents: Child Abuse Through the Ages and Today.* New York: Plenum.

Chagnon, N. A.; Flinn, M. V.; and Melancon, T. F. (1979). "Sex-Ratio Variation Among the Yanomamö Indians." In *Evolutionary Biology and Human Social Behavior: An Anthropological Perspective,* ed. N. A. Chagnon and W. Irons. North Scituate, MA: Duxbury Press.

Chapman, M. (1980). "Infanticide and Fertility Among Eskimos: A Computer Simulation." *American Journal of Physical Anthropology* 53:317–327.

Cowlishaw, G. (1978). "Infanticide in Aboriginal Australia." *Oceania* 48:262–283.

Daly, M., and Wilson, M. (1984). "A Sociobiological Analysis of Human Infanticide." In *Comparative and Evolutionary Perspectives on Infanticide: Introduction and Overview,* ed. S. B. Hrdy and G. Hausfater. New York: Aldine.

Denham, W. W. (1974). "Population Structure, Infant Transport, and Infanticide Among Pleistocene and Modern Hunter-Gatherers." *Journal of Anthropological Research* 30:191–198.

Devereaux, G. (1976). *A Study of Abortion in Primitive Societies,* revised edition. Madison, CT: International Universities Press.

Dickemann, M. (1975). "Demographic Consequences of Infanticide in Man." *Annual Review of Ecology and Systematics* 6:107–137.

Dickemann, M. (1979). "Female Infanticide, Reproductive Strategies, and Social Stratification: A Preliminary Model." In *Evolutionary Biology and Human Social Behavior: An Anthropological Perspective,* ed. N. A. Chagnon and W. Irons. North Scituate, MA: Duxbury Press.

Dickemann, M. (1984). "Concepts and Classification in the Study of Human Infanticide: Sectional Introduction and Some Cautionary Notes." In *Comparative and Evolutionary Perspectives on Infanticide: Introduction and Overview,* ed. S. B. Hrdy and G. Hausfater. New York: Aldine.

Divale, W. T. (1972). "Systemic Population Control in the Middle and Upper Paleolithic." *World Archeology and Anthropology* IV:65–68.

Divale, W. T., and Harris, M. (1976). "Population, Warfare, and the Male Supremacist Complex." *American Anthropologist* 78:521–538.

Fjellman, S. M. (1979). "Hey, You Can't Do That: A Response to Divale and Harris's 'Population, Warfare, and the Male Supremacist Complex.' " *Behavior Science Research* 14:189.

Fukasaku, M. (1975). "The Psychology of Infanticide." *Japan Interpreter* 10:205–208.

Granzberg, G. (1973). "Twin Infanticide: A Cross-Cultural Test of a Materialistic Explanation." *Ethos* 1:405–412.

Hansen, E. (1979). " 'Overlaying' in 19th-Century England: Infant Mortality or Infanticide?" *Human Ecology* 7:333–352.

Harris, M. (1977). *Cannibals and Kings: The Origins of Culture.* New York: Random House.

Hirschfeld, L. A.; Howe, J.; and Levin, B. (1978). "Warfare, Infanticide, and Statistical Inference: A Comment on Divale and Harris." *American Anthropologist* 80:110–115.

Hrdy, S. B., and Hausfater, G. (1984). *Comparative and Evolutionary Perspectives on Infanticide: Introduction and Overview.* New York: Aldine.

Hughes, A. L. (1981). "Female Infanticide." *Ethnology and Sociobiology* 2:109–111.

Jefferey, R.; Jefferey, P.; and Lyon, A. (1984). "Female Infanticide and Amniocentesis." *Social Science and Medicine* 19:1207–1212.

Kang, G.; Horan, S.; and Reis, J. (1979). "Comments on Divale and Harris's 'Population, Warfare, and the Male

Supremacist Complex.'" *Behavior Science Research* 14:201–211.

Kellum, B. (1974). "Infanticide in England and in the Later Middle Ages." *History of Infanticide Quarterly* 1:367–388.

Lancaster, C., and Lancaster, J. (1978). "On the Male Supremacist Complex: A Reply to Divale and Harris." *American Anthropologist* 80:115–117.

Langer, W. (1974). "Infanticide: A Historical Survey." *History of Childhood Quarterly* 1:353–365.

Lund, N. (1985). "Infanticide, Physicians, and the Law: The 'Baby Doe' Amendments to the Child Abuse Prevention and Treatment Act." *American Journal of Law and Medicine* 11:1–29.

Miller, B. D. (1981). *The Endangered Sex.* Ithaca, NY: Cornell University Press.

Minturn, L. (1989a). "The Birth Ceremony as a Rite of Passage into Infant Personhood." In *Abortion Rights and Fetal Personhood*, ed. E. Doerr and J. W. Prescott. Long Beach, CA: Centerline Press.

Minturn, L. (1989b). "This Child Is Ours: A Cross-Cultural Study of Definitions of Personhood." In *Heterogeneity in Cross-Cultural Psychology*, ed. D. M. Keats, D. Munroe, and L. Mann. Rockland, MA: Swets and Zeitlinger.

Minturn, L. (1993). *Sita's Daughters: Coming Out of Purdah.* Oxford, Eng.: Oxford University Press.

Minturn, L., and Stashak, J. (1982). "Infanticide as a Terminal Abortion Procedure." *Behavior Science Research* 17:70–90.

Neel, J. V. (1970). "Lessons from a 'Primitive' People." *Science* 170:815–822.

Riches, D. (1974). "The Netsilik Eskimo: A Special Case of Active Female Infanticide." *Ethnology* 13:351–361.

Schrire, C., and Steiger, W. L. (1974). "A Matter of Life and Death: An Investigation into the Practice of Female Infanticide in the Arctic." *Man* 9:161–184.

Scrimshaw, S. C. M. (1984). "Infanticide in Human Populations: Societal and Individual Concerns." In *Comparative and Evolutionary Perspectives on Infanticide: Introduction and Overview*, ed. S. B. Hrdy and G. Hausfater. New York: Aldine.

Whyte, M. K. (1978). "Codes Dealing with the Relative Status of Women." *Ethnology* 17:211–237.

Williamson, L. (1978). "Infanticide: An Anthropological Analysis." In *Infanticide and the Value of Life*, ed. M. Kohl. Buffalo, NY: Prometheus.

Leigh Minturn

INFERTILITY

The inability to conceive a child is a heartrending tragedy that many couples increasingly face. An estimated 2.4 million American couples fail to achieve a pregnancy within one year of unprotected intercourse, and only 80 percent of couples achieve a first pregnancy within that year. These statistics have increased since the 1960s because of two major social trends.

As women have shifted pregnancy from their twenties to their late thirties, there has been an increase in maternal age among married couples. In any one cycle of attempted pregnancy, the fecundity rate (chance of a conception) of American couples is 20 percent to 25 percent. This rate, against which all treatments must be judged, is age-related. If one looks at mean conception rates, one-half of women in their twenties will have conceived in three months, one-half of women in their early thirties will have conceived by five months, and one-half of women in their late thirties will have conceived by eight to nine months. In addition, there has been a marked increase in pelvic inflammatory disease (PID) as part of the wide spread of venereal diseases. Approximately 850,000 cases are diagnosed yearly in the United States, with each episode of this disease leading to a 20 percent chance of infertility.

To understand the diagnosis and treatments of infertility, a short review of basic biology is needed. To fertilize an egg, the male must produce a sufficient number of functional sperm. These must be deposited into the female and must survive in the relatively hostile vagina. They must then be able to enter the protected environment of the cervix and survive the filtering function of its mucus; only about 10 percent of the viable sperm will then enter the upper genital tract. They will pass through the uterine cavity and await the released ovum in the far end of the fallopian tubes. The female must ovulate (release the egg) and the tube must pick up the egg from the peritoneal cavity and provide an environment for the egg to be fertilized. Sperm may survive in the cervix for three to four days, but the released egg must be fertilized within twelve to twenty-four hours.

If conception occurs, the newly formed zygote (fertilized egg) floats through the tube, reaching the uterus and implanting itself on a receptive lining. This trip takes five days; interruption may result in an ectopic pregnancy (implantation and development outside the uterus). In the case of a normal pregnancy, the uterus maintains the newly formed and growing embryo, under the direction of hormones produced by the ovary. Infertility implies that at least one of these steps did not occur. Approximately 40 percent of the time the problem is due to male factors, and 60 percent of the time it is due to female factors. In 30 percent of infertile couples, there are mutual and multiple factors.

Before treatment can be undertaken, a diagnosis must be made, based on six to eight weeks of testing at various times in the woman's cycle. Ovulation is identified by one or more tests. A basal body temperature (BBT) chart, on which a woman plots her oral temperature each morning before rising, will demonstrate a characteristic shift of three-quarters of a degree around the time of ovulation. This is an inexpensive way to demonstrate retroactively that ovulation has occurred, with the most fertile period being just before the rise in temperature. Daily urine testing enables proactive demonstration of ovulation and its timing through the detection of the leutenizing hormone (LH) surge, the pituitary gland's message to the ovary to release the egg. Blood measurement of the hormone progesterone, which the ovary makes after ovulation, is commonly done in the third week of the cycle, and a biopsy of the uterus lining late in the menstrual cycle is done to document both the occurrence of ovulation and the adequacy of progesterone production to maintain the early pregnancy.

The patency (openness) of the genital tract is ascertained by a procedure (hysterosalpingogram) in which radio-opaque dye is injected into the uterus and X rays of the dye's passage are taken. This test shows the anatomy of the uterus as well as the patency of the tubes. If no other factor is found, the final test done on the woman is an operative procedure called laparoscopy, which requires an anaesthetic and is commonly a same-day procedure. A small telescope is placed into the abdominal cavity through a small incision below the umbilicus. With the abdominal cavity well distended with gas to aid in visualization, the outer surfaces of the fallopian tubes, ovaries, and uterus can be explored. For conception to occur, a fallopian tube must be free to move and catch the released egg as it is expelled from the ovarian surface. Laparoscopy commonly reveals adhesions (immobilizing scar tissue) or endometriosis (deposits of uterine lining tissue in inappropriate locations). However, the procedure is not just diagnostic. With the advent of laser and other technologies, findings can be both diagnosed and corrected during a single operation.

Male-factor problems are tested with a semen analysis. Laboratory examination of freshly ejaculated semen collected by masturbation can provide documentation for parameters such as sperm quantity and concentration, percentage of live sperm, sperm shape, and swimming velocity. Sperm counts of greater than 20 million per milliliter, 60 percent alive with good forward progression, and 60 percent shaped normal are indicative of normal fertility potential. Testing has become more sophisticated, and sperm can now be tested for function rather than just numbers. For example, there is the hamster penetration assay, where an actual inability to fertilize or penetrate an egg may identify more subtle problems. A postcoital test examining the woman's cervical mucus for live sperm two to ten hours after intercourse completes the evaluation and looks at the combined interaction of the couple in their attempt to conceive.

Through completion of this evaluation, one is better able to arrive at a diagnosis and begin treatment. If irregular menses or problems with ovulation are diagnosed, other endocrine systems (e.g., adrenal, thyroid, or pituitary) are examined and corrected if abnormal. The treatment of ovulation problems typically involves the use of clomiphene citrate (Clomid), a false hormone that "tells" the pituitary gland to stimulate the ovary to work harder and thereby release an egg. Other drugs, such as Pergonal, Metrodin, or Lutrepulse, are used in cases where Clomid fails or is inappropriate.

Tubal or uterine factors of infertility identified during these evaluations commonly require surgery performed via major or endoscopic procedures for correction. Cervical factors require further testing to identify infections and frequently require bypassing the cervix with sperm washed from the semen and placed by artificial insemination into the uterus. Male-factor problems require urologic evaluation and can be treated by hormones, surgery, or artificial insemination as indicated. Approximately 10 percent of infertile couples will go through this entire evaluation and no specific factors will be identified. This frustrating diagnosis of unexplained infertility is a reflection of the current limitations of medical science. Treatment, in this case, is to induce production of multiple eggs coupled with artificial insemination. Overall, more than 50 percent of infertile couples will be helped with these methods.

No discussion of infertility practices would be complete without a discussion of assisted reproductive technology. The ability to take an egg or eggs by insertion of a fine needle through the vagina under ultrasound guidance and combine the retrieval with suitably prepared sperm represents the most exciting progress of infertility science. Whether reimplanting the combined sperm-egg mixture into the fallopian tube (gamete intrafallopian transfer), allowing fertilization in the dish and reimplanting the newly formed zygote into the tube (zygote intrafallopian transfer), or allowing fertilization and embryo development and then transferring the embryo into the uterus (in vitro fertilization–embryo transfer), these new technologies hold the future for all infertile couples.

Combinations of other techniques, such as donated sperm, donated eggs, borrowed uteri, and surrogate parenting, are rapidly expanding the horizon of infertility treatment options.

(*See also:* Conception: Medical Aspects; Conception: Legal Aspects; Family Planning; Pregnancy and Birth)

BIBLIOGRAPHY

American Fertility Society. (1993). "Assisted Reproductive Technology in the United States and Canada: 1991 Results from the Society for Assisted Reproductive Technology Generated from the American Fertility Society Registry." *Fertility and Sterility* 59:956–962.

Hammond, M., and Talbert, L. (1985). *Infertility.* Oradell, NJ: Medical Economics Books.

Silber, S. (1985). *How to Get Pregnant.* New York: Warner Books.

Speroff, L.; Glass, R.; and Kase, N. (1989). *Clinical Gynecologic Endocrinology and Infertility.* Baltimore: Williams & Wilkins.

Richard J. Kates

INHERITANCE

The law of inheritance determines who is entitled to receive what a property owner owns on that owner's death if that owner dies intestate. An owner dies intestate if that person (the decedent) dies without a will or will substitutes effective at the time of death to dispose of all property.

History of Intestacy Law

The roots of the American laws of inheritance—each state has its own—go back to early English law. The institution of English feudalism produced a twofold law of inheritance; a bifurcated vocabulary accompanied that twofold law. Under feudalism, all land ownership was derived from the king directly or from a pyramid of lords and sublords who, themselves, derived land ownership directly or indirectly from the king. Therefore, one set of laws, with its accompanying vocabulary, applied to land or real property; another applied to personal property—that is, to everything else.

Real property was governed by the law of descent, and personal property was governed by the law of distribution. Real property descended at the owner's death to the heirs; personal property was distributable to the next of kin. When English law, in the seventeenth century, finally permitted a landowner to dispose of property by will, the will devised that land. The transfer of land by will was a devise and the recipient was a devisee. However, a will bequeathed personal property by legacy or bequest to a legatee.

At first, after the Norman conquest of England and in the eleventh to thirteenth centuries, land could not be transferred during the owner's lifetime without permission of the king or of the lord or sublord to whom the landowner owed allegiance.

Originally, land descended by law, and not by the will of the owner. There could be only one heir, one person entitled to the land at the owner's death. That heir, generally, was the oldest living son, because of the law of primogeniture (from the Latin, for first to be born).

The interest of the owner's surviving spouse was a life interest only. The widow had the protection of dower (from whence the word "dowager" derives), which gave her an interest in only one-third of her deceased husband's land, for her lifetime only. The widower, generally, had an interest, called curtesy, for his lifetime in all of his deceased wife's land (Kempin 1990; McGovern, Kurtz, and Rein 1988; Scoles and Halbach 1993).

The precept of the twelfth-century treatise commonly known as Glanvill, that "only God can make an heir" (Biancalana 1988), has echoed down the centuries, well past the demise of feudalism with its strictures against disposition of land by will, and in favor of primogeniture. Until recently, the echoes of this precept have limited the rights of illegitimate children and of adopted children (Fuller 1992; Rein 1984). They have also limited the freedom of renunciation of intestate interests, usually attempted to thwart creditors or the tax collector (Lauritzen 1953).

In 1660, England abolished feudalism and almost the last of the restrictions on the disposition of land. However, primogeniture lingered on in England until 1925 (Scoles and Halbach 1993), although the law was rejected by the New England colonies almost immediately upon their settlement in America and, later, in the eighteenth century, by the southern colonies (Clignet 1992; Salmon 1986).

The pattern of disposition of personal property at death for the intestate decedent was set in 1670 by the English Statute of Distributions. Wills and post-obit gifts (gifts effective after death) of personal property had been permitted, with the encouragement and supervision of the Church of England, or ecclesiastical courts, rather than the king's courts, which administered the laws affecting land to protect the feudal interests of the king (Scoles and Halbach 1993).

In the past 100 years, the split of the law of descent and distribution between real property and personal property has been almost obliterated in all of the states of the United States, although the split vocabulary lingers on in some legal documents and state statutes. The principal prejudices built into the law of descent of land—prejudices against the surviving spouse, younger sons, daughters, and ancestors—have disappeared. However, other odd distinctions, based on the obsolete feudal rationale that treated land differently from other property, surprisingly remain in the substantive and procedural law of decedents' estates. Some states, for instance, retain preference for land by directing that a decedent's creditors be paid first from the decedent's personal property and, only after that is exhausted, from the decedent's real property.

With the distinction between real and personal property almost obliterated, the 1670 Statute of Distributions has provided the model for American statutes on intestacy or inheritance for more than 300 years. Under this statute, a widow received one-third of her deceased husband's personal property, later to be extended to real property as well, if he was also survived by issue, and one-half if he was not. This statute applied to the personal property of a husband who died intestate but not to a wife's, since her personal property was considered to belong to her husband upon their marriage. This was just one of the several consequences of the law of coverture, which deprived women of legal capacity once married, consequences overruled, gradually, by the Married Women's Property Acts enacted in the nineteenth and twentieth centuries (Chused 1983; Salmon 1986; Warbasse 1987; Wenig 1990).

Under the Statute of Distributions, a decedent's children received the balance of the decedent's property equally, with a deceased child's share passing to that child's issue/descendants.

If the intestate decedent was survived by his widow but no issue, or no widow and no issue, the rest, or all, of his personal property was distributable equally to his brothers and sisters. Again, for equality of the "stocks" or lines of relationship, the issue of a deceased brother or sister stepped into the shoes of their deceased parent to receive that parent's share of the decedent's intestate estate.

If no brothers or sisters or their issue survived the decedent, his intestate estate passed in equal shares to his next of kin "in equal degree." To determine the "degree" of kinship, one in effect climbs up the steps of a two-sided ladder and then down the other side; count the number of steps *up* from decedent to his and his living relative's common ancestor and then count the number of steps down to the decedent's living relative (see Figure 1). For instance, a decedent may be survived only by an uncle on his father's side and by first cousins, children of the decedent's deceased paternal aunt. The decedent's uncle is related to the decedent in the third degree, determined by counting from the decedent up to his father (1) and then up to his father's parents (2) and then down to his uncle (3). The decedent's first cousins are in the fourth degree, determined by counting the two steps up to the decedent's paternal grandparents and then down to their daughter, the decedent's father's de-

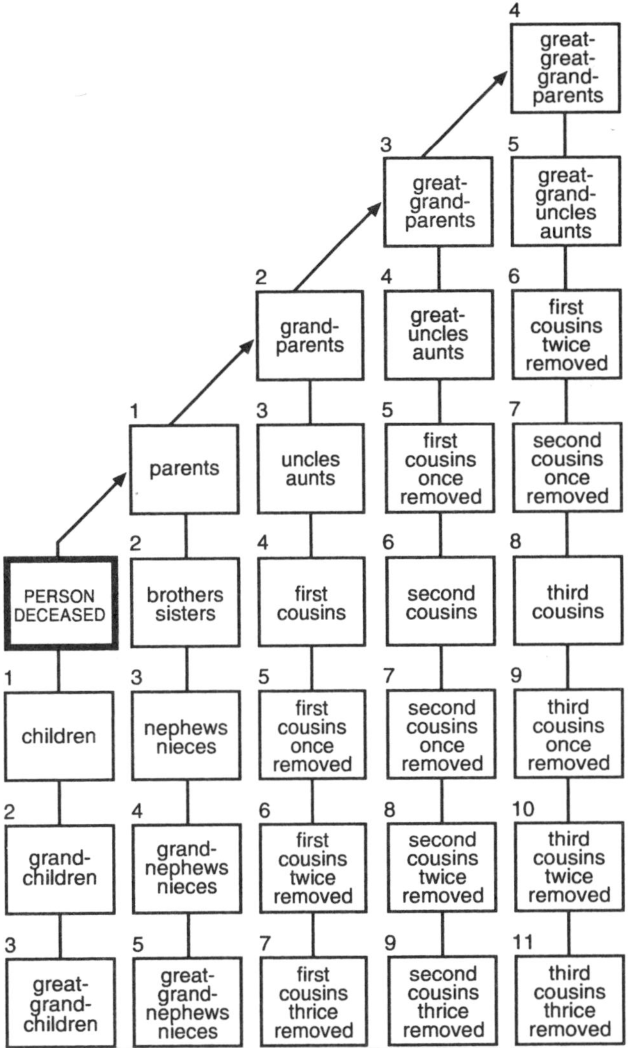

Figure 1 Illustration of consanguinity showing the degrees of relationships (numbered).

ceased sister (3) and then down to that aunt's children (4), who are the decedent's first cousins. The decedent's uncle, who is in the third degree, inherits from the decedent; his first cousins, in the fourth degree, do not.

Changes in Intestacy Law

Step by step, intestacy law changed, with changes beginning in the early nineteenth century and accelerating in the second half of the twentieth century. The changes have enlarged the family of intestate takers in some respects and have decreased the size of the family in other respects.

The changes have to be described broadly because the different states of the United States do not always agree on the timing of the changes nor on the substance of all the changes. However, the broad picture of changes can be said to reflect a sociological history of the family in the twentieth century. This history is one of the growing importance of the spouse, whether husband or wife; of the belief in equality, whether of the sexes or of all of the grandchildren; of "serial polygamy" and the mingled family—the family with "his" children, "her" children, and "their" children; of the fact that neither marriage nor procreation is required for a child to be "ours"; and of the diminished relevance of the extended family.

An early nineteenth-century statute in England, adopted by all of the states of the United States sooner or later, permitted surviving parents (or grandparents, or great-grandparents) to be included among the possible intestate takers if the intestate died with no children or descendants of children. Now, in most states, the decedent's surviving parents are preferred over the decedent's brothers and sisters, though in some states the decedent's siblings share with the decedent's parents under a variety of formulas (McGovern, Kurtz, and Rein 1988).

Relatively recent changes in the laws of inheritance in various states of the United States include the substantial increase in the intestate share of the surviving spouse, even to the exclusion of issue—if the statutory amount, which can be as high in some states as $200,000, for the surviving spouse subsumes the entire estate, or if the only issue are "their" issue, issue both of the deceased and of the surviving spouse, and there are no "his" issue and no "her" issue. Some state statutes reduce the size of parents' intestate shares if the spouse survives and eliminate brothers' and sisters' intestate shares if the decedent's spouse or parent survives. Illegitimate and adopted children are included in the definition of the decedent's children or the decedent's relatives' children. State intestate statutes no longer give preference to decedent's relatives of the whole-blood over relatives of the half-blood. The preference of the common law for equality of "stocks," for family lines, is giving way to the division of intestate shares that pass to children's or sibling's descendants equally among surviving descendants of the same degree. State intestate laws are beginning to eliminate "laughing heirs" (i.e., distant relatives, relatives beyond the decedent's grandparents and their descendants) as intestate takers even though these distant relatives are the decedent's next of kin. Finally, in recognition of the mingled family, some states have begun to provide for decedent's stepchildren as intestate takers if the decedent has no other intestate takers.

The intestate statutes, and the changes to these statutes, embody guesses about the directions a decedent might have given for the distribution of his or her property if the decedent had bothered to give such directions. These guesses might not in fact fulfill the wishes of the decedent.

Protection of Family

The decedent's directions in his or her will can supersede the directions of the intestate statute. Save for usually minimal homestead rights, family allowances, and exempt property for surviving spouse or minor children, a decedent is not required to provide for anyone except his or her surviving spouse. Almost all of the states provide the surviving spouse with one or another kind of protection against disinheritance.

None of the states, except Louisiana, protects children or other descendants against intentional disinheritance. No state protects other relatives against intentional disinheritance.

No state in the United States permits the court, as Great Britain does, to rewrite a decedent's will or ignore the application of the intestate law for the purpose of making "reasonable financial provision" for the decedent's spouse, ex-spouse, child, stepchild, or any other person if "maintained, either wholly or partly," by the decedent immediately before his or her death (Shapo 1993).

Importance of Will Substitutes

Inheritances may be received other than by will or the intestate statutes. Not all transfers on death must be by will or intestacy (Langbein 1984, 1988).

A decedent's will trumps intestacy law, but a decedent's will substitutes trump both his or her will and intestacy law, and except in a small minority of the states, will substitutes also trump the protection that state law might provide surviving spouses against disinheritance.

The term "will substitutes" refers to all assets with pay-on-death or transfer-on-death beneficiary designations, including life insurance; U.S. saving bonds and Treasury obligations; IRAs and some other pension accounts; lottery and sweepstakes winnings payable in installments over a period that may last beyond the owner's lifetime; other contracts providing for death benefits; and, where state law permits, bank accounts and securities.

Will substitutes also include bank accounts in the name of the depositor "in trust for" a named beneficiary, funded revocable trusts, and bank and brokerage accounts in joint name. These will substitutes are the functional equivalent of pay-on-death beneficiary designations.

Will substitutes that result in partial irrevocable transfers during the owner's lifetime and in complete transfers at the owner's death are joint tenancies with right of survivorship in real property, securities, automobiles and other vehicles, or other tangible personal property with registered ownership.

Both the will and the intestacy system are irrelevant to will substitutes with designated beneficiaries who survive the death of the owner. As an individual's will substitutes proliferate, the beneficiary designations multiply and supplant both the decedent's will and the backup intestate statutes. Each life insurance or accidental death policy, provided by employer, credit card, or direct purchase; each IRA, acquired annually from different banks, brokerage firms, or mutual funds; each Treasury note or U.S. bond; and each pay-on-death account will have its own beneficiary-designation form. Each of these forms may be completed at different times, but all must be individually rewritten and transmitted separately to the various financial institutions if the owner wants to change beneficiary designations.

Inheritance, whether looked at from the point of view of the inheritance provider or the inheritance recipient, is no longer tied up in one neat package of either a will or the default alternative of the intestacy system.

(*See also:* Family Law; Kinship; Marital Property and Community Property)

BIBLIOGRAPHY

Atkinson, T. E. (1953). *Handbook of the Law of Wills and Other Principles of Succession*, 2nd edition. St. Paul, MN: West Publishing.

Baker, J. H. (1979). *An Introduction to English Legal History*, 2nd edition. Woburn, MA: Butterworth.

Batts, D. A. (1990). "I Didn't Ask to Be Born: The American Law of Disinheritance and a Proposal for Change to a System of Protected Inheritance." *Hastings Law Journal* 41:1197–1270.

Biancalana, J. (1988). "For Want of Justice: Legal Reforms of Henry II." *Columbia Law Review* 88:433–536.

Bigelow, M. M. (1909). "The Rise of the English Will." In *Select Essays in Anglo-American Legal History*, ed. Association of American Law Schools. Boston: Little, Brown.

Chused, R. (1983). "Married Women's Property Law, 1800–1850." *Georgetown Law Journal* 71:1359–1425.

Clignet, R. (1992). *Death, Deeds, and Descendants: Inheritance in Modern America.* Hawthorne, NY: Aldine.

Fellows, M. L. (1993). "The Law of Legitimacy: An Instrument of Procreation Power." *Columbia Journal of Gender and Law* 3:497–534.

Friedman, L. M. (1977). "The Law of Succession in Social Perspective." In *Death, Taxes, and Family Property*, ed. E. C. Halbach, Jr. St. Paul, MN: West Publishing.

Fuller, L. A. (1992). "Note: Intestate Succession Rights of Adopted Children: Should the Stepparent Exception Be Extended?" *Cornell Law Review* 77:1188–1232.

Gross, C. (1909). "The Mediæval Law of Intestacy." In *Select Essays in Anglo-American Legal History*, ed. Association of American Law Schools. Boston: Little, Brown.

Kempin, F. G., Jr. (1990). *Historical Introduction to Anglo-American Law.* St. Paul, MN: West Publishing.

Langbein, J. H. (1984). "The Nonprobate Revolution and the Future of the Law of Succession." *Harvard Law Review* 97:1108–1140.

Langbein, J. H. (1988). "The Twentieth-Century Revolution in Family Wealth Transmission." *Michigan Law Review* 86:722–750.

Lauritzen, C. M. (1953). "Only God Can Make an Heir." *Northwestern University Law Review* 48:568–589.

McCauliff, C. M. A. (1992). "The Medieval Origin of the Doctrine of Estates in Land: Substantive Property Law, Family Considerations, and the Interests of Women." *Tulane Law Review* 66:919–1013.

McGovern, W. M., Jr.; Kurtz, S. F.; and Rein, J. E. (1988). *Wills, Trusts, and Estates.* St. Paul, MN: West Publishing.

Rein, J. E. (1984). "Symposium: The Winds of Change in Wills, Trusts, and Estate Planning Law." *Vanderbilt Law Review* 37:711–810.

Salmon, M. (1986). *Women and the Law of Property in Early America.* Chapel Hill: University of North Carolina Press.

Scoles, E. F., and Halback, E. C., Jr. (1993). *Decedents' Estates and Trusts*, 5th edition. Boston: Little, Brown.

Shapo, H. S. (1993). "A Tale of Two Systems: Anglo-American Problems on the Modernization of Inheritance Legislation." *Tennessee Law Review* 60:707–781.

"Uniform Probate Code." (1983, suppl. 1994). *Uniform Laws Annotated:* Vol. 8, *Estate, Probate, and Related Laws.* St. Paul, MN: West Publishing.

Warbasse, E. B. (1987). *The Changing Legal Rights of Married Women, 1800–1861.* New York: Garland.

Wenig, M. M. (1990). "The Marital Property Law of Connecticut: Past, Present, and Future." *Wisconsin Law Review* 1990:807–879.

Wigmore, J. H. (1935). "Symposium on Succession to Property by Operation of Law: Introduction." *Iowa Law Review* 20:181–184.

MARY MOERS WENIG

IN-LAW RELATIONSHIPS

Relationships with in-laws are a special category within kinship systems that has not been widely studied. Generally, kin relationships are defined by either blood (consanguine) ties or marriage (affinal) ties. Blood relationships are bound together by genetic lines, but relationships based on marriage are bound together by law and a code of conduct that accompanies them. In-law relationships are unique in that they are defined through a third party by both a marriage and a blood relationship. Some anthropologists have argued that in-law relationships are important to societies, both past and present, because they represent an alliance between two groups of blood relations (Wolfram 1987). In these cultures, in-law relationships are clearly defined and circumscribed by explicit institutional arrangements and prescribed and proscribed behaviors (Goetting 1990). In Western ideology, however, the husband–wife marital bond is the central family tie and supersedes claims of the extended family. Despite agreement about the rules of membership, the codes of conduct associated with in-law relationships remain nebulous. The actual interactions and sentiments assigned to these relationships are subject to individuals' definitions (Goetting 1990). The few patterns that do exist and have been observed are restricted to relationships between parents-in-law and children-in-law. Other in-law relationships, such as that between sisters- or brothers-in-law, appear to be solely based on friendship or idiosyncratic relations (Finch 1989).

Very little research has been conducted on affective relationships between parents and children-in-law, but there is ample evidence in the popular culture of negative attitudes toward mothers-in-law. These negative attitudes have also been documented in psychological studies wherein children report a perception of greater interpersonal distance and more negative attitudes toward mothers-in-law than mothers (Denmark and Ahmed 1989). The problematic nature of the relationship is also underscored in studies of early years of marriage that focus on adjustment of in-laws and the influence of in-laws on the marital relationship.

The bulk of research on in-law relationships has focused on assistance and support patterns. These patterns reflect the distinctive feature of in-law relations, which is that they are generally conducted through and, in a sense, for the sake of a third party (Finch 1989). Children-in-law primarily receive support from parents-in-law as indirect beneficiaries of parental aid to married children. Hence, the primary patterns of contact and support between children-in-law and their parents-in-law reflect customary patterns of parent–child relationships.

Studies demonstrate that over the life cycle, aid between parents and children tends to be unidirectional, from parents to children, and that parental aid is most concentrated in the early years of children's marriages and decreases over time (Goetting 1990). Although financial aid most often begins and is concentrated in early years of marriage, aid in the form of services reaches a peak during preschool years of grandchildren. Both gender and class differences have been observed in provision of parental aid (Adams 1964). The wife's parents tend to be a source of greater aid in terms of service, while sons' parents tend to provide financial aid. More frequent financial help is given to middle-class than to working-class children and children-in-law. Working-class parents, when they live close by, give what they can in terms of services.

The presence of grandchildren also appears to influence in-law relationships. The birth of the first child has been reported to transform the mother-in-law–daughter-in-law relationship into one involving significant support patterns. Lucy Fischer (1983) notes that daughters with preschool children needed and received more help from both mothers and mothers-in-law. Mothers-in-law were more likely to give things, whereas mothers were more likely to do things. Daughters-in-law tended to seek help and advice more frequently from their mothers than from their mothers-in-law and were more likely to express ambivalence about help from their mothers-in-law.

Just as there is little evidence of direct support from parents-in-law to their children-in-law, so research is consistent in demonstrating that children-in-law make a minimal direct contribution to the care of their elderly parents-in-law. The flow of support for in-laws from the child generation to the parent generation is indirect and reflects patterns of gender differences associated with parental care. Parents are more likely to turn to daughters and, thereby, sons-in-law for help than to sons and daughters-in-law. However, help to the elderly, which does not usually entail financial support, is more restricted to services and help with household tasks and personal care (Powers and Kivett 1992; Schorr 1980). This type of support is primarily performed by daughters, not sons or sons-in-law.

Although daughters are the preferred caregivers for elderly parents, geographic proximity also influences parental care. When daughters are not available or geographically close, parents turn to sons and daughters-in-law for help when there is illness (Powers and Kivett 1992). In these situations, daughters-in-law often provide more direct service than their husbands, reflecting women's role as kin keepers (Finch 1989). In the hierarchy of sources of support for the elderly, daughters-in-law take precedence over sons (Schorr 1980). Moreover, children-in-law are often more functional in the kin network than are consanguine kin who are more distantly related, such as grandchildren or siblings (Kivett 1985). There is some evidence, however, that caring for mothers-in-law is perceived as more stressful and requiring more tasks than caring for a mother (Steinmetz 1988).

Support for parents-in-law can also take place in the form of coresidence. Again, the stronger kinship tie of women appears to dictate a greater number of mothers living with daughters and sons-in-law than with sons and daughters-in-law. Social class also has been observed to be associated with different patterns of support. There is a greater flow of financial aid from middle-class children to parents and parents-in-law than is true of working-class families, but a greater flow of service and coresidence exists among the working class.

The requirement of a third party as a defining factor for an in-law relationship makes these relationships uniquely vulnerable to dissolution when the marriage of the third party is dissolved by divorce or death. Along with gender differences, the presence or absence of children from the dissolved marriage appears to influence the continuance of in-law-relationships. Once a marriage has produced offspring, in-laws become affinal relatives who are defined not only by the order of law but also by their recognition of a biological link to the child. Hence, when the legal basis of the relationship is dissolved, there remains a relationship based on a common biological link (Johnson 1989). It is this tie, combined with the tendency in Western culture for mothers rather than fathers to retain custody of the children after a divorce, that appears to influence in-law relationships after divorce. Overall, divorce decreases in-law contact and support to various degrees. The extent of these decreases differs by gender and the presence or absence of grandchildren. There is greater interaction and support given between divorced women and their former in-laws than is true for men (Goetting 1990; Johnson 1989). It has been suggested that this greater contact may be motivated by the desire of grandparents to maintain access to grandchildren. Maternal grandparents have less contact with ex-sons-in-law than do paternal grandparents with ex-daughters-in-law, and the extent of contact between the paternal grandparents and ex-daughters-in-law tends to diminish over time as grandchildren grow and their needs diminish (Johnson 1989).

In-law relationships are perhaps the kin relationships most subject to voluntary definitions and individual interpretations. Most often, "in-laws serve as a reservoir of supplemental resources to be tapped as social norms dictate and practicalities allow" (Goetting 1990, p. 86). It must be underscored, however, that research focused on in-law relationships has been limited, and the patterns reported here apply mainly to mainstream American culture. Although researchers have observed and reported variation by social class, they have virtually ignored other demographic factors, such as ethnicity and regional residence.

(*See also:* Filial Responsibility; Grandparenthood; Intergenerational Relations; Kinship; Widowhood)

BIBLIOGRAPHY

Adams, B. N. (1964). "Structural Factors Affecting Parental Aid to Married Children." *Journal of Marriage and the Family* 26:327–331.

Anderson, T. B. (1984). "Widowhood as a Life Transition: Its Impact on Kinship Ties." *Journal of Marriage and the Family* 46:105–114.

Brody, E. M., and Schoonover, C. B. (1988). "Patterns of Parent-Care when Adult Daughters Work and When They Do Not." *Gerontologist* 5:372–381.

Denmark, F. L., and Ahmed, R. A. (1989). "Attitudes Toward Mother-in-Law and Stepmother: A Cross-Cultural Study." *Psychological Reports* 65:1194.

Finch, J. (1989). *Family Obligations and Social Change.* Cambridge, Eng.: Polity Press.

Fischer, L. R. (1983). "Mothers and Mothers-in-Law." *Journal of Marriage and the Family* 45:263–290.

Goetting, A. (1990). "Patterns of Support Among In-Laws in the United States: A Review of Research." *Journal of Family Issues* 11:67–90.

Johnson, C. L. (1989). "In-Law Relationships in the American Kinship System: The Impact of Divorce and Remarriage." *American Ethnologist* 16:87–99.

Kivett, V. R. (1985). "Consanguinity and Kin Level: Their Relative Importance to the Helping Network of Older Adults." *Journal of Gerontology* 40:228–234.

Lopata, H. Z. (1970). "The Social Involvement of Widows." *American Behavioral Scientist* 14:4–57.

Powers, E. A., and Kivett, V. R. (1992). "Kin Expectations and Kin Support Among Rural Older Adults." *Rural Sociology* 57:194–215.

Schneider, D. (1968). *American Kinship: A Cultural Account.* Englewood Cliffs, NJ: Prentice Hall.

Schorr, A. L. (1980). *Thy Father and Thy Mother: A Second Look at Filial Responsibility and Family.* Washington, DC: U.S. Government Printing Office.

Spicer, J., and Hempe, C. (1975). "Kinship Interaction After Divorce." *Journal of Marriage and the Family* 37:113–119.

Steinmetz, S. K. (1988). *Duty Bound: Elder Abuse and Family Care.* Newbury Park, CA: Sage Publications.

Townsend, A. L., and Poulshock, S. W. (1986). "International Perspectives on Impaired Elders' Support Networks." *Journal of Gerontology* 41:101–109.

Wolfram, S. (1987). *In-Laws and Out-Laws: Kinship and Marriage in England.* London: Croom Helm.

RHONDA J. V. MONTGOMERY

INTERGENERATIONAL RELATIONS

Intergenerational relations refers to the formal and informal associations and bonds between members of different age groups and birth cohorts. Such connections can be visualized in terms of the components of the relationship (e.g., their structure, norms, rules), in terms of how they change or endure across historical time, or in terms of how they vary cross-culturally. These elements provide an important framework for the associations between family members.

Family Structure

Family structure refers to the actual design of relational networks due to demographic changes and variation in social rites such as birth, death, and marriage, as well as through informal activities of association. While some elements of family structure are common cross-culturally, others vary. Moreover, paradigmatic family formation patterns for any one culture often change over time.

Historically, the dominant forms of intergenerational family structure have been (1) the "nuclear family formation," two-generational formations in which married parents reside with one or more minor and/or unmarried offspring and (2) the "extended family formation," composed of two, minimally, but more likely three or more generations. Many analysts also distinguish between the "family of orientation" into which one is born and with whom one grows up and the "family of procreation" one forms as an adult with a partner for the purpose of child rearing.

While members may or may not share residency in extended families, these units are composed of substantial numbers of individuals of the same generation (horizontally) and/or across generations (vertically). However, family structure is dynamic, and new and evolving forms such as, in the United States, the growing prominence of single-parent families, female-headed families, "couple only" families, and "lone adult" families reflect changing social and demographic trends, each with implications for intergenerational relations.

Historical data suggest that nuclear family formations predominated well into the nineteenth century. Short life expectancies limited, for most, the probability of individual survival much past fifty years of age, making extensive three- or more generation family networks the exception. At the same time, the need for a large number of offspring for labor-intensive agriculturally based family economic production put a premium on nuclear family life. Peter Laslett's (1972) study of mean household size in one hundred communities in England between 1574 and 1821 indicated that nuclear families with an average of five individuals predominated; in the United States, household size in 1850 averaged 5.6 persons (Bane 1976).

By 1930, average American household size had declined to 4.1 persons (Bane 1976). Declines in nuclear family size in the United States and Europe since the late nineteenth century are generally attributed to (1) a steep decline in mortality (Uhlenberg 1980), (2) lower birthrates because of the increased probability of survival to adulthood, and (3) the growing emphasis on industrially based, rather than agriculturally based, family economic production (Watkins, Menken, and Bongaarts 1987). By the last quarter of the twentieth century, nuclear families composed fewer than a third of all households in the United States (White and Tsui 1986).

During the first half of the twentieth century, many analysts of family behavior maintained that increased urbanization and industry-based economic support led to the social isolation of the nuclear family because of the need to move, on demand, to seek better employment opportunities (Parsons 1966). Others have argued that this emphasis on nuclear family isolation, if valid at all, is most likely to characterize white, urban, middle-class Americans, since race and ethnic, rural/urban, and socioeconomic status distinctions are likely to moderate isolation, particularly from extended kin systems (Sussman and Burchinal 1968).

Some analysts maintain that, as a result of increased life expectancy and declining birth rates, the most consistent and important change in family structure during the twentieth century in most industrialized societies was the growing "verticalization" of the family. This refers to the increase in family membership *across* generations at the same time that the family network is experiencing a decrease in membership horizontally—*within* any one generation (George and Gold 1991; Hagestad 1986). As a result, families in many industrialized societies are often "topheavy," with larger proportions of members in the older generations than in the younger ones. Also, there is now a much greater likelihood than at the beginning of the twentieth century, in many industrialized societies, that members of the youngest generation in a family will have a living grandparent for a sizable part of their lifetime. Conversely, by the mid-1980s in the United States, about one-half of all individuals sixty-five years or older were great-grandparents in four-generation families, and there is evidence that up to 20 percent of women who live to be eighty or older are members of five-generation families (Hagestad 1986, 1988).

Along with increased verticalization of the extended family, gender-related differences in family composition increased throughout the twentieth century. Mortality declines have resulted in sexual distinctions in life expectancy, with age-specific life expectancy for females greater than for males in nearly every age range. As a consequence of this difference and the tendency for women to marry men older than themselves, the probability that the older members of a family will be female has increased greatly.

A number of trends mark late-twentieth-century family structure in the United States. Linda M. Burton's research has indicated that the occurrence of teenage pregnancy over multiple generations within a family network will create an "age-condensed" family structure with as few as fifteen years separating generations. This narrow span between generations may serve to blur the identification and roles of mothers and daughters and lead to grandmotherhood at an early age for women in the third generation of the family (Burton 1985; Elder, Caspi, and Burton 1987). On the other hand, a growing trend toward delayed childbearing among some women who have postponed parenthood until their mid-thirties or later has increased the number of "age-gapped" intergenerational family patterns (Bengtson, Rosenthal, and Burton 1990). The most abbreviated intergenerational family structure is one characterized by childlessness, whereas greater complexity in structure marks the growing number of "reconstituted" families with stepchildren, stepparents, and stepgrandparents.

Changes in the duration of marriage have greatly affected twentieth-century family structure. Because of increases in life expectancy, the average length of a marriage in the United States, before the death of one spouse, increased from twenty-eight years at the end of the nineteenth century to more than forty-three years by the 1970s (Goldman and Lord 1983). Nevertheless, more marriages in the United States terminated due to divorce than by death by 1974, and almost half of new marriages are expected to end in divorce. Moreover, both divorce and family reconstitution in the event of remarriage greatly alter, in differing ways, the family networks of men, women, and offspring (Glick 1980; Hagestad 1986).

Trends in family structure in the United States vary across ethnic groups. For example, in contrast with the white population in the United States, African Americans are more likely to be in families headed by a single female. African Americans are also more likely to experience marital disruption in both a first and a second marriage and are less likely to remarry—particularly African-American women. As a result, African Americans are also less likely to be part of step-family formations (Taylor et al. 1990).

Living Patterns

Linked closely to the structure of families are their living arrangements, particularly the formation of household units. In the United States during the early decades of the twentieth century, three-generation households (typically older individuals living with their adult children and grandchildren) were quite common (Juster and Vinovskis 1987). Changes in familial living patterns over the ensuing decades have been a function of several factors, including increased life expectancy, social norms, and economic status. For instance, the increased rate of divorce among those in their twenties and thirties has resulted in greater numbers of Americans returning to the homes of their parents, at least for the short term, following that major personal change. Intergenerational living patterns also vary somewhat by race and ethnicity, both in the United States and elsewhere.

By the mid-twentieth century, social theorist Talcott Parsons (1966) maintained that the demand for occupational and geographic mobility inherent in modern, industrial society had resulted in the physical isolation of the nuclear family from the greater, extended family. He claimed, moreover, that this isolation promoted the decline of the extended family. In fact, investigations have revealed that while the frequency of interpersonal contacts is more limited among family members not living in the same vicinity, the number of intergenerational contacts of all kinds (including through telephone calls and letters) can be substantial when family members remain close emotionally (DeWit and Frankel 1988).

Living arrangements vary considerably across cultures and ethnic groups. For example, in comparison with white families, African-American families are somewhat less likely to be headed by a married couple and much more likely to be headed by a single female; by the mid-1980s, half of all African-American children under age eighteen lived in households with their mothers but not their fathers (Jaynes and Williams 1989). African Americans are also more likely than white Americans to live in extended family households. Research has shown that for African-American women, this is primarily a result of the larger proportion of African-American women with grandchildren in their households (Beck and Beck 1989; Farley and Allen 1987).

Older Americans are much more likely than in the past to live alone or with a spouse only (Treas and Bengtson 1987). Indeed, the growth of one-person households in the United States from 5 percent of all households in 1900 to 18 percent by 1973 was due primarily to the increase in women fifty-five years of age or older who were living alone (Kobrin 1976). Contrary to enduring popular myth, however, older Americans have not been abandoned by younger family members who have moved to other communities. In fact, older individuals generally choose to live separately from their children, preferring what German analyst Leopold Rosenmayr has named "intimacy at a distance"—having at least one child physically nearby for frequent in-person interactions (Shanas et al. 1968). When they do live with an adult child, it tends to be with a daughter and as a result of a crisis, such as serious illness or disability (Lopata 1973).

Some of the most interesting trends in living patterns are evident in Sweden, which is often on the leading edge of social change in the Northern Hemisphere and, therefore, highly illustrative. Sweden has the lowest marriage rates among industrialized countries as well as the highest average age for entry into a first marriage for both men and women. As a result, married-couple households are being replaced in large numbers by nonmarried, cohabiting-couple households. Sweden also has, among Western countries, the lowest average household size and the highest percentage of single-person households (Popenoe 1987).

In more traditional societies, increasing life expectancy, especially for females, coupled with long-standing culturally imposed maintenance of home-based, nurturing roles for wives, has led to new living arrangements in midlife for many women. For example, women in Iran now spend an average of one-third of their lives in widowhood. Since they are expected to depend financially on male relatives throughout their lives, most of the widows spend this long period of their lives in the households of sons or other male relations (Aghajanian 1985).

Intergenerational Norms

Norms refer to widely shared expectations and beliefs about behavior and events considered typical or standard for a certain group of people. While some family norms (e.g., commitment to the nurturing of young children by parents) endure over time and cross-culturally, others (e.g., the timing of transitional events such as leaving home and age at first marriage) are substantially affected by changing demographic patterns and social trends.

Tamara K. Hareven (1977) has noted that, across historical time, a society's values influence what are considered "appropriate" rather than "deviant" family-related events and behavior. For instance, the circumstances in which being an "old maid" is socially appropriate and acceptable have varied considerably over the years.

One of the more striking influences on family norms since the late 1800s has been change in the experience of family deaths. In 1860, for example, 84 percent of Canadians who had reached fifty years of age could expect to have lost both parents, a figure that had decreased to 40 percent a century later (Gee 1987). In the United States, while the loss of a young child was a normative event for parents as recently as 1900, it is uncommon today.

Intergenerational norms can vary or remain fairly constant cross-culturally. Teenage marriage, for instance, may be considered acceptable in some societies but deviant in others, and ethnic subcultures within a larger societal context may vary considerably regarding the acceptable timing of family events. Hareven (1977) points out, for example, that during the late nineteenth century, Irish immigrants to the United States married later than did some other cultural groups, and they also had larger numbers of children over a longer time period.

Intergenerational Roles

The roles (identifiable set of behaviors typically attached to a particular status) that various family members play have also changed over historical time. Hareven has pointed out, for instance, that, in contrast with current family life, in the nineteenth century the interval between the date of marriage and the birth of the first child was much shorter than it is today, thus linking the onset of the two roles in time very closely for the new couple. Moreover, since, historically, child rearing occurred over a much greater proportion of one's adult life, few of one's later years were spent outside the parental role (Hareven 1977). The increased verticalization of family structure, resulting from greater life expectancy, also has affected the length of time spent in particular family roles. Moreover, the joint effect of having fewer offspring while living longer has resulted in the assumption of a greater number of intergenerational roles—for example, one woman can simultaneously be a grandparent, great-grandparent, and great-aunt.

Many roles in the family have been and continue to be gender-related. Women in families have been primarily or exclusively responsible for kin care activities, such as child rearing and the care of family members who are sick or old and frail. These roles are standard for women cross-culturally also. In many economically developing societies, where women have only recently begun to enter the urban labor force in great numbers, there is often confusion within the family regarding whether to conform to the traditional model regarding the gender distribution of domestic roles or to renegotiate the distribution and percentage of effort they require (Ramu 1987). Also, for all cultures experiencing a substantial increase in life expectancy, the role of adult children of both sexes in the provision of care to old and frail parents has expanded in both scope and duration. Moreover, with lower birthrates, this caregiving role often has become the responsibility of a smaller generation of adult children in the family.

Intergenerational Exchanges

Within the context of both the family and society, resources of various kinds are transferred between members of different generations, birth cohorts, and age groups. Societal-level intergenerational exchanges may be the material outcomes of public policy or the private sector, or they may be the products of creative activity (e.g., research, music, literature, or systems of jurisprudence).

Family-based resource exchanges often take the form of emotional support or material goods, as in the case of inheritances. A hallmark of change in familial intergenerational exchanges in industrialized societies since the late 1800s has been the shift from economically based instrumental exchanges among family members to those stressing expressive and emotional needs. This shift occurred at the same time that the focus in family life moved from fulfilling the requirements of the family as an economic operating unit to the wishes and choices of individual family members. At the same time, family ties became more voluntary, and emotional support became a highly valued intergenerational exchange given and received across the life course (Hagestad 1986; Riley 1983). In particular, the increase in life expectancy within old age augmented markedly the emotional support from adult child to frail, older parent.

Analysts have developed several theoretical perspectives of the ways in which resources flow within the family. Exchange theory, for instance, considers the array of social interactions within the family as the exchange of resources between members where those with the greater amount of social power design and direct the exchange process (Dowd 1975). Another view portrays a reciprocity of exchanges among family members, where the reciprocity itself is seen as a motivator of interdependence over the family life course, at different locations within the family structure (e.g., between parent and child; between grandparent and grandchild), and in terms of how much particular family members perceive each member to have given and received in the past (Sussman 1965). Others see the flow of resources to older family members, specifically, in terms of the "credits earned" by these individuals for providing resources in the past to family members now on the giving end (Horowitz and Shindelman 1983).

The life cycle model maintains that there is a curvilinear shape to the intergenerational distribution of resources: Those in the middle generation or generations in the family provide the bulk of family resources to those who are either younger or older (Hill 1965, 1970; Sussman 1965). A contrasting view, the role continuity model, claims that, unless financially strained, older generations in the family distribute their resources to younger, successive generations (Kalish 1975; Riley and Foner 1971). Finally, others see the giving and receiving of familial resources as a series of hierarchical/sequential activities. Here, individuals first seek assistance from members of the nuclear family; failing that, from extended family members; and, as a last resort, from institutional sources such as government programs and banks (Morgan 1983).

Despite the emphasis on emotional support, inheritance remains a prime mechanism for intergenerational exchanges within the family. In many Western societies prior to industrialization, inheritance was the prime method by which the means of family economic support (typically the farm or a small business) was passed from father to son. With industrialization and the movement of economic support for most families to the factory or office, inheritance has become a means of funneling a broader variety of goods to younger family members. While the transfer of monetary and property goods is still routine, more symbolic effects, such as cherished heirlooms and mementos, are bequeathed to younger family members as well (Schorr 1980; Sussman, Cates, and Smith 1970).

On the societal level, intergenerational transfers occur across large groups of people of different age groups and birth cohorts. In many instances, societal-level transfers are the products of public policy. Indeed, many outcomes of public policy affect everyone in that society (e.g., the building of roads from funds derived from federally mandated tax revenues). In other instances, some components of a public policy may direct resources to a subset of individuals but not to others, while other components serve as a more inclusive resource transfer mechanism. For example, Social Security legislation in the United States contains measures to provide income in retirement to most older Americans through its Old Age and Survivors Insurance program. Yet it also includes a means of support for those of any age who have become disabled, an unemployment insurance component for those who have recently lost their jobs, and the public assistance Supplemental Security Income (SSI) program for those meeting the criteria who have chronic financial difficulties.

Often, when there is disagreement over the procedure for and/or direction of intergenerational resource transfers, contention focuses upon one or more of these factors: (1) the concept of who and what constitutes a "generation," (2) the issue of the individual's or group's "absolute" versus "relative" gain or loss as a result of a resource transfer, in comparison with the lot of others, (3) the perception of the resource allocation "pie": Is its size constant? expandable?, and (4) the notion of "distributive justice," or fairness, in the decision rule for resource allocation (Hirshorn 1991).

In the United States, a public debate arises periodically regarding the equity of intergenerational resource transfers stemming from public policies—with much of the concern centered on these issues. Particularly during the 1980s, some observers maintained that there was considerable inequity in the allocation of public sector resource transfers, particularly resources affecting the welfare of the young (those under eighteen years of age), in contrast with those affecting the elderly (those over sixty-five years of age). This "intergenerational inequity" perspective contends that the well-being of the young has not only diminished considerably but also has done so as a direct result of the enhancement of the well-being of older Americans. Older Americans, then, are seen as a monolithic group, accumulating much of the nation's personal wealth while receiving a larger than appropriate share of public resources in the form of Social Security—chiefly Medicare health insurance and Social Security retirement funds (Lamm 1985; Preston 1984).

A contrasting view that arose during that period states that all generations/birth cohorts/age groups have a "common stake" in intergenerational exchanges, since over the life course, most people will both give and receive a multitude of resources to and from both society and their families. Moreover, any age group is composed of individuals who are heterogeneous in a wide array of statuses (e.g., economic, health, and family support). Therefore, the forms and amounts of public support individuals require to sustain themselves will vary widely.

This perspective emphasizes, furthermore, that any intergenerational transfer will affect some individuals directly but others indirectly, particularly when one examines how it is disseminated within the family context. For example, a grandparent's SSI is likely to be used to purchase clothing and food for a grandchild living in the same household as well as help directly to underwrite the needs of the grandparent. Therefore, this view of intergenerational transfers maintains that current and future generations of older persons have a "common stake" in the welfare of the young and vice versa (Kingson, Hirshorn, and Cornman 1986).

Another societal-level intergenerational transfer stems from private-sector endeavors that affect both the "active working population," comprised primarily of those who are in their twenties through their fifties, and the "dependent population"—children, youth, and much of the older population. These transfers take place primarily in the form of wages earned by the active working population and the tax revenues that these workers provide. It is important to note that the age ranges for the active, in contrast with the dependent, population vary from one society to another. Moreover, within the age range comprising the dependent population are many school-age children and retirees who are part of the labor force at least part-time or part-year, while many middle-agers, willingly or unwillingly, are not.

Finally, an enduring form of societal-level transfer is comprised of the products of scientific and artistic endeavor (e.g., research, music, literature, and jurisprudence). These benefit not only the multiple generations living at the time of the products' creation but also generations to come.

(*See also:* Demography; Elders; Entitlements; Ethnicity; Exchange Theory; Extended Family; Family Gender Roles; Grandparenthood; Inheritance; In-Law Relationships; Nuclear Family)

BIBLIOGRAPHY

Aghajanian, A. (1985). "Living Arrangements of Widows in Shiraz, Iran." *Journal of Marriage and the Family* 47:781–784.

Bane, M. J. (1976). *Here to Stay.* New York: Basic Books.

Beck, R. W., and Beck, S. H. (1989). "The Incidence of Extended Households Among Middle-Aged Black and White Women: Estimates from a Five-Year Panel Study." *Journal of Family Issues* 10:147–168.

Bengtson, V.; Rosenthal, C.; and Burton, L. (1990). "Families and Aging: Diversity and Heterogeneity." In *Handbook of Aging and the Social Sciences*, 3rd edition, ed. R. H. Binstock and L. K. George. New York: Academic Press.

Burton, L. M. (1985). "Early and On-Time Grandmotherhood in Multigenerational Black Families." Ph.D. diss. University of Southern California.

DeWit, D. J., and Frankel, B. G. (1988). "Geographic Distance and Intergenerational Contact: A Critical Assessment and Review of the Literature." *Journal of Aging Studies* 2:25–43.

Dowd, J. J. (1975). "Aging and Exchange: A Preface to Theory." *Journal of Gerontology* 30:584–594.

Elder, G. H., Jr.; Caspi, A.; and Burton, L. M. (1987). "Adolescent Transitions in Developmental Perspective: Sociological and Historical Insights." In *Minnesota Symposium on Child Psychology*, Vol. 21, ed. M. Gunnar. Hillsdale, NJ: Lawrence Erlbaum.

Farley, R., and Allen, W. R. (1987). *The Color Line and the Quality of Life in America.* New York: Russell Sage Foundation.

Gee, E. M. (1987). "Historical Change in the Family Life Course of Canadian Men and Women." In *Aging in Canada*, 2nd edition, ed. V. Marshall. Markham, Ont.: Fitzhenry & Whiteside.

George, L. K., and Gold, D. (1991). "Life Course Perspectives on Intergenerational and Generational Connections." *Marriage and Family Review* 16:67–88.

Glick, P. (1980). "Remarriage: Some Recent Changes and Variations." *Journal of Family Issues* (Dec.):455–478.

Glick, P. (1984). "Marriage, Divorce, and Living Arrangements." *Journal of Family Issues* 5:7–26.

Goldman, N., and Lord, G. (1983). "Sex Differences in Life Cycle Measures of Widowhood." *Demography* (May): 177–195.

Hagestad, G. O. (1986). "The Aging Society as a Context for Family Life." *Daedalus* 115:119–139.

Hagestad, G. O. (1988). "Demographic Change and the Life Course: Some Emerging Trends in the Family Realm." *Family Relations* 37:405–410.

Hareven, T. K. (1977). "Family Time and Historical Time." *Daedalus* (Spring):57–70.

Hill, R. (1965). "Decision Making and the Family Life Cycle." In *Social Structure and the Family*, ed. E. Shanas and G. Streib. Englewood Cliffs, NJ: Prentice Hall.

Hill, R. (1970). *Family Development in Three Generations.* Cambridge, MA: Schenkman.

Hirshorn, B. (1991). "Multiple Views of the Intergenerational Flow of Society's Resources." *Marriage and Family Review*, special edition on intergenerational relations.

Horowitz, A., and Shindelman, L. (1983). "Reciprocity and Affection: Past Influences on Current Caregiving." *Journal of Gerontological Social Work* 5:5–20.

Jaynes, G. D., and Williams, R. M., Jr., eds. (1989). *A Common Destiny: Blacks and American Society.* Washington, DC: National Academy Press.

Juster, S., and Vinovskis, M. (1987). "Changing Perspectives on the American Family in the Past." *Annual Review of Sociology* 13:193–216.

Kalish, R. (1975). *Late Adulthood.* Monterey, CA: Brooks/Cole.

Kingson, E. R.; Hirshorn, B. A.; and Cornman, J. M. (1986). *Ties That Bind: The Interdependence of Generations.* Report from the Gerontological Society of America. Washington, DC: Seven Locks Press.

Kobrin, F. (1976). "The Fall in Household Size and the Rise of the Primary Individual in the United States." *Demography* 13:127–138.

Lamm, R. D. (1985). *Mega-Traumas: America at the Year 2000.* Boston: Houghton Mifflin.

Laslett, P., and Wall, R. (1972). *Household and Family in Past Time.* Cambridge, Eng.: Cambridge University Press.

Lopata, H. Z. (1973). *Widowhood in an American City.* Cambridge, MA: Schenkman.

Morgan, J. N. (1983). "The Redistribution of Income by Families and Institutions and Emergency Help Patterns." In *Five Thousand American Families: Patterns of Economics Progress*, ed. G. J. Duncan and J. N. Morgan. Ann Arbor: University of Michigan Press.

Parsons, T. (1966). *Societies: Evolutionary and Comparative Perspectives.* Englewood Cliffs, NJ: Prentice Hall.

Popenoe, D. (1987). "Beyond the Nuclear Family: A Statistical Portrait of the Changing Family in Sweden." *Journal of Marriage and the Family* 49:173–183.

Preston, S. H. (1984). "Children and the Elderly: Divergent Paths for America's Dependents." *Demography* 21:435–457.

Ramu, G. N. (1987). "Indian Husbands: Their Role Perceptions and Performance in Single- and Dual-Earner Families." *Journal of Marriage and the Family* 49:903–916.

Riley, M. W. (1983). "The Family in an Aging Society: A Matrix of Latent Relationships." *Journal of Family Issues* 4:439–454.

Riley, M. W., and Foner, A. (1971). "Social Gerontology and the Age Stratification of Society." *Gerontologist* 11:79–87.

Schorr, A. (1980). *Thy Father and Thy Mother: A Second Look at Filial Responsibility and Family Policy.* Washington, DC: U.S. Government Printing Office.

Shanas, E.; Townsend, P.; Wedderburn, D.; Friis, H.; Millhoj, H. P.; and Steuhower, J. (1968). *Old People in Three Industrial Societies.* New York: Atherton.

Sussman, M. B. (1965). "Relationships of Adult Children with Their Parents in the United States." In *Social Structure and the Family: Generational Relationships*, ed. E. Shanas and G. Streib. Englewood Cliffs, NJ: Prentice Hall.

Sussman, M. B., and Burchinal, L. (1968). "Kin Family Network: Unheralded Structure in Current Conceptualizations of Family Functioning." In *Middle Age and Aging: A Reader in Social Psychology*, ed. B. L. Neugarten. Chicago: University of Chicago Press.

Sussman, M. B.; Cates, J.; and Smith, D. (1970). *The Family and Inheritance.* New York: Russell Sage Foundation.

Taylor, R. J.; Chatters, L. M.; Tucker, M. B.; and Lewis, E. (1990). "Developments in Research on Black Families: A Decade of Review." *Journal of Marriage and the Family* 52:993–1014.

Treas, J.; and Bengtson, V. L. (1987). "Family in Later Years." In *Handbook on Marriage and the Family*, ed. M. Sussman and S. Steinmetz. New York: Plenum.

Uhlenberg, P. (1980). "Death and the Family." *Journal of Family History* 5:313–320.

Watkins, S. C.; Menken, J. A.; and Bongaarts, J. (1987). "Demographic Foundations of Family Change." *American Sociological Review* 52:346–358.

White, M. J., and Tsui, A. O. (1986). "A Panel Study of Family-Level Structural Change." *Journal of Marriage and the Family* 48:435–446.

Barbara A. Hirshorn

INTERMARRIAGE

Contrary to the old saying, love is not blind. It is possible to predict fairly accurately the kind of person one will marry. In the United States, marriage usually occurs between individuals who resemble each other in social class, education, religion, and in various personal traits. An exception to these patterns is what is called intermarriage. These are unions between people with different cultural backgrounds. Because marriages involving religious, national, or ethnic differences have received extensive attention, this entry will center on interracial marriages and the children of these marriages.

Historically, interracial marriage has received mixed reactions. There were antimiscegenation laws in the United States until 1967, when they were overturned by the Supreme Court. Although these unions have been legalized, they are still viewed as unacceptable by most Americans. In fact, it was not until 1992 that a Gallup Poll reported for the first time that a slight majority of Americans said they were against antimiscegenation laws (Gallup 1993).

Although interracial marriage is a popular topic of discussion, these relationships remain clouded in myth. According to the U.S. Bureau of the Census, there were more than 310,000 interracial unions in 1970, climbing to almost 651,000 in 1980 and 964,000 in 1990. Cross-racial joinings remain a small segment of the U.S. population (1.8 percent of all marriages in 1990). Between 1960 and 1990, 74 percent of interracial marriages were between whites and non-African Americans. During that same time period, African-American–white unions were only 24 percent of all interracial marriages, peaking at 26 percent in 1980. Even then, only about 2.2 percent of all marriages involving African Americans were interracial (U.S. Bureau of the Census 1989, 1990).

According to the 1990 census, 71 percent of the African-American–white unions involved an African-American man and a white woman; among whites, men were more likely than women to intermarry, 497,000 versus 434,000 (U.S. Bureau of the Census 1990). In contrast, Asian-American, Native-American, and Hispanic-American women are the prime candidates for interracial marriage. According to the 1980 census, the interracial marriage rate averaged 25 percent among Asians and America; Japanese Americans were most likely to marry outside their group (34%), followed by Korean Americans (32%) and Filipino Americans (30%) (Kitano et al. 1984). Generally, when Asian Americans marry out of their ethnic groups, they do so first with Hawaiians or whites; individuals from a different Asian background are a distant third (Lee and Yamanaka 1990).

Data on Hispanic and Native-American intermarriage are unclear. The 1970 census revealed that 33 percent of married Native-American males had white wives, and 35 percent of married Native-American women had white husbands (Passel 1976). Data from the 1976 Survey of Income and Education showed 40 percent of married Native-American men between the ages of twenty-four and fifty-four had white wives (Sandefur and Scott 1983). Among Mexican Americans in California, studies reveal that more than half their marriages were interracial (Moore and Pachon 1985). Census data show that for Hispanics intermarriage occurs most often with Filipino Americans, African Americans, and whites (Lee and Yamanaka 1990).

Because interracial marriage is unusual, many commentators have asked why they occur at all. There are three sets of reasons offered: social-psychological, normative, and structural.

Social-Psychological Factors

Social-psychological approaches explore motives that are typically described as involving peculiar psychological reasoning. For example, the frequent occurrence of unions between Asian females and American males is often explained by male attraction to the stereotype of compliant and submissive Asian females; these qualities clash with the independent and dominant picture offered of American women (Thornton 1983).

Using exchange theory, the role of physical appearance can help explain the formation of African-American–white relationships. Exchange theory suggests that partners must offer something of value in trade for a relationship. Typically, money or social status is the object of exchange. Thus, in a racially prejudiced society, African Americans must offer, according to exchange theory, more to whites than vice versa to take part in interracial relationships. In one study, impartial judges rated twenty interracial couples in terms of physical attractiveness, and the couples involved, in turn, rated themselves and each other. The African Americans were predicted to exceed their white partners in ratings of physical attractiveness. It was found that the couples did not think this was the case while the judges did (Murstein, Merighi, and Malloy 1989).

Other work is concerned with clinical settings and highlights troubled individuals. John Brown (1987) cautioned counselors that African-American–white couples were "at risk populations." While nonclinical, studies of Asian-American–white marriages find parallel results. Gyung Jeong and Walter Schumm (1990) found that the time since the last visit to Korea and the level of education were the only two factors associated with marital satisfaction for Korean-American wives.

There has also been work on the perceptions of interracial marriages. One study found sociality, sex, and race unrelated to college students' attitudes about them; however, tolerance scores were associated with disapproval of white–Iranian and African-American–white unions (Sones and Holston 1988). Other work on attitudes presents inconsistent results. African-American women are found to be less favorable than white women toward interracial marriages but more favorable toward interracial dating (Paset and Taylor 1991; Korolewicz and Korolewicz 1985).

Normative Factors

At the normative level, research highlights the social acceptance of minorities by the wider society, often measured by levels of assimilation. In this view, the United States is a melting pot where children of immigrants become in time socially, culturally, and economically integrated. While opportunities for immigrants are understood to be limited, their descendants, having become acculturated, achieve upward mobility. Intermarriage is a function of declining socioeconomic and cultural differences between whites and minorities.

In this perspective, researchers are interested in comparing how much like the mainstream these alternative marriages are. In this light, work has focused on the sex of the partners, the generation of residence in America among racial minorities, previous marital status, and the age of the spouses.

A key ingredient to the idea of assimilation is length of residence, which is an important concern to Asian Americans and Hispanics, because most of them arrived in the United States after 1970. The data support an association between intermarriage and generational status, although the pattern is not uniform. Among Asians in the United States, the native-born are more prone to intermarriage than are recent immigrants (Wong 1989; Lee and Yamanaka 1990; Sung 1990). Japanese women in interracial marriages are more likely foreign-born (Lee and Yamanaka 1990). Harry Kitano and his colleagues (1984) found in Los Angeles County that most outmarriages occurred after the first generation of immigration. Morrison Wong (1989) found a peculiar pattern of post-1965 Chinese immigrants being more involved in interracial marriage than pre-1965 immigrants. Foreign-born Hispanics and blacks are more likely than native compatriots to marry out of the group (Macpherson and Stewart 1992).

There are also norms concerning the appropriate age at marriage, and again, the role of age in the process differs by group. Younger women are reported to be among those most likely to intermarry (Macpherson and Stewart 1992). Among Asians in the United States, U.S.-born Japanese and foreign-born Vietnamese women below age thirty-five were most likely to be in an interracial union in 1980. A similar pattern is evident among intermarried Asian-American men, who are generally younger when they marry (Lee and Yamanaka 1990). Betty Lee Sung (1990) described older Chinese Americans as more likely to intermarry.

The American norm is that couples will be similar in age, with males typically slightly older. Analysis of census data revealed that intermarried African Americans (both male and female) were either significantly older or much younger in age than their spouses (Tucker and Mitchell-Kernan 1990). Using exchange theory, the authors of one study explored whether intermarried Latinos failed to follow the age norm of slightly older male–younger female. They found that Mexican-American females were more likely to be much younger than their white husbands (Kearl and Murguia 1985). Couples entering interracial marriages are likely to have been previously married, a pattern that might explain findings that some groups of intermarrieds are older than the norm (Tucker and Mitchell-Kernan 1990).

Structural Factors

Certain factors outside the person provide boundaries to experience. How much contact there is with other racial groups depends on geographic location, socioeconomic similarities, and levels of discrimination. If, because of isolation or discrimination, members of various groups are unlikely to interact, intermarriage is rare. Certain regions—for example, the South—exert greater control over mate selection than do others (Tucker and Mitchell-Kernan 1990). These demographic factors are of concern to those who use structural approaches to study interracial marriage.

Peter Blau (1977) developed a theory suggesting that the chance of interracial marriages occurring depends mostly on the extent of group intersections. In this theory, group size is the primary determinant of intergroup relations. The probability that intermarriage will occur, in part, depends on having available partners from another group, which is in turn determined by that group's relative size. Members of large groups can find partners from within, while members of small groups must look elsewhere.

The theory also suggests that if two groups are isolated from each other, chance meetings are unlikely and intermarriage rates will be low. With little chance of meeting, fortuitous encounters are slim, as is the potential for establishing more meaningful bonds. High levels of income inequality also dampen group blending, while an imbalanced sex ratio encourages contact.

Structural studies tend to support these propositions. Intermarriage rates are much higher for those Asian Americans living outside areas of large Asian concentration (Wong 1989; Sung 1990; Lee and Yamanaka 1990). In contrast, Native-American–white marriages occur more often in states with large Native-American populations (Sandefur and McKinnell 1986).

However, region is not the complete explanation of intermarriage patterns. One study found that African-American–white unions occurred most often in the West (Macpherson and Stewart 1992). That attitudes about interracial contact and improvement of African-American conditions are more favorable toward African Americans in the West than elsewhere could explain this pattern (Campbell 1971). However, intermarried couples did not grow up there; many moved to the West from the North or another country. This suggests that racially tolerant environments are insufficient explanation for higher rates of intermarriage. A better understanding of the role society plays in constraining "unconventional" marriages is needed (Tucker and Mitchell-Kernan 1990).

Education is another structural factor deemed important in explaining the incidence of interracial marriage in the United States. The couples typically are well educated (Macpherson and Stewart 1992; Sung 1990; Wong 1989; Sandefur and McKinnell 1986), especially young African-American men in interracial marriages (Tucker and Mitchell-Kernan 1990). However, not all interracial couples are equally well educated. Women in African-American–white interracial marriages, in general, have significantly higher levels of education than women in Native-American–white unions (Sandefur and McKinnell 1986).

The normal pattern is for people of similar social class, usually measured by occupation and income, to marry. For Asian Americans, there are no simple relationships between social class and intermarriage. Among Asian-American women who intermarry, only Chinese, foreign-born Indian, and U.S.-born Koreans earn higher incomes than their intramarried counterparts. Intermarried men were found in the top category of administrative and professional occupations. Only U.S.-born Chinese and Indians and foreign-born Japanese and Vietnamese did not follow this pattern (Lee and Yamanaka 1990; Wong 1989). Native Americans who marry other Native Americans are poorer than those married interracially (Sandefur and McKinnell 1986). Work outside the home may be related to the higher social class standing found among intermarried couples. Women in African-American–white unions are more likely to be in the work force than are intramarried women (Macpherson and Stewart 1992).

Research provides a limited understanding of interracial marriage. Most researchers are interested in explaining deviations from normal patterns, typically depicted as personal or cultural shortcomings in these relationships. Movement toward the "white" pattern is expected as the only appropriate option. There are, nevertheless, other options. Studies of Mexican-American–white intermarriage suggest that marital quality need not be based on movement toward mainstream culture and does not automatically result in assimilation into that mainstream culture (Fernandez and Holscher 1983). Fixating on one kind of experience excludes other equally viable realities. Research must take a broader view of these relationships than can be gleaned by a focus on one model of family life or highlighting these unions as at-risk populations. The most important direction for future work is to develop a more complex description of the varieties of patterns among such a diverse population. Relating personal to structural factors would be an especially fruitful, although difficult, task.

Multiracial People

Although the number of interracial unions is easier to estimate than is the number of interracial children, it is calculated that approximately 2 million children live in multiracial households (Chew et al. 1989). They live primarily in California, Texas, New York, Illinois, Washington, and Hawaii. Most live in Asian–white or Hispanic–white households.

Throughout American history, the presence of offspring from interracial unions has created dilemmas for the racial system. Popular definitions of race are dichotomous, suggesting "either/or," bipolar schemes that clearly delineate people into mutually exclusive categories (Daniel 1992). Historically, the term "mixed race" referred to people of black–white mixture who were viewed as part of a two-tiered race system: whites and blacks, with racially mixed people considered to be superior blacks. Revisionist histories on race relations highlight the nature of racial boundaries and clearly show that they are at best arbitrary (Fernandez 1992).

This bimodal thinking about race remains a legacy found in research on identity and multiracial people. Monoracial identification and social belonging cast multiracial people as deviant, with intrinsically problematic identities. As the basis for many social-psychological theories on multiracial people, Maria Root (1992) notes that these models present racial boundaries as rigid. For example, monoracial and monocultural perspectives provide the foundation for models of assimilation and acculturation (Phinney 1990). These theories argue that people should identify with one group. Attempts among multiracial people to move back and forth between color lines are typically viewed in a pejorative manner rather than as a creative strategy in coping with the artificial boundaries created by dichotomous thinking on race (Daniel 1992).

Thus, the debate on multiracial people revolves around whether they should maintain single-heritage or multiple-heritage identities. Proponents of single-heritage identity view multiple identity as untenable, while defenders of multiple-heritage identity suggest that it is no less viable than any other self-image. Emerging work suggests that individuals can have multiple fluid identities with various groups. This may be especially true among minority–minority mixtures such as Asian-American–African-American and Native-American–African-American. Three types of conclusions are typical of this research area: Multiple identities are problematic, resemble others, or are a unique phenomenon.

The problematic approach. This perspective assumes that multiracial adolescents face special problems and therefore are an at-risk group. The children examined are typically patients of mental-health professionals or are involved with social service agencies (Gibbs and Moskowitz-Sweet 1991; McKelvey, Mao, and Webb 1993). Biracial children in the child welfare system were found to receive no special treatment even though they encountered racism from extended families and had mothers who expressed mixed feelings about them (Folaron and Hess 1993).

The equivalent-pattern approach. The theme for this research tradition is that identity development is similar for all populations; multiracials are, hence, not at-risk populations. Kwai Grove (1991) compared the identity of mixed Asian-American–white students with their Asian-American and white counterparts. All identity statuses were similar. The one difference was that the multiracials saw race as less important than did Asian-American respondents.

There were other slight differences between monoracial and biracial children. Many biracials struggle with how to follow two sets of cultural rules and with where they fit in racially. However, the nature of this conflict is not homogeneous. Ronald Johnson and Craig Nagoshi (1986) found that biracial males revealed higher socially desirable traits than monoracial males; biracial females were more extroverted than their monoracial counterparts.

For some, the context of development is important (Jacobs 1992). Ana Cauce and her colleagues (1992) found in adolescent self-reports that biracials did not differ from control groups on aspects of family and peer relations (support, trust, alienation), life stress, psychology distress, or self-worth. They differed in that they had less restrictive mothers. Jewelle Gibbs and Alice Hines (1992) found biracial children holding positive identities were most likely from intact upper-class families, attending integrated schools and living in integrated neighborhoods. Those with less positive identities were more likely from single-parent families and lacked contact with the noncustodial parent's family and friends.

The variant approach. Multiracial researchers have provided an important impetus for the emergence of the variant view. This approach presumes that the identities/perspectives developed from multiracials' experiences are unique and no less intrinsically valid than those found in other populations. Cookie Stephan and Walter Stephan (1989, 1991) found that identification for biracials is highly subjective, with people of similar biological heritage proclaiming different identities, and that most biracials identified with several groups and yet did not suffer ill effects. While the extent of the exposure to their heritages is important in the nature of identification, it was not a necessary and sufficient condition for identification. The Stephans' work describes bicultural socialization generally leading to intergroup tolerance, language facility, enjoyment of cultures of minority groups, and better relationships with single-heritage groups than the latter hold with each other. Consistent with this research is the work of Christine Kerwin and her colleagues (1993). They found that biracial children were sensitive to both cultures and parents, instead of being marginal. They also found that parents who saw the children as multiracial were secure in their own identities.

Other work suggests that even while the stages of development may resemble that of other adolescents, the final stage is unique (Kich 1992). Some work in this vein describes stages of development based on models produced for African-American adolescents (Poston 1990). The tendency to use models from one group's experience and transfer them for use for another group has drawn criticism in other contexts.

Conclusion

While intermarriage is a popular topic of public debate, research on the subject is all too rare. Past efforts were dominated by a focus on African-American–white families and views of interracial families and people as marginal. While this legacy has continued, there are also counterbalancing perspectives, with a particularly notable focus on how multiracial status can be mentally healthy. In this way, interracial research remains dominated by political agendas. Thus, mundane aspects of interracial people's lives, such as the dynamics of normal family life, peer pressure, and how this group feels about topics other than race, are as yet unexplored issues.

Work is beginning on previously unexamined areas. Divorce, custody, and foster parenting have come under focus. Researchers are exploring how ideas about race and sex are linked to perspectives on interracial relationships and the nature of minority–minority intermarriages. However, a lack of access to numbers of interracial families will severely hamper this research effort. Popular sources for study are still college students and mental-health clients; these are hardly average citizens. Multiracial people are rarely in identifiable areas, and consequently, it is difficult to gather information from enough of this population to say anything that would be representative.

Clearly, the phenomenon of intermarriage will grow in importance and will influence society by provoking questions about the nature of race and race relations.

(*See also:* Ethnicity; Exchange Theory; Mate Selection; Personal Relationships)

BIBLIOGRAPHY

Blau, P. (1977). *Inequality and Heterogeneity.* New York: Free Press.

Brown, J. (1987). "Casework Contacts with Black–White Couples." *Social Casework* 68:24–29.

Campbell, A. (1971). *White Attitudes Toward Black People.* Ann Arbor: Institute for Social Research, University of Michigan.

Cauce, A.; Hiraga, Y.; Mason, C.; Aguilar, T.; Ordonez, N.; and Gonzales, N. (1992). "Between a Rock and a Hard Place: Social Adjustment of Biracial Youth." In *Racially Mixed People in America*, ed. M. Root. Newbury Park, CA: Sage Publications.

Chew, K.; Eggebeen, D.; and Uhlenberg, P. (1989). "American Children in Multiracial Households." *Sociological Perspectives* 32:65–85.

Daniel, G. (1992). "Passers and Pluralists: Subverting the Racial Divide." In *Racially Mixed People in America*, ed. M. Root. Newbury Park, CA: Sage Publications.

Fernandez, C. (1992). "La Raza and the Melting Pot: A Comparative Look at Multiethnicity." In *Racially Mixed People in America*, ed. M. Root. Newbury Park, CA: Sage Publications.

Fernandez, C., and Holscher, L. (1983). "Chicano–Anglo Intermarriage in Arizona, 1960–1980: An Exploratory Study of Eight Counties." *Hispanic Journal of Behavioral Sciences* 5:291–304.

Folaron, G., and Hess, P. (1993). "Placement Considerations for Children of Mixed African-American and Caucasian Parentage." *Child Welfare* 72:113–125.

Gallup, G. (1993). *The Gallup Poll: Public Opinion, 1992.* Wilmington, DE: Scholarly Resources.

Gibbs, J., and Hines, A. (1992). "Negotiating Ethnic Identity: Issues for Black–White Biracial Adolescents." In *Racially Mixed People in America*, ed. M. Root. Newbury Park, CA: Sage Publications.

Gibbs, J., and Moskowitz-Sweet, G. (1991). "Clinical and Cultural Issues in the Treatment of Biracial and Bicultural Adolescents." *Families in Society* (December):579–592.

Grove, K. (1991). "Identity Development in Interracial, Asian/White Late Adolescents: Must It Be So Problematic?" *Journal of Youth and Adolescence* 20:617–628.

Jacobs, J. (1992). "Identity Development in Biracial Children." In *Racially Mixed People in America*, ed. M. Root. Newbury Park, CA: Sage Publications.

Jeong, G., and Schumm, W. (1990). "Family Satisfaction in Korean/American Marriages: An Exploratory Study of the Perceptions of Korean Wives." *Journal of Comparative Family Studies* 21:325–336.

Johnson, R., and Nagoshi, C. (1986). "The Adjustment of Offspring of Within-Group and Interracial/Intercultural Marriages: A Comparison of Personality Factor Scores." *Journal of Marriage and the Family* 48:279–284.

Kearl, M., and Murguia, E. (1985). "Age Difference of Spouses in Mexican-American Intermarriage: Exploring the Cost of Minority Assimilation." *Social Science Quarterly* 66:453–460.

Kerwin, C.; Ponterotto, J.; Jackson, B.; and Harris, A. (1993). "Racial Identity in Biracial Children: A Qualitative Investigation." *Journal of Counseling Psychology* 40:221–231.

Kich, G. (1992). "The Developmental Process of Asserting a Biracial, Bicultural Identity." In *Racially Mixed People in America*, ed. M. Root. Newbury Park, CA: Sage Publications.

Kitano, H.; Yeung, W.-T.; Chai, L.; and Hatanaka, H. (1984). "Asian-American Interracial Marriage." *Journal of Marriage and the Family* 46:179–190.

Korolewicz, M., and Korolewicz, A. (1985). "Effects of Sex and Race on Interracial Dating Preferences." *Psychological Report* 57:1291–1296.

Lee, S., and Yamanaka, K. (1990). "Patterns of Asian-American Intermarriage and Marital Assimilation." *Journal of Comparative Family Studies* 21:287–305.

Lyles, M.; Yancey, A.; Grace, C.; and Carter, J. (1985). "Racial Identity and Self-Esteem: Problems Peculiar to Biracial Children." *Journal of the American Academy of Child and Adolescent Psychiatry* 24:150–153.

McKelvey, R.; Mao, A.; and Webb, J. (1993). "Premigratory Expectations and Mental Health Symptomology in a Group of Vietnamese Amerasian Youth." *Journal of the Academy of Child and Adolescent Psychiatry* 32:414–418.

Macpherson, D., and Stewart, J. (1992). "Racial Differences in Married Female Labor Force Participation Behavior: An Analysis Using Interracial Marriages." *Review of Black Political Economy* 21:59–68.

Moore, J., and Pachon, H. (1985). *Hispanics in the United States.* Englewood Cliffs, NJ: Prentice Hall.

Murstein, B.; Merighi, J.; and Malloy, T. (1989). "Physical Attractiveness and Exchange Theory in Interracial Dating." *Journal of Social Psychology* 129:325–334.

Paset, P., and Taylor, R. (1991). "Black and White Women's Attitudes Toward Interracial Marriage." *Psychological Reports* 69:753–754.

Passel, J. (1976). "Provisional Evaluation of the 1970 Census Count of American Indians." *Demography* 13:397–409.

Phinney, J. (1990). "Ethnic Identity in Adolescents and Adults: Review of Research." *Psychological Bulletin* 108:499–514.

Poston, W. C. (1990). "The Biracial Identity Development Model: A Needed Addition." *Journal of Counseling and Development* 69:152–155.

Root, M. (1992). "Back to the Drawing Board: Methodological Issues in Research on Multiracial People." In *Racially Mixed People in America*, ed. M. Root. Newbury Park, CA: Sage Publications.

Sandefur, G., and McKinnell, T. (1986). "American Indian Intermarriage." *Social Science Research* 15:347–371.

Sandefur, G., and Scott, W. (1993). "Minority Group Status and the Wages of Indian and Black Males." *Social Science Research* 12:44–68.

Scott, R. (1987). "Interracial Couples: Situational Factors in White Male Reactions." *Basic and Applied Social Psychology* 8:125–137.

Sones, D., and Holston, M. (1988). "Tolerance, Sociability, Sex, and Race: Correlates of Attitudes Toward Interracial Marriage." *Psychological Reports* 62:518.

South, S., and Messner, S. (1986). "Structural Determinants of Intergroup Association: Interracial Marriage and Crime." *American Journal of Sociology* 91:1409–1430.

Stephan, C. (1991). "Ethnic Identity Among Mixed-Heritage People in Hawaii." *Symbolic Interaction* 14:261–277.

Stephan, C., and Stephan, W. (1989). "After Intermarriage: Ethnic Identity Among Mixed-Heritage Japanese-Americans and Hispanics." *Journal of Marriage and the Family* 51:507–519.

Stephan, W., and Stephan, C. (1991). "Intermarriage: Effects on Personality, Adjustment, and Intergroup Relations in Two Samples of Students." *Journal of Marriage and the Family* 53:241–250.

Sung, B. L. (1990). "Chinese-American Intermarriage." *Journal of Comparative Family Studies* 21:337–352.

Thornton, M. C. (1983). "A Social History of a Multiethnic Identity: The Case of Black Japanese Americans." Ph.D. diss. Ann Arbor: University of Michigan.

Thornton, M. C. (1992). "The Quiet Immigration: Foreign Spouses of U.S. Citizens, 1945–1985." In *Racially Mixed People in America*, ed. M. Root. Newbury Park, CA: Sage Publications.

Tucker, M. B., and Mitchell-Kernan, C. (1990). "New Trends in Black American Interracial Marriage: The Social Structural Context." *Journal of Marriage and the Family* 52:209–218.

U.S. Bureau of the Census. (1989). *Statistical Abstract of the United States*, 109th edition. Washington, DC: U.S. Government Printing Office.

U.S. Bureau of the Census. (1990). "Household and Family Characteristics: March 1990 and 1989." *Current Population Reports*. Series P-20, no. 447. Washington, DC: U.S. Government Printing Office.

Wong, M. (1989). "A Look at Intermarriage Among the Chinese in the United States in 1980." *Sociological Perspectives* 32:87–107.

MICHAEL CHARLES THORNTON
SUZANNE WASON

INTIMACY

A growing body of evidence suggests that intimacy promotes human well-being, while its absence has deleterious effects. People who lack intimate relationships have higher mortality rates, more accidents, and higher risks for developing illnesses than those who have intimate relationships. People who lack intimate relationships also are more vulnerable to feelings of loneliness and more likely to develop symptoms of psychological disturbance.

Intimate relationships not only have directly beneficial effects, but also seem to buffer people from the pathogenic effects of stress. This buffering effect can be observed with a variety of stressors (e.g., births, illnesses, deaths) and with various stress-related outcomes (e.g., depression, anxiety, illness). People who have satisfying intimate relationships are less likely to experience the negative outcomes of stress than those who do not.

When close relationships function poorly, however, the partners seem to incur an increased risk of distress, illness, and poor adjustment. Poorly functioning relationships with parents, spouses, friends, and other peers have been associated with both short-term and long-term negative outcomes, such as poor self-efficacy, depression, and physical complaints.

As evidence of the beneficial effects of intimate relationships accumulates, scholars are perceiving the need for a deeper understanding of how these effects are realized. This deeper understanding requires that scholars first establish a clear conception of what intimacy entails. Second, it requires further exploration of how and under what circumstances intimate interactions create positive experiences for those who participate in them. Third, the successful functioning of intimate relationships needs to be understood better, and factors that contribute to successful relationships need to be identified. The issues addressed by research on intimate relationships thus far depend on the life stage and the type of relationship (friendship, marital relationship, parent–child relationship) being studied. Life stage and relationship type, along with individual traits, individual life histories, gender, and other subgroup norms, are contextual factors that shape people's experiences of intimacy within their interactions and relationships. A growing appreciation for the importance of context is becoming apparent in the research on intimacy.

Conceptions of Intimacy

Conceptions of intimacy usually address one or more of three phenomena: (1) intimate interactions, (2) intimate experiences, and (3) intimate relationships. Intimate interactions are communicative exchanges between people. In line with the etymological origins of the word "intimacy," most definitions of intimate interaction converge on a notion of sharing the personal (innermost, private) aspects of the self. Sharing can include both verbal and nonverbal behaviors. Verbal sharing can involve self-disclosure of personal facts, opinions, and beliefs. It can also include the verbalization of feeling and emotion. Nonverbal sharing can include a shared meaningful glance, affectionate touching, shared emotional expressions, and sexual activity. Sharing the personal means sharing vulnerable aspects of the self.

Intimate relationships, in contrast, "impl[y] a series of interactions between two individuals known to each other. . . . [Within a relationship, an] interaction is affected by past interactions [and] is likely to influence future ones" (Hinde 1981, p. 2). Intimate experiences are the feelings and thoughts people have during and as a result of their intimate interactions.

Conceptions of intimate interactions have historically emphasized intimate behavior. Self-disclosure, the verbal sharing of personal, private information about oneself to another, has long been a central focus of research on intimate interaction. Verbal responsiveness has also been of interest to those studying intimate interactions. Verbal responsiveness says to one's interaction partner that one is "interested in an understanding of that communication" (Miller and Berg 1984, p. 193).

Intimate behavior can be nonverbal as well as verbal. Intimate nonverbal behavior includes maintaining forward-leaning eye contact, and close physical proximity during interaction. These behaviors are critical to people's perceptions of which interactions are intimate (Burgoon et al. 1991).

Most conceptions of intimate interactions also include intimate experience. Karen Prager (1995) distinguishes an affective and a cognitive/perceptual component of intimate experience. The affective component consists of each individual's involvement or interest in the interaction, and his or her positive feelings about the partner and the interaction. Conversations that generate negative affect between the partners are not usually considered intimate (Derlega and Chaikin 1975). The cognitive/perceptual component refers to the partners' perceptions that they have understood one another or that they have been understood. A similar though not identical concept is validation (Sullivan 1953).

Some theorists have emphasized the role of affect in intimate experience. Robert J. Sternberg (1988) viewed emotional intensity as a critical part of intimate experience. He argued that intimate interactions within recently established relationships are likely to be the most emotionally intense because of uncertainty and novelty. As partners get to know and become increasingly predictable to one another, the emotional intensity of their interactions may wane (Berscheid 1983). Because intense emotion is central to intimate experience, longtime relationship partners may come to believe that they are not as "intimate" as they once were.

Gordon J. Chelune, Joan T. Robison, and Martin J. Kommor (1984) have emphasized the cognitive aspects of intimate interaction. They suggest that intimate experience arises from the meaningfulness of intimate interaction, which in turn facilitates mutual understanding between partners. They suggest further that the repetition of intimate interactions over time creates in partners an expectation of rewarding interaction in the future. It also creates an expanding base of mutual knowledge. These likely become important ingredients in intimate relationships.

Most conceptions of intimacy focus on intimate relationships. An intimate relationship is, minimally, one in which intimate interactions occur on a frequent (or at least regular) basis; partners have a history of repeated intimate interactions, and each partner in the relationship can count on and expect intimate interactions with the other at acceptable intervals. Harry T. Reis and Phillip R. Shaver (1988) have noted that theorists rarely imply so narrow a definition of intimate relationships, however. Rather, relational conceptions of intimacy often attempt to capture the complexity of intimate relating over time. Those who take this approach offer comprehensive descriptions of intimate relationships via multidimensional models. Mark Schaefer and David Olson (1981) suggested that partners in intimate relationships could share seven kinds of intimacy: emotional, social, intellectual, sexual, recreational, spiritual, and aesthetic.

Affectively oriented conceptions define intimate relationships according to the feelings partners have about one another within the relationship. In one example, intimate relationships are defined by the emotional accessibility, naturalness, and nonpossessiveness the partners feel (Dahms 1972). In another definition, a relationship is intimate if the partners feel they can confide in each other (O'Connor 1992).

Steve Duck (1994) has suggested that a mutual striving for meaningfulness is the defining component of intimate relationships. In his view, people seek intimate interactions and relationships to develop "shared symbolic universes." He argues that because the creation of meaning from perception is so basic to human activity, the realization that another shares that meaning becomes the cornerstone of the relationship's foundation. Relationships are intimate when partners engage in the striving for meaningfulness together.

Intimate Interactions and Experiences

It is likely that intimate relationships exert beneficial effects on the partners' health because intimate partners confide in each other. Investigations into the association between intimate interactions and intimate experiences may reveal how intimate interactions exert their propitious effects. Research has examined the impact of intimate behavior on experiences such as attraction, liking, mood, and enjoyment of the interaction (e.g., Kleinke 1986). Each of these seems directly enhanced by and increases the likelihood of verbally intimate interaction. However, the positive effects of intimate relating should always be viewed in context. The effect of intimate behavior in one setting may be quite different from its effect in another. For example, confiding might be welcome from a friend over dinner but not from a stranger on an airplane. Increasingly, scholars wish to learn under what conditions people are likely to engage in intimate interactions (Snell 1989) and under what conditions will intimate behavior lead to intimate experiences (Lazowski and Anderson 1990).

Nonverbal intimacy. Nonverbal intimate behavior (i.e., immediacy behavior) is closely linked to intimate experience. Behaviors such as mutual gazing and forward leaning have been associated with positive affect, friendship, and romantic involvement.

Touch is especially likely to be perceived as intimate. Stanley E. Jones and Elaine Yarbrough (1985) identified three types of touch that nearly always elicited intimate experience in one sample of college students. Inclusion touches, such as legs, knees, or shoulders that touched, conveyed tactile statements of togetherness. Sexual touches involved extended holding and caressing. Affectionate touches covered the widest range of touches and were neither inclusion nor sexual touches.

Contextual factors seem to modify the association between nonverbal intimate behavior and experiences of intimacy. Most scholarly work in this area has concentrated on the immediate context (i.e., contextual factors close in time and space to the interaction itself). For example, the seating arrangement in a room can be conducive (or not) to intimate interaction (Argyle and Dean 1965). When seating is moderately close (neither too close nor too far), strangers are most likely to exhibit immediacy behaviors and talk about more personal topics. The attractiveness of the interaction partner may also modify the relationship between intimate behavior and experience. For example, the touches of attractive people seem to convey more intimacy than those of unattractive people. Other contextual factors that modify the impact of intimate nonverbal behavior include the nature of the occasion, the gender composition of the dyad, and dyad partners' relationship to one another.

More distal or remote contextual factors (i.e., those more distant in time and space from the interaction) can also modify associations between nonverbal intimate behavior and intimate experience. Sociocultural norms exemplify these contextual factors. Peter A. Andersen (1993) notes that the amount of eye contact required to convey attentiveness varies from culture to culture. The same amount of eye contact can facilitate intimate experience with one partner yet be perceived as intrusive and/or rude to another. Groups also can have different norms for nonverbal intimacy and, thus, alter its impact among members of the group. For example, in the United States, boys' and girls' same-sex peer groups have different norms regarding how much intimate contact is appropriate for friends. Based on a review of the literature, Eleanor E. Maccoby (1990) described the norms of boys' groups as discouraging the communication of vulnerability, while the norms of girls' groups encouraged such communication. Deborah Tannen's (1990) research supported Maccoby's contention. Tannen found that boys often trivialized or joked about personal matters, while girls talked about them more earnestly. Further, girls maintained more eye contact, faced one another more, and sat closer together than boys did.

Verbal intimacy. Self-disclosure has received the most attention in research on verbal intimacy. When interaction participants reveal vulnerable aspects of themselves through self-disclosure, and when they express feelings about what they have disclosed, their interaction partners perceive their disclosures to be more personal. Self-disclosure may also be experienced as more intimate when it addresses issues that are immediate to the time and place of the interaction and salient to the discloser and recipient.

Contextual factors modify the relationship between self-disclosure and intimate experience. The most powerful contextual influence on self-disclosure is, most likely, the type of relationship shared by the partners. Research has reliably shown that higher levels of both breadth and personalness of information are disclosed when partners are closer friends or romantic partners rather than simply acquaintances (Miller 1990). People are also more expressive of their emotions with close friends than with casual friends or acquaintances. The presence of confiding interactions has been found to most distinguish close relationships from more casual ones.

Intimacy in interactions between close friends is observable in other ways as well. Relative to casual friends, close friends display more nonverbal involvement when conversing, are more deliberate in arranging to have conversations with one another, and seek more exclusivity and privacy when they do converse. Beginning in adolescence, interactions between close friends are experienced as more beneficial and enjoyable than other interactions. They are more likely to be described as emotionally supportive and meaningful than interactions with casual friends.

People's personality characteristics are part of the context that affects whether people will engage in intimate behavior. There is evidence that individual differences in intimacy motivation predict people's behavior when opportunities for intimate interaction arise. Dan P. McAdams (1982) proposed that people who desire and seek out opportunities for intimate interaction with others would, when given the opportunity to tell an imaginative story, imbue it with intimacy-related themes. Both sets of behavior, in his view, were manifestations of an underlying intimacy motivation. Research has largely upheld this notion. For example, college students who were high in intimacy motivation (i.e., whose imaginative stories contained intimacy-related themes) encouraged more reciprocal spontaneous dialogue in a group setting. In addition, they were more likely to engage in self-disclosure and responsive listening than those who were lower in intimacy motivation.

The gender of interaction participants is a widely studied contextual factor. Kathryn Dindia and Mike Allen (1992) concluded that most research shows females disclose more personal information to others than males do. Efforts to explain sex differences have mostly focused on gender-related individual differences, with mixed results. Researchers need to move beyond the study of gender-related individual differences and explore gender-specific pressures that prevail within interactions themselves (Geis 1993).

Along those lines, some research suggests that intimate interactions between same-sex friends must operate within the intimacy norms of the larger same-sex peer groups. For example, it is within the context of same-sex friendships that females most consistently report sharing more personal, private disclosures than males, and doing so more frequently. In contrast, male and female partners in heterosexual romantic relationships report similar patterns of self-disclosure. Perhaps heterosexual relationships provide boys and men with an opportunity to share their vulnerabilities without risking the ridicule and rejection that their same-sex peers are likely to visit upon them. Individual differences may, however, interact with situational factors. Androgynous adolescent boys (i.e., who have as many feminine as masculine traits) may have intimate interactions with their same-sex friends that are similar to girls' interactions.

Intimate Relationships

Because most of the research on intimate relationships addresses adolescence, early adulthood, and (to a lesser extent) middle adulthood, this review draws principally from that literature. While the literature on other life stages examines important aspects of intimate relationships that have implications for intimacy (e.g., attachment, social support, and companionship), intimacy has rarely been mentioned.

The literature on intimate relationships is also largely confined to certain relationship types. Discussions of friendship and marital relationships frequently consider the importance of intimacy. There is little or no mention of intimacy in the literature on parent–child relationships, however, despite evidence that parents are children's most frequent conversation partners before adolescence. The systematic study of intimacy in lesbian and gay relationships (of any type) is also in its infancy.

Friendship. Intimacy becomes an increasingly important aspect of friendship as children get older. Children mention intimacy as an important aspect of their friendships, beginning in preadolescence. For adolescents, the ability to share one's personal thoughts and feelings is a top priority in choosing a friend. In fact, an increase in the frequency of open, frank discussions of private concerns between friends is observable between the middle-childhood and adolescent stages.

At each life stage, intimate friendships can assist individuals in their efforts to address the normative issues and concerns of that life stage. Adolescents may experience their intimate friendships as havens from pressures to conform to the peer group. With friends, adolescents can just be themselves. For young adults, intimate interactions with friends may serve an important self-clarifying function. Young friends can help one another to formulate the goals, values, and ideals that will become the foundation of their new adult identities. Older adults look to intimate friends for emotional support and validation following the death of a spouse. Reminiscences shared by longtime friends may assist older adults with their efforts to develop a sense of integrity.

The middle adult years, in contrast, seem to witness decreases in contact between intimate friends. In the United States, men are especially likely to report a lack of intimate friendship. A combination of extensive work and family obligations and male sex-role restrictions may combine to decrease men's opportunities for building and maintaining intimate friendships during the middle years. This decline in friendship intimacy is not as pronounced for women.

Marriage. Marital relationships have been the focus of most research dealing with the processes that contribute to satisfying intimate relationships. Perhaps this is because marriage is the centerpiece of the intimate relationship network for most adults in the United States (O'Connor 1992) and is a major source of stability (or lack thereof) for a couple's children.

Although marriage is an important source of intimate contact, marital intimacy tends to decline over time. Both husbands and wives report a drop in the pleasing things their partners do for them, in the time they spend on joint leisure, in their sexual activity, and in their expressions of affection.

Frequent (or at least regular) intimate contact is associated with marital satisfaction. Conversely, disagreement about how much intimate contact is desirable in the marriage produces dissatisfaction. It may also fuel discordant, dysfunctional interaction and increase the likelihood that couples will seek marital therapy.

Marital partners probably have an easier time establishing a mutually satisfying pattern of intimate relating when they have compatible intimacy needs and preferences. It is unlikely, however, that difficulties with intimacy are due solely to partners entering the marriage with incompatibilities between traitlike needs for intimacy. In addition, partners' negotiations about how much intimate contact they share may intensify apparent incompatibilities. Incompatibilities can appear to get worse because certain kinds of conflict negotiation strategies seem to create instead of solve problems.

It is reasonable to hypothesize that skillful negotiations can reduce conflict about intimacy in marriage. Some strategies for negotiating solutions to conflict are more likely to be associated with discordant, unsatisfying marriages. Conflicts about intimacy may be associated with a commonly observed dysfunctional communication pattern called rejection-intrusion or demand-withdraw. Demand-withdraw describes a pattern of marital interaction in which one spouse (most often the husband) withdraws from interaction and the other spouse (most often the wife) makes concerted efforts to engage the withdrawn spouse. The negative affect that this pattern of interaction generates likely contributes to problems with intimacy. While research suggests that more skillful negotiations would reduce intimacy-related conflict, this has yet to be determined.

Conclusion

A deeper understanding of the processes by which intimate relationships affect, for good or ill, the health and well-being of the individuals involved in them is needed. This understanding should come, in part, from further exploration of the processes by which dyadic intimate interactions result in intimate experiences for individuals. Intimate experiences may ultimately be linked to physiological processes that enhance immune functioning. Whether or not such links are identified, however, it seems likely that benefits can accrue to those whose intimate partners learn the skills involved in intimate interaction.

It is relatively well established that people who can form and maintain satisfying intimate relationships enjoy higher levels of well-being and fewer symptoms of stress-related illnesses. To the extent that research on intimate relationships explores the processes within intimate relationships that contribute to their success, practitioners should be better equipped to advise people in troubled relationships.

(*See also:* Attachment; Communication; Friendship; Gender; Love; Marital Quality; Personality Development; Personal Relationships; Self-Disclosure; Trust)

BIBLIOGRAPHY

Andersen, P. A. (1993). "Cognitive Schemata in Personal Relationships." In *Individuals in Relationships*, ed. S. Duck. Newbury Park, CA: Sage Publications.

Argyle, M., and Dean, J. (1965). "Eye Contact, Distance, and Affiliation." *Sociometry* 28:278–304.

Berscheid, E. (1983). "Emotion." In *Close Relationships: Development and Change*, ed. H. H. Kelley, E. Berscheid, A. Christensen, J. H. Harvey, T. L. Huston, G. Levinger, E. McClintock, L. A. Peplau, and D. R. Peterson. New York: W. H. Freeman.

Burgoon, J. K.; Buller, D. B.; Hale, J. L.; and deTurck, M. A. (1991). "Relational Messages Associated with Nonverbal Behaviors." *Human Communication Research* 10:351–378.

Chelune, G. J.; Robison, J. T.; and Krommor, M. J. (1984). "A Cognitive Interactional Model of Intimate Relationships." In *Communication, Intimacy, and Close Relationships*, ed. V. J. Derlega. Orlando, FL: Academic Press.

Dahms, A. M. (1972). *Emotional Intimacy*. Boulder, CO: Pruett.

Derlega, V. J., and Chaikin, A. L. (1975). *Sharing Intimacy*. Englewood Cliffs, NJ: Prentice Hall.

Derlega, V. J., and Grzelak, J. (1979). "Appropriateness of Self-Disclosure." In *Self-Disclosure: Origins, Patterns, and Implications of Openness in Interpersonal Relationships*, ed. G. J. Chelune. San Francisco: Jossey-Bass.

Dindia, K., and Allan, M. (1992). "Sex Differences in Self-Disclosure: A Meta-Analysis." *Psychological Bulletin* 112:106–124.

Duck, S. W. (1994). *Meaningful Relationships: Talking, Sense, and Relating*. Newbury Park, CA: Sage Publications.

Geis, F. L. (1993). "Self-Fulfilling Prophecies: A Social-Psychological View of Gender." In *The Psychology of Gender*, ed. A. E. Beall and R. J. Sternberg. New York: Guilford.

Hinde, R. A. (1981). "The Bases of a Science of Interpersonal Relationships." In *Personal Relationships*, ed. S. W. Duck and R. Gilmour. London: Academic Press.

Jones, S. E., and Yarbrough, E. (1985). "A Naturalistic Study of the Meanings of Touch." *Communication Monographs* 52:19–56.

Kleinke, C. L. (1986). "Gaze and Eye Contact: A Research Review." *Psychological Bulletin* 100:78–100.

Lazowski, L. E., and Anderson, S. M. (1990). "Self-Disclosure and Social Perceptions: Impact of Private, Negative, and Extreme Communications." *Journal of Social Behavior and Personality* 5:131–154.

Maccoby, E. E. (1990). "Gender and Relationships." *American Psychologist* 45:513–520.

McAdams, D. P. (1982). "Intimacy Motivation." In *Motivation and Society*, ed. A. Stewart. San Francisco: Jossey-Bass.

Miller, L. C. (1990). "Intimacy and Liking: Mutual Influence and the Role of Unique Relationships." *Journal of Personality and Social Psychology* 59:50–60.

Miller, L. C., and Berg, J. (1984). "Selectivity and Urgency in Interpersonal Exchange." In *Communication, Intimacy, and Close Relationships*, ed. V. J. Derlega. Orlando, FL: Academic Press.

O'Connor, P. (1992). *Friendships Between Women: A Critical Review.* New York: Guilford.

Prager, K. J.; Fuller, D. O.; and Gonzalez, A. S. (1989). "The Function of Self-Disclosure in Social Interaction." *Journal of Social Behavior and Personality* 4:563–580.

Prager, K. J. (1995). *Intimacy.* New York: Guilford.

Reis, H. T., and Shaver, P. (1988). "Intimacy as Interpersonal Process." In *Handbook of Personal Relationships: Theory, Relationships, and Interventions*, ed. S. Duck. New York: Wiley.

Shaefer, M., and Olson, D. (1981). "Assessing Intimacy: The Pair Inventory." *Journal of Marital and Family Therapy* 7:47–60.

Snell, W. E. (1989). "Willingness to Self-Disclose to Female and Male Friends as a Function of Social Anxiety and Gender." *Personality and Social Psychology Bulletin* 15:113–125.

Sternberg, R. J. (1988). "Triangulating Love." In *The Psychology of Love*, ed. R. J. Sternberg and M. L. Barnes. New Haven, CT: Yale University Press.

Sullivan, H. S. (1953). *The Interpersonal Theory of Psychiatry.* New York: W. W. Norton.

Tannen, D. (1990). "Gender Differences in Topical Coherence." *Discourse Processes* 13:73–90.

KAREN JEAN PRAGER

J

JEALOUSY

Often called the "green-eyed" monster, jealousy has been a literary theme for centuries. It was not until the 1970s that it became the focus of systematic social science research, however.

Most contemporary conceptualizations of jealousy focus on situational antecedents to define it. This makes it possible to distinguish jealousy from envy, since different situations evoke these two emotions. Jealousy is precipitated by a threat from an agent to a person's relationship with someone, whereas envy is a negative reaction that is precipitated when someone else has a relationship to a person or object (Bringle and Buunk 1985).

Distinguishing between jealousy and envy does not mean that they cannot occur in the same situation; they can. However, the overlapping occurrence of the two phenomena does not suggest that one can be reduced to the other.

Jealousy is best viewed as a compound emotion, resulting from the situational labeling of one or more of the primary emotions, such as fear or anger. Society teaches individuals to label the primary emotions they experience in specific situations that threaten significant relationships as jealousy. In other words, the primary emotion words such as "anger" and "fear" *describe* the emotional state, while the compound emotion word "jealousy" *explains* the emotional state (Hupka 1984).

Since individuals learn "explanations" during the socialization process, this conceptualization of jealousy assumes that jealousy is a social phenomenon. It is at least partially learned, and it is manifested in response to symbolic stimuli that have meaning to the individual. The social aspects of jealousy have been noted by a number of writers. Kingsley Davis (1936), who is among the most prominent, argues that a comprehensive conceptualization of jealousy must include the public or community element.

The distinction between primary emotions and the compound emotion of jealousy is illustrated by the following example of sexual jealousy. A husband confesses to his wife that he recently had a one-time sexual relationship with another woman while away from home on a trip. Depending on a variety of cultural, personal, and relational factors, the wife may experience either anger, fear, disgust, sadness, or a combination of such primary emotions. If the woman is typical of most individuals in Western society, she will interpret her husband's extramarital relationship as a threat to their marriage and will have learned that people experience jealousy in such situations. As a result, she will explain her anger, fear, and other primary emotions in terms of jealousy. Since extramarital sex is incompatible with many people's moral values, this example illustrates Eugene Mathes's (1991) point that the situations in which jealousy is experienced are determined by a person's beliefs about morality as well as by social expectations.

Jealousy is defined in a variety of ways in the literature. Gordon Clanton (1981) defines it as a protective reaction to a perceived threat to a valued relationship. Gerald W. McDonald (1982), taking a structural exchange perspective, views marital jealousy as the perceived threat of diminution or loss of the valued resources of the spouse. Robert Bringle and Bram Buunk (1985) define it as an aversive emotional reaction that occurs as the result of a partner's extradyadic relationship that is real, imagined, or considered likely to occur. Ira L. Reiss (1986) presents a sociological or group perspective by defining jealousy as a boundary-setting mechanism for what the group feels are important relationships. Finally, Gary L. Hansen (1991) expands upon Clanton's definition and views jealousy as a protective reaction to a perceived threat to a valued relationship, arising from a situation in which the partner's involvement with an activity and/or another person is contrary to the jealous person's definition of their relationship.

Dual-Factor Conceptualization

These definitions imply that two factors are necessary for a person to be jealous. First, the person must perceive his or her partner's actual or imagined involvement with an activity and/or another person as contrary to her or his definition of their relationship (Factor 1). Second, the person must perceive the relationship as valuable (Factor 2). Factor 1 acknowledges that how one subjectively defines a relationship is important in understanding jealousy. As Carolyn Ellis and Eugene Weinstein state (1986, p. 343), "Jealousy occurs when a third party threatens the area of identification that *specifically defines the relationship* [emphasis in original]." The partner's behavior referred to in Factor 1 need not be sexual. Jealousy can arise from one's partner's involvement with children, professional colleagues, or solitary activities if such behavior is contrary to the jealous person's definition of their relationship and if the relationship is valued. Factor 2, the importance of viewing the relationship as valuable, is demonstrated by the cross-cultural findings that the importance of marriage or the value society places on it is related to jealousy.

This conceptualization focuses on the social psychological and sociological aspects of jealousy. There are others. There is the psychoanalytic speculation that early sibling conflicts may increase the intensity of jealousy in adult romantic relationships (Freud 1955). There is also John Bowlby's (1969, 1973, 1980) attachment theory, which postulates that ill-formed or disrupted attachments with early caretakers often result in "anxious attachment." The anxiously attached person remains excessively sensitive to the possibility of separation or loss of love and is especially susceptible to adult jealousy. A study by Clanton and David J. Kosins (1991) designed to test these two perspectives found little support for them and concluded that a sociological view emphasizing jealousy's role as a protector of valued relationships is a theoretical framework with greater utility.

Types of Jealousy

Various attempts have been made to distinguish between different types of jealousy. One important distinction is between "normal" and "abnormal" jealousy (Pines 1992). Normal jealousy has its basis in a real threat to a person's relationship with another. Most "normal" people experience intense jealousy when a valued relationship is threatened. On the other hand, jealousy is abnormal in two circumstances. First, jealousy is abnormal when it is not related to a real threat to a valued relationship, but to some inner trigger of the jealous individual; such jealousy is also called "delusional" jealousy. Second, jealousy is abnormal when the response is dramatically exaggerated or violent.

A similar distinction is made by Gerrod W. Parrott (1991), who believes that the most important distinction concerns the nature of the threat to the relationship. Jealousy may occur when the threat is only suspected and its nature is unclear. On the other hand, it may occur when the threat is unambiguously real and its effects are known. When the threat is unclear or only suspected, the result is "suspicious" jealousy, and the predominant reactions concern fears and uncertainties. When the threat to the relationship is unambiguous and damaging, the result is fait accompli jealousy, and the reactions are to a threat that is an accomplished fact.

Finally, Gregory L. White and Paul E. Mullen (1989) differentiate three major classes of jealousy. "Symptomatic" jealousy is a consequence of a major mental illness such as paranoid disorder, schizophrenia, substance abuse, or organic brain disorder. Because of personality disorder or strong sensitizing experiences, some people are especially sensitive to self-esteem or relationship threat and experience "pathological" jealousy. "Normal" jealousy, on the other hand, occurs in people who are neither sensitized nor suffering from a major mental illness. These three classes of jealousy differ according to the relative influences of biology, personality, and relationship on the development of jealousy; in the jealous person's capacity for reality testing; and in suggested treatment approaches.

Correlates of Jealousy

Research has identified a number of factors associated with jealousy. While both females and males experience jealousy, there are differences in the ways they experience and react to it. Men are more reactive to sexual involvement or threats, while women are more distressed by emotional involvement, loss of time and attention, and the prospect of losing a primary relationship (Buss et al. 1992; Teismann and Mosher 1978). Women are more likely to try to change to please their partners to avoid the threat of another relationship, whereas men are more likely to seek solace or retribution in alternative relationships (White and Mullen 1989). In addition, women are more likely to test a relationship by deliberately attempting to make their partners jealous (Adams 1980).

Researchers have consistently found gender-role traditionalism to be related positively to jealousy for one or both sexes. The division of labor in traditional gender roles may foster dependency and a sense of personal inadequacy. The resulting fear of facing the world alone increases jealousy. Similarly, positive associations have been found between jealousy and low self-esteem, insecurity, relationship dependency, and/or lack of alternatives for one or both sexes.

While they have been the focus of fewer studies, findings on how some other factors relate to jealousy are of interest. There is evidence that jealousy is negatively related to postconventional moral reasoning among women (Mathes and Deuger 1985) and that males in heterosexual couples are more sexually jealous than males in homosexual relationships (Hawkins 1990). Other findings are of interest for what they fail to show. Both romanticism and trust have been found not to be related to jealousy (Hansen 1982, 1985b). These results fail to support the belief that jealousy and romantic love are intimately linked as well as the assumption that trust decreases the probability of jealousy.

Responses to and Coping with Jealousy

People respond to jealousy-producing situations in a number of ways. One of the more comprehensive attempts to classify them comes from Jeff Bryson (1991), who identified eight modes of response: emotional devastation, reactive retribution (get even), arousal (intensify ardor or interest in partner), need for social support (intensify interaction with friends), intropunitiveness (blame and punish oneself for being jealous), confrontation (confront the situation directly), anger, and impression management (make others think one does not care, get drunk or high). These eight responses comprise a variety of cognitive, emotional, and behavioral reactions that are independent of each other. A person may experience all of them, some of them, or only a single reaction in response to a particular jealousy-producing situation.

In addition to identifying the ways in which people respond, research has also focused on how people cope with jealousy. Buunk (1982) examined the ways in which people cope with extramarital relationships of their spouses and identified three strategies: avoidance (of the spouse), reappraisal (of the situation), and communication. Avoidance includes such things as considering the possibility of leaving the spouse and retreating. Reappraisal refers to cognitive attempts to reduce one's jealousy and includes developing a critical attitude toward one's own jealousy as well as direct attempts to get the jealousy under control by relativizing the whole situation. Communication, the most common strategy, can reduce jealousy if it results in a redefinition of the relationship or a changed perception of the partner's behavior. Buunk (1982) found that communication is positively related to marital satisfaction, while avoidance is negatively related to it. Janice L. Francis (1977) reached a similar conclusion when she identified the development of communication skills as the appropriate treatment mode for sexual jealousy.

There is evidence that some people also cope with jealousy by devaluing their relationship. Peter Salovey and Judith Rodin (1985) found that "selective ignoring," defined as simply deciding that the desired object is not that important, is a coping strategy used by some.

While many studies of jealousy do not investigate the extreme techniques of coping with jealousy such as use of physical force or homicide, studies of family violence leave little doubt that they occur frequently. Martin Daly, Margo Wilson, and Suzanne J. Weghorst (1982) reviewed several studies of spousal homicide that used data beyond those found in police files and concluded that male sexual jealousy may be the major source of conflict in an overwhelming majority of spousal homicides in North America. There also is evidence that one of the groups among principal perpetrators of murder/suicide is composed of young males with intense sexual jealousy (Marzuk, Tardiff, and Hirsch 1992). Similarly, studies have noted the prevalence of jealousy as a motive in nonfatal wife abuse (Dobash and Dobash 1979) and courtship violence (Bookwala et al. 1992).

Finally, a number of social-psychological studies provide insight into some of the cognitive processes that may be involved as people cope with jealousy by changing their perceptions of their partners' behavior. Studies by White (1981) and Buunk (1984) indicate that perceived motives or attributions for the partner's behavior are related to jealousy. Therefore, changes in perceived motives or attributions can reduce jealousy. In addition, Bernd H. Schmitt (1988) found that jealous people derogate their rival on attributes they perceive to be important to their partners, but not on attributes they perceive as less important to their partners.

Conclusion

Jealousy has emerged as a legitimate area of social scientific study since the 1970s. In that time, considerable progress has been made in understanding the nature of jealousy, in identifying factors associated with it, and in examining some of the ways people respond to and cope with jealousy. However, because there is much more to learn, jealousy, which is a major issue in many intimate relationships, should remain a significant focus of scientific investigation.

(*See also:* ATTACHMENT; ATTRIBUTION IN RELATIONSHIPS; COMMUNICATION; EXTRAMARITAL SEX; FAMILY VIOLENCE; LOVE; PSYCHIATRIC DISORDERS; SPOUSE ABUSE AND NEGLECT)

BIBLIOGRAPHY

Adams, V. (1980). "Getting at the Heart of Jealous Love." *Psychology Today* 13:38–47, 102–106.

Bookwala, J.; Frieze, I. H.; Smith, C.; and Ryan, K. (1992). "Predictors of Dating Violence: A Multivariate Analysis." *Violence Victimology* 7:297–311.

Bowlby, J. (1969). *Attachment and Loss:* Vol. 1, *Attachment.* New York: Basic Books.

Bowlby, J. (1973). *Attachment and Loss:* Vol. 2, *Separation.* New York: Basic Books.

Bowlby, J. (1980). *Attachment and Loss:* Vol. 3, *Loss.* New York: Basic Books.

Bringle, R., and Buunk, B. (1985). "Jealousy and Social Behavior: A Review of Person, Relationship, and Situational Determinants." In *Review of Personality and Social Psychology:* Vol. 6, *Self, Situations, and Social Behavior*, ed. P. Shaver. Newbury Park, CA: Sage Publications.

Bryson, J. B. (1991). "Modes of Response to Jealousy-Evoking Situations." In *The Psychology of Jealousy and Envy*, ed. P. Salovey. New York: Guilford.

Buss, D.; Larsen, R. J.; Westen, D.; and Semmelroth, J. (1992). "Sex Differences in Jealousy: Evolution, Physiology, and Psychology." *Psychological Science* 3:251–255.

Buunk, B. (1982). "Strategies of Jealousy: Styles of Coping with Extramarital Involvement of Spouse." *Family Relations* 31:13–18.

Buunk, B. (1984). "Jealousy as Related to Attributions for the Partner's Behavior." *Social Psychology Quarterly* 47:107–112.

Clanton, G. (1981). "Frontiers of Jealousy Research: Introduction to the Special Issue on Jealousy." *Alternative Lifestyles* 4:259–273.

Clanton, G., and Kosins, D. J. (1991). "Developmental Correlates of Jealousy." In *The Psychology of Jealousy and Envy*, ed. P. Salovey. New York: Guilford.

Daly, M.; Wilson, M.; and Weghorst, S. J. (1982). "Male Sexual Jealousy." *Ethology and Sociobiology* 3:11–27.

Davis, K. (1936). "Jealousy and Sexual Property." *Social Forces* 14:395–405.

Dobash, R. E., and Dobash, R. (1979). *Violence Against Wives: A Case Against the Patriarchy.* New York: Free Press.

Ellis, C., and Weinstein, E. (1986). "Jealousy and the Social Psychology of Emotional Experience." *Journal of Social and Personal Relationships* 3:337–357.

Francis, J. L. (1977). "Toward the Management of Heterosexual Jealousy." *Journal of Marriage and Family Counseling* 3:61–69.

Freud, S. (1955). "Some Neurotic Mechanisms in Jealousy, Paranoia, and Homosexuality." In *The Standard Edition of the Complete Psychological Works of Sigmund Freud*, Vol. 18, ed. and trans. J. Strachey. London: Hogarth Press.

Hansen, G. L. (1982). "Reactions to Hypothetical, Jealousy-Producing Events." *Family Relations* 31:513–518.

Hansen, G. L. (1985a). "Dating Jealousy Among College Students." *Sex Roles* 12:713–721.

Hansen, G. L. (1985b). "Perceived Threats and Marital Jealousy." *Social Psychology Quarterly* 48:262–268.

Hansen, G. L. (1991). "Jealousy: Its Conceptualization, Measurement, and Integration with Family Stress Theory." In *The Psychology of Jealousy and Envy*, ed. P. Salovey. New York: Guilford.

Hawkins, R. O., Jr. (1990). "The Relationship Between Culture, Personality, and Sexual Jealousy in Men in Heterosexual and Homosexual Relationships." *Journal of Homosexuality* 19:67–84.

Hupka, R. B. (1984). "Jealousy: Compound Emotion or Label for a Particular Situation." *Motivation and Emotion* 8:141–155.

Marzuk, P. M.; Tardiff, K.; and Hirsch, C. S. (1992). "The Epidemiology of Murder-Suicide." *Journal of the American Medical Association* 267:3179–3183.

Mathes, E. W. (1991). "A Cognitive Theory of Jealousy." In *The Psychology of Jealousy and Envy*, ed. P. Salovey. New York: Guilford.

Mathes, E. W., and Deuger, D. J. (1985). "Jealousy and Moral Development." Paper presented at the annual meeting of the Midwest Psychological Association, Chicago.

McDonald, G. W. (1982). "Marital Jealousy: A Structural Exchange Perspective." Paper presented at the National Council on Family Relations Preconference Theory Construction and Research Methodology Workshop, Washington, DC.

Parrott, W. G. (1991). "The Emotional Experiences of Envy and Jealousy." In *The Psychology of Jealousy and Envy*, ed. P. Salovey. New York: Guilford.

Pines, A. M. (1992). *Romantic Jealousy: Understanding and Conquering the Shadow of Love.* New York: St. Martin's Press.

Reiss, I. L. (1986). *Journey into Sexuality: An Exploratory Voyage.* Englewood Cliffs, NJ: Prentice Hall.

Salovey, P., and Rodin, J. (1985). "The Heart of Jealousy." *Psychology Today* (Sept.): 22–29.

Schmitt, B. H. (1988). "Social Comparison and Romantic Jealousy." *Personality and Social Psychology Bulletin* 14:374–387.

Teissman, M. W., and Mosher, D. L. (1978). "Jealous Conflict in Dating Couples." *Psychological Reports* 42:1211–1216.

White, G. L. (1981). "Jealousy and Partner's Perceived Motives for Attraction to a Rival." *Social Psychology Quarterly* 44:24–30.

White, G. L., and Mullen, P. E. (1989). *Jealousy: Theory, Research, and Clinical Strategies.* New York: Guilford.

GARY L. HANSEN

JOINT CUSTODY *See* CHILD CUSTODY

JUVENILE DELINQUENCY

In assigning responsibility for child rearing to parents, Western cultures place a heavy burden on families. Families in such cultures must transmit values so as to lead children to accept rules that they are likely to perceive as arbitrary. It should be no surprise, therefore, to find that family life bears a strong relation to juvenile delinquency.

Family life can be viewed from three general perspectives. The first is structure: Who lives within a household? The second is interaction: How do the family members treat one another? The third is social setting: What is the nature of the community in which the family can be found? Each of these perspectives contributes information relevant to understanding the impact of family life on juvenile delinquency.

Family Structure

When anthropologists discuss family structure, they consider normative patterns. That is, they consider ideal households—or at least widely respected households—in terms of membership. Societies that idealize households with one adult man and one adult woman plus their offspring (nuclear family societies) can be contrasted with those in which one man lives with several women and their children (called polygynous) or several men live with one woman and their children (called polyandrous).

In contemporary Western societies, a nuclear family structure has been idealized. Conversely, deviations from this structure have been blamed for a variety of social problems, including delinquency. Although both the popular press and participants in the legal system blame "broken" homes for failures to socialize children as willing participants in an ordered social system, their conclusion goes well beyond the facts.

Claims that single-parent households produce delinquents fit well with several theories. Some assume that children learn how to become adults by association with parents of their own sex. Boys reared without a resident father, according to this assumption, would be deprived of the association necessary for appropriate maturation. As a result, children are said to overreact by asserting "masculinity" through delinquent behavior. This opinion has been buttressed by reports suggesting that typical delinquents lack the guidance of a father.

A conviction that lack of paternal guidance causes delinquency dominated early research in the field. High rates of broken homes among incarcerated youths were taken to evidence support for the assumption. In the 1920s, for example, boys in New York State reformatories were shown to be twice as likely to come from broken homes as boys in New York City public schools (Slawson 1923). Studies in London, Chicago, Boston, and rural California followed. These, too, showed that broken homes were more common among incarcerated delinquents than among unselected populations. In 1965, convinced that broken homes cause crime, Daniel Moynihan suggested that crime could be reduced by altering family structure among African Americans. Despite the publicity given to the Moynihan Report, however, research has not shown a causal connection.

If poverty causes crime and if the incidence of broken homes is greater among the poor, then broken homes might be "taking a bum rap" as causing crime. In addition, official records for delinquency may inflate a connection because they reflect decisions by authorities regarding how to treat delinquents. When deciding what to do with a delinquent, representatives of the criminal justice system who believe that broken homes cause crime are more likely to place those from broken homes in institutions.

Simple comparisons of the proportions of delinquents from broken homes with the proportions of nondelinquents from such homes confound many factors associated with family structures in the comparisons. Both social class and ethnicity are among the confounding factors.

Several studies that went beyond comparing the incidence of broken homes among criminals with the incidence in the general population fail to show a link between broken homes and delinquency. For example, among African Americans in St. Louis, boys from broken homes were not more likely to become delinquent than those from two-parent homes (Robins and Hill 1966). Careful analyses of juvenile court cases in the United States during 1969 showed that economic conditions rather than family composition influenced children's delinquency (Chilton and Markle 1972). In studies of London schoolboys and of American schoolchildren of both sexes, delinquency was not more prevalent, within social class, among children from single-parent homes.

Children in single-parent families are likely to have been exposed to such criminogenic influences as parental conflict and alcoholism. To detect effects on sons' criminality, one study divided both broken and united families according to whether the father was an alcoholic or a criminal (McCord 1982). The study showed that alcoholic or criminal fathers were more likely to have sons convicted of serious crimes whether or not the father was present. There was no association between criminal behavior and broken homes regardless of whether the sons had alcoholic or criminal fathers.

Single parents often find it hard to get assistance. If they must work to support themselves and their families, they are likely to have difficulty providing supervision for their children. Poor supervision, like alcoholism and criminality, seems to generate delinquency.

Careful study of the impact of differences in household composition shows that in homes that lack fathers, grandmothers appear to be protective against delinquency (Ensminger, Kellam, and Rubin 1983). This evidence further undermines theories that rely on same-sex adults as explanation for successful socialization in families.

Knowledgeable observers have concluded that the evidence fails to support a conclusion that broken homes cause crime. Asking whether broken homes are good or bad is misleading; the answer must depend in part on the available alternatives. Family conflict is particularly criminogenic, and the choice to divorce must typically be made by parents who do not get along. Convincingly, David P. Farrington (1978) found that among boys who had not been previously aggressive, marital disharmony of parents when the boys were fourteen predicted subsequent aggressive behavior. Furthermore, effects of living with a single parent vary in relation to the emotional and economic climate in the home.

Family Interaction

Perhaps the best grounds for believing that family interaction influences conduct disorder comes from programs that alter parental management techniques and thereby benefit the children (Arnold, Levine, and Patterson 1975; Klein, Alexander, and Parsons 1977). Consistent and reasonable guidance forms the foundation for such programs.

Social control theory postulates that bonds between parents and children provide a basis for children to give up their immediate pleasures in exchange for receiving distal rewards attached to socialized behavior. Consistent discipline and supervision add social control to the internalized bonds on the route toward forming well socialized adolescents. The theory gains support from a series of studies showing absence of parental affection to be linked with delinquency. Furthermore, reductions in delinquency between ages fifteen and seventeen appear to be related to friendly interaction between teenagers and their parents, a reduction that seems to promote school attachment and stronger family ties (Liska and Reed 1985). In their review of many studies investigating the relationships between socialization in families and juvenile delinquency, Rolf Loeber and Magda Stouthamer-Loeber (1986) conclude that parental neglect had the largest impact.

Parental rejection may affect the ways in which children regard both themselves and others. Parents who fail to provide consistent guidance deprive their children of opportunities to gain approval by choosing to behave in accordance with parental rules. If parents treat their offspring with disdain, the offspring are likely to regard themselves as unworthy of care.

Symbolic interaction theories suggest that roles assigned within families can importantly affect how children define others with whom they are likely to have contact. A variety of types of evidence suggests that delinquents have little self-esteem. Other studies suggest that delinquents lack empathic responses to those around them.

Whether family rejection or neglect affects tendencies toward delinquency through failures in attachment or through role concepts may appear to be merely an interesting academic debate. Yet designs for intervention strategies have depended on these theories to decide what approaches to take.

Prevention programs that successfully developed bonds between counselors and youths have failed to prevent delinquency, as have some carefully designed programs aimed toward building self-esteem. The Cambridge-Somerville Youth Study successfully established close bonds between young boys and counselors over several years. Nevertheless, boys who formed such bonds were not less likely to become delinquents than matched boys who were not assigned to program counselors (McCord 1992).

One of many programs aimed at improving self-esteem identified aggressive boys in sixth grade and provided a randomly selected group of the vulnerable children with special classes in remedial reading and lessons that provided models for behavior the next school year. Although the boys in these special classes reported that the program had been helpful, neither school nor police records supported a judgment that the program had reduced delinquency (Reckless and Dinitz 1972). Similarly discouraging results come from attempts to build self-confidence among adjudicated delinquents between ages fifteen and seventeen (Empey and Erickson 1972) and students in public schools (Gottfredson 1987).

Programs that help parents become adequate guides for their children seem to be more effective when started before kindergarten (Weikart and Schweinhart 1992), and changes in self-esteem appear more likely to reduce aggressive behavior when begun in primary grades (Tremblay et al. 1992). Once personalities have become fairly stable, the evidence suggests, intervention programs may be ineffective if they rely either on attempts to establish internal bonds or to increase self-esteem.

In sum, parental affection and reasonable parental control have been shown to promote socialized behavior. Yet when children fail to receive these early in their lives, substitutions have typically been ineffective. The failures of intervention programs suggest a weakness in theory and indicate that more needs to be learned regarding the mechanisms by which family interactions influence the behavior of offspring.

Community

Where a family lives affects the nature of opportunities that will be available to its members. In some communities, public transportation permits easy travel for those who do not own automobiles. Opportunities for employment and entertainment extend beyond the local boundaries. In other communities, corner gatherings open possibilities for illegal activities. Lack of socially acceptable opportunities leads to frustration and a search for alternative means to success. Community-based statistics show high correlations among joblessness, crime, household disruption, housing density, infant deaths, and poverty (Sampson 1992).

Community variations may account for the fact that some varieties of family life have different effects in terms of delinquency in different communities (Larzelere and Patterson 1990; Simcha-Fagan and Schwartz 1986). In general, consistent friendly parental guidance seems to protect children from delinquency regardless of neighborhoods. However, poor socialization practices seem to be more potent in disrupted neighborhoods.

Neighborhoods influence children's behavior by providing the values that lead to perceiving how to act. The theory of differential association suggests that people acquire their behavioral orientations by learning to define experiences through the eyes of their associates (Sutherland and Cressey [1924] 1974). This theory and the related social learning theory place a premium on the idea that peer groups shape the behavior of adolescents. In general, the influence of peers is greater among those who interact less with their parents.

Communities in which criminal activities are common tend to establish criminal behavior as acceptable. Tolerance for gang activities varies by community. In neighborhoods in which gangs are respected, gang membership may generate loyalties that increase the likelihood of violence. Friendships among delinquents seem to involve closer ties as well as greater mutual influence than do friendships among nondelinquents (Bowker and Klein 1983; Giordano, Cernkovich, and Pugh 1986). Through ties of friendship, communities have multiplying effects.

Conclusion

This brief review of the research indicates that a popular opinion about family impact is wrong; parental absence is *not* importantly related to juvenile delinquency. Family life is the more relevant influence on delinquency; children reared by competent, affectionate parents are unlikely to commit serious crimes either as juveniles or as adults. On the other hand, children reared by parents who neglect or reject them are likely to be greatly influenced by their community environments, which may offer opportunities and encouragement for juvenile delinquency.

(*See also:* Adolescence; Adolescent Sexuality; Child Abuse and Neglect: Emotional and Psychological Aspects; Divorce: Effects on Children; Gangs; Parent Education; Peer Pressure; Poverty; Runaway Children; Self-Esteem; Truancy)

BIBLIOGRAPHY

Arnold, J. E.; Levine, A. G.; and Patterson, G. R. (1975). "Changes in Sibling Behavior Following Family Intervention." *Journal of Consulting and Clinical Psychology* 43:683–688.

Bowker, L. H., and Klein, M. W. (1983). "The Etiology of Female Juvenile Delinquency and Gang Membership." *Adolescence* 18:739–751.

Chilton, R. J., and Markle, G. E. (1972). "Family Disruption, Delinquent Conduct, and the Effect of Subclassification." *American Sociological Review* 37:93–99.

Empey, L. T., and Erickson, M. L. (1972). *The Provo Experiment: Evaluating Community Control of Delinquency.* Lexington, MA: Lexington Books.

Ensminger, M. E.; Kellam, S. G.; and Rubin, B. R. (1983). "School and Family Origins of Delinquency: Comparisons by Sex." In *Prospective Studies of Crime and Delinquency*, ed. K. T. Van Dusen and S. A. Mednick. Boston: Kluwer-Nijhoff.

Farrington, D. P. (1978). "The Family Backgrounds of Aggressive Youths." In *Aggression and Antisocial Behaviour in Childhood and Adolescence*, ed. L. A. Hersov and M. Berger. Oxford, Eng.: Pergamon.

Giordano, P. C.; Cernkovich, S. A.; and Pugh, M. D. (1986). "Friendships and Delinquency." *American Journal of Sociology* 91:1170–1202.

Gottfredson, G. D. (1987). "Peer Group Interventions to Reduce the Risk of Delinquent Behavior: A Selective Review and a New Evaluation." *Criminology* 25:671–714.

Klein, N. C.; Alexander, J. F.; and Parsons, B. V. (1977). "Impact of Family Systems Intervention on Recidivism and Sibling Delinquency: A Model of Primary Prevention and Program Evaluation." *Journal of Consulting and Clinical Psychology* 45:469–477.

Larzelere, R. E., and Patterson, G. R. (1990). "Parental Management: Mediator of the Effect of Socioeconomic Status on Early Delinquency." *Criminology* 28:301–323.

Liska, A. E., and Reed, M. D. (1985). "Ties to Conventional Institutions and Delinquency: Estimating Reciprocal Effects." *American Sociological Review* 50:547–560.

Loeber, R., and Stouthamer-Loeber, M. (1986). "Family Factors as Correlates and Predictors of Juvenile Conduct Problems and Delinquency." In *Crime and Justice*, Vol. 7, ed. M. Tonry and N. Morris. Chicago: University of Chicago Press.

McCord, J. (1982). "A Longitudinal View of the Relationship Between Paternal Absence and Crime." In *Abnormal Offenders, Delinquency, and the Criminal Justice System*, ed. J. Gunn and D. P. Farrington. Chichester, Eng.: Wiley.

McCord, J. (1992). "The Cambridge-Somerville Study: A Pioneering Longitudinal-Experimental Study of Delinquency Prevention." In *Preventing Antisocial Behavior: Interventions from Birth Through Adolescence*, ed. J. McCord and R. E. Tremblay. New York: Guilford.

Moynihan, D. (1965). *The Negro Family: The Case for National Action.* Washington, DC: U.S. Government Printing Office.

Reckless, W. C., and Dinitz, S. (1972). *The Prevention of Juvenile Delinquency: An Experiment.* Columbus: Ohio State University Press.

Robins, L. N., and Hill, S. Y. (1966). "Assessing the Contribution of Family Structure, Class, and Peer Groups to Juvenile Delinquency." *Journal of Criminal Law, Criminology, and Police Science* 57:325–334.

Sampson, R. J. (1992). "Family Management and Child Development: Insights from Social Disorganization Theory." In *Facts, Frameworks, and Forecasts: Advances in Criminological Theory*, Vol. 3, ed. J. McCord. New Brunswick, NJ: Transaction.

Simcha-Fagan, O., and Schwartz, J. E. (1986). "Neighborhood and Delinquency." *Criminology* 24:667–699.

Slawson, J. (1923). "Marital Relations of Parents and Juvenile Delinquency." *Journal of Delinquency* 8:280–283.

Sutherland, E. H., and Cressey, D. R., eds. ([1924] 1974). *Criminology*, 9th edition. Philadelphia: Lippincott.

Tremblay, R. E.; Vitaro, F.; Bertrand, L.; LeBlanc, M.; Beauchesne, H.; Boileau, H.; and David, L. (1992). "Parent and Child Training to Prevent Early Onset of Delinquency: The Montreal Longitudinal-Experimental Study." In *Preventing Antisocial Behavior: Interventions from Birth Through Adolescence*, ed. J. McCord and R. E. Tremblay. New York: Guilford.

Weikart, D. P., and Schweinhart, L. J. (1992). "High/Scope Preschool Program Outcomes." In *Preventing Antisocial Behavior: Interventions from Birth Through Adolescence*, ed. J. McCord and R. E. Tremblay. New York: Guilford.

JOAN MCCORD

KINSHIP

All human beings are connected to others by blood or marriage. Connections between people that are traced by blood are known as consanguineal relationships. Relationships based upon marriage are affinal relationships. These connections are described by genealogies, which trace the consanguineal and affinal relationships among individuals. Theoretically, the kinds of relationships that genealogies describe are the same for all individuals in all cultures—that is, any person can in principle trace a relationship to a spouse, children, children's children, parents, parents' siblings, the spouses and children of parents' siblings, and so on. However, people in different societies customarily calculate genealogical connections differently, recognizing some kinds of relationships and ignoring others. The culturally determined genealogies turn objective relationships of blood and marriage between people into kinship. In no culture are all genealogical relationships recognized as kin relations. All people have genealogical relations about whom they know nothing, and everyone knows of relatives who have no importance in their lives. Genealogical relationships that have no social significance, either because the individuals whom they designate are unknown or because they are known but ignored, are not kin in the social sense. Genealogical ties that a culture chooses to recognize are what constitute an individual's kin.

Kinship relations have routinely captured the attention of students of human culture. This is especially true of anthropologists, whose major focus has traditionally been upon kin-based societies. Kinship, once a primary focus of cultural anthropology, has faded in centrality since the 1970s as many traditional societies have been drawn into the world system. The significance of kin relations begins to diminish only in large societies with mobile populations and money-based economies. By contrast, kin relations in most nonindustrial cultures underlie such critical domains as place of residence, inheritance customs, religious obligations, political power, economic relations, domestic life, and choice of spouse. People across cultures are more likely to turn to kin than to nonkin for help and are more likely to give aid and comfort to kin than to nonkin (Broude 1994).

If kin relations are the result of the selective exploitation and interpretation of genealogies by cultures, how do societies accomplish this transformation of biological fact into social reality? The transformation is achieved in part by the way in which a particular culture establishes recognized kin groups and in part by the way in which a society comes to label relatives with respect to some target person, or "ego." Recognized kin groups are established by and reflected in what are called descent rules. The labeling of relatives is described by a culture's kinship terminology. Further, in all societies, human beings often reside near or with kin. Different cultures, however, follow different rules regarding which kin will live with whom. The three major elements of kinship are rules of descent, kinship terminology, and residence rules. The incest taboo, rules governing marriage choice, and family structure are also important (Fox 1967).

Descent

Descent rules define socially recognized kin groups by tracing connections through chains of parent–child ties. A society may focus exclusively on connections traced through the male parent (patrilineal) or through the female parent (matrilineal). In either case, the culture is employing a unilineal, or single-line, descent system.

When descent is patrilineal, the descent group is composed of people of either sex whose fathers belong to the group. Siblings belong to the descent group of their father, but their mother belongs to a different descent group, the group to which her father belongs. Therefore, a man's children will belong to his descent group, but a woman's children will not belong to her descent group. Analogously, if descent is matrilineal, siblings belong to the mother's group but their father does not. A woman's children will belong to her descent group, but a man's children will not belong to his. Sometimes a society will assign individuals to one unilineal descent group for one purpose and to the other for another purpose, resulting in a system of double descent. For example, the person's patrilineal descent group may be in charge of political functions, while inheritance operates through the matrilineal descent group.

In contrast to societies that trace descent unilineally, individuals in some cultures such as the United States are characterized by bilateral descent rules, tracing relationships through both parents. In these societies, other institutions, such as governments, churches, businesses, and voluntary organizations, provide the structure and perform the functions of other societies' kin-based groups. In some societies, descent is traced through one parent for some people and through the other parent for other people; this is ambilineal descent. For instance, males may trace descent through their fathers, and females may trace descent through their mothers.

Because unilineal descent rules produce bounded and nonoverlapping groups, unilineal descent is a more powerful organizing principle than bilateral descent in that unilineal descent groups are able to act as corporate groups on behalf of their members in a way that bilateral descent groups cannot. Each patrilineal descent group in a society that traces descent through the father has a particular identity and membership that is entirely different from the identity and membership of any other partilineal descent group in the same society. Where descent is traced bilaterally, by contrast, only full siblings belong to precisely the same descent group because only full siblings have the same parents. Where descent is reckoned bilaterally, a person tends to single out some relatives within his or her kin group as more important than others. This close circle of kin is referred to as one's kindred. Who is included in one's kindred and who is not is a matter of individual choice based upon individual preference and sentiment. What is more, the definition of kindred shifts, depending upon circumstances. For instance, Americans are likely to count a smaller number of relatives as close when planning the guest list for Christmas dinner than when they are writing wedding invitations. In either case, because bilateral descent groups fan out indefinitely, it becomes hard to decide where to draw the line between kin who are close and kin who are not. Since each person belongs to a unique descent group and different bilateral descent groups in the same society have somewhat overlapping but also somewhat different memberships, these groups cannot function effectively as representatives of their members.

Unilineal descent, specifically patrilineal descent, is the most common system of reckoning (Ember and Ember 1988). Therefore, the majority of cultures around the world exploit blood and marriage connections to maximize the power and effectiveness of the kin group in supervising a wide variety of activities in which individuals participate. Unilineal descent groups are important sources of political power in many societies. The leaders can arbitrate disputes between individuals within the descent group or between different descent groups. They can go to war in support of a group member and retaliate for wrongs done to one of their own. Unilineal descent groups can delegate land rights and often act as a kind of government vis-à-vis the members. Unilineal descent groups also have important economic roles. Such groups can own land, money, houses, religious places and objects, songs, economic capital, and even personal names. Property is often inherited through the unilineal descent group. Unilineal descent groups can lend money and maintain members who have no other means of support. The unilineal descent group is also commonly the center of religious activity. Often a descent group is identified with supernatural beings who may be ancestors or claimed ancestors of members of the group. Supernaturals may be believed to protect and otherwise affect the members of the group, and the members may, in turn, be required to engage in particular activities in an effort to influence the actions of the supernatural.

Particular descent groups can also be associated with particular sets of taboos that the members of the group are obligated to honor. Marriages, often regulated by the unilineal descent group, may be prohibited or preferred between members of the same descent group, depending upon the norms of the group. Unilineal descent groups may also take over the burden of providing what are sometimes very costly payments to the bride or bride's family when a member of the group is married.

Kinship Terminology

Cultures transform cross-culturally equivalent genealogies into socially defined kin relations by the way in which they name categories of individuals who are members of the kin group. Such naming results in the kinship terminology of the culture. In all cultures, one or more of nine basic criteria are used in the system of kinship terminology particular to that culture (Kroeber 1909; Murdock 1949). These are generation, lineality and collaterality, sex, affinity, polarity, bifurcation, relative age, speaker's sex, and address versus reference. In the United States and most other Western societies, the first five criteria are commonly used. Americans customarily distinguish among kin and assign kin terms on the basis of a person's generation, directness of relationship, sex, ties of blood versus marriage, and the use of different terms by interacting kin.

Different cultures collapse different relatives under one name that allows kinship terminology to transform objectively identical genealogies into different social constructions of kinship. For instance, the kinship terminology employed by Americans uses the term "aunt" to refer to all of the sisters of a person's mother but employs a different term for the mother herself. In some other cultures, by contrast, a person's mother and the mother's sister are referred to by the same term. Relatives who are called by the same label tend to be identified with similar roles, responsibilities, and privileges with regard to ego. Similarly, relatives who are distinguished from each other terminologically also tend to play distinctive roles with respect to ego. Kin names, therefore, act to reinforce cultural expectations about how kin will behave toward one another. While classificatory kin terms emphasize similarities in the relationships of different kin to ego, individuals distinguish between relatives who are called the same name and respond to them differently in a myriad of ways. Thus, in societies where mother and mother's sisters are called by the same term, children know the difference between their mothers and aunts, treat them differently, and feel differently about them. The collapsing of different categories of relatives under one label facilitates certain kinds of interactions between kin but does not eradicate an individual's ability to appreciate that people called by the same name are, nevertheless, not the same people.

While kin terminology is not uniform across cultures, there are a number of systems of kin naming that appear over and over from one culture to the next. Six such systems of kinship terminology have been identified, based on the manner in which cousins and siblings are classified: Hawaiian, Eskimo, Sudanese, Iroquois, Crow, and Omaha (Murdock 1949). American kin terms are of the Eskimo type. Cousins are distinguished from brothers and sisters, but cousins on the father's side are not distinguished from those on the mother's side—they are all referred to as "cousin."

Cultures that share systems of kinship terminology also tend to be similar in residence patterns, descent rules, and family organization (Levinson and Malone 1980). These similarities in important features of social structure are thought to account for shared kin terminology systems. Societies with similar patterns of descent, residence, and family organization are likely to allocate roles, rights, and responsibilities similarly.

A shared system of kin terminology reflects and reinforces these similar role assignments. For example, in societies that trace descent through the father, a greater number of terminological distinctions are made regarding relatives from different generations for kin traced through the father than for kin traced through the mother. This may be because role, rights, and responsibilities depend upon the age of the relative vis-à-vis ego. As the interactions between an individual and the father's kin are more finely enumerated and distinguished in cultures where descent is traced through the male parent, the generation-based name distinctions on the father's side of the genealogy that are typical of these cultures reflect generation-based role distinctions. As interactions between an individual and relatives traced through the mother are not so finely drawn, terminological distinctions also tend to be less finely distinguished.

In societies that trace descent through the father, married couples also tend to live with or near the husband's family. This means that children of both sexes as well as married males will be interacting daily with relatives traced through the father, while no individuals will ever live where there is a concentration of relatives traced through the mother. The finer distinctions between the father's kin on the basis of age may reflect the far greater number of interactions that an individual will have with these relatives and, therefore, the greater need to distinguish these relatives on the basis of age. Societies that reverse this pattern of kin naming, distinguishing between mother's but not father's kin on the basis of generation, tend to trace descent through the female parent. In cultures of this kind, married couples are more likely to live with or near the wife's family. The greater role of the mother's kin in the life of the individual is mirrored in the more clearly differentiated kin labeling with respect to relatives traced through the mother.

Residence Rules

In all known cultures, at least some people—usually the majority—live near or with kin. Which kin live together differs from one society to the next and from family to family within a culture, but one particular kind of household tends to predominate in a given society. This is in part because many cultures have explicit rules that specify where a married couple will establish their new home.

In most societies around the world, newly married people are required or expected to live with or near the husband's family. This patrilocal residence pattern is found in 70 percent of a sample of 1,153 cultures (Levinson and Malone 1980). Residence is matrilocal in 11 percent of these societies, with a married couple living with or near the wife's family. Couples live apart from both the husband's and the wife's families in 5 percent of cultures. Husbands and wives are expected to live with or near the husband's mother's brother in 4 percent, a pattern known as avunculocality, or the uncle's place. Residence rules that require a couple to live with or near the family of one or the other spouse are known a unilocal rules. In 7 percent of cultures, a married couple can live with or near the family of either spouse, based on bilocal residence rules. Sometimes couples change households over the course of their marriage. Patrimatrilocal residence rules require couples to live first with the husband's family and then with the wife's parents. In matripatrilocal cultures, the opposite occurs.

Particular rules of residence seem to occur more frequently in some kinds of cultures than in others. Neolocal residence is most common in societies whose economies depend upon money. The introduction of money into a culture means that individuals can obtain what they need on a flexible schedule, so that a husband and wife are no longer as dependent upon kin for the necessities of life. Further, in money-based economies, people are not as free to remain in one place; they may be required to move to where a job is available. Moving entire households composed of parents, aunts, uncles, and cousins is impractical. Therefore, as money economies make couples more independent and also more mobile, living with relatives becomes less necessary and less realistic (Ember and Ember 1983).

In most cultures, people live with relatives. Some theorists have suggested that the particular choice of relatives with whom to live is influenced by which sex makes the greater economic contribution in the culture (Levinson and Malone 1980; Murdock 1949). Residence would be patrilocal where men make the greater economic contribution and matrilocal where the contribution of women is greater. This theory is intuitively attractive, but in fact residence rules are not predictably related to the roles of men and women in the economy. However, residence rules are predictably related to warfare (Ember and Ember 1983). In particular, where wars tend to be waged between groups who live far apart from each other, interfering with the subsistence activities of the men, residence rules tend to be matrilocal. Perhaps this is because matrilocality allows a closely related and therefore cohesive group of women to take charge of subsistence tasks when the men are away. Where enemies are close to home, societies are more likely to be patrilocal. Perhaps under these circumstances, families wish to keep the men at home as a kind of militia. Bilocality also occurs in particular kinds of cultures. Societies that allow a married couple to live with either set of parents have often been recently depopulated by disease. Dramatic population reductions of this sort may mean that one parent or set of parents has died. The flexibility of the bilocal residence means that a particular couple can choose to live with whichever parents have survived (Ember and Ember 1983).

In most cultures around the world, people live in the company of kin. The particular patterning of household differs dramatically from culture to culture, but in all cultures, households are composed of relatives. This means that the most fundamental challenges of living are met with the help of kin. Human beings give and receive food from kin, accept the support of kin in the rearing of their children, go to kin when in need of help, and help kin who are in need. Human beings also treat kin preferentially and are, in turn, treated preferentially by kin. For instance, among the Philippine Ilongot, kin ties regulate all important interactions between people (Rosaldo 1980). Kin hunt together and cooperate in the performance of other subsistence activities. A man who must make a marriage payment receives contributions from his kin. Relatives visit each other, provide each other with food and medical knowledge, take care of one another, and tend each other's children. A man will request help from his nephew because he views the child as his own, and a woman will give a sister rice for her family because sisters should feed each other's children. This pattern of nepotism is captured in the familiar homily that "blood is thicker than water." Just as kin are favored over nonkin, closer kin are favored over those who are more distantly related. None of this is surprising. Biological evolutionary theory suggests that because relatives share genes, they should be disposed to be good to each other; contributing to the survival and reproduction of a blood relative results in the proliferation of genes identical to one's own. This is entirely consistent with the Darwinian claim that animals, including the human animal, act in ways that promote the representation of their own genes in the gene pool of their kind.

In the United States and other Western societies, the idealized kinship customs are monogamous marriage, neolocal residence, nuclear families, incest prohibitions within the nuclear family, bilateral descent, and Eskimo kinship terminology. However, there are often important intrasocietal variations in the overall importance of kinship and kin and specific customs, with the most notable ones involving social class and ethnic variation (Schneider 1973).

(*See also:* Extended Family; Fictive Kinship; Genealogy; Incest Taboo; Inheritance; Nuclear Family)

BIBLIOGRAPHY

Barnes, J. A. (1971). *Three Styles in the Study of Kinship.* Berkeley: University of California Press.

Broude, G. (1994). *Marriage, Family, and Relationships.* Santa Barbara, CA: ABC-CLIO.

Ember, C., and Ember, M. (1988). *Anthropology,* 5th edition. Englewood Cliffs, NJ: Prentice Hall.

Ember, M., and Ember, C. (1983). *Marriage, Family, and Kinship: Comparative Studies of Social Organization.* New Haven, CT: HRAF Press.

Fox, R. (1967). *Kinship and Marriage.* London: Penguin Books.

Kroeber, A. L. (1909). "Classificatory Systems of Relationship." *Journal of the Royal Anthropological Institute of Great Britain and Ireland* 39:77–84.

Levinson, D., and Malone, M. J. (1980). *Toward Explaining Human Culture.* New Haven, CT: HRAF Press.

Murdock, G. P. (1949). *Social Structure.* New York: Macmillan.

Rosaldo, M. Z. (1980). *Knowledge and Passion: Ilongot Notions of Self and Social Life.* Cambridge, Eng.: Cambridge University Press.

Schneider, D. M. (1973). *American Kinship: A Cultural Account.* Chicago: University of Chicago Press.

Stephens, W. N. (1963). *The Family in Cross-Cultural Perspective.* New York: Holt, Rinehart and Winston.

Gwen J. Broude

L

LATER-LIFE FAMILIES

Within the marriage and family field, the focus is often directed toward the formation of families and the expansion of the nuclear family unit. The study of later-life families directs attention to the latter portions of family life and examines the contraction of the nuclear family unit. Given the changing family networks in the middle and later years, the maintenance of family relationships within and beyond the nuclear unit is a concern. Maintaining long-term marriages; launching children; developing relationships with sons- and daughters-in-law; reorganizing marriages after retirement; developing grandparent relationships; providing care for less healthy family members; and dealing with divorce, widowhood, and other marital changes are some of the topics addressed in the study of later-life families. Scholarship on later-life families examines the family from the vantage point of the mature years of family life rather than the initiation of such families.

Grounded in the developmental perspective, later-life families have been defined as "families who are beyond the child-rearing years and have begun to launch their children" (Brubaker 1983, p. 9). The developmental perspective examines families as changing over time, and stages in family development can be identified as the family structure is altered (Rodgers and White 1993). Family structure is changed when the number of persons within a household changes or when the relationships within the households are altered qualitatively; family interaction patterns are altered because the individuals no longer share a common domicile; and identifiable transition events occur to indicate the change within the family unit (Rodgers and White 1993). For example, the launching of children through the establishment of an independent household by the younger family member or the retirement of a parent or spouse are events that mark movement into the latter stages of family development. Families can usually identify the time when a child moved out of the parental household or the date of retirement. At the same time, these events do not occur without warning or preparation. There is a process (transition) that generally leads up to the event that signifies that a family is experiencing changes associated with later-life families.

The definition of later-life families does not specify a chronological age because the events that signify contraction can occur at varying ages. For example, becoming a grandparent is often associated with later life. In one study of African-American grandmothers, the median age at which a woman became a grandmother was thirty-six years, and the median age for becoming a great-grandmother was fifty-six years (Burton and Bengtson 1985). A study of college students reported that most of their grandmothers were sixty years of age or older (Thompson and Walker 1987). These studies suggest that there is a wide variation in the chronological age at which an individual experiences the events associated with later-life families. For most situations, individuals either have experienced or are anticipating the experience of events associated with later-life families by the time they are forty to fifty years of age.

Unique Characteristics of Later-Life Families

One unique characteristic of later-life families is that they are multigenerational. Increased longevity suggests that the number of living generations within a family will increase. It is not uncommon for families to have three, four, or five living generations, and interaction among these generations is important when exploring later-life family relationships. Although most later-life families are multigenerational, it is clear that interactions vary from family to family and among generations. Some families feel that they are "caught in the middle" (adult child caught between the older and younger generations) because they are providing assistance to both generations. Other families identify the older family members as resources for younger families. Later-life family researchers explore the reciprocity of multigenerational interactions within everyday life as well as during the changes associated with later life (retirement, widowhood, caregiving).

Another unique characteristic of later-life families is that they share a lengthy family history or track record (Brubaker 1983, 1985). The launching of children generally occurs within the context of a lengthy history of interaction, which may include a strong marriage, divorce, or a wide array of other types of family activities such as decision making, coping, and supporting one another. This lengthy history is obvious in long-term marriages or sibling relationships for older persons, and it is also characteristic of parent–child relationships in the later years. The history of interaction over the years provides families with shared meanings for everyday activities and events. Often these shared meanings are unique to each family network and provide insight to nonfamily members when seeking to understand the way families define situations such as caregiving. For example, the shared meanings may identify who among a group of sons and daughters will provide care to unhealthy parents.

A third unique characteristic is that later-life families are heterogeneous. Differences among later-life families result from varying historical, cultural, racial, and ethnic backgrounds. Older people and their families differ in their historical experiences because they represent different historical periods, and even though they may share the same historical period, they hold various perceptions of what happened within this time frame. Similarly, cultural, racial, and ethnic differences provide considerable variations in the ways older people and their families define the later years. In addition to these differing settings, each later-life family has its own unique experiences and perspectives that contribute to heterogeneity. As families age, their experiences become more heterogeneous. The study of later-life families requires a sensitivity to variations within and among families.

Continuity and Change in Later-Life Families

Continuity as well as change are frequently found within later-life families. The families' history of interaction provides a setting for the changes associated with the later years. Continuity is evidenced within the way families deal with the challenges of the later years, and a recognition of these consistencies is helpful in understanding how families define the later years. One example of the continuity versus change paradox in the study of later-life families is marriage in the later years. In most cases, marriage in the later years is based on a history of interaction that can be characterized as positive or negative. When children leave home, it is likely that a marriage that has been unfulfilling will become even more unfulfilling. A marriage that has been fulfilling will probably become more fulfilling. The continuity of relationships provides insight into the strategies families employ to address the changes associated with the later years.

Marriage in the Later Years

Marriages in the later years experience a number of changes that challenge both the married persons as well as their families. For example, as children leave home to establish their independent households, the nuclear unit contracts. This is a process for most middle-aged couples because many have more than one child, and they become independent at different times. As the children leave home, the couple may need to develop revised divisions of household tasks as well as different ways of communicating. Retirement is another event that provides a time for change within the marriage.

Gender differences in marital status are obvious because the majority of men are married and the proportion of married women declines with age. According to the U.S. Bureau of the Census (1988), the majority of men (more than 80%) and women (approximately 66%) aged sixty-four years or younger are married; among those sixty-five to seventy-four years old, most of the men (about 80%) and approximately half of the woman are married; and for those seventy-five years of age or older, two-thirds of the men are married and less than one-quarter of the women are married. These demographics clearly illustrate the gender differential in longevity.

Research on long-term marriages suggests that couples married for many years report high levels of marital satisfaction (Sporakowski and Axelson 1989). There is some evidence that satisfaction with marriage may increase as the children leave home and as the number of years of marriage increases. It is likely that couples with less than positive feelings of satisfaction divorced before they entered the later years and those who continued their marriages experienced improved levels of satisfaction after the children became independent.

The couple may experience a reorganization of tasks within the household as the children leave home and as one or more of the spouses becomes retired. Research (Brubaker and Hennon 1982) indicates that couples seem to continue the patterns of household activities they had established before they retired (for most couples, it is a traditional gender-differentiated division of household tasks). These patterns seem to continue even though they expected to share more of the responsibility for the activities after they retired. While there may be some change in household activities, it is likely that these changes will result in more time spent in the activities usually performed by the individual rather than in an increased sharing of the activities.

The timing of retirement may have a differing influence on later-life marriages. In marriages in which both partners are employed, both can retire at approximately the same time (synchronized), or the husband may retire before his wife (desynchronized–husband initially), or the wife may retire before her husband (desynchronized–wife initially) (Brubaker 1985). Marital satisfaction seems to be lower in the desynchronized–husband initially situations, and women have a more difficult time with retirement than men. The traditional types of retirement in which only one partner has been employed may result in lower levels of satisfaction for the partner who has not previously been employed.

Marriage in the later years is grounded in a history of interaction and continuity. Partners seem to provide support to one another as they experience the changes associated with later life. As health of married persons changes and as there is need to provide care, it is likely that spouses will provide extraordinary assistance as primary caregivers. Even though these caregiving partners report stress and burden associated with the provision of care, their marital satisfaction scores remain high. Marriage for many older persons is a relationship of support and satisfaction, while there are a number of challenges to address in later life.

Sexuality in the Later Years

Although interest in sex and participation in sexual activity decline with age (Palmore 1981), research indicates that older persons are sexual; older men and women are interested and participate in sexual activity. Erdman Palmore's (1981) study demonstrated that married men and women expressed more interest in sex than the amount of activity they reported. Few were not sexually active. Often sexual activity is defined as participating in sexual intercourse, but older persons often defined sexual interest and activity broadly (e.g., caressing, massaging, holding hands). The research indicates that older persons are sexual beings who have experienced a decline in sexuality in the later years and who express their sexuality in a wide range of activities.

Continuity in sexual interest and activity is an important issue in later life. Persons who are sexual in the middle years are likely to be sexual in the later years. The decline in sexual participation seems to be related to the husband's desire and health situation. Often couples cease sexual activity because a health problem temporarily limits activity; however, in many cases sexual activity can be resumed after the health situation improves. Sexuality is a natural experience that is lifelong, and while there may be some changes in frequency and definitions in later life, older men and women are likely to continue to express their sexuality throughout their lives.

Divorce in Later Life

Approximately 7 percent to 9 percent of men and women fifty-five to sixty-four years of age enter the later years in the divorce status, and with increasing age the proportion of divorced older persons declines (less than 3% at age seventy-five years or older) (U.S. Bureau of the Census 1988). Older divorced persons may be "newly divorced" (married for many years and divorced in later life), "career divorced" (married and divorced early in life and has not remarried), or "serial divorced" (married and divorced more than twice and may or may not be divorced in later life) (Brubaker 1985). Older divorced women report more emotional disruption than men (Chiriboga 1982). The newly divorced have seldom expected to be unmarried in later life, and the divorce changes the financial plans and social networks of older persons. The career divorced may have the opportunity to continue the financial and social relationships they have developed in their earlier years as an unmarried person. The serial divorced feel a disruption because they expected to be married in their later years, but they also have experienced divorce previously in their lifetime. Although research seldom distinguishes among the different types of divorced, it is no doubt that there are variations among the divorced in later life.

Research indicates that divorced persons are less financially, socially, and emotionally advantaged than married persons in the later years (Hennon 1983). For example, divorced elderly experienced a decline in financial resources, while married persons increased their resources over a five-year period (Uhlenberg and Myers 1981). Compared to widowed and never married persons, Pat M. Keith (1986) reported that divorced women had lower incomes than widowed women, while divorced men reported higher incomes than widowed or never married men. Socially, a larger proportion of divorced older persons had not maintained contacts with friends when compared with never married persons. Older divorced persons expressed feelings of unhappiness, isolation, pessimism, and emotional problems when compared to younger divorced persons (Chiriboga 1982).

The divorced in later life seem to be vulnerable to financial difficulties and a limited social network. Consequently, it is not surprising that they are often unable to help their children (Hennon 1983). Research on gender differences suggests that divorced women are more vulnerable than divorced men. While there are a sizable number of divorced persons in later life, it is likely that the number will not increase substantially in the future.

Widowhood in Later Life

Widowhood is an event that many people experience in later life. Before age sixty-five, a small portion of the men (less than 4%) and women (approximately 17%) are widowed. However, for those between sixty-five and seventy-four years of age, about 8 percent of the men and more than 36 percent of the women are widowed. For those seventy-five years of age or older, nearly 25 percent of the men and 66 percent of the women are widowed. Thus widowhood is more likely to be experienced by women, although a sizable portion of men are widowed in later life (U.S. Bureau of the Census 1988).

Widowhood marks a change in nearly every aspect of a person's life. One's economic, physical, emotional, and social situations are altered by the death of a spouse. After the death of a spouse, it is likely that the financial resources will decline for both men and women. Over time, the financial situation seems to level off or improve. Improvement is most often related to remarriage, which is more likely for men than for women.

Research indicates that physical and emotional health declines after the loss of a spouse. Recently widowed men and women exhibit forms of depression (sadness, dissatisfaction with self, insomnia, appetite and weight loss), but over time these symptoms lessen and the widowed person's physical and emotional health improves (Feinson 1986).

Primary relationships with children, grandchildren, siblings, and friends are particularly important for the widowed. Even though the size of the social network may decrease, there is a continuation in social contact for both men and women. There may be an increase in amount of social interaction for women. For example, widows increased their contact with family members, especially sisters (O'Bryant 1988). The continuation of family relationships and friendships may provide a buffer when the widowed, especially women, deal with the changes associated with the loss of a spouse.

While there appears to be little difference between widows and widowers, it is likely that the path to widowhood may affect adjustment to the loss of a spouse. For example, widowhood may be sudden and unexpected, sudden after some health difficulties, or expected after a lengthy period of caregiving. For all individuals, the first few months of widowhood are particularly difficult. After several months, widows and widowers begin to readjust their lives and eventually organize to adapt to the loss of a spouse (Heinemann and Evans 1990). Within eighteen to twenty-four months, most of the widowed have adjusted to the loss of a spouse. However, it is likely that the widowed seldom "get over" the loss of a spouse because marriage is such an intimate relationship.

Grandparenthood

Grandparenthood is an important intergenerational relationship in later life. Approximately three-fourths of older persons are grandparents and half are great-grandparents (Hagestad 1988). The age at which a person becomes a grandparent varies widely; some are in their thirties, while others are in their fifties. In any case, the grandparent relationship marks an event associated with the transition into later life.

While there are few normative definitions of grandparents, and the types of grandparents vary considerably, grandparents provide a stability and continuity within the family network. It is a relationship that is meaningful for both older men and women, although women express more satisfaction with the grandparenting role and men feel more responsibility for caretaking.

Grandparent–grandchild interaction is related to the age of the grandchild. The younger the grandchild, the more likely the adult parent will be a mediator between grandparent and grandchild. This is particularly important if a divorce occurs in the middle generation. Stepgrandparent relationships are also related to the age of the grandchild. Younger grandchildren (age ten years or less) are more likely to perceive the stepgrandparent relationship as important (Sanders and Trygstad 1989).

Caregiving in Later-Life Families

Women (wives, daughters, daughters-in-law) most frequently provide the primary care for older family members (Stone, Cafferata, and Sangl 1987). Elaine M. Brody (1990) has observed that caregiving may be a career for women within the family. Families provide care that could not be provided by secondary organizations such as government because the cost of such care would be too great.

Husbands and wives provide similar amounts of assistance to their spouses, but wives seem to be more depressed about their caregiving responsibilities. Wives also report more difficulty within the marital relationship than do husbands. Another gender difference is that caregiving wives initially seem to be more emotionally involved in the caregiving activities, while husbands are more detached and instrumentally involved in providing assistance. Differences in spousal caregiving may be related to differences in definitions of masculinity and femininity. Husband and wife caregivers express their love to their needy partners by providing care in the manner that is consistent with their sex role expectations.

Adult children are also caregivers for elderly parents. Some daughters feel "in the middle" because they are caregivers for their own children as well as their parents (Brody 1981); sons may be "on the periphery" (Brubaker 1990). For example, daughters are involved in routine caregiving activities, and sons are more likely to assist in specific, narrowly defined areas. Adult children develop patterns of caregiving that are unique to each individual family history. Married caregiving adult women report that the responsibilities of providing care have negatively affected their marriages. There is little doubt that caregiving for elderly family members is related to stress and burden, but the provision of care occurs within a family context. The type of dependency, family history, and other responsibilities of the caregiver are some of the issues that need to be considered when assessing the amount of stress or burden within each family situation.

Conclusion

Later-life families provide an example of the continuity and change of family relationships. As children leave home and parents address the challenges in later life the strengths and weaknesses of the family relationships become evident. For most families, there is a viable family network in later life that becomes a source of support in dealing with the changes associated with widowhood, caregiving, and other situations associated with the later years. The family is important to older people, and younger persons also value the elderly relatives. The history of family relationships is particularly relevant to understanding later-life family interactions. In providing support to later-life families, it is important to recognize the positive and negative aspects as well as the diversity of family relationships.

(*See also:* Death and Mourning; Divorce: Emotional and Social Aspects; Elders; Filial Responsibility; Grandparenthood; Intergenerational Relations; Marital Quality; Retirement; Sexuality in the Life Cycle; Widowhood)

BIBLIOGRAPHY

Brody, E. M. (1981). "Women in the Middle and Family Help to Older People." *Gerontologist* 25:19–29.

Brody, E. M. (1990). *Women in the Middle.* New York: Springer-Verlag.

Brubaker, T. H., ed. (1983). *Family Relationships in Later Life.* Newbury Park, CA: Sage Publications.

Brubaker, T. H. (1985). *Later-Life Families.* Newbury Park, CA: Sage Publications.

Brubaker, T. H. (1990). "Families in Later Life: A Burgeoning Research Area." *Journal of Marriage and the Family* 52:959–981.

Brubaker, T. H. (1993). "Family Life Education for the Later Years." *Family Relations* 42:212–221.

Brubaker, T. H., and Hennon, C. B. (1982). "Responsibility for Household Tasks: Comparing Dual-Earner and Dual-Retired Marriages." In *Women's Retirement: Policy Implications of Recent Research,* ed. M. E. Szinovacz. Newbury Park, CA: Sage Publications.

Burton, L. M., and Bengtson, V. L. (1985). "Black Grandmothers: Issues of Timing and Continuity of Roles." In *Grandparenthood,* ed. V. L. Bengtson and J. F. Robertson. Newbury Park, CA: Sage Publications.

Chiriboga, D. A. (1982). "Adaptation to Marital Separation in Later and Earlier Life." *Journal of Gerontology* 37:109–114.

Feinson, M. C. (1986). "Aging Widows and Widowers: Are There Mental Health Differences?" *International Journal of Aging and Human Development* 23:241–255.

Hagestad, G. O. (1988). "Demographic Change and the Life Course: Some Emerging Trends in the Family Realm." *Family Relations* 37:405–410.

Heinemann, G. D., and Evans, P. L. (1990). "Widowhood: Loss, Change, and Adaptation." In *Family Relationships in Later Life*, 2nd edition, ed. T. H. Brubaker. Newbury Park, CA: Sage Publications.

Hennon, C. B. (1983). "Divorce and the Elderly: A Neglected Area of Research." In *Family Relationships in Later Life*, ed. T. H. Brubaker. Newbury Park, CA: Sage Publications.

Keith, P. M. (1986). "Isolation of the Unmarried in Later Life." *Family Relations* 35:403–409.

O'Bryant, S. L. (1988). "Sibling Support and Older Widows' Well-Being." *Journal of Marriage and the Family* 50: 173–183.

Palmore, E. (1981). *Social Patterns in Normal Aging: Findings from the Duke Longitudinal Study.* Durham, NC: Duke University Press.

Rodgers, R. H., and White, J. M. (1993). "Family Development Theory." In *Sourcebook of Family Theories and Methods*, ed. P. G. Boss, W. J. Doherty, R. LaRossa, W. R. Schumm, and S. K. Steinmetz. New York: Plenum.

Sanders, G. F., and Trygstad, D. W. (1989). "Stepgrandparents and Grandparents: The View from Young Adults." *Family Relations* 38:71–75.

Sporakowski, M. J., and Axelson, L. V. (1989). "Long-Term Marriages: A Critical Review." In *Lifestyles of the Elderly: Diversity in Relationships, Health, and Caregiving*, ed. L. Ade-Ritter and C. B. Hennon. New York: Human Sciences Press.

Stone, R.; Cafferata, G. L.; and Sangl, J. (1987). "Caregivers of the Frail Elderly: A National Profile." *Gerontologist* 27:616–626.

Thompson, L., and Walker, A. J. (1987). "Mothers as Mediators of Intimacy Between Grandmothers and Their Young Adult Granddaughters." *Family Relations* 36:72–77.

Uhlenberg, P., and Myers, M. A. P. (1981). "Divorce and the Elderly." *Gerontologist* 21:276–282.

U.S. Bureau of the Census. (1988). "Marital Status and Living Arrangements: March 1988." *Current Population Reports.* Series P-20, no. 431. Washington, DC: U.S. Government Printing Office.

TIMOTHY H. BRUBAKER

LAW AND THE FAMILY *See* FAMILY LAW

LIFESTYLE *See* CELIBACY; COMMUNES; GAY AND LESBIAN PARENTS; SEXUAL ORIENTATION; UTOPIAN COMMUNITIES

LONELINESS

> Nature did not construct human beings to stand alone. . . . Those who have never known the deep intimacy and intense companionship of happy mutual love have missed the best thing that life has to give. Love is something far more than desire for sexual intercourse; it is the principal means of escape from loneliness which afflicts most men and women throughout the great part of their lives.
>
> —Bertand Russell (1929, pp. 122–123)

Complementing Russell's affliction view, contemporary social scientists have defined loneliness as the unpleasant experience that occurs when a person's network of social relationships is deficient in some important way, either quantitatively or qualitatively (Peplau and Perlman 1982, p. 4). These social scientists conceptualize loneliness as stemming from a discrepancy between the level of social contact a person needs or desires and the amount he or she has. The deficits can be in the individual's broader network of relationships, leading to social loneliness, or in the person's intimate relationships, leading to emotional loneliness (Weiss 1973). In either case, loneliness is a subjective experience—people can be alone without being lonely, or lonely in a crowd. It is also a common experience in modern societies: When polled, roughly one-fourth of Americans say they have felt "lonely and remote from others" within the past two weeks (Weiss 1973, p. 23).

In thinking about loneliness in a family and life cycle perspective, several questions come to mind: Does being married protect an individual from becoming lonely? Is the quality of the husband–wife and parent–child relationships associated with loneliness? How are family life transitions such as parenthood and becoming widowed intertwined with loneliness? Since the mid-1970s, social scientists have published a growing number of studies addressing these very questions.

Marital Status

Not surprisingly, loneliness is less common among married than among nonmarried individuals. This is a well-established finding, shown in the United States, Canada, the Netherlands, and Sweden. When the unmarried are divided into categories, the results vary somewhat by study. The general tendency appears to be for single people to be less lonely than the divorced or widowed (Essex and Nam 1987; Perlman 1988, Table 3). In at least one Dutch sample, single parents were also a group high in loneliness (de Jong-Gierveld 1982).

Differences in loneliness as a function of marital status can be explained either in terms of selection (i.e., the distinctive characteristics of people who do and do not marry) or what marital relationships provide. If selection is operating, it means that the people who marry are different and would avoid loneliness even in the absence of getting married. This explanation is, unfortunately, difficult to test. The second view implies that the more the marital relationships provide, the less lonely the partners should be. Consistent with this explanation, low marital satisfaction is associated with greater loneliness. Similarly, compared with individuals who confide in their spouses, married individuals who talk most openly about the joys and sorrows of their lives with somebody besides their spouse are more prone to being lonely.

Even in the initial stages of marriage, these qualitative differences can operate. Stan W. Sadava and Cheryl Matejcic (1987) studied 38 couples in the initial stage of marriage before they had children. Several aspects of their marriages were associated with the respondents' loneliness. For example, looking at the results for just one partner, lonely men had more apprehension about communicating with their wives than did nonlonely men. Between partners, the husbands of lonely wives engaged in little self-disclosure within their marriages.

Parent–Child Relations

After passing through the initial stages of marriage, couples following a traditional sequence of family development will likely have children. In the transition to parenthood, women who are lonely during their pregnancy are at higher risk for postpartum depression (Cutrona 1982).

Be it via genetic determinism or socialization, children bear resemblances to their parents in several domains; loneliness is no exception. Judith Lobdell and Daniel Perlman (1986) administered questionnaires to 130 female undergraduates and their parents. Preliminary analyses showed that the fathers and mothers in this study manifested greater than chance similarity to their loneliness scores. As expected, the main analyses demonstrated that the parents' loneliness scores were modestly correlated with those of their daughters.

Lobdell and Perlman also had these university students rate their parents' marriages and child-rearing practices. Lonely students depicted their parents as having relatively little positive involvement with them. This is one of several studies showing the cold, remote picture of parent–child relations reported by lonely young adults. They also saw their parents as having lower than average marital satisfaction. This finding complements other studies showing that children whose parents divorce are at risk for loneliness, especially if the divorce occurs early in the child's life.

In infancy, children are highly dependent on parents and caretakers. As they get older, peer relations become more important. Along with this shift comes a shift in what type of relations are most closely linked with loneliness. In the middle elementary years, it is the quality of children's relationships with their mothers. In late adolescence, it is the quality of university students' relationships with their peers.

Pauline Bart (1980) has analyzed how children's leaving home affects middle-aged mothers. She interviewed 22 women and examined the case records of 533 more. Based on these sources, Bart concluded that women who adopt the traditional role of being homemakers devoted to their children are prone to experience greater loneliness and depression when their children leave home than are women less invested in a maternal, homemaker role.

Relational Transitions

In addition to the departure of children, other relational transitions are associated with loneliness. Charles T. Hill, Zick Rubin, and L. Anne Peplau (1976) studied the ending of 103 dating relationships. As these relationships ended, presumably both partners experienced a decline in the social aspects of their lives, but in many couples one person initiated the breakup while the other was "left behind." Hill, Rubin, and Peplau found that the initiators suffered significantly less loneliness than the partners who were spurned. Perhaps having control over such life changes helps reduce the distressing effects of losing a partner. Of course, individuals who initiated the breakup may have lost less from the termination and/or had alternative relationships pending. But then, either or both of these circumstances may be associated with having greater control.

As discussed, divorced individuals tend to have high loneliness scores. John C. Woodward, Jackie Zabel, and Cheryl Decosta (1980) asked 59 divorced persons when and under what circumstances they felt lonely. For these respondents, the period of greatest loneliness occurred before (rather than after) the divorce decree became final. Both ex-husbands and ex-wives felt lonely when they felt out of place at a particular social event or excluded by others. For ex-wives, loneliness was also triggered when they wanted to join an activity but were unable to do so; they had no one with whom to share decision-making responsibilities and daily tasks; they felt stigmatized by being divorced; and they had financial problems.

A University of Tulsa study (Jones and Adams 1978) involving 74 men and women compared the divorce experiences of lonely versus nonlonely individuals. Lonely individuals blamed more of the marriage's problems on their former spouses. They also had more difficulties in their relationships with their ex-partners. They argued more over child rearing, felt less affection, and had less friendly interactions. In terms of adjusting to separation, lonely respondents drank more, experienced greater depression, felt more cut off from their friends, spent more time with their children, and were less likely to become romantically involved with a new partner.

For many North Americans, marriage lasts "till death do us part," but what about those left behind at the death of a spouse (a situation faced predominantly by women)? Helena Z. Lopata (1969) has identified several ways in which widows miss their husbands. For example, when their spouses die, women lose

- a partner who made them feel important;
- a companion with whom they shared activities;
- an escort to public encounters as well as a partner in couple-based socializing;
- a financial provider who enabled them to participate in more costly activities and enjoy a more expensive lifestyle.

With such losses, it is not surprising that loneliness is a major problem in bereavement.

Robert O. Hansson and associates (1986) found a general tendency for greater loneliness to be associated with a maladaptive orientation toward widowhood. Prior to the death of their husbands, the lonely widows engaged in less behavioral rehearsal (e.g., finding jobs, getting around on their own) for widowhood and instead engaged in more rumination about the negative consequences of the spouse's impending death. At the time of the spouse's death, subsequently lonely widows experienced more negative emotions and felt less prepared to cope. Lonely widows were also less likely to engage in social comparison with widowed friends.

If a spouse dies unexpectedly, loneliness is especially pronounced. To overcome loneliness, widows typically turn to informal supports (e.g., friends, children, and siblings), as opposed to formal organizations or professionals (e.g., their church, psychotherapists). In widowhood as in other transitions, time heals: Feelings of loneliness are greatest shortly after the loss of a spouse but decline over the months and years. As widows continue their lives, the quality of their closest friendship is more likely to be associated with their experiences of loneliness than is the quantity or quality of their closest kin relationships (Essex and Nam 1987).

Conclusion

The picture of loneliness is more complex than it would seem. At various ages and positions in life, kin relationships, friendships, and other factors differ in their importance in the loneliness equation. In addition, marriages and other intimate relationships throughout adulthood have the potential for both greater satisfaction and greater loneliness. Therefore, it is not simply the relationships, but what happens in them that counts.

(*See also:* Death and Mourning; Divorce: Emotional and Social Aspects; Single Parents; Singles; Widowhood)

BIBLIOGRAPHY

Bart, P. (1980). "Loneliness of the Long-Distance Mother." In *The Anatomy of Loneliness*, ed. J. Hartog, J. R. Audy, and Y. A. Cohen. New York: International Universities Press.

Cutrona, C. E. (1982). "Depressive Attributional Style and Nonpsychotic Postpartum Depression." Ph.D. diss. University of California, Los Angeles.

de Jong-Gierveld, J. (1982). "Loneliness and the Degree of Intimacy in Personal Relationships." Paper presented at the Madison Conference on Personal Relationships, Madison, WI.

Essex, M. J., and Nam, S. (1987). "Martial Status and Loneliness Among Older Women: The Differential Importance of Close Family and Friends." *Journal of Marriage and the Family* 49:93–106.

Hansson, R. O.; Jones, W. H.; Carpenter, B. N.; and Remondet, J. H. (1986). "Loneliness and Adjustment to Old Age." *International Journal of Aging and Human Development* 24:41–53.

Hill, C. T.; Rubin, Z.; and Peplau, L. A. (1976). "Breakups Before Marriage: The End of 103 Affairs." *Journal of Social Issues* 32:147–168.

Jones, W., and Adams, L. (1978). "Loneliness and Divorce." Paper presented at a meeting of the Southwestern Psychological Association, New Orleans.

Lobdell, J., and Perlman, D. (1986). "The Intergenerational Transmission of Loneliness: A Study of College Females and Their Parents." *Journal of Marriage and the Family* 48:589–595.

Lopata, H. Z. (1969). "Loneliness: Forms and Components." *Social Problems* 17:248–261.

Peplau, L. A., and Perlman, D., eds. (1982). *Loneliness: A Sourcebook of Current Theory, Research, and Therapy.* New York: Wiley.

Perlman, D. (1988). "Loneliness: A Lifespan, Developmental Perspective." In *Families and Social Networks*, ed. R. M. Milardo. Newbury Park, CA: Sage Publications.

Russell, B. (1929). *Marriage and Morals.* New York: Liveright.

Sadava, S. W., and Matejcic, C. (1987). "Generalized and Specific Loneliness in Early Marriage." *Canadian Journal of Behavioral Science* 19:56–65.

Weiss, R. S. (1973). *Loneliness: The Experience of Emotional and Social Isolation.* Cambridge, MA: MIT Press.

Woodward, J. C.; Zabel, J.; and Decosta, C. (1980). "Loneliness and Divorce." *Journal of Divorce* 4:73–82.

DANIEL PERLMAN

LOVE

The song lyrics "Love and marriage go together like a horse and carriage" illustrate the significance of the concept of love in North American society, where it is regarded as a necessary prerequisite for marriage. For example, when young adults are asked, "If a man (woman) had all the other qualities you desired, would you marry this person if you were not in love with him (her)?" at least 80 percent answer "No" (Simpson, Campbell, and Berscheid 1986). In addition to regarding love as the basis for marriage, North Americans view love as essential for the continuation of marriage. Research has found that a substantial proportion of young adults believe the disappearance of love is a sufficient reason to end a marriage (Simpson, Campbell, and Berscheid 1986).

Given the importance that is placed on love in making major life decisions, such as whether to marry someone or whether to stay married, a critical question is: What do people mean when they use the word *love?* Even though research and theorizing related to this question has a relatively short history in the social sciences, these efforts have already produced significant strides in the knowledge of love.

Social Scientists' Views of Love

Social scientists have defined love in a variety of ways. Table 1 provides examples of definitions that appear in the literature. As is evident from the table, a commonly accepted, precise definition of love has not yet been found. It is not surprising, therefore, that there has been considerable debate about whether it is even possible to define love (e.g., Fehr and Russell 1991). Some social scientists have taken the view that a complex concept such as *love* does not lend itself to a single, simple definition, and have instead turned their attention to developing models or theories of love. Four such theories are especially prominent in the close-relationships literature: Elaine Hatfield and G. William Walster's (1978) companionate/passionate love typology; Robert J. Sternberg's (1986, 1988) triangular theory of love; John A. Lee's (1973) and Susan S. Hendrick and Clyde Hendrick's (1986) love styles; and Cindy Hazan and Phillip Shaver's (1987) conceptualization of love as attachment.

Hatfield and Walster's companionate/passionate love. Hatfield and Walster (1978) were among the first social psychologists to study the concept of love. They developed a typology in which a distinction was made between companionate and passionate love. Companionate love was defined as "the affection we feel for those with whom our lives are deeply entwined" (p. 9). Passionate love was defined as "a wildly emotional state, a confusion of feelings: tenderness and sexuality, elation and pain, anxiety and relief, altruism and jealousy" (p. 2). According to Sharon S. Brehm (1985), there are three major differences between these two forms of love. The most striking is the emotional intensity that is experienced. Companionate love, as evident from its definition, is a calm, steady, relaxed state; passionate love is an emotional roller coaster, with intense highs and lows. The person who is passionately in love reports feelings of

Table 1 Definitions of Love

Love is an *attitude* held by a person toward a particular other person, involving a predisposition to think, feel, and behave in certain ways toward that other person [Rubin 1970, p. 265].
"Love" refers to a sentiment—it involves affect (feeling, emotion), libido, and cognition (an idea, knowledge, conscious awareness) [Lasswell and Lasswell 1967, p. 212].
Love . . . the personal experience and manifest expression of being attached or bonded to another person [Money 1980, p. 218].
Love . . . is a complex syndrome composed of . . . biological, psychological, and social factors, but no component by itself is a necessary or sufficient condition for the entire syndrome [Averill 1985, p. 88].
Love is an emotion, just an ordinary, non-cosmic, luxurious but not essential emotion [Solomon 1981, p. xxiv].

euphoria and excitement as well as periods of extreme anxiety and depression. There is a tendency for the passionate love experience to dominate the person's life, whereas companionate love leaves room for other interests and pleasures.

The two types of love also differ in the emphasis placed on sexuality. While both kinds may include a sexual component, passionate love is much more highly sexualized. Feelings of sexual attraction are strong, and sexual experiences are characterized by greater intensity.

Finally, companionate love is presumed to be much more stable than passionate love. When Hatfield and Walster (1978) first introduced their ideas about love, they stated that the intensity of passionate love could not be sustained over a long period of time. In contrast, companionate love was regarded as a sturdy, enduring kind of love. As will be seen, research has shown that passionate love may last longer than had been thought. While further investigation is necessary before this issue is resolved, most psychologists would agree that the experience of passionate love is much more likely than companionate love to be accompanied by feelings of insecurity and fears that the relationship will end. Companionate love feels much less fragile because it is based on a foundation of respect, trust, and caring.

A comparison of the research findings across several studies conducted by Hatfield and her colleagues concerning the theory of companionate/passionate love was published by Jane Traupmann and Hatfield (1981). In these studies, dating couples, newlyweds, and "long-marrieds" were asked how much passionate love and companionate love they felt for their partner. The authors found that levels of both passionate and companionate love were very high in the samples of steady daters and newlywed couples. Both types of love also remained high in the longer-married groups. However, there was a slight decrease in passionate love reported by the women who were married thirty-four years or more, which was accompanied by a similar, small decline in the amount of companionate love reported. Thus, contrary to the expectation that passionate love would diminish over time, Traupmann and Hatfield reported that both kinds of love remained very high from the steady-dating stage onward. Importantly, the slight decrease found in the oldest group was equal for both passionate and companionate love.

Sternberg's triangular theory of love. A somewhat different view of love is taken by Sternberg (1986). According to his theory, love is comprised of three components, which can be pictured as forming the vertices of a triangle: intimacy, passion, and decision/commitment. Intimacy is defined as "feelings of closeness, connectedness, and bondedness in loving relationships" (p. 119). Passion refers to feelings of arousal, physical attraction, and sexual activity. The decision/commitment component includes the short-term decision that one loves another person as well as the longer-term commitment to maintain the relationship. Sternberg proposes that different combinations of these three components produce different kinds of love. For example, infatuation is seen as the presence of passion along with the absence of intimacy and commitment. Companionate love is conceptualized as a combination of intimacy and commitment, minus passion. The theory also addresses the time course of these components. Specifically, Sternberg predicts that commitment in a relationship will increase over time, while passion and intimacy will diminish.

There is a scarcity of research on Sternberg's model, given that he has just begun to develop scales to measure the three components. However, Michele Acker and Mark H. Davis (1992) administered a preliminary version of the scale to more than 200 adults in order to test Sternberg's predictions. Consistent with the theory, scores on the commitment scale were higher for people who were in more serious relationships; the scores were lowest in the casually dating group and then increased systematically from the exclusively dating group to the engaged/living together group, with the highest commitment scores in the married group. Sternberg's prediction of a decline in passion over time was supported only in the women's data. Finally, there was no evidence that intimacy diminished over time, contrary to the theory.

Acker and Davis also explored which of the three components best predicted relationship satisfaction. Their analyses revealed that the most consistent and powerful predictor of satisfaction was commitment, particularly in the longest relationships. Thus, in long-term relationships, the level of commitment determined satisfaction more than the level of intimacy or passion. These interesting results must be regarded as tentative, however, until they can be replicated with an established, validated measure of the three components.

Hendrick and Hendrick's love styles. Hendrick and Hendrick's (1986) model of love is based on Lee's (1973) typology of love styles. Based on analyses of literature and interviews with people, Lee delineated the following six forms of love:

1. *Eros* is a romantic, passionate kind of love, largely based on physical attraction.
2. *Ludus* is seen as a game-playing love in which one plays the field and does not commit to a single relationship.
3. *Storge* is friendship-based love, where love is seen as growing out of a solid, close friendship rather than intense passion and infatuation.
4. *Mania* is an intense, possessive, dependent love in which the person becomes obsessed with the loved one, becomes jealous easily, and needs constant assurances that he or she is loved.
5. *Pragma* is a very practical, shopping-list kind of love; a relationship is considered only if the other person comes from a similar family background, has promising career prospects, would be a good parent, and so on.
6. *Agape* is a selfless, altruistic love that is gentle, caring, dutiful, and given without the expectation of receiving anything in return.

Hendrick and Hendrick (1986) developed scales to measure each of these six love styles, and have summarized the research conducted using these scales in *Romantic Love* (1992).

To provide further research into Hendrick and Hendrick's love scales, Nancy K. Grote and Irene H. Frieze (1992) administered their Friendship-Based Love scale (a measure of the Storge love style) and Hendrick and Hendrick's eros and ludus love-style scales to more than 700 middle-aged adults. They found that women and men who were married or dating scored higher on friendship-based love and eros than those who were separated or divorced. Married people also scored lower on ludus than those who were dating or separated/divorced. A related finding was that respondents with high ludus scores were more likely to have had an extramarital affair than those with high eros or friendship-based love scores. Finally, when the researchers compared whether friendship-based love, eros, or ludus was most highly correlated with relationship satisfaction, friendship-based love emerged as the strongest predictor. It was also more highly correlated than the other two love styles with variables such as importance of the relationship, respect for one's partner, and feelings of closeness to one's partner.

Love as attachment (Hazan and Shaver). Developmental psychologists have had a longstanding interest in the nature of infant–caregiver attachment. Specifically, it has been postulated that children develop different attachment styles, depending on the availability and responsiveness of their primary caregiver. Based on observations of interactions between mothers and their children, Mary Ainsworth and her colleagues (1978) classified children as secure, avoidant, and anxious/ambivalent. Secure children had mothers who were responsive to the children's needs and provided comfort in times of distress. Avoidant children had mothers who consistently rejected their attempts to seek comfort or make physical contact; these children were withdrawn and avoided their mothers. Anxious/ambivalent children had mothers who unnecessarily intruded or interfered with the children's activities and were reticent or inconsistent in responding in times of distress. Hazan and Shaver (1987) explored whether evidence of these different attachment styles would be found in adult love relationships. They presented adults with three attachment-style descriptions and asked them to choose the one that best characterized them: secure (comfortable with dependency and closeness to others), avoidant (uncomfortable with others' desires for closeness and dependency), or anxious/ambivalent (desiring a high level of closeness to others, but anxious that others will not reciprocate). Remarkably, the proportion of adults endorsing each style was similar to the proportion of infants who are classified into each style in the developmental literature (56% secure; 25% avoidant; 19% anxious/ambivalent). These and other findings led Hazan and Shaver (1987) to suggest that "romantic love is an attachment process—a biosocial process by which affectional bonds are formed between adult lovers, just as affectional bonds are formed earlier in life between human infants and their parents" (p. 511).

In addition, Hazan and Shaver (1987), by analyzing the responses of 620 adults to a questionnaire published in their local newspaper, were able to point out differences among the three attachment types. They found that people who classified themselves as secure portrayed their most important love relationship in very positive terms (e.g., happy, trusting). Those who chose the avoidant style described their most significant love experience less positively. These relationships were characterized by a fear of intimacy, ups and downs, and jealousy. The anxious/ambivalent respondents reported obsession, intense sexual attraction, emotional highs and lows, and a desire for extreme closeness in their love relationships. These differences were also reflected in the questions on relationship stability. Those in the secure group reported an average relationship length of more than ten years, compared with less than six years for avoidants and less than five years for anxious/ambivalents. (The average age in each of the three groups was thirty-six years.) Similarly, the divorce rate was approximately twice as high in the insecure groups (10% of anxious/ambivalents; 12% of avoidants) than in the secure group (6%).

Hazan and Shaver also reported that the three groups differed in their perceptions of their parent–child relationships. Secures reported warmer, more caring, affectionate relationships with their parents and between their parents than the other groups. Avoidants saw their mothers as cold and rejecting, and anxious/ambivalents described their fathers as unfair.

Since the publication of Hazan and Shaver's pioneering study, there have been many investigations of the adult love relationships of people with different attachment styles (for reviews, see Shaver and Hazan 1993; Bartholomew and Perlman 1994).

Is integration of these theories possible? Attempts at integration of the various theories of love have already begun. For example, Hendrick and Hendrick (1989) asked nearly 400 university students to complete a number of scales. They then conducted a factor analysis (a statistical technique that groups items on the basis of similarity) to determine which of the scales would cluster or group together. The pattern of findings was rather complex. However, generally it appeared that the scales clustered in accordance with Hatfield and Walster's distinction between passionate and companionate love.

Ordinary People's Conceptions of Love

While some social scientists have developed definitions and theories of love, others have been interested in discovering how ordinary people view love. Beverley Fehr began investigations of this topic by asking 141 laypeople (students at a large university on the Canadian West Coast) to list the features or characteristics of love (Fehr 1988). The responses revealed that the lay conception of love is very rich and complex; sixty-eight features of love were identified. These features included, among others, caring, respect, devotion, sexual attraction, thinking about the other all the time, and excitement. As the first three features suggest, some of the responses were highly similar to Hatfield and Walster's descriptions of companionate love. As the last three features suggest, other responses closely matched Hatfield and Walster's depiction of passionate love. This raised an important question: Which do ordinary people see as capturing the true meaning of love—companionate love, passionate love, or both?

To answer this question, Fehr conducted another study in which the sixty-eight features from the first study were presented to a new group of respondents, who rated each according to whether it was a good or poor feature of love (Fehr 1988). The highest ratings were assigned to the kinds of features that best described companionate love (trust, caring, honesty, friendship, and respect). The lowest ratings were given to features that referred to passionate love (sexual passion, excitement, thinking about the other all the time, energy, and gazing at the other). Therefore, Fehr concluded that ordinary people see love in both companionate and passionate terms. However, it is companionate love that is regarded as the essence of love; passionate love is seen as less important.

This conclusion was supported in further studies. For example, it was found that an increase in companionate features was taken as an indication that a relationship had become more loving, whereas an increase in passionate features was not seen as diagnostic of increased love (Fehr 1988). Conversely, a violation of companionate features (e.g., feeling one could no longer trust a partner) was taken as a sign of relationship deterioration, whereas a violation of passionate features (e.g., no longer gazing into a partner's eyes) was not.

Thus, according to ordinary people, companionate features lie at the heart of love, whereas passionate features are much more peripheral. Similar results have been reported by other researchers who have replicated these studies on the American West Coast and the Canadian East Coast, using students and nonstudents as research participants (see Fehr 1993).

Do Women and Men See Love Differently?

One of the questions that has intrigued love researchers is whether women and men have different views of love. One social scientist has commented, "Probably the most powerful individual difference that affects how we experience love is that of gender" (Brehm 1985, p. 99). Consequently, it is not surprising that love researchers have examined gender differences in conceptions and the experience of love.

Companionate love. Who has a more companionate or friendship-based approach to love, women or men? This question has been addressed from a number of perspectives. However, the answer that emerges is quite consistent; women hold a more companionate view of love. For example, in the love-styles research, women usually score higher than men on the storge scale, which measures friendship-based love (e.g., Hendrick and Hendrick 1986; Hendrick,

Hendrick, and Adler 1988). Women also score higher than men on Zick Rubin's (1973) liking scale, which has been regarded as a measure of companionate love. Similarly, in Grote and Frieze's (1992) sample of middle-aged married adults, women scored higher on the friendship-based love scale than men.

Romantic/passionate love. Who has a more romantic or passionate approach to love, women or men? The stereotype is that women are the ones concerned with romance. However, the research shows that men are the more romantic sex. Evidence to support this comes from a variety of sources. For example, since the mid-twentieth century, social scientists have been constructing scales to assess romanticism. These scales typically measure the extent to which someone holds romantic beliefs such as: There is one (and only one) person who is "right" for you; the person who is right for you will match all of your ideals; love conquers all; and love at first sight can be "true" love. Men consistently score higher on these kinds of scales than women. In addition, studies with both dating couples and newlyweds have found that men report falling in love more quickly than women (e.g., Huston et al. 1981).

In contrast to men's more romantic orientation to love, women are more pragmatic or practical. For instance, women usually score higher than men on the pragma love-style scale. Women are more cautious about falling in love than are men and also fall out of love more quickly (e.g., Hill, Rubin, and Peplau 1976). Finally, some romanticism scales also include nonromantic items such as, "Economic factors should be given careful consideration when choosing a mate." Women tend to agree, whereas men tend to disagree, with such statements.

The finding that women are more companionate than men and that men are more romantic than women has led some researchers to conclude that when it comes to love, women and men live in completely different worlds. However, research by Fehr and Ross H. Broughton (1993) invites a somewhat different interpretation. In a series of studies, university students were presented with descriptions of fifteen different kinds of love (e.g., maternal love, sisterly love, friendship love, romantic love, infatuation). Subjects were asked to read each description and rate how closely each captured their own view of love. Consistent with past research, women rated the description of friendship love as portraying their view of love to a greater extent than did men. Also, consistent with past research, men gave higher ratings than women to the description of romantic love. This also extended to a whole family of romantic/passionate kinds of love, including infatuation, puppy love, sexual love, and passionate love. However, it was found that even though women assigned higher ratings than men to the friendship-love description, this was still the description that men rated highest. In other words, men regarded the description of friendship love (and related companionate types of love such as familial love) as representing what love means to them. In contrast, men gave the *lowest* ratings to the romantic/passionate varieties (while women's ratings of these types were still lower). Thus, it would appear that there is greater similarity in women's and men's conceptions of love than had been assumed. Despite differences in their ratings, both women and men see companionate love as more central to their view of love than romantic/passionate love. Thus, once again, the theme is repeated—companionate love seems to capture what love means to people, whereas passionate love plays a more minor role.

Conclusion

The research on everyday views of love has revealed that both companionate (friendship) love and passionate love are included in ordinary people's conception of love, with companionate love seen as more important. However, the issue that has not been addressed fully is whether companionate love figures more prominently than passionate love in research driven by the social science theories. A preliminary answer was provided by Grote and Frieze's (1992) study. They reported that middle-aged adults who were married or dating scored higher in friendship (companionate) love than those who were separated or divorced. Also, friendship-based love was found to be a stronger predictor of relationship satisfaction than romantic, passionate love (eros). A study by Hendrick and Hendrick (1993) complements these findings. They asked two groups of young adults in dating and marital relationships to provide a personal account (story) of their romantic relationship. The stories were then coded according to which of the six love styles was portrayed. Interestingly, friendship-based love (storge) was the dominant category. For example, in one group, 72 percent of the stories were classified as storge, whereas only 22 percent were classified as eros. Similar findings were reported in the other group. The authors comment that "What is perhaps most important to conclude from this research is that there is a strong friendship component to love, even in the romantic relationships of young adults who are merely dating" (p. 464). Thus there is evidence that companionate love lies at the heart of love, for ordinary people and social scientists alike.

(*See also:* Attachment; Commitment; Friendship; Gender; Intimacy; Jealousy; Mate Selection; Trust)

BIBLIOGRAPHY

Acker, M., and Davis, M. H. (1992). "Intimacy, Passion, and Commitment in Adult Romantic Relationships: A Test of the Triangular Theory of Love." *Journal of Social and Personal Relationships* 9:21–50.

Ainsworth, M. D. S.; Blehar, M. C.; Waters, S.; and Wall, S. (1978). *Patterns of Attachment: A Psychological Study of the Strange Situation.* Hillsdale, NJ: Lawrence Erlbaum.

Averill, J. A. (1985). "The Social Construction of Emotion: With Special Reference to Love." In *The Social Construction of the Person,* ed. K. J. Gergen and K. E. Davis. New York: Springer-Verlag.

Bartholomew, K., and Perlman, D., eds. (1994). *Attachment Processes in Adulthood.* London: Jessica Kingsley.

Brehm, S. S. (1985). *Intimate Relationships.* New York: Random House.

Fehr, B. (1988). "Prototype Analysis of the Concepts of Love and Commitment." *Journal of Personality and Social Psychology* 55:557–579.

Fehr, B. (1993). "How Do I Love Thee? Let Me Consult My Prototype." In *Individuals in Relationships,* Vol. 1, ed. S. Duck. Newbury Park, CA: Sage Publications.

Fehr, B., and Broughton, R. H. (1993). *Individual Differences in Views of Love.* University of Winnipeg.

Fehr, B., and Russell, J. A. (1991). "Concept of Love Viewed from a Prototype Perspective." *Journal of Personality and Social Psychology* 60:425–438.

Grote, N. K., and Frieze, I. H. (1992). "Friendship-Based Love in Intimate Relationships." Paper presented at the International Conference on Personal Relationships, Orono, ME.

Hatfield, E., and Rapson, R. L. (1993). *Love, Sex, and Intimacy: Their Psychology, Biology, and History.* New York: HarperCollins.

Hatfield, E., and Walster, G. (1978). *A New Look at Love.* Reading, MA: Addison-Wesley.

Hazan, C., and Shaver, P. (1987). "Romantic Love Conceptualized as an Attachment Process." *Journal of Personality and Social Psychology* 52:511–523.

Hendrick, C., and Hendrick, S. S. (1986). "A Theory and Method of Love." *Journal of Personality and Social Psychology* 50:392–402.

Hendrick, C., and Hendrick, S. S. (1989). "Research on Love: Does It Measure Up?" *Journal of Personality and Social Psychology* 56:784–794.

Hendrick, S. S., and Hendrick, C. (1992). *Romantic Love.* Newbury Park, CA: Sage Publications.

Hendrick, S. S., and Hendrick, C. (1993). "Lovers as Friends." *Journal of Social and Personal Relationships* 10:459–466.

Hendrick, S. S.; Hendrick, C.; and Adler, N. L. (1988). "Romantic Relationships: Love, Satisfaction, and Staying Together." *Journal of Personality and Social Psychology* 54:980–988.

Hill, C. T.; Rubin, Z.; and Peplau, L. A. (1976). "Breakups Before Marriage: The End of 103 Affairs." *Journal of Social Issues* 32:147–168.

Huston, T. L.; Surra, C. A.; Fitzgerald, N. M.; and Cate, R. M. (1981). "From Courtship to Marriage: Mate Selection as an Interpersonal Process." In *Personal Relationships:* Vol. 2, *Developing Personal Relationships,* ed. S. Duck and R. Gilmour. New York: Academic Press.

Lasswell, T. E., and Lasswell, M. E. (1976). "I Love You but I'm Not in Love with You." *Journal of Marriage and Family Counseling* 2:211–224.

Lee, J. A. (1973). *The Colours of Love.* Don Mills, Ontario: New Press.

Money, J. (1980). *Love and Love Sickness.* Baltimore: Johns Hopkins University Press.

Rubin, Z. (1970). "Measurement of Romantic Love." *Journal of Personality and Social Psychology* 16:265–273.

Rubin, Z. (1973). *Liking and Loving.* New York: Holt, Rinehart and Winston.

Shaver, P., and Hazan, C. (1993). "Adult Romantic Attachment: Theory and Evidence." In *Advances in Personal Relationships,* Vol. 4, ed. D. Perlman and W. H. Jones. London: Jessica Kingsley.

Simpson, J. A.; Campbell, B.; and Berscheid, E. (1986). "The Association Between Romantic Love and Marriage." *Personality and Social Psychology Bulletin* 12:363–372.

Solomon, R. C. (1981). *Love: Emotion, Myth, and Metaphor.* Garden City, NY: Anchor/Doubleday.

Sternberg, R. J. (1986). "A Triangular Theory of Love." *Psychological Review* 93:119–135.

Sternberg, R. J. (1988). *The Triangle of Love.* New York: Basic Books.

Sternberg, R. J., and Barnes, M. L., eds. (1988). *The Psychology of Love.* New Haven, CT: Yale University Press.

Traupmann, J., and Hatfield, E. (1981). "Love and Its Effect on Mental and Physical Health." In *Aging: Stability and Change in the Family,* ed. R. W. Fogel, E. Hatfield, S. B. Kiesler, and E. Shanas. New York: Academic Press.

Beverley Fehr

MARITAL INTERACTION *See* COMMUNICATION; CONFLICT; INTIMACY; MARITAL QUALITY

MARITAL POWER

Power is the ability to change the behavior of another member of a social system. It is a fundamental aspect of all human relationships, including family relationships. In addition to its theoretical importance, the balance of power in marriage is also an important variable for therapists and family life educators.

Theories Explaining Power Differentials

Theories and research explaining couple-to-couple and society-to-society differences in the balance of power in marriage appear to be inconsistent and contradictory. Much of the seeming contradiction stems from assuming that the various explanations are alternatives to each other. Instead, power should be viewed as having multiple determinants, and each theory identifies one or more of the many determinants. This multiple-determined theoretical perspective was formulated in a classic paper by J. R. P. French and Bertram Raven (1959) that identified six "bases" (determinants or explanations) of power: coercion, reward, legitimacy or the right to compliance, identification with the person seeking compliance, expertise or experience, and information or knowledge. Almost all subsequent research on the determinants of power can be classified under one of these six categories, although often other terminology is used. For example, much of the research on the ability of one person to provide valued rewards uses the term "resources" to refer to economic rewards, and much of the research on legitimacy uses the term "culture" or "cultural context" to refer to culturally scripted legitimacy.

Economic resources. The term "resources" was introduced by Robert Blood and Donald Wolfe (1960) for the idea that the spouse who provides the most valued resources to a marriage will have the most power. The original formulation emphasized economically important resources such as income, education, and occupational status. A sizable body of research in the ensuing two decades confirmed the findings of Blood and Wolfe's study but also demonstrated that the ability to provide economic reward by itself is not a sufficient explanation for which partner has the most power. Resource theory in the sense of an exclusive focus on economic resources became discredited. However, the fundamental tenant of the theory continues to be supported, even as new research modified it by expanding the range of determinants to include more of the six bases for power identified by French and Raven (1959). These other bases of power interact with economic resources. For example, Martin King Whyte (1990) concluded that when couples pool their income and other economic resources, the greater contribution of one partner to the pool does not influence marital power. These findings are not necessarily a refutation of the idea that economic resources influence power in marriage. Rather, they indicate specifications that must be included as part of the theory.

Interpersonal skills and relationships. Differences between couples in marital power have also been related to differences in interpersonal skills and relationships of the partners. These studies illustrate what French and Raven (1959) identify as expertise as a basis of power. Marc DeTurck and Gerald Miller (1986), for example, found that skill in communicating with a spouse affects marital power. Similarly, Jan Pahl (1983) found that money management skills influence power in decision making. What George Conklin (1979) calls the theory of primary interest and presumed competency also illustrates expertise as a basis of power.

The "primary interest" aspect of Conklin's theory is the idea that the spouse who has the most interest in a certain decision will tend to have the power to make that type of decision. This seems to contradict the principle of least interest (Waller 1951)—the idea that the spouse who is least interested in maintaining the relationship will have greater power in the marriage. This principle is illustrated by Francesca Cancian's (1987) argument that because of the "feminization of love" women need love and tenderness more than men. This makes women more emotionally dependent on marriage and, consistent with the principle of least interest, reduces their power. Both principles are correct. Some spouses can exercise power by taking the initiative, and others by the explicit or implicit coercion of threatening to leave.

Power strategies (in French and Raven's theory, power based on expertise and knowledge) can also be considered an aspect of the interpersonal skill theory of power. Strategies, in turn, can depend on circumstances. Rodney Cate, James Koval, and James Ponzetti (1984) and Christine Sexton and Daniel Perlman (1989) found that husbands and wives in dual-career couples use more and different types of strategies than single-career couples to gain power in the marriage. Ethnic culture and circumstances also influence power strategies, as shown by Mwalimu Burgest and Mary Goosby (1985), who identified four "games of power" used in African-American families to gain or maintain the upper hand.

Social structural theories. In addition to expanding the scope of resources beyond those tied to economic contributions to the family, resource theory underwent another major change in response to findings from cross-cultural and cross-class research. Mirra Komarovsky (1964), for example, found that among working-class couples the husbands with the highest income and education did *not* have the most power. Studies in some other societies also often failed to show a strong relationship between resources and power. These cross-class and cross-cultural discrepancies led Hyman Rodman (1972) to formulate a "resources in cultural context" theory. He argued that individual resources are relatively unimportant in societies where the cultural context institutionalizes male dominance in the family. Rodman's theory seems to exemplify what French and Raven (1959) had earlier called legitimacy as a basis of power.

A feminist version of marital power based on legitimacy derived from cultural norms was put forth by Dair Gillespie (1971). She theorized that marital power can best be described as a caste/class system because husbands as a class have power in marriage as a result of discrimination against women in society, not because of the specific resources they contribute to the marriage. The feminist perspective overlaps with conflict theory as applied to the study of marital power by Randall Collins (1971) and Pauline Boss and her colleagues (1993). This approach holds that power differentials within families are a result of sex stratification in the larger society and that family members with the most power in the larger society are more able than others to advance their interests within the family.

Research by Rosemary Cooney and her colleagues (1982) on Puerto Rican families tested the theory that normative ascription of power overrides resource contribution. They found that the decision-making power associated with the contribution of resources changed as predicted between generations, depending on the level of assimilation and acceptance of modern values.

Rebecca Warner, Gary Lee, and Janet Lee (1986) found that women had more power in societies characterized by cultures that specify matrilocal residence, nuclear rather than extended families, and matrilineal descent. These aspects of social organization affect marital power regardless of whether or not they are normative. The influence of nonnormative social oganization was illustrated by a study of families in Bombay, India, which found that despite strong norms specifying male dominance, wives in nuclear households had more power than wives in extended households (Straus 1975). A comparative study of couples in Bombay and Minneapolis also found that economic and interpersonal skill resources and the resource of kin support influenced marital power in both cities (Straus 1988). Similarly, a study of 122 societies did not find support for the overriding importance of normative ascription of power (Lee and Peterson 1983). It was found that even in strongly patriarchal societies, wives' resources increased the likelihood that they would have marital power.

Other social organization variables that have been shown to influence the balance of power in marriage include whether the couple is married or cohabiting, whether it is a second marriage, whether there are minor children, and the age of the partners.

Multidetermined theories. Rather than thinking of individual resource theories and social structural theories as competing, it is more fruitful to think of them as parts of a multidetermined system. For example, Komarovsky's (1964) theory encompassed both types of determinants, including systems of mate selection, willingness to take advantage of a spouse's vulnerabilities, manipulative skills, social rank in the community, lower emotional involvement, and cultural norms vesting power in men. Komarovsky was also one of the first to point out that violence is a noneconomic resource through which men gain power in marriage. Rae Lesser Blumberg and Marion Tolbert Coleman (1989) also developed a multidetermined model to explain marital power.

Trends in Marital Power

Research on trends in marital power since the early 1980s has mostly been under the influence of feminist scholarship in the form of studies of the changing roles of women. These studies have found a trend toward more egalitarian marriages. Explanations of the trend seem to fall under the same headings as in studies of marital power done in the 1960s and 1970s.

Some authors, such as Phyllis Moen (1992), note the economic resources women acquired with the increase in the percentage of women in paid employment. For example, the percentage of women with paid jobs and with children under six years of age increased from 13 percent in 1950 to 52 percent in 1987.

Other authors have emphasized the normative shift brought about by the feminist movement, which campaigned for equality between men and women as a societal goal. Despite these gains, traditional roles and power imbalances remain (Moen 1992). The review by Paula England and Diane Swoboda (1988) concluded that although women are taking on more traditional male roles (e.g., careers, sports, and criminal activities), husbands are not taking on traditional female roles (e.g., housework and child care), and this preserves inequality in marital power.

Consequences of Power Distribution

Much of the research since 1980 has focused on the consequences of the unequal distribution of marital power. These studies uncovered a wide array of consequences. Empirical research has generally confirmed Jessie Bernard's (1972) idea that, as a result of greater power, husbands are more satisfied with their marriage than are wives (Aida and Falbo 1991; Fowers 1991). Mark Whisman and Neil Jacobson (1990) found that marital satisfaction is greatest for the spouse with the greatest power. However, Bernadette Gray-Little (1982) found that marital satisfaction is greater in traditional marriages.

The mental health of spouses is also linked to power. Wives who have greater power report higher levels of self-esteem (DeTurck and Miller 1986) and lower rates of depression (Mirowsky 1985). Gladis Kaufman (1988) found that egalitarian marriages result in the least stress for wives and that both egalitarian and husband-dominated (as opposed to wife-dominated) relationships result in the least stress for husbands.

The distribution of power in marriage is related to the division of household labor. Glenna Spitze (1988) argued that the spouse with the most power and resources used his or her power to pass the household work on to the other spouse. Arlie Hochschild (1989) confirmed this hypothesis for men but not for women. Women continued to do the majority of the housework regardless of their economic contribution. Beth Anne Shelton (1990) found that although women with paid employment do less housework, their husbands did little more than husbands of women without paid jobs.

Physical violence is more likely to occur in marriages where the power is unequally distributed (Straus, Gelles, and Steinmetz 1980). One explanation is what Craig Allen and Murray Straus (1984) call the "ultimate resource theory." When husbands lack economic or interpersonal skill resources to maintain a dominant position in the marriage, they tend to fall back on a resource that, on average, husbands have more than wives: physical size and strength.

A number of other consequences of marital power have been studied. For example, spouses in egalitarian relationships tend to evaluate each other more highly and perceive that the spouse evaluates them more highly than in husband-dominant relationships (Lundgren, Jergens, and Gibson 1982). Regardless of sex, traditionally male characteristics were attributed to the partner perceived as the leader, and traditionally female characteristics tended to be attributed to the partner with less power (Gerber 1988). Success in losing weight by wives is related to their having an income and control of the checkbook (Hamilton and Zimmerman 1985).

The studies cited indicate that inequality in marriage has serious negative effects. However, some studies suggest that when the inequality is in the form of female dominance, the negative effects are less severe. Both male dominance and female dominance are associated with a higher risk of violence than in egalitarian marriages, but the risk is greatest in male-dominant marriages (Straus, Gelles, and Steinmetz

1980). Some studies have found no harmful consequences of female dominance (Gray 1984; Henggeler et al. 1988).

As a result of these studies, it is known that unequal power in marriage is not merely contrary to democratic and humanistic values; it also has a variety of harmful effects, including lowered marital satisfaction and an increased probability of conflict, stress, depression, and violence.

Measuring Power

Although there is agreement on the importance of understanding and measuring marital power, how to measure it is a subject of controversy. This can be illustrated by the controversy over Blood and Wolfe's (1960) Decision Power Index. This index measures power by asking who had the final say in respect to a series of decisions, such as what house or apartment to take, or how much money to spend per week on food. It stimulated a great deal of research because it is brief and can be included in survey research. Ironically, the Decision Power Index is probably also the most frequently criticized aspect of the research it stimulated. These criticisms do not necessarily mean that other measures are better. In fact, the criticisms apply to at least an equal or greater extent to other measures. In addition, much of the criticism of this instrument is based on plausible assumptions rather than empirical research that compared the Decision Power Index with some other measure and found the other measure to be better. An example is the assumption that, since the Decision Power Index was developed for use in the United States, it is not valid to use it for other societies. Despite the plausibility of this assumption, when it has been used in cultures as diverse as those of Japan and India, the findings tend to parallel those obtained for American couples or to differ in ways that reflect the unique features of that culture and, therefore, show the ability of the Decision Power Index to provide culturally meaningful findings (Allen 1984; Allen and Straus 1984).

Large discrepancies have been found between data provided by a wife and data provided by her husband (Monroe et al. 1985). It has been assumed that this will also result in findings that are different when the analysis uses data from interviewing husbands as compared to findings when the analysis uses data provided by wives. Janet Bokemeier and Pamela Monroe (1983), for example, deplore the fact that most of the eighty studies they reviewed used a single family member as the informant, but they do not discuss any studies that compare the results of testing the same hypothesis using data provided by wives with data provided by husbands. In fact, the few studies that have actually investigated this issue found that the results tend to be parallel (Allen 1984; Allen and Straus 1984; Straus, Gelles, and Steinmetz 1980). The empirical data on reliability do show the Decision Power Index to be low relative to tests with fifty or a hundred items, ignoring the fact that it is not lower than the reliability of other instruments with only eight items (Allen 1984; Allen and Straus 1984). There does not seem to have been research that compares the reliability of the Decision Power Index to other measures of marital power.

The problems of "final say" measures of marital power are serious, and research to develop better measures is needed. However, the available empirical evidence does not show any alternatives that are more valid or more reliable. Different measures do yield different findings, but probably more because they measure different aspects of marital power, not because one is valid and the other is not.

Conclusions

Research from a feminist perspective reinvigorated research on marital power by focusing on gender-based differences in power. This should not obscure the fact that in addition to normative ascription of superior power to husbands and gender bias in economic opportunities, many other characteristics of the partners and the marriage affect the balance of power. Despite considerable progress in understanding the determinants of power in marriage, there is much still to be learned. For this reason, the balance of power in marriage will continue to be an important issue to study. Power will also continue to be an important quality-of-life issue, because research shows that inequality has many harmful effects and because, despite progress toward equality, inequality remains predominant. Thus, it is important that steps to achieve greater equality in marriage be a focus of family life education and family therapy. However, important as these efforts are, it is equally important to keep in mind the research that shows that much of the inequality in marriage has its roots in the inequality between men and women in the larger society. Consequently, an essential part of national family policy is to reduce the inequality between men and women, which is at the heart of much of the imbalance in power between husbands and wives.

(*See also:* Conflict; Dual-Earner Families; Equity and Close Relationships; Family Gender Roles; Family Life

EDUCATION; FAMILY POLICY; FAMILY THERAPY; FAMILY VIOLENCE; GENDER; MARITAL QUALITY; MEASURES OF FAMILY CHARACTERISTICS; RESOURCE MANAGEMENT)

BIBLIOGRAPHY

Aida, Y., and Falbo, T. (1991). "Relationships Between Marital Satisfaction, Resources, and Power Strategies." *Sex Roles* 24:43–56.

Allen, C. M. (1984). "On the Validity of Relative Studies of 'Final Say' Measures of Marital Power." *Journal of Marriage and the Family* 46:619–629.

Allen, C. M., and Straus, M. A. (1984). " 'Final Say' Measures of Marital Power: Theoretical Critique and Empirical Findings from Five Studies in the United States and India." *Journal of Comparative Family Studies* 15:329–344.

Bernard, J. (1972). *The Future of Marriage.* New York: World Publishing.

Blood, R. O., and Wolfe, D. M. (1960). *Husbands and Wives: The Dynamics of Married Living.* New York: Free Press.

Blumberg, R. L., and Coleman, M. T. (1989). "A Theoretical Look at the Gender Balance of Power in the American Couple." *Journal of Family Issues* 10:225–250.

Bokemeier, J., and Monroe, P. (1983). "Continued Reliance on One Respondent in Family Decision-Making Studies: A Content Analysis." *Journal of Marriage and the Family* 45:645–652.

Boss, P. G.; Doherty, W. J.; LaRossa, R.; Schumm, W. R.; and Steinmetz, S., eds. (1993). *Sourcebook of Family Theories and Methods: A Contextual Approach.* New York: Plenum.

Burgest, M. D. R., and Goosby, M. (1985). "Games in Black Male/Female Relationships." *Journal of Black Studies* 15:277–290.

Cancian, F. M. (1987). *Love in America.* New York: Cambridge University Press.

Cate, R. M.; Koval, J. E.; and Ponzetti, J. J., Jr. (1984). "Power Strategies in Dual-Career and Traditional Couples." *Journal of Social Psychology* 123:287–288.

Collins, R. (1971). "A Conflict Theory of Sexual Stratification." *Social Problems* 19:3–21.

Conklin, G. H. (1979). "Cultural Determinants of Power of Women Within the Family." *Journal of Comparative Family Studies* 10:35–54.

Cooney, R. S.; Rogler, L. H.; Hurrell, R. M.; and Ortiz, V. (1982). "Decision Making in Intergenerational Puerto Rican Families." *Journal of Marriage and the Family* 44:621–631.

DeTurck, M. A., and Miller, G. R. (1986). "The Effects of Husbands' and Wives' Social Cognition on Their Marital Adjustment, Conjugal Power, and Self-Esteem." *Journal of Marriage and the Family* 48:715–724.

England, P., and Swoboda, D. (1988). "The Asymmetry of Contemporary Gender-Role Change." *Free Inquiry in Creative Sociology* 16:157–161.

Fowers, B. J. (1991). "His and Her Marriage." *Sex Roles* 24:209–221.

French, J. R. P., and Raven, B. H. (1959). "Bases of Social Power." In *Studies in Social Power,* ed. D. Lartinght. Ann Arbor: University of Michigan Press.

Gerber, G. L. (1988). "Leadership Roles and the Gender Stereotype Traits." *Sex Roles* 18:649–668.

Gillespie, D. L. (1971). "Who Has the Power? The Marital Struggle." *Journal of Marriage and the Family* 33:445–458.

Gray, J. P. (1984). "The Influence of Female Power in Marriage on Sexual Behaviors and Attitudes: A Holocultural Study." *Archives of Sexual Behavior* 13:223–231.

Gray-Little, B. (1982). "Marital Quality and Power Processes Among Black Couples." *Journal of Marriage and the Family* 44:633–646.

Hamilton, N., and Zimmerman, R. (1985). "Weight Control: The Interaction of Marital Power and Weight Loss Success." *Journal of Social Service Research* 8:51–64.

Henggeler, S. W.; Edwards, J. J.; Hanson, C. L.; and Okwumabua, T. M. (1988). "The Psychosocial Functioning of Wife-Dominant Families." *Journal of Family Psychology* 2:188–211.

Hochschild, A. (1989). *The Second Shift.* New York: Avon Books.

Kaufman, G. M. (1988). "Relationship Between Marital Power and Symptoms of Stress Among Husbands and Wives." *Wisconsin Sociologist* 25:35–44.

Komarovsky, M. (1964). *Blue-Collar Marriage.* New York: Random House.

Lee, G. R., and Peterson, L. R. (1983). "Conjugal Power and Spousal Resources in Patriarchal Cultures." *Journal of Comparative Family Studies* 14:23–38.

Lundgren, D. C.; Jergens, V. H.; and Gibson, J. L. (1982). "Marital Power, Roles, and Solidarity and Husbands' and Wives' Appraisals of Self and Other." *Sociological Inquiry* 52:33–52.

Mirowsky, J. (1985). "Depression and Marital Power: An Equity Model." *American Journal of Sociology* 91:557–592.

Moen, P. (1992). *Women's Two Roles.* New York: Auburn House.

Monroe, P. A.; Bokemeier, J. L.; Kotchen, J. M.; and McKean, H. (1985). "Spousal Response Consistency in Decision-Making Research." *Journal of Marriage and the Family* 47:733–738.

Pagelow, M. (1984). *Family Violence.* New York: Praeger.

Pahl, J. (1983). "The Allocation of Money and the Structuring of Inequality Within Marriage." *Sociological Review* 31:237–262.

Rodman, H. (1972). "Marital Power and the Theory of Resources in Cultural Context." *Journal of Comparative Family Studies* 3:50–69.

Sexton, C. S., and Perlman, D. S. (1989). "Couples' Career Orientation, Gender-Role Orientation, and Perceived Equity as Determinants of Marital Power." *Journal of Marriage and the Family* 51:933–941.

Shelton, B. A. (1990). "The Distribution of Household Tasks: Does Wife's Employment Status Make a Difference?" *Journal of Family Issues* 1:115–135.

Spitze, G. (1988). "Women's Employment and Family Relations: A Review." *Journal of Marriage and the Family* 50:595–618.

Straus, M. A. (1975). "Husband–Wife Interaction in Nuclear and Joint Households." In *Women: A Feminist Perspective*, ed. J. Freeman. Mountain View, CA: Mayfield.

Straus, M. A. (1988). "Exchange and Power in Marriage in Cultural Context: Bombay and Minneapolis Comparisons." In *Family and Support Systems Across the Life Span*, ed. S. K. Steinmetz. New York: Plenum.

Straus, M. A.; Gelles, R. J.; and Steinmetz, S. K. (1980). *Behind Closed Doors: Violence in American Families.* Garden City, NY: Doubleday.

Waller, W. (1951). *The Family: A Dynamic Interpretation*, rev. R. Hill. New York: Dryden.

Warner, R. L.; Lee, G. R.; and Lee, J. (1986). "Social Organization, Spousal Resources, and Marital Power." *Journal of Marriage and the Family* 48:121–128.

Whisman, M. A., and Jacobson, N. S. (1990). "Power, Marital Satisfaction, and Response to Marital Therapy." *Journal of Family Psychology* 4:202–212.

Whyte, M. K. (1990). *Dating, Mating, and Marriage.* New York: Walter de Gruyter.

MURRAY A. STRAUS
CARRIE L. YODANIS

MARITAL PROPERTY AND COMMUNITY PROPERTY

The term "marital property" has been defined as any interest that arises in one spouse, with respect to property owned or acquired by the other spouse, solely by virtue of the existence of the marriage (Marsh 1952).

These interests may be involuntary. Involuntary marital property exists or arises by operation of law during the ongoing marriage or upon the termination of marriage on divorce or on the death of one of the spouses. These involuntary marital interests may be modified or relinquished by a couple's agreement or by one spouse's written waiver, sometimes signed only under the law's careful safeguards of disclosure and informed consent, and sometimes carelessly and unknowingly signed.

Other marital property interests may exist by default. The default interests exist by operation of law, but only in the absence of action by the spouse who owns the property. For instance, if a wife dies with a will that disposes of her property, her will may give her surviving husband a smaller share of her property than the law would have provided if she had died intestate—that is, without a will.

One spouse or the other can create still another kind of marital property. Voluntary marital property is created by the gratuitous unilateral act of husband or wife who, by gift, converts "his" property or "her" property into "their" property. A couple's jointly held and jointly titled bank account or home can be called "their" voluntary marital property.

For couples whose marriages end in divorce, marital property is the pot of assets divisible on divorce. What constitutes that pot varies from state to state and sometimes within individual states depending on barely perceived stereotypes of judges and lawyers whose job it is to state what the law is.

The notion of what is the marital property of a married couple may be that of the spouses themselves, sociologists of marriage, or newspaper and magazine advice columnists. These groups are more likely to agree with each other than with the law's characterization. What the law, or, rather, the multifold and simultaneously applicable laws identify for a couple as "their" property, rather than "his" property or "her" property, may often not square with the understanding of the couple or, at least, of one of the two spouses.

One Dear Abby column printed a letter from a wife who complained that her husband had lent $10,000 to his brother; the brother was now driving around in a brand-new car, refusing to pay back any of the $10,000, and her husband refused to try to collect the loan. Dear Abby's response was "Go after the money. It's your money, too." But the wife lived in Oklahoma, and Dear Abby was wrong. If the wife lived in the neighboring state of Texas, Dear Abby would have been right.

In the United States, federal law provides a few of the marital property rules. One example is the federal requirement that the surviving spouse be provided for by the deceased spouse's employment-provided tax-qualified pension plan (Moss 1991). But except for such a limited preemptive override, states' laws govern. American society is a geographically mobile society, with, each year, millions of married couples moving from one state to another. The rules of involuntary marital property interests and of default marital property interests will change for the couple who does not stay put. Even for the couple who never moves, the legislature may, from time to time, enact changes in the rules that affect involuntary or default interests. These rules are, more often than not, enacted inconsistently and without any thought given to what marriage is (or should or could be) or to the ways in which today's marital partnerships can be embodied in the laws of marital property.

What exists is a crazy quilt of marital property laws from state to state within the United States and, for most of the states, even within each state. To understand the why and the what of that crazy quilt, it is necessary to look to history.

History of Marital Property Law

For more than 500 years, there have existed among the Western nations two different concepts of marital property. For these centuries, there have been countries that recognize a system of joint ownership between husband and wife and countries that recognize a system of separate ownership (Donahue 1979; Holdsworth 1903–1972; Maitland [1898] 1978).

Under separate ownership—the "his" or "hers" system—husband and wife own all property separately, whenever or however acquired, except for those items that one or the other or both expressly agree to hold jointly. The husband owns "his" property and the wife "hers," with the quantum of the separately owned interests rarely approaching equality. This is the common-law or separate-property system of the countries where Anglo-American common law is in force.

Under joint ownership—the "theirs" or "ours" system—husband and wife own jointly the property either has acquired during the marriage, unless they have expressly agreed to hold the property separately. This is the community property or marital partnership system of most of the countries of continental Western Europe and of the Western Hemisphere. (The "community" of community property is the marital community—that is, the community of husband and wife.) The common-law countries of Canada and the United States have within them their community property jurisdictions: Quebec in Canada, and Arizona, California, Idaho, Louisiana, Nevada, New Mexico, Puerto Rico, Texas, Washington, and Wisconsin in the United States (McClanahan 1982).

Why are there two different systems? In the Middle Ages, the fundamental division between the separate-property system and the community property system was by no means clear. The idea of a "community of goods" between husband and wife began to exist in countries ranging from Iceland to Portugal; there are intimations of its existence in Britain before the Norman Conquest in 1066 and the growth of the common law of England.

Just across the English Channel, in much of France and in most of the rest of Western Europe, the law was that of community property. The wife was co-owner with her husband of all community property. Under the continental law system, the wife shared with her husband all assets, save perhaps for gifts and inheritances, that were acquired during marriage and could look forward, *whether or not she survived,* to her share of the common pot. The husband was the manager of the community property, but he managed it as agent of the marital community or partnership, for the benefit of both himself and his wife.

However, for reasons of the politics and the law of English feudalism, under which all land whatsoever was held of some lord, and ultimately of the Crown, in a chain-linked pyramid, with links of reciprocal duties of protection and service, English law took the route of separate property.

The English law of "his" property and "her" property incorporated the chain links of feudalism, and its insistence that there could be only one landowner to satisfy the reciprocal obligations, with the result that all property was primarily "his."

In any lands owned by a wife before the marriage or that came to her during the marriage, her husband had an "estate by right of the marriage." He was, in effect, the owner of the lands of his wife for the period of the marriage and, if a child was born to the marriage, for his full lifetime if he survived his wife. The wife's property other than land was even less hers than her land was. Save for the wife's "necessary clothes" or "paraphernalia," as of the moment of marriage her personal property and debts owed her were not hers but her husband's, with his full power to dispose of that property during his lifetime or by will, and subject, therefore, to the claims of the husband's creditors.

What the wife was given, in return for all that was taken from her, was dower, the protective device for the wife who lived to be a widow. A widow was entitled to enjoy, but only for her life, one-third of all lands that her husband himself owned at any time during the marriage. To protect the wife who survived her husband, her dower right attached to and followed the husband's land and could not be extinguished without her agreement. But dower was an inchoate right that ripened for the wife only when she became a widow.

The common law of England gave a wife none of the assets acquired by the husband during marriage, except for the protective dower interest that was hers to enjoy only for her life and only if she survived to be a widow. The common law of England, in addition, took from the wife the assets she had on entering the marriage, giving her back only some of these assets, and only again, if she survived her husband.

The great legal code of sixteenth-century Spain was the source of the law of community property for most of the Western European countries and the Western Hemisphere countries. This code makes explicit that the core and, hence, the raison d'être of the regime or system of community property is the concept of partnership. Legal historians suggest that in England during feudalism "the habits of the great folk are more important than the habits of the small" and, therefore, "the law for the great becomes the law for all" (Maitland [1898] 1978). In England, the wife was thought of as subservient and in need of support and the protection of dower. But other countries, looking at the merchants or the farmers, with family sharing one bread and pot, said that the wife is entitled to half of the marital property because of the marital partnership (Donahue 1979).

In time, and very gradually, the English common law of coverture (defined as the condition or state of a married woman) that, upon marriage, made husband and wife one and that one the husband, lifted. At first, this cover of coverture, which eclipsed the married woman, lifted only for the wealthy.

As the law of trusts developed in England, the courts of equity (but not of law) recognized for the women with lands the concept of a married woman's separate estate. This concept permitted married women fortunate enough to have property to manage their own financial affairs. However, the separate estate did not necessarily provide for the total financial independence of the wealthy wife. Her separate estate, created by a third person for her benefit, might not direct that she be given complete authority to manage and dispose of her property. The disabilities of coverture that denied the married woman legal capacity, including the capacity to contract with respect to her property, did not begin to disappear until the nineteenth century (Chused 1983, 1988; Salmon 1986).

The equitable device of the wife's separate estate benefited only the propertied woman made wealthy by gifts from others. The wife who acquired what little property she had by working for it had no separate estate. The wife who was a boardinghouse keeper, seamstress, farmwife with butter and eggs earnings, storekeeper, shop girl, or factory worker could not claim her earnings as her own, free from her husband's dominion.

The Married Women's Property Acts

During the nineteenth and twentieth centuries, the Married Women's Property Acts were enacted. These acts carried forward the English common-law system into a world that, gradually, dispensed with the husband's estate by marital right; disbursed the eclipse of coverture; and recognized the wife's separate rights and dominion over her own property and, finally, over her earnings.

The Married Women's Property Acts came piecemeal and in fits and starts over more than a century, beginning in Arkansas and Mississippi in the 1830s. These acts were passed in at least three waves, each wave arising for a somewhat different reason. The earliest statutes were enacted primarily to free married women's property from their husband's debts. By and large, these first sets of statutes left untouched the traditional marital estate rules; the eclipse of the wife by coverture continued. The next wave of legislation, before and after the Civil War, established separate estates for married women, without the assistance of equity. Starting in the last third of the nineteenth century, the third wave brought statutes that gave to wives their own earnings. Not until well into the first half of the twentieth century was the last of these statutes enacted. For some few states, restrictions on a wife's power to contract, to engage in business activity, to enter into a commercial partnership with her husband, and to convey her own real property without her husband's consent continued until the 1960s or later (August 1990; Chused 1983, 1988; Warbasse 1987; Wenig 1990).

Finally, as a consequence of the equal rights movement of the 1970s came legislative and judicial action degenderizing marital property laws. Protective rights afforded wives were applied to husbands as well. The inchoate right of dower, or its metamorphosis into the right not to be disinherited, became the husband's right as well as the wife's. In 1979, the U.S. Supreme Court declared unconstitutional a state statute that provided for alimony for the wife but not for the husband. State laws were amended to impose the obligation of support of spouse and children, formerly only the husband's obligation, on the wife as well.

The Married Women's Property Acts, and the subsequent cases and statutes that degenderized marital property law, conferred upon wives no property right enforceable against their husbands. The full-blown separate-property regime, the "his" and "hers" system, looks to title: What is in the wife's name belongs to the wife; what is in the husband's name belongs to the husband. The absoluteness of separate property may be modified in separate-property states, with substantial variations from state to state, by laws of involuntary marital property interests such as the right not to be disinherited, and by laws of default marital property interests such as intestate law. Whatever relief the involuntary and default marital property rules may provide, it is clear that the laws of the separate-property states reject the principle that, during marriage and on the death of a spouse, husband and wife are, because of the marriage, a partnership, with property acquired by either during the marriage constituting "their" or "our" property, rather than "his" or "her" property.

History of Community Property Law

The "our" property jurisdictions of the United States are the states of Arizona, California, Idaho, Louisiana, Nevada, New Mexico, Texas, Washington, and Wisconsin, plus Puerto Rico. All nine community property states, except Wisconsin, recognized the partnership of husband and wife by state constitution or statute early in these states' history. These eight community property states were admitted to statehood over a span of 100 years, from 1812 to 1912.

Only Louisiana arrived with a full-blown civil law system in place, from its French and Spanish heritage, including the community property regime. New Mexico was close. During its long territorial period, New Mexico's laws reflected a strong Spanish influence. The influence of Spanish law was so well accepted that no marital property statutes were deemed necessary for many years, the community property laws being determined by the laws of Spain and Mexico.

The remaining six community property states, by constitution or by legislative act, adopted the English common law. But, at the same time or after the intervention of several years, they carved out an exception to their adoption of common law. They rejected the English laws of property of husband and wife—the husband's estate by marital right and dower—in favor of adoption of community property (August 1990; McClanahan 1982).

Legal historians suggest that in some of these states the climate that produced the Married Women's Property Acts also promoted the adoption of community property law. Some of the newcomers from the East who participated in the California constitutional convention in 1849 believed only that they were enacting a Married Women's Property Act, relieving coverture's disabilities. However, besides having the advantage of the knowledge and experience of some of the debaters of the civil law community property regime, California, in its post-Gold Rush year, had an additional reason; the state needed women. The community property system made much more sense for women, so it was adopted (August 1990; Prager 1976; Wenig 1990).

In the 1970s, the equal protection clause of the U.S. Constitution's Fourteenth Amendment and the equal rights amendments added to some state constitutions were employed in women's quest for equality under the law. Federal and state legislation was scrutinized for discriminatory provisions, and piecemeal or omnibus bills were passed to scour the language of gender discrimination from the law. The then eight community property states changed the husband's "head and master" role as sole manager of the couple's community property by enacting joint management and control statutes, or, for Texas, a separate and equal system of management.

Some among the proponents and opponents of the federal equal rights amendment suggested that enactment would require the equality of ownership of property acquired during marriage that the community property regime provides. Others recognized that a choice could be made and proposed that that choice be the sharing or marital partnership mode.

Wisconsin acted upon that choice. After the defeat in 1974 of a referendum for a Wisconsin equal rights amendment, efforts commenced for marital property reform. The culmination was the 1984 Wisconsin Marital Property Act (WMPA), based on the Uniform Marital Property Act (UMPA). Effective as of 1986, the WMPA converted Wisconsin into the ninth community property state, and the tenth community property jurisdiction, of the United States.

American Community Property Laws

What is the law of community property in the nine community property states? None of these states agree on all aspects of their community property laws, though they have much more in common among themselves than do the common-law or separate-property states. All of the community property states agree that both husband and wife are co-owners of all property that is community property. Each of these states agrees that each spouse has an immediate undivided one-half interest in the marriage's community property. Each of these states agrees also that there can exist separate property, property that may be owned by only one spouse or the other.

There is more agreement than disagreement among the community property states on the basic principles of community property and separate property:

> Separate property is property that is acquired prior to marriage and that property's traceable proceeds and reinvestments, plus gifts and inheritances of a spouse from third persons.

- Community property is almost everything else.
- The general presumption favors the community; property acquired during marriage is presumed to be community property.
- A particular item of property—for instance, a home, pension, or business owned by one spouse prior to the marriage—can, in time, become "mixed" property, part separate and part community.
- By transmutation (by agreement or gift) or commingling, separate or mixed property can become community property.
- By premarital agreement and, for most of the community property states, by agreement entered into after the marriage, a couple can elect out of the community property regime (McClanahan 1982; Mennell 1988).

The major divergence comes with respect to the "fruits" or income rule. Income of community property is, of course, community property. But in five of the community property states—Arizona, California, New Mexico, Nevada, and Washington—"rents, issues, and profits" of separate property are separate. This is the "American" rule, ushered in in 1860 by the California Supreme Court in an "infamous decision" written by a man who was a recent judicial importation to California from an eastern state and who had no knowledge of, or fondness for, community property (Reppy and DeFuniak 1975).

Texas, faced with the language of its law that replicated the California statute mauled by the eastern judge, adhered to the correct rule. This is the rule of Texas's ancestral Spain, and of all the other community property countries, that separate property income during marriage is community property. This "fruits" rule is also the law in Idaho, Louisiana, Wisconsin, and Puerto Rico, the four other community property jurisdictions that ignored or rejected California's misinterpretation.

The community property laws of the ten jurisdictions may vary from each other in other details as well. Since this is an area of state law, there is only the community property law of each particular jurisdiction, as laid down by its own statutes and interpreted by the decision of its own courts.

The methods of characterization of increase in value during marriage of separate property vary from state to state and from case to case within some states, with respect to different kinds of property, such as home or other real property, life insurance or retirement benefits, or business enterprise or investment properties (Wenig 1989). For instance, if a woman owns a home before her marriage, that home starts out as separate property. But the marital community—that is, both wife and husband, or either of them—contributes mortgage payments, or cash or labor toward capital improvements to the home. A few of the community property states apply a reimbursement rule that either allocates to the marital community the amount of the contribution during marriage or allocates to the original owner the value of the separate home upon the marriage. Other community property states identify the portion of the value of "mixed" property that is community and the portion that is separate property by use of an apportioning fraction.

The community property states may differ from each other on the characterization of funds recovered for personal injuries or disability payments.

For some but not all of the community property states, spouses' joint ownership with right of survivorship, an important *voluntary* marital property interest in the separate-property states, may be considered incompatible with community property.

Some of the community property states hold that the marital community and, hence, the ongoing accrual of community property interests cease once a couple is "living separate and apart." Other community property states hold that only divorce or death terminates the marital community.

Because both husband and wife are equal co-owners of their community property (unless both agree to the contrary), in all of the community property states, on the death of either husband or wife, their community property is divided equally between the estate of the deceased spouse and the surviving spouse. There is no such unanimity on divorce. Only a few of the community property states insist on equal division of the divorcing couple's community property. Some of the community property states permit the divorce court to divide the spouses' community property equitably, and not necessarily equally, between them. One or two community property states also permit the divorce court to divide equitably not only the couple's community property but also the separate property of one spouse or the other (McClanahan 1982; Mennell 1988).

Some of the community property states apply a "quasi-community property" concept to protect the nonpropertied spouse of the couple who has migrated from a separate-property state. For instance, a married couple may move from a northern, separate-property state down to a retirement community in California. During their residence in the north, most of the property may have been accumulated by the wife and titled in her name only. By use of the quasi-community property concept, on the death of the wife, survived by the husband, property titled in the wife's name will be treated as if it were community property and divided between her estate and the husband; on divorce, that property will be treated as if it were community property, equally owned by both the husband and the wife. But, because quasi-community property is not community property, if the husband predeceases the wife, the husband's estate cannot share in these quasi-community property assets.

Separate-Property States

"No-fault divorce" was officially ushered in by a California statute in 1969 and by the promulgation in 1970 by the National Conference of Commissioners of Uniform State Laws of its Uniform Marriage and Divorce Act (UMDA) (Kay 1990).

Equitable distribution of property on divorce did not start with the no-fault divorce revolution. Some of the separate-property states did provide for property settlement, as well as alimony, on divorce. However, there were no guidelines, standards, or definitions to aid the divorce court. It was the 1970 UMDA that introduced the concept and definition of marital property to the separate-property states.

The original version of the UMDA directed the court to divide marital property in just proportions and defined marital property as including all property acquired by either spouse subsequent to the marriage, with the principal exception of gifts and inheritances. However, the Family Law Section of the American Bar Association (ABA) opposed the UMDA's marital property provision and fought for and won reversion to "kitchen sink" equitable distribution without characterization of property as marital or separate, with each case to "depend on its own facts."

Nonetheless, despite the rejection of the UMDA's marital property concept on divorce, that concept now predominates. The equitable-distribution statutes of the separate-property states can be categorized as dual property systems (systems that at divorce characterize property as marital property and separate property) with untouchable separate property, dual property systems with reachable separate property, and kitchen sink systems. Half of the noncommunity property states are in the first category, the one rejected by the ABA Family Law Section; the rest of the noncommunity property states are almost equally divided between those that characterize property as marital and separate but permit division of separate property if needed and those that need not characterize property to divide it but are, in fact, beginning to do so (Wenig 1989, 1990). In addition, deferred or quasi-community property has arrived in the separate-property states.

What exists now, in all of the states of the United States, is recognition that marriage is an economic partnership. But it is only with respect to, and at the end of, the pathological marriage—the marriage that ends in divorce—that the marital partnership is recognized by the separate-property states. Community property states, on the other hand, also recognize the partnership during marriage and upon the termination of the marriage on the death of a spouse.

(*See also*: Divorce: Legal Aspects; Divorce: Economic Aspects; Inheritance; Premarital Agreements)

BIBLIOGRAPHY

August, R. (1990). "The Spread of Community Property Law to the Far West." *Western Legal History* 3:35–66.

Baker, J. H. (1979). *An Introduction to English Legal History*, 2nd edition. London: Butterworth.

Berman, H. J. (1994). "The Origins of Historical Jurisprudence: Coke, Selden, Hale." *Yale Law Journal* 103:1651–1738.

Blumstein, P., and Schwartz, P. (1983). *American Couples.* New York: William Morrow.

Cheadle, E. A. (1981). "The Development of Sharing Principles in Common-Law Marital Property States." *University of California at Los Angeles Law Review* 28:1269–1313.

Chused, R. (1983). "Married Women's Property Law, 1800–1850." *Georgetown Law Journal* 71:1359–1425.

Chused, R. (1988). *Cases, Materials, and Problems in Property.* New York: Matthew Bender.

Donahue, C. (1979). "What Causes Fundamental Legal Ideas? Marital Property in England and France in the Thirteenth Century." *Michigan Law Review* 78:59–88.

Holcomb, L. (1983). *Wives and Property—Reform of the Married Women's Property Law in Nineteenth-Century England.* Oxford, Eng.: Martin Robertson.

Holdsworth, W. (1903–1972). *A History of English Law*, 17 vols. London: Methuen.

Jacob, H. (1988). *Silent Revolution: The Transformation of Divorce Law in the United States.* Chicago: University of Chicago Press.

Kay, H. H. (1990). "Beyond No-Fault: New Directions in Divorce Reform." In *Divorce Reform at the Crossroads*, ed. S. D. Sugarman and H. H. Kay. New Haven, CT: Yale University Press.

Maitland, F. W. ([1898] 1978). *The History of English Law Before the Time of Edward I*, 2nd edition. Cambridge, Eng.: Cambridge University Press.

Marsh, H., Jr. (1952). *Marital Property in Conflict of Laws.* Seattle: University of Washington Press.

McClanahan, W. S. (1982). *Community Property Law in the United States.* Rochester, NY: Lawyers Cooperative Publishing.

Mennell, P. L., and Boykoff, T. M. (1988). *Community Property in a Nutshell,* 2nd edition. St. Paul, MN: West Publishing.

Moss, A. (1991). *Your Pension Rights at Divorce.* Washington, DC: Pension Rights Center.

Prager, S. W. (1976). "The Persistence of Separate Property Concepts in California's Community Property System 1849–1975." *University of California at Los Angeles Law Review* 24:1–82.

Reppy, W. A., Jr., and DeFuniak, W. Q. (1975). *Community Property in the United States.* Indianapolis, IN: Bobbs-Merrill.

Salmon, M. (1986). *Women and the Law of Property in Early America.* Chapel Hill: University of North Carolina Press.

Siegel, R. B. (1994). "Home as Work: The First Women's Rights Claims Concerning Wives' Household Labor, 1850–1880." *Yale Law Journal* 103:1073–1217.

Warbasse, E. (1987). *The Changing Legal Rights of Married Women, 1800–1861.* New York: Garland.

Wenig, M. M. (1989). "The Increase in Value of Separate Property During Marriage: Examination and Proposals." *Family Law Quarterly* 23:301–337.

Wenig, M. M. (1990). "The Marital Property Law of Connecticut: Past, Present, and Future." *Wisconsin Law Review* 1990:809–879.

MARY MOERS WENIG

MARITAL QUALITY

When Americans are asked to rate or rank their life goals, having a happy marriage is always among the most important. People in most other modern societies seem to be somewhat less enamored of marriage than Americans, but with the possible exception of Scandinavians, who have often chosen nonmarital cohabitation over marriage, most adults throughout the modern world devote much effort to striving for a happy and satisfying marriage. Given the prominence and prevalence of this goal, family social scientists and psychologists could hardly avoid trying to assess the extent of its attainment and to identify the conditions under which it is likely to be attained. These efforts have been extensive, and the academic and clinical literature that deals with marital happiness and/or satisfaction is huge, with the number of relevant books, articles, and chapters published in the United States alone since the 1960s numbering in the thousands.

The terms "marital happiness" and "marital satisfaction" are closely related, but not synonymous (Campbell, Converse, and Rodgers 1976). Both refer to positive feelings that a spouse derives from a marriage, and both happiness and satisfaction are broader and more global in their meaning than such concepts as enjoyment, pleasure, and contentment. According to Angus Campbell, Philip Converse, and Willard Rodgers (1976), marital happiness is based on an affective evaluation, whereas marital satisfaction seems to have a more cognitive basis that involves a relation of one's circumstances to some standard. They found that marital happiness varied positively with formal education, while the most highly educated persons reported somewhat less marital satisfaction than those with less education. However, marital happiness and satisfaction are highly correlated and generally have been found to bear a similar relationship to other variables; thus, the common practice of using the two terms interchangeably in literature reviews is sloppy, but not a very serious error. This entry uses "marital quality" as a blanket term to cover either or both.

Marital quality is often used in a sense that includes marital adjustment as well as happiness and satisfaction. However, it is better to conceive of marital adjustment as something that may affect marital quality but is not part of it, since adjustment is an aspect of the relationship between spouses rather than a feeling experienced by each of them. Such indicators of adjustment as conflict, communication, and sharing of activities may relate differently to the spouses' feelings in different marriages, or even differently to the husband's and wife's feelings in the same marriage. The literature on marital adjustment is quite closely related to that on marital happiness and adjustment; the two literatures cannot be cleanly separated, since some marital quality scales (e.g., the widely used Dyadic Adjustment Scale) mix elements of adjustment with spouses' evaluations of their marriages (Spanier 1976). However, the focus in this entry is only on marital quality, as indicated by husbands' and wives' evaluations.

Measurement Issues

Marital happiness and satisfaction are often measured by single, straightforward questions that ask respondents to rate their marriages on a scale of happiness or satisfaction. There may be up to ten points on the scale, but often there are only three or four.

The prevailing view in family social science is that such single-item indicators of marital quality are unsophisticated, and they are shunned by many researchers in favor of scales and multiple-item indices. Nevertheless, the best evidence on trends in and correlates of marital quality are based on responses to one, two, or three questions, since more complex measures have very rarely been used with large and representative samples. Furthermore, several critics have argued for the use of global measures of marital quality rather than multidimensional scales and indices that include variables that may influence or be influenced by spouses' evaluations of their marriages (e.g., Fincham and Bradbury 1987; Huston, McHale, and Crouter 1986; Huston and Robins 1982; Norton 1983). One may go beyond these critics and argue that one-item measures are sometimes superior to even two- and three-item scales and indices.

If a question has high face validity, as the straightforward questions about marital happiness and satisfaction do, then any other questions will have a lower face validity and perforce must deal with something other than simply happiness or satisfaction. The purpose of multiple-item scales is to measure "latent" variables for which no direct measurement is possible and for which several indirect measures produce a higher degree of validity than a single one can. The usual assumption seems to be that there can be no simple, direct, and straightforward measure of feelings or other psychological characteristics, although single-item measures of date of birth, gender, and various demographic characteristics are routinely used. However, the correctness of this assumption is not self-evident, and the preference for multiple-item indicators for all psychological characteristics may grow primarily out of the researchers' need to feel sophisticated.

Nevertheless, most questions used to gauge marital happiness and satisfaction provide only crude measurement, if only because they offer only a few response alternatives, and the distribution of responses is usually highly skewed. For instance, the question about marital happiness most often used on national surveys in the United States offers only three degrees of happiness—"very happy," "pretty happy," and "not too happy"—and up to two-thirds of the respondents select the highest degree. Much of the variance in marital happiness must be among those who select the "very happy" alternative, but the measure is not finely calibrated enough to capture that variance. Furthermore, there is probably a systematic overreporting of marital happiness and satisfaction, due not only to social desirability considerations—the most commonly discussed source of response bias—but also due to denial and a stoic tendency to put up a happy front. The extent of any such bias is unknown, and perhaps unknowable, but the likelihood that it is substantial is high enough to make it unwise to take reports of marital happiness and satisfaction at face value. Generally, only trends in the reports, and differences among categories of married persons, are worthy of interpretation. Of course, changes and differences in response bias may occasionally affect trend and comparative data.

Trends in Reported Marital Happiness

An essential part of the task of assessing the state of marriage in a modern society is to gauge change in the overall level of reported marital quality. Unfortunately, the data necessary for this task are quite limited for most societies, the United States being no exception. Until the early 1990s, about the only published evidence on this issue for the United States was from the Americans View Their Mental Health Surveys, conducted with national samples in 1957 and 1976. Joseph Veroff, Elizabeth Douvan, and Richard A. Kulka (1981) compared responses at the two dates to the question, "Taking things all together, how would you describe your marriage—would you say that your marriage was very happy, a little happier than average, just about average, or not too happy?" The "very happy" responses increased from 47 to 53 percent, and the combined "average" and "not too happy" responses declined from 32 to 20 percent—an indication of a moderate increase in marital happiness. The importance of not combining evaluations of specific aspects of marriages with global evaluations is illustrated by the fact that the percent of respondents who said "nothing" in response to a question about "not so nice things" about their marriage declined from 31 to 23, and the percent who reported problems with their marriage rose from 46 to 61. There apparently were specific aspects of marriages not covered by the questions that tended to improve from 1957 to 1976.

The most common reason given for the 1957–1976 increase in average marital happiness is that the steep increase in divorce beginning in 1965 improved the speed and effectiveness of the removal of persons in poor marriages from the married population. Since the divorce rate continued to rise after 1976 before leveling off at a very high level in the 1980s, there are reasons to suspect that the increase in marital happiness continued after 1976—a suspicion often voiced by commentators on American marriage.

The best relevant data, however, indicate otherwise. The General Social Surveys conducted by the

National Opinion Research Center have asked a simple marital happiness question of its married respondents annually since 1973, except in 1979, 1981, and 1992 (Davis and Smith 1993). The question is worded, "Taking things all together, would you say that your marriage is very happy, pretty happy, or not too happy?" Fewer than 5 percent of the respondents have typically chosen the "not too happy" alternative, so the data are often collapsed into "very happy" versus less favorable responses. The 1973–1993 trend is shown in Figure 1, the linear trend line being distinctly downward, though only at the rate of .32 points per year.

The important thing about these findings is not that reported marital happiness declined moderately, but that it did not increase substantially, as it should have done if the main reason for the increase in divorce in recent decades was, as the sanguine view of American marriage would have it, an increased reluctance of persons to endure poor marriages. Assuming the validity of the reports of marital happiness, the sanguine view is clearly indefensible; the increase in divorce must have resulted to a large extent from an increased tendency for marriages to go bad. This point is illustrated by the other two linear trend lines in Figure 1. The decline in the percent of persons in very happy marriages was steeper for all ever-married, nonwidowed persons (.60 points per year) and for all persons age thirty or older (.73 points per year) than for those currently married. Data on the trend in percent of ever-married, nonwidowed persons in marriages in which they reported to be "very happy" at various lengths of time after the first marriage indicate that a decreasing proportion of the persons in the United States who marry at least once are finding the marital happiness they seek (Glenn 1991, 1993). In addition, the increase in divorce has not even decreased the proportion of persons who say they are in less than happy marriages at various lengths of time after the first marriage.

One might speculate that the apparent decline in the prospects of achieving a good marriage is illusory and has resulted from an increased tendency of persons in unsatisfactory marriages to report the quality of their marriages honestly. There is no definitive evidence that this explanation is not correct, but if the validity of reports of marital happiness had increased, the relationship of reported marital happiness to variables likely to be affected by marital happiness should have increased; that did not happen. For instance, the relationship of reported marital happiness to reported global (personal) happiness remained virtually stable from 1973 to 1993.

Why has the probability of attaining happy and satisfying marriages in the United States declined? Since few commentators have recognized such a change or conceded that it has probably occurred, little has been written on the topic. Norval D. Glenn (1991) has speculated that a decline in the ideal of marital permanence has made persons less willing and less able to

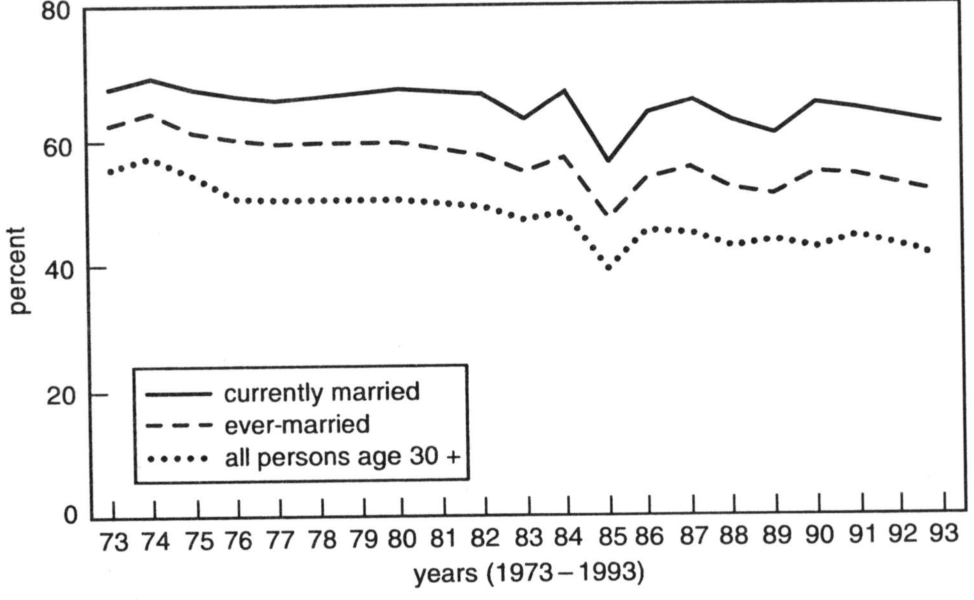

Figure 1 Percent of currently married persons, ever-married and not widowed persons, and all persons age thirty or older who reported being in a very happy marriage.

make the commitments, sacrifices, and "investments" of energy, time, and lost opportunities that are necessary to make marriages succeed. The breakdown in consensus about marital roles, whereby the terms of the marriage must be negotiated by each married couple and often must be renegotiated during the course of the marriage, has almost certainly contributed to the change, as have increased expectations of marriage. Disagreement over the division of household responsibilities has also emerged as a major cause of trouble in American marriages (Berk 1985; Booth et al. 1984).

Bases of Marital Quality

Marriage counselors, ministers, various custodians of the folklore, and perhaps even family social scientists and psychologists may possess a great deal of wisdom about how to achieve and maintain happy and satisfying marriages. Many people probably know a great deal about how to achieve a happy marriage, but that knowledge is based hardly at all on systematic research. In spite of the enormous amount of research devoted to the topic, truly scientific evidence on the bases of marital happiness and satisfaction is meager. One reason may be that marital quality is inherently hard to study, but a more certain reason is that most of the research has been seriously deficient.

Consider, for instance, the many cross-sectional studies of samples of married persons in which various demographic and social variables have been related to the respondents' reports of their marital happiness or satisfaction. These studies have amassed a large body of evidence on the correlates of the measures of marital quality and have often inferred cause and effect from the correlational data. Even though some of the studies have used apparently sophisticated causal modeling, virtually none of the research has met the requirements for valid causal inference. An inherent limitation of studies concentrating on currently married persons, especially in a society with very high divorce rates, is that many of the persons among whom negative influences on marital quality have been the strongest have been selected out of the sampled population through divorce. Therefore, the effects of the negative influences will be underestimated or not detected at all in analyses of data on married persons, or positive effects may even be attributed to the influences.

There are two aspects of the problem. First, divorce lessens the variance of marital quality, thus attenuating estimates of effects on that variable. Second, if variables that affect marital quality affect the probability of divorce in ways other than via marital quality, the estimates of the effects can be substantially biased in either direction. A hypothetical case will illustrate the point. Suppose that celebrity status typically has negative effects on marital quality and that it increases the probability of divorce (by providing numerous alternatives to the current marriage) at each level of marital quality. If the latter effect is very strong and the former is relatively weak, a causal analysis with cross-sectional data that does not take the selection factor into account will estimate the effect of celebrity status on marital quality to be positive. Suppose that adherence to a particular religious ideology typically exerts positive influence on marital quality but decreases the probability of divorce at each level of marital quality. In this case, the straightforward testing of a simple causal model may indicate a negative effect of religious adherence on marital quality, or at least it will yield an attenuated estimated positive effect.

It is theoretically possible, of course, to incorporate selection processes into causal models to obtain unbiased estimates of effects (Berk 1983; Heckman 1979), but the methods developed to do this have been criticized as inadequate, and in any event, they require information the researcher rarely has. Given the limitations of corrections for "sample selection bias," it is hardly lamentable that they have rarely been used in studies of the bases of marital quality.

A more promising solution to the problems posed by the use of cross-sectional data from samples of married individuals to infer effects on marital quality is to use longitudinal data or cross-sectional data from samples including formerly married as well as currently married individuals. Except in those rare studies in which marital quality has been assessed at frequent intervals before divorces have occurred, such research requires the assumption that marital quality becomes low before divorce occurs, but that assumption seems generally justified. Overall, longitudinal data are, of course, better for the purpose at hand, but cross-sectional data can be used to assess the effects of background variables that can be measured with reasonable accuracy through retrospective reports. Unfortunately, research with these designs has been rare, and such research with data from large and representative national samples is only in its infancy. As it increases, a substantial increment in credible evidence on the effects of several demographic and social variables on marital quality can be expected.

In the meantime, the evidence on the bases of marital happiness and marital satisfaction from "mainstream" quantitative social science consists almost entirely of a body of weak correlations and estimates of weak effects. The lack of strong relationships no doubt results in large measure from some of the most important influences on marital quality not being amenable to measurement on large-scale surveys and thus not being taken into account. Individuals' feelings about their marriages are also subject to considerable short-term fluctuation, and the variance resulting from this fluctuation will not be explained by the major long-term influences on marital quality. There is also the attenuation of measured relationships resulting from the selection of many of the people with the least satisfactory marriages out of the population of married persons.

These limitations of the evidence do not mean that it is worthless, but only that it should be interpreted with caution. Most of the estimates of effects are probably in the right direction, and theory, common sense, and what is known about the phenomena studied from sources other than the data at hand (side information) can provide strong clues about when to suspect that the estimated direction is wrong. When theory and common sense suggest that the direction of the estimated effects is right, it should often be suspected that the real world effects are stronger than the estimated ones. Since correlational data not used to test explicitly specified causal models can suggest effects on marital quality, it is useful to discuss briefly some of the frequently found correlates.

One of the most frequent findings concerning marital quality is that it bears a nonmonotonic relationship to family life stage, being high in the preparental stage, lower in the parental stages, and relatively high in the "empty nest" or postparental stage. Although every few years someone publishes an article challenging the existence of this nonmonotonic relationship, its cross-sectional existence is hardly in doubt; it has been found by numerous studies conducted over more than twenty years, and the data from large national samples reported in Table 1 clearly show it. The reasons for and meaning of this cross-sectional relationship are not clear, however, and it is much less than certain that marriages that survive through all of the stages typically follow the down-up pattern suggested by the cross-sectional data (Vaillant and Vaillant 1993).

Most of the data on family life stage and marital quality confound any effects of presence–absence of children with those of duration of marriage. However, research has shown that each of these variables bears a relationship to measures of marital quality when the other is held constant (e.g., Glenn 1989; McLanahan and Adams 1989; White and Booth 1985; White, Booth, and Edwards 1986). That average marital quality drops during the first few years of marriage is hardly in doubt, especially in view of the fact that a high divorce rate during those years eliminates many of the worst marriages and prevents many marital failures from being reflected in the cross-sectional data. That reported marital quality is typically lower after the birth of the first child than earlier is also not in doubt, but in spite of numerous studies of the transition to parenthood (e.g., Belsky, Spanier, and Rovine 1983; Feldman and Nash 1984; Goldberg, Michaels, and Lamb 1985; McHale and Huston 1985), it still is not certain that the addition of a child to the family typically brings about any permanent reduction in marital quality. At least one study has found evidence that the cross-sectional association of the presence of a child or children with low marital quality results to a large extent, though not totally, from the fact that children tend to prevent or delay divorce and keep unhappily married couples together, at least temporarily (White, Booth, and Edwards 1986). The apparent upturn in marital quality in the postparental stage is probably real, though small, but the existence of positive duration-of-marriage effects beyond the middle years is not at all certain, since the cross-sectional data confound any effects of marital duration with those of cohort membership and the divorces of unhappily married persons.

Some of the other data in Table 1 suggest influences stronger than those of family stage or duration of marriage. Since reported marital happiness varies directly with frequency of attendance of religious services and strength of identification with a religious group or denomination and is higher for persons who report a religious preference than for those who say they have no religion, religiosity is probably a rather strong positive influence on marital quality, especially since indicators of religiosity are also associated with low divorce rates (Glenn and Supancic 1984). However, more than religiosity may be involved in the relationship between frequency of attendance of religious services and marital quality. Such attendance is an indicator of social participation and social integration as well as religiosity, and there are many suggestions in literature that social integration is conducive to marital success. The data in Table 1 indicating that frequency of association with extended family members is positively related to marital happiness are also consistent with the social integration explanation of marital happiness.

The literature on African-American–white differences in the probability of marital success is exten-

Table 1 Percent of Married Persons Who Reported Very Happy Marriages

Characteristic	*Husbands*	*(n)*	*Wives*	*(n)*
Hours per Week Wife Worked Outside Home				
0–9	68.4	(4,120)	63.7	(4,627)
10–29	65.9	(705)	63.1	(841)
30 or more	66.2	(2,580)	63.1	(2,836)
Race				
White	68.6	(6,691)	65.1	(7,482)
African American	54.5	(595)	48.3	(654)
Education				
Less than high school	66.4	(2,194)	56.7	(2,135)
High school	67.9	(3,503)	64.8	(4,761)
Junior college	61.4	(233)	62.4	(272)
Bachelor's degree	68.4	(938)	71.6	(844)
Graduate degree	69.1	(548)	67.6	(275)
Husband's Occupational Prestige*				
Low	64.9	(3,153)	60.2	(3,597)
Medium	69.3	(3,095)	64.9	(3,430)
High	70.8	(745)	74.6	(748)
Age at First Marriage†				
12–19	65.2	(741)	62.6	(2,690)
20–22	69.6	(2,005)	65.7	(2,284)
23–39	67.5	(3,274)	65.0	(1,912)
Years Since First Marriage†				
0–2	75.0	(323)	78.8	(391)
3–5	63.8	(575)	66.6	(623)
6–8	63.2	(493)	64.4	(543)
9–11	63.7	(393)	61.6	(490)
12–14	68.2	(349)	64.1	(473)
15–19	63.5	(600)	58.5	(681)
20–24	63.6	(584)	59.6	(732)
25–29	69.3	(647)	62.0	(713)
30–39	68.6	(1,040)	67.1	(1,225)
40 or more	74.0	(1,074)	64.0	(1,046)
Family Life Stage				
Preparental	70.8	(994)	74.4	(1,094)
Parental	64.5	(3,771)	59.6	(4,375)
Postparental	70.2	(2,659)	65.1	(2,823)
Spend a Social Evening with Relatives				
Never or infrequently	59.9	(484)	51.8	(463)
Several times a year	62.0	(876)	61.8	(880)
About once a month	64.5	(828)	62.8	(785)
Once or twice a week/several times a month	69.3	(2,139)	65.2	(2,534)
Almost daily	72.6	(246)	66.3	(334)
Religious Preference				
Protestant	68.1	(4,743)	63.9	(5,493)
Catholic	69.5	(1,864)	62.6	(2,172)
Jewish	68.4	(152)	68.6	(188)
None	53.5	(518)	56.8	(337)
Identification with a Religion or Denomination				
Strong	75.1	(2,333)	69.1	(3,436)
Somewhat strong	65.3	(702)	62.5	(755)
Not very strong	64.0	(3,114)	57.5	(2,946)
Attendance of Religious Services				
Never	57.8	(978)	58.9	(855)
Infrequently	62.8	(1,792)	58.7	(1,418)
Several times a year	67.5	(1,006)	61.1	(1,067)
One to three times a month	67.8	(1,117)	59.2	(1,343)
Weekly or almost weekly	73.0	(1,968)	68.0	(2,746)
Several times a week	77.6	(532)	71.2	(836)

* Hodge-Siegel-Rossi scores: Low = 9–39; Medium = 40–59; High = 60–82.

† Persons in first marriages only.

SOURCE The 1973–1991 General Social Survey Cumulative File (Davis and Smith 1993). Data are weighted on number of persons age 18 or older in the household.

sive, yet there is no definitive evidence as to why reported marital quality is higher among whites (see Table 1) and divorce rates are lower. The measures of socioeconomic status usually included on social surveys do not account for much of the difference and in fact do not relate strongly to either reported marital quality or the probability of divorce (Glenn and Supancic 1984). Of course, this does not mean that past differences in economic conditions or differences in economic security are not important reasons for the racial difference in the probability of marital success, but their influence may be largely through such variables as the lower sex ratio among African Americans (Guttentag and Secord 1983).

The lack of even a moderately strong relationship between reported marital happiness and two of the independent variables included in Table 1 illustrates the danger of concluding that there is no effect on marital quality on the basis of cross-sectional data. The indicated differences in marital happiness by age at first marriage (shown only for persons in their first marriages) are quite small, which might lead to the conclusion that early marriages are almost as successful on average as marriages of more mature persons. However, the divorce rate *does* vary substantially by age at marriage—an indication that early marriages are unusually likely to have failed, either by ending in divorce or being less than satisfactory (Bumpass and Sweet 1972; Schoen 1975). It appears that persons who find themselves in less than satisfactory marriages within a few years after marriage are more likely to divorce if they were married early, and this results in a very small difference in marital quality between early and late marriers in intact first marriages.

The data in Table 1 show virtually no relationship between the number of hours the wife worked outside the home and the reported marital happiness of either the wife or the husband. There is no definitive evidence that the wife's working outside the home *does* affect marital quality, but these cross-sectional data do not prove that it does not. Suppose that at each level of marital quality, the probability of divorce varies directly with the number of hours the wife works outside the home—not an unlikely relationship. If so, poor marriages will be more quickly ended among couples in which the wife works more hours outside the home, thus raising the average marital quality in the remaining marriages in that category. If so, marital quality should vary positively with number of hours worked by the wife unless wives' working outside the home has a negative effect on marital success.

Dozens of other variables have been related to measures of marital happiness and satisfaction, but the ones discussed here are among those to which the greatest attention has been devoted. The deficiencies in the evidence of the causal importance of these variables is illustrative of the weakness of the body of "scientific" study concerning the bases of marital quality.

Consequences of Marital Quality

In contrast to the literature on the bases of marital quality, that on its consequences is quite sparse. About the only variables likely to be affected by marital quality to which strong relationships have been shown to exist are global happiness and life satisfaction (Andrews and Withey 1976; Campbell, Converse, and Rodgers 1976; Glenn and Weaver 1981). Data from the 1982–1991 General Social Surveys show that the percent of married persons who said they were personally very happy varied from 57.2, for those who said they had "very happy" marriages, to 11.2 and 2.6, respectively, for those reporting "pretty happy" and "not too happy" marriages. Although this relationship may be partially spurious, it is likely to be largely causal, since theory and common sense predict strong effects of marital quality on life quality. If so, the data indicate that having a good marriage is virtually necessary, though not sufficient, for global happiness.

Research on the effects of marital quality is likely to increase along at least two different lines. There is already a great deal of evidence on the probable effects of marital status on physical and mental health (Umberson 1987; Verbrugge 1979), and researchers are beginning to perceive the need to do equally extensive and sophisticated research on the health effects of marital quality. Simply stated, the main question is: How bad does a marriage have to be before it is worse than no marriage at all? There is also much discussion, especially in the journalistic and policy literature, about the effects of marital quality on children, as conservatives and communitarians have challenged the orthodox liberal belief that it is better for the children if the parents divorce when a marriage goes bad. Virtually everyone agrees that a violent or extremely hostile marriage is bad for children, but how bad does a marriage have to be for the children to benefit from the parents' separation? Excluding the most hostile and conflict-ridden marriages, is there any close relationship between the quality of the parents' marriage and the children's well-being? So far, well-conducted research has provided hints, but no compelling evidence.

(*See also:* Communication; Conflict; Demography; Division of Labor; Divorce: Emotional and Social Aspects; Dual-Earner Families; Family Gender Roles; Measures of Family Characteristics; Remarriage)

BIBLIOGRAPHY

Andrews, F. M., and Withey, S. B. (1976). *Social Indicators of Well-Being: Americans' Perceptions of Life Quality.* New York: Plenum.

Belsky, J.; Spanier, G.; and Rovine, M. (1983). "Stability and Change in Marriage Across the Transition to Parenthood: A Second Study." *Journal of Marriage and the Family* 45:567–577.

Berk, R. A. (1983). "An Introduction to Sample Selection Bias in Sociological Data." *American Sociological Review* 48:386–398.

Berk, S. F. (1985). *The Gender Factory.* New York: Plenum.

Booth, A.; Johnson, D. R.; White, L.; and Edwards, J. N. (1984). "Women, Outside Employment, and Marital Instability." *American Journal of Sociology* 90:567–583.

Bumpass, L. L., and Sweet, J. A. (1972). "Differentials in Marital Instability: 1970." *American Sociological Review* 37:754–766.

Campbell, A.; Converse, P.; and Rodgers, W. (1976). *The Quality of American Life: Perceptions, Evaluations, and Satisfactions.* New York: Russell Sage Foundation.

Davis, J. A., and Smith, T. (1993). *The General Social Surveys, 1972–1993: Cumulative Data File.* Chicago: National Opinion Research Center.

Feldman, S., and Nash, C. S. (1984). "The Transition from Expectancy to Parenthood: Impact of the Firstborn Child on Men and Women." *Sex Roles* 11:84–92.

Fincham, F. D., and Bradbury, T. N. (1987). "The Assessment of Marital Quality: A Reevaluation." *Journal of Marriage and the Family* 49:797–809.

Glenn, N. D. (1989). "Duration of Marriage, Family Composition, and Marital Happiness." *National Journal of Sociology* 3:3–24.

Glenn, N. D. (1991). "The Recent Trend in Marital Success in the United States." *Journal of Marriage and the Family* 53:161–270.

Glenn, N. D. (1993). "The News is Bad, But Not Quite as Bad as First Reported: A Correction." *Journal of Marriage and the Family* 55:242–243.

Glenn, N. D., and Supancic, M. (1984). "The Social and Demographic Correlates of Divorce and Separation in the United States: An Update and Reconsideration." *Journal of Marriage and the Family* 46:563–575.

Glenn, N. D., and Weaver, C. N. (1981). "The Contribution of Marital Happiness to Global Happiness." *Journal of Marriage and the Family* 43:161–168.

Goldberg, W. A.; Michaels, G. Y.; and Lamb, M. E. (1985). "Husbands' and Wives' Patterns of Adjustment to Pregnancy and First Parenthood." *Journal of Family Issues* 6:483–504.

Guttentag, M., and Secord, P. F. (1983). *Too Many Women: The Sex Ratio Question.* Newbury Park, CA: Sage Publications.

Heckman, J. J. (1979). "Sample Selection Bias as a Specification Error." *Econometrica* 45:153–161.

Huston, T. L.; McHale, S. M.; and Crouter, A. C. (1986). "When the Honeymoon is Over: Changes in the Marital Relationship Over the First Year." In *The Emerging Field of Close Relationships*, ed. R. Gilmour and S. Duck. Hillsdale, NJ: Lawrence Erlbaum.

Huston, T. L., and Robins, E. (1982). "Conceptual and Methodological Issues in Studying Close Relationships." *Journal of Marriage and the Family* 44:901–925.

McHale, S. M., and Huston, T. L. (1985). "The Effect of the Transition to Parenthood on the Marriage Relationship: A Longitudinal Study." *Journal of Family Issues* 6:409–434.

McLanahan, S., and Adams, J. (1989). "The Effects of Children on Adults' Psychological Well-Being: 1957–1976." *Social Forces* 68:124–146.

Norton, R. (1983). "Measuring Marital Quality: A Critical Look at the Dependent Variable." *Journal of Marriage and the Family* 45:141–151.

Schoen, R. (1975). "California Divorce Rates by Age at First Marriage and Duration of First Marriage." *Journal of Marriage and the Family* 37:348–555.

Spanier, G. B. (1976). "Measuring Dyadic Adjustment: New Scales for Assessing the Quality of Marriage and Similar Dyads." *Journal of Marriage and the Family* 42:15–27.

Umberson, D. (1987). "Family Status and Health Behavior: Social Control as a Dimension of Social Integration." *Journal of Health and Social Behavior* 28:306–319.

Vaillant, C. O., and Vaillant, G. E. (1993). "Is the U-Curve of Marital Satisfaction an Illusion? A 40-Year Study of Marriage." *Journal of Marriage and the Family* 55:230–239.

Verbrugge, L. M. (1979). "Marital Status and Health." *Journal of Marriage and the Family* 41:267–285.

Veroff, J.; Douvan, E.; and Kulka, R. A. (1981). *The Inner American: A Self-Portrait from 1957 to 1976.* New York: Basic Books.

White, L. K., and Booth, A. (1985). "Transition to Parenthood and Marital Quality." *Journal of Family Issues* 6:435–450.

White, L. K.; Booth, A.; and Edwards, J. N. (1986). "Children and Marital Happiness: Why the Negative Correlation?" *Journal of Family Issues* 7:131–147.

Norval D. Glenn

MARITAL RAPE *See* Rape

MARITAL ROLES *See* Family Gender Roles

MARITAL SATISFACTION *See* MARITAL QUALITY

MARITAL SEX

Although many individuals now engage in sexual activity prior to marriage, marriage remains the only fully socially legitimate forum for sexual activity. Traditionally, the wedding night and honeymoon period were considered important rites of passage during which sexual activity for the couple was expected to begin and was socially sanctioned. Furthermore, with the exchange of wedding vows in which men and women promise to "forsake all others," it was (and still is) expected that the marital partners will engage in sexual activities only with each other.

However, marital sexuality per se has been the topic of very few social scientific studies. Indeed, one social scientist, Cathy Greenblat (1983, p. 289), commented that marital sex "remains more the topic of jokes than of serious social scientific investigation." For example, of 553 scholarly articles on human sexuality that were published between 1987 and 1992 and included in the psychological literature database (Psychlit), there was only one specific article on marital sexuality (i.e., Strong and DeVault 1994). This lack of research may be due in part to the fact that social scientists have tended to focus on aspects or types of sexuality that are considered potentially problematic (such as adolescent sexuality, teenage pregnancy, risk factors associated with sexually transmitted diseases and AIDS, and contraceptive behavior); because marital sex is both monogamous and socially sanctioned, it has not been viewed as a "social problem" that needs to be investigated.

Although research articles focused exclusively on marital sex may be difficult to find (for exceptions, see Donnelly 1993; Greenblat 1983), data on marital sexuality are available from other sources. Large-scale sex studies conducted on the general population and published in various books constitute one source. Alfred Kinsey and his associates conducted the first of these large-scale studies in the 1940s and 1950s (Kinsey, Pomeroy, and Martin 1948; Kinsey et al. 1953) and provided the first major source of information about marital and other forms of sexuality.

The results of the National Health and Social Life Survey (NHSLS), a more recent large-scale study on sexuality, have appeared in both popular book form, *Sex in America: A Definitive Survey* (Michael et al. 1994), and academic book form, *The Social Organization of Sexuality* (Laumann et al. 1994). The NHSLS, which was headed by sociologists Edward Laumann and John Gagnon, was based on a random sample of the American population.

Information on marital sexuality can also be obtained from research articles that focus on nonsexual aspects of the marital relationship (e.g., communication, relationship satisfaction) and include analyses relating these variables to sexual behaviors or feelings. Several magazine surveys have been conducted on marital and adult sexuality (e.g., Levin and Levin 1975), but the results, while they may make interesting reading, are often not that accurate because the samples that are used are not representative of the general population.

Sexual Frequency and Variety

The data reported by Kinsey and his colleagues (Kinsey, Pomeroy, and Martin 1948; Kinsey et al. 1953) suggested that the typical adults getting married in the 1940s lacked variety in their sex lives. They engaged in sexual intercourse, but primarily in the missionary position (man on top). Although they used a variety of preintercourse petting techniques (including kissing and some genital fondling), it is unlikely that they engaged in oral-genital sex, unless they were well educated and relatively nonreligious. They probably had to abstain from sex for long periods each month because they relied on the "rhythm method" of birth control (a method of contraception in which the partners abstain from intercourse during the period in which the woman is likely to be fertile). The husband initiated sex, and the wife was expected to be responsive but not too passionate.

Social changes occurred in the 1960s and 1970s that liberalized marital sexuality. There was the sexual revolution, the women's liberation movement, the introduction of the birth control pill, the advent of sex therapy, and the commercialization of sex. Many sex researchers in the 1960s and 1970s concluded that married couples were having more active and varied sexual relationships than they had previously had as a result of these social changes (Hunt 1974).

However, the NHSLS study suggests that marriages may not be as sexually erotic as they were previously imagined to be. In fact, one much-publicized finding is that American couples are not having frequent sex. According to NHSLS data, married couples have sex an average of seven times a month (this amounts to fewer than two times a week). Only 7 percent of the married respondents reported having sex four or more times each week, but 12 percent to 13 percent reported having sex only a few times per year. Similar results were found in another national study of more than 6,000 married people, the National Survey of Families and Households (NSFH), which contained a question on sexual frequency (Call, Sprecher, and Schwartz 1992; Donnelly 1993).

Although married couples may not be having sexual intercourse any more frequently than married couples did in the 1940s, they do seem to be engaging in a greater variety of sexual activities. Certainly, married couples in the 1980s and 1990s have been more comfortable with oral-genital sex than married couples a generation or two earlier. Studies in the 1980s and 1990s indicate that a majority of married couples engaged in oral-genital sex at least occasionally (e.g., Blumstein and Schwartz 1983; Gagnon and Simon 1987; Michael et al. 1994). Anal intercourse is also tried by about 10 percent of American couples (e.g., Michael et al. 1994; Voeller 1991). Positions other than missionary are also frequently used (Blumstein and Schwartz 1983), and many couples report experimenting with new sexual techniques or activities at least some of the time (Greeley 1991).

The frequency with which couples engage in sex—and what they do—is affected by the partners' ages and by the duration of their marriage. All studies that have examined this issue have shown that the frequency of sexual intercourse declines with the length of the relationship (i.e., the longer couples have been married, the fewer times they have sex). However, social scientists have had difficulty determining whether it is the partners' ages that cause the decline or if the critical factor is boredom due to being with the same partner year after year. Most researchers agree that both factors probably are operating (e.g., Blumstein and Schwartz 1983). Specifically, there are decreases in sexual frequency due to age-related factors (declines in physical abilities, increased incidences of illness, and negative attitudes about sex in the elderly) *and* the loss of novelty that results from having sexual intercourse with the same person. According to the latter argument, remarried individuals should have more frequent sex than individuals of about the same age who are still in their first marriages; this hypothesis has been supported by data (Call, Sprecher, and Schwartz 1992). There are also certain times over the lifespan when sexual frequency may decline due to lack of opportunities. For example, involvement in other roles, such as demanding jobs and parenthood (especially when there are many children and/or the children are very young), decreases marital sexuality (Greenblat 1983).

Sexual Satisfaction

Modern American couples expect that marital sexual activity will be pleasurable and fulfilling. Research indicates that most couples are in fact satisfied with their sex lives. For example, Andrew Greeley (1991) found that approximately one-third of the husbands and wives he surveyed reported "a very great deal" of sexual satisfaction, and another one-third reported "a great deal" of satisfaction. A majority of the respondents in the NHSLS study also reported that they were happy with their sex lives. "Many said that sex with their partner made them feel wanted, satisfied, loved, and cared for, which indicates that even if they do not have sex as often as [researchers] might have suspected, many couples still enjoy sex when they have it [Michael et al. 1994, p. 123]." The study also showed that married people were more physically pleased and emotionally satisfied with their sex lives than single people were with theirs. However, it is important to recognize that couples who are dissatisfied with their sex lives do not usually end up in survey studies of marital couples. Instead, they may be in divorce court or engaging in illicit sexual liaisons. Sex problems are reported to be one of the reasons—although usually not the most important one—for marital separation and/or divorce (Cleek and Pearson 1985).

Research shows that couples who are sexually satisfied are more likely than couples who are less satisfied to be having frequent sex, to be having oral-genital sex (especially important to husbands' rating of sexual satisfaction), and to be engaging in other varieties of sexual activities (Blumstein and Schwartz 1983; Greeley 1991). Women, who do not have orgasms as consistently as men (Masters and Johnson 1966), have increased sexual satisfaction when they have orgasms (Pinney, Gerrard, and Denney 1987), especially if they have orgasms before their partner (Darling, Davidson, and Cox 1991). The association between sexual activities and sexual satisfaction probably occurs because specific pleasurable sexual interactions lead to sexual satisfaction, but also because a feeling of sexual satisfaction leads to the desire for specific sexual interactions.

Despite an overall high level of sexual satisfaction, some couples do develop sex problems. One or both partners may have difficulty with any of the following: lack of desire for or interest in sex, arousal difficulties (lack of lubrication for women and erectile difficulties for men), orgasm/ejaculation difficulties (premature ejaculation for men and inability to have orgasm for women), and painful intercourse (Masters and Johnson 1970). Sex therapies have been developed to deal with these problems. Of these, lack of sexual desire is the most difficult to treat (Kaplan 1979). In some cases, this lack of sexual desire may indicate that something is wrong with the marriage.

Sexuality and Relationship Experiences

A married couple's relationship inside the bedroom is often related to their relationship outside the bedroom; that is, couples who are happy with their sex lives tend to be happy with other, nonsexual aspects of their marriage (Greeley 1991; Hatfield et al. 1982; Hunt 1974). The frequency with which a couple has sexual intercourse is also related to relationship satisfaction. Denise Donnelly (1993) found that marriages in which partners reported a high level of mutually satisfying interactions had higher rates of sexual activity.

Other relationship experiences, including equity, power, love, and how a couple resolves conflict, are also associated with marital sexual satisfaction and frequency. For example, social psychologist Elaine Hatfield and her colleagues (1982) found that people who feel that their marriages are fair and equitable are more satisfied with their sex lives and report having sex more often than those who feel that their relationships are inequitable. Couples who enjoy spending time together and who share social activities and hobbies also have sex with greater frequency than couples who share few outside activities (Blumstein and Schwartz 1983), as do couples who perceive that the spouse is as loving as he or she used to be—that is, earlier in the marriage (Edwards and Booth 1976). Conversely, marriages filled with conflict and those in which one or both partners have threatened to leave are characterized by low frequencies of sexual intercourse (Donnelly 1993; Edwards and Booth 1976).

However, it is important to recognize that the occurrence of arguments and conflicts is virtually inevitable in any marital relationship, yet the majority of married men and women continue to have enjoyable sex. Research suggests that as long as a couple continues to have more pleasant than unpleasant interactions (whether those interactions are sexual or nonsexual), they will tend to be happy with each other (Gottman et al. 1976; Howard and Dawes 1976).

It makes intuitive sense that a good sex life is strongly related to a good overall relationship. What is less intuitive is the direction of that relationship—that is, does unsatisfying sex lead to an unsatisfying marriage, or does a bad marriage lead to bad sex? On the one hand, it seems likely that an unhappy partner—one who is preoccupied, worried, or angry about various nonsexual aspects of the marital relationship—may have difficulty becoming sexually interested in and aroused by the other partner, especially if that partner is viewed as causing the conflict. On the other hand, it seems equally likely that a person who is not satisfied with either the quantity or the quality of marital sex may in turn become dissatisfied with other aspects of the marriage. After examining the data from their large-scale sex survey, Philip Blumstein and Pepper Schwartz (1983, p. 201) concluded that "it looks as if other problems come into the bedroom and eventually corrode the entire relationship." In their examination of sexual satisfaction in the first five years of marriage, Alexander Clark and Paul Wallin (1965) also concluded that the quality of a marriage predicts whether a couple will have a satisfactory sexual relationship to a greater degree than the reverse. Whatever the direction of the relationship between sexual satisfaction and overall satisfaction in marital relationships, most researchers agree that the two are intimately connected.

Sexual Communication

As seen from the reviewed research, good overall communication between spouses is positively related to the quality of their sexual relationship. Not surprisingly, good communication about sex also appears to promote positive interpersonal outcomes. Specifically, the quantity and the quality of a couple's communication about sex—whether that communication is about their sexual desires, expectations, preferences, attitudes, or standards—play an important role in determining their sexual satisfaction. For example, married individuals who believe that they communicate well with their partners about sex also feel more sexual satisfaction (Cupach and Comstock 1990).

One important aspect of sexual communication that has been studied by social scientists is the initiation and refusal of sexual intercourse. Several researchers have discussed the existence of "sexual scripts" that prescribe specific, socially acceptable sexual behaviors for men and women (Gagnon and Simon 1973). According to the traditional sexual script, men are expected to seek sexual opportunities and to be the initiators of sexual activity, whereas women are expected to wait for the male partner to initiate sexual activity and then either to accept or to refuse his sexual invitation. Many married couples subscribe to this traditional sexual script (which was established by men!)—that is, they follow a pattern of sexual interaction in which the husband initiates sexual activity and the wife responds to his initiation (Byers and Heinlein 1989; Carlson 1976; Rubin 1976). However, additional research indicates that this may change over the course of the relationship as each partner becomes more comfortable with nontraditional roles (Brown and Auerback 1981). For example, a woman may become more likely over the duration of the marriage to initiate sexual activity herself rather than waiting for her spouse to do so, and a man may become more comfortable in the role of the recipient rather than the initiator of sexual activity.

As long as both partners in the marriage share the same sexual script, whether it is traditional or nontraditional, they are likely to be satisfied with their sexual interactions. However, conflict and decreased sexual satisfaction may result if one or both partners deviate from or become unhappy with their usual sexual script (Cupach and Metts 1991). For example, if the wife subscribes to the traditional sexual script and expects the husband to initiate all sexual activity, but he wishes to share the role of initiator with her, they are likely to experience some degree of tension and sexual dissatisfaction. Alternatively, if the husband subscribes to the traditional sexual script, but the wife does not and so takes on the role of initiator, the husband may feel threatened by the wife's sexual invitations.

A shared sexual script is not the only part of communication that is related to sexual satisfaction. How couples talk about sex—the specific words or phrases they use to communicate sexual interest to each other or to indicate a preference for a particular type of sexual activity—is also associated with how satisfied they are with the sexual aspects of their relationships. Research indicates that couples may develop their own special phrases, terms, or names for sexual body parts, activities, and preferences. For example, a wife may ask her husband if he would like to have some "afternoon delight" rather than asking him in a more formal manner if he would like to "engage in sexual intercourse" with her. The development of a special sexual vocabulary and the use of pet names, phrases, and euphemisms may enhance a couple's feelings of emotional intimacy, love, and commitment (Bell, Buerkel-Rothfuss, and Gore 1987; Cornog 1986).

Although married couples may develop their own idiosyncratic sexual vocabularies, additional research has revealed that the majority tend to employ indirect techniques (e.g., kissing, suggestive glances or physical contact, playing music) rather than direct, verbal techniques (e.g., "I want to have sex") for communicating sexual interest to the partner (Brown and Auerback 1981; Byers and Heinlein 1989). In addition, several gender differences exist. Specifically, when communicating with their spouses or lovers, men and women often use different vocabularies for referring to male and female genitalia and the act of intercourse. Women are more likely than men to use formal terms for genitalia and intercourse rather than slang or euphemistic terms (Sanders 1978; Simkins and Rinck 1982). Men and women also appear to have different motives for communicating sexual interest to their partners. Specifically, women primarily initiate sexual intercourse to receive "love, intimacy, and holding," whereas men primarily initiate intercourse to achieve "sexual release" (Brown and Auerback 1981; Hatfield et al. 1988).

Sex and Cohabiting Couples

Researchers have also turned their attention to the sexual experiences of couples involved in two other types of long-term, committed relationships: cohabiting heterosexual couples and homosexual couples. In general, homosexual male (gay) couples and heterosexual cohabiting couples tend to have sexual intercourse more frequently than married couples (Blumstein and Schwartz 1983; Call, Sprecher, and Schwartz 1992; Michael et al. 1994). Homosexual female (lesbian) couples, on the other hand, have sex less frequently than all other couple types, although they engage in more nongenital physical contact (e.g., cuddling, hugging). Like married couples, homosexual couples and heterosexual cohabitors have sex less frequently over the course of their relationship.

Gay, lesbian, and heterosexual cohabiting couples also may use or prefer different types of sexual activities than those typically used by married couples. For example, lesbian couples engage in more kissing, caressing, holding, and breast stimulation during lovemaking than do other couples; gay couples, in turn, incorporate more body contact, including nipple stimulation and caressing, into their lovemaking than do heterosexual couples (Blumstein and Schwartz 1983; Masters and Johnson 1979). Although oral-genital sex and anal intercourse have increased among married couples, these particular sexual activities are more likely to be used by homosexual couples. For example, approximately 50 percent of gay couples and 39 percent of lesbian couples report usually or always using oral sex during lovemaking, compared to 30 percent of heterosexual couples; gay men are also more likely to have anal sex than are heterosexual couples (Blumstein and Schwartz 1983).

While most married couples are sexually satisfied (e.g., Greeley 1991; Michael et al. 1994), most nonmarried homosexual and heterosexual couples appear equally sexually satisfied. As with married couples, this sexual happiness is likely to be associated with satisfaction with the overall relationship (Hunt 1974). For example, psychologist Lawrence Kurdek (1991) surveyed gay, lesbian, heterosexual cohabiting, and heterosexual married couples about various aspects of their sexuality. His results indicated that couples who reported feeling satisfied with their sexual relationship were also satisfied with their relationship as a whole—regardless of the type of couple. However, other research suggests that homosexual couples may be more satisfied with their sexual interactions than are heterosexual couples (Coleman, Hoon, and Hoon 1983; Masters and Johnson 1979).

The quantity of sex is as important to homosexual and heterosexual cohabiting couples as it is to married couples in determining their sexual and relationship satisfaction. Gay men and male cohabitors who have sex frequently report having a good sex life and a good relationship. However, lesbians and female cohabitors are less likely to associate sexual frequency with satisfaction; that is, they do not feel less sexually satisfied or less satisfied with the relationship when sexual frequency is low (Blumstein and Schwartz 1983). Particular types of sexual activities—especially oral-genital sex—also are associated with sexual satisfaction. For example, unlike heterosexual women (but like gay and heterosexual men), the more often lesbian couples give and receive oral sex, the happier they are with both their sex life and their relationship in general. This may be due to the fact that sexual activity results in orgasms more often for women in homosexual relationships than for women in heterosexual relationships (Bressler and Lavender 1986; Coleman, Hoon, and Hoon 1983). Gay men, on the other hand, tend to be more satisfied the more often they engage in a variety of sexual activities, including oral sex, anal sex, and mutual genital manipulation (Blumstein and Schwartz 1983).

With regard to sexual communication, Blumstein and Schwartz (1983) reported that sexual initiation—which partner makes the first sexual overture—is less likely to follow the traditional sexual script in cohabiting relationships. However, although heterosexual cohabiting women initiate sex more frequently than heterosexual married women, their cohabiting male partners still initiate more. In lesbian and gay couples, it is often the more emotionally expressive partner who makes more sexual initiations, perhaps because expressive people are sensitive about how to approach a sexual partner (Blumstein and Schwartz 1983).

Conclusion

Sexuality plays an important role in marital and other types of long-term, committed relationships. The amount of sex partners have, the kinds of sexual activities in which they engage, and how they communicate with each other about their needs, desires, preferences, and attitudes can have an enormous impact not only on what takes place in the bedroom but what happens in the rest of the house as well.

(*See also*: Communication; Extramarital Sex; Sexuality; Sexuality in the Life Cycle; Sexual Orientation; Sexual Problems)

BIBLIOGRAPHY

Bell, R. A.; Buerkel-Rothfuss, N. L.; and Gore, K. E. (1987). "'Did You Bring the Yarmulke for the Cabbage Patch Kid?' The Idiomatic Communication of Young Lovers." *Human Communication Research* 14:47–67.

Blumstein, P., and Schwartz, P. (1983). *American Couples.* New York: William Morrow.

Bressler, L. C., and Lavender, A. D. (1986). "Sexual Fulfillment of Heterosexual, Bisexual, and Homosexual Women." *Journal of Homosexuality* 12:109–122.

Brown, M., and Auerback, A. (1981). "Communication Patterns in Initiation of Marital Sex." *Medical Aspects of Human Sexuality* 15:105–117.

Byers, E. S., and Heinlein, L. (1989). "Predicting Initiations and Refusals of Sexual Activities in Married and Cohabiting Heterosexual Couples." *The Journal of Sex Research* 26:210–231.

Call, V. R. A.; Sprecher, S.; and Schwartz, P. (1992). "The Frequency of Sexual Intercourse in American Couples: A National Sample." Paper presented at the annual meeting of the National Council on Family Relations, Orlando, FL.

Carlson, J. (1976). "The Sexual Role." In *Role Structure and Analysis of the Family*, ed. F. I. Nye. Newbury Park, CA: Sage Publications.

Clark, A. L., and Wallin, P. (1965). "Women's Sexual Responsiveness and the Duration and Quality of Their Marriages." *American Journal of Sociology* 21:187–196.

Cleek, M. G., and Pearson, T. A. (1985). "Perceived Causes of Divorce: An Analysis of Interrelationships." *Journal of Marriage and the Family* 47:179–183.

Coleman, E. M.; Hoon, P. W.; and Hoon, E. F. (1983). "Arousability and Sexual Satisfaction in Lesbian and Heterosexual Women." *The Journal of Sex Research* 19:58–73.

Cornog, M. (1986). "Naming Sexual Body Parts: Preliminary Patterns and Implications." *The Journal of Sex Research* 22:393–398.

Cupach, W. R., and Comstock, J. (1990). "Satisfaction with Sexual Communication in Marriage: Links to Sexual Satisfaction and Dyadic Adjustment." *Journal of Social and Personal Relationships* 7:179–186.

Cupach, W. R., and Metts, S. (1991). "Sexuality and Communication in Close Relationships." In *Sexuality in Close Relationships*, ed. K. McKinney and S. Sprecher. Hillsdale, NJ: Lawrence Erlbaum.

Darling, C. A.; Davidson, J. K.; and Cox, R. P. (1991). "Female Sexual Response and the Timing of Partner Orgasm." *Journal of Sex and Marital Therapy* 17:3–21.

Donnelly, D. A. (1993). "Sexually Inactive Marriages." *The Journal of Sex Research* 30:171–179.

Edwards, J., and Booth, A. (1976). "Sexual Behavior In and Out of Marriage: An Assessment of Correlates." *Journal of Marriage and the Family* 38:73–81.

Gagnon, J. H., and Simon, W. (1973). *Sexual Conduct: The Social Sources of Human Sexuality.* Chicago: Aldine.

Gagnon, J. H., and Simon, W. (1987). "The Sexual Scripting of Oral-Genital Contacts." *Archives of Sexual Behavior* 16:1–25.

Gottman, J.; Notarius, C.; Markman, H.; Banks, S.; Yoppi, B.; and Rubin, M. E. (1976). "Behavior Exchange Theory and Marital Decision Making." *Journal of Experimental Social Psychology* 34:14–23.

Greeley, A. M. (1991). *Faithful Attraction: Discovering Intimacy, Love, and Fidelity in American Marriage.* New York: Doherty.

Greenblat, C. S. (1983). "The Salience of Sexuality in the Early Years of Marriage." *Journal of Marriage and the Family* 45:289–299.

Hatfield, E.; Greenberger, R.; Traupman, P.; and Lambert, M. (1982). "Equity and Sexual Satisfaction in Recently Married Couples." *The Journal of Sex Research* 18:18–32.

Hatfield, E.; Sprecher, S.; Pillemer, J. T.; Greenberger, D.; and Wexler, P. (1988). "Gender Differences in What Is Desired in the Sexual Relationship." *Journal of Psychology and Human Sexuality* 1:39–52.

Howard, J. W., and Dawes, R. M. (1976). "Linear Prediction of Marital Happiness." *Personality and Social Psychology Bulletin* 2:478–480.

Hunt, M. (1974). *Sexual Behavior in the 1970s.* Chicago: Playboy Press.

Janus, S. S., and Janus, C. L. (1992). *The Janus Report on Sexual Behavior.* New York: Wiley.

Kaplan, H. S. (1979). *Disorders of Sexual Desire.* New York: Simon & Schuster.

Kinsey, A. C.; Pomeroy, W. B.; and Martin, C. E. (1948). *Sexual Behavior in the Human Male.* Philadelphia: Saunders.

Kinsey, A. C.; Pomeroy, W. B.; Martin, C. E.; and Gebhard, P. H. (1953). *Sexual Behavior in the Human Female.* Philadelphia: Saunders.

Kurdek, L. A. (1991). "Sexuality in Homosexual and Heterosexual Couples." In *Sexuality in Close Relationships*, ed. K. McKinney and S. Sprecher. Hillsdale, NJ: Lawrence Erlbaum.

Laumann, E. O.; Gagnon, J. H.; Michael, R. T.; and Michaels, S. (1994). *The Social Organization of Sexuality.* Chicago: University of Chicago Press.

Levin, R., and Levin, A. (1975). "Sexual Pleasure." *Redbook* 145:42–56.

Masters, W. H., and Johnson, V. E. (1966). *Human Sexual Response.* Boston: Little, Brown.

Masters, W. H., and Johnson, V. E. (1970). *Human Sexual Inadequacy.* Boston: Little, Brown.

Masters, W. H., and Johnson, V. E. (1979). *Homosexuality in Perspective.* Boston: Little, Brown.

Michael, R. T.; Gagnon, J. H.; Laumann, E. O.; and Kolata, G. (1994). *Sex in America: A Definitive Survey.* Boston: Little, Brown.

Pinney, E. M.; Gerrard, M.; and Denney, N. W. (1987). "The Pinney Sexual Satisfaction Inventory." *The Journal of Sex Research* 23:233–251.

Rubin, L. B. (1976). *Worlds of Pain: Life in the Working-Class Family.* New York: Basic Books.

Sanders, J. S. (1978). "Male and Female Vocabularies for Communicating with a Sexual Partner." *Journal of Sex Education and Therapy* 4:15–18.

Simkins, L., and Rinck, C. (1982). "Male and Female Sexual Vocabulary in Different Interpersonal Contexts." *The Journal of Sex Research* 18:160–172.

Sprecher, S., and McKinney, K. (1993). *Sexuality.* Newbury Park, CA: Sage Publications.

Strong, B., and DeVault, C. (1994). *Human Sexuality.* Mountain View, CA: Mayfield.

Voeller, B. (1991). "AIDS and Heterosexual Anal Intercourse." *Archives of Sexual Behavior* 20:233–276.

PAMELA C. REGAN
SUSAN SPRECHER

MARITAL TYPOLOGIES

Part of the process of science is description. Thus, sociologists, psychologists, home economists, and others who study marriage relationships use the scientific method to study and describe marriages. As an aid in this description process, some scholars have classified marriages into different patterns or typologies. Typologies, used in all fields of science, are artificial categories developed to demonstrate the similarities that exist within a group and highlight the differences between groups. Those who study marriage use typologies to put marriages into a series of groups based on shared characteristics. For example, Walter F. Willcox (1892) identified two types of marriage: despotic and democratic. The despotic type of marriage, based on Roman law, viewed the wife as the property of the husband and, therefore, subject to him in all matters. The democratic type of marriage arose under the Teutones. They honored women and viewed the husband and wife as equals who made decisions on a democratic basis. This typology was developed as a simple way of bringing order to the study of marriage relationships.

Scholars have since developed numerous typologies in an attempt to describe marriages more clearly. In the 1940s, sociologists noted two types of marriage: institutional and companionate (Burgess and Locke 1948). The traditional institutional marriage emphasized the separate roles that husbands and wives played within the family. Husbands were the primary wage earners and decision makers. They also served as the link between the family and the larger society. Wives were usually responsible for child rearing and homemaking and were subordinate to the desires of their husbands. However, a trend was noted toward companionate marriages, which emphasized shared, rather than separate, roles and decision-making responsibilities. In companionate marriages, wives often earned an income and husbands assisted with care of the children. The specific roles and responsibilities carried out within the companionate marriage were not based on a person's gender, but on a mutual agreement between two equals.

Later scholars criticized the institutional/companionate typology because it was not adequate for describing many of the differences that existed within marriage relationships. Therefore, John F. Cuber and Peggy B. Harroff (1965) studied enduring marriages and developed one of the best known marital typologies. They proposed three institutional (conflict-habituated, devitalized, passive-congenial) and two companionate (vital, total) types of marriage.

Conflict-habituated marriages were those where couples engaged in high levels of conflict. The conflict was not out of control but frequent enough that the entire marriage was influenced by a climate of friction. Devitalized marriage partners had a strong sense of enthusiasm in the early part of their marriage but grew apart and became distant from each other in later life. Passive-congenial marriages were those in which couples shared numerous common interests and responsibilities and seldom argued. Spouses in vital marriages shared numerous important activities and were to a large extent involved in each other's lives. In total marriages, there were few areas of tension; individuals shared all of the important events of their lives.

A Good Typology of Marriage

If a typology is to be useful in describing marriage, it must include six important characteristics. The typology must be able to economize thought, exhaustive, mutually exclusive, a reliable means of assigning couples to a type, developed through a systematic process, and useful in improving the marriage.

A good typology should be able to economize thought. It should describe a great deal about a marriage concisely. The typology should group together into one type all marriages sharing similar characteristics and separate into different types those marriages that differ from one another.

Exhaustive means that all of the important dimensions of a marriage relationship are included when couples are assigned to a marital type. If communication is an important component of a marriage, then "communication" must be one of the criteria used to assign couples to a marriage type. However, if the typology is to be exhaustive, it must include *all* other important dimensions of marriage relationships, not merely communication.

Mutually exclusive means that a couple should be assigned only to one type of marriage. Thus, a couple should be classified as either a vital or a total marriage, not a mixed type including characteristics common to both vital and total marriages.

A reliable method of assigning couples means there must be no uncertainty in the typology assignment. A good typology will clearly outline why the marriage is assigned a specific type.

The typology should be developed through a systematic process rather than merely by intuition or logic. However, some typologies have been developed in a fairly informal fashion when scholars, based on their own understanding of marriage, developed what they thought were the most important and logical characteristics to describe all marriages. For example, some scholars assumed that marital stability (how likely the couple is to stay married) and marital satisfaction (the degree of happiness within the marriage) were the best two dimensions to describe all marriages (Levinger 1965; Lewis and Spanier 1979), and as a result, these two characteristics were used to develop a typology. On the other hand, some scholars use sophisticated systematic scientific procedures to observe marriages and, as a result of their observations, develop a typology. For instance, John M. Gottman (1993b) and his colleagues observed marital partners as they discussed real relationship problems, and then they developed five marital types based on their observations. Therefore, Gottman's marital types are derived from systematic observations rather than mere impressions and beliefs about marriage.

Finally, a good typology should be useful for improving the marriages. Information about the types should help counselors and marriage therapists in their work to improve marriage relationships.

Using Logical Methods to Create Typologies

As noted, some scholars develop a typology based on what they *believe* are the most important characteristics that describe marriage relationships. The basis for the marital typology is therefore the scientist's *personal* logic and reason. Most of the marriage typologies that have been developed have used this informal logical process.

George Levinger (1965) believed that marital stability and satisfaction were two of the most significant dimensions to consider when developing marital types; marriages could be either high or low on stability and either high or low on marital satisfaction. He used these two dimensions of marriage to describe four different marital types. Full-shell marriages had high levels of satisfaction and stability; these couples rarely if ever considered divorce and were very happy with the relationship. No-shell marriages had low levels of stability and satisfaction; these couples were having difficulty staying together and were not happy with the relationship. Empty-shell marriages were low on satisfaction, yet there were high levels of stability; while these couples were not happy with their relationships, there was no thought of divorce. Half-shell marriages had high levels of satisfaction, yet the couples were likely to terminate the marriage.

Using Scientific Methods to Create Typologies

In more recent works, an effort has been made to classify marriages into one type or another based on systematic scientific observations of the marriages (Fitzpatrick 1988; Gottman 1993a, 1993b; Gottman and Levenson 1992; Snyder and Smith 1986).

Douglas K. Snyder and Gregory T. Smith (1986) developed a typology of marriage based on marital satisfaction. They administered a 280-item questionnaire to one group of couples in marital counseling and another group of couples from the general population who were not in counseling. Based on the responses to the questionnaire, the marriages were classified into one of five different marital types.

Type 1 marriages had little distress. Husbands and wives shared the responsibilities for child rearing. Minor problems focused on dissatisfaction with the children and conflict over parenting. Type 2 marriages were those where partners reported no marital difficulties even though problems likely did exist. These marriages were viewed as "perfect" because the partners lacked the ability to evaluate their relationship critically. Type 3 marriages had moderate levels of marital conflict. Husbands reported conflict in areas of finances, parenting, and conflict resolution. Women reported conflict in the same areas but also expressed dissatisfaction because of a lack of spousal affection, a lack of leisure time with their husbands, and the children's interference with their marriage and personal goals. Type 4 marriages had high levels of dissatisfaction with the relationship. Relationships with children and the parenting role were the partners' only satisfaction. Type 5 marriages were also characterized by high levels of marital dissatisfaction, but the partners were also very dissatisfied with their children and their parenting roles.

Another scientifically developed typology (Fitzpatrick 1988) focused primarily on the couple's communication. Married couples responded to a 184-item questionnaire that measured how they organized their time, space, and energy, displayed power and affection, and attained a sense of meaning in their lives. Three marital types were identified: traditionals, independents, and separates.

One type, the traditionals, stressed a very conventional outlook on life and believed husbands should be more dominant than wives. Wives took their husbands' last names in marriage, and extramarital sex was not at all acceptable. Traditional couples were good companions and shared most of their time and space with each other; little time was left for individual interests and activities. Even when conflict occurred, traditionals were not assertive. Of all three types, traditionals were the most satisfied with their marriages. Independents were almost the opposite of the traditionals. They supported a more equal sharing of roles and opposed a traditional way of life. They valued a more independent use of their time and space than traditionals but still considered themselves emotionally close to their spouses. Like traditionals, they did not avoid conflict. They were more assertive than traditionals, but they were still highly satisfied with their marriages. The third type, the separates, held to conventional views like the traditionals yet stressed the freedom to lead separate lives. They kept a regular daily schedule, yet had less sharing in their marriages than traditionals. They typically avoided conflict but were somewhat more assertive than traditionals.

Probably the most comprehensive marriage typology was developed using a computer-scored questionnaire (Lavee and Olson 1993). David H. Olson and his colleagues used a questionnaire called ENRICH to evaluate marriage relationships along nine dimensions: personality issues, communication, conflict resolution, financial management, leisure activities, the sexual relationship, children and parenting, family and friends, and religious orientation. The results were computer-scored and computer-analyzed using a sophisticated statistical technique called cluster analysis. The couples' responses to the questionnaire were also used to help the couple understand which aspects of their relationship were strengths and which were weaknesses. This study yielded a list of seven different types of marriages: devitalized, financially focused, conflicted, traditional, balanced, harmonious, and vitalized.

The first and most common was labeled a devitalized marriage, which was primarily characterized by dissatisfaction with all nine dimensions of the relationship. Thus, spouses were dissatisfied with their partner's personality, communication with the partner, the way they dealt with conflict, managed their finances, spent their leisure time, engaged in sexual activities, interacted with their children and family, and the religious dimensions of their lives. The second type of union was labeled a financially focused marriage. Couples in this category were dissatisfied with each aspect of their relationship except the way they handled their finances. Agreement on finances seemed to be the sole strength of these marriages. The third type was characterized as a conflicted marriage. Partners in these marriages were dissatisfied with communication, conflict resolution, their partner's personality, and their sex life. However, they were satisfied with their children, religious life, and the use of leisure time within their marriage. Dissatisfaction stemmed most often from things within the relationship, and satisfaction was obtained from things outside the relationship. The fourth type of union was characterized as traditional marriage. Traditional couples were dissatisfied with communication, conflict resolution, and sex, yet they were satisfied with family and friends, religion, and leisure time. Partners in the fifth type, balanced marriage, were highly satisfied with their communication, conflict resolution, leisure activities, children, and sex life, but were dissatisfied primarily with their financial management. The sixth type, harmonious marriage, was self-focused and tended to be a union in which the couple was highly satisfied with their sex life, leisure time, and finances. Dissatisfaction within harmonious marriages arose for the most part from interaction with their children and family and their friendships with others. Vitalized marriage demonstrated the highest levels of satisfaction across all nine dimensions.

One strength of this typology is that nine different marital dimensions are evaluated before a couple is assigned to a typology. An additional strength is the ENRICH questionnaire. This measure, used by thousands of couples since 1986, is accepted as a valid and reliable way to examine marital and premarital relationships. This typology can also be useful to clergy and marital counselors who are helping couples improve their marriages, because it highlights specific areas of the relationship that need work. It gives a clear understanding of both the strong and weak areas of a relationship. Finally, this typology demonstrates clearly that couples can be satisfied with some dimensions of their marriage, yet dissatisfied with other aspects.

It is evident by this brief discussion that the study of marriage has generated many different typologies that all attempt to describe marriage. Only one typology has been practically useful in not only describing marriage but predicting marital stability, whether a couple will divorce or whether they will stay together (Gottman 1993b).

Gottman and his colleagues observed the actual conflict of couples, and from their observations of conflict, couples were divided into five different types (Gottman 1993a, 1993b; Gottman and Levenson 1992). Three of these marriage types (validating, volatile, and conflict-minimizing) were stable and, thus, not likely to divorce. The other two types (hostile and hostile detached) were unstable and on the path toward divorce.

Validating couples avoided conflict unless there was a very serious issue in the marriage. When conflict did arise, there were high levels of validation. Validation was defined as minimal vocal responses from the listener such as "mmmmhmmm" or "yeah" that provided feedback that the speaker should continue; the listener was listening and wanted to understand the point of view of the speaker. Volatile couples valued their individuality more than the marriage, and they allowed each partner more time for privacy. They thrived on conflict and were free to express their disagreements. Husbands and wives expressed high levels of both positive and negative feelings within their conflict. Conflict-minimizing couples avoided all marital conflict. They were distant from each other, with low levels of sharing and companionship. They valued their own separate space and desired high levels of independence. In all three of the stable types of marriages, partners had both positive and negative interactions with each other. However, the stable couples had much higher levels of positive than negative interaction.

Hostile couples engaged in high levels of conflict. One partner complained and criticized, and the other responded defensively. Neither seemed to understand the point of view of the partner. Hostile detached couples engaged in a type of guerrilla warfare. While they typically led very emotionally separate and independent lives, they got into brief encounters of attack and defend. When not attacking, the listener would nonverbally communicate disinterest, coldness, and disapproval of the conflict. Disinterest was referred to as stonewalling, typically a male behavior showing a lack of interest in the message of the speaker.

The unstable couples resolved their conflicts in primarily negative ways. They rated their conflicts as more serious and felt more negative during their conflicts than the stable couples. Unstable couples were less satisfied with their marriages, more likely to have been thinking about divorce, and more likely to have already separated than were the stable couples.

Gottman's typology demonstrates that not all stable marriages are alike, and neither are all unstable marriages. Neither intense conflict nor conflict avoidance is necessarily a problematic marital pattern. However, for a marriage to be stable, negative communication must be offset by about five times as much positive communication. Still, a high level of negative interaction will not in itself lead to divorce unless there is nothing positive in the relationship. Even withdrawal and expressions of disgust, contempt, and defensiveness do not lead to divorce when they are combined with a very high level of positive interaction with the spouse. Therefore, professionals may use this final typology to teach couples to fight in ways that will resolve the conflict and not lead to divorce.

Problems with Typologies

While numerous typologies have been developed, no single one has been widely adopted. Typologies are useful because they group similar types of marriages into one category and bring order to the study of marriage. However, no typology seems to be able to meet all of the characteristics of a good typology; all typologies have problems.

For example, when researchers assign a marriage to a typology, they lose sight of the uniqueness of the marriage within that typology. A group of marriages will differ along many dimensions, so they are not all the same. Thus, some scholars believe that typologies actually blur reality rather than describe it more clearly (Hall and Lindzey 1985). While a typology does help to describe marriage in an understandable way, it may simplify the complexity of marriage too much.

Most of the previously discussed typologies focused on two or three dimensions of marriage and in doing so made those few dimensions the most important characteristics of marriage. Even though Gottman and his colleagues used a very systematic process to assign couples to a type, their observations focused solely on the couple's conflict. Olson's typology was the only exception, since it examined nine different dimensions of marriage. Focusing on so many dimensions of the marriage relationship strengthens the typology because it assumes all nine dimensions are important in describing marriage.

An additional problem arises with typologies when the spouses disagree on which typology best describes their marriage. For example, Snyder and Smith (1986) found that almost 50 percent of couples disagreed about which typology most accurately described their marriage. This may be evidence of the fact that there are really two perspectives of the same marriage—his marriage, as the husband sees it, and her marriage, as the wife sees it. A good typology should place the couple into one category only.

Finally, typologies tend to present only a still-life snapshot of marriage, when in reality a marriage can change over time and across situations. A relationship that is categorized as vital at one point in time may be characterized as conflict-habituated later on because of changes that have taken place. In fact, marriages are typically very dynamic and can change considerably over time. Research done on the first year of marriage indicates that partners' feelings of love for each other (as well as their hugging, kissing, and affection) decrease, while conflict increases (Huston, McHale, and Crouter 1986). Marriages also change when new members are added to the family as a result of a birth or when a spouse retires. Therefore, while a typology is useful to describe a marriage at one point in time, it is not helpful for describing how the marriage changes over time.

Conclusion

Using the scientific method to study and describe marriage relationships is a challenging activity; marriage relationships are by nature very private and personal. Therefore, trying to observe and describe important components of marriage in a scientific way is extremely difficult. Until a more precise and reliable method of studying marriage is designed, however, marital scholars will continue to adapt and use typologies to understand marriage because they do help describe reality. The business of science is description, and a typology is useful in this process. The more a typology can include characteristics of a good typology as described, the more useful it will be in the study of marital relationships.

Typologies do not attempt to state that one type of marriage is better than another. Some of them, however, are used to predict which marital types will remain intact. They are also used to identify which aspects of a relationship need to be addressed. Individuals are then left to use this information, along with their own values and beliefs, to help create and maintain a rewarding marriage.

(*See also:* Communication; Conflict; Family Therapy; Marital Power; Marital Quality)

BIBLIOGRAPHY

Brubaker, T. H. (1985). *Later-Life Families.* Newbury Park, CA: Sage Publications.

Burgess, E. W., and Locke, H. J. (1945). *The Family: From Institution to Companionship.* New York: American Book Company.

Cuber, J. F., and Harroff, P. B. (1965). *Sex and the Significant Americans.* New York: Penguin Books.

Fitzpatrick, M. A. (1988). *Between Husbands and Wives: Communication in Marriage.* Newbury Park, CA: Sage Publications.

Gottman, J. M. (1993a). "The Roles of Conflict Engagement, Escalation, and Avoidance in Marital Interaction: A Longitudinal View of Five Types of Couples." *Journal of Consulting and Clinical Psychology* 61:6–15.

Gottman, J. M. (1993b). *What Predicts Divorce: The Relationship Between Marital Processes and Marital Outcomes.* Hillsdale, NJ: Lawrence Erlbaum.

Gottman, J. M., and Levenson, R. W. (1992). "Marital Processes Predictive of Later Dissolution." *Journal of Personality and Social Psychology* 63:221–233.

Hall, C. S., and Lindzey, G. (1985). *Introduction to Theories of Personality.* New York: Wiley.

Hawkins, J. L.; Weisberg, C.; and Ray, D. L. (1977). "Marital Communication Style and Social Class." *Journal of Marriage and the Family* 39:479–490.

Huston, T. L.; McHale, S. J.; and Crouter, A. C. (1986). "When the Honeymoon's Over: Changes in the Marriage Relationship Over the First Year." In *The Emerging Field of Personal Relationships*, ed. R. Gilmour and S. Duck. Hillsdale, NJ: Lawrence Erlbaum.

Lavee, Y., and Olson, D. H. (1993). "Seven Types of Marriage: Empirical Typology Based on ENRICH." *Journal of Marital and Family Therapy* 19:325–340.

Levinger, G. (1965). "Marital Cohesiveness and Dissolution: An Integrative Review." *Journal of Marriage and the Family* 27:19–28.

Lewis, R. A., and Spanier, G. B. (1979). "Theorizing About the Quality and Stability of Marriage." In *Contemporary Theories About the Family*, Vol. 1, ed. W. R. Burr, R. Hill, F. I. Nye, and I. L. Reiss. New York: Free Press.

Olson, D. H., and McCubbin, H. I. (1983). *Families: What Makes Them Work.* Newbury Park, CA: Sage Publications.

Rausch, H. L.; Barry, W. A.; Hertel, R. K.; and Swain, M. A. (1974). *Communication, Conflict, and Marriage.* San Francisco: Jossey-Bass.

Snyder, D. K., and Smith, G. T. (1986). Classification of Marital Relationships: An Empirical Approach." *Journal of Marriage and the Family* 48:137–146.

Willcox, W. F. (1892). *Studies in History, Economics, and Public Law.* New York: Columbia University.

Edgar C. J. Long

MARRIAGE CEREMONIES

Rituals or ceremonies that celebrate a newly achieved marital status are near universal. Why is that? The assumption of husband and wife roles, before and after the birth of a child, clearly marks the beginning of a new generation. The fulfillment of these roles—husband, wife, and parent—is fundamental to the continuity of a society. Therefore, both the larger social group and individual families have an investment in the institutions of mate selection, marriage, and parenthood. This investment is recognized and acknowledged with a variety of ceremonies, including engagement or betrothal rituals, marriage ceremonies, and christening or naming ceremonies.

Marriage ceremonies range across cultures from very elaborate ceremonies including the performance of religious rituals, dancing, music, feasting, oath taking, and gift exchange over several days to the virtual absence of ceremonies in the relatively few societies where individuals announce their marriage by simply acting married—that is, usually by living together and telling others that they are now married. Marriage ceremonies, along with those marking birth, death, and achievement of adult status in some cultures, are the major rites of passage in cultures around the world. Religion plays a role in ceremonies in most cultures. Prayers, sacrifices, and donations are often made and rituals performed to gain supernatural blessings or to ward off evil forces.

In a few societies, such as rural communities in the Balkans, people from communities, villages, or kin groups that are antagonistic to one another sometimes intermarry. In these situations, the marriage ceremonies often allow for the expression of hostilities between the groups through wrestling matches and the ritualized exchange of insults.

A key component of marriage ceremonies is the symbolic expression of the new status of the bride and groom through an alteration of their physical appearance. Change in clothing style or hair style, as among Hopi women in Arizona, and the exchange and wearing of wedding rings or other types of jewelry such as ankle bracelets are a few of the ways this custom is played out in different cultures.

Marriage ceremonies are common across cultures for a number of reasons. First, marriage is an important emotional and social transition for the bride and groom, and participation of family and friends in the process can be a major source of emotional and financial support for the newlyweds. Second, marriage usually marks a dramatic change in social status for individual newlyweds. In most societies, newlyweds are considered adults and potential parents. The couple is expected to establish a new home apart from their natal families or, in some societies, one spouse is expected to join the community or home of the other spouse's natal family (in most cases, the bride moves to the groom's community). The marriage ceremony emphasizes the importance of these new statuses and the behavioral expectations associated with them, both for the individuals and the community. Third, ceremonies are often paid for by the families of one spouse, sometimes both, and this emphasizes to the couple their parent's investment in them and their parent's expectation that they will produce and raise the next generation in the family. Fourth, in some societies, much wealth is exchanged between families at marriage. This exchange may take the form of bride price, where the groom's family makes a payment to the bride's family or kin group, or dowry, where the bride brings wealth to the marriage. This exchange may also take the form of an expectation of a large inheritance in the future. In these societies, marriage ceremonies are often elaborate affairs, symbolic of the large investment that families have in marriage (Rosenblatt and Unangst 1974).

In the United States, marriage is a civil action licensed by each state, but most people use the occasion for a special ceremony to mark a couple's rite of passage from singlehood to marriage. Most states require the presence of one or more witnesses and a certified individual to oversee the vows. However, the majority of couples (80%) are married by a clergyman (Knox and Schacht 1991), thus ensuring the approval of their religious organization as well as the state. In religious terms, marriage is a sacrament, "an outward and visible sign of inward and spiritual grace" (Saxton 1993). The remaining 20 percent of couples, who forego a religious ceremony, are married by a judge or justice of the peace.

The fifty states have slightly different requirements that must be fulfilled before a couple can marry. Some states require blood tests for venereal disease before a couple may obtain a marriage license, some states require a waiting period, a few states specify who a person can or cannot marry (i.e., close relatives cannot marry), and most states specify the youngest age at which a person can marry without the consent of a parent or guardian. All states require that a couple obtain a marriage license.

There are several rites and rituals that make up the wedding ceremony in the United States. However, it is up to the individual couple whether they incorporate some or all of these in their wedding. Generally, the more formal the wedding, the more traditional it is and the more often these customs are followed. These traditions include the following: a bridal shower in which the bride receives personal gifts or gifts to help establish a household; a party for the groom given by male friends, meant to be a "last fling" before he gives up his state of bachelorhood; an exchange of wedding rings, which symbolize "an unbroken circle of never-ending love" for the couple (Davidson and Moore 1992); and a white bridal gown (symbolizing virginity) with a veil to cover the bride's face. Also worn or carried by the bride is "something old, something new, something borrowed, and something blue." According to David Knox and Caroline Schacht (1991, pp. 217–218), these latter requirements symbolize the following: The old represents the durability of the impending marriage; the new emphasizes the new life that is about to begin; the borrowed represents something that has already been worn by a currently happy bride; and the blue stands for fidelity. Inclusion of children in the wedding party is meant to encourage fertility. Another tradition is for the bride to throw her garter to the single men present at the wedding party and her bouquet to the unmarried women. Throwing away the bouquet symbolizes the end of girlhood, and the woman who catches it is supposed to be the next to marry. Rice thrown upon the departing couple symbolizes fertility (Knox and Schacht 1991). A traditional wedding ends with a reception and/or banquet for the wedding guests. Often, music and dancing accompany the feast, and an important ritual is the cutting of the wedding cake. It reenacts the custom of "breaking bread" and symbolizes the breaking of the bride's hymen to aid in first sexual intercourse and future childbirth (Chesser 1980).

The vows expressed at weddings are variable. Most marriage vows include the promise of a commitment, including permanency and fidelity. However, there have always been couples who create their own vows to express their individual philosophy toward marriage. Christian ceremonies emphasize marriage as a divine sacrament and call attention to the tie between the couple and God. In these cases, marriage is under the jurisdiction of God (Saxton 1993). Religious vows include promises made between the couple that reflect their religion. Americans of different ethnic ancestry, such as Jews, Poles, Italians, Latinos, and African-Americans, sometimes develop ceremonies that feature elements from both American culture and their specific ancestral cultures.

During the early 1990s, the cost of a traditional U.S. wedding ceremony with about 200 guests was between $15,000 and $30,000 (Knox and Schacht 1991). This expenditure for a traditional wedding is often beyond the means of many young people and their families. Therefore, many weddings now take place in ordinary clothing and are held in backyards, civic gardens, and parks.

Marriage ceremonies in the United States are as varied as the couples who marry. They may be formal or informal, religious or secular, expensive or modestly priced. In any case, the ceremony symbolizes a couple's transition from single to married status and represents a willingness on the part of the couple to become a family and begin a new generation.

(*See also:* Family Rituals; Marriage Definition; Religion)

BIBLIOGRAPHY

Broude, G. (1994). *Marriage, Family, and Relationships.* Santa Barbara, CA: ABC-CLIO.

Chesser, B. J. (1980). "Analysis of Wedding Rituals: An Attempt to Make Weddings More Meaningful." *Family Relations* 29:204–209.

Davidson, K. J., and Moore, N. B. (1992). *Marriage and Family.* Dubuque, IA: Wm. C. Brown.

Knox, D., and Schacht, C. (1991). *Choices in Relationships,* 3rd edition. St. Paul, MN: West Publishing.

Rosenblatt, P., and Unangst, D. (1974). "Marriage Ceremonies: An Exploratory Cross-Cultural Study." *Journal of Comparative Family Studies* 5:41–56.

Saxton, L. (1993). *The Individual, Marriage, and the Family,* 8th edition. Belmont, CA: Wadsworth.

David Levinson
Marilyn Ihinger-Tallman

MARRIAGE COUNSELING

Married couples seek counseling because they have not found a way to solve the difficult problems confronting them. They have not found a way to live together in a satisfying manner and therefore do not feel committed to their relationship. They look to a counseling setting, where they can work with a professional, to develop a relationship with their spouse that is more pleasurable and satisfying.

The Marriage Counseling Movement

The marriage counseling movement dates to the post-World War I era in Great Britain, Germany, and Austria, when marital and sexual problems were more readily acknowledged. Attempts were made by various helping professions such as medicine, psychology, education, social work, the ministry, and law to provide answers for people with marital or sexual problems. In this instance, marriage counseling was a secondary activity of a professional with other primary commitments. Only in the United States did a specific profession develop to deal with problems between family members. This is due in part to the American belief that social ills can be addressed by education. As divorce and juvenile delinquency rates increased dramatically, there were an array of responses. Some of these have included the following movements: family life education; social hygiene; child guidance; parent education; women's rights; community mental health; new psychotherapeutic modalities such as group, brief, and cognitive approaches; and marital counseling/therapy and family therapy. These all occurred within a matter of decades as responses to social, cultural, and historical currents in thinking (Broderick and Schrader 1991).

In the early 1930s, two specific but different centers offered marriage counseling in America. One was the American Institute of Family Relations in Los Angeles, a clinic established by Paul Popenoe, a biologist specializing in human heredity. Popenoe claimed that he was the first to introduce the phrase "marriage counseling" into the English language. He translated it from the German *Eheberatungsstellen,* a term used for marital consultation centers in Vienna and elsewhere in Europe. Popenoe popularized the profession of marriage counseling by providing case material to a popular early television semidocumentary, Divorce Court. He also began a monthly column, "Can This Marriage Be Saved?," in *The Ladies' Home Journal.*

The other marriage counseling center, the Marriage Council of Philadelphia, was established in 1932 by

Emily Hartshorne Mudd, who was committed to research on the marriage counseling process. She was also among the first to publish a book in the field.

The first professional organization, the American Association of Marriage Counselors (AAMC), was established in 1945 with standards of practice encouraging both publication and research. Postgraduate professional training centers were established beginning in the 1950s, with a code of ethics—a sign of maturity in a profession—formally adopted in 1962. The first legal recognition of marriage, family, and child counselors occurred in California in 1963. This marked a family-oriented clinical profession that was separate from social work, psychology, and psychiatry. There was a recognition of the importance of family therapy, so the AAMC incorporated "Family" into its title in 1970, becoming the American Association of Marriage and Family Counselors. This was changed to the American Association for Marriage and Family Therapy (AAMFT) in 1978.

Healthy Relationships

Research and clinical experience can be used to evaluate the possible reasons why a couple has a healthy relationship and why their marriage works. Both individuals in a healthy couple believe that their spouse is trustworthy and basically a decent person. They feel they can disagree with their spouse without being isolated or abandoned. There is also the belief that humans are fallible, which means that an absolute answer does not exist and opinions are open to challenge. Neither person in the couple has more power or dominance over the other, which allows them to be intimate with each other. Each person takes responsibility for his or her personal behavior and has a clear notion of what he or she feels and thinks, including individual choices and opinions, which are respected. When a couple does have problems they have the requisite skills to negotiate solutions. This means that there is discussion, they listen to each other, and they resolve differences with the maintenance of positive feelings. Differences that may arise include financial issues; setting priorities; decisions about education, either for the couple or their children; and planning for vacations and for eventual retirement. The individuals express caring feelings. They share the everyday things of life. They respect one another. If they become angry or have other strong feelings, they are able to exercise self-control and express their feelings without attacking the other. If they have children, they try not to argue in front of them, because this is upsetting to the children. If their children know the parents are upset, parents inform their children when they have resolved their issues. The couple's goals are defined, and decisions are made. This is done with a mixture of skill and good humor. The couple feels connected to extended family and to their community so that they are not isolated. It follows that a healthy couple's relationship is a necessary ingredient for a high quality of family functioning (Beavers 1985).

Love is a very important factor in the relationship of a couple, but more is necessary than love if people expect to have a healthy relationship. Individuals need to have personal qualities that include an ability to make and keep a commitment, a sensitivity to the needs of another, an ability to be generous, consideration for another's feelings, loyalty, responsibility for one's actions, and trustworthiness. Additional qualities for the marriage to develop and mature are acceptance, forgiveness, and resilience while tolerating each other's flaws, peculiarities, and mistakes (Beck 1988).

Troubled Relationships

A couple may seek couple counseling or marital therapy in at least three contexts. Preventive intervention, wherein a spouse may accompany a client for educational and supportive reasons, may occur when people are receiving information on reducing stress and increasing wellness to decrease risk factors for mortality and morbidity in a range of diseases (House 1988). Supportive therapy, provided for a couple while one spouse is being treated for a mental or physical illness, involves setting clear boundaries on the illness so the illness does not take over the relationship (Hafner 1986; Rolland 1990, 1994). Intensive treatment of relationship issues can occur with or without concurrent treatment of an individual mental disorder (McDaniel 1992).

In many instances, troubled relationships lead to depression and anxiety in one or both mates. In other circumstances, the depression and anxiety aggravate difficulties already present in the relationship (Beck 1988). Problematic issues that usually are addressed alone or in combination are communication, conflict, sexuality, finances, role relationship, family of origin issues, trust, loyalty, and infidelity. In the midst of these issues is the couple, caught between high expectations and diminishing emotional resources (Dym and Glenn 1993). When these issues are not addressed and resolved, divorce is the usual outcome. Divorce occurs in nearly half of all marriages.

Therapist Roles

The contact for couple therapy is usually initiated by a woman. Sometimes husbands are unwilling to talk to a therapist regarding problematic issues, which may lead a wife to attend by herself. All therapists assess the couple's situation by finding out what the problem is and who is more upset by it. The therapist discovers if and when the problem does not occur and what leads to its absence. There is also a determination if the individuals have a positive regard for each other (Berg 1988). While the questioning and response process is under way the therapist is also developing an alliance with the couple. This is accomplished by having the couple feel welcome. The therapist listens carefully and offers clear feedback. The outcome of the intervention is a shared definition of the problem and of the goals of therapy (Beck 1988).

Sometimes a couple is overwhelmed by the enormity of their problems. They need an objective third person to establish a setting of safety so they can set their priorities. It is important to do this to determine when the problem is solved. A small change in one person's behavior can make profound and far-reaching differences in the behavior of all persons involved (De Shazer 1988). Therapy ends when clients have a sense of competence and control over their lives. This does not mean that all life issues have to be worked out. This therapy process usually does not take a long time. Moshe Talmon (1990) has completed research that indicates it is possible for people to redirect themselves after one session. The more usual course of therapy is eight to ten sessions over three to six months (Budman and Gurman 1988). There are situations that indicate that people should not engage in counseling. It is important that people with chemical dependency problems, which include alcohol and drugs, be treated and in recovery prior to engaging in couple therapy if that therapy is to be successful.

Aaron T. Beck (1988) has identified the following six problems, which may be present alone or in combination, as being the most common problems in marriages:

1. The couple has negative perceptions and negative thoughts leading to provocation and rage, which overwhelm positive aspects of the marriage.

2. There is a change from an earlier time, when the partner was idealized (partner perceived as all good), to the present, when there is disillusionment (partner seen as all bad).

3. Each spouse views the same event in a completely different way.

4. There are rigid rules and expectations, which lead to frustration, anger, and a sense of being controlled or out of control. Sandra P. Thomas (1993) conducted research suggesting that many health problems affecting women, such as depression, obesity, headaches, and autoimmune diseases, may in part result from women's unhealthy reaction to anger. This reaction has been either an explosive release of anger or keeping the anger in rather than discussing the angry feelings, preferably with the person who touched them off.

5. There is a breakdown in making important decisions and a breakdown in the partnership.

6. Partners may believe they are speaking the same language, but what they say and what their mate hears are often very different. Research by linguist Deborah Tannen (1990) indicates that women and men have different styles of conversation, which confound women's and men's attempts to communicate with each other. Problems in communication may aggravate the frustrating and disappointing interactions that many couples experience.

Therapist interventions discussed to this point deal with here-and-now problem solving to bring about change, but there is another school of thought, which focuses on understanding unconscious conflict. The belief is that individual personality is organized by the internalization of family experience. People seek a complementary personality in a mate. If individuals are to change themselves and their relationships, it comes about through an uncovering process by working with dreams and fantasy material to reach and resolve unconscious conflict (D. E. Scharff 1992; J. S. Scharff 1992).

If a couple feels there is hope that they can gain insight into their problems and realize that there are repetitive patterns of problematic interactions, then they can begin to solve them. A crucial part of this process is for people to realize they do have choices; they are not simply victims of a bad relationship, no matter how hopeless it may seem. They can and should take responsibility for their relationship (Beck 1988). Many people cannot do this, for various reasons. They may have sought help too late; they have no positive feelings for their spouse and none can be rekindled. These people usually decide that divorce is their only option.

There is a paucity of longitudinal research on the factors that account for endurance in relationships and what leads a couple to divorce. John M. Gottman

(1993, 1994) has done the most extensive research in this area. He has developed an empirical model that predicts with 94 percent accuracy which couples will and will not divorce over the course of three years. This is accomplished by microanalysis of the communication patterns and subtle emotional exchange between husbands and wives as they discuss a problem. The danger signals are criticism voiced as an accusation or attack on the partner's character; contempt; defensiveness in terms of fault-finding statements; and stonewalling, which means the partner does not respond but there is quiet disapproval. The couple withdraw from each other. They do not know how to de-escalate arguments; therefore, they feel hopeless. By identifying warning signs, Gottman has created a profile that therapists can use to strengthen and improve a couple's marriage.

Conclusion

Martin Grotjahn (1960) described marriage as the stage on which each spouse plays out all the unfinished issues of emotional development from his or her childhood background. On the other hand, progressive and continuous disappointment, leading to feelings of emptiness, loneliness, frustration, and bitter anger, usually ends in emotional numbness and the demise of the marriage. If the couple seeks counseling before the relationship reaches this stage, however, they may become knowledgeable and begin a healing process that can lead to their emotional growth.

(*See also:* Commitment; Communication; Conflict; Family Life Education; Family Systems Theory; Family Therapy; Intimacy; Love; Marital Typologies; Parent Education; Trust)

BIBLIOGRAPHY

Beavers, W. R. (1985). *Successful Marriage: A Family Systems Approach to Couples Therapy.* New York: W. W. Norton.

Beck, A. T. (1988). *Love Is Never Enough.* New York: Harper & Row.

Berg, I. K. (1988). "Couple Therapy with One Person or Two." In *Troubled Relationships*, ed. E. W. Nunnally, C. S. Chilman, and F. M. Cox. Newbury Park, CA: Sage Publications.

Broderick, C. B., and Schrader, S. S. (1991). "The History of Professional Marriage and Family Therapy." In *Handbook of Family Therapy*, Vol. II, ed. A. S. Gurman and D. P. Kniskern. New York: Brunner/Mazel.

Budman, S., and Gurman, A. S. (1988). *Theory and Practice of Brief Therapy.* New York: Guilford.

Charny, I. W. (1992). *Existential/Dialectical Marital Therapy: Breaking the Secret Code of Marriage.* New York: Brunner/Mazel.

De Shazer, S. (1988). *Clues: Investigating Solutions in Brief Therapy.* New York: W. W. Norton.

Dym, B., and Glenn, M. (1993). *Couples: Exploring and Understanding the Cycles of Intimate Relationships.* New York: HarperCollins.

Gottman, J. M. (1993). *What Predicts Divorce: The Relationship Between Marital Processes and Marital Outcomes.* Hillsdale, NJ: Lawrence Erlbaum.

Gottman, J. M. (1994). *Two-Part Harmony: Why Marriages Succeed or Fail.* New York: Simon & Schuster.

Grotjahn, M. (1960). *Psychoanalysis and the Family Neurosis.* New York: W. W. Norton.

Hafner, R. J. (1986). *Marriage and Mental Illness: A Sex-Roles Perspective.* New York: Guilford.

House, J. S.; Landis, K. R.; and Umberson, D. (1988). "Social Relationships and Health." *Science* 241:540–544.

McDaniel, S. H.; Hepworth, J.; and Doherty, W. J. (1992). *Medical Family Therapy: A Biopsychosocial Approach to Families with Health Problems.* New York: Basic Books.

Rolland, J. S. (1990). "Anticipatory Loss: A Family Systems Developmental Framework." *Family Process* 29:229–244.

Rolland, J. S. (1994). *Families, Illness, and Disability: A Biopsychosocial Treatment Model.* New York: Basic Books.

Scharff, D. E. (1992). *Refinding the Object and Reclaiming the Self.* New York: Jason Aronson.

Scharff, J. S. (1992). *Projective and Introspective Identification and the Use of the Therapist's Self.* New York: Jason Aronson.

Talmon, M. (1990). *Single-Session Therapy.* San Francisco: Jossey-Bass.

Tannen, D. (1990). *You Just Don't Understand: Women and Men in Conversation.* New York: William Morrow.

Thomas, S. P., ed. (1993). *Women and Anger.* New York: Springer-Verlag.

Carole M. Mucha

MARRIAGE DEFINITION

The institution of marriage is found in all societies. In the United States, marriage means stabilized patterns of norms and roles associated with the mutual relationship between husband and wife. It joins together a man (or men) and a woman (or women) in a special kind of social and legal arrangement that serves several purposes for a society. While this definition fits what is meant by marriage in the United States and other Western nations, it is not broad enough to encompass the essential features of marriage across all cultures. However, because marriage as an institution may differ in structure, function, dynamics, and meaning from one culture to another, no all-encompassing definition of marriage is possible (Kottak 1991). In almost all societies, it entails a legal contract (written or verbal), and this contract varies in the degree to which it can be broken.

Why People Get Married

In most societies, marriages are formed to produce children. From the perspective of evolutionary biology and sociobiology, all individual human beings, as with other species, are driven to reproduce and invest in their offspring to ensure that their genes are passed on to future generations. For at least two million years and perhaps longer, marriage or some arrangement like it has been the social relationship that has proven most effective for this purpose. It is also in the interest of all social groups to maintain and reproduce themselves so that the group will continue. Through the marital union, a stable living unit is established (a family). In this unit, children are socialized into the society's norms and values. In some societies, the connection between marriage and reproduction is so strong that if conception does not occur a divorce is permissible, and often is automatic. In others, a marriage does not take place until after pregnancy occurs and fertility is proven (Miller 1987). For a society, the institution of marriage ensures the regulation of sexual activity for adults and the socialization and protection of children born as a result of that sexual activity. However, individuals living within a society need not comply with behavior that serves the needs of society. Why do they?

In the United States, the most often stated reason for marrying is for love—that is, a man and a woman perceive a mutual emotional and/or physical attraction that is satisfying enough to both that they decide to contract a lifelong relationship. Marriage is a socially sanctioned relationship from which children are born; thus, many people marry to have children. Some persons are premaritally pregnant, and they choose marriage to provide two parents for their child or to escape the negative sanctions or stigma they feel they may experience as an unwed parent. Other persons report that their motivation for entering into a marriage is for economic security, to escape the living situation they are in, or because the relationship has lasted so long that marriage is viewed simply as the "next logical step" (Knox and Schacht 1991).

The feelings called romantic love are nearly universal culturally. In some 85 percent of cultures, at least some people report feeling "in love" with another at some time in their lives (Jankowiak 1994). Love has not always been the basis for marriage in the United States, and it is not the basis for marriage in some societies around the world today. In the early Colonial period in the United States, marriages were arranged, based on the economic needs and the prospects of two families. Even when mutual attraction was the basis for a couple's desire to marry, social boundaries were rarely crossed among financially well-off families who sought to maintain their positions of status and power through appropriate marriages of their children. Marriages of individuals in other social classes varied according to the family's economic circumstances, whether it was a son or a daughter who wanted to marry, and the number of children in the family who needed a dowry or deed of land for marriage to occur. In the Colonial agrarian economy, fathers deeded land to sons to set up new households. Where sons were located in the sibling group (oldest, middle, youngest) and whether their labor was still needed at home to farm the family's land were strong considerations that determined whether a father would grant permission to marry. However, although marriages were based on economic rather than romantic considerations, this did not mean that romantic love was wholly absent from Colonial society. It was present but not linked directly or consistently to courtship or marriage. It did not become the basis for marriage until the late 1700s (Baca-Zinn and Eitzen 1990).

Rules and Regulations

In the United States, marriage is a legal contract, with the state regulating the economic and sexual exchanges between two heterosexual adults (McIntyre 1994). The fifty states vary somewhat in the regulations or criteria that must be satisfied before a couple can contract to marry. Most states specify that people must get a license to marry; be a specific age before they can marry; marry only people of the opposite sex; must not be married to someone else; cannot marry persons with whom they hold certain kin relationships (e.g., mother, father, sibling, in-laws [in some states]); and must be married by a legally empowered representative of the state with two witnesses present. In some states, the couple must have blood tests made to ensure that neither partner has a sexually transmittable disease in the communicable stage. Some states demand a waiting period between the time of purchasing a marriage license and the marriage ceremony (Knox and Schacht 1991). The nature of the legal contract is such that the couple cannot dissolve their marriage on their own; the state must sanction the dissolution of marriage, just as it sanctions the contracting of it.

In some other parts of the world, marriages are arranged and love is hoped for after the marriage occurs. Arranged marriages are the norm in many parts of the world. One cross-cultural survey indicates that marriages are arranged for girls in 44 percent of cultures and for boys in 17 percent (Broude 1994). Arranged marriages occur through the involvement of two sets of parents or through negotiations by professional marriage brokers with prospective families. However, even in most societies where marriage is arranged, the prospective bride and groom are consulted and have some veto power if they feel the proposed partner is absolutely unacceptable. Even in cultures where marriages are preferably arranged and the wishes of the parents and kin of the prospective couple are important, marriages based on love do occur. They typically take place through elopement followed by the grudging acceptance of the parents and kin. The motivation for arranged marriage is to assure the continuity of the family's political and economic well-being and growth. The desire is to provide the best possible match for the children, so educational level, personal skills, and family resources are all important considerations. Because many family resources may be exchanged through marriage, the reputation, resources, and knowledge of the marriage brokers are important (Saxton 1993).

Types of Marriage

To this point, the institution of marriage has been discussed as if all marriages were the same—a living arrangement legally contracted by or for two people of the opposite sex. However, this description has been limited insofar as it describes monogamous marriage. There are other types of marriage, which include more than one husband or wife at the same time (plural marriage or polygamy), several husbands and wives (group marriage), or ones that are not contracted on the basis of the state's rules and regulations specified earlier (common-law marriage).

Monogamy is the only legal type of marriage permitted in the United States. It is illegal to have more than one spouse at a time (bigamy), and most citizens comply with this rule. There are a few exceptions, however. In some western states, members of some fundamentalist Mormon groups practiced polygamy until the late nineteenth century (Hardy 1992). While those who practice group marriage and those in homosexual unions may wish to call themselves married and hold rites or ceremonies to make a public statement that they are married, the states do not recognize such unions as legal.

While having more than one spouse is illegal in the United States, polygyny (one husband with two or more wives at the same time) is the preferred form of marriage throughout most of the world. Seventy-five percent of the world's societies prefer this type of marriage (Saxton 1993). Preference, however, does not necessarily translate into practice, because the number of men and women of marriageable age in most cultures is about the same, meaning that there are rarely more than a few extra women available as second or third wives. Thus, even when polygyny is preferred, there are only a few men, mostly wealthy ones, who have more than one wife at a time (Broude 1994).

Very few societies have polyandrous marriages. Polyandry refers to one wife having several husbands at the same time. Such marriages occur only in a few cultures—probably no more than a dozen—and often take the form of fraternal polyandry, that is, when the husbands are brothers. The cause of such an arrangement is unclear but may be related to the need to keep scarce resources such as small parcels of land inherited by the brothers under the control of a single household.

Group marriage (when men and women living together consider themselves married to each other) is illegal, but there are examples of it throughout the history of the United States and in other societies as well. However, in no society is this type of marriage the primary form of marriage. It was practiced by members of the Oneida Company in the mid-1800s in Vermont and then in New York when the group was forced to move because of community disapproval. A study of more than 100 group marriages in the early 1970s showed that such arrangements do not last long: only 7 percent of the "multilateral marriages" studied lasted longer than five years (Constantine and Constantine 1973). Most of these groups consisted of two couples who lived together, sharing economic resources, services, and child care as well as sexual access. Communication and personality conflicts were the primary reasons for dissolving the group, and bonds between same-sex members of the group were the primary factor responsible for success.

In the United States, common-law marriage is recognized in twelve states and the District of Colombia. These states are Alabama, Colorado, Georgia, Iowa, Kansas, Montana, Ohio, Oklahoma, Pennsylvania, Rhode Island, South Carolina, and Texas. If a heterosexual couple who are of legal age and legally competent to marry (e.g., they are not already married) make an agreement to live together as husband and wife and actually do cohabit, they are legally married. A ceremony is not necessary, nor is compliance with the other formal requirements governing marriage in their state (Knox and Schacht 1991). This practice stems from the tradition that marriage contracted between two adults was their own or their family's business. Historically in continental Europe and England (societies that are the source of much of U.S. law and custom), marriage needed neither civil nor religious sanction. However, the Catholic Church became more powerful during the Middle Ages and assumed control over marriage (Goody 1988). Even though private arrangements continued, these marriages were not recognized as valid by the church (Saxton 1993). In the United States, marriage became regulated by civil laws in the nineteenth century, but some "states took the position that private marriages were valid so long as they were not expressly forbidden by statute. Such unions were called common law" (Saxton 1993, p. 198). In all societies, a marriage is generally not recognized as such unless the couple is deemed married by the community. However, once a marriage is recognized by one state, it must be recognized by all other states (e.g., a common-law marriage officially recognized by Texas must be recognized in Oregon even though Oregon does not officially sanction common-law marriages).

Finally, some social groups have attempted to organize themselves and function without marriage. These include communes, religious orders, and special social or occupational categories such as warrior castes. In the United States, the best known of such groups are the Shakers, a religious community among whose central rules are celibacy and communal living without marriage. Although the group has lasted since the late 1700s, its numbers have now dwindled from a high of about 4,000 in some sixty communities in the mid-1800s to fewer than a dozen members in one community in 1991 (Foster 1991). Similarly, many communes founded in the 1960s either folded or instituted monogamous marriage. The two types of social groups that have survived without marriage are religious orders and caste or castelike groups such as the Hijras in India. However, all of these groups are institutionalized within a larger society and are able to attract new members from that society.

Conclusion

Marriage represents a multi-level commitment, one that involves person-to-person, family-to-family, and couple-to-state commitments. In all societies, marriage is viewed as a relatively permanent bond, so much so that in some societies it is virtually irrevocable. The stability provided by a life-long promise of remaining together makes marriage the institution most suited to rearing and socializing the next generation of members, a necessary task if the society's norms, values, and goals are to be maintained and if the society itself is to be perpetuated.

(*See also:* Communes; Family Law; Family Rituals; Marriage Ceremonies; Mate Selection; Polyandry; Polygyny; Utopian Communities)

BIBLIOGRAPHY

Baca-Zinn, M., and Eitzen, D. S. (1990). *Diversity in Families.* New York: HarperCollins.

Broude, G. (1994). *Marriage, Family, and Relationships.* Denver: ABC-CLIO.

Constantine, L. L., and Constantine, J. M. (1973). *Group Marriage.* New York: Macmillan.

Foster, L. (1991). *Women, Family, and Utopia.* Syracuse, NY: Syracuse University Press.

Goody, J. (1988). *The Development of the Family and Marriage in Europe.* Cambridge, Eng.: Cambridge University Press.

Hardey, B. C. (1992). *Solemn Covenant: The Mormon Polygamous Passage.* Urbana: University of Illinois Press.

Jankowiak, W., ed. (1994). *Romantic Passion: The Universal Emotion?* New York: Columbia University Press.

Knox, D., and Schacht, C. (1991). *Choices in Relationships.* St. Paul, MN: West Publishing.

Kottak, C. P. (1991). *Cultural Anthropology,* 5th edition. New York: McGraw-Hill.

McIntyre, L. (1994). *Law and the Sociological Enterprise.* Boulder, CO: Westview Press.

Miller, B. (1987). "Marriage, Family, and Fertility." In *Handbook of Marriage and the Family,* ed. M. B. Sussman and S. K. Steinmetz. New York: Plenum.

Saxton, L. (1993). *The Individual, Marriage, and the Family.* Belmont, CA: Wadsworth.

Marilyn Ihinger-Tallman
David Levinson

MASS MEDIA

For thousands of years, the major determinants of attitudes, expectations, and family behavior were largely a function of the limited influences possible from parents or members of a small extended-family structure. In the nineteenth and particularly in the twentieth century, however, the family unit has been exposed to forms of communication that have a "public or social character" well beyond any popular media that might have been a part of human experience throughout all earlier history (Comstock and Paik 1989). These newer media can penetrate the privacy of family units with combinations of information and entertainment in an instantaneous fashion. Such exposure to alternative possibilities of lifestyles, through information often presented in the format of entertainment, may in a variety of subtle and direct ways affect the individual attitudes, desires, and ultimately the overt behaviors of family members. The mass media include newspapers, magazines, books, phonograph records or other audio communication devices (e.g., tapes or compact discs), live theater, radio, film, and television. Finally, there is the computer, which is likely to become a major source of communication in the twenty-first century.

Emergence of Mass Communication

A great step forward in mass media came with the development of the printing press in Mainz, Germany, in the fifteenth century. Still, the accessibility of printed materials remained limited for centuries to small numbers of religious authorities or to ruling nobilities and then gradually to an increasing but very small middle class. It was not until the middle of the nineteenth century, with the combination of industrialization and urbanization of nations such as England, France, Germany, and the United States, that there was sufficient literacy for families to possess their own printed Bibles and to draw, from both the Old and the New Testaments, external information that seemed to bear on family life. Some of the first mass literature that also affected family life was evident with the distribution of serialized fiction and, during the same period, the emergence of family magazines. Charles Dickens perhaps represents the first individual who could, through his serialized novels as well as through his editing of magazines such as *Household Words*, reach thousands of readers month after month and provide portrayals of family life. Dickens's *A Christmas Carol* (1843) ostensibly reflected to thousands of readers a traditional middle-class Christmas dinner and other family practices. It also exposed others to a particular kind of family lifestyle toward which they may not have hitherto aspired. Dickens himself traveled extensively in England and the United States, giving readings from his novels to large audiences. In doing so, he attained a fame that would be comparable to that of a rock star or movie idol of the twentieth century. At the same time as books and magazines or printed music seemed to be proliferating wildly in the nineteenth century, illiteracy was still the rule for the majority of individuals, even in the industrialized countries. In the absence of electric lighting or the telephone, most families still drew almost entirely on their own resources for entertainment and communication.

The twentieth century can be understood as the age of mass media. With the widespread availability of electricity, the development of the phonograph, the wide distribution of newspapers or magazines by means of the railroads and trucks, and the advent of inexpensive moving-picture theaters, what is commonly viewed as mass media truly emerged. In the movies, families, generally attending together, could see examples of a panoply of different family problems and family lifestyles. Greatly increased literacy in the Western industrial nations also led to the emergence of more popular magazines. The fashions shown in the magazines fostered much more rapid changes in styles of dress. During the late 1920s and throughout the 1940s, radio became the primary home-penetrating medium. Its combination of popular music, "soap operas" or serialized fiction, comedy, and of course a vast proliferation of commercial messages reached the family in a way that had never been the case before. In the past, a family might have sat by the fireside exchanging stories, legends, or family history, but by the early 1930s, families sat around a small radio console on Sunday night listening to the jokes of Eddie Cantor. During the week, they tuned in to the portrayal of Jewish family life in the extremely popular "Rise of the Goldbergs" or perhaps to the widely heard "Amos and Andy" series, an unintentionally but extremely prejudicial portrayal of African-American family life.

Although television sets became commercially available in the late 1940s, it was not until well into the 1950s that the medium, with its combination of entertainment shows, news presentations, and commercials, began to penetrate powerfully into American home life. There seems little question now that television—with its availability evident in the fact that practically every home in the United States has at least one set (if not more) and its accessibility increasing throughout the world—is the dominant popular medium with significant impact on the family.

Studying the Impact of Media

To understand how mass media influence the family unit or its individual members, the beginning point must be a modified phrasing of Harold Lasswell's (1932) question, "Who says what to whom through what medium with what effect?" Each form of the mass media penetrates the family in a somewhat different fashion. Print materials, newspapers, magazines, and books are generally individually purchased or delivered to a specific family member. For very young children, the bedtime reading ritual may be a special moment of emotional closeness and an important introduction to reading. Research suggests that preschoolers and relatively young students demonstrating greater imaginative resourcefulness have more regularly been exposed to such parental bedtime reading rituals (D. G. Singer and J. L. Singer 1990). At older ages, reading is generally a private experience. One's own imagery capacities are used to enhance the written words and there is more self-pacing, review, or even opportunity to drift into fairly elaborate fantasy during the process (D. G. Singer 1992). Comparisons across media suggest that reading and radio listening may actually provide "deeper" processing, better comprehension, and more effective recall then watching a televised version of the same material (Beagles-Roos and Gat 1983; Greenfield, Farrer, and Beagles-Roos 1986; Greenfield and Beagles-Roos 1988; Hayes, Kelley, and Mandel 1986).

Radio, which began its role in the family as a somewhat unifying influence, now plays a different role as a consequence of its displacement by television. While once the family might have gathered round to listen to a fictional story or to hear a "fireside chat" by President Franklin D. Roosevelt, today radio consists chiefly of specialized music programming geared to the individual tastes of different family members. It may be listened to via earphones or in the privacy of one's room or automobile. Individually purchased audiotapes or compact discs can also be listened to privately. Storytelling via radio is rare. The news, sporting events, and talk shows on this medium seem more oriented to lonely persons isolated in apartments or driving their cars.

The television medium represents the overwhelmingly influential mass medium of the twentieth century and possibly the twenty-first. Its daily home usage, already 4 hours and 35 minutes by 1950, was consistent at about 7 hours throughout the 1980s (Andreasen 1990). With the increased flexibility and diversity of cable broadcasting, it should be likely to hold or increase that status. The combinations of the visual (the most powerful sense) and auditory representations, the immediacy of impact, and the carefully engineered pacing of material—designed to sustain viewer attention—give it an advantage. Analysis of the psychological features of television viewing suggest that it is easier than dealing with other popular media. Television has a special quality of providing a kind of low-arousal escape from the urgency and complexity of individual ongoing thought processes (Kubey 1990; J. L. Singer 1980). Through the vividness of its visual presentation day after day (in contrast to theatrical films, which are seen only occasionally), television conveys a sense of reality (even when the story is clearly fiction) that penetrates the consciousness and creates special belief-systems or "cultivation" effects (Gerbner et al. 1986) and specifically influences conceptions about family life (Brown and Bryant 1990). Since a large percentage of family units include children, the potential of the medium as a source of imitative behavior is a special concern.

How do social scientists and communications researchers accumulate data about the media? Large-scale surveys are conducted using interviews or regular telephoning of carefully selected national or regional samples to learn of usage frequency, reliance on media for specific purposes, and interest in advertised products. Nielsen ratings identify selected families around the country deemed to be especially representative of national trends and track these families' regular reports of their television viewing hours and program selection. New devices such as Peoplemeters are being tried. Such systems involve tracking ratings based on the button-pressing of keypads supplied to the families, who record their choices while they are actually viewing their shows. The systems can even assess enjoyment or comprehension levels of programs being watched.

Other approaches to studying family viewing include actual observers in the home. In one such study, it was noted that children who had earlier been identified as heavy viewers often sat quietly by the set for several hours with no adult (other than the observer) in the room and with minimal parental communication (Desmond, Singer, and Singer 1990); a link was thus made between viewing and family communication patterns. The use of daily home logs by parents trained to fill out forms that list available programs has been effective in assessing preschool children's television viewing for two-week periods scattered over a year's time (J. L. Singer and D. G. Singer 1981). A method that may be of particular value for adolescents and the adults in a family is the Experience Sampling Method, where each individual carries a paging device and rating cards on which to respond whenever signaled. These "beeper" techniques allow an evaluation of what people were thinking or feeling while using a particular medium (Kubey 1990). This method was able to show in a series of studies that parents seemed in better moods and more lively when engaged in non-television-viewing activities with the children than when watching.

Another approach to understanding how the media might influence families and their individual members is through content analyses. Earlier studies of newspapers' so-called ladies pages and of magazines consistently pointed to an emphasis on the woman as loyal wife and homemaker. The long tradition of women's magazines, going back to the 1837 *Godey's Lady's Book* (the first American mass magazine), established a homemaker, "fashion and food" emphasis that still persists, according to content analyses of *Family Circle* (Philips 1978).

Film content analyses have shown the growing fascination of older children with danger, an effect that may reflect their efforts to cope with the increasing riskiness and conflicts that they are coming to recognize as part of life by reframing such dangers in a clear play or make-believe context (Apter 1990; D. G. Singer and J. L. Singer 1990). Analyses of soap operas (daytime television serials), which are especially attractive to women across socioeconomic levels, indicate that the plots do not reflect either the "ideal" American nuclear family (a unit that reflects perhaps only 30% of actual families) nor do they show distinctive patterns that mirror the families of their viewers (Pingree and Thompson 1990).

Probably the greatest amount of research and systematic observation concerning mass media and families has come in the area of television content, since more than 100 million people in the United States are likely to be watching television on any given night. Much has been made of the fact that in the 1950s and 1960s family situation comedies (usually one-half hour in length) or even family dramas (involving a full hour) were likely to represent the so-called traditional intact nuclear family. In the 1970s and 1980s, broadcasters began experimenting with more varied family portrayals. They shifted from the generally white middle-class families of the "Leave It to Beaver" or "Brady Bunch" genre toward more representations of households run by single parents (usually mothers). In the 1970s and 1980s, portrayals of nonwhite families increased. The networks clearly were making an effort to depict greater diversity. The extremely successful "Cosby" show depicted an upper-middle-class African-American family in which both parents were professionals and lived with their children in an attractive home. This series contrasted with earlier negative images of African Americans (Berry and Asamen 1993). Following the success of the "Cosby" show in the 1980s, the 1990s began to reflect a movement again toward intact traditional nuclear families, according to content analyses. Despite occasional criticism of the networks by political or religious groups, content analyses of family representations on television generally indicate that families are on the whole presented as well-working units (Abelman 1990; Skill, Wallace, and Cassata 1990). If one were to assume that families will, to some extent, try to reshape their behavior whenever possible in relation to the kinds of models shown on the popular medium of television, then the models represented there are salutary from a mental-health standpoint. They emphasize considerable internal effort at conflict resolution and at mutual respect among family members. Whatever negative influences television may have, they do not seem to stem from the content of situation-comedy portrayals of family.

While television on the whole in the United States has not grossly distorted ordinary family living (except in quasi-caricature forms such as "The Simpsons" or "Roseanne"), television's tremendous emphasis on violent content and suggestive sexuality may have over the years affected children somewhat differently than adolescents. From the standpoint of content analyses, adolescents' grasp of sexuality, their attitude toward personal development, and their sense of future vocational goals seem especially influenced by music videos or music television (MTV), which is extremely popular, and of course the bombardment of commercial messages. Both of these have, on the whole, greatly exaggerated the importance of feminine beauty, hypermasculinity, and slim figures; their presentation is a relentless sexual seduction. Family controls that might still affect what is watched regularly on television may lose their impact when the prepubescent or adolescent members of the family have videotapes readily available. (Lindlof and Schatzer 1990). The increased penetration of the American home by MTV and other rock music videos has been documented extensively (Greenfield et al. 1987; Rothschild and Morgan 1987; Signorielli 1987).

There are indications that active parental intervention through discussions, co-viewing, and control of viewing may work. However, such effects are primarily limited to the youngest members of the family (Desmond, Singer, and Singer 1990; Morgan 1987).

A serious question remaining in the research literature is to what extent sheer exposure via film or television will lead to changes in belief systems, attitudes, and overt behavior in family members. One widely accepted theoretical position is the social learning model. Many experiments demonstrate that both adults and children observing certain forms of behavior on film or television incorporate them into their own repertory of responses and show some degree of imitation. This is especially true for younger children, who lack a history of exposure to significant alternatives that can mitigate the impact of one viewing experience.

A second theoretical approach, not inconsistent with the first, derives from extensive research in the field of cognitive psychology. According to this theory, a great deal of human retention is organized for efficiency around particular mental structures called schemas. These schemas, which usually involve classification of observations or experiences around certain key categories, lead to efficient retention and then to efficient recall in appropriate circumstances. Scripts are schemas about sequences of events, and they determine to some extent how individuals interpret or behave in specific social settings (e.g., restaurants and hair salons) or more complex interpersonal transactional situations (e.g., on dates or at parties). Intense vivid exposure such as one experiences in a movie theater or even the less intense but *persistent* exposure one has in home viewing of television can lead to the formation of schemas and scripts that will later determine how one interprets and reacts in similar real-life situations.

In effect, these positions argue (especially for television) that whatever independent moral precepts or advice individuals may have received from parental figures or from religious teachings or school settings, the heavy exposure to television may generate new sets of expectancies and sets of reaction potentials that derive more from the essentially make-believe character of television's show-business structure. To the extent that certain elements are consistently a part of what television presents, children in particular are susceptible to influence. From the standpoint of media's impact on the family, then, more attention must be given to the specific impact that television produces in relation to children.

Television Viewing and Children

Television viewing is generally tolerated by the vast majority of parents as simply a form of entertainment. Yet television may actually represent the intrusion into the daily life of the family of a stranger who is intent, on the one hand, on familiarizing children with commercial products and who, on the other hand, makes use of a great deal of physical violence to sustain excitement in the interests of holding attention. Content analyses over several decades have indicated an extremely high level of violent material as part of the daily fare of television (Huesmann and Malamuth 1986). Imitative aggression may follow exposure to so much violent material.

Other possible consequences of heavy television viewing include the likelihood that it may create a habitual reliance on this "easy" medium, distracting the child from attempting the more difficult tasks of thinking, playing, and reading, as well as doing homework (Postman 1985; J. L. Singer 1980). The rapid pacing that characterizes American commercial television—the frequent fragmentation, short sequences interrupted by commercials, and shifts of focus designed to sustain attention to the set—may conceivably develop a mental set in children that precludes sustained attention to more complex material in the classroom (D. G. Singer and J. L. Singer 1990).

To study the effects of television's penetration into family life and its more direct potential influence on children, one must of course take into account the characteristics of the family atmosphere. Table 1 provides an example of the kinds of variables that need to be considered within a family setting (left column) and the possible effects that heavy television viewing or particular kinds of viewing, especially of violent programs, may have on children's overt attitudes and behaviors (right column). A number of research studies have taken into account family attitudes and particular family settings and how these interact with heavy television viewing to produce the sets of responses listed in the right-hand column of Table 1. Thus, parents who place more value emphasis on social interaction and less on self-control and restraint may not restrict children's viewing, with the result that their children are more likely to be exposed to aggressive television content and to reflect this in their overt behavior (J. L. Singer, D. G. Singer, and Rapaczynski 1984b). Similarly, when parents do not show an emphasis on imaginativeness and, at the same time, do not restrict children's exposure to more aggressive television content, there is evidence that such children will prove to be less imaginative in their spontaneous behavior (J. L. Singer and D. G. Singer 1986; J. L. Singer, D. G. Singer, and Rapaczysnki 1984a). Another feature of the parents' role is the communication style with the child. Some parents primarily engage children by short statements that involve peremptory commands or statements simply indicating disapproval of certain behaviors and fail to communicate at greater length about other subjects. Other parents may show a greater tendency for more extended explanations and a general pattern of filtering the external world of their children. These indi-

Table 1 Variables to Be Considered for Television Viewing in a Family Setting

Independent Variables

- I. Family patterns
  - A. Parental values or traits
    - 1. Resourcefulness and imagination
    - 2. Stability or reliability
    - 3. Sociability
  - B. Parental mediation styles
    - 1. Discussion versus prescription
  - C. Parental disciplinary style
    - 1. Power assertion (physical punishment)
  - D. Level of parental stress
  - E. Daily routines
    - 1. Organization of household
    - 2. Sleep patterns
    - 3. Cultural variety
    - 4. Emphasis on contact sports
  - F. Socioeconomic status
  - G. Home television environment
    - 1. Parents' television-viewing frequency
    - 2. Parents' use of television rules or mediation of child's television viewing
    - 3. Number of sets, cable access, and types of programming available
- II. Child characteristics
  - A. Television-viewing patterns
    - 1. Frequency
    - 2. Type of programming, (e.g., realistic action-adventure, fantasy action-adventure)
    - 3. Alone or with others
    - 4. Identification with characters
  - B. IQ or basic verbal skill
  - C. Gender and age
  - D. Imaginativeness

Dependent Variables

- I. Cognitive functions
  - A. General information
  - B. Reading skills
  - C. Reality–fantasy distinction
  - D. Belief in "scary world"
  - E. Grasp of television
    - 1. Program comprehension
    - 2. Knowledge about commercials
    - 3. Understanding special effects
- II. Imaginativeness
- III. Behavioral patterns
  - A. Cooperation with peers and prosocial or positive affective reactions
  - B. Motoric restlessness
    - 1. Waiting ability in games
    - 2. Waiting-room restlessness
  - C. Aggression
  - D. School behavior adjustment

cations of parents' mediation styles in association with television viewing suggest that those parents who are more oriented toward fuller discussions and explanations have children who seem able to grasp more of the properties of the television medium and show more program comprehension, more knowledge about commercials, and better understanding of the special effects on television.

The disciplinary style of the parents is a critical determinant of overt behaviors. Parental reliance on physical punishment is tied to restlessness and aggression or poor school adjustment in many studies. When such punishment is combined with children's unrestrained television viewing, particularly of more aggressively oriented programming, the children are independently rated as more physically aggressive (J. L. Singer and D. G. Singer 1986). As a matter of fact, there is evidence that individuals who at ten years of age were exposed to considerable aggressive television material are more likely by age thirty to be showing persistent aggressive behavior, including a much greater potential for criminal behavior, than those who as children had watched relatively little aggressive television. Indeed, even though parental variables might have played a role in the initial tendency of the children to watch so much television of this type, these follow-up studies indicate that the special linkage of heavy viewing to overt aggressive behavior cannot be accounted for solely by such family influences. Television's impact on the inclination toward potentially violent or dangerous behavior must be taken seriously (Huesmann 1986; Huesmann and Malamuth 1986).

Of particular importance within the home is how parents structure rules around the television set, how much time they spend with the children explaining things about television, their insistence on monitoring and limiting what children watch, and their engaging in coviewing with children (Abelman 1990; Desmond, Singer, and Singer 1990).

Approaches to moderating the influences of television on children have come through the so-called critical-skills training movement with respect to media usage. Lesson plans have been developed for elementary school and high school (Brown 1991; Desmond, Singer, and Singer 1990; D. G. Singer and J. L. Singer 1991; D. G. Singer, J. L. Singer, and Zuckerman 1990). These plans are designed to assist parents and teachers in providing children with a keener understanding of the nature of the medium to which they are exposed from such early ages. The lesson plans also seek to teach critical evaluation of commercials and even the news, since news programs are often organized with an emphasis on the most dramatic rather than the most socially meaningful content. Moreover, children are helped to understand special effects such as disappearances or amazing superhuman feats and, of course, the nature of fictional aggression.

Various parent-advocacy groups, religious organizations, and journalists have called on the industry and the government to act to reduce some of the hazards of the television medium as regards children and also to enhance the more constructive potential of television. Congressional legislation of the early 1990s responded to many of these concerns. It called for more regulative attention by the Federal Communications Commission to the obligations of local stations in providing better-quality programming for children and in reducing some of the more potentially exploitative features of commercial television. In addition, there are increasing indications that public broadcasting will attempt to provide more balanced programming designed to enhance school readiness and to provide entertainment that is less oriented toward aggression, especially for preschoolers and relatively young students. Ultimately, the control of the television set in the American home depends on recognition by the adult caregivers that the medium has a considerable potency and potential influence that cannot be ignored.

(*See also:* Communication; Family Policy; Family Values; Family Violence; Personality Development; Play; Sexuality Education)

BIBLIOGRAPHY

Abelman, R. (1990). "From the 'Huxtables' to the 'Humbards': Portrayal of the Family on Religious Television." In *Television and the American Family,* ed. J. Bryant. Hillsdale, NJ: Lawrence Erlbaum.

Andreasen, M. S. (1990). "Evolution in the Family's Use of Television: Normative Data from Industry and Academe." In *Television and the American Family,* ed. J. Bryant. Hillsdale, NJ: Lawrence Erlbaum.

Apter, M. (1990). *The Dangerous Edge: The Psychology of Excitement.* New York: Free Press.

Beagles-Roos, J., and Gat, I. (1983). "Specific Impact of Radio and Television in Children's Story Comprehension." *Journal of Educational Psychology* 75:128–137.

Berry, G. L., and Asamen, J. K. (1993). *Children and Television: Images in a Changing Sociocultural World.* Newbury Park, CA: Sage Publications.

Brown, J. A. (1991). *Television "Critical Viewing Skills" Education: Major Media Literacy Projects in the United States and Selected Countries.* Hillsdale, NJ: Lawrence Erlbaum.

Brown, D., and Bryant, J. (1990). "Effects of Television on Family Values and Selected Attitudes and Behaviors." In *Television and the American Family,* ed. J. Bryant. Hillsdale, NJ: Lawrence Erlbaum.

Bryant, J., ed. (1990). *Television and the American Family.* Hillsdale, NJ: Lawrence Erlbaum.

Comstock, G., and Paik, H. (1989). *Television and the American Child.* New York: Academic Press.

Desmond, R.; Singer, J. L.; and Singer, D. G. (1990). "Family Mediation: Parental Communication Patterns and the Influences of Television on Children." In *Television and the American Family,* ed. J. Bryant. Hillsdale, NJ: Lawrence Erlbaum.

Gerbner, G.; Gross, L.; Morgan, M.; and Signorielli, N. (1986). "Living with Television: The Dynamics of the Cultivation Process." In *Perspectives on Media Effects,* ed. J. Bryant and D. Zillmann. Hillsdale, NJ: Lawrence Erlbaum.

Greenfield, P., and Beagles-Roos, J. (1988). "Radio vs. Television: Their Cognitive Impact on Children of Different Socioeconomic and Ethnic Groups." *Journal of Communication* 38:71–72.

Greenfield, P.; Bruzzone, L.; Koyamatsu, K.; Satuloff, W.; Nixon, K.; Brodie, M.; and Kingsdale, D. (1987). "What Is Rock Music Doing to the Minds of our Youth? A First Experimental Look at the Effects of Rock Music Lyrics and Music Videos." *Journal of Early Adolescence* 7:315–329.

Greenfield, P.; Farrer, D.; and Beagles-Roos, J. (1986). "Is the Medium the Message? An Experimental Comparison of the Effects of Radio and Television on Imagination." *Journal of Applied Developmental Psychology* 7:201–218.

Hayes, D. S.; Kelley, S. B.; and Mandel, M. (1986). "Media Differences in Children's Story Synopses: Radio and Television Contrasted." *Journal of Educational Psychology* 78:341–346.

Huesmann, L. R. (1986). "Psychological Processes Promoting the Relation Between Exposure to Media Violence and Aggressive Behavior by the Viewer." *Journal of Social Issues* 42:125–139.

Huesmann, L. R., and Malamuth, N. M. (1986). "Media Violence and Antisocial Behavior." *Journal of Social Issues* 42:1–199.

Kubey, R. (1990). "Television and Family Harmony Among Children, Adolescents, and Adults: Results from the Experience Sampling Method." In *Television and the American Family,* ed. J. Bryant. Hillsdale, NJ: Lawrence Erlbaum.

Lasswell, H. D. (1932). "The Triple Appeal Principle: The Contribution of Psychoanalysis to Political and Social Science." *American Journal of Sociology* 37:523–538.

Lindlof, T. R., and Schatzer, M. J. (1990). "VCR Usage in the American Family." In *Television and the American Family,* ed. J. Bryant. Hillsdale, NJ: Lawrence Erlbaum.

Morgan, M. (1987). "Television, Sex Role Attitudes, and Sex Role Behavior." *Journal of Early Adolescence* 7:269–282.

Philips, E. B. (1978). "Magazine Heroines: Is *Ms.* Just Another Member of the *Family Circle*?" In *Health and Home: Images of Women in the Mass Media,* ed. G. Tuchman, A. K. Daniels, and J. Benet. New York: Oxford University Press.

Pingree, S., and Thompson, M. E. (1990). "The Family in Daytime Serials." In *Television and the American Family,* ed. J. Bryant. Hillsdale, NJ: Lawrence Erlbaum.

Postman, N. (1985). *Amusing Ourselves to Death.* New York: Viking Press.

Rothschild, N., and Morgan, M. (1987). "Cohesion and Control: Adolescents' Relationships with Parents as Mediators of Television." *Journal of Early Adolescence* 7:299–314.

Signorielli, N. (1987) "Children and Adolescents on Television: A Consistent Pattern of Devaluation." *Journal of Early Adolescence* 7:255–268.

Singer, D. G. (1993). "Creativity of Children in a Television World." In *Children and Television: Images in a Changing Sociocultural World,* ed. G. L. Berry and J. K. Asamen. Newbury Park, CA: Sage Publications.

Singer, D. G., and Singer, J. L. (1990). *The House of Make-Believe: Children's Play and the Developing Imagination.* Cambridge, MA: Harvard University Press.

Singer, D. G., and Singer, J. L. (1991). *Creating Critical Viewers.* New York: National Academy of Television Arts and Sciences.

Singer, D. G.; Singer, J. L.; and Zuckerman, D. (1990). *The Parent's Guide: Use Television to Your Child's Advantage.* Reston, VA: Acropolis Books.

Singer, J. L. (1980). "The Power and Limitations of Television: A Cognitive-Affective Analysis." In *The Entertainment Functions of Television,* ed. P. H. Tannenbaum. Hillsdale, NJ: Lawrence Erlbaum.

Singer, J. L., and Singer, D. G. (1981). *Television, Imagination, and Aggression: A Study of Preschoolers.* Hillsdale, NJ: Lawrence Erlbaum.

Singer, J. L., and Singer, D. G. (1986). "Family Experiences and Television Viewing as Predictors of Children's Imagination, Restlessness, and Aggression." *Journal of Social Issues* 42:107–124.

Singer, J. L.; Singer, D. G.; and Rapaczynski, W. (1984a). "Children's Imagination as Predicted by Family Patterns and Television-Viewing: A Longitudinal Study." *Genetic Psychology Monographs* 110:43–69.

Singer, J. L.; Singer, D. G.; and Rapaczynski, W. (1984b). "Family Patterns and Television Viewing as Predictors of Children's Beliefs and Aggression." *Journal of Communication* 34:73–89.

Skill, T.; Wallace, S.; and Cassata, M. (1990). "Families on Prime-Time Television: Patterns of Conflict Escalation and Resolution Across Intact, Nonintact, and Mixed-Family Settings." In *Television and the American Family,* ed. J. Bryant. Hillsdale, NJ: Lawrence Erlbaum.

JEROME L. SINGER

MATE SELECTION

Marriage is very popular worldwide; in the United States, more than 95 percent of people marry at some point in their lives (Glick 1984). In most societies, marriage is preceded by what is called mate selection or courtship, the process by which single people select their marriage partners. Social scientists have found that this premarital phase of relationships is important in predicting how successfully relationships will function after a marriage. This predictability is of interest because marriages that are unhappy result in several undesirable outcomes for families and society. These negative outcomes can include physical illness, divorce, dysfunctional children, abuse between married partners, and child abuse.

Proposed Explanations

Since the early 1900s, social scientists have been attempting to explain how marital partners are selected. Some early Freudian advocates attempted to explain mate selection by assuming that people select partners who are similar to their opposite-sex parent. Research did not find that to be the case. Later, social scientists put forth three possible explanations of the mate selection process. One explanation assumes that people select others for marital partners based on the degree to which they perceive that they will be compatible with the other person. Another proposed explanation alleges that people select mates on the basis of whether the rewards that will come from marrying that person outweigh the costs involved. A third explanation holds that the development of relationships toward marriage is very complex and cannot be adequately understood by focusing only on compatibility or the rewards of a premarital relationship.

Compatibility explanations. Early attempts by social scientists to explain mate selection assumed that people looked for partners with whom they thought they would be compatible. Compatibility was seen to be likely when the partners in a relationship matched each other on various stable psychological and background attributes. However, social scientists differed in how they defined "matching." One group of scientists believed that compatibility between premarital partners was based on the degree to which partners complemented each other's personalities. Another group asserted that compatibility was based on whether people were similar to each other in attitudes, values, and various background factors.

The personality complementarity hypothesis holds that people choose as mates those individuals who are most likely to gratify their personality needs (Winch 1955). Needs of partners can be gratified in two different ways. First, people can be gratified in certain instances by selecting a partner who differs in the intensity of a personality characteristic relative to themselves. For example, it is assumed that a person high in the personality dimension of dominance will prefer to select a partner who is low in the need for dominance. Second, personality need gratification is seen to occur when partners are high on different personality characteristics that complement each other. For example, a person high on dominance is expected to be gratified by a partner who is high on submissiveness. These types of mate selection considerations are quite similar to people's everyday reasoning that holds that "opposites attract." Although most people have observed individual couples who seem to complement each other (e.g., the gregarious, outgoing female who has married the quiet, reserved male), scientific studies have found little evidence suggesting that people pick others who complement their personalities. The one major study (Winch 1955), now quite outdated, that offered support for the theory was later criticized as having inadequately tested the theory. Virtually all subsequent studies have not supported personality complementarity as a significant factor in mate selection. Consequently, researchers and theoreticians give little attention to this potential explanation of mate selection. However, from everyday observation, many people still hold to this explanation.

At about the same time, theoreticians and researchers also were interested in whether similarity between individuals played a role in their selection of a mate. It was proposed that people prefer partners who are similar to themselves. Research does show that people resemble their partners in many different ways. Married partners have been found to be similar in their choice of religious affiliation and in ethnic background, family background, intelligence, attitudes, values, personality, and physical attractiveness. It intuitively makes sense that similarity should be an important factor in selecting a mate. However, while similarity may create good feelings and a personal sense of worth, it may also lead to expectations of personal rewards.

Although this similarity theory is intuitively appealing and seems to be supported by research, closer consideration of the theory has raised questions concerning how accurate it is in explaining mate selection. Some researchers (e.g., Kerckhoff 1974) have suggested that people who marry are similar to each other because the structure of society ensures that similar people will meet each other. For example, people who live close to each other tend to have similar levels of education, to be in the same social class, and to have similar attitudes and values. Consequently, those whom individuals meet daily and are attracted to tend to be quite similar to themselves. Therefore, people may not consciously choose a similar mate; they simply do not have a great number of opportunities to meet people who differ drastically from themselves.

Other social scientists have suggested that the mate selection process is more complicated than suggested by similarity and complementary explanations. It was suggested that several factors may be important in mate selection and that these factors operate in sequence during the courtship. One prominent sequential explanation focused on a more complex process known as the "filter" model of mate selection. This filter explanation emerged from a study that suggested that people first filter out those potential partners who are not similar and then filter out those who do not complement their personalities (Kerckhoff and Davis 1962). This filtering process purportedly resulted in a partner who was both similar to and complementary to the self. However, later research did not support this proposed model of mate selection.

Subsequent sequential explanations of mate selection were proposed. One explanation held that people first select partners on the basis of certain stimulus factors (e.g., physical attractiveness), later on the basis of values, and last on the basis of how well the partners' roles "fit" each other (Murstein 1976). Another explanation proposed several sequential stages that acted as filters in the mate selection process (Lewis 1973). The process of mate selection, according to this explanation, started with filtering first on the basis of partners' perceiving similarities, which led to the following stages of reaching pair rapport, including self-disclosure, role-taking, achieving interpersonal role fit, and finally achieving dyadic crystallization. As of the mid-1990s, these proposed explanations were not generally acknowledged as a good reflection of how couples move to marriage. Many social scientists do not believe that the mate selection process is as orderly as filter models suggested. In addition, there was little research that supported these sequential stage models.

Exchange model. The lack of success by proponents of the filter models in explaining courtship led social scientists to look for other explanations. In step with the psychological thinking of the time, courtship researchers began to examine the behavioral aspects of the movement to marriage. The most prominent of these behavioral frameworks is known as social exchange. Those who hold to an exchange perspective believe that the development of commitment to a particular future marital partner is based on the satisfactory exchange of rewards between partners during courtship (Huston and Cate 1979). According to this framework, people are first attracted to others based on how rewarding they think the other person would be (e.g., physical attractiveness). Once they are initially attracted, people must determine whether the person is likely to see them as a rewarding person. Then, if they think there is mutual attraction (rewardingness), they attempt to move the relationship to deeper levels. Further development will depend on whether the partner is as rewarding as past relationships and whether there are other attractive alternatives to the relationship. So if a person perceives that his or her present partner is equal to or better than what he or she is used to and that that person does not feel he or she can do any better, the relationship will move closer to marriage. According to exchange principles, further movement to marriage would occur if the partners believed that rewards would increase in the future, the division of rewards between partners was fair, kin and friends supported the relationship, and that further movement to marriage was commensurate with how much they had invested in the relationship.

Interpersonal process model. As of the mid-1990s, thinking in the area of mate selection was that the movement to marriage is largely determined by interaction between premarital partners in differing social contexts. This interpersonal process approach assumes that mate selection is a complex phenomenon. Similarity, complementarity, and exchange may be part of the process, especially early in the relationship, but progress to marriage is also influenced by many different factors, both internal and external to the relationship. This complexity, which allows for multiple influences on premarital pairs, can lead to differing pathways to marriage.

One group of researchers has suggested that there are three basic pathways to marriage and that these pathways are influenced by different factors. One research study has examined these possible pathways (Cate, Huston, and Nesselroade 1986). The first pathway to marriage is called prolonged courtship, and it proceeds slowly in an up-and-down fashion (rocky road) to eventual marriage. People who follow this path tend to report more conflict in their courtships than those in other pathways, have more doubt about whether they are making the right decision about the relationship, perceive more parental opposition to marriage, and tend to be younger at the time of marriage. These findings raise questions for future research, such as whether parental opposition causes increased conflict in the couple or whether parents are opposed because they feel their children are too young to marry.

The second pathway to marriage is called the accelerated courtship. The development of this type of relationship is rapid, moving quickly to commitment and marriage, with few ups and downs. Partners in this type of courtship report relatively less conflict in the early stages than those in other pathways, as well as less communication designed to maintain the relationship. People whose courtships follow this path tend to be older than those in other types of courtship pathways, and they perceive that their parents are relatively eager for them to marry. Overall, people in this pathway may have moved to marriage for reasons other than their compatibility with the partner. Research has yet to address whether moving to marriage in this way enhances or is detrimental to later marital satisfaction and stability.

The third type of courtship takes a moderate path to marriage after a time of lower commitment by the partners. This courtship is called the intermediate type. People who follow this path have relatively less conflict throughout the relationship with their partners than those in other types of relationships. They also have more past dating experience, are more likely to have been involved in a serious relationship with another partner before meeting their present partner, and tend to be older when they meet their partner. These attributes suggest some cautiousness by these people, possibly due to their extensive past involvements. However, the movement to marriage goes fairly smoothly, without much conflict over time. Intuitively, these types of courtships seem to have several positive features, such as an older age at marriage, less conflict, and more relationship experience. Thus, these types of relationships might be expected to lead to more stable marriages, but further research is needed to explore that possibility.

Factors Predicting Courtship Stability

Despite dissatisfaction with theoretical and conceptual explanations for courtship, scientists have examined many factors that might lead to premarital relationship stability. Some of the factors that predict stability do support earlier theoretical explanations (e.g., rewards, similarity), but other predictive factors also are important. Factors that promote premarital stability can be classified into five areas: individual factors, the "fit" between partners' individual factors, attitudes and feelings about the relationship, the nature of the partners' interactions, and the social networks in which courtships exist.

Individual factors. Intuitively, most people expect that the personality characteristics (one type of individual characteristic) of courting partners would be very helpful in explaining movement to marriage. Surprisingly, that has not been the case. Only a few isolated factors have been found to predict relationship stability. Since many of these findings come from isolated studies, less confidence can be placed in the idea that they exert strong effects on the course of marriage. However, two studies (Femlee, Sprecher, and Bassin 1990; Hendrick, Hendrick, and Adler 1988) have identified self-esteem as a possible factor in the stability of premarital relationships. The higher the self-esteem, the more likely courtships are to remain stable. It seems likely that when people feel good about themselves, they may bring other characteristics to the relationship that promote compatibility and stability.

The "fit" of the partners' characteristics. As presented earlier, married partners tend to be similar in several characteristics (attitudes, values, age, etc.), suggesting to some researchers that people select each other on the basis of similarity. Although there is doubt about whether similarity is a selection factor during premarriage, it has been found to predict stability of courtships. In the classic Boston couples study (Hill, Rubin, and Peplau 1976), premarital couples who stayed together over a two-year period were more similar in age, involvement, academic achievement, educational aspirations, and physical attractiveness than were the couples who broke up during that period. Other studies have found that similarity in preferences for activities (Surra and Longstreth 1990) and in race (Femlee, Sprecher, and Bassin 1990) were predictive of relationship continuance. From an exchange perspective, it may be that perceiving someone as similar to oneself convinces an individual that the person will be rewarding in the future. Thus, stability would be promoted.

Attitudes and feelings about the relationship. In American society, love is seen as essential to close relationships. However, social scientists cannot totally agree on the definition of love. One definition depicts love as being composed of caring, attachment, and intimacy (Rubin 1973). Another definition sees love as being comprised of caring and attachment, but also includes such factors as commitment, sexual involvement, and uniqueness of the relationship (Braiker and Kelley 1979). Other theorists believe that there are different types of love, such as erotic love, playful love, possessive love, practical love, and giving love (Hendrick, Hendrick, and Adler 1988). Not surprisingly, research that examines these different conceptualizations of love shows that the more people love each other, the more likely their courtships are to be stable. Thus, research shows that relationships are more likely to be stable when love is characterized by (a) a need to care for the partner, (b) attachment to the partner, (c) commitment, (d) confidence that the partner can be disclosed to, (e) uniqueness of the relationship, and (f) a sense of belonging, closeness, and involvement.

Although commitment is sometimes seen as a characteristic of love, it also can be viewed as a distinct concept. There is some agreement that commitment is multifaceted (Johnson 1991), being composed of personal, moral, and structural commitment. When personal commitment is present, people are attracted to their partner and the relationship and perceive the relationship as part of their self-concept. Moral commitment exists when people believe they *ought* to stay in a relationship. This moral obligation exists when people feel they must be consistent in their actions, that society views staying together as the "right" thing, and that they have a personal sense of obligation to their partner. Structural commitment exists when people perceive that they have few alternatives to their partners or when they feel that they have invested too much in the relationship to end it. Again, it is not surprising that people who are highly committed to their partners have more stable dating relationships. Studies mainly have focused on personal and structural commitment. People who are satisfied with their partners (personal commitment) and feel that they do not have many alternatives to their partner or have high investment in the relationship (structural commitment) have more stable courtships than those less committed (Femlee, Sprecher, and Bassin 1990; Hendrick, Hendrick, and Adler 1988).

Partner interaction. The effect of sexual involvement on premarital relationships has been widely debated over the years. Early studies showed that having sexual intercourse prior to marriage was related to lower quality of the later marriage. However, later studies revealed that higher sexual involvement is related to greater stability in premarital relationships (Femlee, Sprecher, and Bassin 1990). Such a finding could be interpreted to mean that engaging in sexual activity with a partner is directly enhancing to a relationship. However, what moves people to marriage may not be sexual involvement in and of itself, but the things that tend to go along with being sexually involved, such as love, commitment, and the amount of time spent together.

Good communication, in the form of basic self-disclosures to the partner, is related to courtship continuance (Sprecher 1987). It is likely that when people tell each other about their innermost values and feelings, they each feel good that their partner would share such things and subsequently that mutual trust would develop. Such trust then encourages more self-disclosure, which leads to more trust, and so on. These positive cycles of communication and trust are enhancing to the general development of premarital relationships.

Contrary to everyday thinking, the amount of conflict in premarital relationships is not necessarily predictive of relationship breakup (Femlee, Sprecher, and Bassin 1990). However, there are aspects of conflict that may lead to the dissolution of courtship relationships. One study suggested that when conflict about a particular issue persisted over time, relationship breakup was more likely (Lloyd 1990). This suggests that there may be something about the way people handle conflict that determines whether conflict will hurt or help a relationship. The findings of an additional study suggested that conflict is detrimental to the continuation of a relationship only when the conflict involves certain relational aspects (Surra and Longstreth 1990). For example, conflicts over sex, partying, and companionship seem to be particularly destructive to premarital relationships.

The frequency with which courting partners see each other is related to the stability of their premarital relationships (Femlee, Sprecher, and Bassin 1990). The more people see each other, the more likely they are to stay together. Although time itself may lead to greater movement to marriage, it is likely that the particular things that transpire between partners during extended periods of time together play a role in relationship continuance. The more time people spend together, the more likely they are to love each other, become committed, get sexually involved, and engage in extensive communication with each other. It makes sense that these factors would in turn cause people to spend more time together. Again, such a cycle of positivity can operate to lead people toward marriage.

Social networks. Little empirical research has looked at how the social networks in which people live affect the development of their premarital relationships. However, from a social exchange perspective, it makes sense that friends and kin who interact with courting couples can provide rewards or costs that would affect their movement to marriage. In the past, it was assumed by many that opposition of kin to a marriage actually pushed people to marry. However, studies show that lack of support from kin and friends deters the movement to marriage (Femlee, Sprecher, and Bassin 1990). Specifically, stable courtships are characterized by increased communication and support (especially for females) from the social network. This supports the interpersonal process model discussed earlier, which assumes that premarital relationships are influenced by factors at many different levels, from the actual interaction of partners to the way they interact with kin and friends.

The Future of Courtship and Marriage

There is no reason to expect that courtship and marriage will not continue to be an important part of social life in the future. Developments in society help to predict how courtship will be affected. Age at first marriage is increasing and probably will continue to do so. It is also possible for women to conceive safely and have children later in life than has been the norm. Therefore, people may not perceive an urgency to marry and have children, as was true of many in the past. This may induce greater equality between men and women, as women who choose to have children later than usual will have the opportunity to establish careers before having children.

The continuing problem of AIDS and the lack of therapeutic measures to alleviate this problem will continue to affect premarital relationships. If this problem cannot be overcome, it is likely that the sexual choices of many single people will continue to be inhibited. On the other hand, if cures and treatments are developed, a trend toward increased sexual "liberalism" may resume.

As women achieve more equality with men, changes in courtship are likely. Equality brings with it the power to determine to a larger extent how relationships operate. As women gain greater equality, they make take a more assertive role in the initiation and maintenance of relationships. Also, as women increase their economic independence from men, they may feel less pressure to marry relatively early. Such a choice might motivate many women to choose other types of relationships, such as cohabitation.

However, courtship and marriage are long established social institutions. It is likely that these institutions will continue to play an important role in world culture.

(*See also:* Attractiveness; Commitment; Communication; Conflict; Exchange Theory; Intimacy; Love; Personal Relationships; Self-Disclosure; Social Networks)

BIBLIOGRAPHY

Braiker, H. B., and Kelley, H. H. (1979). "Conflict in the Development of Close Relationships." In *Social Exchange in Developing Relationships*, ed. R. L. Burgess and T. L. Huston. New York: Academic Press.

Cate, R. M.; Huston, T. L.; and Nesselroade, J. R. (1986). "Premarital Relationships: Toward the Identification of Alternative Pathways to Marriage." *Journal of Social and Clinical Psychology* 4:3–22.

Femlee, D.; Sprecher, S.; and Bassin, E. (1990). "The Dissolution of Intimate Relationships: A Hazard Model." *Social Psychology Quarterly* 53:13–30.

Glick, P. C. (1984). "Marriage, Divorce, and Living Arrrangements." *Journal of Family Issues* 5:7–26.

Hendrick, S. S.; Hendrick, C.; and Adler, N. L. (1988). "Romantic Relationships: Love, Satisfaction, and Staying Together." *Journal of Personality and Social Psychology* 54:980–988.

Hill, C. T.; Rubin, Z.; and Peplau, L. A. (1976). "Breakups Before Marriage: The End of 103 Affairs." *Journal of Social Issues* 32:147–168.

Huston, T. L., and Cate, R. M. (1979). "Social Exchange in Intimate Relationships." In *Love and Attraction*, ed. M. Cook and G. Wilson. Oxford: Pergamon.

Johnson, M. (1991). "Commitment to Personal Relationships." In *Advances in Personal Relationships*, ed. D. Perlman and W. Jones. Greenwich, CT: JAI Press.

Kerckhoff, A. C. (1974). "The Social Context of Interpersonal Attraction." In *Foundations of Interpersonal Attraction*, ed. T. L. Huston. New York: Academic Press.

Kerckhoff, A. C., and Davis, K. E. (1962). "Value Consensus and Need Complementarity in Mate Selection." *American Sociological Review* 27:295–303.

Lewis, R. A. (1973). "A Longitudinal Test of a Developmental Framework for Premarital Dyadic Formation." *Journal of Marriage and the Family* 35:16–25.

Lloyd, S. A. (1990). "A Behavioral Self-Report Technique for Assessing Conflict in Close Relationships." *Journal of Social and Personal Relationships* 7:265–272.

Murstein, B. I. (1976). *Who Will Marry Whom?* New York: Springer-Verlag.

Rubin, Z. (1973). *Liking and Loving: An Invitation to Social Psychology*. New York: Holt, Rinehart and Winston.

Sprecher, S. (1987). "The Effects of Self-Disclosure Given and Received on Affection for an Intimate Partner and Stability of the Relationship." *Journal of Social and Personal Relationships* 4:115–127.

Surra, C. A., and Longstreth, M. (1990). "Similarity of Outcomes, Interdependence, and Conflict in Dating Relationships." *Journal of Personality and Social Psychology* 59:1–16.

Winch, R. F. (1955). "The Theory of Complementary Needs in Mate Selection: Final Results on the Test of the General Hypothesis." *American Sociological Review* 20:552–555.

Rodney M. Cate

MEASURES OF FAMILY CHARACTERISTICS

A 1964 review of tests and scales used in family research found serious deficiencies (Straus 1964), and subsequent reviews showed very little improvement (Straus 1992; Straus and Brown 1978). However, changes in the nature of the field have contributed to an increase in the use of standardized tests to measure characteristics of the family. This is an important development because standardized tests are vital tools for both clinical assessment and research. New tests tend to produce a flowering of research focused on the newly measurable concept. Examples of tests that have fostered much research include measures of marital satisfaction (Spanier 1976), adequacy of family functioning (Olson, Russell, and Sprenkle 1989), and family violence (Straus 1990a). Hundreds of family measures are abstracted or reproduced in compendiums such as *Family Assessment* (Grotevant and Carlson 1989), *Handbook of Measurements for Marriage and Family Therapy* (Fredman and

Sherman 1987), and *Handbook of Family Measurement Techniques* (Touliatos, Perlmutter, and Straus 1990). There is also a growing methodological literature on techniques for constructing measures of family characteristics, such as those by Karen S. Wampler and Charles F. Halverson, Jr. (1993) and Thomas W. Draper and Anastascios C. Marcos (1990). The state of testing in family research, however, is not as healthy as these publications might suggest. In fact, the data indicate that the validity of tests used in family research is rarely known.

For purposes of this entry, the term "measure" includes test, scale (such as Likert, Thurstone, Guttman, and Semantic Differential scales), index, factor score, scoring system (when referring to methods of scoring social interaction such as Gottman 1994 or Patterson 1982), and latent variables constructed by use of a structural equation modeling program. The defining feature is that they "combine the values of several items [also called indicators, questions, observations, events] into a composite measure . . . used to predict or gauge some underlying continuum which can only be partially measured by any single item or variable" (Nie et al. 1978, p. 529).

Advantages of Multiple-Item Measures

Multiple-item measures are emphasized in this entry because they are more likely to be valid than single-item measures. Although one good question or observation may be enough and thirty bad ones are useless, there are reasons why multiple-item measures are more likely to be valid. One reason is that most phenomena of interest to family researchers have multiple facets that can be adequately represented only by use of multiple items. A single question, for example, is unlikely to represent the multiple facets of marital satisfaction adequately.

A second reason for greater confidence in multiple-item measures occurs because of the inevitable risk of error in selecting items. If a single item is used and there is a conceptual error in formulating or scoring it, hypotheses that are tested by using that measure will not be supported even if they are true. However, when a multiple-item test is used, the adverse effect of a single invalid item is limited to a relatively small reduction in validity (Straus and Baron 1990). In a fifteen-item scale, for example, a defective item is only 6.6 percent of the total, so the findings would parallel those obtained if all fifteen items were correct.

Multiple items are also desirable because measures of internal consistency reliability are based on the number of items in the measure and the correlation between them. Given a certain average correlation between items, the more items, the higher the reliability. If only three items are used, it is rarely possible to achieve a high level of reliability. Reliability needs to be high because it sets an upper limit on validity.

Status and Trends in Family Measurement

To investigate the quality of measurement in family research, all empirical studies published in two major U.S. family journals (*Journal of Marriage and the Family* and *Journal of Family Psychology*) were examined. To determine trends in the *Journal of Marriage and the Family*, issues from 1982 and 1992 were compared. For the *Journal of Family Psychology*, issues from 1987 (the year the journal was founded) and 1992 were compared. Of the 161 empirical research articles reviewed, slightly fewer than two-thirds used a multiple item measurement. This increased from 46.9 percent initially to 68.1 percent in 1992. A typical article used more than one such instrument, so that a total of 219 multiple item measures were used in these 161 articles. Reliability was reported in 79.4 percent of these articles. Reliability reporting increased from 53.3 percent initially to 90.6 percent in 1992. Six percent of the articles had as their main purpose describing a new measurement instrument or presenting data concerning an existing instrument.

How one interprets these statistics depends on the standard of comparison. Articles in sociology journals and child psychology and clinical psychology journals are appropriate comparisons because these are the disciplines closest to family studies and in which many family researchers were trained. For sociology, the findings listed above can be compared to those reported in a study by Murray A. Straus and Barbara Wauchope (1992), in which they examined empirical articles from the 1979 and 1989 issues of *American Sociological Review*, *American Journal of Sociology*, and *Sociological Methods and Research*. This comparison shows that articles in family journals pay considerably more attention to measurement than articles in leading sociological journals. None of the 185 articles in sociology journals was on a specific measure, whereas 6 percent of the articles in the family journals were devoted to describing or evaluating an instrument. This portends well for family research because it is an investment in tools for future research. Only one-third of the articles in the sociology journals used a multiple-item measure, compared to more than two-thirds (68%) of articles in the family journals. The record of family researchers also exceeds that of sociologists in respect to reporting reliability. Only about 10 percent of the articles in sociology journals, compared to 80 percent of the articles in family journals, reported the reliability of the instruments. The main problem area is validity; only 12.4 percent of the articles in family journals described or referenced evidence of validity. The fact that this is three times more than in sociology is not much consolation because 12 percent is still a small percentage. Moreover, reporting or citing information on validity did not increase from the base period. Since validity is probably the most crucial quality of an instrument, the low percentage and the lack of growth indicate that more attention needs to be paid to measurement in family research.

There is no comparable study of measures in child or clinical psychological journals.

Reasons for Underdevelopment of Measures

The limited production of standard and validated measures of family characteristics is probably the result of a number of causes. Conventional wisdom attributes it to a lack of time and other resources for instrument development and validation. This is not an adequate explanation because it is true of all the social sciences. Why do psychologists devote the most resources to developing and validating tests, sociologists the least, and family researchers fall in between?

One likely reason is a difference in rewards for measurement research. A related reason is a difference in the opportunities and constraints. In psychology, there are journals devoted to psychological measures in whole or in part, such as *Educational and Psychological Measurement* and *Journal of Clinical and Consulting Psychology*. There are no such journals in sociology or family studies. Moreover, there is a large market for psychological tests, and several major firms specialize in publishing tests. It is a multimillion-dollar industry, and authors of tests can earn substantial royalties. By contrast, sociology lacks the symbolic and economic reward system that underlies the institutionalization of test development as a major specialization in psychology. The field of family studies lies in between. In principle there should be a demand for tests because of the large number of family therapists, but few family therapists actually use tests.

A second explanation for the differences among psychology, family studies, and sociology in attention to measurement is a situational constraint inherent in the type of research done. A considerable amount of family research is done by survey methods—for example, the National Survey of Families and Households. Surveys of this type usually include measures of many variables in a single thirty- to sixty-minute interview. Clinical psychologists, on the other hand, often can use longer and therefore more reliable tests, because their clients have a greater stake in providing adequate data and will tolerate undergoing two or more hours of testing.

Third, most tests are developed for a specific study and there is rarely a place in the project budget for adequate measure development—test/retest reliability, concurrent and construct validity, and construction of normative tables. Even when the author of a measure does the psychometric research needed to enable others to evaluate whether the measure might be suitable for their research, family journals rarely allow enough space to present that material.

Fourth, the optimum procedure is for the author to write a paper describing the test, the theory underlying the test, the empirical procedures used to develop the test, reliability and validity evidence, and norms. This rarely occurs because of the lack of resources indicated above. In addition, most investigators are more interested in the substantive issues for which the project was funded.

Another reason why standardized tests are less frequently used in family research is that many studies are based on cases from agencies. A researcher studying child abuse who draws the cases from child protective services might not need a method of measuring child abuse. However, standardized tests are still needed because an adequate understanding of child abuse cannot depend solely on officially identified cases. It is important also to do research on cases that are not known to agencies, because such cases are much more numerous than cases known to agencies and because general population cases typically differ in important ways from the cases known to agencies (Straus 1990b).

The Future of Family Research Measures

There are grounds for optimism and grounds for concern about the future of family tests. The grounds for concern are, first, that in survey research on the family, concepts are often measured by a single interview question. Second, even when a multiple-item test is used, it is rarely on the basis of empirical evidence of reliability and validity. Third, the typical measure developed for use in a family study is never used in another study. One can speculate that this hiatus in the cumulative nature of research occurs because of the lack of evidence of reliability and validity and because authors rarely provide sufficient information to facilitate use of the instrument by others.

The grounds for optimism are to be found in the sizable and slowly growing number of standardized instruments, as listed in compendiums (e.g., Grotevant and Carlson 1989; Fredman and Sherman 1987; Touliatos, Perlmutter, and Straus 1990). A second ground for optimism is the rapid growth in the number of psychologists doing family research, because psychologists bring to family research an established tradition of test development. Similarly, the explosive growth of family therapy is grounds for optimism, because it is likely that more tests will gradually begin to be used for intake diagnosis.

There is a certain irony in the second source of optimism, because basic researchers usually believe that they, not clinicians, represent quality in science. In respect to measurement, clinicians tend to demand instruments of higher quality than do basic researchers because the consequences of using an inadequate measure are more serious. When a basic researcher uses an instrument with low reliability or validity, it can lead to a Type II error—that is, failing to accept a true hypothesis. This may result in theoretical confusion or a paper not being published. But when a practitioner uses an invalid or unreliable instrument, the worst-case scenario can involve injury to a client. Consequently, clinicians need to demand more evidence of reliability and validity than do researchers. As a result, clinically oriented family researchers tend to produce and make available more adequate measures. Hubert M. Blalock (1982) argued that inconsistent findings and failure to find empirical support for sound theories may be due to lack of reliable and valid means of operationalizing concepts in the theories being tested. It follows that research will be on a sounder footing if researchers devote more attention to developing reliable and valid measures of family characteristics.

(*See also:* Marital Quality; Marital Typologies; Research Methods)

BIBLIOGRAPHY

Blalock, H. M. (1982). *Conceptualization and Measurement in the Social Sciences.* Newbury Park, CA: Sage Publications.

Burgess, E. W., and Cottrell, L. S. (1939). *Predicting Success or Failure in Marriage.* Englewood Cliffs, NJ: Prentice Hall.

Cronbach, L. J. (1970). *Essentials of Psychological Testing.* New York: Harper & Row.

Draper, T. W., and Marcos, A. C. (1990). *Family Variables: Conceptualization, Measurement, and Use.* Newbury Park, CA: Sage Publications.

Fredman, N., and Sherman, R. (1987). *Handbook of Measurements for Marriage and Family Therapy.* New York: Brunner/Mazel.

Gottman, J. M. (1994). *What Predicts Divorce? The Relationship Between Marital Process and Marital Outcome.* Hillsdale, NJ: Lawrence Erlbaum.

Grotevant, H. D., and Carlson, C. I. (1989). *Family Assessment: A Guide to Methods and Measures.* New York: Guilford.

Nie, N. H.; Hull, C. H.; Jenkins, J. G.; Steinbrenner, K.; and Bent, D. H. (1978). *SPSS: Statistical Package for the Social Sciences.* New York: McGraw-Hill.

Olson, D. H.; Russell, C. S.; and Sprenkle, D. H. (1989). *Circumplex Model: New Scales for Assessing Systematic Assessment and Treatment of Families.* New York: Haworth Press.

Patterson, G. R., ed. (1982). *Coercive Family Processes: A Social Learning Approach.* Eugene, OR: Castalia.

Spanier, G. B. (1976). "Measuring Dyadic Adjustment: The Quality of Marriage and Similar Dyads." *Journal of Marriage and the Family* 38:15–28.

Straus, M. A. (1964). "Measuring Families." In *Handbook of Marriage and the Family*, ed. H. T. Christenson. Chicago: Rand McNally.

Straus, M. A. (1990a). "The Conflict Tactics Scales and Its Critics: An Evaluation and New Data on Validity and Reliability." In *Physical Violence in American Families: Risk Factors and Adaptations to Violence in 8,145 Families*, ed. M. A. Straus and R. J. Gelles. New Brunswick, NJ: Transaction.

Straus, M. A. (1990b). "Injury and Frequency of Assault and the 'Representative Sample Fallacy' in Measuring Wife Beating and Child Abuse." In *Physical Violence in American Families: Risk Factors and Adaptations to Violence in 8,145 Families*, ed. M. A. Straus and R. J. Gelles. New Brunswick, NJ: Transaction.

Straus, M. A. (1992). "Measurement Instruments in Child Abuse Research." Paper prepared for the National Academy of Sciences panel of child abuse research. Durham, NH: Family Research Laboratory, University of New Hampshire.

Straus, M. A., and Baron, L. (1990). "The Strength of Weak Indicators: A Response to Gilles, Brown, Geletta, and Dalecki." *Sociological Quarterly* 31:619–624.

Straus, M. A., and Brown, B. W. (1978). *Family Measurement Techniques*, 2nd edition. Minneapolis: University of Minnesota Press.

Strauss, M. A., and Wauchope, B. (1992). "Measurement Instruments." In *Encyclopedia of Sociology*, ed. E. F. Borgatta and M. L. Borgatta. New York: Macmillan.

Touliatos, J.; Perlmutter, D.; and Straus, M. A. (1990). *Handbook of Family Measurement Techniques*, 3rd edition. Newbury Park, CA: Sage Publications.

Wampler, K. S., and Halverson, C. F., Jr. (1993). "Quantitative Measurement in Family Research." In *Source Book of Family Theories and Methods: A Contextual Approach*, ed. P. G. Boss, W. J. Doherty, R. LaRossa, W. R. Schumm, and S. K. Steinmetz. New York: Plenum.

MURRAY A. STRAUS
SUSAN M. ROSS

MENOPAUSE

Menopause refers to the point in a woman's reproductive life when menstrual cycling ceases and relatively abrupt and significant declines in the production of ovarian sex hormones occur. More precisely, the term "menopause" means cessation of menses or the last menstrual cycle, which must be confirmed by twelve months without cycling. The average age of natural menopause is approximately fifty-one years and varies in different studies; menopause can occur at any time between forty and sixty years of age (Greene 1984; McKinlay, Brambilla, and Posner 1992). Cessation of cycling at earlier ages is usually referred to as premature ovarian failure.

The decline in ovarian function that results in menopause typically begins as early as the late thirties, when the regular menstrual intervals become shorter. In the early forties, menstrual intervals begin to vary, and in the late forties just before menopause, intervals are increasingly irregular; there may be intervals of two months or more in which no menses occur (Cutler and Garcia 1992; Treloar 1981). This latter period is called the perimenopause or transition to menopause and ranges in length from two to eight years, with an average length of four years (McKinlay, Brambilla, and Posner 1992). Only about 10 percent of women will have an abrupt cessation of cycling. Tobacco smoking is the one factor that clearly affects the age of menopause, with smokers becoming menopausal almost two years earlier on average and having a shorter transition period (McKinlay, Brambilla, and Posner 1992).

Biological Basis

Basically, menopause occurs because there are no more follicles in the ovaries. At about six months of gestation, human females have all the ovarian follicles that they will ever have. Loss of follicles begins before birth, and at birth there are about 400,000 follicles remaining, of which approximately 400 will actually produce eggs (Richardson and Nelson 1990).

Women's menstrual cycles are the result of a complex negative-feedback system; a brain center called the hypothalamus produces a gonadotropin-releasing hormone (GnRH) that stimulates the pituitary gland (attached to the hypothalamus by a stalk) to secrete pituitary hormones called follical-stimulating hormone (FSH) and luteinizing hormone (LH) or gonadotropins. These pituitary hormones travel in the blood to the ovaries, where they stimulate ovarian follicles such that each month one follicle develops, produces sex hormones, and ovulates while many other follicles are lost. When estradiol, the major sex hormone produced by follicles, is low, FSH and LH levels rise to stimulate the follicles to produce estradiol. By the same token, as estradiol starts to rise, FSH and LH levels decline (Johnson and Everitt 1988).

During the last decade of menstrual life, FSH levels rise to higher than normal levels even though a pool of follicles remains; as a result, loss of follicles accelerates dramatically (Richardson and Nelson 1990). This situation can give rise to abnormally high estradiol levels that exacerbate such problems as fibroids, endometriosis, and fibrocystic breast disease. High FSH levels are commonly used by physicians to confirm a woman's perimenopausal status.

At the time of the last cycle, there are few if any remaining follicles, and most are insensitive to gonadotropic stimulation; this results in extreme high levels of FSH and LH and low levels of estradiol. Within a year of the last cycle, production rates for estrogens drop approximately 85 percent for estradiol and 58 percent for estrone; production rates for androgens drop approximately 67 percent for androstenedione and 29 percent for testosterone (Longcope, Jaffee, and Griffing 1981). The major source of hormones following menopause is androgen production by the outer part (cortex) of the adrenal glands. In a process called "aromatization," some of these adrenal androgens are converted to estrone, the principal estrogen of the postmenopausal woman. In addition, about half of naturally postmenopausal women derive significant amounts of testosterone from their ovaries. Postmenopausal women without ovaries do not have this source of hormone and may have lower levels of adrenal androgens as well (Cummings et al. 1982). Thus, women of menopausal age without ovaries may have both an estrogen and an androgen deficiency. Factors associated with higher postmenopausal hormone levels are weight and body surface area; larger, heavier women will have more aromatization of adrenal androgens to estrone and more available (unbound) hormone.

Physical Effects

Many symptoms have been associated with the peri- and postmenopausal periods (Greene 1984). Among them are heart palpitations, dizzy spells, numbness and tingling, migraines, anxiety, tension, irritability, lack of energy, depressed mood, apathy, memory loss, weight gain, vaginal dryness, joint/ bone aches and pains, hot flashes, night sweats, and insomnia. The only symptoms that increase from the peri- to the postmenopausal period and are clearly associated with estrogen deficiency are the vasomotor symptoms of hot flashes and night sweats and vaginal problems such as dryness or infection (atrophic vaginitis). It has been estimated that 70 percent of women experience hot flashes around the time of menopause (Ginsburg and Hardiman 1991). The vasomotor symptoms are caused by estrogen deficiency affecting the brain, while vaginal symptoms are caused by the effects of estrogen deficiency on the vagina. It is likely that many of the other symptoms listed above arise from abrupt fluctuations in hormone levels during the pre- and perimenopausal periods, but these issues require further research.

The more serious and life-threatening effects of low postmenopausal estrogen levels tend to develop slowly and may go unnoticed for a long time. Before menopause, rates of cardiovascular disease are higher for men than for women, but after menopause, the rates are similar (Sitruk-Ware 1991a). There are at least two ways in which low estrogen levels appear to make women more vulnerable to coronary heart disease. Before menopause, women have lower levels of fats in the blood called low-density lipoproteins (LDL) and higher levels of high-density lipoproteins (HDL) than men. Evidence suggests that LDL promotes deposits of fatty plaques in the arteries (atherosclerosis) that can block blood flow to the heart and brain, while HDL helps to prevent such deposits and is protective. After menopause, HDL levels do not change much, but LDL levels rise, increasing the risk of atherosclerosis (Sacks and Walsh 1990). It has become clear that estrogen also acts immediately and directly on the cardiovascular system (Rosano et al. 1993). Estrogen given to postmenopausal women has a dilative effect and increases blood flow in veins and arteries. Therefore, it appears that postmenopausal estrogen deficiency acts to narrow arteries and decrease blood flow. The relative importance of these different estrogen effects on the cardiovascular system is being investigated.

Estrogen deficiency also affects the skeleton. Low estrogen levels somehow bring about an increased outflow of calcium from bone (osteopoenia) that eventually leaves bones weakened and more easily broken (osteoporosis) (Cutler and Garcia 1992; Luciano 1992). Women's bone mass is maximal at age thirty, when bone formation and resorption are in balance. Loss of bone due to more resorption than formation begins in the premenopausal years but accelerates after menopause. Calcium is also a major constituent of skin collagen, and at the same time that bones weaken, skin becomes thinner and begins to lose its elasticity. Facial skin is more sensitive to estrogens than the skin of the breast or thigh, suggesting that low estrogen levels may have a noticeable effect on facial appearance.

The urethra and neck of the bladder, as well as the breast, genitals, vagina, and reproductive organs, are supported by estrogens, such that low estrogen levels over time result in atrophic changes in these structures (Cutler and Garcia 1992). The surface layer of tissue of the urethra and bladder is maintained by estrogen in much the same way as that of the vagina. Symptoms of estrogen deficiency of the urinary tract are burning and irritation—particularly with sexual intercourse, increased urinary tract infections (cystitis), frequent need to urinate (urgency, frequency), and loss of urine when sneezing and coughing (stress incontinence). The effects of estrogen deficiency on the vagina are progressive and eventually result in vaginal atrophy. At first, low estrogen levels result in vaginal dryness or less vaginal lubrication, as well as a less acidic vaginal environment, which permits growth of anaerobic bacteria and development of odor. With continued estrogen deficiency, the vaginal wall eventually becomes thin and loses its elasticity, such that sexual intercourse may cause pain and vaginal bleeding, and there may be repeated infections. After menopause, the breasts decrease in size and the structure of breast tissue changes.

Psychological Effects

Menopause is a potentially stressful physical event. How stressful it will be for any one woman will depend not only on the nature of her physical experience at that time but on many other factors, including her attitudes and beliefs concerning menopause and aging; her culture's views and treatment of women after menopause; her coping skills or habitual ways of dealing with stress; her physical and psychological health; the quality of her existing relationships—how positive, supportive, and stress-free they are; and the number of stressful events that occur in her life at that time. Such events may include having to care for dependent, elderly parents; anxiety over children; getting a divorce; losing a job; financial problems; or the illness or death of a parent or another close family member.

The "empty nest syndrome" was the typical explanation for women's midlife unhappiness in the past. However, evidence suggests that women whose children have left home are not more prone to depression and that many are relieved, not depressed. In one large study of naturally menopausal women, depression was significantly associated with marital status and education; widowed, divorced, or separated women with fewer than twelve years of education were the most depressed, women who had never been married were the least depressed, and married women fell in between (McKinlay, McKinlay, and Brambilla 1987). Another study found that divorced and childless women, as well as women from lower classes, were more likely to experience mental disorder during this period (Hallstrom and Samuelsson 1985). Several studies have found that women who reported marital dissatisfaction during the peri- and postmenopausal periods were significantly more apt to report symptoms. These marital problems had not arisen at this time but tended to be long-standing. It appears that preexisting marital problems, as well as other stressful life events, can exacerbate symptoms associated with menopause (Ballinger 1990; Green 1984).

It had been generally accepted that there were adverse changes in middle-aged women's psychological characteristics brought about directly by menopause. However, prospective population-based studies from 1984 to 1990 did not support this belief (Greene 1984; Hallstrom and Samuelsson 1985; Matthews et al. 1990; McKinlay, McKinlay, and Brambilla 1987). Neither have the majority of studies demonstrated an increase in the incidence or prevalence of psychiatric disorder. The psychological characteristic most commonly associated with postmenopause has been depression. While depression is not uncommon during women's middle years, research does not show it peaking dramatically at or just after menopause, except in the case of women made menopausal by surgery (McKinlay, McKinlay, and Brambilla 1987). It is likely that very low estrogen and androgen levels, commonly seen in women without their ovaries, depress emotional well-being as well as aspects of cognitive functioning such as short-term memory and ability to concentrate (Sherwin 1988b; Sherwin and Gelfand 1985).

Additionally, it is important not to ignore that the way women experience menopause is heavily influenced by culture or the customs, mores, and values of the society in which they live (Greene 1984). Wide variation exists in attitudes and responses to menopause, both among highly traditional societies and within modern ones. Examples of cultural variables that affect the way menopause is experienced are the stability of the sociocultural milieu, the importance of the childbearing function in women's roles, and the availability of postmenopausal social roles that are useful and carry high status. Other factors that can contribute to these differences are unusual cultural mores; religious beliefs; and the presence of physical, social, or economic hardship. Paradoxically, elevation of social status at menopause most often occurs in cultures where women have low status or are stigmatized before menopause. Depending on the culture, menopause may be associated with a withdrawal from social activities, be viewed as a sign of aging and behavioral decline, give greater freedom, or increase social or "supernatural" power.

Sexual Effects

Social, psychological, and hormonal factors all affect sexuality. Evidence concerning the roles that hormones play suggests that sexual interest in both men and women is related to androgens, particularly testosterone, while women's ability to respond sexually as well as their physical sexual attractiveness are related more to estrogens (McCoy 1991; Morokoff 1988). The effect of testosterone on sexual interest is presumed to take place in the brain, while sexual response and attractiveness depend, for the most part, on the peripheral effects of estrogens.

There have been comparatively few studies of changes in women's sexual interest and behavior associated with menopause, and almost no studies involving couples—whether heterosexual or lesbian (McCoy 1994). The most studied sexual variables have been coital frequency, vaginal dryness, and sexual interest. Of six studies that obtained sexual data at a minimum of two points from pre- to peri- to postmenopause, all found a decrease in frequency of sexual intercourse. Of five studies that obtained data on vaginal dryness and on sexual interest, all found increases in vaginal dryness and decreases in sexual interest. There is less evidence for other aspects of sexuality, but the limited data suggest decreased capacity for orgasm and increased vaginal discomfort during sexual intercourse. Although these changes in sexuality are in a negative direction, they reflect a *relative* change in women's sexuality related to menopause and not the end of women's sexual lives.

Medical Interventions

For many women who choose not to use hormone replacement therapy (HRT), treatment after menopause consists of dietary changes, improved nutrition, and proper exercise (Cutler and Garcia 1992; Greenwood 1992). While these lifestyle changes are extremely helpful, HRT remains the most effective treatment for the symptoms and conditions caused by menopause.

Hormone replacement therapy. HRT can take several forms. The menopausal women may take an estrogen combined with cyclic use of a progesterone for twelve days each month, an estrogen combined with a lesser dose of progesterone every day, or an estrogen alone (Cutler and Garcia 1992; Luciano 1992; Sitruk-Ware 1991b).

Several different estrogens are available for use in HRT and are administered either orally, transdermally (through the skin), by injection, or sometimes implanted under the skin. In the United States, the most commonly prescribed product is an orally administered tablet that contains conjugated equine estrogens derived from pregnant mares' urine. Conjugated estrogens are promoted as natural, but a large percentage of them (equilin, equilenin, and others) are natural only to the horse. Tablets containing *esterified* conjugated estrogens have a smaller percentage (6% to 15%) of these horse estrogens.

The estrogen 17-β estradiol is the major estrogenic human hormone and the most potent physiologic estrogen. It is available either orally, by injection, or transdermally from a patch or an alcohol gel applied to the skin. Another human estrogen, estrone, is available for oral use. All of the replacement estrogens are also available as creams that are designed for vaginal use.

Progestins, structurally unlike those found in humans, as well as micronized progesterone like that of human females, are available for use in HRT. The most commonly used and readily available product is a progestin (medroxyprogesterone acetate). There is some evidence that effects of nonhuman progestins counter some of the beneficial effects of estrogens, but the issue is not resolved. All forms of progesterone have antiestrogenic and antiandrogenic effects and, depending on the dosage, can cause PMS-like complaints as well as decreased sexual interest.

Androgens are not commonly used in HRT in the United States, but they can play an important role in the treatment of surgically menopausal women, as well as women with cancer who have undergone chemotherapy or pelvic radiation (Kaplan 1992; Sherwin 1988a; Sherwin, Gelfand, and Brender 1985). Androgens can also be used effectively with the small number of naturally menopausal women who complain of a major loss of sexual interest. While synthetic oral androgens are available (methyl testosterone), they are not appropriate for long-term use, because they affect liver proteins. The safe way to administer androgens is by injection of testosterone like that found in humans (testosterone cypionate or enanthate) every four to six weeks.

Risks and benefits of HRT. The use of estrogens not natural to the human, as well as the oral administration of estrogen, can result in overproduction of liver proteins. Because of these effects, use of oral conjugated equine estrogens results in a decrease in available testosterone, an increase in clotting factors, an increased probability of gallbladder disease, an increase in a substance that can contribute to high blood pressure, an immediate increase in triglycerides and HDLs, and a decrease in LDLs (Geola et al. 1980; L'Hermite 1990; Mathur et al. 1985). About 3 percent to 4 percent of women using equine estrogens develop high blood pressure, and the risk of undergoing surgery for gallbladder disease is two to four times greater. Because these estrogens decrease available testosterone, they may also contribute to loss of sexual interest. Other oral estrogens (micronized 17-β estradiol and estrone sulfate) have comparatively minor effects on liver proteins. Such effects are totally absent when these estrogens are administered nonorally, except that the positive effect on lipoproteins occurs but is delayed until approximately six months after the start of therapy (L'Hermite 1990).

The use of estrogen by a woman with a uterus increases the risk of uterine cancer four to eight times, and risk is related both to duration of use and dosage of the estrogen (Luciano 1992). However, when a progesterone is used with estrogen, the rate of uterine cancer may actually drop below that of untreated women. Cyclic use of a progesterone results in a monthly bleed; this fact has led many women to choose to use estrogen and progesterone continuously, because in many cases, any bleeding or spotting they experience may stop after three months or so. For a woman who has her uterus and uses estrogen alone, an endometrial biopsy or uterine sonography must be performed regularly so that any negative changes in the uterine lining can be detected and treated immediately.

In contrast to uterine cancer, incidence of breast cancer rises progressively throughout life, and it is estimated that one in ten women will develop it in her lifetime (Brinton 1990; Luciano 1992). While the role of estrogen in uterine cancer is well understood, the role that estrogen plays in the development of breast cancer is not. Risk increases with dosage and duration of use, with an increased risk of 30 percent after fifteen years use of HRT. The survival rate for women who develop breast cancer during or after estrogen use is increased about 40 percent over those not using HRT. Whether the addition of a progesterone or an androgen to HRT makes any difference in the risk is not clear.

The demonstrated benefits of HRT to date are impressive (Luciano 1992; Sitruk-Ware 1991b). A conservative estimate is that the risk of cardiovascular disease is reduced by half in current users. If HRT is begun at menopause, osteoporosis is prevented in all but 2 percent of women as long as use continues. In addition to relieving vasomotor symptoms, HRT helps to maintain thickness and elasticity in skin, prevents vaginal atrophy, reduces the occurrence of urinary problems, and may have positive effects on emotional well-being and cognitive function.

Considerable variation exists in the hormone levels of postmenopausal women, and comparatively little is known about the characteristics of women who do well without therapy. Whether or not a postmenopausal woman uses HRT should be the result of her informed choice. In making this choice, she must weigh the risks and benefits of HRT in the context of her current health status and quality of life, as well as the prevalence of osteoporosis, cardiovascular disease, and cancer in her family history.

(*See also:* Middle Age; Sexuality in the Life Cycle)

BIBLIOGRAPHY

Ballinger, S. (1990). "Stress as a Factor in Lowered Estrogen Levels in the Early Postmenopause." In *Multidisciplinary Perspectives on Menopause*, ed. M. Flint, F. Kronenberg, and W. Utian (Annals of the New York Academy of Sciences, Vol. 592). New York: New York Academy of Sciences.

Brinton, L. (1990). "Menopause and the Risk of Breast Cancer." In *Multidisciplinary Perspectives on Menopause*, ed. M. Flint, F. Kronenberg, and W. Utian (Annals of the New York Academy of Sciences, Vol. 592). New York: New York Academy of Sciences.

Cummings, D. C.; Rebar, R. W.; Hopper, B. R.; and Yen, S. S. C. (1982). "Evidence for an Influence of the Ovary on Circulating Dehydroepiandrosterone Sulfate Levels." *Journal of Clinical Endocrinology and Metabolism* 54:1069–1071.

Cutler, W. B., and Garcia, C.-R. (1992). *Menopause*, revised edition. New York: W. W. Norton.

Geola, F. L.; Frumar, A. M.; Tataryn, I. V.; Lu, K. H.; Hershman, J. M.; Eggena, P.; Sambhi, M. P.; and Judd, H. L. (1980). "Biological Effects of Various Doses of Conjugated Equine Estrogens in Postmenopausal Women." *Journal of Clinical Endocrinology and Metabolism* 51:620–625.

Ginsburg, J., and Hardiman, P. (1991). "What Do We Know About the Pathogenesis of the Menopausal Hot Flush?" In *The Menopause and Hormonal Replacement Therapy: Facts and Controversies*, ed. R. Sitruk-Ware and W. H. Utian. New York: Marcel Dekker.

Greene, J. G. (1984). *The Social and Psychological Origins of the Climacteric Syndrome.* Aldershot, Eng.: Gower.

Greenwood, S. (1992). *Menopause Naturally: Preparing for the Second Half of Life*, revised edition. San Francisco: Volcano.

Hallstrom, T., and Samuelsson, S. (1985). "Mental Health in the Climacteric." *Acta Obstetrica Gynecologica Scandinavica Supplement* 130:13–18.

Johnson, M. H., and Everitt, B. (1988). *Essential Reproduction*, 3rd edition. Oxford, Eng.: Blackwell Scientific.

Kaplan, H. S. (1992). "A Neglected Issue: The Sexual Side Effects of Current Treatments for Breast Cancer." *Journal of Sex and Marital Therapy* 18:3–19.

L'Hermite, M. (1990). "Risks of Estrogens and Progestogens." *Maturitas* 12:215–246.

Longcope, C.; Jaffee, W.; and Griffing, G. (1981). "Production Rates of Androgens and Oestrogens in Postmenopausal Women." *Maturitas* 3:215–223.

Luciano, A. A. (1992). "Hormone Replacement Therapy in Postmenopausal Women." *Infertility and Reproductive Medicine Clinics of North America* 3:109–127.

Mathur, R. S.; Landgrebe, S. C.; Moody, L. O.; Semmens, J. P.; and Williamson, H. O. (1985). "The Effect of Estrogen Treatment on Plasma Concentrations of Steroid Hormones, Gonadotropins, Prolactin, and Sex Hormone-Binding Globulin in Postmenopausal Women." *Maturitas* 7:129–133.

Matthews, K. A.; Wing, R. R.; Kuller, L. H.; Meilahn, E. N.; Kelsey, S. F.; Costello, E. J.; and Caggiula, A. W. (1990). "Influences of Natural Menopause on Psychological Characteristics and Symptoms of Middle-Aged Healthy Women." *Journal of Consulting and Clinical Psychology* 58:345–351.

McCoy, N. L. (1991). "Menopause and Sexuality." In *The Menopause and Hormonal Replacement Therapy: Facts and Controversies*, ed. R. Sitruk-Ware and W. H. Utian. New York: Marcel Dekker.

McCoy, N. L. (1994). "Survey Research on the Menopause and Women's Sexuality." In *Modern Management of the Menopause: Proceedings of the VII International Congress on the Menopause, Stockholm, Sweden, 1993*, ed. G. Berg and M. Hammar. London: Parthenon.

McKinlay, J. B.; McKinlay, S. M.; and Brambilla, D. (1987). "The Relative Contributions of Endocrine Changes and Social Circumstances to Depression in Mid-Aged Women." *Journal of Health and Social Behavior* 28:345–363.

McKinlay, S. M.; Brambilla, D. J.; and Posner, J. G. (1992). "The Normal Menopause Transition." *Maturitas* 14:103–115.

Morokoff, P. J. (1988). "Sexual in Perimenopausal and Postmenopausal Women." *Psychology of Women Quarterly* 12:489–511.

Richardson, S. J., and Nelson, J. F. (1990). "Follicular Depletion During the Menopausal Transition." In *Multidisciplinary Perspectives on Menopause*, ed. M. Flint, F. Kronenberg, and W. Utian (Annals of the New York Academy of Sciences, Vol 592). New York: New York Academy of Sciences.

Rosano, G. M. C.; Sarrel, P. M.; Poole-Wilson, P. A.; and Collins, P. (1993). "Beneficial Effect of Estrogen on Exercise-Induced Myocardial Ischaemia in Women with Coronary Artery Disease." *Lancet* 342:133–136.

Sacks, F. M., and Walsh, B. W. (1990). "The Effects of Reproductive Hormones on Serum Lipoproteins: Unresolved Issues in Biology and Clinical Practice." In *Multidisciplinary Perspectives on Menopause*, ed. M. Flint, F. Kronenberg, and W. Utian (Annals of the New York Academy of Sciences, Vol. 592). New York: New York Academy of Sciences.

Sherwin, B. B. (1988a). "Affective Changes with Androgen and Estrogen Replacement Therapy in Surgically Menopausal Women." *Journal of Affective Disorders* 14:177–187.

Sherwin, B. B. (1988b). "Estrogen and/or Androgen Replacement Therapy and Cognitive Functioning in Surgically Menopausal Women." *Psychoneuroendocrinology* 13:345–357.

Sherwin, B. B., and Gelfand, M. M. (1985). "Sex Steroids and Affect in the Surgical Menopause: A Double-Blind, Crossover Study." *Psychoneuroendocrinology* 10:325–335.

Sherwin, B. B.; Gelfand, M. M.; and Brender, W. (1985). "Androgen Enhances Sexual Motivation in Females: A Prospective Crossover Study of Sex Steroid Administration in the Surgical Menopause." *Psychosomatic Medicine* 47:339–351.

Sitruk-Ware, R. (1991a). "Do Estrogens Protect Against Cardiovascular Disease?" In *The Menopause and Hormonal Replacement Therapy: Facts and Controversies*, ed. R. Sitruk-Ware and W. H. Utian. New York: Marcel Dekker.

Sitruk-Ware, R. (1991b). "Hormonal Replacement Therapy: What to Prescribe, How, and for How Long?" In *The Menopause and Hormonal Replacement Therapy: Facts and Controversies*, ed. R. Sitruk-Ware and W. H. Utian. New York: Marcel Dekker.

Treloar, A. E. (1981). "Menstrual Cyclicity and the Premenopause." *Maturitas* 3:249–264.

Norma L. McCoy

MIDDLE AGE

Aging is not only an organic process, it is also a social process. While aging can be measured simply in terms of the passage of years, the meaning of aging can also be assessed by the passage of normative life events (e.g., graduation, marriage, parenthood, retirement) or through membership in a particular age cohort (e.g., coming of age during the Depression or being a baby boomer). The adage that "you are only as old as you feel" reflects this concept of age as having both social and personal meanings.

The concept of middle age is a cultural artifact, one best illustrated by the negative images of midlife typically held by many Americans. Middle-aged people are generally perceived as being increasingly more concerned with the past than the future, often preoccupied with issues of health care and money, and either stagnating or in the throes of a midlife crisis. As for middle-aged women, they are often portrayed as being consumed with the change of life. As Winifred Gallagher (1993, p. 51) argues, however, these common perceptions are essentially myths "derived not from the ordinary experiences of most people but from the unusual experiences of a few . . . [and] although these make for livelier reading and conversation, they generate an unnecessarily gloomy attitude about the middle years." Research reveals that most middle-aged individuals are physically healthy and productive, and studies of successful middle-aged persons have found that, as a result of their accumulated status and wisdom, these individuals perceive of themselves as more in command of their lives—that is, they feel capable of redefining social roles and moderating their feelings to meet their needs (Grambs 1989; Guttman 1987; Neugarten 1968; Troll 1985).

Societal Interest

The life course is a journey marked by stages. These stages are not fixed; existing ones have expanded and shrunk in length, and new ones have emerged in response to broader social change. The timing of the period of metamorphosis from child to adult, for instance, varies across cultures and time periods (Cohen 1987). Historically, social scientists have focused more on the earlier life stages of human development. Achievement of adult status was thought of as having arrived or as reaching a pinnacle, and the next phase of life was viewed primarily as a plateau until the onset of old age.

Judith Treas and Vern L. Bengston (1982) assert that society's interest with the transitions of middle and old age is a result of three trends: the graying of the population, the rapid pace of social change, and the emergence of the profession of gerontology. Numbers alone may account for curiosity with the second half of life. Not only are there more older persons, but also the elderly are living longer. In 1900, the average American could only expect to live forty-seven years, and only 4 percent of the total U.S. population was sixty-five years or older. By 1990, the average life expectancy had increased to seventy-five years, and almost 13 percent of the U.S. population was sixty-five years or older. Declining fertility and mortality rates shifted the median age of Americans from twenty-two in 1900 to thirty-two in 1990 (U.S. Bureau of the Census 1992a).

The declining mortality trend has led to a democratization of middle and old age (Treas and Bengston 1982). Whereas at the turn of the twentieth century only a relatively small group of citizens experienced the later life-cycle stages, today a majority of Americans reach middle, old, and even advanced old age. Interest in middle age is also spurred by the aging of the baby boomer generation (persons born between 1946 and 1964, the largest age cohort in the United States). Also heightening interest in middle age is the fact that rapid social change has added new variations to the midlife experience. For example, a forty-year-old women in the 1930s had far different experiences and options than a forty-year-old woman in the 1990s. One of the most significant changes for middle-aged women is their increased participation in the labor force. Prior to the 1940s, women workers were typically young and single. In 1940, 28 percent of all women were employed outside the home; of these, more than two-thirds were single women (Blau and Ferber 1986). In the 1990s, married women (57%) were almost as likely to be employed as single women (68%) (U.S. Bureau of the Census 1992b). Women in the 1940s also had fewer reproduction options—whether seeking to achieve, prevent, or terminate pregnancies. Women reaching their forties in the 1990s represent the first cohort to be legally able to exert fertility control (Grambs 1989). Finally, the emergence of the gerontology profession has resulted in the promotion of scientific research and scholarly writing as well as popular literature on the dynamics and nature of the aging experience.

Social and Psychological Meanings

The period called middle age lacks well-defined boundaries. Michael Farrell and Stanley Rosenberg (1981, p. 16) suggest that, "like defining a period of history, no one quite agrees when middle age begins or ends." Although middle age can range from thirty to sixty-four years of age, in the United States age forty is commonly thought of as a watershed. Whereas the twenties and thirties are perceived of as bringing major transitions and representing a high plateau in terms of physical strength and vigor, the forties are marked by a sense of decreasing energy and physical attractiveness (Clausen 1986).

While social scientists often focus on normative life experiences, it is important to underscore that there may not be one universal path, but rather several different paths to aging. Gender does make a difference in many aspects of life; the life histories of men and women are quite distinct. It is increasingly argued that the development of females and males is unique enough so that different frameworks are required to explain the aging experience for each gender. As Jean Grams (1989) asserts, menstruation, childbearing, and menopause denote key physiological occurrences in women's lives of which men have no comparable biological life course markers.

Even within adult male or adult female development there may be great diversity. Social class, ethnicity, religion, and sexual orientation affect images and the way people define themselves as they age. For example, Bernice Neugarten (1968) found that working-class individuals typically experience critical life events such as marriage, the birth of the first child, and middle age at an earlier age than middle-class persons. Working-class men, who are more likely to be concerned with physical strength and vigor, tend to see middle age as beginning at thirty-five. Middle-class men more often place the start of middle age at forty-five. Although working-class men often view middle age as a time of decline, middle-class men view their forties and fifties as a period of peak productivity and income.

As life expectancy continues to increase, the boundaries of middle age may also shift. Projections suggest that the average life expectancy will increase to eighty-one years by 2080 (U.S. Bureau of the Census 1992a). Yet social scientists suggest that the stages of human development should not be linked too closely to a timetable, especially the entry into middle age. While childhood and adolescence are more often marked by formal rites of passage and ceremonies, the transition from young adult to middle age is marked neither by special rites of passage nor by predictable chronological events (Clausen 1986). Social cues, especially role changes in the family and work domains, may be better indicators of developmental change than chronological age alone.

Most of the scientific and popular literature on adult development suggests that the transition to middle age occurs between ages forty and forty-nine. While no formal rite of passage exists, throughout the fifth decade of life there is a gradual accumulation of physiological changes, life problems, and role transitions that lead individuals to define themselves as middle-aged. Being identified by others as someone who is middle-aged carries a message to adults who have just turned forty, whether they feel middle-aged or not. Further, these messages of aging increase during the fifties, causing definitive changes in self-conceptions of aging. For many, the fiftieth birthday, marking half a century of life, is a significant aging benchmark. Despite a double standard of aging for women and men, John Logan, Russell Ward, and Glenna Spitze (1992), in their study of 1,200 adults, found that women did not adopt middle- or old-age identities at either a younger or an older age than men did.

Periods of transition across the life course are characterized by asynchronies in biological, psychological, and/or sociological development (Riegel 1975). The contradictions experienced within this state of asynchrony must be resolved if the individual is to reach a new developmental stage (Tamir 1982). Eric Erikson defined the developmental task for middle adulthood as the crisis of generativity versus stagnation. According to Erickson (1950, p. 231), "generativity is primarily the interest in establishing and guiding the next generation or whatever in a given case may become the absorbing object of a parental kind of responsibility." Generativity is thus a growth-producing development, a desire to both learn and teach about aspects of life that offer challenges. In contrast, stagnation is the acceptance of the status quo and a refusal to grow. This theme of generativity as the task of midlife is echoed in the works of Neugarten (1968) and K. Warner Schaie (1977–1978), who refer to this stage of development as the responsible stage, when individuals' awareness extends beyond themselves as individuals to acceptance of their role in maintaining the social structure or social systems. Carol Gilligan (1982) found that the middle years for women often were a return to unfinished business of adolescence—a time to sort out personal issues of identity and intimacy. Morton Lieberman and Hanley Peskin (1992, p. 133) propose that "periods of adult crises and transitions are times of natural growth and therapeutic efficacy."

A significant portion of the literature on the psychology of aging has focused on individual's views of their sexuality. As men and women grow older, they face a number of myths about aging and sexuality. For women, menopause has been cast as a major turning point or a traumatic event in their lives. Menopausal women are often portrayed as either chronically depressed or as emotionally volatile. The reality is, however, far different. Perimenopause begins on average at about age forty-seven and typically lasts four years. Thus, the median age of last menstrual period is about fifty-one (McKinlay, Brambilla, and Posner 1992). Although women do experience vasomotor symptoms (e.g., hot flashes), the vast majority do *not* experience depression during or after menopause (Matthews 1992). In one of the few longitudinal studies of menopause transition, Sonja McKinlay has found that more than two-thirds of the women report relief or neutral feelings about cessation of menses and that, over a four-year period, changes in women's attitudes toward menopause are in a positive or a neutral direction (Avis and McKinlay 1991; McKinlay, Brambilla, and Posner 1992). It has been suggested that the aging heterosexual woman may experience a growing interest in sexual activities as she is freed from the need to worry about birth control. Longitudinal research, which is less likely to be confounded by generational differences, suggests that, for both men and women, an individual's pattern of sexuality in earlier years it the best predictor of one's sexuality in later life (Whitbourne 1990). The availability of sexual partner, however, affects the frequency of certain types of sexual activity for both men and women.

Unlike women, men do not experience a distinct climacteric phase. They do, however, experience a number of gradual physiological changes, such as in the frequency of orgasm, ease of erection, and length of refractory period. Older men typically have a shorter orgasm, involving fewer contractings of the prostrate and less seminal fluid. Interviews by William Berquist, Elinor Greenberg, and G. Alan Klaum (1993, p. 45) with persons in their fifties revealed that both sexes reported a greater "patience in their sexuality" and "they savored the experience as well as the outcome," suggesting that the sexuality of men and women in their fifties is connected to a newly discovered and deeper quality of intimacy.

Contemporary Family Life and Middle Age

Throughout the twentieth century, major demographic shifts have transformed American families. One of most consistent changes has been the verticalization of the family (Bengston, Rosenthal, and Burton 1990). Increased life expectancy coupled with decreasing fertility have resulted in a pattern of an increasing number of living generations in a family, accompanied by a decreasing number of members within a single generation. As Gunhild Hagestad (1987) asserts, family relationships now have an unprecented duration. Parents and children may now share five decades of life, siblings may share eight decades of life, and the grandparent–grandchild bond may last two or three decades. Unlike their middle-aged predecessors, most baby boomers as they enter their forties have two living parents.

The verticalization of the family has also been accompanied by increased educational and labor force opportunities for women, technological advances in reproductive choice, and public acceptance of divorce, heterosexual and homosexual cohabitation, single lifestyles, and single parenting. Thus, men and women face unprecedented choices about whether and when to marry; whether to remain married, divorce, or remarry; and whether and when to have children (George and Gold 1991).

Two outcomes of these phenomena are that transitions such as marriage and parenthood that were once clear markers of young adulthood are less predictable, and there is a greater diversity in the structure of American families. Although the cultural ideal of the traditional nuclear family consisting of a lifelong married couple and their minor children continues to exist, it has become markedly less prevalent. Intergenerational family structures now include age-condensed, age-gapped, truncated (i.e., childless), single-parent, and stepfamily models (Bengston, Rosenthal, and Burton 1990). These phenomena are of importance in understanding the various stages of the life course. As Glen Elders (1985) asserts, timetables in the life course acquire particular relevance when they are viewed across generations. "The interweave of generational trajectories means that their temporal coordination has noteworthy implications for each life course" (Elders 1985, p. 41).

It is important to stress, however, that these demographic shifts are not distributed equally over the entire population. The magnitude of change varies by factors such as social class, race, and educational attainment. For example, while there is an increasing number of single-parent families across all racial groups, the extent varies. In 1990, single-parent families accounted for 23 percent of all white families, 33 percent of all Hispanic families, and 61 percent of all African-American families (U.S. Bureau of the Census 1992c). It must also be underscored that the effects of these various social trends are different for middle-aged men and women. While there have been changes in masculine and feminine roles within the family, women are still the primary kinkeepers and family nurturers. Moreover, it is the women in the middle generations who are the most centrally involved in maintaining family contact and cohesion. One change, however, has been the erosion of the principle of a family wage system (Ehrenreich 1983). For many families, the concept that a male breadwinner's wages alone should be sufficient to support a family is no longer true.

The family life cycle literature has historically characterized middle age as the time in which parents are concerned with launching their children and confronting the empty nest. Although the empty nest period is typically portrayed as a stressful time for parents, for mothers especially, research suggests just the opposite. For example, Marjorie Lowenthal and David Chiriboga (1972) found that most middle-aged parents favorably anticipated their children's departure. Studies also suggest that marital satisfaction typically increases after the launching of children (Lupri and Frideres 1981; Rollins and Feldman 1970). For a growing number of parents, however, it is either taking longer to launch children or these fledgling adults are returning to the nest. A 1988 national survey revealed that nearly three-quarters of adults aged nineteen to twenty-five had coresided with parents for at least some time after age nineteen and that among parents aged forty-five to fifty-four who had an adult child, nearly half (45%) had an adult child living at home (Aquilino 1991).

The timing and dynamics of launching the children are also influenced by the nature of the family structure. A comparison of the age-condensed family and the age-gapped family, for example, illustrates how different family forms may lead to very different midlife experiences.

The age-condensed family reflects a pattern of multiple-generation childbearing in the teens or early twenties. In this family form, members in their forties and fifties are not only parents but also grandparents. Because the mothers are single, unmarried adolescents in many of these cases, responsibility for the children often falls on the older women in the family. Census data suggest that due to earlier childbearing among African-American women as compared to white woman, the age-condensed family structure is more prevalent in the African-American community. Moreover, African Americans are more likely than whites to live in three-generation households. Ruby W. Beck and Scott H. Beck (1989) found that almost one-half of African-American women lived in a three-generation household at some point between 1969 and 1984. As compared to white grandmothers, African-American grandmothers had a more active role in parenting the grandchild, disciplining the grandchild, and providing child care for the adolescent daughter (Cherlin and Furstenberg 1986). Thus, for a significant proportion of women in age-condensed families, especially women of color, their middle years may involve a return to child rearing. The role of middle-aged men in age-condensed families has been less well explored. While this lack of attention may be partly due to the matrilineal nature of many of these age-condensed families, it may also reflect social scientists' bias of defining families as synonymous with households, which makes men who do not coreside invisible, even though they may be active family participants.

The age-gapped family represents a pattern of multiple generations delaying childbearing until their thirties or forties, a pattern that is more typical of white families than families of color. While the media have popularized the notion that the current cohort of adult daughters is the sandwich generation, national data reveal that only about 7 percent of women in the United States are faced with simultaneously caring for a child under age fifteen and a frail older parent (Cantor 1991). In contrast to the age-condensed family, the generational age difference of thirty or forty years in the age-gapped family may contribute to greater difficulties in building bonds across multiple generations due to different value or life orientations (George and Gold 1991). For example, the middle generation may face difficulties in building connections between grandparents who experienced the Great Depression of the 1930s and grandchildren who entered their adolescence during the excess of the 1980s.

Across diverse family structures, however, one role of middle age has become more predictable. The verticalization of the family has led to the caring of one's aging parents increasingly being viewed as a marker of middle age. Until 1980, the middle generation spent more years with children under eighteen than with parents over sixty-five. "By 1980, the seesaw tipped in the other direction: Years with parents over sixty-five exceeded years with children under eighteen [Watkins, Menken, and Bongaarts 1987, p. 352]." As daughters are involved in parent care more than sons, this shift has a greater impact on middle-aged women's lives. While mothers may now spend a smaller portion of their lives raising children, the freedom they have gained may, in many cases, simply be replaced with parent or grandparent care.

Conclusion

Carl Jung ([1933] 1971) described the onset of middle age as the "afternoon of life." For many it is a time in which they experience greater self-awareness and introspection as well as a growing sense of the finiteness of time. Appreciation for both the wisdom they have gained from life experiences and their greater capacity for coping with complexity is often expressed by those in their middle years.

While social scientists have traditionally focused on normative life experiences, there is increased recognition of the heterogeneity of the life course. The rapid rate of social change has increased differences both between and within cohorts. Social class, gender, race, and sexual orientation are all sources of variation in the aging process. Moreover, the diversification of contemporary American families influences the nature of family roles not only at midlife but also throughout the life course. Rather than considering a singular path to middle age and old age, it is increasingly important to speak of the different paths to successful aging.

(*See also:* Demography; Grandparenthood; Intergenerational Relations; Later-Life Families; Menopause; Sexuality in the Life Cycle)

BIBLIOGRAPHY

Aquilino, W. (1991). "Family Structure and Home Leaving: A Further Specification of the Relationships." *Journal of Marriage and the Family* 53:999–1019.

Avis, N. E., and McKinlay, S. M. (1991). "A Longitudinal Analysis of Women's Attitudes Toward the Menopause: Results from the Massachusetts Women's Health Study." *Maturitas* 13:65–79.

Beck, R. W., and Beck, S. H. (1989). "The Incidence of Extended Households Among Middle-Aged Black and White Women: Estimates from a Five-Year Panel Study." *Journal of Family Issues* 10:147–168.

Bengston, V. L.; Rosenthal, C.; and Burton, L. (1990). "Families and Aging: Diversity and Heterogenity." In *Handbook of Aging and the Social Sciences*, 3rd edition, ed. R. H. Binstock and L. K. George. New York: Academic Press.

Berquist, W. H.; Greenberg, E. M.; and Klaum, G. A. (1993). *In Our Fifties: Voices of Men and Women Reinventing Their Lives.* San Francisco: Jossey-Bass.

Blau, F. D., and Ferber, M. (1986). *The Economics of Women, Men, and Work.* Englewood Cliffs, NJ: Prentice Hall.

Cantor, M. (1991). "Family and Community: Changing Roles in an Aging Society." *Gerontologist* 31:337–346.

Cherlin, A. J., and Furstenberg, F. F., Jr. (1986). *The New American Grandparent.* New York: Basic Books.

Clausen, J. A. (1986). *The Life Course: A Sociological Perspective.* Englewood Cliffs, NJ: Prentice Hall.

Cohen, G. (1987). "Introduction: The Economy, the Family, and the Life Course." In *Social Change and the Life Course*, ed. G. Cohen. New York: Tavistock.

Ehrenreich, B. (1983). *In the Heart of Men: American Dreams and the Flight from Commitment.* Garden City, NY: Anchor Books.

Elders, G. H., Jr. (1985). Perspectives on the Life Course." In *Life Course Dynamics*, ed. G. H. Elders, Jr. Ithaca, NY: Cornell University Press.

Erickson, E. (1950). *Childhood and Society.* New York: W. W. Norton.

Farrell, M. P., and Rosenberg, S. D. (1981). *Men at Midlife.* Boston: Auburn House.

Gallagher, W. (1993). "Midlife Myths." *Atlantic Monthly* (May):51–68.

George, L. K., and Gold, D. T. (1991). "Life Course Perspectives on Intergenerational and Generational Connections." *Marriage and Family Review* 17:67–88.

Gilligan, C. (1982). *In a Different Voice: Psychological Theory and Women's Development.* Cambridge, MA: Harvard University Press.

Grambs, J. D. (1989). *Women Over Forty: Visions and Realities.* New York: Springer-Verlag.

Guttman, D. (1987). *Reclaimed Powers: Toward a New Psychology of Men and Women in Later Life.* New York: Basic Books.

Hagestad, G. O. (1987). "Able Elderly in the Family Context: Changes, Chances, and Challenges." *Gerontologist* 27:417–422.

Jung, C. G. ([1933] 1971). "The Stages of Life." In *The Portable Jung*, ed. J. Campbell. New York: Viking Press.

Lieberman, M., and Peskin, H. (1992). "Adult Life Crisis." In *Handbook of Mental Health Aging*, 2nd edition, ed. J. E. Birren. New York: Academic Press.

Logan, J. R.; Ward, R.; and Spitze, G. (1992). "As Old as You Feel: Age Identity in Middle and Later Life." *Social Forces* 71:451–467.

Lowenthal, M. F., and Chiriboga, D. (1972). "Transitions to the Empty Nest." *Archives of General Psychiatry* 26:8–14.

Lupri, E., and Frideres, J. (1981). "The Quality of Marriage and the Passage of Time: Marital Satisfaction Over the Family Life Cycle." *Canadian Journal of Sociology* 6:283–305.

Matthews, K. A. (1992). "Myths and Realities of the Menopause." *Psychosomatic Medicine* 54:1–9.

McKinlay, S. M.; Brambilla, D. J.; and Posner, J. G. (1992). "The Normal Menopause Transition." *American Journal of Human Biology* 4:37–46.

Neugarten, B., ed. (1968). *Middle Age and Aging.* Chicago: University of Chicago Press.

Riegel, K. F. (1975). "Adult Life Crises: A Dialectic Interpretation of Development." In *Life Span Developmental Psychology: Normative Life Crises*, ed. N. Datan and L. H. Ginsberg. New York: Academic Press.

Rollins, B. C., and Feldman, H. (1970). "Marital Satisfaction Over the Family Life Cycle." *Journal of Marriage and the Family* 32:20–28.

Schaie, K. W. (1977–1978). "Toward a Stage Theory of Adult Cognitive Development." *International Journal of Aging and Human Development* 8:129–138.

Tamir, L. M. (1982). *Men in Their Forties: The Transition to Middle Age.* New York: Springer-Verlag.

Treas, J., and Bengston, V. L. (1982). "The Demography of Mid- and Late-Life Transitions." *Annals of The American Academy of Political and Social Science* 464:11–21.

Troll, L. E. (1985). *Early and Middle Adulthood: The Best Is Yet to Be—Maybe.* Monterey, CA: Brooks/Cole.

U.S. Bureau of the Census. (1992a). *Sixty-Five Plus in America.* Washington, DC: U.S. Government Printing Office.

U.S. Bureau of the Census. (1992b). *Households, Families, and Children: A 30-Year Perspective.* Washington, DC: U.S. Government Printing Office.

U.S. Bureau of the Census. (1992c). *Marriage, Divorce, and Remarriage in the 1990s.* Washington, DC: U.S. Government Printing Office.

Watkins, S. C.; Menken, J. A.; and Bongaarts, J. (1987). "Demographic Foundations of Family Change." *American Sociological Review* 52:346–358.

Witbourne, S. K. (1990). "Sexuality in the Aging Male." *Generations* 14:28–30.

JUDITH G. GONYEA

MILITARY FAMILIES

The U.S. military is comprised mostly of married men and women who have children. This may be surprising to some, who have images of young, single men leaving their parents to fight in World War II or Vietnam. While those images may have been true in the past, the U.S. Congress created an all-volunteer military force in 1971. With the all-volunteer force came the opportunity to make the military a career. Pay and benefits were increased and, as soldiers, sailors, marines, and airmen began marrying and having children, family support services in the military were developed.

History of Military Families

Beginning with the European colonization of North America, the well-being of families has been an integral part of the military. In colonial America, military training was required of every man, and service in the militia was tightly intertwined with family, social, and religious values. In 1636, Plymouth Colony passed the first pension law in the New World, where any man disabled in military service would be "maintained competently by the Colony during his life." By the mid-seventeenth century, all colonies had enacted military pension legislation that included provisions for the financial relief of maimed soldiers and their families, as well as pensions for their widows and orphans (Black 1989).

Within two months of the signing of the Declaration of Independence in 1776, federal laws were enacted providing financial benefits for military veterans and their families. After the Revolution, individual states, which provided most of the military forces for the country in times of war, enacted legislation for the welfare of soldiers and their families (Black 1989).

Following World War I, Congress created the Veterans Bureau. Established in 1921 and restructured into the Veterans Administration (VA) in 1930, it consolidated state and federal fiscal and social benefits for veterans and their families into one federal office (Black 1991). In 1989, the VA was reorganized into the Department of Veterans Affairs (DVA). The DVA offers numerous financial, educational, and domestic benefits for military veterans and their families. With 240,000 federal employees, the DVA is second in size only to the Department of Defense.

Department of Defense Structure

The Department of Defense (DoD) is the largest governmental agency in the United States. In 1993, its budget was $259.1 billion, which accounted for 18.3 percent of all federal outlays. However, the 1993 DoD budget was 31 percent below its 1985 figure, and further reductions in defense spending are projected (Department of Defense 1993).

Within the DoD are four armed service branches: Army, Air Force, Navy, and Marine Corps. The Army, Air Force, and Navy operate independently, while the Marine Corps falls under the Navy's jurisdiction. The U.S. Coast Guard is also part of the armed services, but it is administered by the Department of Transportation, not the DoD. In a war, the president of the United States can transfer the Coast Guard to the Navy.

Demographics

The DoD is staffed by approximately 4.5 million people. As Table 1 shows, there are about 1.7 million men and women serving on active military duty and another 1.1 million serving in the Selected Reserve forces (which includes the National Guard), all of whom are supported by 1 million civilian DoD employees. These persons are assigned to 470 installations located in the United States, eighty-seven installations located in twenty foreign countries, and eight installations in U.S. territories. As the military reduces its size, the number of installations will also shrink. About one-third of all active-duty military forces are stationed outside of the United States (Department of Defense 1993).

An additional 700,000 people belong to the Individual Ready Reserve, the Standby Reserve, or the Inactive National Guard. They do not participate in regular military training, but they can be mobilized in the event of a national emergency.

The armed services are highly structured organizations where rank and responsibility are usually clearly defined. There are two distinct categories of personnel: the enlisted and the commissioned-officer ranks. Enlisted members generally have at least a high school diploma and are trained in combat and technical skill areas. The enlisted force is more than five times larger than the officer force and is responsible for the day-to-day operation of the military. Senior enlisted personnel (noncommissioned officers) are also responsible for the leadership of junior enlisted members. Commissioned officers, on the other hand, generally have at least one college degree. They are primarily responsible for long-range planning and leadership of larger groups of personnel and organizations.

People choose to enter the active-duty military or National Guard or reserve forces for a number of reasons. Many enter out of a sense of patriotism. Other

Table 1 Military Personnel, 1993

	Active Duty				*Selected Reserve*		
	Officer	*Enlisted*	*Academy*	*Total*	*Officer*	*Enlisted*	*Total*
Army	91,036	495,087	4,201	590,324	105,339	624,039	729,378
Navy	67,156	450,506	4,285	521,947	26,973	115,341	142,314
Marine Corps	18,895	162,982	–	181,877	3,508	38,748	42,256
Air Force	84,340	361,805	4,147	450,292	30,393	170,564	200,957
Coast Guard	7,724	30,417	691	38,832	1,536	9,696	11,232

SOURCES Department of Defense (1993, pp. 28–32); Ungerleider, Smith, and Gordon (1993, p. 87).

reasons include educational benefits, job training, and the opportunity to travel. For families, benefits of serving in the military include job and financial security, medical care, retirement pensions, and camaraderie with other military families.

Active-duty forces. People on active duty work full-time on their military responsibilities. These men and women are well educated. To enlist in the service, one usually needs at least a high school diploma or its equivalent. Officers need a college degree. Once in the service, continued education is encouraged.

Table 2 provides select characteristics of military members and their families. The active-duty military is relatively young, with 49.7 percent of all enlisted personnel under the age of twenty-six. Since officers are required to have a college degree before entering the service, they tend to be older. Because 46 percent of the people choose to leave the service after their

Table 2 Characteristics of the Military, 1993

	Active Duty (%)		*Selected Reserve (%)*	
	Officer	*Enlisted*	*Officer*	*Enlisted*
Age of Military Member				
Less than 21 years	<0.1	15.7	<0.1	9.1
21–25 years	12.8	34.0	4.0	25.7
26–30 years	23.7	20.0	14.3	18.5
31–35 years	21.3	15.5	18.4	13.9
36–40 years	19.8	10.4	19.3	10.4
41–45 years	14.4	3.4	20.8	10.0
46–50 years	6.2	0.7	15.9	6.7
More than 50 years	1.7	<0.1	7.0	4.2
Ethnic/Racial Minorities	13.1	32.6	13.1	27.9
Women	12.7	11.5	14.9	13.1
Married	76.5	58.2	78.1	57.8
Life Course Stage of Spouses				
Younger than 29, no child under 19	11.5	16.6	5.6	11.6
Younger than 29, child under 19	76.6	76.7	77.4	75.6
Youngest child 0–5	39.5	50.7	–	–
Youngest child 6–11	22.4	18.4	–	–
Youngest child 12–17	14.8	7.6	–	–
Older than 30, no child under 18	11.7	6.7	17.0	12.9
Months Separated from Spouse in One Year				
None	21.2	28.3	–	–
Less than 1 month	18.3	10.4	–	–
1–2 months	24.4	16.0	–	–
3–4 months	17.8	15.2	–	–
5–6 months	8.0	11.0	–	–
7–8 months	4.6	6.6	–	–
9–10 months	2.5	4.2	–	–
11–12 months	3.1	8.4	–	–
Time at Present Location				
Less than 1 year	33.7	34.0	10.6	14.1
1–2 years	28.2	27.7	12.4	14.0
More than 2 years	38.0	38.5	76.9	71.9
2–3 years	–	–	10.7	10.1
3–5 years	–	–	13.2	10.7
More than 5 years	–	–	53.0	51.1

SOURCES Data extrapolated from Department of Defense (1993); Black (1993); Defense Manpower Data Center (1985); Defense Manpower Data Center (1986).

first term, and because retirement is offered after twenty years of service for those who choose to make the military a career, only 3.4 percent of the enlisted force and 22.3 percent of the officer force is over the age of forty. Around 30 percent of the entire active-duty force is from ethnic or racial minorities and 12 percent is female.

About 61 percent of the 1.7 million men and women on active duty are married. However, most people get married after entering the service. These military families have 1.5 million children (Department of Defense 1993).

Selected Reserve. Most of the 1.1 million men and women in the Selected Reserve hold civilian jobs outside the DoD while participating in military training one weekend per month plus two weeks per year.

As Table 2 shows, the Selected Reserve forces are older than the active-duty forces, with just 34.8 percent of the enlisted force and 4 percent of the officer force age twenty-five or younger. Because 77.8 percent of the Selected Reserve forces reenlist after their first term, and because it takes longer than twenty chronological years to accrue retirement benefits, substantially more people are over the age of forty-one in the reserves than in the active-duty forces. About 26 percent of reservists represent ethnic or racial minorities and 13 percent are women. As with the active-duty force, 61 percent of reservists are married. There are approximately 2.2 million spouses and children attached to the Selected Reserve forces (Black 1993).

Military Family Lifestyle

Active-duty military families live a lifestyle that is different from that of other segments of the general population, and it can be very rewarding. Frequent moves and living in foreign countries provide growth opportunities for the individuals and the entire family, since one is constantly creating new friendships and experiencing different cultures. However, this lifestyle can also be quite demanding.

Spouses consistently rank military-induced family separation as the most difficult aspect of military life (Black 1993). Table 2 shows that 60.5 percent of the active-duty officers and 61.4 percent of enlisted personnel are separated from their families for one or more months during a one-year period; 10.2 percent of the officers and 19.2 percent of enlisted personnel are separated from their families for seven months or longer. These family separations are the result of military deployments, sea duty, and service in remote locations where families are not permitted due to geographic conditions or possible hostilities. These separations can be especially demanding since 76.7 percent of military families have children at home.

Another potential hardship encountered by military families is frequent geographic mobility. This is more pronounced for active-duty than for reserve families. As Table 2 indicates, less than two-fifths (38% of the officers and 38.5% of enlisted personnel) of the active-duty force lived in the same location for more than two years, as compared to about three-quarters of the Selected Reserve (76.9% of the officers and 71.9% of enlisted personnel). Thus, the active-duty force usually lives away from extended family support systems.

Therefore, the major life stressors faced by military families include frequent moves, the potential of being deployed into hostile areas, frequent periods of family separation, geographic isolation from family support systems, young age as compared to the general population, and a high incidence of young children living at home. Each of these military lifestyle stressors might be adequately dealt with by itself, but military families must often deal with them as an aggregate. This stressor pileup can place military families in a vulnerable position (Boss 1986; McCubbin et al. 1980).

The armed services recognize that dealing with the stressors of military life is a learned process and a developmental task. Hence, support services are provided to families early in their military career to help them develop coping skills that will prevent them from falling into crisis. The military is also aware that strong families contribute to successful military careers. As a result, a host of services to assist families have been created.

Services for Military Families

Most active-duty military bases might be thought of as self-contained communities. Whether overseas or in the United States, most installations have base exchanges (small department stores), commissaries (grocery stores), gas stations, churches, schools and colleges, restaurants, banks, movie theaters, medical and dental facilities, youth activity centers, child-care centers, police and fire departments, and housing. In theory at least, it is possible to have all of one's needs met without leaving the installation.

This tight community structure provides comfort for many military families. Because they live in communities where all of their neighbors face the same military lifestyle stressors, military families can support one another.

In addition, there are many formal family support systems built into the military. Department of Defense Directive 1342.17, "Family Policy," was issued in 1988. This directive provides guidance to all of the service branches and requires that comprehensive family support programs be maintained at every installation. A few of the programs are highlighted below.

Family support centers. The Military Family Act of 1985 established the Office of Family Policy under the Assistant Secretary of Defense for Force Management and Personnel. This law initiated the development of family support centers. These centers are called Community Service Centers in the Army, Family Service Centers in the Navy and Marine Corps, and Family Support Centers in the Air Force. Despite the different names, they all provide the same essential services to families.

Family support centers are found on virtually every active-duty or reserve military installation in the world, providing a one-stop source for most services available to families. They can assist with nonmedical emergencies (food, clothing, shelter, transportation, child care, and financial assistance), budget counseling, spouse employment assistance and counseling, family life education, relocation assistance, support for family members during military deployments, and separation and retirement planning.

Mental health services. Most active-duty installations provide psychiatric, psychological, or social work services to individuals and families. Substance abuse programs, inpatient and outpatient, are also offered. In addition, there are family-advocacy services worldwide that not only deal with family violence issues, but also ensure that educational or medical services are available for handicapped children before families are assigned to a specific installation.

Medical facilities. Most active-duty installations have medical services available. If they are not available, the family uses civilian sources under a government insurance plan.

Chaplains. Military chaplains provide pastoral care, counseling and support, premarital and marital counseling and seminars, family enrichment and growth programs, and religious education and worship opportunities.

Select Military Benefits

Literally hundreds of benefit programs are available to active-duty, guard and reserve, retired, and former military members and their families (Department of Veterans Affairs 1992). Some of the major benefits are highlighted here.

Educational and vocational programs. Since the DVA began offering educational benefits to veterans through the GI Bill in 1944, more than 20 million men and women have received a total of more than $70 billion in assistance. Veterans who leave service with an honorable discharge are eligible for up to $350 per month for thirty-six months while pursuing education. Guard and reserve members are eligible for up to $175 per month. Spouses and children of disabled or deceased veterans may also receive benefits. Any person currently on active duty is eligible to have his or her schooling entirely paid for by the DoD.

Retirement benefits. After serving twenty years on active duty, a service member is eligible for retirement. If the person serves less than twenty years, there is no retirement benefit. Members who complete twenty years of active-duty service receive a monthly retirement payment equal to 40 percent of the average of their highest 36 months of base pay. This percentage of base pay is increased 3.5 percent for each year they serve past twenty years, until thirty years of active service, when the maximum retirement benefit reaches 75 percent. There is no minimum age for retirement and payments are made for life. Retirees and their families also maintain eligibility for medical and other military benefits for life (Ungerleider, Smith, and Gordon 1993). Likewise, National Guard and reserve forces who serve a specified number of years (based on a complex point system) are eligible for retirement benefits. However, their retirement payments do not start until they reach age sixty.

Housing. The DVA guarantees loans made to purchase a house, premanufactured home, or condominium. This means that many commercial lenders will make house loans at lower interest rates with little or no down payment to military veterans. To be eligible for the program, a person must have served honorably in the military for 181 days or longer.

Medical care. In addition to active-duty medical care, the DVA operates 172 full-service hospitals in the United States. Veterans who have medical conditions directly related to military service receive first priority for treatment. Nursing homes and residences are also available to elderly veterans.

Death benefits. Veterans are eligible for certain burial expenses in any cemetery in the United States. In addition, the DVA operates 114 cemeteries worldwide that can be used by both veterans and family members.

Counseling services. The DVA operates about 200 Veteran Counseling Centers (commonly referred to as Vet Centers) around the country to help veterans and their families with psychological, emotional, and physical needs.

Conclusion

The majority of men and women in the armed services are married and have children. Life can be very rewarding and exciting for many of these military families, but it can also be challenging. Recognizing this, the services have built a host of formal and informal family support services into the military. Once young families are given tools to use in dealing with stress, they should be able to adapt adequately to military life. However, the military lifestyle is not for everyone, and when some families choose to leave the military, the services assist them in making the transition back to civilian life.

(*See also:* Entitlements; Family Policy; Family Therapy; Retirement; Stress)

BIBLIOGRAPHY

Black, W. G., Jr. (1989). "The Military Origins of Federal Social Welfare Programs: Early British and Colonial American Precedents." Ph.D. Diss. University of Minnesota.

Black, W. G., Jr. (1991). "Social Work in World War I: A Method Lost." *Social Service Review* 65:379–402.

Black, W. G., Jr. (1993). "Military-Induced Family Separation: A Stress Reduction Intervention." *Social Work* 38:273–280.

Boss, P. (1986). "Family Stress: Perception and Context." In *Handbook of Marriage and the Family*, ed. M. B. Sussman and S. K. Steinmetz. New York: Plenum.

Defense Manpower Data Center. (1985). *Description of Spouses of Officers and Enlisted Personnel in the U.S. Armed Forces.* Arlington, VA: Author.

Defense Manpower Data Center. (1986). *Description of Spouses of Officers and Enlisted Personnel in the U.S. Selected Reserve.* Arlington, VA: Author.

Department of Defense. (1993). "Almanac." *Defense 93.* Washington, DC: U.S. Government Printing Office.

Department of Veterans Affairs. (1992). *Federal Benefits for Veterans and Dependents.* Washington, DC: U.S. Government Printing Office.

McCubbin, H. I.; Joy, C. B.; Cauble, A. E.; Comeau, J. K.; Patterson, J. M.; and Needle, R. H. (1980). "Family Stress and Coping: A Decade Review." *Journal of Marriage and the Family* 42:855–871.

Ungerleider, A.; Smith, G. L.; and Gordon, D. M. (1993). *Reserve Forces Almanac.* Falls Church, VA: Uniformed Services Almanac.

William G. Black, Jr.

MISSING CHILDREN

After a series of incidents involving the disappearance and subsequent murder of children in the late 1970s and early 1980s, the issue of missing children became an urgent focus of national concern (Gentry 1988). Generally used to describe children whose whereabouts had become unknown to their parents, the phrase "missing children" ultimately came to embrace a wide range of endangered juveniles under eighteen years of age: children abducted by strangers or taken without permission by noncustodial parents, children temporarily lost by their parents, adolescent runaways, and even children abandoned or "thrown away" by their parents. In part because it concerned so many different kinds of children from so many different walks of life, the plight of these youths came to assume a rare prominence in the American psyche, with pictures of missing children soon staring out from store windows, milk cartons, and even envelopes of congressional mail.

In response to this extraordinary new environment, Congress enacted the Missing Children Act in 1982 and the Missing Children's Assistance Act in 1984 (Weisberg 1984). The first of these acts made the missing persons file of the National Crime Information Center far more accessible than in the past to parents trying to locate their children. The Missing Children's Assistance Act established the National Center for Missing and Exploited Children to provide information and technical assistance to both parents and law enforcement, but more importantly it signaled the intention of the federal government to devote long-term attention and resources to studying and addressing the problem. However, some critics soon began to question the importance of that commitment, based on estimates of the number of missing children; arguably those estimates could not withstand rigorous scrutiny (Best 1988).

Categories of Missing Children

Even as that debate raged, however, a federally funded study was under way that would yield a remarkably multifaceted portrait of the population of children who are at least temporarily beyond the control and protection of their parents. Based on a telephone survey of more than 30,000 randomly selected households nationwide, the National Incidence Study (NIS) estimated the number of children in each of the populations previously lumped together as "missing" during 1988 (Finkelhor, Hotaling, and Sedlak 1990). Of equal significance, the study provided basic but highly useful data about both the children involved and the types of incidents that led to their usually temporary disappearance.

Nonfamily abductions. Closest to the core of public conceptions of the missing child problem are those situations in which someone outside the child's family takes, detains, or lures a child away from parental control, often to commit a crime such as sexual assault. Using the legal definition of abduction, the NIS found that 3,200 to 4,600 such incidents occur annually, with 200 to 300 involving true kidnappings by strangers, and 43 to 147 ending in a child-abduction homicide. About three-quarters of children victimized by nonfamily abduction are girls, and teenagers appear particularly at risk. Perpetrators are overwhelmingly males.

Family abductions. Far more children, by contrast, are victims each year of family abductions, incidents in which a member of their own family takes or holds them in violation of a custody agreement or decree. The NIS found 354,000 children in this category, with almost half of them concealed, transported out of state, or otherwise treated by their abductor in such a way that a long-term deprivation of custody appears to have been intended. In sharp contrast to nonfamily abductions, children missing at the hands of family members seem likely to be younger than thirteen and as often boys as girls. Perpetrators, however, are again overwhelmingly male.

Runaways. Not surprisingly, the largest group of missing children identified by the NIS were *not* abducted from parental custody, but had *voluntarily* left home overnight or longer without parental permission. The NIS found more than 446,000 such runaways under age eighteen in 1988. Almost all of them were teenagers, and a disproportionate number were from stepparent homes. During their time away from home, about one-fourth of the runaways were without a secure and familiar place to stay, and one in ten had not returned home after more than a month away. In its telephone interviews with parents, the NIS found little concrete evidence of harm suffered by runaways during their absence, but other shelter- or clinic-based studies have found such youths to be at high risk of disease, substance abuse, exploitation, physical injury, and clinical depression (Loken and Kennedy 1990; Shaffer and Caton 1984; Yates et al. 1988; Yates et al. 1991).

Thrownaways. At even greater risk is another large group of children "missing" from home—not by their own choice, but by virtue of having been abandoned by their parents or told by their parents to leave home. These thrownaways were found by the NIS to number more than 127,000 in 1988, with more than 44,000 lacking a secure place to stay while away. Though, like runaways, these children are usually in their teens, thousands of very young children are abandoned each year to the foster care system, where they may languish for many years. Adolescent thrownaways are at especially high risk of entering long-term street life, and the risks to their health and safety are far higher than those facing most runaways (Reuler 1991; Yates et al. 1991).

Lost, injured, or "otherwise missing" children. Finally, a surprising number of children every year are "missing" to their parents because they are lost, have suffered an injury, or have had a miscommunication with their parents about their whereabouts. Some 438,000 children a year, according to the NIS, fall into this category. Of those incidents, about a third are serious enough that law enforcement authorities are called to assist in recovering the child. While virtually all children who disappear in one of these ways are recovered by their parents within twenty-four hours, about 20 percent of them suffer some kind of physical harm during the absence.

The Future of the Missing Children Issue

For all its intrinsic value, greater understanding of the variety of ways in which children become "missing" seems likely to exact a price in the clarity, and perhaps the momentum, of the missing children movement. The early phase of legislative activity, including the Missing Children Act, which focused primarily on improvements in law enforcement protection for children, seems to have continuing relevance mainly for abducted, lost, or injured children. Further, the special complications of family abductions often require social service interventions not common in police work (Agopian 1984; Hoff 1985).

Adolescent runaways and thrownaways, by contrast, together constitute the most numerous group of children at risk for lack of parental care. The federal Runaway and Homeless Youth Act provides funding for emergency assistance and transitional living services for these youths, but on a very small scale in comparison to the numbers in need of help (National Network of Runaway and Youth Services 1985). Only a handful of states, most notably New York, have *state* runaway and homeless youth statutes authorizing and funding temporary shelter for youths caught on the street. Under the common law, anyone other than a parent providing shelter to a child could be held civilly, and in some states criminally, liable for "harboring" a runaway. In the meantime, the laws of many states liberally permit parents to "place" their children voluntarily in foster care and provide for punishment of parental abandonment or neglect of children only if the child has not reached adolescence.

What began, then, as an issue focused on injuries to parental *custody* may finally come full circle to an inquiry on why so many children are "missing" adequate parental *care*, and how society can appropriately intervene to protect and nurture them.

(*See also:* Child Abuse and Neglect: Legal Aspects; Child Custody; Gangs; Juvenile Delinquency; Runaway Children; Truancy)

BIBLIOGRAPHY

Agopian, M. (1984). "The Impact on Children of Abduction by Parents." *Child Welfare* 63:511–519.

Best, J. (1988). "Missing Children, Misleading Statistics." *The Public Interest* 92:84–92.

Finkelhor, D.; Hotaling, G.; and Sedlak, A. (1990). *Missing, Abducted, Runaway, and Thrownaway Children in America.* Report to Office of Juvenile Justice and Delinquency Prevention, U.S. Department of Justice.

Gentry, C. (1988). "The Social Construction of Abducted Children as a Social Problem." *Sociological Inquiry* 58:413–425.

Hegar, R., and Greif, G. (1991). "Abduction of Children by Their Parents: A Survey of the Problem." *Social Work* 36:421–425.

Hoff, P. (1985). *Parental Kidnapping.* Washington, DC: National Center for Missing and Exploited Children.

Loken, G., and Kennedy, J. (1990). "Legal Cocaine and Kids: The Very Bitterness of Shame." *Hofstra Law Review* 18:567–606.

National Center for Missing and Exploited Children. (1985). *Investigator's Guide to Missing Child Cases.* Washington, DC: Author.

National Network of Runaway and Youth Services. (1985). *To Whom Do They Belong?: A Profile of America's Runaway and Homeless Youth and the Programs That Help Them.* Washington, DC: Author.

Reuler, J. (1991). "Outreach Health Services for Street Youth." *Journal of Adolescent Health* 12:561–566.

Shaffer, D., and Caton, C. (1984). *Runaway and Homeless Youth in New York.* Report to the Ittleson Foundation, New York.

Spitzer, N. (1986). "The Children's Crusade." *Atlantic* 257:18–23.

Terr, L. (1983). "Child Snatching: A New Epidemic of an Ancient Malady." *Journal of Pediatrics* 103:151–156.

Weisberg, D. K. (1984). "Children of the Night: The Adequacy of Statutory Treatment of Juvenile Prostitution." *American Journal of Criminal Law* 12:1–67.

Yates, G.; MacKenzie, R.; Pennbridge, J.; and Cohen, E. (1988). "A Risk Profile Comparison of Runaway and Non-Runaway Youth." *American Journal of Public Health* 78:820–821.

Yates, G.; MacKenzie, R.; Pennbridge, J.; and Swofford, A. (1991). "A Risk Profile Comparison of Homeless Youth Involved in Prostitution and Homeless Youth Not Involved." *Journal of Adolescent Health* 12:545–548.

Gregory Loken

MOTHERS

Historically, the experience of motherhood has been a central aspect of most women's lives. Until the 1970s, any role for women other than motherhood was considered deviant (Hoffman and Hoffman 1973). Since that time, women have increased the variety of choices available to them, although motherhood is certainly still an option.

Becoming a Mother

When childbearing is a conscious decision, couples assess the direct financial costs of rearing the child and the indirect costs such as disruption of the woman's employment and career opportunities. However, cultural expectations for parenthood are the most influential factors affecting the decision to have a child (Straits 1985). In the United States, there is tremendous pressure for women to bear children (Richardson 1993); women are socialized to believe that having children is natural and necessary. However, an increasing number of women are choosing not to have children. In 1960, 11 percent of women above the age of forty were childless, but 25 percent of the women born in the 1950s and early 1960s are expected to remain childless (U.S. Bureau of the Census 1982). Studies also show that women without children, whether by choice or because of infertility, are as satisfied with their lives as women with children (Baruch, Barnett, and Rivers 1983; Callan 1987). The choice of a child-free marriage has become an acceptable option (Thornton 1989).

An increasing number of couples are delaying childbearing until midlife. Approximately 76 percent of women aged thirty-one to thirty-five in 1978 had given birth to their first child by age twenty-five (U.S. Bureau of the Census 1978). However, in 1985, only thirty-nine percent of ever-married women had become mothers before reaching twenty-five years of age (U.S. Bureau of the Census 1987). This postponement of childbearing is frequently a well-planned choice (Daniels and Weingarten 1988). Some of the women delaying childbearing seek to enjoy an autonomous life for themselves before beginning the tasks of parenting, and others want to achieve career objectives before raising children (Wilkie 1987). However, most of the research examining delayed motherhood has studied a remarkably homogeneous population of predominantly white, married, and middle- to upper-middle-class women (Daniels and Weingarten 1988; Frankel and Wise 1982; Walters 1986). Studies have not focused on the impact of postponed mothering on single women and within diverse cultural communities.

Although contemporary motherhood is often seen as a choice, some women do not make a conscious decision to get pregnant. These pregnancies occur because couples do not use contraceptives or their contraceptive effort fails for various reasons. Research on the consequences of unplanned pregnancies are concentrated in the areas of teenage pregnancy and family violence. For example, poverty is a constant problem for teenage mothers (Hayes 1987), and the abused child is frequently the product of an unwanted pregnancy (Bennie and Sclare 1969). Although these are serious possible consequences, little is known about how women who have unplanned pregnancies fare in their day-to-day mothering roles, compared to those whose pregnancies were planned.

Role in Child Rearing

Once women become parents, they are a constant presence throughout their children's lives. Regardless of children's ages, mothers typically are more involved in the daily lives of their children then are fathers (Clarke-Stewart 1978; Kivett 1988). Attentive, active, hands-on parenting characterizes mothering, but these behaviors are considered optional for fathers (Boulton 1983; Daniels and Weingarten 1988). The tasks of motherhood and fatherhood are also different. David Piachaud (1984) identified three categories of child-care tasks: basic tasks (feeding, washing), educational and entertaining tasks (reading to, playing with a child), and indirect supervisory activity (being on-call). Mothers' child rearing involves basic tasks, the day-to-day activities of looking after children, whereas fathers are involved in more entertaining and educational tasks and indirect supervisory activities (LaRossa and LaRossa 1981).

Mothering is a complicated and conflicting experience: It is irritating, frustrating, and overwhelming, but also exciting and gratifying (Chodorow and Contratto 1982). The constant care of children may interfere with mothers' other activities, such as housework and the pursuit of hobbies, and confine mothers to the home. Employed mothers do a "second work shift" of child-care and household tasks after returning home from their paid work (Hochschild 1989). On the other hand, many mothers express a sense of meaning, purpose, and fulfillment associated with motherhood. In one study that involved fifty married mothers of small children, Mary Boulton (1983) found that about a third of the mothers both enjoyed and found broader meaning in mothering, another third neither enjoyed nor found meaning in mothering, and the remainder had mixed experiences.

Effects of Maternal Employment

One crucial factor affecting contemporary motherhood is women's paid employment. Early research tended to view women's employment as having mostly negative effects on children (Hoffman and Nye 1974). However, numerous studies have concluded that it has not been fully demonstrated that mothers' employment alone has either positive or negative effects on children's development and educational outcomes (Bianchi and Spain 1986; Hayes and Kamerman 1983). This is not surprising, because employment of mothers is a complex issue that goes beyond the mother–child relationship.

Research has shown that employed mothers are likely to have a higher family income and more liberal gender-role attitudes than their nonemployed counterparts. Employed mothers, especially those who are career-oriented, might be older as well, thus more mature but possibly less amenable to the unpredictability involved in parenthood. Many studies also show that daughters are more affected by maternal employment than sons. Daughters of employed mothers are more likely to be independent than are daughters of nonemployed mothers (Hoffman 1974), to plan for their own future employment (Moore, Spain, and Bianchi 1984), to hold egalitarian gender-role attitudes (Wilkie 1987), and to view women and their own mothers as competent (Bloom-Feshbach, Bloom-Feshbach, and Heller 1982).

Although employed mothers spend less time with their children, there is no consistent evidence that children of employed mothers feel deprived. A number of factors may moderate the effects of mothers' employment on children, including class and race of parents, sex and personality characteristics of the children (Moore, Spain, and Bianchi 1984; Wilkie 1987), and occupational status and employment preferences of the mother (Acock, Barker, and Bengston 1982).

Several studies suggest that mothers' employment enhances the academic achievement of girls in all social classes, but not of middle-class boys (Hoffman 1974). Although one study showed small negative effects of mothers' employment on white children's academic achievement (Milne et al. 1986), a re-analysis of the same data showed that the small negative effects were found only among white middle-class children in two-parent families whose mothers worked full-time before the child entered school (Heyns and Catsambis 1986). These effects are reduced even further when mothers have a positive attitude toward work.

Quality of Mothering

Several factors affect the quality of mothering. First, shared parenting reduces certain levels of anxiety and stress related to mothering (Richardson 1993). Historically, men have made only a modest contribution to the daily business of caring for children. Some studies suggest that men's increased participation in housework may encourage more sharing of child care (Ishii-Kuntz and Coltrane 1992). Second, maternal employment seems to have positive effects on children when mothers themselves value their work role (Freeman 1988) and are satisfied with their paid work (Hock and DeMeis 1990). Thus, it is seen as necessary to improve the opportunities for and work conditions of employed women. The first step in this improvement is to increase the availability of quality child care. Paid paternal leaves might be another solution to ensure continuity in women's employment (Volling and Belsky 1993). Also, care must be taken not to identify child-care concerns as inherently those of women. If motherhood is to become a less exhausting and costly experience for women, policymakers must seriously address child-care issues more as a family's rather than a woman's problem. Third, both mothers and fathers need to be educated about what constitutes high-quality parenting that facilitates healthy child development. In particular, the family life educator can contribute greatly toward improving parenting quality among young mothers. Fourth, research findings that reveal that mothers who physically abuse their children tend to be socially isolated (Smith 1975) suggest that it is important for women to have built-in support networks of families and friends. When these are not available, social service agencies might help create a supportive environment for mothers.

Finally, it must be noted that mothers' roles vary cross-culturally. For example, an important role of mothers in Japan is not only to look after their children's needs but also to transmit the father's authority to the children because of his frequent absence from home due to work demands (Ishii-Kuntz 1993). The findings from cross-cultural research expand understanding of the complexities of motherhood. In studying motherhood, not only should the social and material circumstances in which women give birth to and rear children be examined, but also the cultural beliefs and expectations about reproduction and child rearing must be considered.

(*See also:* Child Care; Dual-Earner Families; Fathers; Gay and Lesbian Parents; Pregnancy and Birth; Single Parents; Stepparenting; Teenage Parenting; Work and Family)

BIBLIOGRAPHY

Acock, A. C.; Barker, D.; and Bengston, V. L. (1982). "Mother's Employment and Parent Youth Similarity." *Journal of Marriage and the Family* 44:441–458.

Baruch, G. K.; Barnett, R.; and Rivers, C. (1983). *Lifeprints: New Patterns of Love and Work for Today's Women.* New York: New American Library.

Bennie, E., and Sclare, A. (1969). "The Battered Child Syndrome." *American Journal of Psychiatry* 125:975–979.

Bianchi, S. M., and Spain, D. (1986). *American Women in Transition.* New York: Russell Sage Foundation.

Bloom-Feshbach, S.; Bloom-Feshbach, J.; and Heller, K. A. (1982). "Work, Family, and Children's Perceptions of the World." In *Families That Work: Children in a Changing World*, ed. S. B. Kamerman and C. D. Hayes. Washington, DC: National Academy Press.

Boulton, M. G. (1983). *On Being a Mother: A Study of Women with Preschool Children.* London: Tavistock.

Callan, V. J. (1987). "The Personal and Marital Adjustment of Mothers and of Voluntarily and Involuntarily Childless Wives." *Journal of Marriage and the Family* 48:847–856.

Chodorow, N., and Contratto, S. (1982). "The Fantasy of the Perfect Mother." In *Rethinking the Family: Some Feminist Questions*, ed. B. Thorne and M. Yalom. New York: Longman.

Clarke-Stewart, K. A. (1978). "And Daddy Makes Three: The Father's Impact on Mother and Young Child." *Child Development* 49:466–478.

Daniels, P., and Weingarten, K. (1988). "The Fatherhood Click: The Timing of Parenthood in Men's Lives." In *Fatherhood Today: Men's Changing Role in the Family*, ed. P. Bronstein and C. P. Cowan. New York: Wiley.

Frankel, S., and Wise, M. (1982). "A View of Delayed Parenting: Some Implications of a New Trend." *Psychiatry* 45:220–225.

Freeman, L. B. (1988). "Working Mothers in Dual-Earner Families: Mother Role Orientation, Coping Strategies, and Strain Between the Maternal and Work Roles." Ph.D. diss. Columbia University.

Hayes, C. D. (1987). *Risking the Future: Adolescent Sexuality, Pregnancy, and Childbearing*, Vol. 1. Washington, DC: National Academy Press.

Hayes, C. D., and Kamerman, S. B., eds. (1983). *Children of Working Parents: Experiences and Outcomes.* Washington, DC: National Academy Press.

Heyns, B., and Catsambis, S. (1986). "Mother's Employment and Children's Achievement: A Critique." *Sociology of Education* 59:140–151.

Hochschild, A. (1989). *The Second Shift.* New York: Avon Books.

Hock, E., and DeMeis, D. K. (1990). "Depression in Mothers of Infants: The Role of Maternal Employment." *Developmental Psychology* 26:285–291.

Hoffman, L. W. (1974). "Effects on Child." In *Working Mothers*, ed. L. W. Hoffman and F. I. Nye. San Francisco: Jossey-Bass.

Hoffman, L. W., and Hoffman, M. (1973). "The Value of Children to Parents." In *Psychological Perspectives of Population*, ed. J. Fawcett. New York: Basic Books.

Hoffman, L. W., and Nye, F. I., eds. (1974). *Working Mothers.* San Francisco: Jossey-Bass.

Ishii-Kuntz, M. (1993). "The Japanese Father: Work Demands and Family Roles." In *Men, Work, and Family*, ed. J. C. Hood. Newbury Park, CA: Sage Publications.

Ishii-Kuntz, M., and Coltrane, S. (1992). "Predicting the Sharing of Household Labor: Are Parenting and Housework Distinct?" *Sociological Perspectives* 35:629–647.

Kivett, V. R. (1988). "Older Rural Fathers and Sons: Patterns of Association and Helping." *Family Relations* 37:62–67.

LaRossa, R., and LaRossa, M. M. (1981). *Transition to Parenthood: How Infants Change Families.* Newbury Park, CA: Sage Publications.

Milne, A. M.; Myers, D. E.; Rosenthal, A. S.; and Ginsburg, A. (1986). "Single Parents, Working Mothers, and the Educational Achievement of School Children." *Sociology of Education* 59:125–139.

Moore, K.; Spain, D.; and Bianchi, S. M. (1984). "The Working Wife and Mother." *Marriage and Family Review* 7:77–98.

Piachaud, D. (1984). *Round About Fifty Hours a Week.* London: Child Poverty Action Group.

Richardson, D. (1993). *Women, Motherhood, and Child Rearing.* New York: St. Martin's Press.

Smith, S. M. (1975). *The Battered Child Syndrome.* London: Butterworth.

Straits, B. C. (1985). "Factors Influencing College Women's Responses to Fertility Decision-Making Vignettes." *Journal of Marriage and the Family* 47:585–596.

Thompson, L., and Walker, A. J. (1989). "Gender in Families." *Journal of Marriage and the Family* 51:845–871.

Thornton, A. (1989). "Changing Attitudes Toward Family Issues in the United States." *Journal of Marriage and the Family* 51:873–893.

U.S. Bureau of the Census. (1978). "Fertility of American Women: June 1978." *Current Population Reports.* P-20, no. 341. Washington, DC: U.S. Government Printing Office.

U.S. Bureau of the Census. (1982). "Fertility of American Women: June 1982." *Current Population Reports.* P-20, no. 387. Washington, DC: U.S. Government Printing Office.

U.S. Bureau of the Census. (1987). "Fertility of American Women: June 1987." *Current Population Reports.* P-20, no. 427. Washington, DC: U.S. Government Printing Office.

Volling, B. L., and Belsky, J. (1993). "Parent, Infant, and Contextual Characteristics Related to Maternal Employment Decisions in the First Year of Infancy." *Family Relations* 42:4–12.

Walters, C. A. (1986). *The Timing of Motherhood.* Lexington, MA: Lexington Books.

Wilkie, J. R. (1987). "Marriage, Family Life, and Women's Employment." In *Women Working*, 2nd edition, ed. A. H. Stromberg and S. Harkess. Mountain View, CA: Mayfield.

MASAKO ISHII-KUNTZ

NAMING

Families in all societies provide personal names for the children born into them. Personal names are cultural universals. By naming children, families are inducting them into the family and the society. Further, they are expressing their hopes and desires for those children in the names they select. Names are messages to children about who they are expected to be, as well as messages to the society at large about just who this child is.

While personal names are universal, the components that make up a personal name and the ways names are bestowed vary widely from society to society. Within American society, there is great variation in how children are named from subgroup to subgroup and from one historical period to the next.

Components of American Personal Names

Most American personal names include a given name, a middle name, a surname, and occasionally a suffix (Jr., II, III, etc.). The idea of given names is much too old to have a discernible origin. In the earliest records of the earliest societies, people were provided given names. It is a reasonable assumption that given names probably date from the origin of language itself; when humans began naming their world, they possibly began with themselves. The American stock of given names, however, does have a distinct history.

American given names can be traced back through early American and British history. According to George Stewart (1979), a small, highly traditional stock of Anglo-Saxon names was dominant in England until the Norman Conquest in 1066. Gradually, over the next century, a traditional stock of Norman names (William, Henry, Richard, Robert; Matilda, Heloise, Emma) became prominent in England. By the late Middle Ages the use of saints' names became popular (John, James, Thomas, Stephen; Mary, Elizabeth, Katherine, Margaret). The name pool was too small to distinguish people adequately, however, and nicknames became a common device for distinguishing people. After the Reformation a new pattern emerged. Women were given names from the New Testament and non-Biblical saints' names, while men were given names from the New Testament and traditional Norman names.

The first immigrants to the southern colonies of America brought their naming practices with them. The Puritan immigrants to New England, however, began going to the Old Testament for names, and the traditional Norman names disappeared for a period. At the same time, interaction with two culturally distinct groups had little effect on American naming practices. Although the white settlers had much interaction with the Indians, they did not adopt Indian names. In addition, African Americans brought to America as slaves were given traditional English names, and their naming patterns remained traditional until the early twentieth century.

During the 1800s, Old Testament names began to drop in popularity and non-Biblical names became more popular. The Norman names, which had lost popularity with Puritanism, returned and new names flourished. Some of these new names were introduced by immigrant groups (German, Scotch-Irish), others were family names used as given names, and still others were coined by using diminutive forms of traditional given names. Increasingly for girls, masculine names were transformed by the addition of feminine suffixes (e.g., Roberta, Michelle). The stock of given names was growing dramatically.

In the twentieth century, this expansion of the stock of given names accelerated. The coinage of names by changing the spelling of traditional names (e.g., Debra), by recombining syllables from traditional names (e. g., Kathann), and by making up completely new names picked up the pace. Given names have become part of the fast-changing world of fashion, exhibiting great turnover from one generation to the next.

Although the origin of surnames is unclear, they also have a long history. According to Christopher Andersen (1977), the ancient Greeks, Hebrews, and Romans had surnames. After the fall of the Roman Empire, however, surnames disappeared until the eleventh century. English surnames did not become common until after the Crusades. By 1465, King Edward IV decreed that the Irish should take and transmit surnames. The possession of a surname came to be seen as a sign of modernization. By the twentieth century colonization had spread the use of surnames to many non-Western nations.

English surnames came from numerous different sources, but most were derived from an individual's occupation (Smith, Baker, Taylor), place of origin or residence (London, Washington), or physical characteristics (White, Brown). In addition, many surnames are converted patronyms created by adding an "s" to the father's name (Abrams, Edwards), or by adding a suffix (Johnson). American surnames are transmitted along the male line, and women usually, at marriage, assume their husband's surname. The trend for some women to retain their own surname after marriage or to hyphenate their surname with their husband's reflects the resurgence of feminism in the 1970s.

Middle names, although they existed earlier in the Chinese and Korean cultures, started to be used in the United States and England at the end of the eighteenth century. By the end of the nineteenth century most Americans were given middle names, and today only 1 percent to 4 percent of American children do not have middle names. Middle names are useful in distinguishing one generation from the next when sons are named after their fathers, and sometimes they preserve a mother's maiden name. Middle names, which served to convey status, first became popular among the upper classes and then were adopted by the general population.

Name Selection

In many societies, there are prescribed systems for selecting children's names. In the United States, systems for selecting names exist for two subgroups, Catholics and Jews. American Catholics are theoretically bound by Canon 761, set forth by Pope Benedict XV in 1917, to choose names for their children from the Church's list of acceptable saints' names. If such names are not selected as first names, then they are supposed to at least be recorded as baptismal names. Increasingly, however, American Catholics are ignoring this prescription.

Jewish parents are expected to name their children after deceased relatives, never living relatives. Like American Catholics, American Jews are increasingly ignoring this prescription, although many Jewish parents do try to give their child a name beginning with the same letter as the name of a deceased relative.

Most Americans are not bound by any naming systems. They are free to select their children's names in whatever manner they choose. They may name a child after a family member, living or dead, and they may bestow this name as either a first or middle name. Two different studies of the sources of given names (Rossi 1965; Alford 1988) have estimated that more than half of all children get at least one name from a relative, although it is more likely to be a middle name than a first name. This pattern of drawing a large percentage of given names from relatives is very old and does not appear to be waning. A small percentage of names (maybe 6 to 10 percent) are taken from people special to the parents (friends or famous people). The remainder of names, more than half of all first names, are chosen on the basis of aesthetic preference, usually from the pool of given names available. A small percentage of parents make up new, unique names for their children by changing the spelling of a traditional name or by recombining name elements.

When parents select names, whether on the basis of preference, taste, honor, or emulation, they typically are unaware of the influences underlying their choice. Research has revealed a number of patterns in name preference that suggest the influences underlying name selection in the United States. The most important variable of all is the sex of the child. Because the American pool of given names is sex-typed, names convey someone's sex more effectively than anything else. That so few Americans have names that are sex-ambiguous (names like Leslie, Lynn, Lee, Robin; 1 percent to 3 percent of men and 5 percent to 7 percent of women) suggests the importance of names conveying sex.

Four generalizations are instructive. First, boys are much more likely to be named after a relative than girls. In turn, girls' names are more often selected for their aesthetic appeal. Second, there is a much larger pool of girls' names than boys' names and girls are less likely to share popular names. Stanley Lieberson and Eleanor Bell (1992) found that 20 percent of all girls born in 1985 in New York had the ten most popular girls' names, while 35 percent of all boys born had the ten most popular boys' names (see Table 1); this was 50 percent or higher in the 1800s. Girls' names change more from generation to generation as well. Preferences in boys' names change much more slowly. Third, girls' and boys' names differ phonetically. Lieberson and Bell found that nearly 34 percent of girls' names ended in a "schwa" sound (Jessica, Sarah), while only 1 percent of boys' names ended with that sound. Some 28 percent of girls' names ended in an "ee" sound (Mary, Amy), but only 10 percent of boys' names ended with that sound. In contrast, boys' names usually end in a consonant. Fourth, many popular girls' names (Danielle, Michelle, Stephanie) are adapted from boys' names, but few if any boy's names are adapted from girls' names.

Alice Rossi (1965), Richard Alford (1988), and Lieberson and Bell (1992) have offered some interpretations of these sex differences. Rossi has suggested that boys more than girls are seen as symbolic carriers of family continuity. Therefore, they are more likely to receive family names. Alford and Lieberson and Bell suggest that girls' names, in contrast, are seen as a form of decoration, verbal jewelry. Since the aesthetics of girls' names is more important, girls' names are more fashionable. An apt analogy can be made between sex differences in clothing and sex differences in names. Clothing variation between men is less than that between women. Further, over time men's fashions change more slowly and less dramatically than women's fashions. This analogy can be extended from names and clothes to American gender roles themselves. It can be argued that female gender roles permit greater variation from woman to woman than male gender roles. So too, female gender roles have changed more over time than male gender roles. Despite these changes, however, two important elements of the female role have always been beauty and fashion, while two important elements of the male role have always been stability and tradition.

Social class, measured either by education or occupation, is the second most important factor after sex in determining name selections. Rex Taylor (1974), Rossi (1965), Alford (1988), and Lieberson and Bell (1992) have all uncovered pronounced class differences in naming. First, parents with higher socioeconomic status (SES) are more likely to select more traditional names than parents of lower SES. Lower SES parents have a greater preference for new and unique names than higher SES parents. Higher SES parents are more likely to give family names (especially the father's and grandfather's) to boys and to give less "feminine" names to girls than lower SES parents. Finally, names that first become popular among higher SES parents gradually trickle down to lower SES parents, evidence of status diffusion.

Table 1 Ten Most Popular Names for Boys and Girls*

Girls	*Percent*	*Boys*	*Percent*
Jennifer	4.2	Michael	5.7
Christine	3.1	Christopher	3.4
Jessica	2.3	John	2.7
Melissa	2.0	David	2.6
Michelle	1.9	Matthew	2.6
Nicole	1.8	Joseph	2.6
Sarah	1.7	Brian	2.6
Lisa	1.3	Jason	2.6
Elizabeth	1.3	Daniel	2.4
Amy	1.3	Robert	2.3

*New York State, 1985.

These class differences have stimulated some interesting interpretations. First, it seems clear that higher-status parents use names as a vehicle to convey status to their children. Status is conveyed in the form of a name of a high-status relative or a traditional, high-status name. Higher-status fathers are especially likely to name their firstborn sons after themselves. For example, Taylor (1974) found that 77 percent of lawyers, 52 percent of doctors, and 23 percent of teachers give their names to their firstborn sons. In addition, high-status parents are more likely to bestow traditional names, especially upon boys. These names connote stability and tradition. Lower-status parents, in contrast, choose a different route to status. By less often using names of relatives, and by rejecting more traditional names for new and more unique names, lower SES parents are expressing their desire for change, and for a new status system.

Name Use in the Family

Within the American family, people tend to use either first names, kin terms (e.g., Dad), or kin terms with first names (e.g., Aunt Sue). Which option is used depends on two general, nonexclusive, dimensions of the relationship: intimacy–distance and person–role. In other words, the choice of a term expresses feelings of intimacy, feelings of social distance, or any point in between the two. The same choice of a term also expresses either the person-to-person quality of a relationship (where role expectations are absent, minimal, or negotiable) or a role-dominated relationship (where role expectations are traditional, constraining, and nonnegotiable).

Americans use kin terms with mothers, fathers, grandparents, and, to a lesser extent, with aunts, uncles, and parents-in-law. However, Americans tend to use personal names with sons, daughters, siblings, cousins, grandchildren, husbands, and wives. Role terms are used almost universally with parents, to emphasize their authority and the importance of the roles they occupy. Role terms or role terms plus first names are used with grandparents and aunts and uncles, not so much to emphasize authority, but to show respect for elder kinsmen.

According to David Schneider and George Homans (1955), Americans have a wide variety of alternative terms available for parents (e.g., "Father," "Pop," "Pa," "Dad," "Daddy," etc.), and the election of one term rather than another varies with the situational context and with the quality of the particular relationship. "Father" suggests greater formality, distance, and respect. "Dad" suggests less formality and distance. Shifts in the use of parental terms as one grows up reflect changes in the quality of the relationship. The continued use of the preferred early childhood terms "Mommy" and "Daddy" suggests a relatively unchanging relationship.

With offspring, siblings, spouses, and grandchildren, Americans tend to use first names. In these cases, the role-governed aspects of the relationship are de-emphasized, while the person-to-person aspects of the relationship are emphasized. The use of first names, or sometimes terms of endearment, suggests an open, intimate relationship in which the parameters of the relationship are open and negotiable. For example, the American practice of calling one's spouse by name, a nickname, or a term of endearment is unusual in cross-cultural perspective. In most societies, spouses use kin terms (e.g., wife). Schneider and Homans (1955) suggest that the American practice reflects a new attitude toward marriage, such that the husband–wife relationship is outside the realm of kinship and centers instead on the unique relationship between marriage partners.

(*See also:* Family Gender Roles; Gender; Gender Identity; Kinship)

BIBLIOGRAPHY

Alford, R. (1988). *Naming and Identity: A Cross-Cultural Study of Personal Naming Practices.* New Haven, CT: HRAF Press.

Andersen, C. P. (1977). *The Name Game.* New York: Jove.

Lieberson, S., and Bell, E. O. (1992). "Children's First Names: An Empirical Study of Social Taste." *American Journal of Sociology* 98:511–554.

Rossi, A. S. (1965). "Naming Children in Middle-Class Families." *American Sociological Review* 30:499–513.

Schneider, D. M., and Homans, G. C. (1955). "Kinship Terminology and the American Kinship System." *American Anthropologist* 57:1194–1208.

Stewart, G. R. (1979). *American Given Names.* New York: Oxford University Press.

Taylor, R. (1974). "John Doe, Jr.: A Study of His Distribution in Space, Time, and the Social Structure." *Social Forces* 53:11–21.

Richard Alford

NONMARITAL PREGNANCY

Increasing numbers of births to unmarried mothers began to be a major concern in the United States in the late 1960s. There were about 224,000 children born in 1960 to unmarried mothers (Furstenberg 1991), but by 1991 that number had risen to more than 1.2 million (Ventura and Martin 1993). Births to unmarried women increased from 5.3 percent of all births in 1960 to nearly 30 percent of all births in 1991. It has been suggested that the United States is following a pattern established in Sweden, where more than half of all births in 1989 were nonmarital (Burns and Scott 1994).

Childbearing Trends

Nonmarital births are of two basic types. Some, especially among those who are younger, are to women who have never been married. The second category includes childbearing among women who were previously married, but who were divorced or widowed at the time of the birth. Unwed parenthood became a more visible issue among young, never-married women when the large number of teenagers born during the "baby boom" of the 1940s and 1950s started having babies themselves. Traditionally, most teenage girls who became pregnant were married by the time the child was born. This began to change during the 1960s, when fewer pregnant young women married prior to giving birth. Between 1960 and 1975, the total birthrate for teenage women decreased by nearly one-third, but the birthrate for *unmarried* teenage women increased by more than 50 percent

(Furstenberg 1991). Even though fewer teenagers per 1,000 were getting pregnant, the larger size of the teenage population, and especially the declining rates of marriage among expectant teenagers, resulted in a massive increase in nonmarital teenage births. By the mid-1980s, it was reported that, among all developed societies, the United States had the highest rates of teenage pregnancy, abortion, and births (Jones et al. 1985).

About one-third of all nonmarital births are to teenage mothers, but teenagers are not the only group with increasing out-of-wedlock births. Between 1960 and 1988, the number of births to unwed mothers twenty years old and older jumped more than fivefold from 132,200 to 683,000 (Furstenberg 1991). Larry Bumpass and Sara McLanahan (1989) point out that a major factor in the increased number of such births is that the stigma traditionally attached to unwed motherhood has lessened for two reasons. First, because divorce is so common, a marriage no longer guarantees that a husband will be present to help raise the child anyway. Second, while nonmarital pregnancy is still proof of sexual intercourse outside marriage, it is now recognized that most adults experience premarital intercourse; this recognition has weakened public disapproval of nonmarital pregnancy.

While most nonmarital pregnancies are unintended, an increasing number are intentional. Some couples who live together without being married decide to have children. Many of these cohabiting couples raise their offspring together and share responsibilities as if they were married. Some single women desire children but have no wish to be married. It also has been asserted, based on anecdotal evidence, that some young girls get pregnant as a means to escape from poor or abusive families.

Vital Statistics

The number of nonmarital births in the United States rose from 665,747 in 1980 to 1,213,796 in 1991, an increase of 82 percent over eleven years. In 1991, 29.5 percent of all births were to unmarried women. Only about half of these nonmarital births were first births for the mothers. In 1984, 41 percent of white nonmarital births and 53 percent of African-American nonmarital births were at least the mother's second child (Bumpass and McLanahan 1989).

The percentage of births to unmarried mothers varies significantly by race and cultural heritage. Although racial differences have narrowed, the rate of nonmarital births was still 2.5 times higher for African-American women than white women in 1993. For African-American teenagers, the rate was 3.7 times higher than for their white counterparts. Of all mothers eighteen to forty-four years old who gave birth in 1991, 16.9 percent of white mothers were single, 27.0 percent of Hispanic mothers were single, and 66.7 percent of African-American mothers were single (Ventura and Martin 1993).

In 1992, 65.3 percent of all births to adolescents fifteen to nineteen years of age were to unmarried mothers. Among white mothers in that age group, 55.7 percent were nonmarital births, while the rate for Hispanic adolescent mothers was 59.7 percent and that for African-American adolescent mothers was 93.8 percent (Bachu 1992). For all ethnicities, the likelihood of the mother being married increased with age at time of birth. Among women thirty to forty-four years of age, 9 percent of white mothers, 18.2 percent of Hispanic mothers, and 48.8 percent of African-American mothers were unmarried at the time of the birth.

Of all never-married women in the United States who had borne a child in 1982, about one-third had less than a high school education. By 1992, that proportion had increased to one-half. The proportion of women with one or more years of college who had borne a child out of wedlock almost doubled between 1982 and 1992. About 43 percent of all never-married mothers who gave birth in 1992 were in the labor force during that year. That percentage has remained fairly stable since 1982 (Bachu 1992).

Risk Factors

Since the late 1960s, the average age of first sexual intercourse has decreased and the age of marriage has increased. Increasing rates of sexual intercourse and declining rates of marriage are the two most important proximate determinants of nonmarital childbearing (Nathanson and Kim 1989). As the gap between the age of first intercourse and age of first marriage widens, the window or risk for pre- or nonmarital pregnancy grows. Barbara Mensch and Denise Kandel (1992) reported that nearly one-third of the sexually active white teenage girls in their nationwide study experienced premarital pregnancy by the age of nineteen.

Nonuse, or inconsistent use, of contraception is also a major risk factor in unplanned pregnancy. Mensch and Kandel (1992) found that the risk of pregnancy increased by a factor of seven for adolescents who do not use contraception. At first sexual intercourse, about 35 percent of adolescents used no method of contraception in 1988 (Mosher and Mc-

Nally 1991), and among sexually active adolescents, about 20 percent say that they never used contraception. Nonuse and inconsistent use of contraception probably characterize at least one-third of sexually active adolescents in the United States, leading to about 11 percent of adolescent females becoming pregnant each year (Miller and Moore 1990). Contraceptive use differs greatly by age and marital status. Young unmarried women who are sexually active most often use the pill or their partners use condoms. Most married women also use the pill when they are young, but past age thirty, female and male sterilization become the major means of preventing conception. Sterilization and the birth control pill are also the predominant means of contraception among formerly married women (Mosher 1990).

Research conducted by Mensch and Kandel (1992) discovered several other factors that predicted premarital pregnancy among their sample. In addition to lack of contraception and illicit drug use, they found that a lower level of educational attainment by a woman's parents, living in a nonintact household at age fourteen, low personal educational expectations, being stopped by police, and younger age of first menstruation increased the risk of premarital pregnancy. Bumpass and McLanahan (1989) also found that the risk of premarital birth was substantially reduced by having grown up in an intact family and by the woman's parents having completed high school. The daughter of a teenage mother is more likely to become pregnant herself while a teenager than the daughter of an older mother (Furstenberg, Levine, and Brooks-Gunn 1990).

Robert Plotnick and Sandra Butler (1991) reported that girls with higher self-esteem are less likely to become unwed mothers than girls with lower self-esteem. They also found that the likelihood of nonmarital childbearing decreases for girls who have nontraditional views on family and gender roles, higher education expectations, and stronger commitment to employment.

Social economic status (SES) plays an important role in determining who will or will not become pregnant outside of marriage. Rates of nonmarital pregnancy are only slightly higher for African Americans than for poor whites, indicating that both SES level and ethnicity influence nonmarital childbearing (Vinovskis 1988). Among unmarried women past the age of twenty, birthrates decrease as educational attainment increases (Lewis and Ventura 1990). John Billy and David Moore (1992) found that the educational level of non-African-American mothers of unmarried daughters played a significant role in the childbearing of the daughters. The higher the educational attainment of the mother, the lower the risk of nonmarital birth for the daughter.

Alternative Pregnancy Outcomes

There are a number of possible outcomes for any pregnancy. During 1988, more than 13 percent of all pregnancies resulted in spontaneous fetal losses or miscarriages. Some other alternative pregnancy outcomes are under the control of the pregnant woman (Miller 1993). First, she can decide whether to carry the baby to term and give birth or have the pregnancy terminated. Of all abortions in the United States, 75 percent are performed on unmarried women (Sachdev 1993). During 1988, about 40 percent of pregnancies among women aged fifteen to nineteen were terminated by abortion (Ventura et al. 1992). Women who are white, better educated, have a relatively high income, live in the Northeastern or Western United States, and are either in school or working are more likely to have abortions. The availability of Medicaid funding increases the chance of a low-income woman terminating her pregnancy. Membership in a particular church does not appear to affect the decision to have an abortion, but the higher the degree of personal religiosity, the less likely the mother is to choose the abortion (Stevans, Register, and Sessions 1992).

Less than 50 percent of all teenage pregnancies result in a live birth. If an unmarried woman decides to have the baby, she must then determine who will raise the child. One historically common option was to get married to legitimize the birth. As social attitudes toward unwed mothers have become more permissive, fewer pregnant women have married. Another option is to allow the child to be adopted. Adoption was chosen by more than one-third of unmarried white mothers during the mid-1960s, but only about 2 percent of unwed mothers choose adoption in the 1990s (Bachrach, Stolley, and London 1992). A 1992 study reported significant short-term differences between unwed adolescent mothers who place their babies for adoption and those who do not. Those who placed their children were less satisfied with their decision six months later than those who chose to raise their babies. On the other hand, those who placed babies for adoption were more likely to have higher educational aspirations and to remain in school. They also were less likely to be on public assistance or to be married at a younger age than their counterparts who were raising their babies (Kalmuss, Namerow, and Bauer 1992).

Young women who do not chose abortion, marriage, or adoption must parent the baby themselves. In these cases, the child is usually reared by the mother and/or her family. These choices are often influenced by the relationship between the baby's father and mother. A financial contribution by the father may pay for an abortion, or a commitment of child support may encourage the unmarried mother to give birth. The choice of adoption requires the father's written endorsement in most states. Neil Cervera (1991) reviewed studies of unwed fathers' participation in the childbearing and child-rearing process and concluded that fathers' involvement can reinforce the mother's self-worth, her sense of competency as a mother, and her attachment to the baby. Additionally, children with whom the father was involved have better social and cognitive skills.

Consequences of Nonmarital Childbirth

Many of the social, economic, and developmental consequences of nonmarital childbearing are shouldered by unmarried women and their children. It has been widely accepted that having children at an early age places both the parents and children at long-term social and economic disadvantage (Hayes 1987). Research in the 1970s and 1980s supported the notion that early parenthood resulted in the interruption of schooling, larger family sizes, and lower occupational attainment. Teen mothers are less likely to marry or remain married, and partners of teen mothers have less ability to pay child support than those of older mothers (Miller 1992). All of these factors contribute to lower standards of living for the whole family, but are felt most strongly by women who are single heads of household.

Other researchers suggest that because adolescent premarital childbearing occurs most frequently in disadvantaged, impoverished, and minority populations, the consequences for the mother may not be as dramatic as they first appear. Arline Geronimus (1991, 1992) proposed that teenage childbearing may in fact be an adaptive response to poverty. In general, adolescents from such backgrounds are less likely to gain an education, receive adequate medical care, accumulate wealth, or achieve improved social position. Geronimus suggests that the advantages of giving birth at a young age, such as increased participation by and care from extended family members, might outweigh social or economic disadvantages for impoverished mothers and children.

It has been proposed that economic factors contribute to the number of women who decide to have children out of wedlock. According to this theory, welfare programs make single parenthood economically viable and even economically attractive to those who live in poverty. In a study of African-American women, Greg Duncan and Saul Hoffman (1990) found little evidence to support the hypothesis that welfare promotes out-of-wedlock births. They did find, however, that women who became pregnant and gave birth during their teen years were those who had the least to lose economically.

Children born to adolescent mothers may also suffer some long-term disadvantages. From a study that began in 1976 with a predominantly African-American sample, Frank Furstenberg and his colleagues (1987) concluded that children of adolescent mothers do less well both cognitively and socially by the time they reach school. In 1984, when these same children were in their late teens, 39 percent had been separated from their mothers for a period of two months or more while growing up. While most of the mothers in the study had intended to raise their children, nearly 40 percent reported that they were not the primary caregiver. At least half of the children had repeated at least one grade in school, and a third reported behavioral problems in high school. Alcohol and drug use among these children was higher than among children born to older parents, and they were also likely to begin having sexual intercourse earlier (Furstenberg, Brooks-Gunn, and Morgan 1987).

Less research has been done about the effect of nonmarital parenting on fathers. Furstenberg (1991) reports that while unwed fathers may play an important role in their children's early life, the strength of these early bonds tends to weaken with time. When continuous contact was maintained with their noncustodial fathers, children in single-mother homes developed better both intellectually and emotionally. By the time the children were adolescents, however, few regularly saw their fathers or received support from them (Furstenberg, Brooks-Gunn, and Morgan 1987).

In addition to the parents and the child, the extended family is also affected by nonmarital births among adolescents. This is especially true for the mother's family of origin, which often assumes responsibility for additional expenses related to pregnancy and childbirth. The burden of child rearing often falls to the child's grandmother(s) or other relatives, most often in the mother's family of origin.

(*See also:* Abortion: Medical and Social Aspects; Adolescent Sexuality; Adoption; Birth Control: Contraceptive Methods; Demography; Pregnancy and Birth; Single Parents; Teenage Parenting)

BIBLIOGRAPHY

Bachrach, C. A.; Stolley, K. S.; and London, K. A. (1992). "Relinquishment of Premarital Births: Evidence from a National Survey." *Family Planning Perspectives* 24:27–32.

Bachu, A. (1992). *Fertility of American Women: June 1992.* Washington, DC: U.S. Department of Commerce.

Billy, J. O. G., and Moore, D. E. (1992). "A Multilevel Analysis of Marital and Nonmarital Fertility in the U.S." *Social Forces* 70:977–1011.

Bumpass, L., and McLanahan, S. (1989). "Unmarried Motherhood: Recent Trends, Composition, and Black–White Differences." *Demography* 26:279–286.

Burns, A., and Scott, C. (1994). *Mother-Headed Families and Why They Have Increased.* Hillsdale, NJ: Lawrence Erlbaum.

Cervera, N. (1991). "Unwed Teenage Pregnancy: Family Relationships with the Father of the Baby." *Families in Society: The Journal of Contemporary Human Services* 1991:29–37.

Duncan, G. J., and Hoffman, S. D. (1990). "Welfare Benefits, Economic Opportunities, and Out-of-Wedlock Births Among Black Teenage Girls." *Demography* 27:519–535.

Furstenberg, F. F., Jr. (1976). *Unplanned Parenthood.* New York: Cambridge University Press.

Furstenberg, F. F., Jr. (1991). "As the Pendulum Swings: Teenage Childbearing and Social Concern." *Family Relations* 40:127–138.

Furstenberg, F. F., Jr.; Brooks-Gunn, J.; and Morgan, S. P. (1987). *Adolescent Mothers in Later Life.* New York: Cambridge University Press.

Furstenberg, F. F., Jr.; Levin, J. A.; and Brooks-Gunn, J. (1990). "The Children of Teenage Mothers: Patterns of Early Childbearing in Two Generations." *Family Planning Perspectives* 22:54–61.

Geronimus, A. T. (1991). "Teenage Childbearing and Social and Reproductive Disadvantage: The Evolution of Complex Questions and the Demise of Simple Answers." *Family Relations* 40:463–471.

Geronimus, A. T. (1992). "Teenage Childbearing and Social Disadvantage: Unprotected Discourse." *Family Relations* 1992:244–248

Hayes, C. D., ed. (1987). *Risking the Future: Adolescent Sexuality, Pregnancy, and Childbearing*, Vol. 1. Washington, DC: National Academy Press.

Jones, E.; Forrest, J.; Goldman, N.; Henshaw, S.; Lincoln, J.; Westoff, C.; and Wulf, D. (1985). "Teenage Pregnancy in Developed Countries: Determinants and Policy Implications." *Family Planning Perspectives* 17:53–63.

Kalmuss, D.; Namerow, P. B.; and Bauer, U. (1992). "Short-Term Consequences of Parenting Versus Adoption Among Young Unmarried Women." *Journal of Marriage and the Family* 54:80–90.

Lewis, C., and Ventura, S. (1990). "Birth and Fertility Rates by Education: 1980 and 1985." *Vital and Health Statistics.* Series 21, no. 49. Hyattsville, MD: National Center for Health Statistics.

Mensch, B., and Kandel, D. B. (1992). "Drug Use as a Risk Factor for Premarital Teen Pregnancy and Abortion in a National Sample of Young White Women." *Demography* 29:409–429.

Miller, B. C. (1993). "Families, Science, and Values: Alternative Views of Parenting Effects and Adolescent Pregnancy." *Journal of Marriage and the Family* 55: 7–21.

Miller, B. C. (1992). "Adolescent Parenthood, Economic Issues, and Social Policies." *Journal of Family and Economic Issues* 13:467–475.

Miller, B. C., and Moore, K. A. (1990). "Adolescent Sexual Behavior, Pregnancy, and Parenting: Research Through the 1980s." *Journal of Marriage and the Family* 52:1025–1044.

Mosher, W. D., and McNally, J. W. (1991). "Contraceptive Use at First Sexual Intercourse: United States 1965–1988." *Family Planning Perspectives* 23:108–116.

Mosher, W. D. (1990). "Contraceptive Practice in the United States, 1982–1988." *Family Planning Perspectives* 22:199–205.

Nathanson, C. A., and Kim, Y. J. (1989). "Components of Change in Adolescent Fertility, 1971–1979." *Demography* 26:85–98.

Plotnick, R. D., and Butler, S. S. (1991). "Attitudes and Adolescent Nonmarital Childbearing: Evidence from the National Longitudinal Survey of Youth." *Journal of Adolescent Research* 6:470–492.

Sachdev, P. (1993). *Sex, Abortion, and Unmarried Women.* Westport, CT: Greenwood Press.

Stevans, L. K.; Register, C. A.; and Sessions, D. N. (1992). "The Abortion Decision: A Qualitative Approach." *Social Indicators Research* 27:327–344.

Ventura, S. J., and Martin, J. (1993). Advance Report of Final Natality Statistics, 1991." *Monthly Vital Statistics Report from the Centers for Disease Control* 42(3):1–48.

Ventura, S. J.; Taffel, S. M.; Mosher, W. D.; and Henshaw, S. (1992). "Trends in Pregnancies and Pregnancy Rates, United States, 1980–88." *Monthly Vital Statistics Report from the Centers for Disease Control* 41:1–12.

Vinovskis, M. (1988). *An "Epidemic" of Adolescent Pregnancy? Some Historical and Policy Considerations.* New York: Oxford University Press.

Brent C. Miller
Thom Curtis

NUCLEAR FAMILY

The term "nuclear family" can be defined simply as a wife/mother, a husband/father, and their children. However, this straightforward structural definition is surrounded by a cloud of ambiguity and controversy. Most of the debates have centered around three questions. First, is the nuclear family universal—found in every known human society? Second, is the nuclear group the essential form of family—the only one that can carry out the vital functions of the family (especially, rearing the next generation) or can other family patterns (e.g., single mothers, single fathers, two women, or two men) be considered workable units for fulfilling these functions? The third issue concerns the link between the nuclear family household and industrial society. In the old days, before work moved outside the home to factories and offices, did parents and children live together under one roof with grandparents and other relatives? Did the nuclear family break away from this extended family system as a result of industrialization?

The debate over the universality and necessity of the nuclear family began in the early twentieth century. Pioneer anthropologist Bronislaw Malinowski (1913) stated that the nuclear family had to be universal because it filled a basic biological need—caring for and protecting infants and young children. No culture could survive, he asserted, unless the birth of children was linked to both mother and father in legally based parenthood. Anthropologist George P. Murdock (1949) elaborated on the idea that the nuclear family is both universal and essential: "Whether as the sole prevailing form of the family . . . or as the basic unit from which more complex families form, [the nuclear family] exists as a distinct and strongly functional group in every known society" (p. 2).

The debate about the nuclear family and industrialism centered around the writings of one of the leading sociologists of the post–World War II era, Talcott Parsons (1955). The nuclear unit, he argued, fits the needs of industrial society. Independent of the kin network, the "isolated" nuclear family is free to move as the economy demands. Further, the intimate nuclear family can specialize in serving the emotional needs of adults and children in a competitive and impersonal world.

In more recent years, the assumptions about the family held by Malinowski, Murdock, and Parsons have been challenged by family sociologists as well as by anthropologists, historians, feminist scholars, and others. Research in these fields has emphasized the diversity of family not only across cultures and eras but also within any culture or historical period.

Anthropologists have pointed out that many languages lack a word for the parent–child domestic units known as "families" in English. For example, the Zinacantecos of southern Mexico identify the basic social unit as a "house," which may include one to twenty people (Vogt 1969). In contrast, historical studies of Western family life have shown that nuclear family households were extremely common as far back as historical evidence can reach, particularly in northwestern Europe—England, Holland, Belgium, and northern France (Gottlieb 1993). These countries have long held the norm that a newly married couple moves out of their parents' homes and sets up their own household. Despite the continuity of form, however, different social classes, ethnic groups, religious persuasions, and geographical regions have had different practices and beliefs with regard to parent–child relations, sexuality, family gender roles, and other aspects of family life.

Family life also has changed in response to social, economic, and political change. Many scholars believe that in the eighteenth century and the early nineteenth century, the modernizing countries of Western Europe witnessed a transformation of family feeling that resulted in "the closed domesticated nuclear family." The new family ideal, Lawrence Stone (1977) argued, prescribed domestic privacy and strong emotional attachments between spouses and between parents and children. On the other hand, some scholars have argued that strong emotional bonds between family members have existed for centuries, and others have argued that the "closed domesticated nuclear family" was a middle-class ideal that came to be applied slowly and incompletely outside that class. In Eastern Europe, however, the nuclear norm did not prevail. Households were expected to contain other relatives besides the nuclear unit (i.e., a third generation or a parent's sibling and possibly that person's spouse and children). It is true that in those parts of Europe about half of the households at any particular time were nuclear, but this unit served as just a stage the family might pass through.

As these examples show, it is important to distinguish between the nuclear family as a cultural symbol and as an observable domestic group (Schneider 1968). The nuclear family is a symbol deeply rooted in Western culture; it is represented in art, family photographs, advertising, and television. However, the family ideal of any particular culture does not necessarily describe the social realities of family life. For example, the nuclear family remains the preferred cultural pattern in the United States despite the fact that the proportion of nuclear family households is smaller than in the past (Skolnick 1991). The persistence of this ideal is reflected in the fact that most divorced people remarry. Further, there is no evidence that most single mothers prefer to raise their children by themselves. In most Western nations, particularly the United States, the wish to become a parent at some time in one's life is virtually universal. Today's longevity means that the parent–child relationship can last fifty years or more. It remains a central attachment in most people's lives.

In any particular time and place, families have always been more varied than the prevailing image of what the ideal family should be. However, although family types are even more diverse than in the past, most contemporary families are still variations on the traditional nuclear family pattern (e.g., the two-job family, the empty nest couple with grown children, or the blended family). An unsettled period of family transition has resulted from major shifts in economic, demographic, political, and cultural trends in the industrialized world and beyond. These changes have altered people's lives dramatically, but other institutions of society—government, business, religion—have not yet caught up with the new realities.

The traditional Western concept of the nuclear family as the only normal, natural family has had a profound influence on research, therapy, and public policy. It has encouraged the tendency to define any departure from that arrangement as unhealthy or immoral. This concentration on a single, universally accepted pattern has blinded students of behavior to historical precedents for multiple legitimate family arrangements.

(*See also:* Extended Family; Fictive Kinship; History of the Family; Kinship; Polyandry; Polygyny)

BIBLIOGRAPHY

Gottlieb, B. (1993). *The Family in the Western World.* New York: Oxford.

Malinowski, B. (1913). *The Family Among the Australian Aborigines.* London: University of London Press.

Murdock, G. P. (1949). *Social Structure.* New York: Macmillan.

Parsons, T. (1955). "The American Family: Its Relations to Personality and the Social Structure." In *Family Socialization and Interaction Process*, ed. T. Parsons and R. F. Bales. New York: Free Press.

Schneider, D. M. (1968). *American Kinship: A Cultural Account.* Englewood Cliffs, NJ: Prentice Hall.

Schneider, D. M., and Smith, R. T. (1973). *Class Differences and Sex Roles in American Kinship and Family Structure.* Englewood Cliffs, NJ: Prentice Hall.

Skolnick, A. (1991). *Embattled Paradise: The American Family in an Age of Uncertainty.* New York: Basic Books.

Stone, L. (1977). *The Family, Sex, and Marriage in England, 1500–1800.* New York: Harper & Row.

Vogt, E. Z. (1969). *Zinacantan: A Maya Community in the Highlands of Chiapas.* Cambridge, MA: Harvard University Press.

Arlene Skolnick

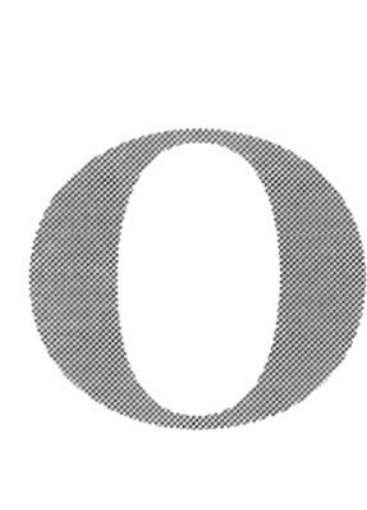

OLD AGE *See* Elder Abuse; Elders; Grandparenthood; Later-Life Families; Retirement; Widowhood

ONLY CHILD

Only children are people who grow up without siblings. They have been stereotyped as "selfish, lonely, and maladjusted." Early in the twentieth century, the emerging discipline of psychology portrayed only children as inevitably pathological. However, since that time, hundreds of studies about only children have been conducted, and the overall conclusion is that only children are no more selfish, lonely, or maladjusted than people who grow up with siblings. Thus, the maturing discipline of psychology no longer views only children as inevitably pathological (Falbo and Poston 1993).

The highest percentage of one-child families in the United States can be found among families formed during the Great Depression. Among white women who began their families during this period, as many as 25 percent had only one child. Immediately after World War II, the average rose to four children per couple. This so-called Baby Boom ended in the late 1960s, and the one-child family gradually became more common again, especially among single-parent families (Falbo 1984).

Researchers have evaluated only children in terms of five main developmental outcomes: intelligence, achievement, personality, sociability, and psychological adjustment. Intelligence (usually measured in terms of standardized ability tests, such as IQ tests) and achievement (measured typically in terms of the number of years of education attained or the prestige of occupations) are the two most commonly studied outcomes. Only children generally score slightly better than others on intelligence when they are young. However, during adolescence, the small advantage in intelligence disappears (Falbo and Polit 1986). On the other hand, only children appear to have and maintain an advantage in achievement. Even when the socioeconomic characteristics of their parents are controlled, analyses indicate that only children tend to complete more years of education than others and are likely to have more prestigious jobs (Blake 1989).

One of the concerns about only children is that their lack of sibling relationships might lead them to have less desirable personalities than those who grew up with siblings. However, the results of hundreds of personality studies suggest that only children are generally like children with siblings in most personality dimensions, including autonomy, generosity, and cooperativeness (Polit and Falbo 1987).

Research into the sociability of only children has yielded mixed results (Falbo and Polit 1986). Although a few large, longitudinal studies suggest that children without siblings may be prone to more solitary recreational activities than children with siblings (Claudy 1984), other studies indicate that only children marry at about the same age as others and are no more likely to divorce (Groat, Wicks, and Neal 1984).

Many studies have also examined the psychological adjustment of only children, typically basing assessments on omnibus adjustment inventories, such as the Junior Eysenck Personality Inventory. Taken as a whole, these studies indicate that only children tend to score much like people with siblings. A few studies have reported that many only children receive services at psychological clinics; however, this type of finding should not be construed to mean that only children are more likely to be maladjusted. Instead, the most plausible interpretation is that the parents of only children are more likely to get services for their children when they need them than are other parents (Falbo and Polit 1986).

In 1979, the People's Republic of China initiated policies that were designed to promote the number of one-child families. These policies were most successful among urban families. In the late 1980s and 1990s, one-child families predominated in urban China. During this time, more than 90 percent of the students in urban elementary schools were only children (Falbo and Poston 1993). Soon after the one-child policy began, Americans and some Chinese predicted that China would become a country filled with "little emperors," Chinese slang for spoiled brats.

Many studies have been done in China about the characteristics of only children to determine if, indeed, they are "little emperors." However, these studies have, in turn, found that only children are similar to, inferior to, and superior to other children (Falbo and Poston 1993). Given the mix of these results, the consequences of the one-child policy on the development of children will likely remain a controversial subject.

(*See also:* CHILDHOOD; PERSONALITY DEVELOPMENT; SIBLING RELATIONSHIPS)

BIBLIOGRAPHY

Blake, J. (1989). *Family Size and Achievement.* Berkeley: University of California Press.

Claudy, J. G. (1984). "The Only Child as a Young Adult: Results from Project Talent." In *The Single-Child Family,* ed. T. Falbo. New York: Guilford.

Falbo, T. (1984). "Only Children: A Review." In *The Single-Child Family,* ed. T. Falbo. New York: Guilford.

Falbo, T., and Polit, D. F. (1986). "A Quantitative Review of the Only Child Literature: Research Evidence and Theory Development." *Psychological Bulletin* 100:176–189.

Falbo, T., and Poston, D. L. (1993). "The Academic, Personality, and Physical Outcomes of Only Children in China." *Child Development* 64:18–35.

Groat, H. T.; Wicks, J. W.; and Neal, A. G. (1984). "Without Siblings: The Consequences in Adult Life of Having Been an Only Child." In *The Single-Child Family,* ed. T. Falbo. New York: Guilford.

Polit, D. F., and Falbo, T. (1987). "Only Children and Personality Development: A Quantitative Review." *Journal of Marriage and the Family* 49:309–325.

TONI FALBO

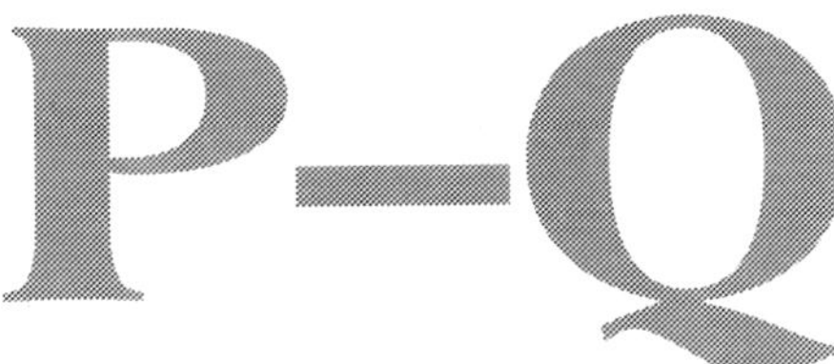

P–Q

PARENT–CHILD RELATIONS *See*

FILIAL RESPONSIBILITY; INTERGENERATIONAL RELATIONS

PARENT EDUCATION

Parent education may be defined as any deliberate effort to help parents be more effective in caregiving for their children. There are many different processes for educating parents, including group meetings, resource centers, newsletters, radio programs, home visits, mentoring, support groups, books, and other media. The contents of these different programs vary substantially, ranging from behavior-management approaches to relationship-enhancement approaches. What the programs have in common is the conviction that parents play a vital role in the development of children and that it is possible to help parents be more effective through training and education.

Social work professionals may call their parent education "parent support" because of the emphasis on helping parents connect with people, information, and resources that will help them be more effective. School professionals including teachers, administrators, and counselors commonly engage in parent education, which they often consider a part of the broader efforts for parent involvement. This approach is based on the premise that more effective parenting will result in more productive students. PTA meetings, newsletters, parent–teacher conferences, and volunteering in the school are some of the methods schools use to foster parent involvement.

There is a growing awareness in society that many social problems are the result of inadequate parenting and that parents are not automatically equipped to deal with the challenges of child rearing. In addition, many social changes are seen as putting additional pressures on families and limiting their supportive connections with family members and others. For example, the increased number of mothers working outside the home, increased rates of divorce, and greater distances from extended family may all make the job of parenting more challenging.

Content of Parent Education

There are many different approaches to parent education, each with different assumptions about the nature of humans and the process of change. Advice to parents given centuries ago emphasized teaching the child to submit to the parents. With the growth of serious research on child development in the twentieth century, the definition of effective parenting has changed dramatically. Since the 1930s, there has been a consistent recognition of the importance of loving, supportive behavior by parents. It has been less clear how much control parents should exercise. At times experts have recommended a very nonrestricting role for parents. Research suggests that some control is necessary, but the kind of control and not just the amount is very important for effective parenting.

Research on parenting behavior shows that parents who are supportive and use helpful discipline are more likely to have children who are socially competent. Social competence includes confidence, independence, responsibility, and achievement. Low levels of parental support are related to low self-esteem, deviance, and risk-taking behaviors. The vital role of parental support is well established.

In research on parenting behavior, discipline has commonly been divided into three kinds. The first kind of discipline is the use of power by parents. Such techniques, in which parents attempt to force or pressure their children to behave in certain ways, are associated with children who are less competent socially. A second kind of discipline is love withdrawal, in which parents show disapproval for behavior that displeases them. It may include ignoring or isolating the child. The use of love withdrawal shows mixed results in its effects on children; some studies found it to be acceptable, while other studies found it resulted in dependent or depressed children. The third type of discipline is called induction. Induction includes reasoning with children and helping them understand the effects of their behavior. Induction is the kind of discipline that is most likely to result in socially competent children.

Each parenting program has a different emphasis. For example, Rudolf Dreikurs (1964) stressed meeting the needs of children, a democratic family, and avoiding power struggles. Thomas Gordon (1970) emphasized the importance of appropriate communication and of allowing children to make their own decisions. Haim Ginott (1965) underscored understanding and respect for the child. A more recent and controversial program developed by Lee Canter and Marlene Canter (1985) has stressed control of behavior.

The content of many parent education programs remains very similar to the roots of the programs in the 1960s. They are largely based on their authors' assumptions about human nature and good-sense recommendations for more effective parenting. Many of the commercial programs have not yet applied more recent research to their curricula. For instance, there is new research on the unique contribution of fathers in a child's development. There is also renewed interest in the role of parental cognitions, including beliefs and attitudes, and their effect on parenting behavior and child outcomes. However, many new findings are often neglected in popular parenting programs.

Many child-rearing issues remain subjects of debate. For example, Sandra Scarr (1992) has suggested that children are born with strong adaptive capacities; if parents provide many opportunities and a good enough environment, children will develop into healthy, capable adults. Some scholars have responded to her statements with a concern that parents need to be intimately involved with their children in order to facilitate their development. This controversy is really just another form of the longstanding nature–nurture debate.

The content of a program should allow for the different needs of different parents. Some of the needs of limited-resource teenage mothers of infants will be very different from the needs of middle-aged parents of teens. Information on feeding, changing diapers, dealing with sickness, and using community resources will be vital for parents of newborns; parents of teens are more likely to be interested in communication, limit setting, and problem solving.

Some scholars encourage parents to select the program that best fits their distinctive needs and values. When parents participate actively in the process of parent education, including the choice of program, they are more likely to be invested in the outcome. In addition, when parents are involved in a program that has assumptions congruent with their own attitudes, the education is likely to be more effective (though there is always a place for checking assumptions and trying new perspectives).

To discuss the content of parenting programs in more detail, it is necessary to divide them into two broad categories: behavior-management approaches and relationship-enhancement approaches.

Behavior-management approaches. Based in social learning theory, these approaches use behavior modification, including reinforcement, punishment, modeling, and contingency. Reinforcers may be material or social rewards. Reinforcers are provided contingent upon appropriate behavior. Punishment, in the form of withheld social attention (e.g., a time-out period) or other reinforcers, is provided in response to inappropriate behavior. The goal is to eventually reduce the frequency of rewards provided so that appropriate behavior will produce its own natural rewards and become internalized.

Gerald R. Patterson (1975), a leader in social learning approaches, asserts that children naturally produce certain undesirable behaviors, which are reinforced when they attract parental attention. Nagging by parents may teach children that they only get attention when they misbehave. It is easy for parents and children to get caught in a destructive cycle: The parents try to control the child; the child resists; the parents become more aversive; the child becomes more resistant or rebellious. Behavior-management approaches attempt to break this cycle with sensible behavior-management tools.

In behavior-management programs, parents commonly target two or three problem behaviors in their children and are taught to reinforce appropriate behavior and to ignore or punish targeted behavior. Parents learn, usually through play sessions, to recognize, acknowledge, and reward appropriate child behavior. Parents receive immediate feedback from trainers. They also learn to communicate clear instructions and to reward the child or give "time-out," depending on child compliance. Evaluation of effectiveness, usually based on parent report or observation of child behavior, generally supports a decrease in targeted problem behaviors.

Behavior modification is accepted as an effective method for controlling specific problem behaviors. Some form of behavior modification is present in most parent education programs. Due in part to its relatively quick results, its systematic focus on changing behavior, and the relative ease with which researchers can evaluate its effects, behavior modification has been a credible model in parent education since the early 1970s. However, the behavioral approaches have also drawn substantial criticism. Some people fault such approaches for making the parent the source of authority: Parents define desirable behavior and manipulate children's experience to assure certain outcomes. Such approaches may not encourage mature autonomy and decision making in children. There are additional problems. Some learning approaches have ignored developmental processes. Sometimes behavior control developed at home does not transfer to other settings or behaviors, and parents may feel burdened with their substantial responsibility in monitoring child behavior.

Because of their ability to manage specific behaviors, behavior-management approaches are likely to have some role in effective parent education, but they may be most effective when combined with relationship-enhancement approaches.

Relationship-enhancement approaches. In contrast to behavior-modification programs, relationship-enhancement approaches place more emphasis on relationship quality and the emotional needs of the parents and their children. Such approaches teach parents to develop an accepting, supportive atmosphere for their children using such skills as reflective listening and active listening. Most of the humanistic, communication, and democratic parenting programs, such as those based on the works of Dreikurs (1964), Ginott (1965), and Gordon (1970), can be seen as relationship-enhancement approaches.

It is common for parents to react to their children's behavior with lectures. Relationship-enhancement approaches suggest a different reaction. Parents who use active listening skills might say things like the following: "I would like to understand how you are feeling. Will you tell me more?" "Let me see if I understand how you feel. Do you feel like . . . ?"

Taking time to understand the child's feelings helps the child feel loved and valued. It also helps the parent and child work together for solutions. It is clear from research that a supportive parent–child relationship as endorsed by relationship-enhancement approaches is very important for the developing child.

Support is more than telling children that they are loved; it is behavior that helps a child feel comfortable and valued. Support might also be called acceptance, affection, love, nurturance, or warmth. One important way to help a child feel support is to understand that child's feelings.

Relationship-enhancement approaches have different strategies for dealing with bad behavior. For example, Ginott (1965) recommended that a parent set clear limits but also take time to understand what the child feels rather than blaming or lecturing. Dreikurs (1964) suggested that parents understand what need the child is expressing in the behavior and help the child meet that need.

In some programs, parents are trained to use "I messages" in order to describe nonjudgmentally the problem behavior and its effects on the parent. The general outline for "I messages" is as follows: "When you (child behavior), I feel (statement of emotion) because (effects)." Together, parent and child identify the problem, list alternatives, choose a solution, decide on an implementation strategy, and evaluate the results.

Control may be maintained by some combination of clear limit setting, reasoning, natural consequences, and helping the child meet needs appropriately, but the development of a warm, trusting relationship is expected to prevent many behavior problems. In addition, parents can improve their management of a child's behavior by being aware of what specific behaviors are developmentally appropriate for that particular child.

Many programs emphasize parents' use of logical consequences for child misbehavior so that children learn to understand the connection between their behavior and the outcomes. An example of logical consequences might be that children who fail to clean their bedrooms suffer messy rooms or they might not be allowed to have friends over until the rooms are in order. Parents are encouraged to reduce their own power by avoiding spanking, shaming, or criticizing children. Parents can facilitate the children's self-control by allowing them to be responsible for their own actions.

It seems clear that effective parenting programs should draw on the sensible response to problem behavior, as suggested in the behavior-management programs, and on the communication and relationship skills, as stressed in the relationship-enhancement approaches.

Other content issues. To better define the essentials of effective parenting, the Cooperative Extension Service gathered a team of parent educators to develop a model of parent education called the National Extension Parent Education Model (NEPEM) that is intended to provide a common ground and common language for any person involved in parent education. The heart of the model (Smith et al. 1994) is a one-page summary of critical parenting practices. Parent educators can draw on this core to structure and guide their program efforts. A comprehensive model might suggest program areas to be developed or that should be evaluated. The model can also lead to research on the interaction of various parenting practices. Finally, the model can guide the thinking of policymakers, helping them develop a functional understanding of and commitment to the purposes and practices of parent education. This model may be the first national effort to establish fundamental content for parent education.

According to the team, there are six categories of critical parenting practices: care for self, understand, guide, nurture, motivate, and advocate. Care for self includes self-knowledge, management of life demands, as well as developing and using support systems; parents who have learned to care for themselves effectively are more likely to provide a secure, supportive, and predictable environment for child rearing. Understand includes the parents' knowledge of child development in general as well as insight into the style and preferences of each of their children; by becoming sensitive to the developmental issues, specific preferences, and circumstantial presses, parents can respond to each child more helpfully. Guide includes behavior that might be considered control or discipline; because flexibility and balance are vital to effective guidance, the most effective parenting will allow the child to make as many decisions as possible. Nurture includes the expression of affection in ways that are effective with each child; basic caregiving, listening, and providing a sense of heritage are also elements of nurture. Motivate includes the stimulation of imagination and curiosity; effective parenting performance in this area is presumed to develop children who are more effective in school and who are more likely to be lifelong learners. Advocate, which stresses the identification and use of community resources to benefit children, recognizes that parents are in a unique role to advocate for their children, and may include working for social change.

The NEPEM is an attempt to focus the content of parent education on a reasonable number of core issues. The model with accompanying discussion and lists of resources is distributed to parent educators through Cooperative Extension Service offices in each county of the United States.

The content of any parent education effort should be sensitive to the needs of the target population. Parents at risk for physically abusing children may need group meetings that emphasize alternatives to violence. Parents at risk for emotionally abusing children seem to benefit from a group format that emphasizes positive discipline and demonstration of affection. Groups that involve extended family in their parenting may need programs that help family members work cooperatively.

As society becomes more diverse culturally, racially, and structurally, program developers need to take into account a growing number of varying populations. Different parents—single, divorced, noncustodial, teen, foster, urban, rural, low-income, and so on—have different patterns of needs.

Process of Parent Education

There are many ways to reach parents with messages on more effective parenting. Group meetings are the traditional way of teaching parents new skills. Meetings may include lectures, discussions, videos, role-playing sessions, and opportunities for practicing skills. It seems likely that, for group meetings to help parents be more caring and understanding, they must be conducted by leaders who are caring and understanding. Although group meetings may be difficult for parents to attend regularly, the group can offer much-needed social support.

Resource centers are another way of providing parenting information. Sometimes a community center, library, or public school develops a special collection of books, tapes, or other materials to help parents. Resource centers are especially likely to be useful when they are easily accessible to parents.

Newsletters make an important contribution to parent education. Commonly, newsletters are used with parents of newborns and include information about development, feeding, and caring for young children. They can be educational, supportive, and cost-efficient. Even the most isolated families can be reached through the use of newsletters. Some researchers report that one issue per month is more effective than one issue every few months. Parents sometimes pass newsletters on to spouses and friends, increasing parents' use of social networks. Advantages of the newsletter include highly relevant information, relatively high use, increased feelings of parent confidence, the flexibility of the format, and its usefulness as a tool for public relations.

Some communities provide radio programs in order to reach the parents who might not otherwise be reached with parenting information. The most effective radio programs carefully target their messages and provide a series of related messages.

Parents at risk for neglecting their children seem to benefit from one-to-one home visits that focus on child-care issues. While home-based parent education may be costly, the visits offer a good opportunity to monitor a child's environment, teach highly relevant skills, and provide support to isolated families.

Parents As Teachers (PAT) is a well-known home-visitation program available statewide in Missouri. PAT offers home visiting, group meetings, developmental screenings, and referral services to parents of preschoolers in an effort to prevent later problems.

Mentoring programs include godparent programs, where trained volunteers visit with mothers of newborns in the hospital. They offer new mothers personal support, information on parenting, and a list of local resources. In many programs, the volunteer checks back with the mother regularly to provide continuing support and guidance.

Support groups provide an opportunity for parents to meet and share experiences and information. Specialized parent-support groups might include parents of children with cerebral palsy, U.S. military families, and so forth. Additionally, family-support programs can link family service organizations, such as the community and the school. Some programs bring parenting classes to work sites during regularly scheduled lunch hours, while others may compile age-paced newsletters for families in the community. Effective support groups facilitate the establishment of support both outside and in the group. They also teach parents ways to use social support in coping, and promote parents' problem-solving abilities.

Books, audio recordings, and videos are increasingly available. They have the advantage of bringing carefully developed information to learners either as a group or individually, and they can be used as part of group meetings to focus the group on real dilemmas and to stimulate discussion.

Family resource programs attempt to provide a variety of services so that families do not need to go from one agency to another. They allow families to become comfortable with staff and maintain better access to services such as parent education, latchkey programs, child care, and social welfare programs. The traditional ideal of a self-supported, closely knit family may generate feelings of isolation for many families. Family resource programs are based on the principles that parenting can be challenging, parents can benefit from parent education, support should focus on family strengths and enhance skills parents already have, and that parents can serve as important sources of support for each other.

A focus on prevention helps avoid the labeling and stigma associated with intervention. Family resource programs facilitate healthy interdependence among parents. Services provided and sponsors of programs are diverse. One important function of family resource programs is to advocate for families, eventually teaching families to advocate for themselves.

Many programs developed by schools emphasize eliminating risk factors and enhancing preventive factors. Suggested guidelines for parent-involvement programs include assessing parents' needs and interests; forming parent networks; allowing parents to recruit other parents; increasing visibility, availability, and friendliness of faculty and staff; emphasizing the potentially positive impact of parent involvement; facilitating active participation in all school events; scheduling events according to the parents' varying needs; encouraging participation at all school levels; establishing a liaison team within school staff; using the school as an activity site; and including the entire community. Parents can assume roles of teacher, partner in school activities and decisions, and/or learner.

Some schools hold monthly workshops for parents. Other approaches to parent education include involving parents in community field trips, tutoring, and parenting-skills training; offering referral services; and cultivating a home–school partnership.

Parent–teacher conferences should assist the parent and improve the parent–child–school relationship. During the conference, teachers can strengthen relationships with parents by demonstrating respect, empathy, knowledge of issues discussed, and skilled communication.

Project Head Start modeled programs with objectives that include changing the attitudes of parents toward schools, school policy, preschool activities, and preschool treatment of children. Programs may teach parents alternatives in child rearing; how to use a child's everyday activities and experiences as learning tools; methods in the facilitation of social, emotional, and language development; effects of social interactions; availability of health and nutrition information; and use of community resources. If possible, father figures are involved. Services are provided at hours convenient to the parents. Staff are paraprofessional, volunteer, or parents. The program can be economical, far-reaching, and effective.

Ideally, objectives of parent education programs should be understood and invested in by the parents; objectives should focus on facilitating development of the total child, increasing parental competence, considering the family and home environment, and identifying developmental problems in a timely fashion. Other goals include improvement of the effectiveness of parents as teachers of their children, better preparation of the children for classroom success, integration of preschool and elementary school philosophy/methods, facilitation of school–community communication, mobilization of support for preventive education, and further understanding of learning in order to improve intervention efforts.

Conclusion

There are problems related to parent education. No established standards exist for parent educators. There is a wide range of approaches and orientations, including some programs that are not in tune with the research. It is difficult for parent education to be sensitive to differences in cultures and values. It is increasingly challenging to motivate parents to participate in group meetings. There is still much to be learned about how to change parent behavior.

One major problem with parent education is lack of quality evaluation. Many studies are nothing more than consumer satisfaction reports. It is difficult to do well-controlled studies because of the many variables that are hard to control (e.g., variations between teachers) and the subtlety of the outcomes. It is probably not reasonable to expect parents' participation in one series of classes to substantially change the broad spectrum of parenting behaviors, and it is not reasonable to expect that improved parenting will result in instant improvement in child behaviors.

Nonetheless, parent education continues to grow. In the challenging tasks of parenting, most parents welcome the help that it offers. As research continues, both the content and process of parent education can be expected to improve, resulting in better family relationships and healthier, more balanced children.

(*See also:* Communication; Discipline; Family Life Education; Personality Development; School; Self-Help Groups; Truancy)

BIBLIOGRAPHY

Abidin, R. R., ed. (1980). *Parent Education and Intervention Handbook.* Springfield, IL: Bannerstone House.

Abidin, R. R. (1992). "The Determinants of Parenting Behavior." *Journal of Clinical Child Psychology* 21:407–412.

Berry, M. (1988). "A Review of Parent Training Programs in Child Welfare." *Social Service Review* 62:302–323.

Canter, L., and Canter, M. (1985). *Assertive Discipline for Parents.* New York: Harper & Row.

Cedar, B., and Levant, R. F. (1990). "A Meta-Analysis of the Effects of Parent Effectiveness Training." *American Journal of Family Therapy* 18:373–384.

Dean, C. (1984). "Parental Empowerment Through Family Resource Programs." *Human Ecology Forum* 14:17–22.

Dickinson, N. S. (1989). "Parent Education Programs: What Works?" *Human Relations* 14:1–6.

Dreikurs, R. (1964). *Children: The Challenge.* New York: Hawthorn Books.

Fine, M. J. (1980). *Handbook on Parent Education.* San Diego, CA: Academic Press.

Fine, M. J. (1990). *The Second Handbook on Parent Education: Contemporary Perspectives.* San Diego, CA: Academic Press.

Ginott, H. (1965). *Between Parent and Child.* New York: Macmillan.

Goddard, H. W., and Miller, B. C. (1993). "Adding Attribution to Parenting Programs." *Families in Society* 74:84–92.

Gordon, T. (1970). *Parent Effectiveness Training.* New York: Peter H. Wyden.

Hamner, T. J., and Turner, P. H. (1990). *Parenting in Contemporary Society.* Englewood Cliffs, NJ: Prentice Hall.

Kurtz, P. D., and Barth, R. P. (1989). "Parent Involvement: Cornerstone of School Social Work Practice." *Social Work* 34:407–413.

Patterson, G. R. (1975). *Families: Applications of Social Learning to Family Life.* Champaign, IL: Research Press.

Peterson, G. W., and Rollins, B. C. (1987). "Parent–Child Socialization." In *Handbook of Marriage and the Family,* ed. M. B. Sussman and S. K. Steinmetz. New York: Plenum.

Rollins, B. C., and Thomas, D. L. (1979). "Parental Support, Power, and Control Techniques in the Socialization of Children." In *Contemporary Theories About the Family,* Vol. 1, ed. W. R. Burr, R. Hill, F. I. Nye, and I. L. Reiss. New York: Free Press.

Scarr, S. (1992). "Developmental Theories for the 1990s: Development and Individual Differences." *Child Development* 63:1–19.

Smith, C. A.; Cudaback, D.; Goddard, H. W.; and Myers-Walls, J. A. (1994). *National Extension Parent Education Model of Critical Parenting Practices.* Manhattan: Kansas State University Press.

Williams, D. K. (1985). *Handbook for Involving Parents in Education.* Atlanta: Humanics Limited.

Wolfendale, S. (1989). *Parental Involvement: Developing Networks Between School, Home, and Community.* London: Cassell Educational.

H. Wallace Goddard

PARENTING *See* Fathers; Foster Parenting; Gay and Lesbian Parents; Grandparenthood; Mothers; Parent Education; Single Parents; Stepparenting; Substitute Caregivers

PEER PRESSURE

"Peer pressure" is a term most often associated with adolescence. Peer pressure is the primary mechanism of transmitting group norms and maintaining loyalties among group members (Clasen and Brown 1985). Peer pressure has well-established roots in the development of adolescents who are exploring their sense of self and holding it up against the mirror of their peer group. In the adolescent stage of life, there is a need for withdrawal from emotional dependence on parents, but a strong need for affiliation also exists. The combination of these needs sets the stage for peer groups and peer pressure to have strong influence on the attitude and behavior of an adolescent.

Research shows that as a natural part of the maturation process the influence of peer pressure is part of what is considered typical development of the adolescent. Development up to the teenage years will most likely have an effect on the peer groups an individual gravitates toward and the peer pressures to which an individual may succumb. Low self-esteem, a high value placed on social interaction, and perhaps family variables are likely to affect an individual's susceptibility to peer pressure. Adolescents face considerable pressure to strive to be popular with and accepted by their peers. As a result, peer pressure can have both positive and negative effects on an adolescent's life.

Peer Pressure and the Developmental Process

The theory of adolescence set forth by Erik Erikson (1968a) identifies the main task of adolescence as building and developing a reasonably stable identity. As adolescents' developmental process of individuating from their parents begins, the use of their peer group seems substantial and possibly greater than the use of their family to explore who they are in the world. Peer influence is essential in the developmental process as adolescents explore interests and ideologies to test their ability to form intimate peer relationships and relinquish dependence on parents while retaining a sense of belonging.

Peer pressure and influence become integral parts in the decision-making process of an adolescent. Perceptions of peer pressure can be significantly associated with dating attitudes, sexual activity, and the use of drugs and alcohol (Brown 1982). As an adolescent seeks out peer group membership, the norms, unspoken attitudes, and behaviors begin to guide the adolescent who desires to belong. Peer pressure can become the price of group membership. Peer pressure is a multidimensional force that varies in strength according to specific behaviors, peer groups, and grades in school. Adolescents are developmentally at a stage where separating from family has begun while at the same time there is a need to belong. Adolescents display much uncertainty with their own judgments, decisions, and choices and so mirror the behaviors of their peers with increased susceptibility to peer pressure. To belong to a peer group there are pressures to dress, behave, and have similar attitudes as those in the group within which the adolescent hopes to belong.

Granville S. Hall (1904) characterizes adolescence by inevitable turmoil, maladjustment, tension, rebellion, dependency conflicts, and exaggerated peer group conformity. Peer pressure as an influence in the process of adolescent development is expectable as the individual attempts to cope with stresses of getting older and to achieve a sense of belongingness. Peggy Giordano, Stephen Cernkovich, and M. D. Pugh (1986) posit three reasons as to how and why the influence of peer pressure becomes attractive and such an important part of peer group formation. The first is rewards of friendship, including intrinsic rewards (e.g., conversation and sharing of confidence, development of intimate interactions), the extrinsic rewards (e.g., money, labor, information, material goods), and identity support (i.e., providing a comfortable arena in which to express identity concerns, talk about problems, and share vulnerabilities). The second concerns the patterns of interaction and influence, such as the amount of time spent with friends, the length of the relationship, and the pressure that friends exert on one another to behave in certain ways. The final dimension deals with the vicissitudes of friendship, including the amount of conflict among friends and the extent of loyalty among friends in the face of trouble.

In a study done at Pennsylvania State University on conception and perceived influence of peer pressure (O'Brien and Bierman 1988), adolescents were more likely to describe peer group influences as global and far-reaching. This means that adolescents perceived the influence of peer pressure to affect many areas in their life, including language, attitude, and behavior. Adolescents acknowledged that to feel they belonged in a peer group, they would mold their behavior, yielding to peer pressure involving such things as dress codes, illicit acts, attitudes, and values. Peer pressure directs adolescents to make decisions and choices that can result in their being part of a peer group or having a feeling of isolation. Older adolescents were also more likely to view peer rejection as an indication of their unworthiness as an individual: "If they do not accept you, you might feel like something's wrong with you—that you are not good enough" (O'Brien and Bierman 1988, p. 1364).

Peer pressure is of genuine concern for adolescents during high school years. The intensity of concern appears to increase slowly at ages eleven through thirteen and begins its decline at ages fifteen through seventeen. The increase of concern at age eleven and the impact of peer pressure are due to adolescents' new awareness that being accepted within a peer group is expected and highly desired. The decline of intensity of concern beginning at age fifteen correlates with adolescents still feeling the impact of peer pressure but feeling more capable of making individual choices as they head toward adulthood, due to the developmental process as adolescents remain aware of socialization within their peer group. Preadolescents and adolescents rely on the norms of their peer group to dictate external behavior patterns. Similarity of interests, values, and opinions are major determinants of interpersonal attraction. Peer pressure, with its goal of conformity within a group, is vital.

Male and Female Responses to Peer Pressure

Peer pressure is a prominent characteristic for both male and female adolescents. Many researchers show that peer pressure appears to be a more dominant and influential feature of high school life for females than for males. It is suggested that this could be due to the fact that traditionally females tend to be more attentive to interpersonal relationships and therefore more vulnerable to the influence of others. Studies have also shown that stereotypic images of masculine and feminine behavior are apparent in both intensity and content of peer influences. Peer pressure appears to have a greater impact for females than for males in the specific areas of appearance and self-evaluation (O'Brien and Bierman 1988). Females are more likely than males to be involved in intimate relationships with peers. Females also tend to be more connected than males with their families throughout the adolescent stage of life. Peer pressure can be influenced by more parental and/or family supervision given to the females.

Peer pressure reported by male adolescents reflected a greater concern with the sexual than with the interpersonal components of heterosexual relationships (Brown 1982). Peer pressure for males appears to be more focused around becoming involved in organizations as well as drug and alcohol use. Peer pressure for males to become involved in organizations can include athletics and clubs, as well as groups that encourage more negative behaviors, such as violent gangs. Males are more susceptible to peer pressure resulting in antisocial behavior.

B. Bradford Brown (1982) reports that males and females differed not only in overall strength they assigned to peer pressures but also in their relative ranking of pressure in various areas. Both females and males agreed that peers seemed most insistent that high school students be socially active. Peer pressure in this area encouraged both female and male peer group members to participate in activity outside of school and family domains. Choices and decisions as to what these activities involved were most times dictated by the norms, interests, and goals of the group. Consistent with findings of other researchers were the issues that adolescents ranked second in terms of peer pressure. Females ranked dress and grooming styles as the second issue. Males ranked the use of drugs and alcohol as the second issue.

Negative Effects of Peer Pressure

Conformity to peer pressure is widely considered a prime factor in an adolescent's engaging in negative behaviors. These behaviors include delinquent acts that the adolescent would not otherwise perform alone. Peer pressure is known to play a role in illicit acts performed by a particular group. Adolescents feeling peer pressure from a group within which they desire to belong can suspend their own better judgment and participate in behaviors they know to be wrong (illegal) and that they may regret later. The influence of peer pressure toward delinquent behavior is conditioned by the frequency (how often the group is together), duration (how long the peer group has been established), priority (how important the peer group is to each individual), and intensity of association with the peer group.

A study done by University of Wisconsin researchers (Brown, Clasen, and Eicher 1986) has shown that adolescents perceive misconduct peer pressures more ambivalently than positive peer pressures; adolescent respondents were more aware of a willingness to yield to peer pressure regarded as having a positive impact. Peer pressure susceptibility for negative behaviors was shown to be less likely identified by the adolescent, but it was prevalent. The more pressure adolescents perceived from friends to engage in misconduct, the more frequent was their self-reported involvement, especially among those with relatively strong antisocial peer conformity disposition. In addition, the stronger that perceived pressures were against negative behaviors, the more adolescents reportedly refrained from misconduct, especially among those with a relatively strong antisocial peer conformity disposition.

Peer pressure with negative effects may range from relatively minor acts to more serious, sometimes tragic incidents, such as rampages and gang violence in school, destruction of property, unplanned and unwanted involvement in sexual experimentation, or harmful acts on innocent bystanders or isolated members of other ethnic groups. Initiation rites into gangs, fraternities, and sororities that are harmful to the individual or others represent another example of the negative effects of peer pressure. Although individual choice plays a role in the decision to participate in negative or harmful acts, research shows that peer pressure to perform an act is often more powerful than individual choice.

Adolescents who smoke marijuana or tobacco; drink beer, wine, or hard liquor; or use psychedelic drugs are more likely than not to be part of a peer group where these behaviors are present and encouraged. Peer pressure within a group that engages in these activities has a higher likelihood to continue regarding these and other behaviors that are established as part of the group culture. Given that certain characteristics and similarities bring individuals into peer groups, yielding to peer pressure remains a factor in maintaining membership.

Positive Effects of Peer Pressure

Socialization and peer pressure appear to enhance friendships over time in peer groups where there are shared and common interests. As a rite of passage, adolescents move toward adulthood, gaining experience within their peer group. Having left the world of childhood for good, but not yet fully admitted to the world of adults, adolescents are virtually forced to create at least a semblance of an "interim culture" of their own (Conger 1977). Peer pressure plays an important role in the development of that culture. Peer pressure can have a positive effect on a group when it has a common goal to maintain and provides a healthy arena in which to grow. A warm, supportive, nonmanipulative group of peers can use peer pressure to help an adolescent through a particularly difficult time. Peer pressure among a peer group can play an important role in helping the male or female adolescent gain a clearer concept of self and learn how to solve problems and set goals.

Athletic teams, study groups, and school clubs are formed on the premise that groups who affiliate toward a common goal can meet success. Peer pressure applied in these groups includes encouragement and support as the group works toward a common goal. Likewise, groups that form with no formal purpose can also apply peer group pressure to help one another with academic problems, family problems, or other interpersonal problems.

Peer pressure is used effectively in psychiatric treatment programs, substance abuse programs, and in some instances correctional facilities for adolescents. In these settings, peer pressure can be used to develop a positive peer culture. With an atmosphere of "we're in this together," peers can use their individual strengths and the strength of the group to solve problems and give mutual support.

(*See also:* Adolescence; Adolescent Sexuality; Friendship; Gangs; Juvenile Delinquency; Personality Development; Play; Truancy)

BIBLIOGRAPHY

Adams, G. R., and Gullotta, T. (1983). "Peer Relations." In *Adolescent Life Experiences*, ed. C. D. Laughton. Monterey, CA: Brooks/Cole.

Berndt, T. J. (1979). "Developmental Changes in Conformity to Peers and Parents." *Developmental Psychology* 15:608–616.

Brown, B. B. (1982). "The Extent of Peer Pressure Among High School Students: A Retrospective Analysis." *Journal of Youth and Adolescence* 11:121–133.

Brown, B. B.; Clasen, D. R.; and Eicher, S. A. (1986). "Perceptions of Peer Pressure, Peer Conformity Dispositions, and Self-Reported Behavior Among Adolescents." *Developmental Psychology* 15:521–530.

Brown, B. B.; Eicher, S. A.; and Petrie, S. (1986). "The Importance of Peer Group ('Crowd') Affiliation in Adolescence." *Journal of Adolescence* 9:73–96.

Campbell, J. D. (1964). "Peer Relations in Childhood." In *Review of Child Development Research*, ed. M. L. Hoffman and L. W. Hoffman. New York: Russell Sage Foundation.

Clasen, D. R., and Brown, B. B. (1985). "The Multidimensionality of Peer Pressure in Adolescence." *Journal of Youth and Adolescence* 14:451–468.

Coleman, J. (1968). *The Adolescent Society.* New York: W. W. Norton.

Conger, J. J. (1977). "Adolescents and Their Peers." In *Adolescence and Youth Psychology Development in a Changing World*, ed. G. Middendorf. New York: Harper & Row.

Costanzo, P. R., and Shaw, M. E. (1966). "Conformity as a Function of Age Level." *Child Development* 37:967–975.

Erikson, E. H. (1968a) *Identity, Youth, and Crisis.* New York: W. W. Norton.

Erikson, E. H. (1968b). "Life Cycle." In *International Encyclopedia of the Social Sciences*, ed. D. L. Sills. New York: Macmillan.

Giordano, P. C.; Cernkovich, S. A.; and Pugh, M. D. (1986). "Friendships and Delinquency." *American Journal of Sociology* 91:1170–1202.

Hall, G. S. (1904). *Adolescence.* New York: Appleton-Century-Crofts.

Hill, P. (1993). "Recent Advances in Selected Aspects of Adolescent Development." *Journal of Child Psychology and Psychiatry* 34:69–99.

Kandel, D. B. (1981). "Peer Influences in Adolescence." Paper presented to the Society for Research in Child Development, Boston.

O'Brien, S. F., and Bierman, K. L. (1988). "Conceptions and Perceived Influence of Peer Groups: Interviews with Preadolescents and Adolescents." *Child Development* 59: 1360–1365.

Pabon, E.; Rodriguez, O.; and Gurin, G. (1992). "Clarifying Peer Relations and Delinquency." *Youth and Society* 24:149–165.

Phelps, H. R., and Horrocks, J. E. (1958). "Factors Influencing Informal Groups of Adolescents." *Child Development* 29:69–86.

Polansky, N.; Lippitt, R.; and Ridl, F. (1950). "An Investigation of Behavioral Contagion in Groups." *Human Relations* 3:319–348.

Scott, S. (1986). *How to Say No and Keep Your Friends: Peer Pressure Reversal for Teens and Preteens.* Amherst, MA: Human Resource Development Press.

Urberg, K. A. (1992). "Locus of Peer Influence: Social Crowd and Best Friend." *Journal of Youth and Adolescence* 21:439–450.

CATHERINE M. LINTON

PERSONALITY DEVELOPMENT

The study of personality development dates from the work of Sigmund Freud ([1895] 1981), and since that time, the term "personality" has been used by psychologists in many ways: referring to an individual's character or qualities, self states, ego traits, emotional expression, and cognitive development. In ordinary usage the term "personality" is used to describe an individual's persona (e.g., heroic, tragic, depressive, manic, virtuous, loyal, courageous, cowardly).

The study of personality focuses on both the observable and nonobservable aspects of the self (including the unconscious, fantasies, daydreams, dreams, motivated hopes and expectations, thoughts, opinions, beliefs, and vague perceptions). Because the nonobservable parts of the self are difficult to quantify, some personality theorists have either ignored or denied their existence (Cattell 1980).

Personality also refers to one's gender role, gender identity, sexuality, and sexual orientation. While one can speak of the self or personality in the abstract, there are no abstract personalities. Gender role and gender identity form the bedrock of a personality. Moreover, each individual's sexuality is unique in terms of having a different threshold for sexual arousal and sexual stimulation; having varied degrees of "sexiness" and seductiveness; being described as active versus passive, masculine versus feminine, strong versus weak—terms that define the frame for one's sexuality; and sexual orientation.

The self emerges from the interplay of biological and social forces, including cultural, ethnic, and religious factors (Buss 1988; Zuckerman 1991). By the second year of life a core gender identity emerges (Stoller 1968), and the toddler proudly announces his or her gender identity with the words "I am a boy" or "I am a girl." Eventually, the child's core gender identity and its nascent gender images coalesce into an adolescent and adult gender identity. The biological underpinnings of personality (including the child's chromosomal, genetic, and hormonal basis for behavior) lead to varied intellectual capacity, developmental conflicts, temperament, affective balance, and level of emotional expressiveness.

The neurobiological sequelae of personality development lead to the formation of specific ego structures including, but not limited to, the following: the child's cognitive capacity; creation of a stimulus barrier to protect the ego from being overwhelmed by internal and external stimuli; the development of ego strength and a competent ego (cf. Brody and Axelrod 1970) whose functions for processing the external world are intact (e.g., attention, concentration, memory, reality testing, perception, and abstract reasoning functions); a predisposition for a gradient of energy expression manifested as temperament; a level of emotional expressiveness; and a biological basis for aggressiveness and sexuality and a threshold for sexual responsiveness.

The study of personality development highlights the nature–nurture controversy, for it is in this unique area of inquiry that the combination of biological and environmental forces are choreographed to produce the beginnings of a nascent self system, one that eventually coalesces into what is labeled as an individual's personality. While the origins of personality development predate birth (as expressed in the parental contributions of unconscious wishes for their child and their physical contribution of genetic material), the child's personality is not a static entity but a dynamic process that changes over one's life cycle. The more individuals know about what motivates behavior the more they can understand personality development.

Theories of Personality Development

Psychologists have explained personality development by appeal to functional and organic theories ranging from, but not limited to, psychodynamic, behavioral, learning, interpersonal, trait versus state, and personal construct theory (L'Abate and Bryson 1993; Millon 1990). Major textbooks on personality typically review fifteen to twenty different theories of personality development (cf. Allen 1994; Ewen 1992; Feshbach and Weiner 1986; Monte 1980).

According to Christopher Monte (1980), all theories of personality attempt to explain the following: (1) What is observable? (i.e., "How did the person come to behave as he or she now does?"); (2) How will a person behave in any situation?; (3) How unique and generalizable is the person's behavior?

Because personality formation is an ongoing developmental process, existing along a continuum and changing with each developmental epoch, a sound personality theory must employ a developmental model and emphasize a biosocial-psychological system (Lidz 1983). A comprehensive personality theory must include reference to developmental psychology, child development, psychoanalytic psychopathology, infant psychology, separation-individuation phenomena, maternal attachment theory, biological bases of behavior (including the effects of fetal hormonal development on behavior), genetic influences on behavior, and the influence of somatic processes on personality development.

Monte (1980) sees four basic schools of thought that represent four different ways of constructing the person, and he has classified the major personality theorists according to these four schools. Psychodynamic theorists (e.g., Sigmund Freud, Anna Freud, Carl G. Jung, Erik H. Erickson, and Erich Fromm) construct the person via inner and outer reality. Cognitive behaviorists (e.g., Neal Miller, John Dollard, Albert Bandura, and Richard H. Walters) construct the person via social learning theory and the person's reality. Radical behaviorists (e.g., Hans J. Eysenck) construct the person via external reality. Humanistic and existentialist theorists (e.g., Robert D. Laing, Gordon Allport, Abraham Maslow, and Carl R. Rogers) see the person as constructing his or her reality.

Personality theories are further divided by Monte (1980) into several types, including trait theory (and type); psychodynamic or psychoanalytic theory (and ego psychology); social learning theory (and behaviorism); and interpersonal theory (and phenomenology). Trait theory states that personality is the dynamic organization within individuals of those psychophysical systems that determine their characteristic behavior and thoughts (Allport 1937, 1955). Psychodynamic or psychoanalytic theory says personality is the certain constancy that prevails in the ways the ego chooses for solving its tasks of drive satisfaction and ethical mediation (Fenichel 1945). Social learning theory claims that personality is the cluster of interrelated responses interacting with stimuli (Bandura and Walters 1963). According to the interpersonality theory, personality is the relatively enduring pattern of interpersonal situations that characterize a human life (Sullivan 1953). This last theory was expanded by Timothy Leary (1957, pp. 15–16), who stated that "personality is the multilevel pattern of interpersonal responses (overt, conscious, or private) expressed by the individual. Interpersonal behavior is aimed at reducing anxiety. All the social, emotional, interpersonal activities of an individual can be understood as attempts to avoid anxiety or to establish and maintain self-esteem."

Each of these theories attempts to explain certain human observations, to make predictions of future behavior based on past behavior (that is, to explain the why of the motivated behavior), and to have their theories generalizable to a large number of individuals. Each personality theory presents a partial understanding of personality. Freud ([1895] 1981), however, was quite ambitious and optimistic and wrote "Project for a Scientific Psychology" to provide a comprehensive and inclusive theory of personality. It was, and still is, the most comprehensive theory of personality.

Process of Personality Development

Even before birth, the parents' unconscious wishes, motivations, hopes, desires, and projections shape the nascent personality formation of their child. Heinz Kohut and Ernest Wolf (1978, p. 416) state that

> when the baby is born, the encounter with the child's actual structural and functional biological equipment will, of course, influence the imagery about its future personality that had been formed by the parents. But the parental expectations will, from birth onwards, exert a considerable influence on the baby's developing self. The self arises thus as the result of the interplay between the newborn's innate equipment and the selective responses of the selfobjects through which certain potentialities are encouraged in their development while others remain unencouraged or are even actively discouraged.

The term "selfobject" is defined by Kohut and Wolf as "objects which we experience as parts of the self; the experienced control over them is, therefore, closer to the concept of control which a grown-up expects to have over his [or her] own body and mind than to the concept of control which he [or she] expects to have over others." This concept of a selfobject revolutionized the way in which cognitive psychologists think about the development of an individual's representational world and the establishment of object relations. The concept of a selfobject links an individual's subjectivity to the world of social relationships.

Donald W. Winnicott (1975), a pediatrician and child psychiatrist from Britain, elaborated on the social basis for developmental psychology when he stated that there is no such thing as a baby without a mother; that is, an infant's identity is inseparable from the mother's identity. All of the infant's early learning (both cognitive and affective) is inextricably bound with the mothering object. For example, the very basis for the infant's self-esteem is rooted in the maternal gaze in which the "gleam in the mother's eyes"—that is, her pride and joy in her infant—is internalized by the infant as the infant's earliest form of self-esteem. Without adequate self-esteem the child's nascent self develops on a bedrock of depression and narcissistic failure.

While the infant's "actual structural and functional biological equipment" provides the "frame" for the picture of "personality," the actual picture (i.e., the child's personality) is a product of the interaction among the child, its caretakers, and the environment.

Some developmental concepts that have been useful in explaining behavior include the concepts of "good enough mothering" and "average expectable environment." These concepts define basic parameters for normative infant growth.

The infant comes into the world as a helpless creature who does not have his or her own food supply; cannot provide himself or herself with protection, shelter, temperature regulation, and survival; and has a neurological substratum that takes up to two decades to mature fully. Indeed, maturational processes in humans are characterized by long delays that lead to an enforced dependency of sometimes up to twenty years. On the other hand, the infant brings to his or her experience a unique perspective.

Joseph Lichtenberg (1983) stated, "The infant begins with genetically endowed schemata that facilitate the organization of experience into units involving elements of self and object, as well as affect and cognition." The infant has a temperament, a native intelligence, a nascent personality, which shape the responses it receives from its world of selfobjects. While the infant learns through interacting with others, he or she also educates the selfobject milieu. In this way, the infant's experience is transformed through its intersubjective encounters with others in what Robert Lang (1976) called the individual's "bipersonal field" and what Lichtenberg (1983) called an "interrelated context" of the sense of self and object.

Although the infant's social-psychological growth follows a developmental path at an equal pace with the maturation of the infant's central nervous system, the infant also contributes to his or her own maturation through social-psychological experiences. The earliest relationship of the infant to the primary caregiver, typically the mother, is a dyadic relationship in which the child's ego develops. The infant is not, however, a passive recipient of experience but actively contributes to his or her development.

The first ego is a body ego (cf. Fliess 1961). The primary caretaker holds and soothes the baby; attends to his or her cooing and vocalization; and interpolates them. If the infant's physical and emotional needs are attended to by the mothering object, then the conditions for an "average expectable environment" and "good enough mothering" are attained. Infants raised in such environments develop the capacity to tolerate frustration and anxiety and learn to be patient and to respond to one's bodily processes with equanimity and not react with catastrophic anxiety.

The caretaker's relationship to the child's body is critical for the child's self-esteem development. For normative development to occur, a child must have the capacity for bodily pleasure, the source of which can be transformed into a buoyant, vitalized self-system. Once the child's body is narcissistically invested (by the parents) with pride and admiration, the child can develop good self-esteem (a critical factor in assuring that the child will develop along normative lines). Lacking good self-esteem, the child will be unable to achieve his or her potential and may become powerless and helpless, unable to respond adaptively and constructively to life's demands. Children with low self-esteem and impaired narcissistic development may become depressed, lethargic, cognitively dull, socially isolated, or aggressive; some, believing they are unworthy, contemplate suicide.

Parents who show joy and pleasurable interest in their child's body (all parts of it, without overstimulating the child) give permission for the child to experience a cohesive bodily identity (body ego) and provide the child with an integrated body schema. Children who do not experience a pleasurable attachment to their bodies may develop a spectrum of psychosomatic disorders, a poor body image, addictions, or self-mutilating behaviors. Those children whose parents denied the existence of their children's sexuality or viewed it and their genitals as bad, may be prone to develop problems with anhedonia, gender role and identity, sexual orientation, or paraphilias (Lothstein 1993).

Developmental psychologists have used a variety of metaphors to describe the early body ego or primitive bodily personality, including "the body envelope," "the skin ego," and "the body ego" (cf. Anzieu 1989). These metaphors describe the infant's earliest identifications as a whole self. The body or skin acts as a container for the infant, establishing a boundary for self–other differentiation and the development of separation-individuation experiences. Unless the child is able to respond normatively to these developmental issues, he or she may become depressed, anxious over issues of separation and loss, and may be unable to achieve autonomy and respond adaptively to change.

Sigmund Freud discussed the way in which bodily zones of pleasure are used by the child during the first four years of life to organize cognitive and affective experiences (i.e., the oral, anal, and phallic phases of development are defined in terms of specific bodily organs, e.g., the mouth, anus, and genitals). Each instinctual zone implied a stage of libidinal organization for psychosexual development.

By the fifth year, all children experience a universal phase of development (the Oedipal phase) in which personality formation is indelibly organized around a particular conflict in the nuclear family. The Oedipal conflict involves a triangulated relationship among the child and his or her parents in which a specific kind of anxiety (castration anxiety) emerges as organizing the child's experience. Castration anxiety arises in response to the child's unconscious motives to usurp the role of the parent of the opposite sex in the context of the child's perceived powerlessness, helplessness, and genital inferiority. The core of the Oedipus complex involves a compromise in which father–son and mother–daughter rivalries, jealousies, and envy take center stage in the relationships (though the real drama was nonobservable—i.e., unconscious). In effect, the Oedipal drama sets the stage for the child's entry into social relationships outside the parental relationship.

During adolescence new conflicts for personality development appear as the surfacing of intense sexual urges promotes the need to resolve the bisexual conflicts of boys and girls.

While Freud focused on the Oedipal phase of psychosexual development, others focused on the pre-Oedipal phase and its relationship to character organization and personality development.

The pre-Oedipal phase of human development focuses on the helpless infant and his or her dyadic bond to the mothering object. During this developmental phase, the anxieties that motivate personality development focus on annihilation anxiety, stranger anxiety, and separation anxiety (Bowlby 1969). Margaret Mahler (1968) provided a unique perspective on the developmental framework for the infant's pre-Oedipal development, stressing the importance of the infant's pre-Oedipal relationships on differentiation of self from others. During this epoch the infant differentiates his or her body and self from the mother and goes through various phases and subphases of separation-individuation (S/I). Mahler described the forerunners of S/I as involving a normal autistic phase (first month) and a normal symbiosis subphase (three to four months), followed by four subphases of separation-individuation that involved a period of differentiation and development of the body image (five to nine months), a practicing subphase (ten to fourteen months), a rapprochement subphase (fourteen to twenty-four months), and an initial consolidation of individuality (two to three years). Themes of separation and symbiosis were identified as core conflicts for the toddler.

Mahler believed that there is a fundamental drive toward individuation in which the child rejects a symbiotic merger with the mother to separate and create an independent identity (i.e., a personality). She rejected the idea that major learning takes place via a process of nonconflictual imprinting. All development involves conflict and change. One may speculate that in later adult development the process of separation and individuation may be transformed into strivings for human potentiality, self-actualization, perfection, and mastery (cf. Maslow 1970).

A second phase of separation-individuation occurs in adolescence and poses a significant threat to the ego or self. At that point the teenager is separating from the parental core and may experience a clinical depression (the experience of object loss acting as a motivator for personality development). A final phase of separation-individuation occurs in old age, when the earlier goals of the self for individuation and autonomy are superseded by dependency needs and a submission to a caregiving environment.

To highlight the complexities of personality development, the second year of life will be focused on as a prototypical model for all phases of development.

The Toddler: "The Magic Years"

The second year of life is a particularly unique epoch for self-development. This is a generative era, representing the period of the birth of the self and the establishment of the ego mechanisms governing gender-self constancy (involving the consolidation and stability of the child's gender-self representation and the experience of the inner continuity and unity of the gender-self representation). At the beginning stage of toilet training, the child is experimenting with issues of autonomy, control, and separateness. Moreover, the child is developing semisymbolic forms of reasoning; undergoing an early genital phase; becoming aware of the anatomical differences between the sexes; revealing a primary femininity or masculinity; having a pre-Oedipal castration reaction; differentiating his or her body image and body schema; showing an increase in negativism, object-loss anxiety, and an increased hostile dependence on the mother; and developing a nuclear self-system and a core gender identity (cf. Lothstein 1983).

In the course of child rearing, it is often difficult to keep in mind all of the challenges and conflicts that the eighteen- to thirty-sixth-month-old child is experiencing. For this period of development, social learning theorists (Bandura 1971; Bandura and Walters 1963) have conceptualized personality development as formed through such mechanisms as imprinting, imitation learning, role modeling, and stimulus-reward systems. Bandura and Walters (1963) stressed the role of modeling on the development of learned social behaviors. By leaving out motivational issues affecting development and denying the efficacy of the unconscious, social learning theorists present only a partial theory of personality development.

In addition to developmental issues, each child also faces a number of environmental challenges that need to be integrated into their developing self-system (Eysenck 1953, 1967). All children vary in levels of physical attractiveness; physical health or illness; intelligence and ego functioning; response to the birth of a new sibling and/or sibling status; number of abandonments and losses, changes, and deaths in the family; the effect of their caregivers; and on the unpredictable or random environmental impingements that may significantly alter their personality formation. While the child appears to be struggling with complex intrapsychic conflicts and attempting to manage severe catastrophic environmental hurdles, to the outside observer the child's apparent quietude may make it appear as if his or her personality development was achieved as if by sleight of hand and not as the result of conflict, crisis, opportunity, or trauma.

Erickson and Stages of Development

Personality is not a static entity. It is a dynamic process that continues throughout the natural course of human development and is shaped and changed by an individual's response to life cycle crises and challenges. In contrast to Freud's focus on instinctual bodily zones for development of ego and psyche, Erickson (1968) focused on universally experienced ego conflicts that are integral to normative personality consolidation. He postulated eight stages of human development that he saw as arising out of life cycle crises. Erickson defined the first core conflicts as involving trust versus mistrust, autonomy versus shame and doubt, initiative versus guilt, and industry versus inferiority. Each of these life cycle stages focuses on a series of sequential ego crises that begin in infancy and extend throughout life to old age (cf. Monte 1980). Erickson's assumption that crisis and conflict are at the core of development is a central tenet of all personality theorists who are psychodynamically oriented.

With the transition to adolescence, the central crisis shifts to one of identity consolidation and the management of role confusion. As the teenager enters adulthood, the core crises for self-development involve intimacy versus isolation, generativity versus stagnation, and ego integrity versus despair. The extent to which an individual responds positively to the challenges around trust, autonomy, initiative, industry, identity, intimacy, generativity, and ego integrity will determine what course personality takes for a given individual. Erickson's schema for personality development underscores the importance of a universal set of ego conflicts that every individual must face to consolidate his or her personality.

Conclusion

While personality is formed in early childhood and consolidated by late adolescence, the development of personality is an ongoing process. Only if individuals become paralyzed by fear or negativism and fail to respond adaptively to life's challenges will they become developmentally arrested and fixed in their behavior. The extent to which individuals maintain strong social relationships and continue to embrace selfobject relationships over the life cycle will determine how successfully those individuals will have adaptively responded to their environment and how accessible they are to changing personality patterns. Even in the elderly, personality can be a fluid and changing process and not a static entity.

The fact that each person has a unique personality attests to the complexity of experience and the idiosyncratic way the various elements of self experience coalesce to form a unique blend of characteristics that have come to be known as one's personality.

(*See also:* ATTACHMENT; GENDER; GENDER IDENTITY; INTIMACY; SELF-ESTEEM; SEXUALITY; SEXUALITY IN THE LIFE CYCLE; SEXUAL ORIENTATION; TRUST)

BIBLIOGRAPHY

Allen, B. P. (1994). *Personality Theories.* Boston: Allyn & Bacon.

Allport, G. (1937). *Personality: Psychological Interpretation.* New York: Henry Holt.

Allport, G. (1955). *Becoming: Basic Considerations for Psychology and Personality.* New Haven, CT: Yale University Press.

Anzieu, D. (1989). *The Skin Ego.* New Haven, CT: Yale University Press.

Bandura, A., ed. (1971). *Psychological Modeling: Conflicting Theories.* Chicago: Aldine.

Bandura, A., and Walters, R. H. (1963). *Social Learning and Personality Development.* New York: Holt, Rinehart and Winston.

Bowlby, J. (1969). *Attachment and Loss:* Vol. 1, *Attachment.* New York: Basic Books.

Brody, S., and Axelrod, S. (1970). *Anxiety and Ego Formation in Infancy.* New York: International Universities Press.

Buss, A. (1988). *Personality: Evolutionary Heritage and Human Distinctiveness.* Hillsdale, NJ: Lawrence Erlbaum.

Cattell, R. (1980). *Personality and Learning Theory.* New York: Springer-Verlag.

Erickson, E. H., ed. (1968). *Identity: Youth in Crisis.* New York: W. W. Norton.

Ewen, R. (1992). *An Introduction to Theories of Personality,* 4th edition. Hillsdale, NJ: Lawrence Erlbaum.

Eysenck, H. J. (1953). *The Structure of Human Personality.* London: Methuen.

Eysenck, H. J. (1967). *The Biological Basis of Personality.* Springfield, IL: Charles C Thomas.

Fenichel, O. (1945). *The Psychoanalytic Theory of Neurosis.* New York: W. W. Norton.

Feshbach, S., and Weiner, B. (1986). *Personality,* 2nd edition. New York: D. C. Heath.

Fliess, R. (1961). *Ego and Body Ego.* New York: Schulte.

Freud, S. ([1895] 1981). "Project for Scientific Psychology." In *The Standard Edition,* Vol. 1, ed. J. Strachey. London: Hogarth.

Jung, C. G. (1968). *Analytical Psychology: Its Theory and Practice.* New York: Pantheon.

Kohut, H., and Wolf, E. (1978). "The Disorders of the Self and Their Treatment: An Outline." *International Journal of Psychoanalysis* 59:413–425.

L'Abate, L., and Bryson, C., eds. (1993). *A Theory of Personality Development.* New York: Wiley.

Lang, R. (1976). *The Bipersonal Field.* New York: Jason Aronson.

Leary, T. (1957). *Interpersonal Diagnosis of Personality.* New York: Ronald Press.

Lichtenberg, J. (1983). *Psychoanalysis and Infant Research.* New York: Analytic Press.

Lidz, T. (1983). *The Person.* New York: Basic Books.

Lothstein, L. (1983). *Female-to-Male Transsexualism.* London: Routledge & Kegan Paul.

Lothstein, L. (1993). "Clinical Management of Gender Dysphoria in Young Boys: Genital Mutilation and DSM IV Implications." In *Gender Dysphoria: Interdisciplinary Approaches in Clinical Management,* ed. W. Bukting and E. Coleman. Binghamton, NY: Haworth Press.

Mahler, M. (1968). *On Human Symbiosis and the Vicissitudes of Individuation:* Vol. 1, *Infantile Psychosis.* New York: International Universities Press.

Mahler, M.; Pine, F.; and Bergman, A. (1975). *Psychological Birth of the Human Infant: Symbiosis and Individuation.* New York: Basic Books.

Maslow, A. (1970). *Motivation and Personality.* New York: Harper & Row.

Millon, T. (1990). *Toward a New Personology: An Evolutionary Model.* New York: Wiley.

Monte, C. (1980). *Beneath the Mask: An Introduction to Theories of Personality.* New York: Holt, Rinehart and Winston.

Stoller, R. (1968). *Sex and Gender: On the Development of Masculinity and Femininity.* New York: Science House.

Sullivan, H. S. (1953). *The Interpersonal Theory of Psychiatry.* New York: W. W. Norton.

Winnicott, D. W. (1975). *Through Pediatrics to Psychoanalysis.* New York: Basic Books.

Zuckerman, M. (1991). *Psychobiology of Personality.* Boston: Cambridge University Press.

L. M. LOTHSTEIN

PERSONAL RELATIONSHIPS

Personal relationships are among the most rewarding elements of most people's lives, but at the same time, they can be among some of the most painful. When relationships are developing, going well, or being well maintained, they are a source of joy and comfort. On the other hand, when they are in turmoil or are breaking up, they can cause some of the most intense grief and psychological pain ever experienced.

The understanding of personal relationships in general has become the focus of a considerable amount of coherent interdisciplinary research attention since the late 1970s. This work explores the ways in which relationships develop, are maintained, and dissolve.

Each of these three elements will be considered in this entry, but the processes involved in each of them are surprisingly similar, with only the outcomes being different. In all cases, the persons carefully process information, attach meaning to it, and interact with one another using symbols and language that convey images of that meaning (Duck 1994; Shotter 1993). Every relationship between two partners inevitably occurs in the context of a network of other relationships and responsibilities. Thus, the partners are involved not only in their own particular relationships but also in other relationships that can influence their thoughts and behavior about the partnership between the two of them. For example, Sally A. Lloyd and Rodney M. Cate (1992) note that dating partners may not persist in developing a relationship with each other because they meet opposition from parents or friends. Alternatively, John La Gaipa (1981) points out that persons may just never consider dating someone from another group or gang because of what members of their own group or gang might think. Or perhaps, two partners may stay in an unhappy engagement, dating, or marital relationship partly because they are worried about the possibly negative opinions of other people, such as, "What would friends or neighbors think if we split up?"

Thus, this entry focuses not only on the thoughts, behaviors, and emotions of the partners but also on some of the general contextual issues that affect the ways in which people relate to one another in a completely functioning social world. The discussion here pays due attention to the social context (Duck 1993) in which relationships are conducted and where people other than the parents themselves may choose to make judgments about "how the partners are doing" (Shotter 1987)—whether they are creating, maintaining, or dissolving their relationship. Also, relationships are conducted in the world of talk, where simple casual conversations can achieve apparently insignificant purposes and yet allow the partners to see themselves in relation to one another (Duck 1991).

Development of Relationships

When relationships develop, it normally means that they grow in intimacy, with the partners becoming closer and more involved as a result of stronger positive emotions or attraction. However, the partners in developing relationships also increase the amount of time spent with one another and do a wider variety of things together. They also seek one another out as companions just for the sake of it rather than to complete tasks or other instrumental activity. This is normally thought to result from an increase in liking.

In line with the suggestions made above, however, researchers have also noted that relationships are emotions put into practice; one's feelings for another person must be put into behavior, and a relationship has to be constructed by negotiating time together, engaging in joint activities, enjoying leisure activities, and completing the chores of living (Duck 1991). A relationship also occurs in a social context in which such feelings and activities have to be conducted. Thus, it is not appropriate for feelings to be expressed in just any old way; the social context has to be taken into account. In fact, people express feelings in ways appropriate in their own culture (e.g., mourners wear black in Western cultures, yet mourners wear white in China). Such points rapidly make clear that a relationship involves multilevel processes of relating, not just emotions and feelings about a partner.

Ted Huston and several of his colleagues (Huston et al. 1981). explored the ways in which couples reflected on their pathway to marriage. In all cases, the process of increasing commitment involved the conjoining of leisure time, the distribution of labor, and the completion of chores together, as well as the development of affection and commitment to each other. Those couples who successfully organized their time in mutually satisfactory ways were the ones who were ultimately the most stable and satisfied, while the amount of affection and love felt for one another was less useful as a predictor of such outcomes. In other words, love is not enough; the management of the minor activities of life has a greater impact on the success of dating relationships as they progress toward marriage.

Carol Werner and her colleagues (1993) further demonstrated that the development of relationships involves the management of time, the creation of special places and rituals, and the celebration of the relationship. For instance, much of relationship building involves the creation of special days and events, the careful attention to partners' birthdays, and rituals together at major holidays and festivals. Such research again suggests strongly that the amount of affection that partners have for one another is not the only basis for success in relationships.

Renate Klein and Bob Milardo (1993) presented other evidence that the development of relationships, and also their management, can be strongly connected to other people and the reactions of those people to the relationship. For example, two persons in a couple do not define their relationship only in terms of their own feelings about the partner; each also has some idea of whether the relationship is "an ideal" relationship—that is, persons adopt notions about the relationship that are derived from the wider culture in which they are situated. When it comes to maintaining a relationship or experiencing conflict in a relationship, the partners are also likely to refer to outsiders' opinions and check with other people to see if they are conducting the relationship wisely or appropriately. Notice, for instance, how often couples who are planning a wedding will not just go ahead with their ideas, but instead will consult manuals, friends, and relatives about how a wedding *should* be done.

In brief, the trend of research on the development of relationships has been to explore the influences outside of the emotional geography of the relationship that affect that emotional interior. Correspondingly, less attention is being paid to the simple emotional factors that make people like one another, as researchers have increasingly realized that a relationship is something that has to be made, not just something that emerges straightforwardly out of feelings and emotions.

Maintenance of Relationships

When a relationship is being maintained, it normally means that the relationship is not developing nor declining in intimacy to any great extent but is held at a stable level. That is, the partners have established a level of intimacy and liking with which they feel comfortable for the time being. However, there are other senses of "relationship maintenance." For example, it can refer to the things that partners do just to keep the relationship in existence, ranging from the occasional letter and the annual Christmas card to the weekly phone call or the daily lunchtime ritual. The term "relational maintenance" is also used to refer to the things that partners do to keep the relationship in good repair or to maintain their relationship satisfaction.

In any case, the maintenance of relationships is not achieved just by the expression of emotions; it depends on the ways in which the partners manage the relationship through their behavior and through the handling of time and the daily hassles of life (Bolger and Kelleher 1993).

Kathryn Dindia and Leslie Baxter (1987) found that couples used a number of strategies to sustain their satisfaction with the relationship and make clear to each other how much they valued the relationship. One set of such strategies depended on the use of memory and reminiscence. The simple action of recalling past events, dramas, turning points, or feelings in a relationship serves to celebrate the existence of the attachment and remind the partners of the value that it has for them. Another strategy related to this is the use of rituals; couples may establish ritual forms of behavior that they follow routinely as a way of celebrating the relationship, such as having a "date night" on Fridays or always going to a particular restaurant each Sunday for lunch. Another such technique is the use of regular phone calls around noon just to find out how the day is going.

Other strategies involve the deliberate attempt to be nice and play up the positive sides of the relationship, to refrain from criticism and be complimentary about the other individual instead; a communicative or "metacommunicative" approach (talking about talk), sharing feelings, talking about the day's events, or focusing specifically on the problems that the couple might have; or merely spending time together, either just "hanging out" or in the completion of shared activities. In all these cases, the research shows that the management of a relationship involves a certain amount of focusing on the relationship itself, as well as on the partner or on one's own feelings. Again, the message is that the management of activities and shared time contributes to the well-being of a relationship; the meaning attached to the activities is more of a contributor to the success of the relationship that is the activity itself (Duck 1994). When the partners are doing things not for their own sake but for the sake of the relationship, it sends a clear signal that the relationship has great significance.

While such messages generate feelings of satisfaction in the relationship, routine maintenance of a relationship is often achieved by means of the little activities of daily life, as Marianne Dainton and Laura Stafford (1993) showed. Their research presented strong evidence that the sharing of tasks is regarded by both men and women as a most important element in sustaining the relationship.

Charlotte Reissman, Art Aron, and Merlynn Bergen (1993) support and extend this idea by showing that relationships and satisfaction are enhanced by the completion of activities that are exciting, rather than simply interesting. In the case of exciting activities, the two partners are aroused by the completion of the activities done together; this contributes to a general sense of growth and development as human beings and to each individual feeling more positively about the situation and the person with whom it was experienced.

Therefore, the maintenance of relationships involves various techniques for sustaining affection, most of which come down to some form of maintenance of the routine behaviors and activities of the relationship, things previously thought to have very little to do with romance or affection. As in much else to do with relationships, the daily practical management of life plays a large part in the satisfactory conduct and maintenance of relationships (Bolger and Kelleher 1993).

Dissolution of Relationships

When a relationship is being dissolved, it normally means that the relationship is not developing in intimacy to any great extent and is in truth declining; the partners are possibly quite antipathetic to each other, there is considerable conflict, and at least one partner is expressing or harboring the desire to leave the relationship. Actually, there are many other elements to relationship dissolution. These involve the fact that the relationship exists in a social network and that the partners have several different issues to consider over and above their own private feelings about the relationship or the partner.

It is important to recognize that even in the discussion of relationship dissolution a relationship is a composite of many parts and processes and not simply the by-product of two persons' liking for one another. Therefore, the unraveling of a relationship is likewise a process that has several parts and it is not simply a consequence of two people coming to like one another less. Gunhild Hagestad and Michael Smyer (1982) pointed out that a "standard" relationship dissolution requires three things. The first is the reduction of affection or liking for the partner. The second is the reduction of commitment to the roles involved in the relationships. For example, a divorcing couple must get used to the idea of not being "married" anymore or not being "a wife" or a "a husband." In present-day Western society, such roles are valued and approved by the majority of the culture. Accordingly, some people like, feel comfortable with, and actually desire the state of being married, in part for its own sake. The third component of a "standard" relationship dissolution is the disentangling from routine ways of doing things as they were set up and carried out in the relationship. Many divorcing couples find it difficult to reorganize their leisure time, their chores, or other activities around the house when they are not doing them in partnership with their former spouse. Where one of the necessary activities of building a relationship is for partners to organize leisure and chores together, one of the unfortunate consequences of breaking up is the necessity first to undo and then to reconstruct some of that organization. Such an undoing of order can cause a sense of loss of structure in a person's life and has to be managed and dealt with in its own right as part of relationship dissolution.

Because any relationship exists in a network of other relationships, the breakup of a particular attachment inevitably involves the network. Other people will be told that the relationship has broken up, and they may have strong reactions to the news. Therefore, people contemplating a breakup tend to become aware of the social consequences of the announcement, in addition to the personal feelings they may be experiencing.

Steve Duck (1982) has suggested that the process of relational breakup has four major phases: the intrapsychic phase, the dyadic phase, the social phase, and the grave-dressing phase.

The intrapsychic phase is where one person considers the difficulties and lack of enjoyment in a relationship, weighs the partner's good and bad points, considers the consequences of leaving and the attractions of alternatives, and so on. At this point, the person does nothing to bring about the end of the relationship; this is basically a complaining, grumbling, self-pitying phase.

The dyadic phase comes when the person confronts the partner with the deficiencies of the relationship and the two of them discuss the issues. Perhaps here they will try to work something out or they may decide to end the relationship. At this point, the partners probably have strong debates or even violent conflicts about one another's behavior and the problems that it seems to create. There is a considerable risk of strongly critical discussion and even unpleasant dispute, but the dyadic phase may also be handled quite calmly and thoughtfully as each person listens to the other intently and constructively. The biggest risk is that the partners will become angry and confrontational, partly as a result of the nature of the situation itself. The very fact of fighting about the relationship could present an extra difficulty that needs special handling.

This phase may, however, result in the two partners becoming more aware of the things that cause problems for one another. The outcome could be a reconciliation. The couple might give the relationship another try in a different shape or use modified behaviors; for example, they may agree to do certain things differently and see how that works out. Perhaps they may use some maintenance strategies to achieve the same desired positive goal.

If the dyadic phase does not help, the next phase is the social phase, where the problems are exposed to other people. These third parties may even become involved in the proceedings and may be asked to help or else to take sides (La Gaipa 1982). The very fact that other people in the network know about the couple's relationship problems inevitably means that the strategies for handling the issues become different. For one thing, a certain amount of impression management begins; each person may want to convince the people in the network that they are in the right and the other person is in the wrong. In this phase, some of the issues of relationship dissolution clearly involve appearances rather than just feelings alone.

The fourth and final phase builds on this last point. This phase is all about appearances and the accounts or stories that are constructed for the ending of a relationship. It occurs when the relationship is beyond revocation and the partners begin "gravedressing." This is, each partner constructs a story about the relationship: their version of its course and history and an account of why it failed. This story is one that each person tells to other people and also to him- or herself as a means of explaining and rationalizing the ending of the relationship. The perfect gravedressing story does not threaten the public image of the person telling the story. For example, if the storyteller revealed that the relationship started only for selfish reasons and was broken off without regard to the partner's feelings, the storyteller would look uncaring, irresponsible, and unsympathetic. On the other hand, a "good story" would indicate the storyteller's recognition of the partner's strong qualities right from the start, coupled with acknowledgment of some key weaknesses that one hoped to overcome with effort, but which ultimately proved insurmountable (Weber 1983).

In the dissolution of relationships, therefore, the concerns of the persons who are breaking up consist of more than the management of feelings for one another. A large part of the work of breaking up consists of managing the "public record" and taking account of the fact that people outside the partnership will be likely to comment on the partners' performance of their relationship and to make moralizing commentaries about it, just as with other aspects of relating (Duck 1990; Shotter 1987, 1992).

Conclusion

In all of the processes involved with personal relationships, the important issues highlighted by recent research have to do with social contexts of relating and the fact that individuals express emotion and conduct relationships against a perpetual backdrop of social expectations and social conventions. In many cases, these expectations and conventions exert a force, at all stages of relating, that modifies and constrains individual feelings. It is this recognition and perhaps the awareness of the powerful force of routine behaviors and everyday talk that defines the research on personal relationships.

(*See also:* Attribution in Relationships; Commitment; Communication; Friendship; Intimacy; Jealousy; Love; Mate Selection; Social Networks; Trust)

BIBLIOGRAPHY

Bolger, N., and Kelleher, S. (1993). "Daily Life in Relationships." In *Understanding Relationship Processes:* Vol. 3, *Social Contexts of Relationships*, ed. S. W. Duck. Newbury Park, CA: Sage Publications.

Dainton, M., and Stafford, L. (1993). "Routine Maintenance Behaviors: A Comparison of Relationship Type, Partner Similarity, and Sex Differences." *Journal of Social and Personal Relationships* 10:255–271.

Dindia, K., and Baxter, L. A. (1987). "Strategies for Maintaining and Repairing Marital Relationships." *Journal of Social and Personal Relationships* 4:143–158.

Duck, S. W. (1982). "A Topography of Relationship Disengagement and Dissolution." In *Personal Relationships:* Vol. 4, *Dissolving Personal Relationships*, ed. S. W. Duck. New York: Academic Press.

Duck, S. W. (1990). "Relationships as Unfinished Business: Out of the Frying Pan and into the 1990s." *Journal of Social and Personal Relationships* 7:5–29.

Duck, S. W. (1991). *Understanding Relationships.* New York: Guilford.

Duck, S. W. (1993). "Preface on Social Context." In *Understanding Relationship Processes:* Vol. 3, *Social Contexts of Relationships*, ed. S. W. Duck. Newbury Park, CA: Sage Publications.

Duck, S. W. (1994) *Meaningful Relationships: Talking, Sense, and Relating.* Newbury Park, CA: Sage Publications.

Duck, S. W.; Rutt, D. J.; Hurst, M. H.; and Strejc, H. (1991). "Some Evident Truths About Conversations in Everyday Relationships: All Communications Are Not Created Equal." *Human Communication Research* 18:228–267.

Hagestad, G. O., and Smyer, M. A. (1982) "Dissolving Long-Term Relationships: Patterns of Divorcing in Middle Age." In *Personal Relationships:* Vol. 4, *Dissolving Personal Relationships*, ed. S. W. Duck. New York: Academic Press.

Huston, T. L.; Surra, C. A.; Fitzgerald, N. M.; and Cate, R. M. (1981). "From Courtship to Marriage: Mate Selection as an Interpersonal Process." In *Personal Relationships:* Vol. 2, *Developing Personal Relationships*, ed. S. W. Duck and R. Gilmour. New York: Academic Press.

Klein, R., and Milardo, R. (1993). "Third-Party Influences on the Development and Maintenance of Personal Relationships." In *Understanding Relationship Processes:* Vol. 3, *Social Contexts of Relationships*, ed. S. W. Duck. Newbury Park, CA: Sage Publications.

La Gaipa, J. J. (1981). "A Systems Approach to Personal Relationships." In *Personal Relationships:* Vol. 1, *Studying Personal Relationships*, ed. S. W. Duck and R. Gilmour. New York: Academic Press.

La Gapia, J. J. (1982). "Rules and Rituals in Disengaging from Relationships." In *Personal Relationships:* Vol. 4, *Dissolving Personal Relationships*, ed. S. W. Duck. New York: Academic Press.

Lloyd, S. A., and Cate, R. M. (1992). *Courtship.* Newbury Park, CA: Sage Publications.

Reissman, C.; Aron, A.; and Bergen, M. (1993). "Shared Activities and Marital Satisfaction: Casual Direction and Self-Expansion Versus Boredom." *Journal of Social and Personal Relationships* 10:243–254.

Shotter, J. (1987). "The Social Construction of an 'Us': Problems of Accountability and Narratology." In *Accounting for Relationships*, ed. R. Burnett, P. McGhee, and D. D. Clarke. London: Methuen.

Shotter, J. (1992). "What Is a 'Personal Relationship?' A Rhetorical-Responsive Account of 'Unfinished Business.' " In *Attributions, Accounts, and Close Relationships*, ed. J. H. Harvey, T. L. Orbuch, and A. L. Weber. New York: Springer-Verlag.

Shotter, J. (1993). *Cultural Politics of Everyday Life.* Toronto: University of Toronto Press.

Weber, A. (1983). "The Breakdown of Relationships." Paper presented to the Nags Head Conference on Social Interaction and Relationships, Nags Head, NC.

Werner, C.; Altman, I.; Brown, B.; and Ginat, J. (1993). "Celebrations in Personal Relationships: A Transactional/Dialectical Perspective." In *Understanding Relationship Processes:* Vol. 3, *Social Contexts of Relationships*, ed. S. W. Duck. Newbury Park,CA: Sage Publications.

STEVE DUCK

PLAY

A question often raised is whether pretend play influences cognitive development in children. Jean Piaget (1962, p. 89) wrote that play relaxes "the effort at adaptation" and that the child engages in activities for the "mere pleasure of mastering them and acquiring thereby a feeling of virtuosity or power." However, Brian Vandenberg (1982, p. 16) likens play to a clown, "culture's way of making fun of itself." Although some other writers regard play as child's "work," Mihalyi Csikszentmihalyi (1982), Brian Sutton-Smith (1982), and Michael Lewis (1982) have all suggested along with Vandenberg that play is just plain fun.

Most researchers in the field of play who have examined animal behavior draw a distinction between play and those animal behaviors that are related to survival and reproduction. Peter Smith (1976) has classified play for young, nonhuman animals into three categories: (1) locomotor play involving jumping, sudden running, dangling, or crawling; (2) play that involves physical objects in a tool-like fashion; and (3) social play, which can include both of the former kinds of activities but also involves contact with siblings. This play is characterized by pouncing, grabbing, playful biting, wrestling, grooming, mounting, or chasing.

Smith (1976) concludes that physical activity of animals is useful as exercise to promote better muscle tone and improves the physical skill and agility needed for escape, survival, and reproduction. Play fighting seems to have little adaptive purpose among animals, although the pouncing play in young cats has proved predictive of the prey-catching skills needed for hunting, and the wrestling in male cubs may be a precursor of the skills needed among lions to assert their authority over other males.

Age Differences in Play

When the play of humans is examined, it is helpful to look at play through a stage approach, recognizing that play serves different purposes at different ages. Piaget (1962) delineated play into three major periods: (1) practice play, which includes imitation, (2) symbolic play, which is pure assimilation or distortion of reality and implies representation of an absent object, and (3) games with rules, such as board games or marbles.

Imitation, the earliest form of play, occurs in the sensor-motor period from birth to approximately twenty-four months. The infant copies the sounds and actions of the persons or animals in the environment. Thus, the words "bye-bye" or a hand wave are reinforced by the adult's smile of approval. Mouth, hands, eyes, and feet are all ready to perform "functional pleasure" games. These movements are pure accommodation, imitation without true understanding of what the act means. A toddler, for example, may pick up a toy telephone and say "goodbye" or wave "bye-bye" to someone entering a room. Only later, as the toddler moves into the stage of symbolic play, will the words and motor movements match appropriately.

Other practice games leading to mastery are evidenced by the infant or toddler swatting a mobile in the crib to make it move, stacking cubes or blocks, or putting plastic sticks into a jar. Fine motor skills are developing as the toddler explores the many objects in the crib or playroom. As the baby gets older, large motor skills are practiced through singing, climbing, riding a tricycle, hopping, running, and jumping.

Symbolic play or pretend play emerges around the age of two, although researchers such as Greta Fein (1981) have found evidence of pretend play among eighteen-month-old toddlers. According to Fein, the following criteria are necessary for symbolic play:

1. A familiar activity may be performed in the absence of necessary material or a social context (washing a doll in a pretend tub).
2. Activities may not be carried out to a logical conclusion (pirates sail away after the pirate boat sinks).
3. Inanimate objects may be treated as real (a stuffed animal is offered food).
4. An object or gesture may be substituted for another (a stick becomes a doll).
5. A child may carry out an activity usually performed by someone else (pretending to be a mail carrier or astronaut).

The period in which symbolic play occurs is called the preoperational period by Piaget. The child in this stage, from ages two to seven, is characterized by confusions of time, space, numbers, and distances. Preoperational children are egocentric, believing that what they feel or think is experienced by others around them. They believe in animism, that is, that everything that moves is alive, such as the blowing wind or a burning candle. The reasoning of a young child is transductive, meaning that simultaneous events have a cause-and-effect relationship (the whistle of a train is responsible for its movement). Children at this stage of development believe in artificialism, the notion that human or humanlike divine architects are responsible for natural formations (a giant's footstep made a hole which became a lake when it rained). The preschooler is unable to understand the notion of conservation, the fact that objects or quantities remain the same despite a change in their physical appearance (four ounces of water poured into a tall thin glass are the same as four ounces poured into a short wide glass where it looks like less).

Because the preoperational child thinks illogically, a certain charm is present that delights caregivers. Play is at peak during this stage, especially from age three to six. In preliminary pretend play, as a child feeds a doll, the child is active while the doll remains passive. Gradually, the doll becomes more active: walking, talking, feeding another doll or the "mommy." Children also move from solitary pretend play to social pretend play, where they interact with other children and take on various roles. In simple solitary pretend play, a child may move a truck along the floor, imitate a cat or dog by crawling along the floor, put a teddy bear to sleep, or rock a doll in a cradle. Two toddlers may even play side by side (parallel play) without playing with each other. They may occasionally exchange a toy or a word, but their major focus is on their own play game.

At about age three, cooperative social pretend play begins and reaches its peak by ages four and five. Carolee Howes (1985) makes a distinction between social play and social pretend play. Social play involves turn-taking and sharing but may not involve the make-believe elements found in symbolic play episodes. In social play, children can hide, play ball with each other, and play finger or movement games, but still not assume roles, change voices, or carry out a story with the numerous transformations of voice, persons, and objects that characterize social pretend play.

Games with rules is the last stage in Piaget's theory of play. At around age seven, the stage of concrete operations, children begin to move away from pretend play and involve themselves with board games. Games with rules are the ludic or playful activities of the socialized being. Some games with rules, such as "Take a Giant Step" and hopscotch, are institutional, having been passed from generation to generation with only minimal changes. Children learn these games either by direct instruction from older children or by observation and imitation. As children move from the preoperational stage to the stage of concrete operations, they begin to think more logically and can understand that rules are constant and cannot be modified. Observation of children in this stage, however, reveals that rules are sometimes changed by the leaders in the game to suit themselves. Only later, as children become older and move into Piaget's last developmental stage of formal operations, do children truly abide by rules and see them as inviolate.

Sex Differences in Play

Advertisers know that there are differences between boys and girls and their attitudes toward toys. When toys are advertised on television, boys are generally the main players of toys geared to both sexes. If a girl is shown as the dominant figure in the scene or viewed playing with a toy with no boys present, boys label it a girl's toy despite a neutral structure such as train set. This was borne out in a study of play themes of preschoolers by Jerome L. Singer and Dorothy G. Singer (1981). Adventure themes, fantasy characters, superheroes, and spacemen were the favored pretend play of boys. Girls indicated a clear preference for family pretend roles (mother, father, baby), playing "house," and dress-up clothes.

Parents may be socializing their children from an early age to choose sex-typed toys and engage in sex-typed play. Rena Repetti (1984), for example, found that children who chose more traditionally sex-linked toys were more likely to be those whose parents responded to gender-role questionnaires in a traditional way. Repetti showed pictures of ten different toys to children ages five-and-a-half to seven-and-a-half and asked them to indicate whether the toy was for boys, for girls, or for both boys and girls. In addition, the children were asked about sixteen adult occupations and whether the job was for men, women, or both. Subjects assigned dolls to girls, jeeps to boys, and toy mixers to girls. The labeling of sex-typed toys was significantly related to a child's tendency to stereotype occupations.

Parents may be influenced by a baby's sex or behavior. Nancy Bell and William Carver (1980) found that when women were asked to offer a baby a toy, those who expressed a belief in sex differences were more apt to choose more masculine-typed toys for an infant boy than were women who expressed little belief in sex differences. If babies were more passive, they were generally offered feminine toys; if more active, they were offered more masculine toys. The infant's behavior was an important factor in illiciting responses from the women, more so than their adult preconceptions based on sex stereotypes.

Children as young as eighteen months have shown preference for sex-stereotyped choices (Caldera, Huston, and O'Brien 1989), and as they get older, this preference for same-sex-typed toys continues (Eisenberg, Tryon, and Cameron 1984). Even when children respond to an opposite-sex-typed toy, they seem to return to the same-sex toy and play with it for longer periods (Schau et al. 1980).

Older children have been studied by Corinne Hutt and Reena Bhavnani (1976), who found that boys were more active and, thus, were classified as inventive explorers when novel toys were introduced into their play environment; girls remained more passive and were labeled nonexplorers. In an earlier study, Sutton-Smith (1968) asked kindergartners to give alternative uses for male- and female-sex-typed toys. The children were familiar with these toys, but their play experiences with them were different. If the toy was same-sex, the child ascribed more unique responses to the toy. Obviously, the child's familiarity and play experience with a toy led to more responses to it than a toy recognized but not used in play. In another experiment of this nature, Erica Rosenfeld (1975) presented children with toys, asking them to suggest novel ways of using them. Both boys and girls offered more interesting and exciting ideas related to the male-typed toy than to the female-typed toy. It appears that toys manufactured for girls tend to be of a more passive nature—dolls, toy stoves, tea sets, carriages—while boys receive the cars, trucks, rocket ships, boats, mechanical sets, minature tools, and toy weapons.

Benefits of Play

Play constitutes a major part of the preschooler's life, but it need not stop as a child gets older. The sensory-motor play of the infant can be found in the adult's enjoyment of trickling sand between the toes or the playful splashing in a pool. Mastery play is in evidence when the adult perfects a tennis or golf stroke or studies a new move in chess. Pretend play is manifested in amateur theatricals, Mardi Gras costume parades, the writing of poetry or prose, and simple daydreaming.

For the child, play has distinct advantages. Compensatory play can allow a child to handle emotions. If a parent has scolded a child, that child can scold its doll or stuffed animal later in the day. If a child is jealous about the arrival of a new baby, a child can enact feelings of anger, jealousy, and later acceptance of this rival through puppet play (D. G. Singer 1993). Some researchers have used play as a means of training children to develop more fantasy skills (Dansky 1980; McCaslin 1984; Rosenberg 1987; D. G. Singer and J. L Singer 1985; Smilansky 1986).

Play can enhance a child's cognitive, physical, social, and emotional development. Cognitive gains can be made in vocabulary through play. When children play "house," they need words for furnishings, utensils, and food. They learn to sequence from big to biggest when they play. Even the baby who uses plastic nesting cubes in the sensory-motor period is beginning to sequence. Children learn colors, shapes, and numbers through play. They need four chairs for children at their tea party. They name the colors of their play objects and differentiate among squares, circles, and triangles in a play "neighborhood" where they learn to recognize the shapes of street signs.

Each form of play has particular benefits. Mastery play leads to development of fine and large motor skills. Pushing a swing or throwing a ball into a hoop leads to feelings of competence and confidence. Social skills are in evidence in all forms of play. Children learn to share, take turns, and cooperate. They learn to concentrate in games with rules, such as board games, or in street games, where rules can be elaborate.

Through sociodramatic play, children learn about roles in society. They can pretend to be a teacher, doctor, firefighter, grocery clerk, or mail carrier. They learn to be flexible through changing roles or by using makeshift materials to substitute for real ones. Emotions are expressed during play when children act out a scary story or play "birthday party" with exclamations of surprise, interest, and joy. Playing pretend games seems to be inductive to positive emotions. Research demonstrates that children who are playing with each other in make-believe games tend to be rated as more joyful than those who are playing in a solitary fashion or at the periphery of the play groupings (D. G. Singer and J. L. Singer 1990; J. L. Singer and D. G. Singer 1981).

Conclusion

Play, especially symbolic or pretend play, may be the training ground for the inventive mind and the attitude toward the possible. Parents or caregivers can foster play through their willingness to give a child space to play in, a few unstructured toys or props to play with, encouragement to use imagination and pretense, and most of all the sanction to enjoy the fantasies and fun of childhood without the threat of shame or embarrassment.

(*See also:* Attachment; Gender; Gender Identity; Personality Development)

BIBLIOGRAPHY

Bell, N., and Carver, W. (1980). "A Reevaluation of Gender Label Effects: Expectant Mothers' Responses to Infants." *Child Development* 51:927.

Caldera, Y.; Huston, A.; and O'Brien, M. (1989). "Social Interactions and Play Patterns of Parents and Toddlers with Feminine, Masculine, and Neutral Toys." *Child Development* 60:70–76.

Csikszentmihalyi, M. (1982). "Does Being Human Matter? On Some Interpretative Problems of Comparative Ludology." *Behavioral and Brain Science* 5:166.

Dansky, J. (1980). "Make-Believe: A Mediator in the Relationship Between Play and Associative Frequency." *Child Development* 51:576–579.

Eisenberg, N.; Tryon, K.; and Cameron, E. (1984). "The Relation of Preschoolers' Peer Interaction to Their Sex-Typed Toy Choices." *Child Development* 55:1044–1050.

Fein, G. G. (1981). "Pretend Play in Childhood: An Integrative Review." *Child Development* 52:1095–1118.

Howes, C. (1985). "Sharing Fantasy: Social Pretend Play in Toddlers." *Child Development* 56:1255–1258.

Hutt, C., and Bhavnani, R. (1976). "Predictions from Play." In *Play*, ed. J. S. Bruner, A. Jolly, and K. Sylvia. New York: Basic Books.

Lewis, M. (1982). "Play as Whimsy." *Behavioral and Brain Sciences* 5:170–171.

McCaslin, N. (1984). *Creative Drama in the Classroom.* New York: Longman.

Piaget, J. (1962). *Play, Dreams, and Imitation in Childhood.* New York: W. W. Norton.

Repetti, R. (1984). "Determinants of Children's Sex Stereotyping: Parental Sex-Role Traits and Television Viewing." *Personality and Social Psychology Bulletin* 10:457–468.

Rosenberg, H. (1987). *Creative Drama and Imagination.* New York: Holt, Rinehart and Winston.

Rosenfeld, E. (1975). "The Relationship of Sex-Typed Toys to the Development of Competency and Sex-Role Identification." Paper presented at the meeting of the Society for Research on Child Development, Denver.

Schau, C. G.; Kahn, L.; Diepold, J.; and Cherry, F. (1980). "The Relationship of Parental Expectations and Preschool Children's Verbal Sex Typing to Their Sex-Typed Toy Play Behavior." *Child Development* 51:266–270.

Singer, D. G. (1993). *Playing for Their Lives: Helping Troubled Children Through Play Therapy.* New York: Free Press.

Singer, D. G., and Singer, J. L. (1985). *Make Believe.* Glenview, IL: Goodyear Books.

Singer, D. G., and Singer, J. L. (1990). *The House of Make Believe.* Cambridge, MA: Harvard University Press.

Singer, J. L., and Singer, D. G. (1981). *Television, Imagination, and Aggression: A Study of Preschoolers.* Hillsdale, NJ: Lawrence Erlbaum.

Smilansky, S. (1986). *The Effects of Sociodramatic Play on Disadvantaged Preschool Children.* New York: Wiley.

Smith, P. K. (1976). "Does Play Matter? Functional and Evolutionary Aspects of Animal and Human Play." *Behavioral and Brain Sciences* 5:139–184.

Sutton-Smith, B. (1968). "Novel Responses to Toys." *Merrill-Palmer Quarterly* 14:151–158.

Sutton-Smith, B. (1982). "The Epistemology of the Play Theorist." *Behavioral and Brain Sciences* 5:170–171.

Vandenberg, B. (1982). "Play: A Concept in Need Definitions?" In *The Play of Children: Current Theory and Research*, ed. D. J. Pepler and K. H. Rubin. Basel, Switzerland: Karger.

Dorothy G. Singer

POLYANDRY

Polyandry, a form of marriage linking a woman to two or more men, exists today in only a few societies, but historical accounts suggest that polyandrous marriage was more common in the past. Continuing declines, which vary from region to region and in their timing, have been attributed to legal codes that outlawed the practice of polyandry, social reformers who worked to eradicate customs seen as "backward" by national populations, and the effect of economic modernization on traditional family organization.

All societies known to have polyandry also recognize marriages with one husband and one wife (monogamy) and marriages with more than one wife (polygyny). The ways in which these marital forms are contracted and combined fall into four distinctive patterns that anthropologists have labeled fraternal polyandry, associated polyandry, Nayar polyandry, and secondary marriage. Moreover, every polyandrous society displays a unique set of rules for and ideas about marriage. The result is cross-societal variation in the incidence of polyandry and the reasons individuals choose one form of marriage over another.

Fraternal polyandry, probably the most common type in incidence, may have been the most widely practiced type on a global basis, so that whereas the other types are localized, fraternal polyandry appeared in widely scattered places. It involves the simultaneous marriage of a family's brothers to one wife. Under special circumstances, the husbands take a second wife, with sisters commonly preferred as cowives (sororal polygyny). Husbands and wives form a single household in the husbands' village. A man without brothers marries monogamously. Researchers have described fraternal polyandry in Tibet, the Himalayas, and Southwest India (Kerala and the Nilgiri Hills).

Associated polyandry has been most thoroughly studied in Sri Lanka, where its practice has also declined. In this system, a second husband is added to a preexisting monogamous union, with brothers preferred as the cohusbands. Although the spouses coreside, property may be held separately, especially if the men are unrelated.

The unique polyandrous system of the Nayars in Kerala was well documented before it disappeared in the early-twentieth century. Nayar households traditionally were formed around siblings rather than married couples. Children were raised by their mothers and maternal uncles, and ancestry was traced through women. A woman maintained concurrent sexual relationships with several men, one of whom would claim paternity when she became pregnant. A man, similarly, would have several wives at a time.

Secondary marriage describes practices found in a number of communities in northern Nigeria and northern Cameroon. The women of these communities are encouraged to contract subsequent marriages while maintaining their first marriages. Unlike the variants of polyandry found in Asia, women coreside with only one husband at a time; the polyandry is never fraternal, and the relationships between the men are distant. Men in these regions, however, marry additional wives in polygyny, and women (who are never sisters) may coreside. Among the consequences of secondary marriage are the very separate marital careers of men and women and the multiplication of in-law relationships across the community.

There also are numbers of societies in which women may have publicly acknowledged extramarital sexual relationships. Such practices must be distinguished from polyandry when they do not involve the rights and obligations customarily associated with marriage, such as economic cooperation between spouses, legitimation of children, and the creation of in-law relationships.

Polyandry has been the focus of anthropological attention since the mid-nineteenth century. However, the anthopologists' explanations for the existence of polyandry have changed over time in response to changing theories in the social sciences. The earliest accounts depicted polyandry as a relic of an earlier stage of human social evolutionary development and asserted that it remained only in socially primitive groups. Other early reports described polyandry as a response to severe resource constraints—which made it difficult for a man to support a wife on his own—or to shortages of women. The problem with these explanations is that polyandry occurs primarily among technologically advanced farming peoples, some of whom occupy ecologically rich environments. Shortages of women in a few polyandrous societies have been attributed to insufficient care of female children, apparently in response to their poorer chances of marrying.

Modern accounts of polyandry have considered how particular marriage customs are integrated with other aspects of social life. Nayar polyandry, for example, may have developed as an adaptation to men's employment in the military and the availability of laborers from other groups to work on the family farm. Tibetan polyandry is reinforced by high demand for male labor and male absences from home. In the Himalayan foothills, where sororal polygyny commonly accompanies fraternal polyandry, men and women are needed equally as workers. Some anthropologists have suggested that economic modernization, which offers employment other than work on the family farm, supports increased monogamy at the expense of polyandry.

Studies have pointed to other advantages of fraternal polyandry under traditional preindustrial socioeconomic conditions. Brothers who jointly marry a single woman need not divide their inheritance and therefore remain wealthier than those who establish separate families. In systems of polyandry where polygyny is rare, relatively fewer women marry and bear children, creating a brake on populating growth.

Throughout the history of studies of polyandry, researchers have noted that polyandry is very deeply ingrained culturally, although some have suggested that living in large, complex households and sharing a wife, as in fraternal and associated polyandry, is psychologically stressful. Data on polyandry in Sri Lanka reveal that such marriages are more stable—and presumably more satisfying—when the cohusbands are brothers. Data on fraternal polyandry in Tibet demonstrate that marriages with two or three brothers are more stable than those including more siblings.

Most recently, evolutionary biologists have begun to take account of variations in human marriage systems. They find polyandry problematic because it appears to constrict men's reproductive opportunities; a man sharing a wife ordinarily has fewer children than a man with one or more wives to himself. Evolutionary biologists argue that polyandry makes greater sense where men find it difficult to support their families. They also explain the preference for brothers as cohusbands in many polyandrous systems in terms of natural selection, which favors altruistic behavior between kin, rather than strangers.

Many topics that would enhance understanding of polyandry remain to be investigated before polyandrous systems decline further. For example, nothing is known of the effects of polyandrous coparenting on child development, and very little is known about the interpersonal relationships between polyandrous spouses.

(*See also:* Kinship; Marriage Definition; Polygyny)

BIBLIOGRAPHY

Beall, C., and Goldstein, M. C. (1981). "Tibetan Fraternal Polyandry: A Test of Sociobiological Theory." *American Anthropologist* 83:5–12.

Berreman, G. D. (1978). "Ecology, Demography, and Domestic Strategies in the Western Himalayas." *Journal of Anthropological Research* 34:326–368.

Crook, J. H., and Crook, S. J. (1988). "Tibetan Polyandry: Problems of Adaptation and Fitness." In *Human Reproductive Behavior: A Darwinian Perspective*, ed. L. Betzig, M. Borgerhoff Mulder, and P. Turke. Cambridge, Eng.: Cambridge University Press.

Fuller, C. J. (1976). *The Nayars Today.* Cambridge, Eng.: Cambridge University Press.

Goldstein, M. C. (1976). "Stratification, Polyandry, and Family Structure in Tibet." *Southwestern Journal of Anthropology* 27:64–74.

Goldstein, M. C. (1978). "Pahari and Tibetan Polyandry Revisited." *Ethnology* 17:325–337.

Gough, E. K. (1959). "The Nayars and the Definition of Marriage." *Journal of the Royal Anthropological Institute* 89:23–34.

Gough, E. K. (1961). "Nayar: Central Kerala." In *Matrilineal Kinship*, ed. D. M. Schneider and E. K. Gough. Berkeley: University of California Press.

Hiatt, L. R. (1980). "Polyandry in Sri Lanka: A Test Case for Parental Investment Theory." *Man* 15:583–602.

Leach, E. (1966). "Polyandry, Inheritance, and the Definition of Marriage—with Particular Reference to Sinhalese Customary Law." Reprinted in *Rethinking Anthropology.* London: Athlone Press.

Levine, N. E. (1988). *The Dynamics of Polyandry: Kinship, Domesticity, and Population on the Tibetan Border.* Chicago: University of Chicago Press.

Levine, N. E., and Sangree, W. H. (1980). "Women with Many Husbands: Polyandrous Alliance and Marital Flexibility in Africa and Asia." *Journal of Comparative Family Studies* (Special Issue) 11.

Muller, J. C., and Sangree, W. H. (1973). "Irigwe and Rukuba Marriage: A Comparison." *The Canadian Journal of African Studies* 7:27–57.

Tambiah, S. J. (1966). "Polyandry in Ceylon—with Special Reference to the Lagala Region." In *Caste and Kin in Nepal, India, and Ceylon*, ed C. von Furer-Haimendorf. London: Asia Publishing House.

Westermarck, E. (1926). *A Short History of Marriage.* London: Macmillan.

Nancy E. Levine

POLYGYNY

Polygyny, the social arrangement that permits a man to have more than one wife at the same time, has been the normatively endorsed form of marriage in more than three-fourths of the world's traditional cultures (Murdock 1957). The two variations of polygyny are sororal (the cowives are sisters) and nonsororal (the cowives are not sisters). Some societies also observe the custom of levirate, making it compulsory for a man to marry his brother's widow.

Historically, polygyny was a feature of the ancient Hebrews, the traditional Chinese, and the nineteenth-century Mormons in the United States, but the modern practice of polygyny is concentrated in Africa, the Middle East, India, Thailand, and Indonesia. The extent to which men are able to acquire multiple wives depends on many factors, including the economic prosperity of the man's family, the prevailing bride price, the differential availability of marriageable females, the need and desire for additional offspring, and the availability of productive roles for subsequent wives. Even in societies that permit polygyny, the conditions of life for the masses make monogamy the most common form of marriage.

Various theories have been advanced to explain the cultural endorsement of polygyny. One of the earliest explanations was based on the notion that men have a greater disposition for variety in sexual partners than do women (Lee 1979). While this theory is of historical interest, there exists no empirical support for the greater sex drive of the male, nor is there any reason to expect the male sex drive to vary from one culture to another.

It has also been suggested that polygyny as a marriage form evolved in response to lengthy postpartum sex taboos because polygyny provides a legitimate sexual outlet for the husband during this period of taboo (Whiting 1964). While men may seek other sexual relationships during the period of a long postpartum taboo, it is not clear why polygyny is the only possible solution to the problem, since the legitimation of sex does not depend exclusively on marriage.

The existence of a low sex ratio, a scarcity of men in relation to women, has also been offered as an explanation for the origin of this practice (Ember 1974). Polygyny maximizes the opportunities for females to marry in a society in which adult males are in short supply. The fact that the sex ratio at the time of young adulthood is numerically balanced in some societies suggests that while a sex ratio imbalance may contribute to the development of polygyny in special cases, it is an incomplete explanation for the existence of polygyny in the majority of societies in the world. For example, plural marriage developed among the Mormons in Utah when, as in most of the western states of the United States, there was an excess of males (Arrington and Bitton 1979).

The theory that has stimulated the most empirical investigation links the existence of polygyny to the productive value of the woman. According to this theory, the occurrence of polygyny is positively related to the extent to which women contribute to the subsistence bases of their respective societies (Boserup 1970; Heath 1958).

However, further research suggests that the relationship between women's economic contribution and marriage form is more complex and that there exists a curvilinear relationship between women's productive value and the existence of polygyny (Lee 1979). Polygyny has been found to be a feature of economic systems where potential female contribution to subsistence is high (such as in gathering and agriculture economies), but the practice has also been found in economic systems where potential female contribution is low (such as hunting and fishing economies). It has been suggested that multiple wives are valued in the first instance, for economic reasons, while in the latter instance, they are valued for reproductive reasons in that the taking of multiple wives maximizes the potential to produce sons, who in turn make an economic contribution (Goody 1973).

While polygyny tends to be viewed by Western cultures as an instrument for the domination of women by men, the degree of autonomy experienced by women in polygynous unions varies within and among cultures. The degree of autonomy of each cowife is influenced by the availability of opportunities outside the home, the degree to which she maintains contact with her family of origin, the availability of gainful employment, the degree of importance attached to the children she has produced, and her life cycle state. Benefits for the wives also include the sharing of economic and domestic responsibilities, the freedom that derives from living apart from the constant supervision of a husband, and the diminished pressure for constant sexual accessibility.

Jealousy, while not an inevitable consequence of polygyny, is reported in many polygynous societies. However, Helen Ware (1979) notes that jealousy among cowives is more a rivalry to secure maximum access to resources for themselves and their offspring than sexual jealousy. To minimize this conflict among cowives, a set of rules is often established that specifies responsibilities and rights in regard to sex, economics, and personal possessions.

Children of polygynous unions may be reared primarily by their mother, under the supervision of the senior cowife, or jointly with a system of rotation. Because the economic claims that many cowives make on their husbands are on behalf of their children, one of the advantages of occupying the position of senior wife is that the position carries with it preferential treatment for the offspring. The notion that mothers in polygynous unions develop extraordinarily close ties with their children as a consequence of the father's absence is not supported (Clignet 1970).

Although antecedents to the occurrence and maintenance of polygyny vary from society to society, ideology and customs develop once polygyny is adopted that contribute to its perpetuation long after the original reason for the practice disappears.

In traditional societies that have encouraged plural marriages in the past, however, the trend is moving toward monogamy. In some cases, this movement occurs in stages (i.e., a gradual reduction in the number of wives permitted), and in other cases, polygyny is permitted but discouraged by recognizing the first marriage as legal and relegating additional wives to the status of concubine.

The explanation most commonly advanced for this movement away from polygyny is that monogamy is more compatible with industrialization. Of course, the role of ideology and the banning of polygyny must also be considered as factors contributing to the decline of the practice.

(*See also:* Kinship; Marriage Definition; Polyandry)

BIBLIOGRAPHY

Arrington, L., and Bitton, D. (1979). *The Mormon Experience.* New York: Alfred A. Knopf.

Boserup, E. (1970). *Women's Role in Economic Development.* London: Allen and Unwin.

Cherian, V. (1990). "Academic Achievement of Children from Monogamous and Polygynous Families." *Journal of Social Psychology* 130:117–119.

Clignet, R. (1970). *Many Wives, Many Powers.* Evanston, IL: Northwestern University Press.

Clignet, R., and Sween, J. (1981). "For a Revisionment Theory of Human Polygyny." *Signs: Journal of Women in Culture and Society* 6:445–468.

Ember, M. (1974). "Warfare, Sex Ratio, and Polygyny." *Ethnology* 13:197–206.

Goody, J. (1973). "Polygyny, Economy, and the Role of Women." In *The Character of Kinship,* ed. J. Goody. London: Cambridge University Press.

Guttentag, M., and Secord, P. (1983). *Too Many Women: The Sex Ratio Question.* Newbury Park, CA: Sage Publications.

Heath, D. (1958). "Sexual Division of Labor and Cross-Cultural Research." *Social Forces* 37:77–79.

Lee, G. (1979). "Marital Structure and Economic Systems." *Journal of Marriage and the Family* 41:701–713.

Mulder, M. (1992). "Women's Strategies in Polygynous Marriage: Kipsigis, Datoga, and Other East African Cases." *Human Nature* 3:45–70.

Murdock, G. (1957). "World Ethnographic Sample." *American Anthropologist* 59:664–687.

Nimkoff, M. (1965). *Comparative Family Systems.* Boston: Houghton Mifflin.

Ware, H. (1979). "Polygyny: Women's Views in a Transitional Society, Nigeria 1975." *Journal of Marriage and the Family* 41:183–195.

Whiting, J. (1964). "Effects of Climate on Certain Cultural Practices." In *Explorations in Cultural Anthropology,* ed. W. Goodenough. New York: McGraw-Hill.

Rose Marie Arnhold

POVERTY

In the United States, people are classified as poor if they live in a family that cannot afford the basic necessities of life—food, clothing, and housing. The amount of money needed to cover the basic necessities—the poverty line or poverty threshold—is set by the federal government according to a predetermined formula.

Measuring Poverty

The official U.S. poverty line consists of a set of different lines, reflecting the fact that different families have different needs. It costs more to feed, clothe, and shelter three people than one person. Thus, the poverty threshold is higher for a three-person family than for a one-person family as shown in Table 1.

The poverty line takes account of economies of scale—the fact that food and housing are less expensive when people share expenses. A three-person family needs more income than a one-person family to maintain the same standard of living, but it does not need three times as much. The poverty threshold also adjusts for age. A family with five adults and no children needs $17,000 to cover basic expenses, whereas a family with one adult and four children needs only $16,000. Similarly, a family headed by an elderly aunt needs somewhat less income than a family headed by a nonelderly person.

The poverty line was developed in the 1960s by Mollie Orshansky (1965), a research analyst at the Social Security Administration. The Johnson administration had declared the War on Poverty in 1964, and the government needed a yardstick against which to measure its progress. To determine a family's basic expenses, Orshansky started with a 1955 consumption survey carried out by the Department of Agriculture, which showed that the average family spent about one-third of its annual income on food. She concluded for this survey that the poverty threshold for a family of four should be three times the cost of food for the family. To determine the cost of food, she used the Department of Agriculture's Economy Food Plan, which met the minimum daily nutritional requirements. With these two pieces of information—the Economy Food Plan and a multiplier of three—Orshansky determined that a family of four at that time needed an annual income of about $3,000 to maintain a minimum standard of living.

Once the poverty lines were set, counting the number of poor families (and poor people) was just a matter of calculating the total annual income of each

Table 1 1992 Poverty Thresholds in Dollars

Size of Family Unit	Weighted Average Thresholds	Related Children Under 18 Years						
		None	One	Two	Three	Four	Five	Six
One person (unrelated individual)	7,143	–	–	–	–	–	–	–
Under 65 years	7,299	7,299	–	–	–	–	–	–
65 years or over	6,729	6,729	–	–	–	–	–	–
Two persons	9,137	–	–	–	–	–	–	–
Householder under 65 years	9,443	9,395	9,670	–	–	–	–	–
Householder 65 years or over	8,487	8,480	9,634	–	–	–	–	–
Three persons	11,186	10,974	11,293	11,304	–	–	–	–
Four persons	14,335	14,471	14,708	14,228	14,277	–	–	–
Five persons	16,592	17,451	17,705	17,163	16,743	16,487	–	–
Six persons	19,137	20,072	20,152	19,737	19,339	18,747	18,396	–
Seven persons	21,594	23,096	23,240	22,743	22,396	21,751	20,998	20,171
Eight persons	24,053	25,831	26,059	25,590	25,179	24,596	23,855	23,085

SOURCE U.S. Bureau of the Census (1993).

family in the United States and comparing it with the appropriate poverty line for that family. If family income was less than the amount needed to cover the cost of food, clothing, and shelter, the family was classified as poor, and everyone living in the family was classified as poor. Information on family income and size was taken from the Current Population Survey, which was carried out each year under the auspices of the U.S. Bureau of the Census. Using the Orshansky thresholds, the government found that in 1964 approximately 7 million families (15 percent of all families) and 35 million people (18 percent of all persons) were living below the poverty line (Danziger and Weinberg 1994).

The poverty thresholds are updated each year to take account of increases in the cost of living. Minor changes have been made in the food budget and family size adjustments since the lines were first developed; for the most part, however, the original thresholds have remained intact. Each year, the Census Bureau collects information on family income and family size, and this information is used, along with the poverty thresholds, to produce an official count of the number of poor persons and poor families in the United States. In 1992, the number of poor families and poor persons was very similar to what they were when the War on Poverty began: 7.098 million families and 37 million people; the poverty rates were 12 percent of all families and 14.5 percent of all individuals (U.S. Bureau of the Census 1993).

Since its creation in the mid-1960s, the official poverty line has been criticized on a number of grounds (Ruggles 1990). Some people object to the way family income is measured. Others are concerned about how the poverty thresholds are determined. These two decisions—what to count and where to draw the line—have important political implications, since they determine the level of poverty at any given time and show how far the country has come and how far it has to go. Sometimes, the poverty thresholds are used to determine eligibility for government benefits.

Critics who believe that the poverty rate is overstated point out that the official measure of family income ignores property, pensions, fringe benefits, and capital gains. If a person owns property or stock or if he or she has substantial savings, the income from these assets is included in the income measure but the value of the assets themselves is not included. Since most individuals who live near the poverty line do not own stocks and do not have substantial savings, the failure to count these assets probably does not have much effect on the poverty rate. Ignoring the value of personal property, such as a home or a farm, however, is probably more important, as is the failure to count fringe benefits.

Another criticism of the income measure is its failure to take account of earnings capacity. Young adults in college may be classified as poor because their earnings are very low. Similarly, some two-parent families have low income because the mother is staying home to care for the children. In these instances, the earnings capacity of the family (or individual) is much higher than current income and may lead to an overestimate of poverty.

Finally, critics claim that failing to count noncash transfers provided by the government, such as free medical care, housing, and food stamps, leads to an overestimate of the poverty rate (Smeeding 1977). They argue that if the cash value of these benefits were counted as part of annual family income, poverty rates would be substantially lower.

On the other side of the debate are those who believe that the official poverty measure underestimates the proportion of people who are poor. They note that the Census Bureau uses pretax income to determine whether family income reaches the poverty threshold. When the original thresholds were developed, ignoring taxes was not a problem because most families near the poverty line did not owe income taxes. Tax liabilities have increased since the 1960s, however, and not subtracting taxes may lead to an overestimate of family income. Changes in the tax code and the Earned Income Tax Credit have reduced the tax liability of poor and near-poor families, making this objection less important today than it was in the mid-1980s.

Economists Sheldon Danzinger and Daniel Weinberg (1994) found that subtracting taxes from family income and adding noncash government transfers, capital gains, and employer-provided health insurance lowered the poverty rate by about 3 percentage points, from 15 percent to 12 percent in 1992. Had they counted earnings capacity and the value of property, the rate would have been even lower.

In addition to criticisms of the income measure, the poverty thresholds themselves have been criticized on several grounds. The main complaint is that the thresholds have not been readjusted to account for increases in the standard of living since the 1950s. When Orshansky set the original thresholds, the average family spent one-third of its annual income on food; today, the average family spends less than one-fifth of its annual income on food. Thus, a poor family today is much worse off, relative to the average family, than a poor family was in the mid-1960s. In 1965, the poverty threshold was about 45 percent of the median family income; in the late 1980s, the poverty threshold was about 37 percent of the median family income (Ruggles 1990).

To address this problem, some people have suggested that the government adopt a relative poverty measure tied to median family income, as opposed to an absolute poverty measure tied to the cost of food. They argue that a relative standard is more appropriate because it defines poverty in terms of a person's ability to participate in mainstream society. Nonparticipation may be a better indicator of poverty in a modern society where most people can afford the basic necessities.

A second criticism of the poverty thresholds is that they do not take account of regional and urban–rural differences in the cost of living. According to poverty threshold guidelines, there is no difference in monetary needs between people who live in New York and Los Angeles and people who live in Tyler, Texas, and Emporia, Kansas. Yet anyone who has ever visited these different parts of the country knows that the cost of living is much higher in the former than in the latter. If regional differences were taken into account, poverty rates would be somewhat higher in large cities and lower in rural areas. They would also be lower in the South.

Poverty Rates

Poverty is unevenly distributed across the population. Some racial and ethnic groups are much more likely to be poor than others, some age groups have a higher risk of poverty than others, and different parts of the country have higher poverty rates than others. Poverty is also correlated with gender.

As Table 2 shows, nearly two-thirds of all poor people in the United States in 1992 were white, less than one-third were African American, and less than one-fifth were of hispanic origin (U.S. Bureau of the Census 1993). Although whites accounted for the bulk of the poverty population, they were underrepresented among the poor. Similarly, African Americans and Hispanics were overrepresented among the poor. African Americans and hispanics were nearly three times as likely as whites to live below the poverty line.

Despite the differences in poverty rates, the trends have been quite similar for African Americans and whites since the 1960s. Both groups experienced large declines in poverty during the 1960s, and both groups stopped improving after the early 1970s. Between 1970 and 1992, poverty increased by 2 percentage points among whites and remained constant among African Americans.

The Hispanic poverty rate grew from 24 percent in 1970 to 29 percent in 1992. Hispanics are a diverse group, made up primarily of Cubans, Mexican Americans, and Puerto Ricans. Cubans have the lowest poverty rate of all Hispanics, and Puerto Ricans have the highest rate. Puerto Ricans experienced the largest increases in poverty during the 1970s and 1980s (Sandefur and Tienda 1988).

Children are greatly overrepresented among the poor. They make up only 26 percent of the population, yet they account for 40 percent of the poor. In contrast, the elderly are slightly underrepresented among the poor. They account for 12 percent of the

Table 2 Population Characteristics and Poverty Rates

	Percent of Population	*Percent of Poor Persons*	*Poverty Rate*
Race and Ethnicity			
Whites	83	68	12
African Americans	13	30	33
Hispanics	9	19	29
Age			
Children	26	41	22
Working-age	61	49	12
Elderly	12	11	13
Sex			
Men	49	43	13
Women	51	57	16
Living Arrangements			
Married couple with children	42	27	10
Female-headed family with children	10	35	48
Region			
Northeast	20	16	12
South	34	41	17
Midwest	24	22	13
West	22	22	14
Central cities	30	43	21
Suburbs	48	32	10
Outside	22	26	17

SOURCE U.S. Bureau of the Census (1993).

population and only 11 percent of the poor. The elderly have a slightly higher poverty rate than working-age adults, 13 percent and 10 percent, respectively. Nearly all elderly adults receive a Social Security pension from the government that lifts them above the poverty line. In contrast, only a small percentage of children receive government transfers and very few are lifted out of poverty through government transfers. Between 1960 and 1970, the poverty rates of children and elderly adults declined dramatically. After 1970, the elderly continued to experience declines in poverty, while children experienced increases in poverty (Preston 1984).

Women are more likely to be poor than men. In 1992, women accounted for 51 percent of the population and for 57 percent of the poor. The ratio of women's poverty rate (16%) to men's poverty rate (13%) was 1.23. The ratio was highest among the elderly (1.78) and lowest among children (1.05). One reason why elderly women have much higher poverty rates than elderly men is that women live longer than men and poverty is highest among the very oldest people. Another reason is that elderly men are much more likely to be married than elderly women, and marriage protects people from poverty (McLanahan, Sorensen, and Watson 1989).

Persons who live in female-headed families with children (families with a female breadwinner and no spouse) are overrepresented among the poor. Ten percent of all people and 35 percent of poor people were living in a female-headed family in 1992. The figures were nearly reversed for married-couple families. The poverty rate of persons in female-headed families was nearly five times as great as the poverty rate of persons in married-couple families, 48 percent versus 10 percent. The proportion of poor people living in female-headed families doubled between 1960 and 1990, leading to a "feminization of poverty" (McLanahan and Sandefur 1994).

Poverty rates vary by geographical location. The South (17%) has the highest poverty rate, followed by the West (14%), the Midwest (13%), and the Northeast (12%). Southerners are overrepresented among the poor, accounting for 41 percent of the poor and for only 34 percent of the population. However, the cost of living is lower in the South than in other parts of the country, as noted, and therefore these statistics may overstate poverty rates in the South. Nearly three quarters of poor people live in metropolitan areas, with more than half of those living in central cities. In 1992, poverty rates were highest in central cities (21%) and lowest in suburban areas (10%). Poverty rates in nonmetropolitan areas (17%) were also above average in 1992 (U.S. Bureau of the Census 1993).

In America, poverty is often concentrated in certain areas of a city or county, which exacerbates its consequences. In 1992, nearly 40 percent of poor people lived in "poverty areas"—census tracts or subdivisions with poverty rates of 20 percent or greater. Most of these areas were in central cities. Concentrated poverty was especially high among African Americans. In the early 1990s, nearly two-thirds of poor African Americans lived in poverty areas. This is not so surprising, since most African Americans live near other African Americans and since the poverty rate for all African Americans was 30 percent (Massey and Denton 1993).

Causes of Poverty

Poverty is a complex phenomenon with many causes. While experts do not agree about which cause is the most important, most people agree that the economy, human capital—education and training, and family structure are important determinants of poverty. There is less consensus about the relationship between culture and poverty (Sawhill 1988).

Poverty rates are sensitive to the performance of the economy. When the economy is strong, people can find work, and wages usually go up. When the economy is weak, as during a recession, people have trouble finding work, wages go down, and poverty rates go up (Blank and Blinder 1986). The close relationship between poverty and the economy can be seen by looking at the trends in the poverty rate and the unemployment rate between 1960 and 1990, as illustrated in Figure 1 (Ellwood 1986).

During the 1960s and early 1970s, the economy did well, unemployment rates were low, and poverty rates went down. In 1974, the country experienced a recession and unemployment rates rose sharply, along with poverty rates. In the late 1970s and early 1980s, there were large back-to-back recessions accompanied by high unemployment and high rates of poverty. After 1983, the economy improved and poverty rates declined, but not to their previous recession levels.

Many people are puzzled by the fact that poverty rates remained high during the 1980s despite economic growth. One reason for this apparent anomaly is that the American economy has been undergoing a fundamental restructuring of work, which has affected both the nature of jobs and the distribution of

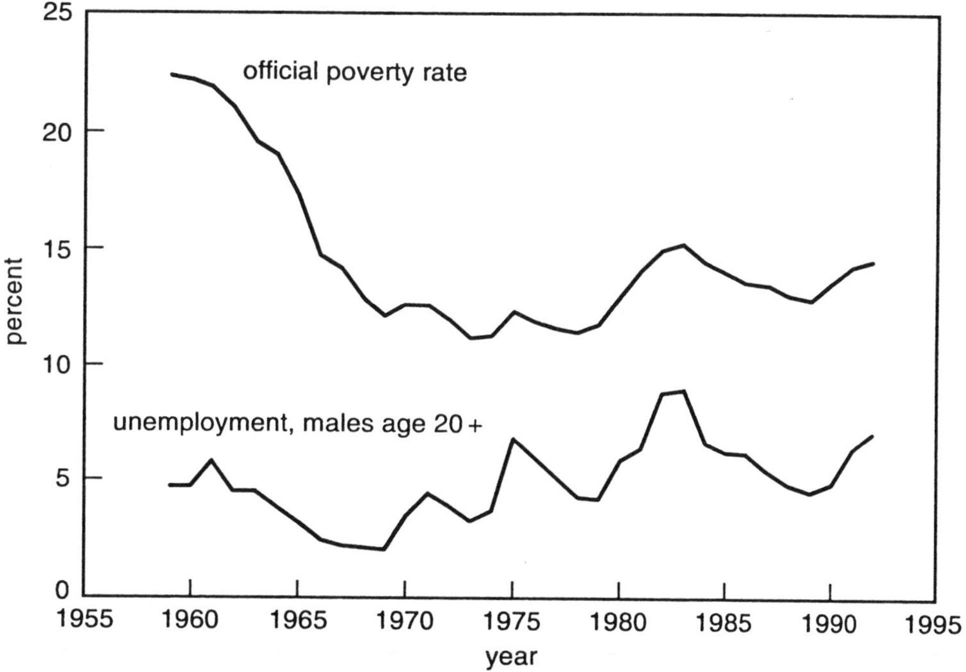

Figure 1 Trends in poverty and unemployment.

earnings (Harrison and Bluestone 1988). Many of the jobs lost during the recessions—particularly the well-paying jobs for low-skilled workers in the industrial sector—never reappeared when the economy began to grow again. Instead, the new jobs that were generated were of two kinds: (1) high-skilled, high-wage jobs for educated workers and (2) low-skilled, low-wage jobs for workers without advanced training. (Kasada 1995). Workers with only a high school diploma had a hard time finding jobs, even when the economy started growing again, and many of those who returned to work were unable to match their prerecession wages. The loss of industrial jobs in the Midwest and Northeast during the 1970s led to high levels of unemployment and concentrations of poverty in the large central cities, which disproportionately affected African-American families and neighborhoods (Wilson 1988).

Lack of education and training also causes poverty. Even in a strong economy, people with minimal skills and no postsecondary education have trouble finding and keeping a steady job. Those who do work often work at low-paying jobs. The close connection between education and earnings can be seen by comparing the poverty rates of people with different levels of education. In 1992, individuals with less than a high school diploma had a poverty rate of 26 percent; persons with a high school diploma but no college degree had a poverty rate of 10 percent; and people with a college degree had a poverty rate of 3 percent (U.S. Bureau of the Census 1993).

The connection between education and economic status can also be seen by comparing the annual earnings of men and women with different levels of education. In 1990, men with less than a high school diploma had earnings of $20,902; men with a high school diploma only earned $26,653; and men with a college degree earned $39,238. For women, the numbers were $14,429, $18,319, and $28,017, respectively (U.S. Department of Education 1993).

The education of the average American increased markedly during the 1960s and remained more or less stable during the 1970s and 1980s (Mare 1995). Thus, the high poverty rates in the late 1970s and throughout the 1980s cannot be blamed on a decline in education. The story is more complicated than this, however. While the absolute level of education did not decline during the 1970s and 1980s, the demand for low-skilled workers fell off sharply, so people needed more and more education just to stay even with the changes in the labor market (Levy 1995).

Poverty is measured as the ratio of family income to family needs; thus, a family may be poor either because its annual income is too low or because its needs are too high. Families with large numbers of children have greater needs than families with few children and thus have a greater chance of being poor, all else being equal. Families with only one parent also have a greater risk of being poor. Almost by definition, a one-parent family cannot make as much money as a two-parent family.

In 1992, the poverty rate of single-mother families was 46 percent, five times as high as the poverty rate of married-couple families (8.4%). The poverty rate for single-father families was 22 percent. One reason why single fathers have lower poverty rates than single mothers is that the former are more likely to be working full time. Even among full-time workers, fathers also earn more money than mothers because men are paid more than women (Bianchi 1995). Finally, families headed by unmarried fathers are much more likely than families headed by unmarried mothers to contain other adults, which increases total family income.

Fertility rates declined after 1960, making family size a less important cause of poverty in the 1990s. In contrast, divorce and nonmarital childbearing increased substantially, making single parenthood a much more important cause of poverty. In 1960, only 9 percent of all children were living in a female-headed family, whereas nearly a quarter of all children were living in such families by 1992 (McLanahan and Casper 1995).

It is important to keep in mind that the causal relationship between family structure and poverty goes in both directions. Family disruption lowers family income, but low income may also be involved in family disruption. Families with low income are more likely to divorce, and women from low socioeconomic backgrounds are more likely to have children outside marriage than are women from more advantaged backgrounds.

The role of culture in determining poverty is controversial and not well understood. Some people see culture as a set of shared values and attitudes that exist more or less independent of the economy. They believe that people are poor because they do not have a strong work ethic, because they are unwilling to delay gratification or plan for the future, or because they lack the commitment to form and maintain stable families. This view of poverty, which is often referred to as the "culture of poverty" argument, was first articulated by liberals during the 1960s and later adopted by conservatives (Wilson 1988).

Culture may also be viewed as a set of institutions, including religious organizations, families, job networks, and political and neighborhood affiliations. Most institutionalists see a close link between culture and the economy. William Julius Wilson (1988), for example, argues that the economic restructuring that took place during the 1970s undermined many of the community and family institutions within African-American neighborhoods, leading to social isolation and the growth of an underclass culture. According to Wilson, culture and social dislocation perpetuate poverty but only because the economy continues to undermine these institutions. These two views illustrate two very different approaches to culture. Conservatives usually argue that culture and values are independent of the economy, while liberals usually argue in favor of the role of the economy in determining culture.

Government Policies

The federal government affects poverty directly by promoting economic growth and keeping unemployment low. In addition, most modern welfare states have social insurance programs that are aimed at preventing poverty by insuring people against the loss of income. A good example of such a program in the United States is Social Security, which provides most elderly people with a pension when they retire. Nearly 75 percent of potentially poor elderly persons have been lifted above the poverty line by Social Security benefits. Without Social Security, the poverty rate of the elderly would have been 51 percent in 1989 instead of 12 percent (Danziger and Weinberg 1994). Other important social insurance programs are unemployment compensation and survivors' insurance.

In addition to insuring people against the risk of poverty, the government provides those who fall below the poverty line with cash transfers, often called "welfare" or "public assistance." These benefits are "income-tested" and are only available to people after they become poor. Welfare benefits are less generous than social insurance benefits and do not move many people above the poverty line. Estimates show that welfare benefits reduced the poverty rate of single-mother families by about 3 percentage points in 1989, from 52 percent to 48 percent. In 1990, the government spent $415 billion on social insurance programs, primarily for the elderly, and $21 billion on Aid to Families with Dependent Children (AFDC), primarily for single mothers (Burtless 1994).

(*See also:* Demography; Divorce: Economic Aspects; Entitlements; Ethnicity; Family Policy; Unemployment; Work and Family)

BIBLIOGRAPHY

Bianchi, S. (1995). "Changing Economic Roles of Women and Men." In *State of the Union*, Vol. 2, ed. R. Farley. New York: Russell Sage Foundation.

Blank, R., and Blinder, A. (1986). "Macroeconomics, Income Distribution, and Poverty." In *Fighting Poverty*, ed. S. Danziger, G. Sandefur, and D. Weinberg. Cambridge, MA: Harvard University Press.

Burtless, G. (1994). "Public Spending on the Poor: Historical Trends and Economic Limits." In *Confronting Poverty*, ed. S. Danziger, G. Sandefur, and D. Weinberg. Cambridge, MA: Harvard University Press.

Danziger, S., and Weinberg, D. (1994). "The Historical Record: Trends in Family Income, Inequality, and Poverty." In *Confronting Poverty*, ed. S. Danziger, G. Sandefur, and D. Weinberg. Cambridge, MA: Harvard University Press.

Ellwood, D. (1986). *Poor Support.* New York: Basic Books.

Garfinkel, I., and McLanahan, S. (1986). *Single Mothers and Their Children: A New American Dilemma.* Washington, DC: The Urban Institute.

Garfinkel, I., and McLanahan, S. (1994). "Single-Mother Families, Economic Insecurity, and Government Policy." In *Confronting Poverty*, ed. S. Danziger, G. Sandefur, and D. Weinberg. Cambridge, MA: Harvard University Press.

Harrison, B., and Bluestone, B. (1988). *The Great U-Turn.* New York: Basic Books.

Hogan, D., and Lichter, D. (1995). "Children and Youth: Living Arrangements and Welfare." In *State of the Union*, Vol. 2, ed. R. Farley. New York: Russell Sage Foundation.

Kasada, J. (1995). "Industrial Reconstruction and the Changing Location of Jobs." In *State of the Union*, Vol. 1, ed. R. Farley. New York: Russell Sage Foundation.

Levy, F. (1995). "Income and Income Inequality." In *State of the Union*, Vol. 1, ed. R. Farley. New York: Russell Sage Foundation.

Mare, R. (1995). "Changes in Educational Attainment and School Enrollment." In *State of the Union*, Vol. 1, ed. R. Farley. New York: Russell Sage Foundation.

Massey, D., and Denton, N. (1993). *American Apartheid.* Cambridge, MA: Harvard University Press.

McLanahan, S., and Casper, L. (1995). "The American Family in the 1990s: Growing Diversity and Inequality." In *State of the Union*, Vol. 2, ed. R. Farley. New York: Russell Sage Foundation.

McLanahan, S., and Sandefur, G. (1994). *Growing Up with a Single Parent.* Cambridge, MA: Harvard University Press.

McLanahan, S.; Sorensen, A.; and Watson, D. (1989). "Sex Differences in Poverty, 1950–1980." *Signs* 15:102–122.

Orshansky, M. (1965). "Counting the Poor: Another Look at the Poverty Profile." *Social Security Bulletin* 28:3–29.

Preston, S. (1984). "Children and the Elderly: Divergent Paths for America's Dependents." *Demography* 21:435–457.

Ruggles, P. (1990). *Drawing the Line.* Washington, DC: The Urban Institute.

Sandefur, G., and Tienda, M. (1988). *Divided Opportunities.* New York: Plenum.

Sawhill, I. (1988). "Poverty in the United States: Why Is It So Persistent?" *Journal of Economic Literature* 26:1073–1118.

Smeeding, T. (1977). "The Antipoverty Effectiveness of In-Kind Transfers." *Journal of Human Resources* 127:360–378.

U.S. Bureau of the Census. (1993). "Poverty in the United States: 1992." *Current Population Reports.* Series P60, no. 185. Washington, DC: U.S. Government Printing Office.

U.S. Department of Education. (1993). *Digest of Educational Statistics.* Washington, DC: National Center for Education Statistics.

Wilson, W. J. (1988). *The Truly Disadvantaged.* Chicago: University of Chicago Press.

SARA MCLANAHAN

PREGNANCY AND BIRTH

A couple's decision to initiate a pregnancy implies the acceptance of the lifelong responsibility of parenthood. Ideally, effective parenting begins even before conception, when the individuals discuss their desire to have a child and seek assurance from a physician or nurse that they are healthy and physically and mentally prepared for the challenges of pregnancy, birth, and parenting.

Pregnancy

Conception occurs when a sperm from the male partner fertilizes an egg from the woman. The product of conception is referred to as an ovum for the first fourteen days. During the next six weeks, it is referred to as an embryo. Thereafter, for the remainder of the pregnancy, it is called a fetus.

The ovum implants in the wall of the woman's uterus (womb) about seven days after fertilization. The ovum then grows through cell division, and a separate structure—called the placenta—develops. The blood vessels of the placenta serve as a link between the woman and the developing baby, bringing oxygen and nourishment to the baby and removing its carbon dioxide and waste products.

Physical and psychological changes. A full-term pregnancy lasts approximately forty weeks or nine calendar months and is divided into three three-month phases called trimesters. During each trimester, the woman experiences various physical and psychological changes.

As the baby grows, the uterus enlarges, producing an obvious change in the shape and appearance of the woman's body. Uterine enlargement is responsible for some of the physical and psychological changes of pregnancy. Other such changes are triggered by the high level of two hormones—estrogen and progesterone—present during pregnancy.

During the first trimester, the woman may have "morning sickness," which refers to persistent nausea and/or vomiting during the morning hours. Sometimes, though, the nausea can occur throughout the day or just in the evening. Other common changes during the first trimester are tender breasts and nipples, fatigue, a desire for more sleep than usual, and frequent urination. Headaches and a sensitivity to odors may also occur. The woman may notice that the skin surrounding her nipples has become darker and that a thin line of darker skin has appeared on her abdomen.

Psychological changes during the first trimester include a feeling of excitement about the pregnancy or anger that an unplanned pregnancy has occurred. The woman may also feel worried or anxious about how she will cope with the birth and the care of a baby.

During the second trimester, many of the physical changes disappear and the woman feels a special sense of psychological well-being. Toward the end of the fifth month of pregnancy, the woman first feels the fetus move, an event called "quickening." Many woman think of quickening as a very special time in the pregnancy, because it helps them feel that the fetus is "a real baby." Food cravings also may occur during the second trimester and continue throughout the pregnancy. As the pregnancy progresses, the woman may have both positive and negative feelings about the changes in the size and shape of her body.

During the third trimester, the woman may have frequent backaches and feel clumsy or awkward due to the change in posture caused by the enlarging uterus. Other third-trimester physical changes include shortness of breath, heartburn or indigestion, more frequent urination, hemorrhoids, leg cramps, swollen ankles, and varicose veins. Shortness of breath is frequently relieved about two to three weeks before birth, when "lightening" occurs, that is, when the uterus moves downward from the abdominal cavity into the pelvic cavity.

The psychological changes of the third trimester may include a return of anxiety about the birth; concerns about changes in relationships with partner, family, and friends; and financial worries. At the same time, the woman may feel excited about the forthcoming birth of her baby and the start of a new phase in her life.

The male partner. The pregnant woman's male partner also may experience physical and psychological changes during the pregnancy. These changes typically mirror the woman's physical and psychological changes and are called the "couvade syndrome."

Physical changes for the male may include indigestion, nausea and/or vomiting, bloating, changes in appetite, food cravings, increased urination, constipation, diarrhea, hemorrhoids, abdominal pain, back pain, headache, toothache, difficulty breathing, sensitivity to odors, skin rashes, itching, fatigue, leg cramps, unintentional weight gain, and even occasional fainting spells.

Psychological changes may include changes in the man's feelings about his body and such mood changes as irritability, restlessness, insomnia, nervousness, inability to concentrate, anxiety, depression, or, conversely, an enhanced sense of well-being.

The presence or absence of a physiological or psychological change in the man is directly related to the presence or absence of that change in his pregnant partner. That is, if the pregnant woman experiences a particular physical or psychological change, her partner most likely will also experience that change, and if the pregnant woman does not experience a particular change, her partner most likely will not either (Fawcett and York 1986).

In addition, research has shown that men who are members of an ethnic minority, have blue-collar jobs, have limited financial resources, had health problems before the pregnancy, and who feel very involved in the pregnancy may be especially susceptible to the couvade syndrome. Men who do not develop the couvade syndrome may feel hostility about the pregnancy or, conversely, may feel a special empathy for the pregnant woman (Clinton 1986; Strickland 1987; Twiggs 1988; Zelles 1989).

There are several theories regarding the couvade syndrome. One proposes that the syndrome is a result of the man's unconscious envy of the woman's ability to create a child. Another suggests that the couvade syndrome results from the man's ambivalence about the pregnancy. Still another theory proposes that the couvade syndrome is a result of the man's identification with his pregnant partner. Research has not, however, supported any of these theories.

Developmental tasks of pregnancy. Pregnancy and the birth of a woman's first child is one way of marking her entry to true adulthood. As pregnancy progresses, the woman faces the challenge of two developmental tasks. One is to accept the fetus as part of her self, yet as a separate being that is a product of her relationship with her partner. The woman achieves this when she accepts her pregnancy, begins to think of herself as a mother, and prepares for childbirth. The second developmental task is to change her child–mother relationship with her own mother to a peer or adult relationship. The woman will accomplish this task more readily when her partner is willing to provide the psychological support previously provided by her mother and when her mother is ready to accept the daughter as an autonomous adult and accept herself as a grandparent.

The pregnant woman, together with her partner, must also face three other developmental tasks. One task for the expectant parents is the commitment to make each other and the coming child a priority in their lives. This may involve adjustments in their usual social life with family members and friends, as well as adjustments in the family budget to provide for another family member. Another developmental task is the division of household responsibilities and career-related responsibilities. The pregnant woman may, for example, need help with household activities, such as heavy cleaning and care of pets. Furthermore, a dual-career couple may decide that one of them will take an extended leave from paid employment after the baby is born. A third developmental task is the formation of a relationship that is emotionally and sexually satisfying to both expectant parents and that is characterized by open, honest communication.

Birth

Birth is the end of the pregnancy. It encompasses two major phases, labor and delivery. Labor typically begins with mild contractions of the uterus that occur five to thirty minutes apart. Each contraction lasts approximately thirty to forty seconds. As labor progresses, the contractions become stronger, occur more frequently, and last up to a minute. Throughout labor, the cervix (the opening of the uterus to the vagina, or birth canal) dilates progressively and the baby moves downward into the birth canal. Delivery occurs when the baby is born by being expelled from the birth canal, with assistance from a physician or nurse-midwife. Shortly thereafter, the placenta detaches from the uterine wall and is discharged through the birth canal.

Throughout labor, the woman experiences sensations ranging from mild discomfort to intense pain. The discomfort and pain can be greatly alleviated by relaxation and breathing exercises, as well as by medications that can be administered by a physician or nurse. The pregnant woman and her partner can learn the proper relaxation and breathing exercises in childbirth-preparation classes taught by trained childbirth educators. These classes foster an understanding of what happens during labor and delivery and provide an opportunity to discuss what is involved when the woman's partner plans to be present at the birth to "coach" her throughout the process.

Although three-quarters of all babies are born through the birth canal, the remaining one-quarter are born by cesarean delivery. This type of delivery occurs when the physician decides that it is the safest method of birth for the mother or the baby.

Cesarean birth requires a cut to be made through the abdominal wall and into the uterus. The woman receives medication so that she does not feel the incision. The physician then removes the baby and the placenta. Most hospitals permit the woman's partner to remain with her during a cesarean delivery.

Conclusion

Pregnancy and birth can be a very special time in the life of a woman and her partner. The many physical and psychological changes, a well as lifestyle changes, involved pose challenges that can be met successfully when both expectant parents share their feelings and experiences with each other and with their physician, nurse, and childbirth educator. The importance of health care throughout pregnancy must be emphasized, because proper health care increases the likelihood of a healthy pregnancy, a healthy baby, and a happy couple.

(*See also:* Birth Control: Contraceptive Methods; Conception: Medical Aspects)

BIBLIOGRAPHY

Belsky, J., and Kelly, J. (1994). *The Transition to Parenthood: How a First Child Changes a Marriage.* New York: Delacorte Press.

Clinton, J. (1986). "Expectant Fathers at Risk for Couvade." *Nursing Research* 35:290–295.

Duvall, E. (1977). *Family Development.* Philadelphia: Lippincott.

Eisenberg, A.; Murkoff, H. E.; and Hathaway, S. E. (1991). *What to Expect When You're Expecting*, 2nd edition. New York: Workman.

Fawcett, J., and York, R. (1986). "Spouses' Physical and Psychological Symptoms During Pregnancy and the Postpartum." *Nursing Research* 35:144–148.

Kitzinger, S., and Bailey, V. (1992). *Pregnancy Day by Day.* New York: Alfred A. Knopf.

Martin, L. L., and Reeder, S. J. (1991). *Essentials of Maternity Nursing: Family-Centered Care.* Philadelphia: Lippincott.

Nilsson, L. (1990). *A Child Is Born.* New York: Delacorte Press/Seymour Lawrence.

Simkin, P.; Whalley, J.; and Keppler, A. (1991). *Pregnancy, Childbirth, and the Newborn: The Complete Guide.* Deephaven, MN: Meadowbrook Press.

Strickland, O. L. (1987). "The Occurrence of Symptoms in Expectant Fathers." *Nursing Research* 36:184–189.

Sullivan, J., and Fawcett, J. (1991). "The Measurement of Family Phenomena." In *Family Theory Development in Nursing*, ed. A. L. Whall and J. Fawcett. Philadelphia: Davis.

Twiggs, F. T. (1988). "Expectant Fathers." *Dissertation Abstracts International* 48:2112B.

Zelles, P. A. (1989). "Social Support and Empathy as Predictors of Couvade Syndrome in Male Partners of Abortion Patients." *Dissertation Abstracts International* 49:2880B.

Jacqueline Fawcett

PREMARITAL AGREEMENTS

Premarital agreements are contracts made by prospective spouses in contemplation and consideration of marriage. They date back to sixteenth-century England, where prospective spouses used them to modify the legal rules that would otherwise apply to them after marriage. By the mid-seventeenth century, such contracts were so important that Parliament required them to be in writing. By 1700, they were so commonplace as to be the subject of jokes in the English popular theater. Today in America, these contracts are still useful; the rich and famous make them, as do other people. The emerging statutes and cases dealing with their validity recognize the differences between them and other contracts and, therefore, treat them differently.

The first difference between premarital agreements and ordinary contracts is their subject matter. Premarital agreements typically deal with one of, or a combination of, three things: property and support rights during marriage and on its dissolution by death of a spouse or divorce; personal rights and obligations of the spouses during marriage; and the education, care, and rearing of children who may later be born to the marrying couple. These subjects are of greater interest to the state than are those of ordinary contracts. The state wishes to protect the welfare of the couple and their children during and after marriage and to preserve the privacy of the family relationship. It passes laws to achieve these goals.

The second difference between premarital agreements and ordinary contracts is the relationship of the parties to each other. Prospective spouses are in a confidential relationship. They are often unevenly matched in bargaining power. The possibility, therefore, that one party may overreach the other is greater than in the case of ordinary contracts.

The third difference between premarital agreements and ordinary contracts is that premarital agreements are to be performed in the future, in the context of a marriage that has not yet begun and that may continue for many years after the agreement is executed and before it is enforced. The possibility that unforeseen events may make enforcement of the agreement unwise, unfair, or otherwise undesirable is greater than in the case of ordinary contracts.

These differences create a dilemma for the law. Prospective spouses have an interest in making their own bargains. As freely made bargains settling rights that might otherwise become a source of litigation, premarital agreements should be encouraged and enforced. To the extent, however, that these agreements vary or diminish the state-prescribed protections for the couple, their children, or their marital status; are likely to be the product of overreaching; or may become unfair by the time they are sought to be enforced, the law is wary of giving them validity. This built-in conflict makes premarital agreements less stable than ordinary contracts and explains why ordinary contract rules alone are insufficient to regulate premarital agreements.

Like ordinary contracts, premarital agreements must be voluntary, made by competent parties, supported by consideration, and consistent with public policy. However, they are subject to a more stringent review for procedural and substantive fairness than that accorded ordinary contracts. Courts review the fairness of ordinary contracts only at the time of execution but review premarital agreements for fairness at the time of enforcement as well.

Subjects of Effective Agreement

The state's interest in the subject matter of premarital agreements makes them more vulnerable to attack than ordinary contracts on the ground that they conflict with public policy. The net result is to limit the subjects on which prospective spouses can effectively contract.

Property and support rights. When a marriage dissolves by death of a spouse, state laws attempt to protect the financial interests of the survivor in a number of ways: provisions for forced shares of each other's estates, homestead rights, exempt property, and family allowances, for example. In most states, couples may alter these protections by premarital agreements. Some states consider certain protections more important than others and thus make it more difficult, or impossible, to waive or alter them—for example, widow's allowance or homestead rights when there are minor or dependent children, intestate shares, or rights to community property.

State law attempts to protect spouses on divorce as well by providing for property division and for continued support in the form of alimony or maintenance. Premarital agreements altering these protections have been slower to win approval than those altering protections on death of a spouse and before 1970 were almost universally held contrary to public policy. Courts thought they promoted divorce and commercialized marriage and that enforcing them would turn economically dependent spouses into public charges.

Since 1970, premarital agreements altering the incidents of divorce have gained wider acceptance. Divorce has become a common occurrence, and many married women have joined the labor force. Courts and legislatures now see these agreements setting forth the parties' expectations and responsibilities as devices for promoting marital stability and accordingly encourage them.

The states that permit premarital agreements altering the incidents of divorce divide on provisions altering support rights. Some consider support a subject that couples cannot control by premarital agreement. Others allow premarital agreements altering support rights but refuse to enforce them if they are oppressive or unconscionable.

Employee benefits. Employee benefits, including pension rights, can be the subject of premarital agreements between prospective spouses except for those emanating from plans covered by ERISA (the Employee Retirement Income Security Act of 1974, as amended by the Equity Retirement Act of 1984). This act of Congress preempts state laws and requires covered employee benefit plans to pay benefits to both the worker and his or her nonparticipating spouse unless the spouse waives them in the manner prescribed by the act. There is doubt about the validity of such waivers in premarital agreements, which are executed before the parties marry, because ERISA requires waiver by a "spouse."

Structure of marriage. Sometimes the contracting couple, instead of or in addition to agreeing to alterations of property and support rights on death or divorce, uses a premarital agreement to structure the relationship by spelling out their personal rights and obligations. Courts have held such agreements unenforceable on the ground that it is improper for the judiciary to intervene in married couples' daily affairs.

Children. Minor children are, of course, subjects of special interest to the state, which stands in the role of *parens patriae* to them. As subjects of premarital agreements, children retain their special status. A number of states have statutes that prohibit couples from making premarital agreements adversely affecting their children's support rights. Provisions for children's custody, care, or education also get careful scrutiny from the courts. Those in derogation of the child's best interests will not survive challenge.

Rules of Fairness

To be upheld, premarital agreements must satisfy local tests of procedural and substantive fairness. As always, procedure and substance are closely related, and legislatures and courts considering the validity of premarital agreements often fail to separate the two. If the substantive terms of an agreement seem fair to the reviewing court, operating with or without statutory guidance, procedural niceties become less important. Conversely, if the agreement seems unfair, the procedures surrounding its execution become more important. The inquiry into procedure is made as of the time the agreement was executed. The question is whether the agreement was fairly procured. The inquiry into substantive fairness may be made at execution or reserved to or repeated at the time of enforcement. It is impossible to reduce the search for substantive fairness, whenever it is made, to a single question; the standards vary considerably from jurisdiction to jurisdiction and sometimes from case to case within a single jurisdiction.

Procuring the agreement. According to most courts, parties to premarital agreements do not deal at arm's length; rather, they are in confidential relationships. In addition they are often ill-matched in terms of bargaining power. Before courts will uphold the validity of premarital agreements, therefore, they must be satisfied that the agreements were fairly procured. As courts and state legislatures describe them, fairly procured agreements are those that the parties enter into voluntarily after making financial disclosure to each other.

The inquiry into voluntariness begins as a review for fraud, overreaching, or sharp dealing but goes deeper than the similar inquiry made in cases of ordinary contracts. Courts typically consider the parties' respective experience, the time between signing the agreement and the wedding, and the parties' representation by independent counsel. Representation by independent counsel is the best evidence that a party made an agreement voluntarily. Yet no state makes consultation with independent counsel an absolute requirement for validity. Some states require only that each party have the opportunity to consult with legal counsel of his or her own choice. In other states, the presence or absence of independent counsel is just another factor to be considered, gaining or losing importance depending on the fairness of the agreement, the adequacy of disclosure, the sophistication of the parties, and other circumstances surrounding execution. When a party signs a premarital agreement despite counsel's advice not to sign, courts may still refuse to enforce the agreement. The result turns on the court's assessment of the financial impact of enforcing the agreement.

The requirement of financial disclosure is closely related to that of voluntariness and follows from the nature of premarital agreements calling for waivers of or alterations in property rights prescribed by the state. These rights take on or lose value on the bases of spouses' earning power and assets. A waiver of or alteration in such rights can hardly be voluntary and therefore fair if the waiving spouse does not know the other's financial status. Accordingly, most jurisdictions require some kind of financial disclosure before the agreement is signed. They describe its extent variously: fair, full, full and fair, full and frank, or fair and reasonable. An agreement that the court finds substantively fair and reasonable may overcome a lack of disclosure; so may a spouse's actual knowledge of the other's assets or a spouse's waiver of the right to disclosure. The extent of required disclosure or knowledge varies from case to case, depending on the relative sophistication of the parties, the apparent fairness or unfairness of the substantive terms of the agreement, and other circumstances unique to the parties and their situation. In every case, disclosure should be enough to give each contracting party a clear idea of the other's property and resources. The best device for proving disclosure is to attach schedules of assets and income to the agreement itself. A mere recital of disclosure in the agreement does not preclude a showing that there was none in fact.

Substantive terms of agreement. In passing on the validity of premarital agreements, courts state that they will not substitute their own notions of what is right for the provisions of the parties' freely made bargains. Yet neither courts nor state legislatures, whose mandates they are obliged to follow, are oblivious to the substantive fairness of these agreements. This is an amorphous concept, which courts determine on a case-by-case basis. Unequal provisions for the parties do not alone make an agreement substantively unfair and therefore invalid.

The standard of substantive fairness, like the extent of required disclosure, is described variously—for example, reasonableness in the circumstances, not so outrageous as to come within unconscionability principles as developed in commercial contract law, fair and equitable, equitable, fair and reasonabale at the time of the making of the agreement, not unconscionable at the time of judgment, and not unconscionable at execution or enforcement. Some states apply different standards to property provisions than those they apply to support provisions. Some distinguish between short marriages and long ones.

The states divide on the appropriate time for measuring substantive fairness—at execution of the agreement, at enforcement, or both. Measuring the substantive fairness of premarital agreements as of the time they were made gives maximum effect to the parties' freedom to contract but does not protect against unforeseen changes in circumstances that may affect the parties' financial status and put one or the other of them at risk if the agreement is enforced. Accordingly, an increasing number of states are assessing the fairness of premarital agreements at the time of enforcement. Provisions waiving or altering support rights are particularly vulnerable under this kind of review. Those that leave a spouse unable to provide for reasonable needs, at a drastically reduced standard of living, or a public charge or close to it will not be enforced; neither will those that are otherwise unconscionable. This does not open the door to a wholesale rewriting of agreements, but it does protect parties against one-sidedness, oppression, or unfair surprise.

The Uniform Premarital Agreement Act

The Uniform Premarital Agreement Act (UPAA), some version of which has now been adopted by nineteen states, lists eight subjects that may be included in premarital agreements. Six deal with property and support rights, a seventh deals with choice of law, and the eighth includes personal rights and obligations and other matters not in violation of public policy or a statute imposing a criminal penalty. It is not clear whether courts will read this provision as overriding earlier judicial decisions refusing to enforce agreements structuring couples' marriages.

UPAA provides for review of procedural and substantive fairness at the time of execution. Under it, an agreement is not enforceable if it either lacked voluntariness or was unconscionable and if the challenging party did not get fair and reasonable disclosure, or waive it, or have adequate actual knowledge of the other's finances. UPAA provides as well for a review of the substantive fairness of spousal support provisions at divorce or separation and empowers courts to modify any such provisions that cause parties to be eligible for support under a public assistance program. This review does not extend to other provisions of the agreement, nor does it extend to agreements effective on the death of a spouse.

Conclusion

The accepted scope of premarital agreements is broad enough to satisfy most couples. However, the developing fairness rules, especially those providing for review at the time of enforcement, pose a serious threat to their ultimate enforceability.

While parties and lawyers have complete control over the circumstances surrounding the execution and contents of their agreements and can, thus, ensure procedural and substantive fairness at time of execution, they cannot control future events. Unforeseen changes in the parties' circumstances may make it unfair to enforce an agreement that was fairly procured and substantively fair at execution. The key to ameliorating the impact of post-execution events is to foresee their possible occurrence and to provide for them. Future events that parties foresee, and freely and knowingly provide for, do not trouble the courts as much as unforeseen events about which the agreement is silent. The more the parties foresee and provide for, the fairer and more stable their agreements become.

(*See also:* Alimony and Spousal Support; Child Custody; Child Support; Divorce: Legal Aspects; Family Law; Marital Property and Community Property)

BIBLIOGRAPHY

Becker, L., and Kosel, J. E. (1987). "Property Disposition, Antenuptial, Postnuptial, and Property Settlement Agreements." In *Valuation and Distribution of Marital Property*. New York: Matthew Bender.

Clark, H. H. (1987). "Antenuptial Agreements." In *The Law of Domestic Relations in the United States*, ed. H. H. Clark. St. Paul, MN: West Publishing.

Lindey, A. (1988). *Separation Agreements and Antenuptial Contracts*. New York: Matthew Bender.

Uniform Laws Annotated, Vol. 9B. (1987). Mineola, NY: E. Thompson.

Winer, E. L., and Becker, L. (1993). *Premarital and Marital Contracts: A Lawyer's Guide to Drafting and Negotiating Enforceable Marital and Cohabitation Agreements.* Chicago: American Bar Association.

Younger, J. T. (1988). "Perspectives on Antenuptial Agreements." *Rutgers Law Review* 40:1059–1091.

Younger, J. T. (1992). "Perspectives on Antenuptial Agreements: An Update." *Journal of the American Academy of Matrimonial Lawyers* 8:1–44.

JUDITH T. YOUNGER

PREMARITAL PREGNANCY *See*

NONMARITAL PREGNANCY; TEENAGE PARENTING

PREMARITAL SEX *See* ADOLESCENT

SEXUALITY; SEXUALITY; SEXUALITY IN THE LIFE CYCLE

PRENUPTIAL AGREEMENTS *See*

PREMARITAL AGREEMENTS

PRIVACY AND CONFIDENTIALITY

The right to privacy is a very broad legal concept. The most well-known, and perhaps most controversial, privacy interest protected by the law is the federal constitutional right of privacy. Many state constitutions also include a right to privacy. In addition, the states have protected privacy and confidentiality through various statutes and under common law.

Constitutional Right to Privacy

The constitutional right to privacy includes the right to make certain decisions (autonomy), the right to bodily integrity, and the right to prevent disclosure of certain private information (*Whalen* v. *Roe* 1977). Cases involving marriage and family life have concerned primarily recognition and definition of the individual's right to make certain personal decisions without undue interference from the state and with protection of certain intimate relationships.

The source of this right to privacy is the due process clause of the Fourteenth Amendment of the U.S. Constitution. Under the due process clause, if a right is found to be "fundamental," the state cannot deprive an individual of that right without complying with procedural and substantive due process. Procedural due process requires that the state provide the individual with notice and a hearing before a judicial tribunal before the right can be infringed. Substantive due process requires that the statute further a compelling state interest and that the means used in the statute be necessary to achieve that interest before a fundamental right can be abridged.

The first case to recognize a fundamental right to privacy explicitly was *Griswold* v. *Connecticut* (1965). The U.S. Supreme Court struck down a Connecticut law that made it a crime to provide contraceptives or information about contraceptives. The parties who challenged the law as unconstitutional had been convicted of violating this law by providing contraceptives and information regarding birth control to married persons. The Court's decision contained several opinions by different justices, reflecting their different views concerning the proper meaning of the due process clause and the proper relationship between that clause and the specific guarantees of the Bill of Rights.

The continuing controversy concerns the central issue of whether the Constitution protects unenumerated rights—rights that are not specifically mentioned in the Constitution—including the right to privacy. The majority of justices in *Griswold* agreed that the Constitution does protect unenumerated rights, and subsequent decisions by the Court have continually reaffirmed this basic principle. However, the dissenters in *Griswold* argued that the Constitution simply does not protect unenumerated rights at all.

Those justices who agreed that the Constitution contained an unenumerated right to privacy initially disputed the source of that right. Justice William O. Douglas found the right to privacy to exist within "penumbras" of the specific guarantees of the Bill of Rights, such as the Fourth Amendment guarantee against unreasonable search and seizure and the Fifth Amendment guarantee against self-incrimination. A majority of the justices expressed the view that has prevailed: The right to privacy exists within the concept of liberty protected by the due process clauses of the Fourteenth and Fifth amendments.

The second major issue concerning the constitutional right to privacy is the scope of that right. Critics of the right to privacy have argued that, once recognized, the scope of the right will be boundless or will be determined by the personal predilections of judges. In *Griswold*, two ideas were set forth as bases for demarcating the contours of the right to privacy. Justice Arthur J. Goldberg stated that fundamental rights were those "rooted" in the " 'traditions and [collective] conscience of our people.' " Justice John M. Harlan found a statute violative of due process if it offended "basic values 'implicit in the concept of ordered liberty.' " Like Justice Goldberg, Justice Harlan believed that history and a system of "basic values" would guide courts in identifying the reaches of the right to privacy. The Court has applied these concepts to privacy cases involving procreation, including contraception, sterilization, and abortion; marriage and child rearing; and sexuality. In doing so, the Court has faced two tasks: (1) determining when history, tradition, or basic values identify conduct as within the protection of the right to privacy and (2) if the conduct is protected, deciding whether the state law seeks to achieve a compelling purpose by means closely related to the purpose that justifies infringing the individual's right.

Procreation

In *Griswold*, the Court struck down a Connecticut statute as an unconstitutional violation of the right to privacy because it unjustifiably infringed on the rights of married persons. Justice Douglas asked, "Would we allow the police to search the sacred precincts of marital bedrooms for telltale signs of the use of contraceptives?" His opinion further emphasized that the "privacy surrounding the marriage relationship-... [was] older than the Bill of Rights—older than our political parties, older than our school system." The essence of the right to privacy recognized in *Griswold* was protection for a realm of private life and a special type of intimate relationship.

In a subsequent case, the Court extended the right to privacy to the use of contraceptives by single persons. Recognizing that *Griswold's* right to privacy was embedded in the marital relationship, the Court nonetheless concluded that privacy included "the right of the *individual*, married or single, to be free from unwarranted governmental intrusion into matters so fundamentally affecting a person as the decision whether to bear or beget a child" (*Eisenstadt* v. *Baird* 1972; emphasis added). The right to privacy was expanded to include individual decision making.

Eisenstadt thus made explicit that the right to privacy encompassed the decision to use contraceptives to avoid bearing a child. Together with *Griswold*, it laid the groundwork for what became one of the Supreme Court's most controversial decisions: *Roe* v. *Wade* (1972).

In *Roe*, the Court held that the right to privacy included a woman's right to decide whether to terminate her pregnancy. This right was not absolute, however. The Court used a trimester framework to balance the competing interests of the state and the woman. During the first trimester of pregnancy, the woman's right to terminate the pregnancy was paramount. During the second trimester, the state could regulate abortion to protect the mother's health. When the fetus became viable (capable of sustaining life outside the womb) at the third trimester, the state's interest in protecting potential life could become compelling and thereby outweigh the woman's privacy interest.

In the years since *Roe* was decided, the Court has had numerous occasions to consider the constitutionality of various regulations on abortion and numerous challenges to the right to privacy. In *Planned Parenthood* v. *Casey* (1992), the Court reaffirmed that the right to privacy extends to the abortion decision up to the point of viability. In a joint opinion written by Justices Sandra Day O'Connor, Anthony M. Kennedy, and David H. Souter, the Court explained that the liberty protected by the Fourteenth Amendment "involv[ed] the most intimate and personal choices a person may make in a lifetime, choices central to personal dignity and autonomy." The justices grounded the decision in the protection for liberty in intimate relationships and autonomous decision making provided by *Griswold* and other cases in the area of procreation and family life. The opinion also found the right stemming from cases recognizing a right to bodily integrity, such as *Cruzan* v. *Missouri* (1990). With *Casey*, the Court could not ignore "the urgent claims of the woman to retain the ultimate control over her destiny and her body, claims implicit in the meaning of liberty."

Casey departed from *Roe* in its formula for balancing the woman's privacy interest against the interests of the state. *Casey* replaced the trimester framework with an undue-burden analysis. The state may now regulate abortion to inform the woman and to persuade her to choose childbirth, as long as the state does not place substantial obstacles in her path if she wishes to terminate the pregnancy. The Court upheld, for example, imposition of a waiting period and special informed consent procedures before allowing an abortion to be performed but found provisions requiring the woman to give notice to her spouse prior to obtaining an abortion to be unduly burdensome and thus unconstitutional.

An earlier case had suggested that the right to bear a child was also fundamental. In *Skinner* v. *Oklahoma* (1942), the Court struck down a law requiring sterilization of certain habitual criminals as a violation of equal protection. Although the Court did not decide the case based on the right of privacy, the Court recognized procreation as a fundamental right.

Marriage and Child Rearing

Although they have not been considered "privacy" rights, the Supreme Court has also recognized marriage and child rearing as fundamental rights protected from unwarranted state interference under the due process clause. Indeed, these rights predated and formed the basis for *Griswold's* recognition of an explicit right of privacy.

In *Loving* v. *Virginia* (1967), the U.S. Supreme Court struck down Virginia's antimiscegenation statute in part as an impermissible infringement on the fundamental right to marry. Similarly, in *Zablocki* v. *Redhail* (1978), the Court invalidated a Wisconsin law that prohibited a person from remarrying if he or she had not met child support obligations because it violated the person's right to marry.

The Court recognized a fundamental right to rear one's child in *Meyer* v. *Nebraska* (1923), which held that the state could not prohibit the teaching of a foreign language because it infringed on the parents' right to control their children's education. Similarly, in *Wisconsin* v. *Yoder* (1972), the Court held that the state could not compel the Amish to send their children to school. However, in this area, as with procreation and marriage, the individual's right is not absolute. The Court upheld a child labor law, against parental objections, in *Prince* v. *Massachusetts* (1944).

The Court has also recognized a fundamental right to parent in a series of cases involving unwed fathers. Beginning with *Stanley* v. *Illinois* (1972), the Court established that fathers who come forward to assume the responsibilities of parenthood and have established a relationship with their children are protected by the due process clause. The Court cut back on this right, however, in *Michael H.* v. *Gerald D.* (1989), when it upheld a presumption that established as a matter of law that the husband of the child's mother was the father of the child if the child was conceived and born during the marriage, even though the biological father was another man.

Sexuality

The Court has most sharply limited the scope of the right to privacy in the area of sexuality. In *Bowers* v. *Hardwick* (1986), a deeply divided Court ruled five to four that a Georgia law making sodomy a crime was constitutional as applied to homosexuals. The Court rejected the petitioner's claim that the law infringed on his fundamental right of privacy. The majority framed the question as whether an individual had a constitutional right to engage in homosexual sodomy and concluded that such an act bore no connection to family, marriage, or procreation and was not " 'deeply rooted in this Nation's history and tradition.' "

The dissenting opinion, written by Justice Harry A. Blackmun, criticized the majority for asking too narrow a question. In Justice Blackmun's view, the right of privacy protected "decisions that are properly for the individual to make . . . [and] certain places" such as the bedroom, both of which were infringed on by the Georgia statute. The rights to family, child rearing, and procreation recognized by precedent were not protected because of their contribution to the public welfare per se, but "because they form so central a part of an individual's life" and identity. Justice Blackmun found sexuality to be protected as part of "the fundamental interest all individuals have in controlling the nature of their intimate associations with others."

Although no federal constitutional protection has been recognized for consenting sexual behavior, a few states have found such a right to exist under their state constitutions (*Texas* v. *Morales* 1992; *Kentucky* v. *Wasson* 1992).

Confidentiality

Many states provide legal protection for certain private aspects of marriage and family life under statutes or common law. The states generally recognize a marital privilege under evidence law that protects against disclosure of confidential marital communications in civil and criminal court proceedings ("Developments" 1985). The privilege applies to information and, in some cases, private acts performed in the spouse's presence that are intended to be confidential. Disclosure of information to or the presence of a third party may destroy the privilege (Feldman and Reed 1987). The most common rationale for the privilege is to promote the social welfare by "encouraging marital confidences." Others have suggested a privacy rationale for the privilege, emphasizing respect for individual rights and for the sanctity of the marital relationship. Courts have consistently resisted any attempt, though, to ground the privilege in the constitutional right to privacy. The courts have also largely rejected attempts to extend this kind of evidentiary protection to other intimate relationships, although a few states have recognized a parent–child privilege ("Developments" 1985).

The courts may also protect the privacy of parties to family law disputes, such as divorce, custody, or paternity proceedings, by closing court proceedings, sealing records, or using anonymous case titles. Most states recognize a strong presumption in favor of open judicial proceedings and records (Hubener 1989). In some cases, though, a litigant's right of privacy under the state constitution may overcome that presumption only where there are compelling reasons to prevent disclosure (*Keene* v. *Sentinel* 1992). In a case decided by the Florida Supreme Court, *Barron* v. *Florida Freedom Newspapers, Inc.* (1988), the court outlined circumstances justifying closure. These reasons might include the need "to avoid substantial injury to innocent third parties," including, for example, children in a divorce, although the court did not find it necessary to seal the records in the divorce case at issue.

Some states limit access to family law proceedings by statute. The most common type of proceedings protected are adoption, paternity, and juvenile cases. Some states, such as California and Delaware, provide this protection for divorce proceedings as well. Statutes sealing adoption records have come under attack, but they have largely withstood challenge. Nonetheless, most states will allow adult adoptees access to their records if they can demonstrate good cause; many states provide for access upon mutual consent; and a few states provide an absolute right of access (Hollinger 1993; Rucker 1983).

(*See also:* Abortion: Legal Aspects; Adoption; Birth Control: Legal Aspects; Children's Rights; Family Law; Family Policy)

BIBLIOGRAPHY

"Developments in the Law—Privileged Communications." (1985). *Harvard Law Review* 98:1450–1665.

Feldman, J. H., and Reed, C. S. (1987). "Silences in the Storm: Testimonial Privileges in Matrimonial Disputes." *Family Law Quarterly* 21:189–241.

Hollinger, J. H. (1993). "Adoption Law." *The Future of Children* 3:43–61.

Hubener, L. F. (1989). "Rights of Privacy in Open Courts—Do They Exist?" *Emerging Issues in State Constitutional Law* 2:189–205.

Rucker, C. A. (1983). "Texas Adoption Laws and Adoptees' Rights of Access to Confidential Records." *St. Mary's Law Journal* 15:153–183.

CASES

Barron v. *Florida Freedom Newspapers, Inc.*, 531 So. 2d 113 (Florida, 1988).

Bowers v. *Hardwick*, 478 U.S. 186 (1986).

Cruzan v. *Missouri*, 497 U.S. 261 (1990).

Eisenstadt v. *Baird*, 405 U.S. 438 (1972).

Griswold v. *Connecticut*, 381 U.S. 479 (1965).

Keene v. *Sentinel*, 612 A.2d 911 (New Hampshire, 1992).

Kentucky v. *Wasson*, 842 S.W.2d 487 (Kentucky, 1992).

Loving v. *Virginia*, 388 U.S. 1 (1967).

Meyer v. *Nebraska*, 262 U.S. 390 (1923).

Michael H. v. *Gerald D.*, 491 U.S. 110 (1989).

Planned Parenthood v. *Casey*, 112 S. Ct. 2791 (1992).

Prince v. *Massachusetts*, 321 U.S. 158 (1944).

Roe v. *Wade*, 410 U.S. 113 (1973).

Skinner v. *Oklahoma*, 316 U.S. 535 (1942).

Stanley v. *Illinois*, 405 U.S. 645 (1972).

Texas v. *Morales*, 826 S.W.2d 201 (Texas, 1992).

Whalen v. *Roe*, 429 U.S. 589 (1977).

Wisconsin v. *Yoder*, 406 U.S. 205 (1972).

Zablocki v. *Redhail*, 434 U.S. 374 (1978).

STATUTES

Cal. Civ. Code 4360 (Deering's 1984 and Supp. 1993).

Del. Code Ann. § 1516 (1993).

Or. Rev. Stat. § 7.211 (1988).

Or. Rev. Stat. § 7.215 (1988).

Or. Rev. Stat. § 419.567 (1987 and Supp. 1992).

Deborah L. Forman

PSYCHIATRIC DISORDERS

Mental illnesses, that is, psychiatric disorders, have been described since ancient times. References to depression, emotional instability, and unrealistic thinking can be found in biblical writings. Greek and Roman cultures believed that mental illnesses were the result of physical disorders. Melancholia, for example, was thought to be caused by an excess of black bile. Hysteria was thought to be due to a wandering uterus.

During medieval times, mental illnesses were believed to be the result of religious difficulties. Misfortunes and suffering were often perceived as divine punishments for sinful behavior; a person who fell into a depression, for instance, was seen as having a spiritual problem. Those who behaved strangely were considered witches, possessed by demons, and were dealt with more severely. Witches were burned at the stake, a practice that continued in the United States in Salem, Massachusetts, where witches were burned until as late as 1692.

When the mentally ill were no longer perceived as spiritually ill or witches, they were simply removed from society and sent to asylums. During the seventeenth and eighteenth centuries, the mentally ill were often placed in chains and incarcerated with the poor and with criminals. In 1793, Phillipe Pinel, director of the hospital in Paris for insane men, issued his famous directive to remove the chains that bound patients to the walls and instituted a new form of treatment referred to as "moral treatment."

In the United States, the "moral treatment" philosophy became the foundation of many private psychiatric facilities. Moral treatment emphasized treating patients decently and sensitively and was a method of reeducating patients. There was an emphasis on building self-esteem and self-control in a proper, supportive environment. Pinel and others, such as Benjamin Rush (the "father of American psychiatry"), observed patients and described what was observed (i.e., the empirical method) to collect information for future use. This eventually led to categorizing mental illnesses by signs, symptoms, and course of illness. A more scientific approach to mental illness emerged.

However, the attitudes that have persisted for centuries about mental illness have not been abolished by recent understanding of psychiatric disorders; beliefs that these illnesses are caused by demons, spiritual deficiencies, weakness of character, and divine punishments for evil deeds continue to have influences in modern times. Prejudice, misunderstanding, shame, and guilt about mental illness still exist. These influences affect the individual suffering from a mental illness as well as that person's family and friends.

Defining Psychiatric Disorders

Psychiatry is a specialty of medicine that focuses on the diagnosis and treatment of mental illness. Mental health professionals differ widely in their training and in their beliefs about the causes and treatments of mental illness. No one definition of a mental disorder would be accepted by all the various mental health professionals (e.g., psychiatrists, psychologists, social workers, psychotherapists, and counselors). However, the *Diagnostic and Statistical Manual of Mental Disorders*, fourth edition (American Psychiatric Association 1994), commonly referred to as DSM IV, has been widely accepted in the United States and many other countries as a common language for defining mental disorders. DSM IV describes the signs and symptoms of more than 200 disorders, and it is the basis for describing mental disorders in this entry.

This then leads to a definition of psychiatric disorders that influenced the American Psychiatric Association to include certain conditions as mental disorders and to exclude others. Each of the psychiatric disorders in DSM IV is conceptualized as a syndrome or pattern of behavioral or psychological signs and symptoms that occur in a person and are associated with present distress; with impaired social or occupational functioning; with a significant increased risk of suffering, death, pain, disability; or an important loss of freedom. In addition, this pattern must not be merely an expectable response to a particular event (i.e., mourning the death of a loved one).

However, there is no "cookbook" method for diagnosing and treating mental disorders. Although signs and symptoms may be presented in as objective a manner as possible, only a qualified professional can make a meaningful diagnosis and recommend an appropriate treatment plan for any of these disorders.

Schizophrenia and Related Disorders

Schizophrenia is probably the most devastating of mental illnesses. Schizophrenia and related disorders have been recognized in almost all cultures, and references to individuals suffering from its symptoms have been described throughout much of recorded time. Modern concepts of the illness date back to 1896, when Emil Kraepelin, a German psychiatrist, applied the term "dementia praecox" to the syndrome that is now referred to as schizophrenia. He believed that dementia praecox was a progressively deteriorating mental disease that affected the young. In 1911, Eugene Bleuler, a Swiss psychiatrist, coined the term "schizophrenia," which means splitting of psyche. He used the word because he believed that schizophrenia was the result of fundamental disturbances in psychic processes. These included disturbances of emotions, thoughts, and volition. Schizophrenia refers to these disturbances in psychic processes and not to "split personality," as is often mistakenly thought.

Kurt Schneider, another German psychiatrist, argued in the early 1950s that certain symptoms were crucial for diagnosing schizophrenia. He listed "first rank symptoms" such as auditory hallucinations of hearing voices arguing or commenting on one's behavior or delusions of having thoughts or feelings controlled by outside sources. He believed that first-rank symptoms were essential for making the diagnosis of schizophrenia. DSM IV takes into account the essential features of a deteriorating course, disturbances in psychic processes, and certain bizarre symptoms, in defining schizophrenia.

The diagnosis of schizophrenia can only be made if there is an active phase of illness during which there are bizarre beliefs that the person's culture would regard as totally implausible, such as one's thoughts being overheard by others or being controlled by outside forces such as computers or spirits. There also could be prominent hallucinations, usually auditory but also visual, olfactory, or tactile, and marked difficulty in communicating coherently so that a person does not make sense any longer. There could also be changes in affect (i.e., the range of mood and feelings expressed, such as a totally flat affect resembling a robot, or inappropriate affect, such as giggling when speaking about the death of relatives or personal tragedy). This acute phase must be of at least one month in duration but very often lasts much longer.

In addition to the active phase, there must also be continued evidence of the disorder for a period of at least six months. This may be either in a prodromol phase (i.e., prior to the acute phase) or in a residual phase (i.e., after the acute phase). During a six-month period, the individual may have marked social isolation, withdrawal, or continued impairment in role functioning at work or school. There may also be pronounced impairment in self-care and hygiene, marked lack of initiative, loss of interest, lack of energy, continued flat affect or inappropriate affect, odd beliefs, delusions, or hallucinations. The illness, of course, must not be the result of drug or alcohol use, not the result of a primary mood disorder, and not the result of a medical condition.

Schizophrenia is certainly a devastating illness but by no means rare; the lifetime prevalence of the disorder is estimated to be about 1 percent, with more than 2 million Americans suffering from the disorder. The sex distribution is equal in males and females, but the age of onset is usually earlier in males. The most common age of onset is between fifteen and thirty-five years of age, around age twenty-one in males and twenty-seven in females. The prevalence reported is higher among African Americans and Hispanics than in whites, but this finding may be due to racial bias. There is equal incidence of new cases across socioeconomic classes but an increased prevalence of schizophrenia in lower socioeconomic groups. This finding is attributed to "the downward drift" in socioeconomic status resulting from impaired social and occupational functioning.

Persons with schizophrenia tend not to marry and are less likely to have children; this is probably due to the illness, which impairs motivation and is associated with social withdrawal. They have a high suicide rate, and life expectancy is shorter than in the general population because of the increased suicide rate and death from a variety of other causes. Rates of homicide and other violent crimes are probably no higher for persons with schizophrenia than for the general population, but there is often much more media attention when a schizophrenic is involved in a violent crime.

There is a familial pattern in individuals with schizophrenia. Although the overall incidence in the general population is 1 percent, the incidence is 12 percent for first-degree relatives (i.e., people who have a sibling or parent with schizophrenia). There is a 40 percent chance that a child will be schizophrenic if both parents are schizophrenic. If one monozygotic twin has schizophrenia, the other has a risk of 45 percent to 50 percent. These figures have been confirmed in adoption studies that demonstrate that children who are first-degree relatives have the same risk for schizophrenia whether they are raised by adoptive parents or by their biological parents. However, nine out of ten persons with schizophrenia have no first-degree relatives with schizophrenia. These figures tend to support a stress/diathesis model, which states that there is a biological vulnerability (diathesis) that is triggered by stress and leads to the symptoms of schizophrenia.

The full course of schizophrenia is one of deterioration over time. Full remissions do occur, but this is rare. Medication is often helpful in decreasing the rate of relapse, but the more common course of the illness is one of acute exacerbations with residual impairments in functioning between episodes. In addition to medication, treatment that focuses on support and social-skills development has proven to be most helpful. Family therapy, which can help diminish interactions with high expressed emotions, has also been shown to help lower relapse rates (Leff et al. 1983).

Schizophrenia should be distinguished from delusional disorder and other psychotic disorders. The main difference between schizophrenia and delusional disorder is that the latter lasts for more than one month and involves beliefs or delusions that occur in real life, such as being followed, being loved at a distance, having inflated self-worth, or having an illness. In delusional disorders, the basic personality of the individual remains intact. The incidence is more rare than schizophrenia, with a prevalence rate of about 0.03 percent, and age of onset is usually older, about age forty. A person with a schizo-affective disorder demonstrates symptoms of schizophrenia and a mood disorder that cannot be diagnosed as either one separately. Schizophreniform disorder presents with symptoms identical to schizophrenia except that the symptoms resolve in less than six months and there is a return to normal functioning. In a brief reactive psychosis, symptoms of the acute schizophrenia occur with emotional turmoil but resolve in less than one month.

Mood Disorders

Mood disorders, depression in particular, are some of the most common syndromes encountered. While mood variations are normal and everyone has a down day or two, especially following a setback, mood disorders occur when there is a change of mood that is constant and persists for more than a two-week period. A persistent, depressed, sad mood is present in a depressive episode. A persistent euphoric or irritable mood is present in mania. Wide swings between depression and euphoria are present in bipolar disorder.

References to depression can be found in the Old Testament. Later, Hippocrates described depression in the fourth century and called it melancholia, which means black bile, reflecting his belief that the state was caused by a chemical imbalance in the body. Sigmund Freud ([1917] 1959) differentiated grieving from depression in one major way by describing the thoughts of the person with melancholia as being self-critical and self-blaming and directing anger toward the self.

DSM IV describes depression as a persistent depressed or irritable mood lasting most of the day, nearly every day, for a period of more than two weeks. The depressed mood is not the result of a medical illness or induced by substance abuse. The depressed mood is accompanied by loss of interest or pleasure in activities and changes in appetite, weight, and sleep patterns. There may also be agitation, fatigue, loss of energy, feelings of worthlessness, excessive guilt, difficulty concentrating, indecisiveness, and recurrent thoughts of death or suicide.

Depression is very common, and it is estimated that between 8 percent and 20 percent of the general population will experience a significant depression at some time (Andreasen and Black 1991). Depression is also much more common in women than men by a ratio of 2 to 1. The average age of onset, according to DSM IV, is in the late twenties, but a major depression can occur at any age. Many psychiatrists emphasize that the symptoms of depression are caused by physical illnesses (Gold 1987). A good physical examination and laboratory studies are necessary in the evaluation of the depressed individual to rule out any physical illnesses, such as thyroid disease, anemia, diabetes, kidney disease, and others. A type of depression that occurs repeatedly during a certain season has been identified. It is called depression with a seasonal pattern or seasonal affective disorder. Bright light phototherapy has been recommended for the winter seasonal depression (Rosenthal 1989). Depression is frequently treated with psychotherapy. This could be interpersonal therapy, which focuses on improving relationships, or cognitive therapy, which focuses on decreasing negative thoughts (Beck 1976). Many depressions are also treated with medications called antidepressants.

Mania is the opposite of depression. It is characterized by an irritable mood or a persistent, elevated, euphoric mood lasting at least one week. There is decreased need for sleep, increased talkativeness, and a flight of ideas, which is the subjective experience that one's thoughts are racing. The state of mania involves distractibility, increased goal-directed activity, and excessive involvement in pleasurable activities that have a high potential for painful consequences, such as buying sprees and sexual indiscretions. The individual must demonstrate impairment in functioning occupationally or socially as a result of the mood disorder and may require hospitalization. To be diagnosed as mania, the episode cannot be the result of substance abuse or a medical illness.

Mania is less common than depression and occurs in men and women equally. Age of onset is usually in the early twenties. An important aspect of manic episodes is that in addition to the gregarious, outgoing, socially active, hypertalkative symptoms, many individuals become psychotic with grandiose or even paranoid delusions. It is important to differentiate mania from schizophrenia.

Bipolar disorder is characterized by both depressive episodes and manic episodes. Its prevalence is estimated to be between 0.4 percent and 1.6 percent of the population. Mania and bipolar disorder are treated with mood-stabilizing medications, which are taken prophylactically when a person is well to prevent future episodes.

It is important to remember that mood disorders also cause significant impairment in functioning. Simple "moodiness" or "blues" without impaired ability to function in school, work, or social settings is not a mood disorder.

Anxiety Disorders

Anxiety is a pathological state characterized by dread, fear, and apprehension that is accompanied by avoidance behavior. Anxiety is differentiated from fear, which is a response to a known cause and would be considered a rational response to a particular situation. Anxiety symptoms may be characterized by physical signs such as shortness of breath, dizziness, palpitations, tachycardia (rapid heart rate), trembling, sweating, numbness, flushes, chills, or chest pain. There also may be psychological symptoms such as fear of dying, fear of going crazy, or fear of passing out. Again, the symptoms must be severe enough to interfere with a person's ability to function or there must be marked distress about having the problem. The symptoms are not due to the direct physiological effects of a drug or a general medical condition.

There are six categories of anxiety disorders: panic disorder, generalized anxiety disorder, phobic disorder, obsessive/compulsive disorder, post-traumatic stress disorder, and acute stress disorder. Panic disorder is characterized by sudden-onset massive attacks. Panic attacks are often associated with agoraphobia (fear of leaving home, being in a crowd, standing in line, being on a bridge, or traveling in a car, bus, train, etc.). Generalized anxiety disorder is characterized by chronic fear and worry. Phobic disorder is distinguished by anxiety symptoms related to situations or objects and can be divided into specific phobias (i.e., fear of certain objects) and social phobia (fear of social interactions that expose a person to scrutiny, i.e., public speaking or eating in public). Obsessive/compulsive disorder involves the persistent need to repeat thoughts or behaviors, and distress if a person is unable to perform these rituals. Post-traumatic stress disorder occurs when anxiety symptoms follow a major stressor in the individual's life. This could occur shortly after the stressful event, but it could also have a delayed onset. Acute stress disorder occurs either during or immediately following a traumatic event and lasts up to one month.

Anxiety disorders are common in the general population, but it is difficult to give accurate figures, and prevalence rates can only be estimated (Andreasen and Black 1991). Panic disorder is estimated to be more common in women (2% to 3%) than in men (0.5% to 1.5%). Generalized anxiety disorder is thought to be present at one time or another in roughly 6.4 percent of the population, with a slight male preponderance. Social phobias occur in 3 percent to 5 percent of the general population, and specific phobias affect up to 25 percent of the population at some point in life. Obsessive/compulsive disorder is estimated to occur in 2 percent to 3 percent of the general population at some point in life. Post-traumatic stress disorder is thought to occur in roughly 0.5 percent of males and 1.2 percent of females.

Anxiety disorders have been effectively treated with psychotropic medication and psychotherapy using behavioral techniques.

Dementia

One of the most common organic mental disorders is dementia, an impairment in memory and cognitive functioning accompanied by personality changes. The disability caused by dementia is severe and this differentiates dementia from mild memory changes that occur during normal aging. Dementia is extremely common, affecting about 5 percent of those over age sixty-five and up to 20 percent of those over age eighty. The most common type of dementia is Alzheimer's disease, followed by vascular dementia. Both are progressive and irreversible. These two dementias account for 80 percent to 90 percent of dementias in the elderly. The remainder are caused by other factors (e.g., infections, vitamin deficiencies, endocrine disorders, heart disease, renal disease, pulmonary disease, and side effects of medication, drugs, or alcohol), many of which are reversible.

Personality Disorders

Personality disorders are long-standing patterns of maladaptive behavior that persist over a person's lifetime. The patterns are usually recognized early in life, often in adolescence or before. DSM IV divides personality disorders into three clusters. The dramatic, emotional, erratic cluster includes antisocial personality disorder, borderline personality disorder, histrionic personality disorder, and narcissistic personality disorder. The anxious, fearful cluster includes obsessive/compulsive personality disorder, avoidant personality disorder, and dependent personality disorder. The odd, eccentric cluster includes paranoid personality disorder, schizoid personality disorder, and schizotypal personality disorder.

The personality disorders are deeply ingrained, rigid, persistent, maladaptive patterns that interfere with social and occupational functioning. The prevalence rate is estimated to be 6 percent to 9 percent of the general population (Kaplan and Sadock 1989). Treatment usually involves psychotherapy.

Disorders of Childhood and Adolescence

Many of the psychiatric disorders discussed so far can occur in childhood or adolescence. DSM IV, however, sets aside a category for disorders that typically arise during that period of life and have their onset in infancy, childhood, or adolescence. It is important to bear in mind that this period of life is one of rapid change and development. Knowledge of normal development and the boundaries and flexibility of "norms" is necessary for accurate assessment.

Mental retardation occurs in about 1 percent of the general population (Kaplan and Sadock 1989), with a male to female ratio of 1.5 to 1. Mental retardation is described as significantly subaverage intellectual functioning, with an IQ of less than 70. These individuals also have impaired adaptive skills in areas of work, socialization, daily living, and self-sufficiency. The vast majority of individuals with the diagnosis are in the mild mental-retardation range, with an IQ of 50 to 70; they are considered "educable" and usually attend special classes. Most individuals with mental retardation are able to hold some type of job and to live in the community. Only a small percentage, perhaps 4 percent to 5 percent, are considered to have severe or profound mental retardation and require institutional care.

Pervasive developmental disorders are characterized by qualitative impairment in reciprocal social interaction, qualitative impairment in verbal and nonverbal communication, and impairment in imaginative activity. The individual's intelligence may or may not be affected, but 70 percent of these individuals are also mentally retarded.

DSM IV also describes specific developmental disorders. These include learning disorders in arithmetic, reading, and expressive writing; communication disorders in expressive language and receptive language; and motor skills disorder (developmental coordination disorder).

Attention-deficit hyperactivity disorder (ADHD) is characterized by hyperactivity, difficulty focusing and maintaining attention, and impulsiveness. Estimates are that this disorder occurs in 3 percent to 5 percent of preschool- and school-age children, with a male to female ratio of 4 to 1. The majority of children diagnosed with this disorder have diminished symptoms with age. However, some individuals continue to have difficulties with attention and impulsiveness as adults, and many are diagnosed with adult attention-deficit disorder.

Disruptive behavior disorders include conduct disorders and oppositional defiant disorders. Conduct disorders are marked by patterns of behavior that violate the rights of others, such as stealing, lying, or aggressive behavior. Oppositional defiant disorder was introduced as a diagnosis in 1980. It is a diagnostic category for children and adolescents who demonstrate "difficult" behavior such as often losing their temper, arguing with adults, or doing things that deliberately annoy others. It is important to remember that the diagnosis requires that the behavior is considerably more frequent than that of most people of the same age. The flexibility and variability of norms must be taken into consideration. Other disorders of childhood and adolescents include separation anxiety disorders, tic disorders (including Tourette's disorder), and elimination disorders (including encopresis and enuresis).

Other Disorders

There are many other psychiatric disorders included in DSM IV. Somatoform disorders are characterized by a preoccupation with the body, physical illness, pain, or fear of disease. Dissociative disorders are marked by sudden changes in level of awareness or identity (Ross 1989). Sexual disorders include paraphilias, such as exhibitionism, pedophilia, or voyeurism, and sexual dysfunction disorders, such as male erectile disorders and female sexual-arousal disorders. Sleep disorders include primary insomnia, primary hypersomnia, sleep/wake schedule disorders, breathing related sleep disorders, and parasomnias such as nightmares, sleep terror disorders, and sleepwalking. Impulse-control disorders involve out-of-control impulses and include intermittent explosive disorder characterized by sudden aggressive acts, kleptomania characterized by repetitive stealing, pyromania characterized by fire setting, and pathological gambling. Factitious disorders are marked by feigning physical or mental symptoms in order to assume the "patient role."

(*See also:* Codependency; Dysfunctional Family; Eating Disorders; Family Therapy; Health and the Family; Self-Help Groups; Sexual Problems; Stress; Substance Abuse; Suicide)

BIBLIOGRAPHY

American Psychiatric Association. (1994). *The Diagnostic and Statistical Manual of Mental Disorders*, 4th edition. Washington, DC: American Psychiatric Press.

Andreasen, N. C., and Black, D. W. (1991). *Introductory Textbook of Psychiatry.* Washington, DC: American Psychiatric Press.

Beck, A. T. (1976). *Cognitive Therapy and the Emotional Disorders.* New York: International Universities Press.

Borbely, A. (1986). *Secrets of Sleep.* New York: Basic Books.

Freud, S. ([1917] 1959). "Mourning and Melancholia." In *Collected Papers*, Vol. 4. New York: Basic Books.

Gold, M. S. (1987). *The Good News About Depression.* New York: Villard Books.

Gold, M. S. (1989). *The Good News About Panic, Anxiety, and Phobias.* New York: Villard Books.

Kaplan, H. I., and Sadock, B. J., eds. (1989). *Comprehensive Textbook of Psychiatry*, 5th edition. Baltimore: Williams & Wilkins.

Leff, J. P.; Kupers, L.; Berkowitz, R.; Vaughn, C. E.; and Sturgeon, D. (1983). "Life Events, Relatives Expressed Emotion, and Maintenance Neuroleptics in Schizophrenic Relapse." *Psychological Medicine* 13:799–806.

Rosenthal, N. E. (1989). *Seasons of the Mind.* New York: Bantam.

Ross, C. A. (1989). *Multiple Personality Disorder.* New York: Wiley.

Sadavoz, J.; Lazarus, L. W.; and Jarvick, L. F., eds. (1991). *Comprehensive Review of Geriatric Psychiatry.* Washington, DC: American Psychiatric Press.

Selzer, M. A.; Sullivan, T. B.; Carsky, M.; and Terkelsen, K. G. (1989). *Working with the Person with Schizophrenia.* New York: New York University Press.

Stoudemire, A., and Fogel, B. S., eds. (1987). *Principles of Medical Psychiatry.* Orlando, FL: Grune & Stratton.

Torrey, E. F. (1983). *Surviving Schizophrenia: A Family Manual.* New York: Harper & Row.

LAWRENCE N. ROSSI

QUALITY OF RELATIONSHIPS *See*

MARITAL QUALITY; PERSONAL RELATIONSHIPS

RAPE

When people hear the word "rape," they often get a mental image: perhaps a stranger with a knife jumping out of the bushes at night and forcing a woman to engage in sexual intercourse. Defining rape is no easy matter, however. Definitions come from the law, the media, research, and political activism. Even within any one of these domains, definitions vary.

Historically, in English common law, rape was defined as a man's engaging in sexual intercourse with a woman other than his wife against her will and without her consent by using or threatening force. Today, the U.S. government and all fifty states each have their own rape laws. Legal reforms have eliminated the marital exemption; in the United States, marital rape is now illegal in all fifty states and on federal land. Reformed laws are often gender-neutral (i.e., someone of either sex could be a rape victim or a rapist), and they often include sexual behaviors other than penile–vaginal intercourse. Reformed laws sometimes redefine force and consent, such as not requiring the victim to resist physically (Estrich 1987).

Media images of rape in effect create definitions learned by everyone who watches movies or television. These images tend to be stereotyped, such as the previously mentioned stranger jumping out of the bushes. Only recently have the media begun to define forced sex between dating partners or spouses as rape.

Researchers studying rape must decide what definition to use. Some researchers rely on the legal definition used in a particular state. Others, however, decide that the legal definitions are too narrow—for example, Diana Russell (1984) used a definition similar to California state law, but she included marital rape, whereas California law did not at the time.

Some feminist political activists have offered political definitions of rape to highlight the social and economic pressures placed on women to engage in sex. Catharine MacKinnon (1987, p. 82) stated, "Politically, I call it rape whenever a woman has sex and feels violated." If a woman consents to sex because she is economically dependent on a man or because she is afraid of the consequences if she says no, MacKinnon does not consider this to be real consent.

Incidence and Prevalence

"Incidence" refers to the number of rapes occurring during a given period of time; "prevalence" refers to the percentage of persons who have been raped. Estimates of the incidence and prevalence of rape depend on the definition of rape used, the population studied, and the methods used to gather data.

The *Uniform Crime Reports* (*UCR*s), published by the Federal Bureau of Investigation (FBI), provide incidence data. The FBI's definition of forcible rape includes both completed and attempted "carnal knowledge of a female forcibly and against her will" (FBI 1993, p. 23). *UCR*s include only rapes that were reported to the police, and they indicated that there were 84 rapes per 100,000 females in 1992 (FBI 1993). This number is an extreme underestimate, however, because most rapes are never reported to the police.

The U.S. government's Bureau of Justice Statistics (BJS) conducts National Crime Victimization Surveys (NCVSs). Interviewers ask randomly selected respondents if they have been victims of various crimes during the previous six months, regardless of whether the crimes were reported to the police. The BJS statistics indicated that in 1991 there were approximately 70 rapes (20 completed and 50 attempted, including heterosexual and homosexual rape) per 100,000 males and females age 12 or older (BJS 1994). Unfortunately, the NCVSs are poor sources of data regarding rape. Respondents are asked if they were attacked or threatened but not directly asked if they have been raped. Nor are they told that threats or attacks by their intimates are germane to the survey (BJS 1994). Interviews are not necessarily confidential; other family members may be present. If someone is raped three or more times and cannot recall the details of each rape, which is likely in marital rape, those rapes are excluded from the study (BJS 1994; Koss 1992).

There have been better studies, however. Russell (1984) conducted a survey of 930 randomly selected women aged 18 to over 85 in San Francisco. Using her definition of rape based on California law but including marital rape, Russell found that 24 percent of the women had been raped in their lifetime; this figure was 44 percent when attempted rape was included. Fewer than one-tenth of these rapes had been reported to the police. The overwhelming majority of the rapes were committed by men the women knew; only 11.8 percent were committed by strangers, compared with 22.6 percent committed by husbands or ex-husbands, 4.0 percent by other relatives, 14.6 percent by lovers or ex-lovers, 13.0 percent by dates or boyfriends, 8.0 percent by friends, 2.5 percent by friends of the family, 6.5 percent by authority figures, and 17.0 percent by other acquaintances.

Mary Koss and her colleagues (Koss et al. 1988; Koss, Gidycz, and Wisniewski 1987) conducted a nationwide survey of 3,187 female and 2,792 male college students. They based their definition of rape on Ohio law. They found that 15.4 percent of the women had been raped since they turned 14; this figure was 27.5 percent when attempted rape was included. Of the women who were raped, 11.1 percent were raped by strangers, compared with 22.0 percent raped by casual dates, 31.4 percent by steady dates, 9.4 percent by husbands or other family members, and 26.1 percent by other acquaintances. Few of the rapes had been reported to the police.

Based on these and other studies, it is clear that date rape and marital rape are widespread. More than half the rapes found in Koss's study of college women, most of whom were single, occurred in dating situations. Although the stereotype is that date rape occurs on first dates between people who hardly know each other, more women were raped by steady dating partners than by casual dating partners. Some date rapes are "gang rapes" in which several rapists rape the same victim (Sanday 1990).

In the general population, not restricted to college students, marital rape is the most common form of rape. Approximately 10 percent to 12 percent of married or previously married women have been raped by their husbands or ex-husbands. In about one-third to one-half of these cases, the woman had been raped by her husband twenty or more times (Finkelhor and Yllo 1985; Muehlenhard et al. 1991; Russell 1990).

Most information about the prevalence of rape pertains to men raping women. It is possible for men to rape men and for women to rape women or men, but little information about incidence or prevalence is available (Sarrel and Masters 1982).

Characteristics of Rape Victims and Rapists

Girls and women are at greater risk for being raped than are boys and men. Although boys and men can be raped, little research exists on characteristics of male victims.

African-American women and European-American women seem to be at similar risk for being raped. In comparison, Native-American women may be at greater risk, while Hispanic-American and Asian-American women may be at lower risk, although more research is needed. While girls and women of all ages can be raped, the greatest risk occurs in their teens and early twenties. Women's attitudes and personalities have little effect on their risk for rape. Several studies, however, have found that women who were sexually abused as girls are at greater risk for rape than are those who were not abused (Harney and Muehlenhard 1991; Koss, Gidycz, and Wisniewski 1987; Russell 1984; Sorenson and Siegel 1992; Wyatt 1992).

Most rapists are male, although women sometimes rape (Brand and Kidd 1986; Sarrel and Masters 1982). Most rapists are below age thirty and are slightly older than their victims. Rape occurs mainly between members of the same ethnic group. Compared with other men, men who rape tend to have different attitudes, characteristics, and experiences.

Causes of Rape

Different rapists commit rape for different reasons, and any one rapist may rape for different reasons at different times. Thus, no one theory can explain all rapes.

Many aspects of American culture promote rape. Commonly held myths contribute to date and marital rape. "A man must have sex to prove his masculinity." "When women say no to sex, they really mean yes, so men should ignore women's refusals." "If a woman engages in kissing or petting, she is obligated to engage in sexual intercourse, or else she is a tease." "If a man spends money on a woman, he is entitled to have sex with her." "What goes on between a husband

and a wife is no one else's business." "The man should be the head of the household." "A husband is entitled to have sex with his wife whenever he wants." These are dangerous myths that can lead to rape (Burt 1991).

Language can promote rape. Language used to discuss sex implies that women are objects ("Check *that* out"), that sex is a commodity ("I hope I get *some*"), and that sex is competitive and antagonistic ("I hope I *score*") (Beneke 1982).

Traditional gender roles prescribing female submission and male dominance are linked to rape. Men who accept traditional gender roles are more likely than other men to regard rape as justifiable, to report that they would commit rape if they could get away with it, and—according to some but not all studies—to commit rape. Rape is more common in cultures that promote the ideology of male toughness, that have a high level of interpersonal violence, or that are frequently at war (Muehlenhard 1988; Muehlenhard and Falcon 1990; Sanday 1981).

Pornography frequently pairs sex and violence and shows rape victims as enjoying rape. This kind of pornography encourages rape fantasies and eroticizes sexual violence. Such portrayals make men more callous to rape and more likely to report that they would rape if they could get away with it (Finkelhor and Yllo 1985; Russell 1984, 1993; Warshaw 1988).

Characteristics of the culture and gender role socialization, however, do not explain why most men do not rape, why some women rape men, or why rape occurs in gay and lesbian relationships in which both persons have experienced similar gender role socialization. Individual differences are also important.

Some people hold beliefs justifying rape more strongly than others. Men who rape tend to have more negative views about relationships between men and women, greater tolerance of violence against women, and increased acceptance of rape myths. Often, men who rape become more sexually aroused to depictions of violent sex than do nonrapists (Barbaree and Marshall 1991). Compared with other men, rapists drink more heavily, begin having sexual experiences earlier, and are more likely to have been physically or sexually abused as children (Berkowitz 1992; Burt 1991; Russell 1984, 1990; Warshaw 1988). Other explanations include emotional problems (e.g., anger and hostility) and personality problems (e.g., antisocial personalities) (Hall and Hirschman 1991).

Consequences of Rape

Rape victims suffer from postassault depression, feelings of betrayal and humiliation, problems with trust and intimacy, guilt, anxiety, fears, anger, physical problems, and sexual difficulties (Muehlenhard et al. 1991). Rape victims can contract sexually transmitted diseases from rapists, and female victims may become pregnant. The consequences of rape have been conceptualized as posttraumatic stress disorder (PTSD), which focuses on the victim's repeatedly reexperiencing the rape (e.g., in dreams or flashbacks); feeling numb and attempting to avoid stimuli associated with the rape; and increased physiological arousal (e.g., difficulty sleeping or concentrating, outbursts of anger, or an exaggerated startle response) (American Psychiatric Association 1994; Herman 1992).

Male and female rape victims experience many of the same consequences (Mezey and King 1989). Although both genders may have difficulty seeking help from crisis intervention services or the police, men may have more difficulty than women because being a rape victim is inconsistent with the male stereotype. Gay and lesbian rape victims may have greater difficulty than heterosexuals obtaining help from social service agencies, which are often not publicized for or geared toward gay and lesbian clients (Waterman, Dawson, and Bologna 1989).

Despite the stereotypes, in some ways the consequences of acquaintance rape are even more traumatic than those of stranger rape. Acquaintance rape is more likely to occur repeatedly, whereas stranger rape is usually a single episode. The more often women are raped by their spouses, the more likely they are to experience severe long-term consequences (Russell 1990). Being raped by a date or husband involves a violation of trust and leaves victims unsure about whom they can trust and about their ability as a judge of character.

Rape by a spouse is often the most violent of all rapes. Women who are raped by their husbands may also be physically battered by them. With continual rape and humiliation, marital rape victims may fear their husbands as hostages fear their captors; they do not know when the next rape will occur. Their children may be aware of the rapes and may even overhear or witness them, which instills fear in the children and negatively affects their attitudes about sex and relationships. The legal system is often of little help (Finkelhor and Yllo 1985; Jeffords 1984; Kilpatrick et al. 1987).

Women who experience marital rape must decide whether to leave their husbands or to live with their rapists. If they choose to stay, they are at risk for subsequent rapes. If they choose to leave, they must adjust economically, socially, and emotionally to separation or divorce; furthermore, rape by ex-husbands is common.

Rape Prevention

There are many approaches to rape prevention. One approach has been to warn women not to go out alone at night, talk to strangers, or wear certain types of clothing. Unfortunately, such advice limits women's freedom and is ineffective because it is based on the myth that most rapists are strangers.

Another approach involves self-defense training. This approach has the advantage of helping women defend themselves while not limiting their freedom. Active resistance strategies such as physically fighting, yelling, screaming, and fleeing are generally more effective in resisting rape attempts than more passive strategies such as begging, pleading, crying, reasoning, or offering no resistance; furthermore, these active strategies do not seem to increase a woman's chance of being injured (Ullman and Knight 1992; Zoucha-Jensen and Coyne 1993). No strategy is absolutely effective, however, and even attempted rape can be traumatic.

Most important is the need to address the causes of rape. Working for gender equality and against the ideas that violence against women is sexy and that violence is a good way to solve problems could help to decrease the prevalence of rape. Both men and women can work for changes in the media, laws and law enforcement, and public opinion so that rape is treated as unacceptable, even when it occurs within dating or family relationships.

(*See also:* CONFLICT; FAMILY VIOLENCE; GENDER; MARITAL POWER; SPOUSE ABUSE AND NEGLECT)

BIBLIOGRAPHY

American Psychiatric Association. (1994). *Diagnostic and Statistical Manual of Mental Disorders*, 4th edition. Washington, DC: Author.

Barbaree, H. E., and Marshall, W. L. (1991). "The Role of Male Sexual Arousal in Rape: Six Models." *Journal of Consulting and Clinical Psychology* 59:621–630.

Beneke, T. (1982). *Men on Rape.* New York: St. Martin's Press.

Berkowitz, A. (1992). "College Men as Perpetrators of Acquaintance Rape and Sexual Assault: A Review of Recent Research." *Journal of American College Health* 40:175–181.

Brand, P. A., and Kidd, A. H. (1986). "Frequency of Physical Aggression in Heterosexual and Female Homosexual Dyads." *Psychological Reports* 59:1307–1313.

Bureau of Justice Statistics (BJS). (1994). *Sourcebook of Criminal Justice Statistics, 1993.* Washington, DC: U.S. Government Printing Office.

Burt, M. R. (1991). "Rape Myths and Acquaintance Rape." In *Acquaintance Rape: The Hidden Crime*, ed. A. Parrot and L. Bechhofer. New York: Wiley.

Estrich, S. (1987). *Real Rape.* Cambridge, MA: Harvard University Press.

Federal Bureau of Investigation (FBI). (1993). *Uniform Crime Reports for the United States, 1992.* Washington, DC: U.S. Government Printing Office.

Finkelhor, D., and Yllo, K. (1985). *License to Rape: Sexual Abuse of Wives.* New York: Free Press.

Hall, G. C. N., and Hirschman, R. (1991). "Toward a Theory of Sexual Aggression: A Quadripartite Model." *Journal of Consulting and Clinical Psychology* 59:662–669.

Harney, P. A., and Muehlenhard, C. L. (1991). "Factors That Increase the Likelihood of Victimization." In *Acquaintance Rape: The Hidden Crime*, ed. A. Parrot and L. Bechhofer. New York: Wiley.

Herman, J. L. (1992). *Trauma and Recovery.* New York: Basic Books.

Jeffords, C. R. (1984). "Prosecutorial Discretion in Cases of Marital Rape." *Victimology* 9:415–425.

Kilpatrick, D. G.; Best, C. L.; Saunders, B. E.; and Veronen, L. J. (1987). "Rape in Marriage and in Dating Relationships: How Bad Is It for Mental Health?" *Annals of the New York Academy of Sciences* 528:335–344.

Koss, M. P. (1992). "The Underdetection of Rape: Methodological Choices Influence Incidence Estimates." *Journal of Social Issues* 48(1):61–75.

Koss, M. P.; Dinero, T. E.; Seibel, C. A.; and Cox, S. L. (1988). "Stranger and Acquaintance Rape: Are There Differences in the Victim's Experience?" *Psychology of Women Quarterly* 12:1–24.

Koss, M. P.; Gidycz, C. A.; and Wisniewski, N. (1987). "The Scope of Rape: Incidence and Prevalence of Sexual Aggression and Victimization in a National Sample of Higher Education Students." *Journal of Consulting and Clinical Psychology* 55:162–170.

MacKinnon, C. A. (1987). *Feminism Unmodified: Discourses on Life and Law.* Cambridge, MA: Harvard University Press.

Mezey, G., and King, M. (1989). "The Effects of Sexual Assault on Men: A Survey of 22 Victims." *Psychological Medicine* 19:205–209.

Muehlenhard, C. L. (1988). "Misinterpreted Dating Behaviors and the Risk of Date Rape." *Journal of Social and Clinical Psychology* 6:20–37.

Muehlenhard, C. L., and Falcon, P. L. (1990). "Men's Heterosocial Skill and Attitudes Toward Women as Predictors of Verbal Sexual Coercion and Forceful Rape." *Sex Roles* 23:241–259.

Muehlenhard, C. L.; Goggins, M. F.; Jones, J. M.; and Satterfield, A. T. (1991). "Sexual Violence and Coercion in Close Relationships." In *Sexuality in Close Relationships*, ed. K. McKinney and S. Sprecher. Hillsdale, NJ: Lawrence Erlbaum.

Muehlenhard, C. L.; Powch, I. G.; Phelps, J. L.; and Giusti, L. M. (1992). "Definitions of Rape: Scientific and Political Implications." *Journal of Social Issues* 48(1):23–44.

Russell, D. E. H. (1984). *Sexual Exploitation: Rape, Child Sexual Abuse, and Workplace Harassment.* Newbury Park, CA: Sage Publications.

Russell, D. E. H. (1990). *Rape in Marriage*, revised edition. Bloomington: Indiana University Press.

Russell, D. E. H. (1993). "Pornography and Rape: A Causal Model." In *Making Violence Sexy: Feminist Views on Pornography*, ed. D. E. H. Russell. New York: Teachers College Press.

Sanday, P. R. (1981). "The Socio-Cultural Context of Rape: A Cross-Cultural Study." *Journal of Social Issues* 37(4):5–27.

Sanday, P. R. (1990). *Fraternity Gang Rape: Sex, Brotherhood, and Privilege on Campus.* New York: New York University Press.

Sarrel, P. M., and Masters, W. H. (1982). "Sexual Molestation of Men by Women." *Archives of Sexual Behavior* 11:117–131.

Sorenson, S. B., and Siegel, J. M. (1992). "Gender, Ethnicity, and Sexual Assault: Findings from a Los Angeles Study." *Journal of Social Issues* 48(1):93–104.

Ullman, S. E., and Knight, R. A. (1992). "Fighting Back: Women's Resistance to Rape." *Journal of Interpersonal Violence* 7:31–43.

Warshaw, R. (1988). *I Never Called It Rape.* New York: Harper & Row.

Waterman, C. K.; Dawson, L. J.; and Bologna, M. J. (1989). "Sexual Coercion in Gay Male and Lesbian Relationships." *Journal of Sex Research* 26:118–124.

Wyatt, G. E. (1992). "The Sociocultural Context of African-American and White-American Women's Rape." *Journal of Social Issues* 48(1):77–91.

Zoucha-Jensen, J. M., and Coyne, A. (1993). "The Effects of Resistance Strategies on Rape." *American Journal of Public Health* 83:1633–1634.

CHARLENE L. MUEHLENHARD
BARRIE J. HIGHBY

RELATIONSHIPS *See* ATTRIBUTION IN RELATIONSHIPS; EQUITY AND CLOSE RELATIONSHIPS; FRIENDSHIP; IN-LAW RELATIONSHIPS; INTERGENERATIONAL RELATIONS; PERSONAL RELATIONSHIPS; SIBLING RELATIONSHIPS

RELIGION

Religion may be defined as (1) a recognition of or belief in a superhuman power or god(s) commanding obedience and worship; (2) a feeling of reverence or spiritual awareness of such a power expressed in life conduct and/or ritual observances; and (3) a system of faith including beliefs, worship, conduct, and perhaps a code of ethics or philosophy. In the United States, some of the major "systems" or religions are Christianity, Judaism, and Islam. Individuals with an awareness of a divine or higher power develop a world view of life that is different from those who have no faith position. All of life may be affected by religion because of the perspective individuals use to interpret life experiences, to set personal goals, and to make decisions.

C. Daniel Batson and W. Larry Ventis (1982) identified a religious orientation they called "quest" for persons searching for truth, a comprehensible faith. People may focus on living in a relationship with God as an end in itself, sometimes referred to as intrinsic religion, or upon using religion for their own purposes, sometimes referred to as extrinsic religion (Allport and Ross 1967). James Davidson (1972, 1975) found that behavioral outcomes of religion correlated with the religious emphasis adopted by individuals. An emphasis on a personal relationship with God was expressed in worship and private devotions, but an emphasis on God's expectations of an individual's relationships with others was more often expressed in social action, such as helping the poor and needy. People who emphasized both were called "true believers" (Davidson 1975). The particular ways in which religion will influence or be influenced by life depend on many factors or dimensions, including but not limited to the importance of religion to the individual (salience), specific beliefs and emphases, the degree of support given by the religious community, devotional practices, attendance at worship services, shared activities of the faith community, the rewards expected for faith, and views of significant others (family, friends, teachers, etc.).

How religion interacts with family life is important. Controversial issues (abortion, right to die, divorce and custody concerns, adoption) affecting families are being decided by Congress, states, and courts, with both advocates and opponents presenting religious arguments. In the realm of personal family living, aspects of religion may act individually or collectively to shape family members' values, decisions, and actions. Marriage and family therapists deal with clients' ways of interpreting their world, which includes their religious frameworks and relationships (Burton 1992).

Family members also influence religion. Families are a primary source of transmitting faith and religiously socializing new generations. Impersonal economic and demographic realities increase persons' desire for religious groups to provide unconditional emotional support that is often in tension with faith institutions' moral guidance/sanctioning roles (D'Antonio and Aldous 1983). Acceptance or rejection of religious doctrine and social/moral mandates affects the societal power, growth, or decline of religious institutions. The willingness of some church members to disagree with church doctrines erodes some of the power of the church's influence (Thornton 1985; D'Antonio 1985).

Icek Ajzen and Martin Fishbein (1980) theorized that behavior is predicted by an intention to act formed by evaluating the relative importance of one's personal attitude and the subjective norms of persons significant to the individual. In the following research, attitudinal and normative (religious, family, and peer-group) factors as well as behavioral outcomes of studies involving religion and family issues are reported. Each type of factor has a place in a study of the interaction of religion and family life.

Two general avenues of religious–family life research have been used. One involves the use of large, often national, data samples, with few detailed items to represent religious dimensions. The other style of research uses measurements of distinct religious aspects connected theoretically to the specific family areas being studied. The first way allows advanced statistical analysis, because of large random population samples, and is often more representative of the population. It identifies correlations with few clues to the processes involved. The second may be more theoretically sound and provides more precise variable conceptualization, but it is usually restricted to smaller samples and is less generalizable to the general population. The use of more detailed data helps distinguish differences that might statistically cancel each other out with less complex survey instruments. These differences help researchers identify processes of interaction between religion and family life. Conclusions drawn from samples of specific groups (e.g., denominations, age or income groups, college students, ethnic associations) may differ from other research about the relationship of family life and religion because of the influence of specific group factors, but those differences help to clarify the complex interaction of dimensions of religion and family life processes.

Religion and Family Composition

Several issues involving family composition appear to be influenced by religious variables: mate selection, interfaith or intrafaith marriage, fertility, and abortion. Mate selection obviously depends somewhat on the number and characteristics of persons met. If persons belong to a small religious group, have an unbalanced sex ratio (few persons to choose from), and develop cultures and values similar to those outside the religious group, they are more likely to intermarry than those who have a larger selection of marital candidates from within their own faith community. Kip Jenkins's (1991) review of research indicated that marriages within the faith were more common if persons attended worship frequently, had a devout childhood home and were devout themselves, and were in close contact with their own family of origin. Having interfaith parental marriages increases the likelihood of interfaith marriages of adult children, but intensive education in the faith decreases the probability of interfaith matches.

William Sander (1993) highlighted the probability that subjective feelings about one's own group and the views of one's own group toward others can also affect relationships leading to intermarriage. High levels of education promote wider selection, resulting in greater opportunities for intermarriage. Sander's study of the General Social Survey data from 1987 to 1991 raised questions of interpretation for this issue. Since the survey asked for persons' current religious affiliation, the researchers could not identify whether or not spouses reared in different religions but reporting the same current one had changed affiliation for the sake of a united family or if they had truly been converted. The study clearly indicated that intermarriages were more rare for subjects born before 1930.

In American society, cohabitation is increasingly common. Religious participation appears to decrease with this living arrangement and tends to increase with marriage (Thornton 1992). Research indicated that high levels of religious participation and commitment are more important predictors of marriage than religious affiliation. Low levels of religious participation and commitment correlated with higher rates of cohabitation.

Fertility (the birthrate of various groups) has historically been higher for Roman Catholics and Mormons than for mainline Protestants, but more recently the birthrate for Roman Catholics has become closer to that of other religious faiths. Tim Heaton (1986) hypothesized that the high rate of Mormon fertility is influenced by a theology that emphasizes eternal rewards for marriage and parenthood, socialization in a Mormon subculture, and frequent contact (regular attendance) with a reference group supporting pronatal attitudes. It was noted that Mormon women who did not attend worship frequently and were not reared in homes led by Mormon parents had a lower birthrate than the national population. Socioeconomic factors may have an effect on fertility.

A corresponding concern is the growth of voluntary childlessness among married couples. According to the 1987–1988 data from the National Survey of Families and Households, a low but consistent inverse relationship existed between individuals' expectation of childlessness and religious participation, religious affiliation, belief in the Bible, and a religious wedding ceremony (Heaton, Jacobson, and Fu 1992). When multiple religious variables were tested together statistically, the only significant correlation was with women's frequency of attending worship. A Canadian study using data from 1980 (Krishnan 1993) indicated that non-Catholic wives in homogamous marriages who frequently attended worship were less likely to restrict family size. Young women or those who married late in life and who attended worship services infrequently were more apt to be childless. Well-educated wives' employment and husbands' low income were also correlated with childless marriages.

Strong abortion attitudes appear to be predicted best by religious variables (Jenkins 1991). Religious variables that had a significant negative relationship with abortion attitudes included frequent worship attendance and religiosity (quality of being religious).

Religion and the Marital Relationship

Two of the most common areas of family research deal with marital quality (satisfaction and adjustment) and stability (whether marriages remain intact or end in divorce). Most studies consider only cross-sectional data rather than longitudinal approaches dealing with the same people over a period of time. Howard Bahr and Bruce Chadwick (1985) surveyed people studied fifty years earlier in Muncie, Indiana. They found that religious affiliation had no relationship to marital satisfaction but that increased worship attendance did correspond with an increase in satisfaction as well as a higher fertility rate.

Since satisfaction is a subjective matter, persons sometimes exaggerate in the direction of the valued norms. To guard against creating biased results, a social desirability of marital conventionalization scale can be used to identify questionable data. Walter Schumm, Steven Bollman, and Anthony Jurich (1982) found that religiosity was still an important predictor of marital satisfaction after controlling for biased answers. Erik Filsinger and Margaret R. Wilson (1984) agreed and theorized that religiosity aids the process of adaptation. Heaton (1984) used national data to show couples with the same religious affiliation were likely to have higher marital satisfaction than those who did not. Jenkins (1991) identified studies showing (1) the religiosity level of wives varied in the same direction as marital satisfaction; (2) a positive relationship existed between religious affiliation and marital adjustment, with conservative groups having high adjustment levels; and (3) Bible reading, prayer, and frequent attendance of services had a positive correlation with satisfaction. However, not all research agrees.

Michael Anthony (1993) analyzed data about religious orientations and marital adjustments in groups of couples, husbands, and wives. Anthony's hypothesis that the mature, intrinsically motivated persons would have high marital satisfaction was confirmed. The surprise was that the indiscriminantly antireligious persons had the second highest marital satisfaction level. The researcher offered a possible explanation: Both groups tend to live by their beliefs without being hypocritical. The lowest level of marital quality correlated with the extrinsic orientation defined as "subordination of one's religious practices and beliefs to the satisfaction of personal needs and wants" (p. 104).

Marital stability seems affected by spouses' level of commitment to one another. Lyle Larson and J. Walter Goltz (1989) explored two types of marital commitment: structural and personal. The concept of structural commitment includes four components: investment that cannot be retrieved, procedures involved in termination, social pressures to remain together, and the degree of attraction to other alternatives. Personal commitment was related to personal satisfaction with marriage and family life. Results indicated no significant correlation between religious homogamy and either personal or structural commitment. The lack of a significant relationship with religious homogamy may mean it is not an important factor, or it may mean that one partner converted, decreased participation, or requested a divorce over differences. Because Catholic and conservative husbands who were active participants had higher levels of structural commitment, the authors suggested that social-control functions of religion affect marital commitment. Family satisfaction, not religion, was wives' major consideration. Larson (1989) concluded better theoretical conceptualization and measurements need to be found to identify what specific aspects of religion affect marital commitment. Attendance, religious affiliation, beliefs, and time spent in devotional practices explain neither the inner complexity of religious experience nor the ways it influences persons' relationships.

Actual divorce rates are primary measures of marital instability. Bahr (1981) indicated highest divorce rates in Utah were for persons with no religious preference or specific interfaith combinations. Research indicates that factors involving affiliation may have some effect, since Mormons have lower-than-average divorce rates (Jenkins 1991).

Parenting and Family Relationships

General consensus affirms that parents influence children. Two specific areas related to religious variables are styles of parenting, particularly regarding discipline, and the transmittal of values and faith heritage. Christopher Ellison and Darren Sherkat (1993) reasoned that parents with conservative faith views would be likely to value children's obedience and endorse authoritarian parenting styles more than religiously liberal parents. Research confirmed this hypothesis with conservative Protestants and Catholics. In summarizing data from the 1988 General Social Survey of the general population, Ellison and Sherkat (1993) indicated that 23 percent of the respondents valued obedience most highly of five variables and 49 percent most valued children's thinking for themselves.

Parents influence their children's religion, values, and behavior. Family religiosity is one of the strongest predictors of faith among teens and adults. Family expressions of faith include talking of faith, family devotional periods, and family projects to help others (Strommen 1993). Seventy-nine percent of college students in one study reported that parents were most influential in developing their religious values (Anderson and Palkovitz 1993). Review of research indicates the religiosity of the parents predicts similar religiosity in children, positive parental communication promotes positive images of God, and high religiosity in the home and shared religious activities encourage family happiness and success (Jenkins 1991).

One way parents help their children's socialization is by "channeling them into other groups or experiences" (Himmelfarb in Cornwall 1989, p. 577). By encouraging organizational activities with those sharing similar values, a supportive network reinforces values taught at home.

Parental and religious influences also affect moral issues. In some research, premarital sex was discouraged by parents, supportive networks, adolescent religiosity, and a high intrinsic religious orientation (Jenkins 1991). J. Timothy Woodroof (1986) highlighted the influence of parents' example, both parents' religious affiliation, and best friends' abstinence.

There are other positive effects of religion. Substance abuse, at least in early stages, is deterred by parental monitoring, youth's high religiosity, and peer-group support (Jenkins 1991). Highly religious women have less psychological distress and better adjustment (Crawford, Handal, and Wiener 1989). Religious persons are able to find hope and courage when facing difficult realities such as terminal illness (Pruyser 1986). Members of faith communities are aided by having a supportive network in place to help in times of need (Taylor and Chatters 1988).

Conclusion

Religion is a multidimensional concept that has often been used simplistically by researchers to show some correlation with family life, even though the connection was not always understood. The interactive processes involved in the complex relationship of religion and family life will become more clear as researchers increase their understanding of the dynamics of each. Social scientists need to identify and develop ways to measure how religious beliefs, attitudes, and devotional practices achieve sufficient importance to be translated into actions. The processes by which the social, cognitive, emotional, and spiritual aspects of religion are translated into behavior in the family context need to be discovered.

(*See also:* ABORTION: MEDICAL AND SOCIAL ASPECTS; BIRTH CONTROL: SOCIOCULTURAL AND HISTORICAL ASPECTS; CELIBACY; COHABITATION; COMMITMENT; ETHNICITY; FAMILY VALUES; INTERMARRIAGE; MARITAL QUALITY; MATE SELECTION)

BIBLIOGRAPHY

Ajzen, I., and Fishbein, M. (1980). *Understanding Attitudes and Predicting Behavior.* Englewood Cliffs, NJ: Prentice Hall.

Allport, G., and Ross, J. M. (1967). "Personal Religious Orientation and Prejudice." *Journal of Personality and Social Psychology* 5:432–443.

Anderson, S. L., and Palkovitz, R. (1993). *A Perspective on Intergenerational Religious Value and Behavior Patterns.* Paper presented at the National Council on Family Relations, Baltimore.

Anthony, M. J. (1993). "The Relationship Between Marital Satisfaction and Religious Maturity." *Religious Education* 88:97–108.

Bahr, H. M. (1981). "Religious Intermarriage and Divorce in Utah and the Mountain States." *Journal for the Scientific Study of Religion* 20:251–261.

Bahr, H. M., and Chadwick, B. (1985). "Religion and Family in Middletown, USA." *Journal of Marriage and the Family* 47:407–414.

Batson, C. D., and Ventis, W. L. (1982). *The Religious Experience: A Social-Psychological Perspective.* New York: Oxford University Press.

Burton, L. A., ed. (1992). *Religion and the Family: When God Helps.* New York: Haworth Press.

Cornwall, M. (1987). "The Social Bases of Religion: A Study of Factors Influencing Religious Belief and Commitment." *Review of Religious Research* 29:44–56.

Cornwall, M. (1989). "The Determinants of Religious Behavior: A Theoretical Model." *Social Forces* 68:572–592.

Crawford, M. E.; Handal, P. J.; and Wiener, R. L. (1989). "The Relationship Between Religion and Mental Health/ Distress." *Review of Religious Research* 31:16–22.

D'Antonio, W. (1985). "The American Catholic Family: Signs of Cohesion and Polarization." *Journal of Marriage and the Family* 47:395–405.

D'Antonio, W., and Aldous, J. (1983). *Families and Religions.* Newbury Park, CA: Sage Publications.

Davidson, J. (1972). "Religious Beliefs as an Independent Variable." *Journal for the Scientific Study of Religion* 11:65–75.

Davidson, J. (1975). "Glock's Model of Religious Commitment: Assessing Some Different Approaches and Results." *Review of Religious Research* 16:83–93.

Davis, J. A., and Smith, T. W. (1989). *The General Social Surveys: Cumulative Codebook, 1972–1989.* Chicago: National Opinion Research Center.

Ellison, C. G., and Sherkat, D. E. (1993). "Obedience and Autonomy: Religion and Parental Values Reconsidered." *Journal for the Scientific Study of Religion* 32:313–329.

Filsinger, E., and Wilson, M. R. (1984). "Religiosity, Socioeconomic Rewards, and Family Development: Predictions of Marital Adjustment." *Journal of Marriage and the Family* 46:663–670.

Heaton, T. B. (1984). "Religious Homogamy and Marital Satisfaction Reconsidered." *Journal of Marriage and the Family* 46:729–733.

Heaton, T. B. (1986). "How Does Religion Influence Fertility?: The Case of the Mormons." *Journal of the Scientific Study of Religion* 25:248–258.

Heaton, T. B.; Jacobson, C. K.; and Fu, X. N. (1992). "Religiosity of Married Couples and Childlessness." *Review of Religious Research* 33:244–255.

Jenkins, K. W. (1991). "Religion and Families." In *Family Research: A Sixty-Year Review, 1930–1990,* Vol. 1, ed. S. J. Bahr. New York: Free Press.

Krishnan, V. (1993). "Religious Homogamy and Voluntary Childlessness in Canada." *Sociological Perspectives* 36:83–93.

Larson, L. E. (1989). "Religiosity and Marital Commitment: 'Until Death Do Us Part' Revisited." *Family Science Review* 2:285–302.

Larson, L. E., and Goltz, J. W. (1989). "Religious Participation and Marital Commitment." *Review of Religious Research* 30:387–400.

Pruyser, P. W. (1986). "Maintaining Hope in Adversity." *Pastoral Psychology* 35:120–131.

Sander, W. (1993). "Catholicism and Intermarriage in the United States." *Journal of Marriage and the Family* 55:1037–1041.

Schumm, W.; Bollman, S.; and Jurich, A. (1982). "The Marital Conventionalization Argument: Implications for the Study of Religiosity and Marital Satisfaction." *Journal for the Scientific Study of Religion* 10:236–241.

Strommen, M. P. (1993). "Rethinking Family Ministry." In *Rethinking Christian Education,* ed. D. S. Schuller. St. Louis, MO: Chalice Press.

Sweet, J.; Bumpass, L.; and Call, V. (1988). "The Design and Content of the National Survey of Families and Households." Working Paper NSFH-1. Madison: Center for Demography and Ecology, University of Wisconsin.

Taylor, R. J., and Chatters, L. M. (1988). "Church Members as a Source of Social Support." *Review of Religious Research* 30:193–203.

Thornton, A. (1985). "Reciprocal Influences of Family and Religion in a Changing World." *Journal of Marriage and the Family* 47:381–394.

Thornton, A. (1992). "Reciprocal Effects of Religiosity, Cohabitation, and Marriage." *American Journal of Sociology* 98:628–651.

Woodroof, J. T. (1986). "Reference Groups, Religiosity, and Premarital Sexual Behavior." *Journal for the Scientific Study of Religion* 25:436–460.

RUTH CORDLE HATCH

REMARRIAGE

Estimates suggest that four of every ten marriages in the United States involve a second or higher-order marriage (National Center for Health Statistics 1991). Another way to look at these figures is to understand that for about 21 percent of all married couples, the current marriage represents a remarriage for at least one of the marital pair. Additionally, 61 percent of remarried men and women marry someone for whom the current marriage also represents a remarriage (Wilson and Clarke 1992).

Most remarriages follow divorce rather than the death of a spouse, and many who elect to remarry do so fairly quickly following divorce, with some variation by age and sex. About 30 percent of divorced men and women remarry within 12 months of their divorce. In 1988, divorced men who remarried did so after 3.6 years on average. Men between 20 and 24 years of age spent about 1.3 years between marriages. In contrast, for men 65 years or older, the interval between marriages was 7.1 years. For previously divorced women, the average interval was 3.9 years, ranging from 1.5 years for those 20 to 24 years of age to 11.2 years for those 65 years or older. At every age, however, the interval between marriages was longer for women than for men. This disparity increased with increasing age (Wilson and Clarke 1992).

Like first marriages, many remarriages end in divorce. Estimates suggest that about 72 percent of recently separated women will eventually remarry (Bumpass and Sweet 1989), and about 60 percent of those who remarry will eventually redivorce (Norton and Miller 1992). Remarriages that consist of a remarriage for both spouses are more likely to end in divorce than those in which it is a remarriage for only one spouse (Wilson and Clarke 1992). However, when the level of education and the age at first marriage are controlled, the likelihood of ending the marriage in divorce is about the same regardless of whether the marriage is a first marriage for both spouses or a remarriage for one or both spouses (Martin and Bumpass 1989).

At the same time, remarriages that end in divorce do so more quickly than first marriages. The median duration of a first marriage was 6.3 years for women aged 20 to 54 in 1990; this figure represented a decline since 1980. For example, women aged 25 to 29 in 1990 had spent a median of 3.4 years in a first marriage. In 1980 the median was 4.0 years. For older women aged 40 to 44, the median duration of first marriage was 9.7 years in 1980; this fell to 7.6 years in 1990. The median duration of a remarriage is about 4.5 years (Norton and Miller 1992).

Factors Affecting Remarriage After Divorce

Several factors have been associated with the probability of remarriage. One factor—age at first marriage—affects the probability of both divorce and remarriage, such that women under twenty years of age at first marriage are most likely to divorce and remarry (Norton and Miller 1992). It follows that as women age, they are less likely to remarry. Men at all ages are more likely to remarry than are women.

Most persons who remarry are older at the time of remarriage than those in first marriages and often begin their marital career before twenty years of age. The age disparity between spouses is greater when a previously divorced male marries a never-married woman. Some racial differences occur regarding age at remarriage. African-American men and women are typically older at remarriage than white men and women, and the interval between marriages is longer. White men and women are less likely to select a never-married partner (Wilson and Clarke 1992).

General racial differences are apparent in that about 72 percent of white women are likely to remarry, whereas fewer than half of African-American women are likely to do so. Not only are white women more likely to remarry than African-American women, white women remarry more quickly. Remarriage is least common among women of Hispanic origin. The racial differences are not compensated for by increases in cohabitation among African Americans and those of Hispanic origin (Bumpass, Sweet, and Martin 1990).

The presence of children from the prior marriage also affects the probability of remarriage, especially for women. Women with children are less likely to remarry than those without children, and those with three or more children are the least likely to remarry.

Socioeconomic status is another factor affecting remarriage. Men in higher socioeconomic statuses are more likely to remarry than are men in lower statuses. Such is not the case for women. Women in higher socioeconomic statuses are less likely to remarry than women in lower socioeconomic statuses (Bumpass, Sweet, and Martin 1990). Income is another indicator of socioeconomic status. For remarriages that result in the formation of stepfamilies, data from the National Survey of Families and Households show that only 37 percent of stepfamilies had a household income of $50,000 or more in 1988. Forty-five percent of first-marriage families reported this same income category. In other words, stepfamilies are more likely to be poorer than first-married families (Larson 1992).

Level of education per se is not associated with remarriage rates. However, women with incomplete education (e.g., those women who failed to complete twelve years of education or four years of college) are most likely to divorce and remarry. In contrast, women who complete exactly twelve or sixteen years of school are less likely to divorce than those who complete either eleven years, thirteen to fifteen years, or seventeen years of school (Moorman and Miller 1992), so they are less likely to be candidates for remarriage. Both men and women who marry never-married partners have more education than those who marry previously married partners (Wilson and Clarke 1992).

Other correlates of remarriage include geographic area and the timing of conception and childbirth. The lowest remarriage rates occur in the Northeast. Rates in the North-Central and the West are about two-thirds higher than those in the Northeast. Remarriage rates in the South are twice as high as those in the Northeast (Bumpass, Sweet, and Martin 1990). Lastly, premarital conceptions and premarital births are associated with a high probability of divorce and remarriage for white women. This trend does not hold for African-American women and women of Hispanic origin (Moorman and Miller 1992).

It is evident that remarriage after divorce occurs most frequently among women who ended their first marriages by divorce at relatively young ages and who had been divorced for a short time. In 1990, almost 78 percent of all women who divorced by ages twenty to twenty-four had remarried, compared with fewer than 45 percent of all women who divorced between ages thirty-five and thirty-nine. This trend was similar for white women, African-American women, and women of Hispanic origin (Norton and Miller 1992).

Remarriage After Death of Spouse

Widowed men and women who remarry present a different picture from those who divorce. The remarriage rate for widowed men is almost five times higher than that for widowed women, although there has been a drop overall in the remarriage rate since 1980. This drop has been accompanied by an increase in cohabitation among widowed persons (U.S. Bureau of the Census 1980, 1989). Remarriage rates decrease with increasing age. Widowed men who marry widowed women are older than those who marry divorced women, a trend similar for widowed women. Moreover, widowed men remarry more quickly than do widowed women (Wilson and Clarke 1992). For example, widowed men spend 3.9 years between marriages on average, compared to 6.4 years for widowed women. Widowed women take about 2.5 times longer to remarry than divorced women do. Some differences in remarriage rates occur by level of education. For widowed men, higher level of education is associated with greater likelihood of remarriage; for women, the effect of level of education is slightly negative (Smith, Zick, and Duncan 1991).

Marital Quality

Much of the literature on remarriage has focused on the married couple and has examined differences in marital quality, happiness, or satisfaction between first-married and remarried couples. In a comparison of thirty-four studies of marital satisfaction in remarriage, few differences were found between individuals in first marriages and those in remarriages. In addition, no differences in marital satisfaction were found between stepfather and stepmother families, those with residential and nonresidential children, nor those in simple and complex remarried family structures (Vemer et al. 1989).

Several factors have been identified as influencing marital quality. The simple fact of bringing children into marriage does not appear to lower the odds of marital success (Martin and Bumpass 1989). However, the way in which family members resolve issues around the stepparent–stepchild relationship does. A consistent finding from the research is that the quality of the stepparent–stepchild relationship affects the marital relationship (Bray, Berger, and Boethel 1994). Some research finds that the presence of a stepchild enhances relationship quality for both spouses, but only in couples where the marriage was a remarriage for only one spouse. For stepmothers in particular, perceived inequities in child-care arrangements (i.e., she believes she assumes too much responsibility for his children) decreases their marital satisfaction over time (Guisinger, Cowan, and Schuldberg 1989). The presence of a "common" child (a child born to the remarriage) positively affects marital quality, although these children may affect other relationships, such as that of the stepmother and stepchild, differently (Ganong and Coleman 1994). There is some evidence that a common child also affects marital stability for at least ten years into the remarriage (Wineberg 1992).

Whereas age of the child has little effect on marital quality (Kurdek 1990), clarity and satisfaction with the stepparent role do (Roberts and Price 1989). Also, spousal consensus about the role of the stepparent and consensus over issues pertaining to child rearing affect the quality of the remarriage (Bray, Berger, and Boethel 1994).

Much of the clinical literature suggests that financial issues negatively affect the remarriage; however, little empirical support has been offered. Pooling resources, as opposed to separate financial arrangements for spouses, is associated with closer adult–child relationships, but it appears to have little effect on the marital relationship (Pasley, Dollahite, and Edmundson 1994).

Conclusion

Remarriage will continue to be a pervasive family form, as the divorce rate is not expected to decline. However, as the remarriage rate declines, cohabitation may become more popular among divorced men and women. This will be an important family form to examine, especially among African Americans, who are the most likely to divorce and the least likely to remarry of any racial group.

(*See also:* Cohabitation; Demography; Divorce: Emotional and Social Aspects; Marital Quality; Remarriage and Children; Stepparenting; Widowhood)

BIBLIOGRAPHY

Bray, J. A.; Berger, S. H.; and Boethel, C. L. (1994). "Role Integration and Marital Adjustment in Stepfather Families." In *Stepfamilies: Current Issues in Theory, Research, and Practice,* ed. K. Pasley and M. Ihinger-Tallman. Westport, CT: Greenwood Press.

Bumpass, L. L., and Sweet, J. A. (1989). "National Estimates of Cohabitation: Cohort Levels and Union Stability." *Demography* 26:615–625.

Bumpass, L. L.; Sweet, J. A.; and Martin, T. C. (1990). "Changing Patterns of Remarriage." *Journal of Marriage and the Family* 52:747–756.

Ganong, L. H., and Coleman, M. (1994). *Remarried Family Relationships.* Newbury Park, CA: Sage Publications.

Guisinger, S.; Cowan, P. A.; and Schuldberg, D. (1989). "Changing Parent and Spouse Relations in the First Years of Remarriage of Divorce Fathers." *Journal of Marriage and the Family* 51:45–456.

Kurdek, L. A. (1990). "Effects of Child Age on Marital Quality and Psychological Distress of Newly Married Mothers and Stepfathers." *Journal of Marriage and the Family* 52:81–85.

Larson, J. (1992). "Understanding Stepfamilies." *American Demographics* 14:36–40.

Martin, T. C., and Bumpass, L. L. (1989). "Recent Trends and Differential in Marital Disruption." *Demography* 25:37–51.

Moorman, J. E., and Miller, L. F. (1992). "Marriage, Divorce, and Remarriage in the 1990s." *Current Population Series.* Series P-23, no. 180. Washington, DC: U.S. Government Printing Office.

National Center for Health Statistics. (1991). "Advance Report of Final Marriage Statistics, 1988." *Monthly Vital Statistics Report.* Vol. 40, no. 4, suppl. Hyattsville, MD: U.S. Public Health Service.

Norton, A. J., and Miller, L. F. (1992). "Remarriage Among Women in the United States: 1985." *Studies in Household and Family Formation.* Series P-23, no. 169. Washington, DC: U.S. Government Printing Office.

Pasley, K.; Dollahite, D.; and Edmundson, M. E. (1994). "The Effects of Financial Management Strategies on Quality of Family Life in Remarriages." *Journal of Family and Economic Issues* 15:53–70.

Roberts, T. W., and Price, S. J. (1989). "Adjustment in Remarriage: Communication, Cohesion, and Marital and Parental Roles." *Journal of Divorce* 13:17–43.

Smith, K. R.; Zick, C. D.; and Duncan, G. J. (1991). "Remarriage Patterns Among Recent Widows and Widowers." *Demography* 28:361–374.

U.S. Bureau of the Census. (1980). "Marital Status and Living Arrangements: March 1980." *Current Population Reports.* Series P-20, no. 433. Washington, DC: U.S. Government Printing Office.

U.S. Bureau of the Census. (1989). "Marital Status and Living Arrangements: March 1988." *Current Population Reports.* Series P-20, no. 433. Washington, DC: U.S. Government Printing Office.

Vemer, E.; Coleman, M.; Ganong, L. H.; and Cooper, H. (1989). "Marital Satisfaction in Remarriage." *Journal of Marriage and the Family* 51:713–725.

Wilson, B. F., and Clarke, S. C. (1992). "Remarriages: A Demographic Profile." *Journal of Family Issues* 13:123–141.

Wineberg, H. (1992). "Childbearing and Dissolution of the Second Marriage." *Journal of Marriage and the Family* 54:879–887.

Kay Pasley
Amy Lofquist

REMARRIAGE AND CHILDREN

Nearly one-fifth of all children in the United States reside with a remarried parent and a stepparent (Glick 1989), and many children who live with a single parent also have a nonresidential parent who has remarried. If the rates of divorce and remarriage recorded in the 1980s continue, more than one-third of all children in the United States will become stepchildren before they reach the age of eighteen (Glick 1989). The effect of remarriage on these children is an important question.

Although remarriage and the formation of stepfamilies have been common in most cultures of the world throughout history, there were fewer than twelve studies of stepchildren and their families prior to 1980 (Coleman and Ganong 1990). Interest by social scientists has soared since then, however. Stepparents were originally considered to "replace" deceased parents, returning the family to nuclear status. In fact, the early meaning of the word "step" was related to bereavement and replacement. However, remarriage generally follows divorce rather than death. A stepparent is no longer a replacement for a deceased parent, but instead is an additional adult who may or may not take a parental role with the children. This is a profound shift with many implications for children. The surge of interest in stepfamily research may be a result of the change in the most frequent precursor of remarriage from death to divorce.

Researchers have tended to adopt the deficit-comparison assumption that stepchildren will have poorer outcomes than children in nuclear families, an assumption influenced by generalizations drawn from clinical writings and from the prevailing belief in society that the nuclear family is the best family structure in which to raise children (Ganong and Coleman 1994b). Theoretical reasons for expecting poorer outcomes for stepchildren include the hypotheses that stress related to family transitions negatively affects children, that divorce and remarriage disrupt children's access to parents as important role models, and that stepparents are less motivated to excel at raising children to whom they are not genetically related. Another hypothesis is that remarried families lack societal guidelines for role performance, which leads to ambiguity, stress, and confusion regarding raising children (Cherlin 1978).

Although a parent's remarriage almost always creates a substantial disruption in a child's life, remarriage does not have uniform psychological and emotional effects, partly because there are wide variations in remarried family structures and partly because remarriage is not a uniform process. There is no single remarried family structure. Researchers have identified fifteen types of remarried family structures based only on the residence of children from the prior unions of both adults (Wald 1981). Following remarriage, children may live all of the time with a stepparent and a parent, they may live part-time in a stepparent–parent household and part-time in a single-parent household, they may live all of the time with one parent but have a remarried parent and a stepparent elsewhere, or they may split time in two stepparent–parent households. In addition, stepchildren may reside full-time or part-time with any combination of siblings, stepsiblings, and half-siblings, or they may never live with the other children in their family. Diverse outcomes for children from such structurally varied and often complex family configurations are not surprising.

Parental remarriage is not a discrete event experienced similarly by all children. Instead, the formation of a remarried family is a process beginning well before legal remarriage and extending for years. The nature of remarried family processes depends on several factors, some related to demographic and structural characteristics (e.g., family income, presence of stepsiblings), and some related to personal characteristics of children, parents, and stepparents (e.g., mental health) and their interpersonal dynamics.

Researchers often have ignored the structural complexity and processual heterogeneity of remarried families, treating stepchildren as a homogeneous group. A common research design is to compare stepchildren to children living in nuclear families or single-parent households. Although findings differ from study to study, overall stepchildren tend to have slightly lower self-esteem, somewhat more internalizing problems (e.g., depression, anxiety), and more externalizing behavioral problems (e.g., fighting) than children in nuclear families. Stepchildren generally are more similar to children in single-parent families on these outcome variables (Ganong and Coleman 1993). Group differences tell only part of the story, however, because most stepchildren are not harmed psychologically by parental remarriage.

In the behavioral realm, some investigators report earlier intercourse and cohabitation, earlier leaving of the home, more substance abuse, and more illegal activities for stepchildren, whereas other investigators report no differences between stepchildren and other children. Studies of cognitive functioning (e.g., school performance, intelligence) generally have not found that parental remarriage has negative effects. Nor does parental remarriage seem to affect attitudes toward marriage and parenthood, although stepchildren's attitudes toward divorce are more positive than those of other children (Coleman and Ganong 1990).

A common finding is that children do not feel as emotionally close to stepparents as they do to biological parents. Nevertheless, most stepchildren develop a reasonably positive relationship with their stepparents. It has been argued that the expectation that stepparent–stepchild relationships be similar in closeness to parent–child relationships is inappropriate and based on a nuclear family ideology.

Although some conclusions may be drawn about the impact of remarriage on children, looking for overall effects generally has been fruitless. The effect sizes (the magnitude of differences between groups) in studies comparing stepchildren to other children tend to be small. This means that the impact of parental remarriage on children is not predictable, but varies as a function of factors that accompany remarriage. Such factors as socioeconomic status, amount of contact with the nonresidential parent and/or the stepparent, number of children in the household, presence of stepsiblings and half-siblings, race, the degree of conflict in the parents' marriage, child temperament, stepfamily conflict and stress levels, and the custody arrangements are potentially important mediators of the effect of parent remarriage on children. Not all of these factors have been studied in depth, but three have: age of the child, sex of the child, and sex of the stepparent.

Clinicians contend that younger children adapt better than older children and adolescents (Visher and Visher 1988). However, few researchers have examined child age at parental remarriage, and most samples have consisted of children from a relatively narrow age range. In the few studies that examined age, the findings were inconsistent.

In contrast, the findings related to sex differences have been quite stable. For girls, outcomes are worse following parental remarriage, and for boys they are better (Needle, Su, and Doherty 1990; Peterson and Zill 1986). Girls are more likely than boys to have conduct problems and to engage in antisocial behaviors. One proposed explanation is that girls in remarried families may be disciplined more than boys and that boys are allowed more freedom (Ganong and Coleman 1994a). On the other hand, girls may have different standards for family relationships, expecting more closeness, warmth, and understanding than boys do. When their expectations are not met, they are more disappointed and upset. Additionally, girls often are closer than boys to custodial mothers following divorce, so they may see the stepfather as an intruder, while boys may welcome a male role model.

There is more information about children who live with stepfathers than those who live with stepmothers; there are more than five times as many stepfather households, since children are usually in their mother's custody after a divorce. Children living with stepfathers often do not fare much differently than children living with both biological parents, perhaps because the heart of family processes in all family structures, at least pertaining to outcomes for children, is the mother–child relationship; stepfathers tend to be more peripheral (Acock and Demo 1994).

Children who live with stepmothers have more overall behavior problems than children in other family structures, including children living with stepfathers, with single mothers, and with both parents. This may be due to more problems in stepmother–stepchild relationships; stepmothers are less satisfied with their relationships with stepchildren than stepfathers (Hobart 1987) and display more negative behaviors toward stepchildren than stepfathers do (Hetherington 1989). Some of these problems are thought to be due to expected family roles for women, which pressure stepmothers to assume a greater amount of child-rearing responsibilities than stepfathers, giving them more opportunities for conflict. The lack of guidelines and role models for stepmothers, along with stigma about "wicked" stepmothers, force stepmothers to function without much social support.

There have been mixed findings concerning the predictions that stepchildren will fare worse than children living with both biological parents. Some studies find that stepchildren experience more stress and more behavioral and psychological problems than other children, and other studies find no differences. Children may be survivors, losers, or winners as a result of parental remarriage (Hetherington 1989).

(*See also:* Child Custody; Divorce: Effects on Children; Remarriage; Sibling Relationships; Single Parents; Stepparenting)

BIBLIOGRAPHY

Acock, A., and Demo, D. H. (1994). *Family Structure and Family Relations.* Newbury Park, CA: Sage Publications.

Cherlin, A. (1978). "Remarriage as an Incomplete Institution." *American Journal of Sociology* 84:634–650.

Coleman, M., and Ganong, L. (1990). "Remarriage and Stepfamily Research in the '80s: New Interest in an Old Family Form." *Journal of Marriage and the Family* 52:925–940.

Ganong, L., and Coleman, M. (1984). "Effects of Remarriage on Children: A Review of the Empirical Literature." *Family Relations* 33:389–406.

Ganong, L., and Coleman, M. (1986). "A Comparison of Clinical and Empirical Literature on Children in Stepfamilies." *Journal of Marriage and the Family* 48:309–318.

Ganong, L., and Coleman, M. (1993). "A Meta-Analytic Comparison of the Self-Esteem and Behavior Problems of Stepchildren to Children in Other Family Structures." *Journal of Divorce and Remarriage* 19:143–163.

Ganong, L., and Coleman, M. (1994a). "Adolescent Stepchild–Stepparent Relationships: Changes over Time." In *Stepparenting: Issues in Theory, Research, and Practice,* ed. K. Pasley and M. Ihinger-Tallman. Westport, CT: Greenwood Press.

Ganong, L., and Coleman, M. (1994b). *Remarried Family Relationships.* Newbury Park, CA: Sage Publications.

Glick, P. (1989). "Remarried Families, Stepfamilies, and Stepchildren: A Brief Demographic Analysis." *Family Relations* 38:24–27.

Hetherington, E. M. (1989). "Coping with Family Transitions: Winners, Losers, and Survivors." *Child Development* 60:1–14.

Hobart, C. W. (1987). "Parent–Child Relations in Remarried Families." *Journal of Family Issues* 8:259–277.

Ihinger-Tallman, M. (1988). "Research on Stepfamilies." *Annual Review of Sociology* 14:25–48.

Needle, R. H.; Su, S. S.; and Doherty, W. J. (1990). "Divorce, Remarriage, and Adolescent Substance Use: A Prospective Longitudinal Study." *Journal of Marriage and the Family* 52:157–169.

Peterson, J., and Zill, N. (1986). "Marital Disruption, Parent–Child Relationships, and Behavior Problems in Children." *Journal of Marriage and the Family* 48:295–307.

Visher, E. B., and Visher, J. S. (1988). *Old Loyalties, New Ties: Therapeutic Strategies with Stepfamilies.* New York: Brunner/Mazel.

Wald, E. (1981). *The Remarried Family.* New York: Family Service Association of America.

LAWRENCE H. GANONG
MARILYN COLEMAN

REPRODUCTION *See* ABORTION: MEDICAL AND SOCIAL ASPECTS; BIRTH CONTROL: CONTRACEPTIVE METHODS; CONCEPTION: MEDICAL ASPECTS; INFERTILITY; PREGNANCY AND BIRTH

RESEARCH METHODS

Four characteristics shape the research methods family scholars use. First, family scholarship has conceptual roots in a variety of disciplines, including anthropology, demography, family and consumer science, economics, history, human ecology, psychology, and sociology. Second, the subject matter studied by family scholars overlaps the subject matter studied by a variety of content specialty areas such as women's studies, adolescence, early childhood, gerontology, education, deviance, nutrition, and counseling. Third, while other fields often focus on isolated individuals, family scholars study individuals who are embedded in family systems. Fourth, families have a shared past and future (Copeland and White 1991). The result is an extraordinary mixture of quantitative and qualitative methods, experimental and survey methods, and cross-sectional and longitudinal methods (Miller, Rollins, and Thomas 1982).

Some family scholars approach their study of the family from a macro/historical perspective or a macro/comparative perspective. Others approach it from an individual perspective. Some scholars seek to discover family patterns in ancient cultures; others seek to solve current social ills. The unit of analysis—that is, the smallest unit about which a scholar draws a conclusion—may be an individual (child, mother, nonresident father), a dyad (husband and wife, siblings), a family (nuclear, stem), a culture, or a historical period.

A researcher may want to explain how a hyperactive child influences outcomes for the family such as conflict or chance of divorce. Other researchers may explain hyperactivity in children in terms of family or cultural factors. For the first researcher, the child's hyperactivity is the independent variable (predictor). For the second researcher, the child's hyperactivity is the dependent variable (outcome).

The intricate relationship between root disciplines and specialty areas on the one hand, and research methodology of groups of scholars on the other hand has been detailed in a more complete exposition by Robert E. Larzelere and David M. Klein (1987).

Strategies for Data Collection

Data is the empirical information researchers use for drawing conclusions. Often a cross-sectional design is used where data is collected just once. This is a snapshot of how things are at a single point in time. Less common are longitudinal designs, where the data is collected at least twice. While each collection point provides a snapshot, it is possible to make inferences about changes. With time series design you have many snapshots and usually more than thirty data collection points.

Cross-sectional design. A cross-sectional design, which gathers data at a single point, can be used in a survey, experiment, in-depth interview, or observational study. The justification for this design is usually cost.

Suppose researchers are interested in the effects of divorce on children. A cross-sectional design could take a large sample of children and measure their well-being. The children would be divided by whether they experienced divorce. If the children who had experienced divorce fared worse on well-being, the researcher would conclude that divorce had adverse effects.

Cross-sectional analysis requires the examination of covariates (related situational variables) to minimize alternative explanations. Children who experienced divorce probably lived in families that had conflict, and they may fare worse on well-being because of this conflict rather than because their parents divorced. Researchers would ask for retrospective information about marital conflict before the divorce, income before the divorce, and so on. These covariates would be controlled to clarify the effects of divorce, as distinct from the effects of these other variables, because each covariate is an alternative explanation for the children's well-being.

Longitudinal design. By collecting data at different times, causal order is clear; the variables measured at time one can cause the variables at time two, but the reverse is not the case. When variables are measured imperfectly, however, the errors in the first wave are often correlated with the errors in the second and third waves. Therefore, statistical analyses of longitudinal data are typically very complex.

The question concerning the influence of divorce on the well-being of children illustrates advantages and disadvantages of longitudinal strategies. The well-being of children is measured at one time. Five years later the researcher would contact the same children and measure their well-being. Some of the children's parents would have gotten divorced. Children who experienced divorce could have their well-being at time two compared to time one. The difference would be attributed to the effects of divorce. By knowing the well-being of these children five years earlier, controls for the influence of conflict on well-being would automatically be incorporated.

Although longitudinal designs are very appealing, there are some basic problems. After five years, the researcher may be able to locate only 60 percent to 70 percent of the children. Those who vanished in the interval might have altered the researcher's conclusions. Second, five years is a long time in the life of a child; if the child was twelve at time one, she or he would be seventeen at time two. Marriages also swing in their well-being. Statistically these problems can be minimized, but the analysis is quite complex.

Time series design. Although some people use time series and longitudinal labels interchangeably, measures are made many times, usually thirty times or more, for time series analyses, which focus on the process of change. By tracking the respondents over time, changes are attributed to their life events.

Using the example of the effects of divorce on children, a researcher may be interested in how effects vary over time. Perhaps there is an initial negative effect that diminishes over time. Alternatively, initial adverse effects may decrease over time for girls but increase for boys.

Designs for Collecting Data

Researchers have a wide variety of approaches and designs to choose from for collection of data. Three common designs are surveys, experiments and quasi-experiments, and observation and in-depth interviews.

Surveys. The most common data collection strategy is the survey. One example, the National Survey of Families and Households, is a sample of more than 13,000 U.S. households conducted in the late 1980s (Sweet, Bumpass, and Call 1988). Such surveys allow researchers to generalize to a larger population, such as that of the United States. Because these surveys are large, researchers can identify special populations such as cohabiting partners, marriages where spouses are unhappy but do not become divorced, or single-parent families headed by fathers. These are "general purpose" surveys, and the data are available for independent scholars, who had nothing to do with the data collection, to analyze the results.

A second type of survey focuses on special populations. Researchers with a particular interest—for example, middle-age daughters caring for aged mothers—focus all of their resources on collecting data about a special group. In many cases, these surveys are not probability samples. Credibility for generalizing comes from comparing the profile of respondents to demographic information. An advantage of these surveys is that they can ask questions the researcher wants to ask. There might be a twenty-item scale to measure the physical dependency of an aged mother. Such detailed measurements are not usually available in general-purpose surveys.

Experiments and quasi-experiments. Experimental designs are used when internal validity is critical (Brown and Melamed 1990). A survey is limited in showing a causal effect; experiments provide stronger evidence because an experiment involves random assignment of subjects to groups and the manipulation of the independent variable by the researcher. On the other hand, experimental designs give up some external validity as they gain internal validity. Because of the difficulty or impossibility of locating subjects who will volunteer to be assigned randomly to groups, many experiments are based on "captive" populations such as college students. Captive populations are fairly homogeneous regarding age, education, race, and socioeconomic status, making it difficult to generalize to a broader population. Experiments that involve putting strangers together for a short experience provide groups that differ qualitatively from naturally occurring groups such as families (Copeland and White 1991).

Many research questions are difficult to address using experiments. Suppose a survey result shows a negative correlation between husband–wife conflict and child well-being. A true experiment requires both randomization of subjects and manipulation of the independent variable. The researcher cannot randomly assign children to families. Nor can the level of husband–wife conflict be manipulated.

Observation and in-depth interviews. Both qualitative and quantitative researchers use observation and in-depth interviews. This may be done in a deliberately unstructured way. For instance, a researcher may observe the interaction between an African-American mother and her child when the child is dropped off at a child-care facility, comparing this to the mother–child interaction for other ethnic and racial groups. The researcher may structure this observation by focusing on specific aspects such as counting tactile contact (i.e., touching or hugging). For many qualitative researchers, however, the aspects of interaction that are recorded emerge after a long period of unstructured observation.

A quantitative researcher may have an elaborate coding system for observing family interaction. This may involve videotaping either ordinary or contrived situations. A researcher interested in family decision making might give each family a task, such as deciding what they would do with $1,000. Alternatively, the researcher might record family interaction at the dinner table. The videotape would be analyzed using multiple observers and a prearranged system. For example, the observers might record how often each family member spoke, how often each member suggested a solution, how often each member tried to relieve tension, and how often each member solicited opinions from others (Bales 1950).

Observational studies often focus on nonverbal behavior. Several researchers have shown that social desirability and reactivity are more likely with verbal behavior than they are with nonverbal behavior. There are many clues in research studies that subjects and respondents use to make predictions about what the study involves and what the researcher is trying to prove. Subjects and respondents often try to please the researcher. By focusing on nonverbal behavior, observational studies may be less biased by social desirability and reactivity (Vincent et al. 1979).

In-depth interviews are widely used by qualitative researchers. When someone is trying to understand how families work, in-depth interviews are an important resource. In-depth interviews vary in their degree of structure. A white researcher, who is married, has a middle-class background and limited experience in interracial settings, may want to understand the relationship between nonresident African-American fathers and their children. Such a researcher would gain much from unstructured in-depth interviews with nonresident African-American fathers and their children, including knowledge to replace assumptions and stereotypes. It may take a series of extended, unstructured interviews before the researcher is competent to develop a structural interview, much less design a survey or an experiment.

Many scholars would limit in-depth interviews and observational studies to areas where knowledge is limited. A major advantage of such designs, however, is that they open up research to new perspectives precisely where survey or experimental researchers naively believe they have detailed knowledge. By grounding research in the behavior and interactions of ordinary people, researchers may be less prone to impose explanations developed by others.

Two major problems are evident with observation and in-depth interviews. First, these approaches make it extremely costly to have a large or representative sample. Second, there are dangers of the researcher losing objectivity. When a researcher spends months with a group either as a participant or an observer, there is a danger of identifying so much with the group that objectivity is lost.

Selected other strategies. Case studies are used on rare populations such as families in which a child has AIDS. Content analysis is often used to identify emergent themes. For example, a review of the role of fathers in popular novels of the 1930s, 1960s, and 1990s will tell much about the changing ideology of family roles. Historical analysis is increasingly important in family scholarship (Elder 1981), as evidenced by a major journal, the *Journal of Family History*. Demographic analysis is sometimes done to provide background information (economic well-being of continuously single families—see Acock and Demo 1994), document trends (increase in the frequency of continuously single families—see Teachman, Polonko, and Scanzoni 1987), and compare studies (division of household chores in Japan and the United States—see Kamo 1988). Increasingly, studies are using multiple approaches: quantitative, qualitative, historical, and so on.

Measurement

All methodological orientations share a common need for measurement. Scientific advancement in many fields is built on progress in measurement (Draper and Marcos 1990). Good measurement is critical to family studies because of the complexity of the variables being measured. Most concepts have multiple dimensions and a subjective component. A happy marriage for the husband may be a miserable marriage for the wife. A daughter may have a positive relationship with her father centered on her performance in sports but a highly negative relationship with her father centered on her sexual activity.

Because of the importance of measurement, it would be easy to assume that all researchers use highly sophisticated measurement models. This is not always the case. A professor trying to measure how much students know on a subject may create a fifty-item test. When doing family research, the same professor wanting to know how happy mothers are in their marriage may use just a single item:

> How would you rate your marital happiness? Would you say you are: (a) very happy, (b) somewhat happy, (c) somewhat unhappy, or (d) very unhappy?

A global response can mask areas of specific concern (husband does no housework), of specific satisfaction (husband is an excellent sexual partner), or specific personality issues (respondent is clinically depressed).

Scales. A number of measurement approaches have been developed. The most common, the Likert scale, gives the respondent a series of statements about a concept, and the respondent checks whether he or she strongly agrees, agrees, does not know, disagrees, or strongly disagrees with each of the statements. Often fewer than ten questions are asked, but they are chosen in a way that represents the full domain of the concept. Thus, to measure marital happiness, several items would be used to represent various aspects of the marriage.

The following is becoming a minimum standard for evaluating a scale. First, a factor analysis is done to see if the several questions converge on a single concept. Second, the reliability of the result (whether the scale gives a consistent result when administered again) is measured. This is done by using the scale twice on the same people and seeing if their answers are consistent or by using the alpha coefficient as a measure on reliability. The alpha coefficient indicates the internal consistency of the scale and should have a value of .70 or greater. This minimum standard has been emerging since the early 1980s. A review of articles in the November 1983 issue of the *Journal of Marriage and the Family* showed that reliability was reported in only five of twenty-two articles. A review of the articles in the November 1992 issue reported reliability in eleven of the twenty-two articles.

Additional procedures are done to assess the validity of the scales—that is, whether a scale measures what it is intended to measure (Carmines and McIver 1979). This is most often evaluated by correlating a new scale with various criteria such as existing scales of the same concept or outcomes that are related to the concepts.

Family scholars are paying increasing attention to measurement. There are now several books that provide scales for measuring key concepts. To varying degrees, these sources provide information on the reliability and validity of the scales (e.g., McCubbin and Thompson 1991). The information on the reliability and validity of these scales is useful but does not replace providing this information for the particular sample being studied. For instance, a scale that was developed on a sample that is middle-class, white, and participating in marriage counseling may or may not be reliable and valid for a different population.

Not all variables are measured by scales. Some variables are adequately measured with a single question. These include variables such as gender and race. Researchers doing observational studies often measure variables as "counts." Count variables are represented, for example, by the number of times a child interrupts a parent, the number of times a person went to church in the past month, and how often the family had meals together in the past week.

Questionnaires and interviews. Questionnaires are the most commonly used methods of measuring the variables in a study. A questionnaire may be designed so it can be self-administered by the respondent, asked in a face-to-face interview, or administered by telephone.

Computer-assisted interviews can be used for all three collection procedures. Self-administered questionnaires are now completed by putting the respondent in front of a computer. After a question is answered, the computer automatically goes to the next appropriate question. This allows each respondent to have an individually tailored questionnaire.

Computer-assisted interviews are becoming the standard for telephone surveys. Some organizations run telephone surveys continuously. This lets researchers locate extremely rare populations such as single-parent fathers, Native-American families, or cohabiting partners who have adolescent children and have cohabited for at least twelve years with the same partner. Each time a person who falls into the target population is identified, she or he is asked the appropriate series of questions. The telephone lab is often administering many different surveys simultaneously.

In the past, researchers felt that face-to-face interviews were uniformly superior to self-administered questionnaires and telephone surveys. Interviews allow the researcher to ask fairly complex questions that may require some explanation. They also provide a measure of quality control because the interviewer will know when the respondents are distracted. At the same time, interviews are highly reactive environments. Interviewers are chosen to match the characteristics of the respondents (sex, race) as much as practical, and the interviewers are trained to minimize asking questions or providing explanations that bias responses.

Missing data. Regardless of the approach to measurement or research design, missing data is a problem. In longitudinal strategies missing data often comes from subjects dropping out of the studies. In cross-sectional strategies missing data often comes from respondents refusing to answer questions. Readers should pay special attention to the amount of missing data. It is not unusual for studies to have 20 percent or more of the cases missing from the analysis. If those who drop out of a study or those who refuse to answer questions are different on the dependent variable, then the results will be biased.

There is no simple solution to missing data. Researchers often impute a value for missing cases. For example, if 10 percent of the respondents did not report their income, the researchers might substitute the median income of those who did report their income. A slightly better solution is to substitute the median for a homogeneous subgroup. Instead of using the overall median, the researcher might substitute a different median, depending on the respondent's gender and education. There are many other imputation methods, involving more complex statistical analysis (Rubin 1987). In any case, it is important to report information about respondents who have missing data.

Quantitative Analysis

The variety of statistical analysis techniques seems endless. To get some notion of the range of analysis procedures used, a review of the 1992 volume of the *Journal of Marriage and the Family* was done. The following list of procedures is shown to demonstrate the range of procedures used during that single year:

- Univariate: means, standards, deviations, percentages.
- Bivariate: Chi-square on contingency tables, ANOVA (analysis of variance), correlations, repeated measures ANOVA, paired t-test.
- Multivariate: MANOVA (multivariate analysis of variance), repeated measures MANOVA, ANCOVA (analysis of covariance), logistic regression, probit regression, ordered probit regression, proportional hazard models with covariates hazard rate modeling, hierarchical analysis of variance, factor analysis, principal components analysis, confirmatory factor analysis, structural equation modeling, path analysis, OLS (ordinary least squares) regression, trend analysis, event history analysis, Chow test, interaction analysis.

This is a very long list, but some commonalties need to be noted. Most analysis involves several independent variables. OLS regression is widely used as a basic statistical model. It allows researchers to include multiple independent variables (predictors) and systematically control for important covariates. Many of the procedures are either special cases of OLS regression (e.g., ANOVA, ANCOVA) or extensions (e.g., logistic regression, probit regression). There is also clear evidence that factor analysis procedures and their extensions, such as confirmatory factor analysis, play a major role in evaluating how well variables are measured.

Special Problems and Ethical Issues

Family researchers study the issues that concern people the most—factors that enhance or harm the well-being of people and families. This often involves asking sensitive questions. Most studies have a high compliance rate, with 80 percent to 90 percent of the people answering most questions. When studies begin by asking questions that respondents are willing to answer, the respondents buy into their role and later report intimate information. The reality is that respondents will tell a stranger personal information they would never share with members of their own family.

While researchers can get people to cooperate with studies, a crucial question is how the researchers should limit themselves in what they ask people to do. All universities have committees that review research proposals where human subjects are involved. Researchers need to demonstrate that the results of their study are sufficiently promising to justify any risks to their subjects. Researchers must take precautions to minimize risks. Sometimes this involves anonymity for the participants (no name or identification associated with respondents or subjects); sometimes it involves confidentiality (name or identification known only to the project's staff). It also involves informed consent, wherein respondents agree to participate after they are told about the project. Informed consent is a special problem with qualitative research. The design of qualitative research is emergent in that the researcher does not know exactly what is being tested before going into the field. Consequently, it is difficult to have meaningful informed consent. The participants simply do not know enough about the project when they are asked to participate.

Even with the best intentions, subjects can be put at risk. Asking adolescents about their relationship with a nonresident father may bring to life problems that had been put to rest. In some cases, the effect of this can be positive; in some cases, it can be negative. Observational studies and participant observation studies are especially prone to risks for subjects. A scholar interested in interaction between family members and physicians when a family member is on an extraordinary life support system is dealing with very important questions. Who decides to turn the machine off? What is the role of the physician? What are the roles for different members of the family? All these are important questions. The presence of the researcher may be extremely intrusive and may even influence the decision-making process. This potential influence involves serious ethical considerations.

Another special risk for qualitative work is unanticipated self-exposure (LaRossa, Bennett, and Gelles 1985). As the project develops, the participant may reveal information about self or associates that goes beyond the original informed consent agreement.

Feminist methodology is not a particular research design method or data collection method (Nielsen 1990). It is distinguished by directly stating the researchers' values, explicitly recognizing the influence research has on the researcher, having sensitivity to how family arrangements are sources of both support and oppression for women, and having the intention of doing research that benefits women rather than simply being about women (Allen and Walker 1993). Given this worldview, feminist methodology presents complex ethical issues to researchers, and it demands that all family scholars be sensitive to these concerns.

Conclusion

The diversity of strategies, designs, and methods of analysis used by marriage and family researchers reflects the equally diverse root disciplines and content areas that overlap the study of marriage and the family. In view of this, cross-sectional surveys remain the most widely used strategy and quantitative analysis is dominant in the reporting of research results in the professional literature. However, experiments, longitudinal, time-series, and qualitative strategies also remain crucial tools for research.

(*See also:* Divorce: Effects on Children; Marital Quality; Measures of Family Characteristics)

BIBLIOGRAPHY

Acock, A. C., and Demo, D. (1994). *Family Diversity and Well-Being.* Newbury Park, CA: Sage Publications.

Allen, K. R., and Walker, A. J. (1993). "A Feminist Analysis of Interviews with Elderly Mothers and Their Daughters." In *Qualitative Methods in Family Research,* ed. J. F. Gilgun, K. Daly, and G. Handel. Newbury Park, CA: Sage Publications.

Bales, R. F. (1950). *Interaction Process Analysis: A Method for the Study of Small Groups.* Cambridge, MA: Addison-Wesley.

Brown, S. R., and Melamed, L. E. (1990). *Experimental Design and Analysis.* Newbury Park, CA: Sage Publications.

Carmines, E. G., and McIver, J. P. (1979). *Reliability and Validity Assessment.* Newbury Park, CA: Sage Publications.

Copeland, A. P., and White, K. M. (1991). *Studying Families.* Newbury Park, CA: Sage Publications.

Draper, T. W., and Marcos, A. C. (1990). *Family Variables: Conceptualization, Measurement, and Use.* Newbury Park, CA: Sage Publications.

Elder, G. H., Jr. (1981). "History and the Family: The Discovery of Complexity." *Journal of Marriage and the Family* 43:489–514.

Gilgun, J. F.; Daly, K.; and Handel, G., eds. (1992). *Qualitative Methods in Family Research.* Newbury Park, CA: Sage Publications.

Kamo, Y. (1988). "Determinants of the Household Division of Labor: Resources, Power, and Ideology." *Journal of Family Issues* 9:177–200.

LaRossa, R.; Bennett, L. A.; and Gelles, R. (1985). "Ethical Dilemmas in Qualitative Family Research." *The Psychosocial Interior of the Family,* ed. G. Handel. New York: Aldine.

Larzelere, R. E., and Klein, D. M. (1987). "Methodology." In *Handbook of Marriage and the Family,* ed. M. B. Sussman and S. K. Steinmetz. New York: Plenum.

McCubbin, H. I., and Thompson, A. I., eds. (1991). *Family Assessment Inventories for Research and Practice.* Madison: University of Wisconsin Press.

Miller, B. C.; Rollins, B. C.; and Thomas, D. L. (1982). "On Methods of Studying Marriages and Families." *Journal of Marriage and the Family* 44:851–873.

Nielsen, J. M. (1990). "Introduction." In *Feminist Research Methods,* ed. J. M. Nielsen. Boulder, CO: Westview Press.

Rubin, D. B. (1987). *Multiple Imputation for Nonresponse in Surveys.* New York: Wiley.

Sweet, J.; Bumpass, L.; and Call, V. (1988). "The Design and Content of the National Survey of Families and Households." Working Paper NSFH-1. Madison: Center for Demography and Ecology, University of Wisconsin.

Teachman, J. D.; Polonko, K. A.; and Scanzoni, J. (1987). "Demography of the Family." In *Handbook of Marriage and the Family,* ed. M. B. Sussman and S. K. Steinmetz. New York: Plenum.

Vincent, J. P.; Friedman, L. S.; Nugent, J.; and Messerly, L. (1979). "Demand Characteristics in Observations of Marital Interaction." *Journal of Consulting and Clinical Psychology* 47:557–566.

Alan C. Acock

RESOURCE MANAGEMENT

Resource management is the process through which people use what they have to get what they want. Families have many demands, from the need to provide food, clothing, and shelter for the members, to the goal of planning for retirement. Through creating and then implementing plans, families use their resources to meet their demands.

Conceptual Framework

During the 1960s, theorists in family resource management began viewing the family as a social system, and resource management as one of the many functions of that system (Knoll 1963; Maloch and Deacon 1966). The systems approach to resource management was more fully developed in the 1970s and 1980s and continues to dominate the field. Following the conceptualization of Ruth E. Deacon and Francille M. Firebaugh (1988), the family's values, demands, and resources are defined as inputs to the system. The inputs are transformed through planning and implementing into outputs of spent resources and met demands. Information regarding both the outcomes and the processes is used to direct future managerial efforts. Decision making and communication are essential processes for using resources to meet demands.

Inputs. Values, defined as what is important or desirable, serve as underlying motivators for managing resources and as guidelines by which alternatives are evaluated. A family's values determine its goals. A family who deems economic security important may have a detailed plan for saving and investing. A family who values independence and autonomy may require that children take responsibility at earlier ages than families who do not hold such values.

Families respond to two types of demands: goal demands and event demands (Deacon and Firebaugh 1988). Goals are objectives that stem from the family's values. They may be explicit, as in financial goals, or they may be implicit, as are many goals revolving around meeting family needs. A family often does not say, for example, "One of our goals is to consume nutritious food." Yet the goal of adequate nutrition guides both food purchase and preparation activities.

Goals may be long- or short-term. Long-term goals often require the accomplishment of several intermediate short-term goals. The long-term goal of a good job may be preceded by short-term goals of education or training coupled with practical experience.

Reasoning that there are some things to which a family must respond that are not goals, Deacon and Firebaugh (1975, 1988) added the idea of events as demands. Events are unexpected occurrences that require action. They may be small, everyday happenings, such as breaking one's eyeglasses, or life-threatening occurrences, such as natural disasters. They may also be positive incidents such as unexpectedly encountering an old friend.

A common characteristic of events is that they require a response, however small, that uses resources earmarked for other purposes. Obviously, responding to a natural disaster would require resources. Having one's eyeglasses repaired or spending time with an old friend would require last-minute rearrangement of one's schedule.

Resource management can be viewed as a process through which the inevitable event demands are handled satisfactorily while the family continues to make progress toward its goals. Having savings or insurance for emergencies and planning for interruptions are ways of preparing to deal with events without irrevocably disrupting goal attainment. Such arrangements, of course, require some level of human and material resources, resources that low-income families may not have. Homeless families (c.f. Bulman 1993; Kozol 1988) frequently note that a single event occurred—job loss, an accident, an illness—for which they were unprepared, causing them to lose their home.

Human and material resources are assets that individuals and families have at their disposal that can be arranged in a variety of combinations to meet demands. Although humans may control material resources, such resources are not characteristics of individuals. Human resources, on the other hand, are attributes of people: knowledge, skills, and human energy. Material resources are depleted when they are used, whereas human resources increase with use. When skills and knowledge are used to change the oil in a car, for example, the individual has more skill and knowledge at the end of the job than at the beginning. Human energy is also enhanced through use; the individual who exercises regularly has more energy rather than less.

"Development of human capital" is used by economists (e.g., Schultz 1981) to describe efforts that increase and enhance human resources. Included are educational and training programs designed to develop skills and knowledge, and health-care and nutrition programs to enhance human energy.

Time is often considered a "resource," frequently the resource that is the scarcest in U.S. families. In a relative sense, time is a constant for everyone, with each individual having exactly twenty-four hours each day. Time is "spent" like money; time spent in one activity is not available for other activities, just as a dollar spent for one item is not available to be spent for another.

Time in and of itself, however, is not truly a resource. Rather, time is required if other resources are to be used (Linder 1970). It is the other resources—energy, skills, knowledge, goods, money—that are used to meet demands. Time, along with money, provides a way of measuring the use of other resources. How long will it take a family member to change the oil and filter in the automobile (to use his or her human resources, along with tools, an oil filter, and a supply of fresh oil)? What is the value of the individual's time compared to the time of a garage mechanic? Such assessments are crucial to managing resources successfully because they provide the benchmarks needed to compare different alternatives available for meeting demands.

The connection between values and goals is explicit; goals are value-based demands. The connections between values and events and between values and resources are just as important. What one family terms a crisis may hardly faze another family. Resources that one family hoards may be spent without a thought by another family. The differences are related to differences in the families' values.

Transformation. Resources are used to meet demands through the processes of planning and implementing the plans (Deacon and Firebaugh 1988). Planning is a series of decisions about the order in which future actions will be carried out and the criteria to be used to judge the outcomes of those actions.

Deacon and Firebaugh (1975, 1988) suggest that standards a family tries to attain are not imposed from outside the family. Rather, the development of appropriate standards involves a series of conscious decisions by those involved. Standard setting is a process of examining demands, on the one hand, and the resources available, on the other, and deciding appropriate criteria for goods and services within resource constraints. Given a goal of a place to live, for instance, the family first must decide the amount of resources that can be devoted to this goal. Initial resource assessment usually involves money, as the family decides how many dollars per month can be devoted to rent or a mortgage payment. The family then decides which of the many aspects of a decent place to live are the most important and, of those, which can be achieved given the funds available. Other resources may be considered as well. Does the family have the human resources needed to purchase an older dwelling and make alterations and additions themselves?

Gradually, a set of criteria emerges as the family balances its goals with its resources: "a two-bedroom apartment within walking distance of a grocery store and the rapid transit system"; "an older house, in an established neighborhood, that could be remodeled or expanded to create the sort of space desired"; "a three-bedroom house in a suburban school district."

Standard setting is often much more straightforward. The standards for a particular project are often determined by the time available—the best that can be done in two weeks. "Of the coats available this year within my price range, which colors and styles look good on me?" Standards, the products of standard setting, specify the quality and/or quantity of products or services desired. They are, essentially, a resolution of demands and resources.

Action sequencing is the process of deciding the activities that need to be done and the order in which the activities will be carried out. Having decided standards for housing, what actions will the family take to find a dwelling that meets their standards?

Rosemary J. Avery and Kathryn Stafford (1991) carry action sequencing further in their "Scheduling Congruity Theory." They suggest that plans to achieve multiple family goals simultaneously depend on the congruity of schedules. Scheduling involves establishing an order or sequence of activities and fitting the activities into a time framework so that one knows the time period when the activity needs to be accomplished. Congruity suggests that the schedules for the achievement of various goals must fit together relatively harmoniously for the goals to be accomplished.

The outcome of planning is a plan containing both standards and sequences of action. Plans have four important attributes: clarity, flexibility, realism, and complexity (Deacon and Firebaugh 1988). Clarity refers to the degree of specificity with which both standards and sequences are delineated. Standards and sequences that are relatively vague can be used when the planner will also be carrying out the plan; they pose difficulties when someone other than the planner will be implementing the plan.

Flexibility refers to the range of acceptable standards and sequences permitted by the plan. Families in which all adults are employed outside the home or are engaged in income-generating activities within the home often find that flexibility in standards and sequences is the key to accomplishing required household tasks (Winter et al. 1993).

Reality reflects the degree to which the standards and sequences included in the plan can actually be accomplished. An individual may be quite realistic about the time needed to accomplish planned sequences but set impossibly high standards for himself or herself. An example is a college student who wishes to maintain an A average, participate in many extracurricular activities, work part time, and have an active social life.

Complexity reflects the combination of people, resources, and scope of the task. A simple plan is one in which a single individual has adequate resources to accomplish a specific goal. A complex plan is one that involves many people, relatively few resources, and a task that is broad in scope. In general, the more complex the plan, the more the need for clarity, flexibility, and realism.

Implementing is simply carrying out the plan. Planning can be entirely mental; implementing requires some physical activity, however minimal. Writing and mailing a check to complete a planned purchase, for example, is implementing a plan with a minimum amount of activity.

Controlling a plan during its implementation assures that the standards and sequences specified in the plan will be accomplished. Controlling involves checking, either comparing actions carried out against those planned or comparing the quality or quantity of a good or service to the standards outlined in the plan. When standards or sequences are not as planned, adjusting has to occur. Either the standards and/or sequences in the plan are adjusted, or the situation is altered to meet the standards or sequences specified. The family who has searched for months for the house that meets their standards, but has been unable to locate such a house, may be forced to rethink their standards to attain their goal of finding a dwelling.

Outcomes. The managerial process can be evaluated by the degree to which demands are met and resources are used as planned (Sharpe and Winter 1991). Effective managers usually succeed in attaining their goals and in responding to events successfully, as measured by the level of satisfaction with the outcomes.

The use of material resources results in a decrease in the resources available for the next managerial problem; the use of human resources results in an increase in available resources. The assessment of resource use is a process of deciding whether the use of human and material resources has been effective in relation to the preceding managerial process and what the implications are for future managerial behavior.

Information about the degree to which demands have been met and the use of resources is an essential part of feedback, information used by the family to guide future actions. If demands are not met to the family's satisfaction, the family may renew its efforts to meet the demands. Alternatively, it may change the demands. Likewise, information about resource use guides future resource development efforts.

Processes in resource management. Decision making permeates all phases of management, from deciding priorities among competing goals to assessing whether demands have been met satisfactorily. Decision making is what occurs between the recognition that a decision is needed and the selection of an alternative. The process may be conscious and deliberate, involving the generation and careful weighing of alternatives; it may also be intuitive, characterized by a subconscious "feeling" about the selection of an alternative. The outcome is the same: A goal is selected, a standard set, a comparison made.

Successful resource management in families requires communication among family members. Like decision making, communication permeates all parts of the managerial process, from establishing demands and appraising resources, through making plans and implementing them, to assessing outcomes. Information is exchanged among family members through verbal and nonverbal means. Problems in communication among family members can result in resource management that is not satisfactory to all members.

Issues in the Study of Resource Management

The foregoing discussion makes the process seem much more straightforward than it actually is. In reality, the process is very complex. Families have competing goals and a scarcity of resources; deciding how to allocate resources among the goals may be very difficult. For example, resource development may be required before some goals can be achieved.

Planning is largely a mental process, often accomplished when an individual is engaged in a physical activity that does not require constant attention, such as commuting to work or engaging in routine household tasks (Winter 1986). Plans made at such times need to be shaped and revised through communication with other family members.

All family managerial activities are not accomplished through family-wide efforts. Rather, role specialization is important, with some family members assuming responsibility for some areas of family life and other members assuming responsibility for different areas. A family may use one managerial style for the management of one resource and a different style for the management of another. In a similar fashion, one style may be used on one life domain and a second style in another domain. Such issues continue to challenge those who study resource management.

(*See also:* Communication; Decision Making and Problem Solving; Entitlements; Family Systems Theory; Homeless Families; Housing; Work and Family)

BIBLIOGRAPHY

Avery, R. J., and Stafford, K. (1991). "Toward a Scheduling Congruity Theory of Family Resource Management." *Lifestyles: Family and Economic Issues* 12:325–344.

Bulman, P. M. (1993). *Caught in the Mix: An Oral Portrait of Homelessness.* Westport, CT: Auburn House.

Deacon, R. E., and Firebaugh, F. M. (1975). *Home Management Context and Concepts.* Boston: Houghton Mifflin.

Deacon, R. E., and Firebaugh, F. M. (1988). *Family Resource Management*, 2nd edition. Boston: Allyn & Bacon.

Gross, I. H.; Crandall, E. W.; and Knoll, M. M. (1980). *Management for Modern Families*, 4th edition. Englewood Cliffs, NJ: Prentice Hall.

Heck, R. K. Z.; Winter, M.; and Stafford, K. (1992). "Managing Work and Family in Home-Based Employment." *Journal of Family and Economic Issues* 13:187–212.

Key, R. J., and Firebaugh, F. M. (1989). "Family Resource Management: Preparing for the 21st Century." *Journal of Home Economics* 81:13–17.

Knoll, M. M. (1963). "Toward a Conceptual Framework in Home Management." *Journal of Home Economics* 55: 335–339.

Kozol, J. (1988). *Rachel and Her Children: Homeless Families in America.* New York: Crown.

Linder, S. B. (1970). *The Harried Leisure Class.* New York: Columbia University Press.

Maloch, F., and Deacon, R. E. (1966). "Proposed Framework for Home Management." *Journal of Home Economics* 58:31–35.

Paolucci, B.; Hall, O. A.; and Axinn, N. (1977). *Family Decision Making: An Ecosystem Approach.* New York: Wiley.

Schultz, T. W. (1981). *Investing in People: The Economics of Population Quality.* Berkeley: University of California Press.

Sharpe, D. L. B., and Winter, M. (1991). "Toward Working Hypotheses of Effective Management: Conditions, Thought Processes, and Behaviors." *Lifestyles: Family and Economic Issues* 12:303–323.

Winter, M. (1986). "Management as a Mental Process: Implications for Theory and Research." Discussion paper presented at North Central Research Group No. 116 Family Resource Management conference, Madison, WI.

Winter, M.; Puspitawati, H.; Heck, R. K. Z.; and Stafford, K. (1993). "Time Management Strategies Used by Households with Home-Based Work." *Journal of Family and Economic Issues* 14:69–92.

Mary Winter

RETIREMENT

Family and work experiences are closely interwoven throughout every adult's life course. During early and middle adulthood, family obligations and events can affect the decision to enter or leave the labor force, the devotion of time and effort to one's occupation, or the acceptance of job-related moves. Similarly, occupational characteristics and demands impinge on a wide variety of family experiences, ranging from the timing of marriage and parenthood to the spending of time with family or the delegation of family responsibilities such as child or elder care to others (Piotrowski, Rapoport, and Rapoport 1987; Spitze 1988). These connections between labor force and family experiences continue into the later years; family obligations affect retirement schedules and retirement benefits as well as postretirement activities. Retirement can, on the other hand, alter relationships with immediate and extended family members. Because knowledge about family–retirement linkages remains limited (Szinovacz, Ekerdt, and Vinick 1992), further scientific exploration of these linkages and their consideration in retirement preparation programs and policy decisions constitutes an important agenda.

Definitions and Trends

The concepts "family" and "retirement" are inherently understood by most, yet scientific definitions of these concepts vary considerably. Definitions of family refer to household composition, common ancestry, childbearing, and child rearing. They can be restricted to nuclear family members (parents and their offspring) or expanded to include other kin. For purposes of this discussion, family is broadly defined to be persons related by blood or marriage, inside and outside the household. Problems in defining retirement arise in regard to the exact timing of the retirement transition and to the distinction between occupational retirement and withdrawal from the labor force (Ekerdt and DeViney 1990). Since many individuals retire gradually, it is difficult to determine when retirement occurred. Was it when a worker changed from full-time to part-time employment or when gainful employment was quit altogether? In addition, some individuals "retire" from one occupation only to take up a second career in later life. Others may receive retirement benefits (Social Security, pensions) even though they are still in the labor force. Moreover, many retirees maintain or even increase their involvement in unpaid work (volunteer work, family-oriented work) after leaving their jobs. Therefore, retirement is defined here as permanent and substantial reduction in gainful employment during late adulthood, regardless of receipt of retirement benefits.

Demographic trends, especially the diversification of family and retirement experiences, are at least partially responsible for the definitional problems. Divorce, single parenthood, early as well as delayed parenthood, voluntary childlessness, multigenerational families, and women's labor force participation have led to considerable variability in family experiences and relationships. This variability will become even more pronounced as the post–World War II birth cohorts reach retirement age. For example, as more and more women participate in the labor force, more couples face the retirement of both spouses, and as the number of divorced women entering old age rises, fewer women will be eligible to rely on spouse benefits as a means of support (O'Grady-LeShane and Williamson 1992).

Retirement as it exists—that is, withdrawal of healthy individuals from the labor force at a certain age (typically between ages fifty-five and seventy) with the expectation of receiving Social Security and/or pension benefits—is a relatively new institution. In the United States, the Social Security Program was enacted in 1935. Although some European nations (e.g., Germany) adopted some Social Security provisions at the end of the nineteenth century, many developing countries still lack public benefits for their elderly (Williamson and Pampel 1993).

Prior to the enactment of the Social Security Program, the minority who were fortunate enough to reach age sixty-five relied primarily on family members and to some extent community support once they were no longer able to work; many others delayed retirement or never retired at all. Old age economic security was often achieved through "family funds" to which unmarried children were required to contribute, forcing some children to delay marriage and many others to forgo further education and the prospect of upward mobility. Those elderly who were unable to work and could not rely on family funds occasionally found support from their communities and charities but were still at considerable risk of poverty (Evans and Williamson 1991; Gratton and Rotondo 1992).

In contrast, most individuals, since the enactment of the program, expect to retire and view retirement as an accepted and deserved life stage. They also count on government-funded economic benefits during their later years, benefits that relieve both families and communities of their previous responsibilities concerning economic care of the elderly. This economic security, accompanied by rising rates of unemployment and early retirement incentives, has resulted in a trend toward earlier retirement, especially among males and single woman (DeViney and O'Rand 1988). This trend has important ramifications for retirees' family activities as well as for the relative timing of retirement and other family events such as grandparenthood.

Family Influences on Retirement

Linkages between family and retirement experiences are complex and must be understood from a life course perspective. For example, early family experiences such as the timing of marriage or parenthood can influence labor force behaviors in early and middle adulthood; these labor force behaviors in turn partially determine retirement benefits and timing. Research has unveiled but a few of these complex and often long-term connections between family and retirement experiences.

In most developed countries, including the United States, retirement benefits (Social Security, private pensions) are based on the labor force history of individuals and their spouses. To be eligible for Social Security or pension benefits, individuals (or their spouses) typically must have been in the labor force (or with a specific company) for a predefined number of years, with the amount of benefits contingent on both number of years in service and lifetime income levels (O'Grady-LeShane and Williamson 1992). Retirement benefits are maximized if at least one spouse maintains continuous and well-paid employment from early adulthood into late adulthood. The jobs and careers of many women are often subject to interruptions, especially during childbearing years. Other women retire early to accommodate their husbands' retirement schedules or to take care of close relatives. Such interruptions can result in substantially reduced retirement benefits (Wolff 1988).

Family responsibilities influence not only retirement income but also the timing of retirement. Women with long-term employment disruptions during their childbearing years and women who have been divorced tend to delay retirement, presumably to achieve higher retirement benefits (Morgan 1992). Economic responsibilities for family members (dependent children or parents) can lead to postponement of retirement, but they may also result in earlier retirement when the demands of employment and family care become incompatible (Scharlach and Boyd 1989). In addition, mounting evidence shows that most spouses opt for joint retirement unless adverse circumstances, including illness of one spouse or substantial sacrifices in one spouse's retirement income, preclude simultaneous retirement (O'Rand, Henretta, and Krecker 1992). To what extent the quality of marital and/or kin relationships affects retirement timing decisions, if at all, remains virtually unknown. It is, for example, conceivable that happily married couples with similar leisure interests are more likely to pursue a joint retirement transition. Similarly, emotional closeness to frail parents may constitute an important factor in the decision to retire early for caregiving reasons.

Despite an abundance of studies, the role family relationships play in adjustment to retirement and well-being in the postretirement years remains unclear. Marriage and marital adjustment contribute to general well-being throughout the lifespan and may become especially important during the retirement years (Atchley 1992). While the quantity of contacts with relatives (including adult children) appears less important for well-being than the quantity of contacts with peers (Lee and Ishii-Kuntz 1987), high-quality enhanced interactions with extended family members could provide support during the retirement transition process and replace former contacts with work colleagues. Proximity to relatives also can motivate relocation after retirement (Cuba and Longino 1991). Since women frequently function as "kinkeepers" (organizing and maintaining kin contacts for the entire family), widowed or divorced men often lack extensive interactions with relatives (Szinovacz 1992), which may render them more vulnerable to the loss of work colleagues after retirement.

Family responsibilities can exert a negative influence on retirees. In addition to prompting mostly women to retire "too early," caregiving needs of close relatives (especially parents) can "spoil" postretirement plans such as travel or desired leisure activities (Vinick and Ekerdt 1991). Furthermore, experiencing negative family events such as illness or death at the time of retirement has been shown to hamper especially women's retirement adjustment (Szinovacz and Washo 1992).

Retirement Influences on Families

Research dealing with retirement effects on families has focused on the marital relationship, and existing studies offer little support for the popular notion that retirement destroys many marriages or at least creates multiple marital problems (Harbert, Vinick, and Ekerdt 1992). Most couples fail to experience significant changes in their marital relationship after retirement, and problems that do occur are typically short-term and not considered serious (Atchley 1992; Ekerdt and Vinick 1991; Vinick and Ekerdt 1991). Nevertheless, retirement can bring about some changes in marital relationships, including changes in the division of household labor, time spent together, and the quality of the relationship.

Many wives expect their husbands to contribute more to household work after the husband's retirement (Ade-Ridder and Brubaker 1988). Whether these expectations are fulfilled is debatable. Certainly, most retired couples divide household labor on a quite segregated basis—husbands perform "male" chores such as repairs and garden work, and wives carry out "female" chores such as cooking, cleaning, and washing the laundry. Wives also continue to carry the major responsibility for and spend considerably more time with household work than do retired husbands. Some studies, on the other hand, indicate that retired husbands, as compared to employed husbands, spend more time with male tasks and in some cases take over chores previously performed by wives (Dorfman 1992). However, enhanced participation of retired husbands in female household tasks may be more common among husbands of housewives than among husbands of retired wives (Szinovacz and Harpster 1994). While many wives appreciate the husbands' efforts, others perceive husbands' help as an interference in their domain and complain that their retired husbands are "underfoot." Such perceptions prevail when the husbands' housework is motivated by lack of other meaningful activities and/or when husbands criticize their wives' performance (Dorfman 1992; Vinick and Ekerdt 1991).

Other problems mentioned by recently retired couples center around the time spouses spend together and their leisure activities. Such problems frequently arise because spouses approach retirement with unrealistic expectations about joint endeavors. Marital interaction styles that have developed over decades are unlikely to undergo drastic changes after retirement (Atchley 1992).

Lowered martial satisfaction also has been noted among couples when the spouses do not retire at the same time. This lowered satisfaction is especially pronounced if the husband retires prior to his wife. Retired husbands whose wives remain in the labor force sometimes "feel lonely at home by themselves" and reject their still-employed wives' demands for more household help. When these husbands exert pressure on their wives to retire as well, wives' marital satisfaction may also decline (Lee and Shehan 1989).

The relationships of some couples improve after retirement. Reduction in work-related stress, elimination of conflict over wives' employment, and implementation of retirement plans such as travel or relocation can revive marriages, at least during the period immediately following retirement (Atchley 1992).

Much speculation but little evidence exists concerning the effects of retirement on relationships to extended kin. A few studies suggest that contacts with relatives are expanded after retirement and that retirees may be expected to take over caregiving obligations from other relatives (Dorfman and Mertens 1990; Vinick and Ekerdt 1991).

Families, Retirement, and Social Change

During the twentieth century, both institutions—retirement and family—have undergone considerable change. Retirement has become a widely accepted and practiced life phase. Public and private retirement benefits guarantee some economic security to retirees, thus creating employment opportunities for younger generations and relieving them at the same time from personal economic support responsibilities for older family members. At the same time, family lifestyles have become more diversified and the life cycle has become less predictable. Perhaps most prominent among the changes in family life are the trends toward gender equality, nonpermanent marriages, and decreased fertility.

Retirement policies pay little tribute to these changes in family lifestyles. Social Security regulations in the United States and many other industrialized countries reflect a male-as-provider ideology that is at odds with today's family values and behaviors. Since work disruptions for child or elder care lead to reduced benefits, many women have to rely on their spouses' benefits to achieve adequate retirement incomes, an option that negates the value of women's own achievements in the labor force and runs counter to values that increasingly endorse gender equality. Furthermore, reliance on spousal benefits is limited for the growing number of retiring divorcees. Only a few countries (e.g., Canada, Germany, France) have started to address this inequity by crediting some child-care years as "work" years in Social Security calculations. Similar adjustments for the care of other relatives, including frail parents, have yet to be implemented (O'Grady-LeShane and Williamson 1992).

In addition, Social Security rules concerning partner benefits presume permanence of marriages and disregard even long-term nonmarital relationships such as heterosexual cohabitants or homosexual couples. In most countries (a notable exception is Canada), persons who are not married or who were divorced do not qualify for partner benefits (O'Grady-LeShane and Williamson 1992).

Lower fertility combined with higher longevity bring about increases in the old-age dependency ratio—the number of people sixty-five or older compared to the entire "working" population. Some people argue that the taxes needed to finance programs and benefits for the increasing elderly population deplete the economic resources of relatively smaller, younger cohorts, often at the expense of programs for children (Longman 1987). Instead, they advocate reductions in government programs for the elderly, including Social Security.

These arguments contain some problematic, if not outright false, assumptions about program financing, the economic burden experienced by younger generations, and the economic well-being of today's elderly. They also disregard the economic benefits that families receive from Social Security and other programs for the elderly. Reductions in these programs, especially in Social Security entitlements, would lead to dramatic increase in economic inequities and poverty among the older population (Kingson, Hirshorn, and Cornman 1986; Quadagno 1991). Adult children would be forced to assume the economic responsibilities for their dying parents, save for their own retirement, and provide for their children's upbringing and education all at the same time.

Most families do not desire a return to intergenerational economic dependencies, and many adults would experience considerable economic hardship if faced with dual economic obligations for dependent children and dependent elderly relatives. Economic dependence of elderly parents on their adult children could also undermine social and emotional bonds between generations (Kingson, Hirshorn, and Cornman 1986; Quadagno 1991).

To assist families struggling to adapt to new societal and economic realties, retirement policies and programs should further gender equality, incorporate alternative family lifestyles, and protect intergenerational ties.

(*See also:* Elders; Entitlements; Family Development Theory; Grandparenthood; Intergenerational Relations; Later-Life Families; Widowhood)

BIBLIOGRAPHY

Ade-Ridder, L., and Brubaker, T. H. (1988). "Expected and Reported Division of Responsibility of Household Tasks

Among Older Wives in Two Residential Settings." *Journal of Consumer Studies and Home Economics* 12:59–70.

Atchley, R. C. (1992). "Retirement and Marital Satisfaction." In *Families and Retirement*, ed. M. Szinovacz, D. J. Ekerdt, and B. H. Vinick. Newbury Park, CA: Sage Publications.

Cuba, L., and Longino, C. F., Jr. (1991). "Regional Retirement Migration: The Case of Cape Cod." *Journal of Gerontology: Social Sciences* 46:S33–S42.

DeViney, S., and O'Rand, A. M. (1988). "Gender-Cohort Succession and Retirement Among Older Men and Women, 1951–1984." *Sociological Quarterly* 29:525–540.

Dorfman, L. T. (1992). "Couples in Retirement: Division of Household Work." In *Families and Retirement*, ed. M. Szinovacz, D. J. Ekerdt, and B. H. Vinick. Newbury Park, CA: Sage Publications.

Dorfman, L. T., and Mertens, C. E. (1990). "Kinship Relations in Retired Rural Men and Women." *Family Relations* 39:166–172.

Ekerdt, D. J., and DeViney, S. (1990). "On Defining Persons as Retired." *Journal of Aging Studies* 4:211–229.

Ekerdt, D. J., and Vinick, B. H. (1991). "Marital Complaints in Husband-Working and Husband-Retired Couples." *Research on Aging* 13:364–382.

Evans, L., and Williamson, J. B. (1991). "Old-Age Dependency in Historical Perspective." In *Growing Old in America*, 4th edition, ed. B. B. Hess and E. Markson. New Brunswick, NJ: Transaction.

Gratton, B., and Rotondo, F. M. (1992). "The 'Family Fund': Strategies for Security in Old Age in the Industrial Era." In *Families and Retirement*, ed. M. Szinovacz, D. J. Ekerdt, and B. H. Vinick. Newbury Park, CA: Sage Publications.

Harbert, E.; Vinick, B. H.; and Ekerdt, D. J. (1992). "Marriage and Retirement: Advice to Couples in Popular Literature." In *Qualitative Methods in Family Research*, ed. J. F. Gilgun, K. Daly, and G. Handel. Newbury Park, CA: Sage Publications.

Kingson, E. R.; Hirshorn, B. A.; and Cornman, J. M. (1986). *Ties That Bind: The Interdependence of Generations.* Washington, DC: Seven Locks Press.

Lee, G. R., and Ishii-Kuntz, M. (1987). "Social Interaction, Loneliness, and Emotional Well-Being Among the Elderly." *Research on Aging* 9:459–482.

Lee, G. R., and Shehan, C. L. (1989). "Retirement and Marital Satisfaction." *Journal of Gerontology: Social Sciences* 44:S226–S230.

Longman, P. (1987). *Born to Pay: The New Politics of Aging in America.* Boston: Houghton Mifflin.

Morgan, L. A. (1992). "Marital Status and Retirement Plans: Do Widowhood and Divorce Make a Difference?" In *Families and Retirement*, ed. M. Szinovacz, D. J. Ekerdt, and B. H. Vinick. Newbury Park, CA: Sage Publications.

O'Grady-LeShane, R., and Williamson, J. B. (1992). "Family Provisions in Old-Age Pensions: Twenty Industrial Nations." In *Families and Retirement*, ed. M. Szinovacz D. J. Ekerdt, and B. H. Vinick. Newbury Park, CA: Sage Publications.

O'Rand, A. M.; Henretta, J. C.; and Krecker, M. L. (1992). "Family Pathways to Retirement." In *Families and Retirement*, ed. M. Szinovacz, D. J. Ekerdt, and B. H. Vinick. Newbury Park, CA: Sage Publications.

Piotrowski, C.; Rapoport, R. N.; and Rapoport, R. (1987). "Families and Work." In *Handbook of Marriage and the Family*, ed. M. B. Sussman and S. K. Steinmetz. New York: Plenum.

Quadagno, J. (1991). "Generational Equity and the Politics of the Welfare State." In *Growing Old in America*, 4th edition, ed. B. Hess and E. W. Markson. New Brunswick, NJ: Transaction.

Scharlach, A. E., and Boyd, S. L. (1989). "Caregiving and Employment: Results of an Employee Survey." *Gerontologist* 29:382–387.

Spitze, G. (1988). "Women's Employment and Family Relations: A Review." *Journal of Marriage and the Family* 50:595–618.

Szinovacz, M. (1992). "Social Activities and Retirement Adaptation: Gender and Family Variations." In *Families and Retirement*, ed. M. Szinovacz, D. J. Ekerdt, and B. H. Vinick. Newbury Park, CA: Sage Publications.

Szinovacz, M.; Ekerdt, D. J.; and Vinick, B. H. (1992). "Families and Retirement: Conceptual and Methodological Issues." In *Families and Retirement*, ed. M. Szinovacz, D. J. Ekerdt, and B. H. Vinick. Newbury Park, CA: Sage Publications.

Szinovacz, M., and Harpster, P. (1994). "Couples' Employment/Retirement Status and the Division of Household Tasks." *Journal of Gerontology: Social Sciences* 49:S125–S136.

Szinovacz, M., and Washo, C. (1992). "Gender Differences in Exposure to Life Events and Adaptation to Retirement." *Journal of Gerontology: Social Sciences* 47:S191–S196.

Vinick, B. H., and Ekerdt, D. J. (1991). "The Transition to Retirement: Responses of Husbands and Wives." In *Growing Old in America*, 4th edition, ed. B. B. Hess and E. Markson. New Brunswick, NJ: Transaction.

Williamson, J. B., and Pampel, F. C. (1993). *Old-Age Security in Comparative Perspective.* New York: Oxford University Press.

Wolff, N. (1988). "Women and the Equity of the Social Security Program." *Journal of Aging Studies* 2:357–377.

Maximiliane Szinovacz

RUNAWAY CHILDREN

Children who run away from home present a serious problem in the United States, yet remain underrecognized, underserved, and poorly understood. An estimated one to two million young people in the United

States run away each year (Tomb 1991). Severe family disturbance, physical and sexual abuse, substance abuse, and legal involvement are characteristics typical of these youths prior to running. Homelessness, increased substance abuse, depression, increased risk for HIV infection and other sexually transmitted diseases, prostitution, rape, and assault are conditions frequently associated with actual running away. However, runaways are not isolated entities; families, child protective and social services, juvenile justice systems, public and mental health systems, educational agencies, and youth shelters all interact with and are affected by the problem of runaways. Multiple factors contribute to the continued underrecognition of the problem. Carrying out accurate studies of runaways is complicated by their mobility and reluctance to speak. There is a lack of public awareness of the causes and risks of runaway behavior and of normal adolescent development. It is also difficult for many people to appreciate the extent of victimization that occurs both before and after these youths run away.

Historical Aspects

An accurate history of runaway behavior begins with clinical and social studies in the twentieth century. One may assume that there have been runaways as long as there have been parents, failed communication, and unhappy children. However, the concepts of childhood, parenting, and family affiliation on which an understanding of runaway behavior is based are recent Western developments. Children (particularly adolescents, who comprise the majority of runaways) running "away" from parents invokes the notion that they belong with parents—legally, emotionally, developmentally, and culturally. The idea that children belong to parents as property in a legal way comes from English common law and underlies the status of running away as a legal offense. The affiliative bonds between children and parents understood in terms of life- and development-sustaining attachment have been present only since John Bowlby's influential work in the 1940s. Prolonged adolescence and late entry into vocational life are relatively recent Western developments. The concept of childhood itself as a stage in life intrinsically different from other stages (i.e., that children are not just like grown-ups socially, emotionally, and cognitively) is an invention or discovery of the nineteenth century. Ideas about the importance of the individual child and family have been shaped by Judeo-Christian heritage, as embodied in the commandment to "honor thy father and mother."

Historical work has revealed that, analogous to modern trends of "throwaway" youths and infants left in dumpsters, children were abandoned in large numbers from Greek antiquity through the Middle Ages by parents from all strata of society. John Boswell (1988) argues convincingly in *The Kindness of Strangers* that the practice of abandoning children was common and reveals different attitudes toward parent–child relations from those previously assumed.

The United States has experienced a dramatic increase in runaways since the 1960s. Before that time, many people viewed running away as a normal variant in healthy adolescent development. Mark Twain's Huckleberry Finn represents a romanticized, literary portrait of a heroic runaway—a mythology underlying the mistaken view of running away as normative. Other people have viewed runaways essentially as rule-breakers who should suffer the consequences.

Demographics

The reality of runaway children stands in stark contrast to both of these views. While running away is defined as being inexplicably absent for twenty-four hours or overnight, only 3 percent of families experience a runaway. Studies indicate that many runaways are never reported. Most runaways are brief, lasting less than six days, but 400,000 runaway children per year remain on the streets for months. Ninety percent of them stay within fifty miles of home (Garbarino, Wilson, and Garbarino 1986).

Runaways come from all socioeconomic and geographic categories, but most are from lower-class families. One quarter of runaways come from single-parent families, and another quarter come from group or foster homes (Garbarino, Wilson, and Garbarino 1986).

The majority of runaway children are between twelve and seventeen years of age. In contrast to adolescents experiencing normal development, runaways differ in important ways. They experience significantly higher probabilities of being sexually active, using drugs, having legal problems, and having been sexually abused (Janus et al. 1987).

Causes

The primary cause of runaway behavior is family or home difficulty. Given the high percentage of runaways who report having been physically or sexually abused at home, one motivation to run is self-preservation by escaping the abuse. Similarly, many runaways run to flee from punitive, neglectful, or rejecting parents. In less overtly disturbed families, verbal abuse, poor communication, and low family cohesiveness can leave the teen feeling unheard and powerless, enhancing vulnerability to running away.

Running away also occurs in the context of family crises such as bankruptcy, divorce, infidelity, or teen pregnancy. Such crises may leave families with limited emotional resources depleted, and a runaway in this context may represent a call for help for the entire family. Running away can be a manipulative attempt by a teenager to get parents to "back down," or it can represent severe rebellion to authority.

Some runaway children have been described as "running to." These restless youths seek the excitement of the street because they have high levels of boredom and a high need for independence. While their home lives may be nonsupportive, these runaways are younger, more impulsive, and tend toward repeated runaways. Predilection toward stimulus-seeking appears to drive the runaway behavior for these individuals (Janus et al. 1987).

However, a significant number of children away from home have neither run away nor "run to." Many have been abandoned or thrown out of their homes, and some have left by "mutual consent." Dubbed "throwaways," these children make up a significant proportion of all runaways. Compared to other runaways, they are older, more traumatized, and have higher levels of individual and family substance abuse. Their families are generally disorganized and dysfunctional. In a few cases, powerful conscious or unconscious motivations have led families to scapegoat a child. It may then become important psychologically, legally, or financially to force the child out of the family.

The psychology of the runaway varies quite significantly from that of normally developing youths. Runaways are demoralized, insecure, and frightened, in contrast to their apparently independent act of leaving home. Running away has many different possible psychological meanings. It can be a means of transforming passive experiences of feeling unheard, powerless, or victimized into an active effort to escape, communicate dramatically, or get revenge. For adolescents with limited coping skills, running away may be an attempt at a seemingly simple solution to a complex personal or family problem.

Runaways often are seeking love, attention, and nurturance. Runaways seek to assuage their own low self-esteem, poor sense of self, and depression. Running away almost invariably expresses despair and anger. A very increased rate of suicidal ideation and behavior is found in runaways. Runaways also often have long histories of failure at school, with peer relations, and in their families. Adopted children who run away may do so because they harbor unresolved fantasies of reuniting with their birth parents.

Parents of runaways can experience high levels of fear and anxiety. The most consistent finding in parents of runaways is a poor relationship with the child. Parents of runaways are often found to be abusive and involved with legal and substance abuse problems. Communicating in negative ways and not being supportive are also characteristic of parents of runaways. In general, the preexisting attachment between a parent and a runaway child is predictive of reunification.

Effects

Benign, self-limited running away does occur. A brief trip to the house of a friend, neighbor, or relative can be concluded by timely return without ill effect to child or family. More prolonged periods of running away, however, are less benign.

Runaways are at very high risk of being traumatized and victimized. Once on the street, survival becomes the sole focus of existence. These youths are in need of immediate food, shelter, and clothing. Their need makes them extremely vulnerable, since they lack trustworthy and safe adults to help them. Their existence among a street culture populated by the criminal, homeless, mentally ill, and disenfranchised further escalates their vulnerability.

Survival skills for the street include theft, hustling, drug dealing, prostitution, and pornography. Most street youths will be victimized by assault or rape. A significant number of runaway girls become pregnant. Health risks are considerable. Hepatitis, tuberculosis, overexposure to the elements, and infections are common. Unprotected sexual intercourse is rampant and homeless youths are at greatly increased risk for HIV infection and other sexually transmitted diseases. Access to health care is limited due to minor status, lack of insurance, and concerns of confidentiality. Worsening depression, suicidality, and substance abuse occur. Being a homeless teenager also confers increased risk toward being a psychiatrically diagnosed homeless adult.

Conclusion

Running away occurs in large numbers, represents a significant departure from normal teenage development, and brings tremendous risk to the runaway. This act often represents a desperate or impulsive solution to a crisis that often involves severe family pathology, such as physical and sexual abuse, family substance abuse, and distorted child–parent relationships. Therefore, running away occurs in the context of the interaction between family dynamics, individual characteristics of the teen, and cultural or social factors that influence teens. Social, legal, clinical, and educational agencies all have an important responsibility to fulfill their roles in servicing this at-risk teenage population.

(*See also:* ADOLESCENCE; CHILD ABUSE AND NEGLECT: SOCIOLOGICAL ASPECTS; CHILDHOOD; COMMUNICATION; DYSFUNCTIONAL FAMILY; FAMILY VIOLENCE; GANGS; INCEST; JUVENILE DELINQUENCY; MISSING CHILDREN; SELF-ESTEEM; SUBSTANCE ABUSE; SUICIDE)

BIBLIOGRAPHY

Blos, P. (1962). *On Adolescence.* New York: Free Press.

Boswell, J. (1988). *The Kindness of Strangers.* New York: Pantheon.

Bowlby, J. (1944). "Forty-Four Juvenile Thieves: Their Character and Home Life." *International Journal of Psychoanalysis* 25:19–52, 107–127.

Bowlby, J. (1966). *Attachment.* New York: Basic Books.

Garbarino, J.; Wilson, S.; and Garbarino, I. (1986). "The Adolescent Runaway." In *Troubled Youth, Troubled Families*, ed. J. Garbarino and J. Sebes. New York: Aldine.

Janus, M. D.; McCormack, A.; Burgess, A.; and Hartman, C. (1987). *Adolescent Runaways.* Lexington, MA: Lexington Books.

Kruks, K. (1991). "Gay and Lesbian Homeless/Street Youth: Special Issues and Concerns." *Journal of Adolescent Health* 12:515–518.

Orten, J., and Soll, S. (1979). "Runaway Children and Their Families." *Journal of Social Issues* 35:101–126.

Rotheram-Borns, M. J. (1993). "Suicidal Behavior and Risk Factors Among Runaway Youths." *American Journal of Psychiatry* 150:103–107.

Sharlin, S. A. (1992). "Runaway Girls in Distress: Motivation, Background, and Personality." *Adolescence* 27:387–405.

Solnit, A.; Nordhaus, B.; and Lord, R. (1992). *When Home Is No Haven.* New Haven, CT: Yale University Press.

Tomb, D. (1991). "The Runaway Adolescent." *Child and Adolescent Psychiatry*, ed. M. Lewis. Baltimore: Williams & Wilkins.

C. PRESTON WILES

S

SCHOOL

American families have experienced some dramatic changes since the early nineteenth century. In 1810, the mean number of children per family was approximately 6.8, compared to 2.3 in 1970 (Risley, Clark, and Cataldo 1976). In 1990, the U.S. Bureau of the Census did not report the mean number of children per family, but instead reported the mean number of persons per household, which was 3.18. This change in reporting reflected extraordinary pressures in society and the resulting effects on the family. Concurrent with changes in families, the overall birthrate declined and the American population as a whole aged. Continuation of this trend will result in an increasingly disproportionate number of adults to young people.

With fewer young people entering the work force, greater emphasis needs to be focused on preparing each youth to be a healthy, educated, and productive adult (Thornburg, Hoffman, and Remeika 1991). However, society may be remiss in fulfilling these responsibilities, according to researchers from the Children's Defense Fund (1988, 1989, 1990). The researchers report distress among American families, and their statistics show that one of every five children lives in poverty, 2.2 million reports of child abuse and neglect occurred in 1987, and about 1.5 million children run away from home annually. Compounding these statistics is the national school dropout rate, which is more than 25 percent; in some urban areas, the range is 50 percent to 75 percent (Doyle 1989).

If dropping out of school could be predicted, then the factors responsible would be obvious, and strategies could be devised to assist students toward graduation. The social factors most often associated with dropping out of school include poverty; lack of family support for study and staying in school; and teen rebellion, deviant peers, and gang influences (Thornburg, Hoffman, and Remeika 1991). Therefore, individual, social, family, and possibly school factors must be considered when estimating the probability of dropping out of school for a single student. Families have two possible ways to influence their children's academic success: directly, by helping their child with schoolwork, and indirectly, by influencing the content and process of education within the school setting.

Poverty and Dropout

Although poverty is associated with school dropout, it is not a sufficient explanation alone to account for the dropout rate among Latino youths. Students from Latino families drop out more than twice as often as students from other ethnic groups regardless of socioeconomic status (Steinberg, Blinde, and Chan 1984).

Olga Reyes and Leonard A. Jason (1993) endeavored to identify the factors associated with academic success for urban Latino high school students rather than the typical focus on dropouts. Their rationale for this approach was to identify the factors that might account for the success of a few students and the lack of success by many others. The authors selected two groups: a low-risk-for-dropout group and a high-risk-for-dropout group, based on grades and attendance. Each student was interviewed by a bilingual and bicultural interviewer. The students were asked a series of questions about their family life, satisfaction with school, if they were recruited by gangs, and if they carried weapons to school. Each student also was given the Piers-Harris Self-Concept Scale to complete (see Piers and Harris 1964 for scale details). Reyes and Jason found the two groups to have similar self-concept scores and similar scores on all family measures. However, unlike the more successful "low risk" students, the "high risk" students were very dissatisfied with school, were often recruited by gangs, and were more than four times as likely to carry a weapon to school. The most common criticism, mentioned by both groups, was the perceived disrespect that teachers and administrators displayed toward students who were struggling with their studies. Unlike many other studies, this study did not find individual factors or family background factors as important contributors to school success, but it did find school personnel's treatment of students to be an important factor.

Lack of Family Support for Education

There is evidence in the literature that parental involvement with children's schooling and time spent on studies are essential components for academic success (Comer and Haynes 1991; Hess and Holloway 1984; Lightfoot 1978). Family support for academic achievement may take various forms, such as praising good grades, privileges granted contingently for high marks, or parental time spent helping their children with studies.

Carla M. Leone and Maryse H. Richards (1989) were interested in the relationship between academic achievement and the amount of time spent doing schoolwork and homework. The students who participated in their study were randomly selected, attending grades five through nine, and were equally divided by sex. The authors found that the amount of time devoted to studies actually declined for underachieving and average students. This trend was especially evident among girls as they progressed to the upper grades. However, higher-achieving students reported that their study time did not change. In ninth grade, boys reported more time spent on their studies than girls, and for both sexes, greater levels of academic success coincided with greater amounts of time spent on homework with parents. Thus, time spent on studies with structure and parental involvement was more focused and therefore more effective. Academic success does not guarantee that a student will graduate, but it does remove a powerful reason for avoiding an unpleasant daily situation at school.

Thomas E. Smith (1990), contrary to Leone and Richards (1989), asserted that time spent on studies was essentially unrelated to achievement. He stated that an antiacademic "adolescent subculture" promoted through the media, music, and peers was far more influential on the use of study time than family encouragement or parental involvement. Two years later, Smith (1992) followed up on his original study and came to the same conclusions. Unfortunately, neither of Smith's studies included any measures of school variables nor asked the students or parents for assessment of school performance. Without these measures of school performance one must assume, as did Smith, that the antiacademic adolescent subculture simply exists as adolescent rebellion.

Teenage Turmoil and Stereotypes

The third major factor often cited for dropping out of school is adolescent rebellion resulting from the physical, emotional, and social turmoil believed typical of adolescence (Smith 1990). Christy M. Buchanan and her colleagues (1990) were interested in some of the prevailing notions about adolescents and have noted that, as a developmental period, adolescence is often laden with many cultural myths conveyed by the media (e.g., "Teen Rage" 1987). These stereotypes portray adolescents in terms of rebelliousness, emotionality, and unbridled biological and hormonal upheavals. The authors noted that few controlled studies have sampled adult views of adolescents, and those that have usually approached healthcare professionals. Many of these adults rarely see adolescents who are not in crisis; therefore, the published reports usually supported the stereotypes. Similarly, early opinion polls of teachers characterized adolescence as a time of great emotional disturbance in which complete personality changes were to be expected.

Buchanan and her colleagues (1990) reported that adults viewed adolescents in two dimensions: adolescents as teenagers (members of a developmental group) and individually (reflecting a history with a specific adolescent). The authors suggested that these views may influence how an adult might initiate an interaction with a previously unknown adolescent. They found that experienced teachers were more likely to adhere to stereotypes of adolescent instability than newer teachers. Regardless of teaching experience, however, all teachers held positive views about adolescents and that adults can have a good influence on them. Likewise, parents acknowledged hearing of the stereotype of adolescence as a turbulent time, but they optimistically reported about good relationships they had with their children. In conclusion, the authors suggested that the teen years are no more vexing than any other child-rearing period; however, they asserted that parents' and teachers' behavior toward adolescents may set the occasion for good or bad interactions. While these conclusions seem to contradict Smith's assertions of an antiacademic adolescent subculture, they do indicate that a stereotype of adolescence does exist.

Social Relevance of Schools

Schools, like families, are facing changing sets of social and economic pressures. Schools emphasize the acquisition of behavior rather than its maintenance, unlike other social institutions. The presumed justification for continuous behavior acquisition (learning) is based on the anticipated need for a broad array of useful behavior in future work settings (Skinner 1953). Unfortunately, for many poor inner-city families and students, the probability of becoming involved in violent crime may be higher than the chances of getting a good job. Therefore, a major issue for many schools is convincing poor youths of the relevance of an education for their future.

The relevance of education is hard to sell when many studies have shown that U.S. students spend substantially less time on schoolwork than students in other industrialized nations. Schools in the United States usually have fewer hours per day and fewer days per year than many other countries. U.S. students spend an average of twenty-one hours on academic subjects in a school week, only fifteen of which could be considered "on task," and homework typically occupies less than six hours a week.

Employment projections predict an increase in the number of jobs available, but more than half of all new jobs are expected to require more than a high school education (Thornburg, Hoffman, and Remeika 1991). Those new jobs requiring only a high school diploma will be more service-oriented, lower-paying, and probably without benefits. Therefore, fewer good opportunities for underskilled adults in a highly technological job market will exist ("Special Report" 1989). These employment projections underscore the importance of good educational preparation.

In summary, schools, like families, are confronting social, economic, and community issues they may not be able to transcend, and, according to Thomas M. Sherman (1992), expecting schools to change society is unreasonable. A possible strategy might involve acknowledging the types of pressures that schools are subjected to and some alternative roles that parents, teachers, and community members might adopt.

Institutional Inertia

Henry S. Pennypacker (1994) suggests that schools, as social institutions, may be struggling to resolve mutually exclusive goals. Schools were originally chartered to improve society through educating youths, and as society grew, so did schools. As schools became larger, less time and fewer resources were available for individual students, teachers, and families. Rationing the resources to match the needs of increasing numbers of students, teachers, and staff promoted a more bureaucratic approach; as a result, process and procedure took priority over people, products, and outcomes. Don Bushell and Donald Baer (1994) assert that teachers are now more accountable for keeping daily attendance, lunchroom counts, number of students needing special education classes, and classroom size than educational outcome data for students because the former numbers have vigilant, dollar-conscious audiences. School funding is based on daily attendance, of vital importance to administrators and school boards; the lunch count is important to cafeteria managers; and special education administrators understand that students with special needs qualify for higher funding allocations. Finally, classroom size is the collective bargaining chip used by labor union negotiators for wage and benefit contracts with school boards (Bushell and Baer 1994). Pennypacker (1994) noted that when schools do assess educational outcomes, the assessment results are often used as justification for increased funding. Ironically, this process demonstrates that failure to meet goals is often more profitable than success.

Bushell and Baer (1994) suggest a possible strategy to alter some of the contingencies maintaining the status quo by focusing on the role of parents and families as an audience. A first step might be to consider the audience as an array of participant observers with different issues of priority and different levels of influence within the community. Families are an excellent example of an audience composed of participant observers, because issues that affect one member ultimately affect all members. The most direct and accessible contact with schools for most families is with teachers; therefore, the first institutional issue to address might be the role of teachers.

Schoolteachers are not often recognized as professionals, even though they depend on adequate tools and sensitive measures to provide effective services just like other professionals. Professionals select tools based on goals and the needs of their clients. Although professionals may appear to work autonomously, they must be sensitive to subtle cues from the situation, results from tests and measures, and other forms of feedback to adjust their interventions for maximum effectiveness. Similarly, teachers must study their student's performance to adjust their educational strategies for maximum effectiveness. Unfortunately, most teachers do not have the professional autonomy to choose instructional tools that are maximally effective (Carnine 1992). Effective instructional methods with integral feedback systems have been available for many years—for example, personalized systems of instruction (PSI) (Keller 1968); peer tutoring on a classroom basis (Greenwood et al. 1988); direct instruction (Becker 1988); precision teaching (Lindsley 1992); and other applications of behavior change technology for students of all ages and abilities (Selinske, Greer, and Lodhi 1991; Sulzer-Azaroff 1986)—but most of these methods have been ignored by schools (Axelrod, Moyer, and Berry 1990). Ironically, computer fluency, often a prerequisite for many entry-level occupations, is well suited to many of these teaching methods, but less than half of all students use computers at school (U.S. Bureau of the Census 1989).

Family Involvement in Schools

Traditional reforms designed for schools usually involve an outsider who does something to the teachers, the students, or the classrooms; the resources needed for implementation are either commandeered or supplied exclusively for the short duration of the project (Fantuzzo and Atkins 1992). There have been some noteworthy exceptions.

Patricia P. Olmstead (1991) described the national Follow Through program as a social action program that became an education program in 1967. The national Follow Through program was inconsistent in quality, but two programs within it proved to be effective: the Behavior Analysis model at the University of Kansas and the Direct Instruction model at the University of Oregon (Pennypacker 1994). Although the Follow Through program was an inconsistent educational intervention, aspects of it may serve as a useful example of parental involvement and audience building. Follow Through has been in existence since 1967, primarily because of parental involvement; therefore, this is not a short-term intervention. An integral part of the program has been advocacy training for parents to learn to become vocal supporters of their children, the program, and the schools. These advocacy skills have been effective at the national level, the local program administration level, and the individual family/student level. Effective parent advocacy skills on behalf of the program at the national level occurred with marches to the U.S. Capitol in the 1970s and again in the 1980s when the program was threatened by budget cuts (Hodges et al. 1980).

Effective parent advocacy skills at the local program level occurred when an appointed program director was not demanding high performance from the program. The parents met with the director, expressed their concerns, and set a six-month trial period, at the end of which the director agreed to resign if the parents were still dissatisfied. Thus, the parents were influential on the program administration level in shaping educational goals deemed appropriate for their children (Olmstead 1991).

In a school district, a disproportionate number of Follow Through students were being assigned to special education classes (Olmstead 1991). The parents, who were concerned about why so many of their children were being placed in special education, asked to speak with the school administration. The director of the special education program met with the parents, explained the placement process, and worked with the parents to help their children make progress. As a result the Follow Through children remained in special education classes half as long as their older siblings who had not been in the program (Szegda 1986). Thus, parental advocacy and involvement on behalf of their children's schooling may have contributed to the shorter duration in special education placements (Olmstead 1991).

Conclusion

Community organizations that are similar to Follow Through programs address the unique needs of communities by involving families, teachers, students, and community members in setting goals, taking action, and using local people to address local concerns. Implicit in community organization efforts is the development of an active audience, who will assess the acceptability, relevance, and effectiveness of an educational program. A focused, organized, and active audience of parents can be instrumental in the shaping of schools to improve the lives of students, families, the community.

(*See also:* Adolescence; Ethnicity; Gangs; Home Schooling; Juvenile Delinquency; Peer Pressure; Poverty; Runaway Children; Truancy)

BIBLIOGRAPHY

Axelrod, S.; Moyer, L.; and Berry, B. (1990). "Why Teachers Do Not Use Behavior Modification Procedures." *Journal of Educational and Psychological Consultation* 1:309–320.

Becker, W. C., ed. (1988). "Direct Instruction." Special Issue. *Education and Treatment of Children* 11:297–402.

Buchanan, C. M.; Eccles, J. S.; Flanagan, C.; Midgley, C.; Feldlaufer, H.; and Harold, R. D. (1990). "Parents' and Teachers' Beliefs About Adolescents: Effects of Sex and Experience." *Journal of Youth and Adolescence* 19:363–394.

Bronfenbrenner, U. (1974). *Is Early Intervention Effective? A Report on Longitudinal Evaluations of Preschool Programs.* Washington, DC: U.S. Department of Health, Education, and Welfare.

Bronfenbrenner, U. (1979). *The Ecology of Human Development: Experiments by Nature and Design.* Cambridge, MA: Harvard University Press.

Bushell, D., Jr., and Baer, D. M. (1994). "Measurably Superior Instruction Means Close Continual Contact with Relevant Outcome Data. Revolutionary!" In *Behavior Analysis in Education*, ed. R. Gardner III, D. M. Sainato, J. O. Cooper, T. E. Heron, W. L. Heward, J. W. Eshelman, and T. A. Grossi. Belmont, CA: Brooks/Cole.

Carnine, D. (1992). "Expanding the Notion of Teachers' Rights: Access to Tools that Work." *Journal of Applied Behavior Analysis* 25:13–19.

Children's Defense Fund. (1988). *A Children's Defense Fund Budget.* Washington, DC: Author.

Children's Defense Fund. (1989). *A Vision for America's Future.* Washington, DC: Author.

Children's Defense Fund. (1990). *S.O.S. America: A Children's Defense Budget.* Washington, DC: Author.

Comer, J. P., and Haynes, N. M. (1991). "Parent Involvement in Schools: An Ecological Approach." *The Elementary School Journal* 91:271–277.

Doyle, D. (1989). "Endangered Species: Children of Promise." *Business Week*, Special Bonus Issue.

Fantuzzo, J., and Atkins, M. (1992). "Applied Behavior Analysis for Educators: Teacher-Centered and Classroom-Based." *Journal of Applied Behavior Analysis* 25:37–42.

Greenwood, C. R.; Carta, J. J.; Kamps, D.; and Hall, R. V. (1988). "The Use of Tutoring in Classroom Management and Educational Instruction." *School Psychology Review* 17:258–275.

Hess, R. D., and Holloway, S. D. (1984). "Family and School as Educational Institutions." In *Review of Child Development Research*, ed. R. D. Parke, R. M. Emde, H. P. McAdoo, and G. P. Sackett. Chicago: University of Chicago Press.

Hodges, W.; Branden, A.; Feldman, R.; Follins, J.; Love, J.; Sheehan, R.; Lumbley, J.; Osborn, J.; Rentfrow, R. K.; Houston, J.; and Lee, C. (1980). *Follow Through: Forces for Change in Primary Schools.* Ypsilanti, MI: Scope Foundation.

Keller, F. S. (1968). "Good-Bye, Teacher . . ." *Journal of Applied Behavior Analysis* 1:79–89.

Leone, C. M., and Richards, M. H. (1989). "Classwork and Homework in Early Adolescence: The Ecology of Achievement." *Journal of Youth and Adolescence* 18:531–548.

Lightfoot, S. L. (1978). *Worlds Apart: Relationships Between Families and Schools.* New York: Basic Books.

Lindsley, O. R. (1992). "Why Aren't Effective Teaching Tools Widely Adopted?" *Journal of Applied Behavior Analysis* 25:21–26.

Olmstead, P. P. (1991). "Parent Involvement in Elementary Education: Findings and Suggestions from the Follow Through Program." *The Elementary School Journal* 91:221–231.

Pennypacker, H. S. (1994). "A Selectionist View of the Future of Behavior Analysis in Education." In *Behavior Analysis in Education*, ed. R. Gardner III, D. M. Sainato, J. O. Cooper, T. E. Heron, W. L. Heward, J. W. Eshelman, and T. A. Grossi. Belmont, CA.: Brooks/Cole.

Piers, E., and Harris, D. (1964). "Age and Other Correlates of Self-Concept in Children." *Journal of Educational Psychology* 55:91–95.

Reyes, O., and Jason, L. A. (1993). "Pilot Study Examining Factors Associated with Academic Success for Hispanic High School Students." *Journal of Youth and Adolescence* 22:57–71.

Risley, T. R.; Clark, H.; and Cataldo, M. F. (1976). "Behavioral Technology for the Normal Middle-Class Family." In *Behavior Modification and Families*, ed. E. J. Mash, A. Hamerlynck, and L. C. Handy. New York: Brunner/Mazel.

SCAN Executive Committee. (1980). *SCAN: Sponsors, Sites, States, Communication Advisory Network.* Ypsilanti, MI: Scope Foundation.

Selinske, R.; Greer, R. D.; and Lodhi, S. (1991). "A Functional Analysis of the Comprehensive Application of Behavior Analysis to Schooling." *Journal of Applied Behavior Analysis* 24:107–117.

Sherman, T. M. (1992). "School Reform." *Journal of Applied Behavior Analysis* 25:27–30.

Skinner, B. F. (1953). *Science and Human Behavior.* New York: Free Press.

Smith, T. E. (1990). "Time and Academic Achievement." *Journal of Youth and Adolescence* 19:539–558.

Smith, T. E. (1992). "Time Use and Change in Academic Achievement: A Longitudinal Follow-Up." *Journal of Youth and Adolescence* 21:725–747.

"Special Report: The Status of Black Children." (1989). *Black Child Advocate* 15:3–7.

Steinberg, L.; Blinde, P. L.; and Chan, K. S. (1984). "Dropping Out Among Language Minority Youth." *Review of Educational Research* 54:113–132.

Sulzer-Azaroff, B. (1986). "Behavior Analysis and Education: Growing Achievements and Crying Needs." *Division 25 Recorder* 21:55–65.

Szegda, M. J. (1986). "School Success and the Parent Education Program: A Long-Term Follow-Up." Ph.D. diss. University of North Carolina, Chapel Hill.

"Teen Rage." (1987). *Detroit Free Press*, Mar. 19, p. 1B.

Thornburg, K. R.; Hoffman, S.; and Remeika, C. (1991). "Youth at Risk; Society at Risk." *The Elementary School Journal* 91:200–208.

U.S. Bureau of the Census. (1989). *School and Home Computer Use.* Washington, DC: U.S. Department of Commerce.

U.S. Bureau of the Census. (1990). *How We Live.* Washington, DC: U.S. Department of Commerce.

JOHN G. YOUNGBAUER

SELF-DISCLOSURE

Ask a self-disclosure researcher what is meant by "self-disclosure" and the answer may be "Who wants to know?" Sidney M. Jourard's original concept of "making the self known to other persons" has evolved into at least four distinct theoretical concepts and even more practical applications. At the most basic level of analysis, self-disclosure can describe exchange of information, expression of private experience, development of relationships, and accomplishment of conversational goals.

The new student of self-disclosure should recognize these conceptual differences to avoid the research problem of applying the wrong tool to the problem at hand. It would not do well, for example, to encourage distraught therapy clients to self-disclose their deepest secrets (which has therapeutic value by way of emotional catharsis) on first or second dates with potential romantic partners (where self-disclosure can regulate intimacy and relationship development).

History of Self-Disclosure

Jourard (1971) believed that the process of revealing oneself to specific others was both a mark of and a contributor to a healthy personality. A sixty-item questionnaire asked each respondent to report the extent to which they discussed various everyday topics (e.g., attitudes, money, body) with specific recipients (parents, friends, spouse). Later questionnaires also measured disclosers' "willingness to disclose," the context of specific situations, relationships to target persons, and specific self-disclosure behaviors, as well as recipients' perceptions of the disclosers. While measurement and validity issues were highly troubling (Chelune 1979), these self-report methods are common in research as measures of one's sense of openness about personal information.

W. Barnett Pearce and Stewart M. Sharp (1973) introduced the concept of self-disclosure as a communicative behavior. Self-disclosure is not just a general experience; it is accomplished by disclosing personal information with specific utterances in a specific conversational context. These utterances can be analyzed for content for the sake of gaining insight into a person's expressive behavior in a variety of conversational settings. While coding systems based on content are reliable, the actual experience of the conversational partners cannot be measured by coders, and research continues to examine the differences in perception people have about self-disclosing statements in conversation.

Definitional problems have haunted self-disclosure research from the start; consequently, it has spawned many related concepts and found many applications. Self-disclosure as a process of giving information to others has been researched as openness in organizational communication. The process of revealing one's personal experience or secrets has been studied through more specific variables such as emotional expressiveness and painful self-disclosure. Nondisclosure has been studied in the form of taboo topics, secrets, privacy, and closedness. Counseling therapists use therapist self-disclosure as a tool for eliciting client self-disclosure for catharsis, exploration, and healing. Marital counselors study self-disclosure as a tool for resolving conflict and building intimacy. Communication researchers study self-disclosure as a regulator of initial interaction and the development of intimacy in close relationships. Gender researchers search for differences in male and female talk through self-disclosure, and psychologists study its relationship to such variables as loneliness, private self-consciousness, and self-monitoring. Organizational researchers study its role in superior–subordinate relationships and information management.

At a broader level, self-disclosure has found a niche in a dialectical theory of openness–closedness in relationships (a theory of interpersonal regulation of intimacy through the regulation of personal privacy), in structural analyses of conversational interaction, and in theories of information exchange.

Self-Disclosure as Personal Experience

Jourard described the experience of a person who makes himself or herself open and available to others as having a healthy personality. Such an expressive person can cope with emotional stress without personal shame. Two major research areas continue under this approach: self-disclosure as catharsis and self-disclosure as a personality variable.

Self-disclosure as catharsis. The proposition that people tend to disclose when they are distressed is "a fever model of disclosure" (Stiles 1987). The analogy to a body's fever in the presence of illness illustrates that self-disclosure is both a symptom of a person's state of stress and a healing response to the stress itself. Jourard believed that people who hide their troubling thoughts from potentially supportive listeners do not find emotional health. Case studies are numerous of clients whose medical problems declined or disappeared as closely guarded secrets were slowly revealed in a progression from secrecy to openness through unfolding self-disclosure.

The fever model of disclosure studies "expressiveness," the ability to express one's feelings and experiences to others. The classic form of a fever model self-disclosure is an "I statement," an utterance in the first person (directly or reflexively) that indicates one's current mood or emotion. "I feel angry" and "It's been really lonely at night for me" would each be regarded as emotionally expressive, whereas "I think you're being unfair," although phrased in the first person, would not be considered to express personal emotion.

The relationship between disclosure and distress may be related to private self-consciousness; the person who is more aware of inner condition and experience is more likely to self-disclose to another than will a person who is more focused on external situations and events (Davis and Franzoi 1987). The distressed person, being more self-conscious, discloses the source of the stress to others. However, while distressed people report that they confide more in others, there is no systematic evidence that their actual behavior includes more self-disclosure. Their self-reports thus may not match their behavior, a common problem in self-disclosure research.

Several explanations exist for the benefit of self-disclosing distress to others:

1. Self-understanding: By putting one's distress into words, one begins the rational process of exploring the source of the stress and its experience, resulting in better understanding of the problem and its resolution.
2. Social support: Disclosure of personal stress or difficulty may allow supportive friends, family, or relationship partners to offer help or support.
3. Direct catharsis: Grief or anger may lose potency as they are converted from feeling into words. Applying symbolic names to the experiences may relieve the feelings themselves of hidden force. Shame may be especially susceptible to this cathartic effect. The very process of speaking aloud of personal shame to another person demonstrates that the topic is not as shameful as it seemed, and the response received may provide a less-than-distressing answer to the unasked question "What's the worst thing that could happen if you disclosed your secret?"

While disclosure of distress may seem to have universally healthy benefits, there are limits to its usefulness (Coates and Winston 1987).

Self-disclosure as a personality variable. Even though Jourard's conception of self-disclosure was an act shared between two people, early research examined the variables that formed a picture of a self-disclosing person, a personality type of the tendency to self-disclose. Hundreds of studies examined variables that might predict high and low disclosure tendencies. The limited success of the findings are illustrated by a meta-analysis of the gender studies, which showed that although females are generally reported to disclose more than males, the difference between the genders is actually quite small, in some cases unnoticeable (Dindia and Allen 1992). Other variables studied include type of relationship between discloser and recipient, valence of the disclosure (positive or negative), intimacy or privacy of the information being disclosed, and topics being disclosed.

In addition to the disclosing personality, research has also identified the opener, a person who is more likely to receive disclosure from others, particularly from those who otherwise are low disclosers (Miller, Berg, and Archer 1983).

Other personality variables are linked to the disclosing personality. Effective self-disclosure is theorized to relate to private self-consciousness (Davis and Franzoi 1987) and self-monitoring. Self-disclosure is therefore connected to the concept of face; one controls the impression formed by others through monitoring the information one shares with others (Holtgraves 1990). As a result, high but not excessive levels of self-disclosure are connected to liking from others, and low levels of self-disclosure are correlated with loneliness. Jourard therefore referred to "optimum" levels of self-disclosure in relationships.

Self-Disclosure for Relationship Development

Self-disclosing talk influences relationships. It is a key factor in developing intimacy in initial interaction, in forming relationships, and in regulating social distance within established relationships.

Intimacy and social penetration. The earliest comprehensive theory that evolved around self-disclosure was social penetration theory, which described a link between intimacy of the relationship and self-disclosure (Altman and Taylor 1973). Self-disclosure is measured both across various topics (breadth) and at various levels of privacy or intimacy (depth); as a relationship becomes more intimate, the dyadic partners will disclose at greater breadth and depth. This model suggests a simple linear correlation between intimacy and self-disclosure; as one increases, the other follows; likewise, as intimacy decreases, self-disclosure becomes less frequent and less personal.

Self-disclosure in early stages of relationship development is different than in later stages (Derlega et al. 1993). First meetings and dates may involve a flurry of self-disclosure, but after a couple has shared much knowledge, relationship behaviors become more predictable and the need for self-disclosure diminishes. However, new experiences can still be shared through self-disclosure. Some partners may continue in high rates of disclosure to preserve novelty and change in a relationship, while others may think of the relationship as more predictable and in less need of ongoing self-disclosure.

Finally, contrary to the linear relationship model, self-disclosure may actually increase as intimacy in a relationship decreases; this is most likely in the event of relational disengagement. A person preparing to exit a relationship may choose to disclose large amounts of information about accumulated frustration, anger, or disappointment to make clear the reasons for the breakup and to convince the other partner of the certainty of the decision.

Self-disclosure as uncertainty reduction. Uncertainty reduction theory describes self-disclosure as a tool for developing relationships during initial interaction. Uncertainty is an unsettling condition that hinders liking; information about others reduces one's uncertainty about them and thus increases liking for them. Self-disclosure offers the needed information to others that will reduce uncertainty and therefore lead to liking (Berger and Calabrese 1975). Positive outcome value theory adapted this theory with the variable of personal expectations; reduced uncertainty only leads to liking in the presence of a "positive outcome value," the anticipation that further interaction with this person will have desirable rewards (Sunnafrank 1986).

Openness, etiquette, and privacy. Early applications of Jourard's work generated popular self-help books that advocated frequent and personal self-disclosure in all of one's relationships. But reckless self-disclosure violates the sense of personal privacy of the recipient, resulting in discomfort and dislike toward the excessive discloser. Etiquette books are clear in demanding respect for others' privacy. In fact, natural conversations contain question–answer sequences that allow partners to regulate their own privacy boundaries by regulating the level of detail and intimacy of a particular topic. Other studies suggest that complete openness and honesty in marital relationships may not be as important to marital satisfaction as has been otherwise commonly advocated.

Self-Disclosure as Conversational Behavior

Self-disclosing talk is not easy to study in natural conversation. What may look like an "I statement" may not contain revelation of personal experience, while other statements that have no apparent disclosive value are quite revealing from the perspective of either participant. Nevertheless, self-disclosure does occur within conversations, and it appears in a variety of patterns.

Reciprocity and self-disclosure sequences. The "dyadic effect" is the tendency for two people to self-disclose at similar levels of intimacy and frequency in a conversation. This pattern of reciprocity, however, only describes the fact that people find similar and acceptable levels of self-disclosure to share in a conversation (Dindia 1994).

Conversational sequences shape the occurrence of self-disclosure in ways other than reciprocal self-disclosure. Self-disclosures may be elicited by direct or indirect questions by the recipient, out of some conversational context, or for a discloser's own purposes. Disclosures themselves are followed by statements that encourage or inhibit further disclosure; follow-up questions and sympathetic comments are more likely to be followed by a second self-disclosure than are statements of opinion, value judgments, or changing the topic (Coupland et al. 1988). Self-disclosure in family talk appears to be more often proactive (self-selected) than reactive (elicited by the other person).

Modeling, a therapeutic tool. The reciprocity phenomenon brings with it a conversational strategy for eliciting self-disclosure from others. Some people feel obligated to return a self-disclosure upon receiving one. It is therefore possible to give a "seed" self-disclosure with the expectation that the other person will reciprocate. Although this can be a manipulative interpersonal strategy, it is also commonly used by higher-status relationship partners such as parents and therapists. Parents may "model" a self-disclosure by disclosing information in a way that says to the child or adolescent, "If you were to self-disclose about this topic, I would not be unkind or intolerant" (Spencer 1994). Similarly, many therapists begin therapy programs by modeling self-disclosures for clients so they will begin to feel comfortable sharing their own experiences with therapists (Hendrick 1987).

Conclusion

Self-disclosure means many things to many people. It can be a sign of intimacy experienced within a personal relationship, a way of exchanging information with others to regulate relationships, or a response to an inner need for social support during stressful times. Therefore, how one explains "self-disclosure" obviously depends on "who wants to know" and for what research or practical purpose the question is being raised.

(*See also:* COMMUNICATION; FRIENDSHIP; INTIMACY; LONELINESS; LOVE; PERSONAL RELATIONSHIPS; TRUST)

BIBLIOGRAPHY

Altman, I., and Taylor, D. A. (1973). *Social Penetration: The Development of Interpersonal Relationships.* New York: Holt, Rinehart and Winston.

Berger, C. R., and Calabrese, R. J. (1975). "Some Explorations in Initial Interaction and Beyond: Toward a Developmental Theory of Interpersonal Communication." *Human Communication Research* 1:99–112.

Chelune, G. J., ed. (1979). *Self-Disclosure.* San Francisco: Jossey-Bass.

Coates, D., and Winston, T. (1987). "The Dilemma of Distress Disclosure." In *Self-Disclosure: Theory, Research, and Therapy*, ed. V. J. Derlega and J. H. Berg. New York: Plenum.

Coupland, J.; Coupland, N.; Giles, H.; and Wiemann, J. (1988). "My Life Is in Your Hands: Processes of Self-Disclosure in Intergenerational Talk." In *Styles of Discourse*, ed. N. Coupland. London: Croom Helm.

Davis, M. H., and Franzoi, S. L. (1987). "Private Self-Consciousness and Self-Disclosure." In *Self-Disclosure: Theory, Research, and Therapy*, ed. V. J. Derlega and J. H. Berg. New York: Plenum.

Derlega, V. J.; Metts, S.; Petronio, S.; and Margulis, S. T. (1993). *Self-Disclosure.* Newbury Park, CA: Sage Publications.

Dindia, K. A. (1994). "The Intrapersonal-Interpersonal Dialectical Process of Self-Disclosure." In *Dynamics of Relationships*, ed. S. Duck. Newbury Park, CA: Sage Publications.

Dindia, K. A., and Allen, M. (1992). "Sex Differences in Self-Disclosure." *Psychological Bulletin* 112:106–124.

Hendrick, S. S. (1987). "Counseling and Self-Disclosure." In *Self-Disclosure: Theory, Research, and Therapy*, ed. V. J. Derlega and J. H. Berg. New York: Plenum.

Holtgraves, T. (1990). "The Language of Self-Disclosure." In *Handbook of Language and Social Psychology*, ed. H. Giles and W. P. Robinson. New York: Wiley.

Jourard, S. M. (1971). *The Transparent Self*, 2nd edition. New York: Van Nostrand-Reinhold.

Miller, L. C.; Berg, J. H.; and Archer, R. L. (1983). "Openers: Individuals Who Elicit Intimate Self-Disclosure." *Journal of Personality and Social Psychology* 44:1234–1244.

Pearce, W. B., and Sharp, S. M. (1973). "Self-Disclosing Communication." *Journal of Communication* 23:409–425.

Spencer, T. (1994). "Transforming Relationships Through Ordinary Talk." In *Dynamics of Relationships*, ed. S. Duck. Newbury Park, CA: Sage Publications.

Stiles, W. B. (1987). " 'I Have to Talk to Somebody': A Fever Model of Disclosure." In *Self-Disclosure: Theory, Research, and Therapy*, ed V. J. Derlega and J. H. Berg. New York: Plenum.

Sunnafrank, M. (1986). "Predicted Outcome Value During Initial Interactions: A Reformulation of Uncertainty Reduction Theory." *Human Communication Research* 13:3–33.

TED SPENCER

SELF-ESTEEM

Self-esteem refers to the evaluative and affective aspects of the self, to how "good" or "bad" people feel about themselves. It is a consequence of the self's capacity for reflexivity, that is, the ability to look at oneself and to evaluate one's actions or appearance. Self-evaluations typically give rise to positive or negative self-feelings, such as pride or shame. These various self-feelings make self-esteem important both experientially (i.e., they constitute some of the strongest emotions) and motivationally (i.e., people are motivated to seek positive self-feelings and to avoid negative ones).

The motivation to maintain and enhance a positive conception of oneself is a major dynamic of many contemporary self-theories (see Wells and Marwell 1976; Gecas 1982, 1991). Various self-theories suggest that people's self-conceptions are valued and protected, and a low self-evaluation (on criteria that matter) is an uncomfortable condition that people are motivated to avoid. This may occur through increased efforts at self-improvement or (more typically) through such self-serving activities as selective perception and memory, various strategies of impression management, and restructuring the environment and/or redefining the situation to make it reflect a more favorable view of self (Rosenberg 1979). These manipulations and distortions may raise self-esteem, but at the price of self-deception. There may also be an optimum level of self-esteem beyond which the consequences for individuals are negative, that is, overly low levels of self-esteem are associated with depression, but overly high self-esteem may be associated with arrogance and conceit.

Development of Self-Esteem

Several processes are important to the development of self-esteem: reflected appraisals, social comparisons, and self-attributions. The most critical one within sociology is reflected appraisals.

The reflected-appraisals process states that individuals come to see themselves and to evaluate themselves as they think others see and evaluate them. Based on Charles H. Cooley's (1902) influential concept of the "looking-glass self" and George H. Mead's (1934) theory of role-taking as a product of symbolic interaction, reflected appraisals emphasize the essentially social character of the self, that is, that self-conceptions reflect the appraisals of others, especially significant others, in an individual's environment. Empirically, however, there is not much congruence between self-appraisals and the actual appraisals by others (Gecas and Burke 1994). This suggests that the appraisals of others are not very accurately perceived, and if accurately perceived may not be believed. There are a number of reasons for this disparity. One is the difficulty of getting honest feedback from others, especially if it is negative (Felson 1980). The norms of social interaction typically emphasize tact and proper demeanor, which serve to protect self-esteem. Another reason is the feedback from "significant others" may be suspect. For example, parents and teachers may overemphasize the importance of praise in developing self-esteem in children. While praise and encouragement may be important for children's self-esteem, successful performance at activities that children value may be more important because they constitute more credible evidence of competence and worth. It should also be noted that the self-esteem motive has a distorting effect on all three processes of self-esteem development, including reflected appraisals. To the extent that the self-esteem motive is operative, individuals are more likely to selectively perceive and remember favorable feedback and ignore or discredit unfavorable feedback from others. For these and other reasons, it must be emphasized that the reflected-appraisals process operates primarily through *perceptions* of the appraisals of others.

Social comparison is the process by which individuals assess their own abilities and virtues by comparing them to those of others. According to Leon Festinger's (1954) theory of social comparisons, the main function of this process is reality-testing. This is most likely to occur in situations where knowledge about some aspect of oneself is ambiguous or uncertain. Local reference groups of persons are most likely to be used as standards for these comparisons, especially under conditions of competition, such as athletic contests and classroom performance. As with reflected appraisals, the reality-testing that occurs by means of social comparisons is biased by the self-esteem motive; individuals are likely to seek out favorable comparisons, avoid unfavorable comparisons, or to try to neutralize unavoidably unfavorable comparisons with various disclaimers and excuses.

Self-attributions refer to the tendency to make inferences about the self from direct observation of personal behavior and its consequences. Daryl Bem's (1972) "self-perception theory" proposes that individuals acquire knowledge about themselves in the same way they acquire knowledge about others, namely, by observing behavior and making inference about internal dispositions and states (e.g., motives, attitudes, self-esteem) from these observations. Self-perception theory can be subsumed under the more general attribution theory, which deals with how individuals make causal attributions about their own and others' behavior. Here as well, people are hardly neutral observers of what they see. Research suggests that causal attributions tend to be self-serving; for instance, individuals are more likely to make internal causal attributions for behavioral successes and external attributions for failures.

While all three of these processes contribute to the development and maintenance of self-esteem, at any particular time one may be more relevant to self-esteem than the others. Also, it is evident that the self does not passively respond to processes that affect it. Rather, it actively shapes and influences these processes in the interests of protecting self-esteem and other self-motivations (see Gecas 1991). In this sense, self-esteem is both a product of social forces and an agent in its own development.

Family Interaction and Self-Esteem

One of the most important social contexts for the development and expression of self-esteem is the family. For children, the family is the most crucial context, since its major function is the socialization and care of children. The family is the first primary group that children experience—the place where they develop their initial sense of self and self-esteem. It is the place where some of the most basic identities—male/female, boy/girl, son/daughter, brother/sister—take shape. Assessments of role performances based on these identities become early sources of self-esteem. Mead's (1934) discussion of the early stages of role-taking and role-playing, processes essential in the development of the self, occur within the context of family interactions. Parents typically serve as mentors and as significant others for children. The intimate, extensive, and relatively enduring relationships characteristic of the family as a primary group make it an important context for the self-esteem of children as well as adults.

All three processes of self-esteem formation are pervasive in family life. Self-attributions are frequently made on the basis of role performances and interactions with family members, feeling good or bad about the self depending on what inferences are drawn. Social comparisons are also a common feature of family life, particularly among siblings. Notions of fairness or injustice initially develop within sibling relations, as do comparisons of various competencies and virtues, with inevitable implications for self-esteem. Reflected appraisals are ubiquitous among family members. All family members have opinions about one another and are typically less reticent to express them to each other than is the case outside of family relations. Siblings, especially, may be only too eager to give critical feedback regarding each other's behavior, appearance, and other matters. Not all of these appraisals, of course, are equally significant for one's self-esteem. Both what is being appraised (with regard to its importance for one's self-concept) and who does the appraising are important qualifiers. For children, the reflected appraisals of their parents may matter much more than those of their siblings, on most things.

Reflected appraisal has been the main process examined in studies of self-esteem within families. The bulk of this research has focused on the effects of parental behavior on children's self-esteem. In general, these studies find that parental support and encouragement, responsiveness, and use of inductive control are positively related to children's self-esteem (Gecas and Seff 1990). Most of these parental variables could be considered indicators of positive reflected appraisals of the child. They are also the parental behaviors found to be associated with the development of other positive socialization outcomes in children (e.g., moral development, prosocial behavior, and school achievement).

Expectedly, these relationships are much stronger for the child's or adolescent's *perceptions* of parental behavior than for actual parental behavior or parental reports of their behavior (Gecas and Schwalbe 1986). Furthermore, this research indicates that there is not much overlap between parental reports of their behavior and children's perceptions of this behavior. Evidently, a good deal of selectivity and bias in recall and perception is reflected in these studies.

Birth order and sibling relations may also be consequential for children's self-esteem. On the basis of both reflected appraisals and social comparisons, firstborns would be expected to have higher self-esteem than children born later. The greater attention and encouragement from parents should contribute to firstborns' greater sense of worth and importance, and firstborns' typically greater power and competence compared with younger siblings should result in more favorable social comparisons. Research, however, provides only modest (and inconsistent) support for these expectations (Adams 1972). Oldest and only children do seem to have higher self-esteem than later-born children, but the differences are not very large. The effects of birth order may be suppressed or mitigated by the influence of several other features of the sibling system, such as sex composition of the sibling order, child spacing, family size, age and sex of target child, age and sex of next oldest sibling. Without taking into account the effect of these other variables, the influence of birth order on self-esteem may largely disappear (Gecas and Pasley 1983).

Other structural variations within families (e.g., single-parent families, stepparent families, extended families) may affect children's self-esteem if they have an impact on reflected appraisals, social comparisons, or self-attributions. There has not been much research on the effects of these family structural variations on children's self-esteem. What research there is does not report much variation. The quality of family relations does not seem to vary consistently enough across these structural variations for them to show significant and consistent differences in children's self-esteem.

Family relations are also important for parents' and spouses' self-esteem, although these have not received nearly the attention given to children's self-esteem. Husbands and wives are typically "significant others" for each other, and the reflected appraisals received within this partnership should matter a great deal for spouses' self-esteem, even more so now than in the past. As the institution of marriage/family continues to evolve from a "traditional" pattern, characterized by multiple functions and a segregated division of labor, to a "companionship" pattern, with fewer functions and an emphasis on love, emotional support, and nurturant socialization, the quality of the marital bond becomes increasingly relevant for the self-esteem of husbands and wives. But relying on this bond as a "haven in a heartless world" (Lasch 1975) is an increasingly fragile emotional anchor for the self in contemporary society, as the high divorce rate attests. Along with the loss of functions (e.g., economic, educational), there has also been a decline of traditional social supports for marriage and family. Consequently, a premium is placed on love and affection. They become the raison d'être for marriage. When they decline, as often happens under the stresses of contemporary life, divorce is a common solution. This too can have serious consequences for self-esteem.

Along with the marital bond, the parental bond is a major source of self-conception and self-esteem for most adults. It may even be a more enduring source of self-definition than marriage, since people do not divorce their children (although some may wish this option were available). The identities of "mother" and "father" are among the most important in the self-conceptions of parents. How parents perform the roles associated with these identities, how their children respond to them, and the quality of the parent–child relationship have major implications for parents' self-esteem.

Research on parenthood suggests that it is a rocky road for parents' self-esteem. The transition to parenthood is itself a major event, typically a source of joy and stress, with significant consequences for the marital bond and for family patterns (White and Booth 1985). Children provide numerous occasions for parental satisfaction as well as distress. They are a source of parental pleasure and pride, increasing parents' self-esteem, as well as a source of frustration, anger, and distress, decreasing parents' self-esteem. Research on parental satisfaction across the various stages of parenthood suggests that the positive experiences are more frequent when the children are young, and the negative experiences increase in frequency when children get older, with adolescence reported as the most difficult time for parents (Pasley and Gecas 1984). There are, of course, numerous factors that qualify or mitigate this pattern, such as number and sex of children, personalities of the children and the parents, and economic and occupational stresses on the family.

Is There Too Much Emphasis on Self-Esteem?

Self-esteem has become the most popular aspect of personality studied and a major emphasis of various family and individual therapy programs. The popularity of the subject is due largely to its perceived salutary consequences for both individual and group functioning and to the perceived strength and pervasiveness of the self-esteem motive. In the minds of many (scholars as well as the general public), high self-esteem has come to be associated with numerous "good" outcomes for individuals (e.g., academic achievement, popularity, personal success, health and happiness), while low self-esteem is associated with various "bad" outcomes (e.g., delinquency, academic failure, and depression). For example, the California Task Force to Promote Self-Esteem and Personal and Social Responsibility (1990, p. 4) concludes:

> Self-esteem is the likeliest candidate for a social vaccine, something that empowers us to live responsibly and that inoculates us against the lure of crime, violence, substance abuse, teen pregnancy, child abuse, chronic welfare dependency, and educational failure. The lack of self-esteem is central to most personal and social ills plaguing our state and nation.

Research on self-esteem gives a much more qualified and equivocal picture. While there is a tendency for high self-esteem to be associated with some positive outcomes and low self-esteem to be associated with negative outcomes, the relationships tend to be modest, often mixed or nonsignificant, and specific to certain conditions (Wells and Marwell 1976; Mecca, Smelser, and Vasconcellos 1989; Gecas 1982). Reasons for the low associations and mixed results are common to much of the research in the social sciences: problems of measurement (validity and reliability); problems of conceptualization (relating a global variable to a specific behavioral outcome); failure to control for other, confounding variables; and reliance on cross-sectional research designs.

Nevertheless, self-esteem has come to be perceived, particularly by family practitioners, as the key to the solution of most personal and interpersonal problems. Programs to "raise self-esteem" are common in society—in classrooms, rehabilitation centers, workplaces, and, of course, families. The research evidence by itself would not seem to warrant this kind of advocacy in the applied sphere. This emphasis on self-esteem within family therapy is probably less a consequence of persuasive scientific research than an expression of some central cultural values, such as individualism (Bellah et al. 1985). Some scholars have expressed concern about this overemphasis on self-esteem, viewing it as detrimental to the maintenance of interpersonal and family bonds. Wesley R. Burr and Clark Christensen (1992) argue that the emphasis on self-esteem in the helping professions may contribute to selfishness, self-centeredness, and excessive individualism, which undermine commitment to families and health of family processes.

Self-esteem is a significant aspect of individual experience, and it does have consequences for individual and family functioning. But it is no panacea for personal or social ills. No variable is. Self-esteem should be viewed in the proper scientific perspective—as an important social psychological variable, which, like a number of others (e.g., commitment, altruism, gender identity), has been found to affect individual functioning and family relations.

(*See also:* Attachment; Attribution in Relationships; Marital Quality; Only Child; Peer Pressure; Personality Development; Sibling Relationships; Social Networks; Symbolic Interactionism)

BIBLIOGRAPHY

Adams, B. (1972). "Birth Order, A Critical Review." *Sociometry* 35:411–439.

Bellah, R. N.; Madsen, R.; Sullivan, W.; Swindler, A.; and Tipton, S. (1985). *Habits of the Heart.* Berkeley: University of California Press.

Bem, D. (1972). "Self-Perception Theory." In *Advances in Experimental Social Psychology*, ed. L. Berkowitz. New York: Academic Press.

Burr, W. R., and Christensen, C. (1992). "Undesirable Side Effects of Enhancing Self-Esteem." *Family Relations* 41:460–464.

California Task Force to Promote Self-Esteem and Personal and Social Responsibility. (1990). *Toward a State of Self-Esteem.* Sacramento: California State Department of Education.

Cooley, C. H. (1902). *Human Nature and the Social Order.* New York: Scribner.

Felson, R. B. (1980). "Communication Barriers and the Reflected Appraisal Process." *Social Psychology Quarterly* 43:223–233.

Festinger, L. (1954). "A Theory of Social Comparison Processes." *Human Relations* 7:117–140.

Gecas, V. (1982). "The Self-Concept." *Annual Review of Sociology* 8:1–33.

Gecas, V. (1991). "The Self-Concept as a Basis for a Theory of Motivation." In *The Self–Society Dynamic*, ed. J. A. Howard and P. L. Callero. Cambridge, Eng.: Cambridge University Press.

Gecas, V., and Burke, P. (1994). "Self and Identity." In *Sociological Perspectives on Social Psychology*, ed. K. Cook, G. A. Fine, and J. House. Needham Heights, MA: Allyn & Bacon.

Gecas, V., and Pasley, K. (1983). "Birth Order and Self-Concept in Adolescence." *Journal of Youth and Adolescence* 12:521–535.

Gecas, V., and Schwalbe, M. (1986). "Parental Behavior and Adolescent Self-Esteem." *Journal of Marriage and the Family* 48:37–46.

Gecas, V., and Seff, M. A. (1990). "Families and Adolescents: A Review of the 1980s." *Journal of Marriage and the Family* 52:941–958.

Lasch, C. (1975). *Haven in a Heartless World.* New York: Basic Books.

Mead, G. H. (1934). *Mind, Self, and Society.* Chicago: University of Chicago Press.

Mecca, A. M.; Smelser, N. J.; and Vasconcellos, J., eds. (1989). *The Social Importance of Self-Esteem.* Berkeley: University of California Press.

Pasley, K., and Gecas, V. (1984). "Stresses and Satisfactions of the Parental Role." *Personnel and Guidance Journal* 2:400–404.

Rosenberg, M. (1979). *Conceiving the Self.* New York: Basic Books.

Wells, L. E., and Marwell, G. (1976). *Self-Esteem.* Newbury Park, CA: Sage Publications.

White, L. K., and Booth, A. (1985). "The Transition of Parenthood and Marital Quality." *Journal of Family Issues* 6:435–449.

Viktor Gecas

SELF-HELP GROUPS

Self-help groups, also known as mutual help, mutual aid, or support groups, are groups of people who provide mutual support for each other. In a self-help group, the members share a common problem, often a common disease or addiction. Their mutual goal is to help each other to deal with, if possible to heal or to recover from, this problem. While Michael K. Bartalos (1992) has pointed out the contradictory nature of the terms "self-help" and "support," the former U.S. surgeon general C. Everett Koop has said that self-help brings together two central but disparate themes of American culture, individualism and cooperation ("Sharing Solutions" 1992).

In traditional society, family and friends provided social support. In modern industrial society, however, family and community ties are often disrupted due to mobility and other social changes. Thus, people often choose to join with others who share mutual interests and concerns. In 1992, almost one in three Americans reported involvement in a support group; more than half of these were Bible study groups ("According to a Gallup Poll" 1992). Of those not involved in a self-help group at the time, more than 10 percent reported past involvement, while another 10 percent desired future involvement. It has been estimated that there are at least 500,000 to 750,000 groups with 10 million to 15 million participants in the United States (Katz 1993) and that more than thirty self-help centers and information clearinghouses have been established (Borman 1992).

Basic Group Models

Self-help groups may exist separately or as part of larger organizations. They may operate informally or according to a format or program. The groups usually meet locally, in members' homes or in community rooms in schools, churches, or other centers.

In self-help groups, specific modes of social support emerge. Through self-disclosure, members share their stories, stresses, feelings, issues, and recoveries. They learn that they are not alone; they are not the only ones facing the problem. This lessens the isolation that many people, especially those with disabilities, experience. Physical contact may or may not be part of the program; in many support groups, members informally hug each other.

Using the "professional expert" model, many groups have professionals serve as leaders or provide supplementary resources (Gartner and Riessman 1977). Many other groups, using the "peer participatory" model, do not allow professionals to attend meetings unless they share the group problem and attend as members or unless they are invited as speakers (Stewart 1990).

Comparing the self-help peer participatory model with the professional expert model, experiential knowledge is more important than objective, specialized knowledge in the peer model. Services are free and reciprocal rather than commodities. Equality among peers, rather than provider and recipient roles, is practiced. Information and knowledge are open and shared rather than protected and controlled.

Peers can model healing for each other. By "the veteran helping the rookie," the person who has "already 'been there' " helps the newer member (Mullan 1992). Through peer influence, the newer member is affected (Silverman 1992). Although the newer member learns that the problem can be dealt with and how, the older member who helps also benefits (Riessman 1965).

One possible effect of this peer model is empowerment. Self-help group members are dependent on themselves, each other, the group, perhaps a spiritual power. Together they learn to control the problem in their lives.

Those who share a common shame and stigma can come together, without judging, to provide an "instant identity" and community (Borman 1992). They can give emotional, social, and practical support to each other. They can explore and learn to understand and to combat the shame and stigma together, enhancing their self-esteem and self-efficacy. Through participation, they can enhance their social skills, promoting their social rehabilitation (Katz 1979).

Through "cognitive restructuring" (Katz 1993), members can learn to deal with stress, loss, and personal change (Silverman 1992).

Recovery Programs

The original model self-help group was Alcoholics Anonymous (AA), founded in 1935 by "Bill W." (William Griffith Wilson) and "Dr. Bob" (Robert Holbrook Smith). It is now estimated that 1 million people attend more than 40,000 groups in 100 countries (Borman 1992). AA has come to be known as a "twelve-step group" because its program for sobriety involves the following twelve steps:

1. We admitted we were powerless over alcohol—that our lives had become unmanageable.
2. Came to believe that a Power greater than ourselves could restore us to sanity.
3. Made a decision to turn our will and our lives over to the care of God *as we understood him.*
4. Made a searching and fearless moral inventory of ourselves.
5. Admitted to God, to ourselves, and to another human being the exact nature of our wrongs.
6. Were entirely ready to have God remove all these defects of character.
7. Humbly asked Him to remove our shortcomings.
8. Made a list of all persons we had harmed and became willing to make amends to them all.
9. Made direct amends to such people wherever possible, except when to do so would injure them.
10. Continued to take personal inventory and when we were wrong promptly admitted it.
11. Sought through prayer and meditation to improve our conscious contact with God *as we understood Him,* praying only for knowledge of His will for us and power to carry that out.
12. Having had a spiritual awakening as the result of these steps, we tried to carry this message to alcoholics and to practice these principles in all our affairs.

There are numerous twelve-step groups modeled after AA, including Adult Children of Alcoholics, Al-

Anon, Alateen, Cocaine Anonymous, Codependents Anonymous, Debtors Anonymous, Divorce Anonymous, Emotions Anonymous, Gamblers Anonymous, Narcotics Anonymous, Neurotics Anonymous, Overeaters Anonymous, and Workaholics Anonymous. Families Anonymous is a fellowship of relatives and friends of people involved in the abuse of mind-altering substances. These "anonymous" groups help their members to recover from their various addictive behaviors while maintaining member confidentiality. This confidentiality extends to not recognizing members as members when they meet outside meetings. Most groups are self-supporting, do not have dues, and decline all outside support to maintain their independence; they do not engage in any controversy, and they neither endorse nor oppose any cause.

Increasingly, there are groups that work toward recovery from addictions but reject certain tenets of twelve-step programs. Charlotte Davis Kasl (1992) has written about the need to fashion different models for recovery for people with different needs. For example, Rational Recovery Systems (affiliated with the American Humanist Association) and Secular Organization for Sobriety both reject AA's emphasis on spirituality.

Several self-help groups that specifically work with families are Parents Anonymous (for family members, to combat child abuse and neglect), Al-Anon (for relatives and friends of persons with alcoholism), and Alateen (for teenage relatives of persons with alcoholism).

Parents Anonymous (PA), founded in 1971 by "Jolly K." and Leonard Lieber (Borman 1979), assures anonymity but is not a twelve-step group. There is no religious commitment. Members provide suggestions and referrals to each other and may work toward solving problems together. PA is the oldest and only national parent self-help program with specialized groups for children. Approximately 15,000 parents and 9,200 children participate in its support groups in the United States each week. There are specialized groups in various states—for example, groups for homeless families. In several states there are groups for grandparents and grandchildren. Weekly meetings are representative of the communities in which they are held (Parents Anonymous 1993).

Al-Anon and Alateen, twelve-step groups affiliated with AA, welcome and give comfort to families of persons with alcoholism and give understanding and encouragement to the person with alcoholism. Meetings are held weekly. "The Al-Anon Family Groups are a fellowship of relatives and friends of alcoholics who share their experience, strength and hope in order to solve their common problems," believing that "alcoholism is a family illness and that changed attitudes can aid recovery" (Al-Anon 1981).

Support and Information Groups

Another type of self-help group focuses on medical diseases or problems. Examples of such groups that help families include AFTER AIDS (for people who have lost a loved one to AIDS), Candlelighters (for parents of young children with cancer), Make Today Count (for persons with cancer and their families), Mended Hearts, Inc. (for persons recovering from heart surgery, and their family and friends), the National Alliance for the Mentally Ill (for families and friends of persons with serious mental illness), National Federation of the Blind (for blind persons and their families), and National Society for Children and Adults with Autism (for children with autism and their families).

The Compassionate Friends (for bereaved parents), Parents Without Partners (for single parents and their children), and Tough Love (providing support and mutual problem solving for parents troubled by teenage behavior) are examples of other types of family-oriented groups.

Many of these organizations have other services in addition to self-help groups, such as information and referral, advocacy and lobbying, grant funding, research support, and practical assistance (e.g., providing hospital beds for home care).

Conclusion

Leonard D. Borman (1992, p. xxv) has written that "the underlying mechanism" of the self-help group is love, "a selfless caring." However, dangers that the self-help "movement" must guard against include dependence, victim-blaming, antiprofessionalism, further medicalization, and co-optation by the medical system.

Nevertheless, Victor W. Sidel and Ruth Sidel (1976, p. 67) have called self-help groups "the grassroots answer to our hierarchical, professionalized society," to its alienation and depersonalization.

(*See also:* Codependency; Dysfunctional Family; Social Networks; Substance Abuse)

BIBLIOGRAPHY

"According to a Gallup Poll." (1992). *The Self-Help Reporter* (Summer):1.

Al-Anon. (1981). *This is Al-Anon: Al-Anon Family Groups.* New York: Al-Anon Family Group Headquarters.

Alcoholics Anonymous. ([1939] 1976). *Alcoholics Anonymous: The Story of How Many Thousands of Men and Women Have Recovered from Alcoholism.* New York: Alcoholics Anonymous World Service.

Bartalos, M. K. (1992). "Illness, Professional Caregivers, and Self-Helpers." In *Self-Help: Concepts and Applications,* ed. A. H. Katz, H. L. Hedrick, D. H. Isenberg, L. M. Thompson, T. Goodrich, and A. H. Kutscher. Philadelphia: Charles Press.

Borman, L. D. (1979). "Characteristics of Development and Growth." In *Self-Help Groups for Coping with Crisis,* ed. M. A. Lieberman and L. D. Borman. San Francisco: Jossey-Bass.

Borman, L. D. (1992). "Introduction: Self-Help/Mutual Aid Groups in Strategies for Health." In *Self-Help: Concepts and Applications,* ed. A. H. Katz, H. L. Hedrick, D. H. Isenberg, L. M. Thompson, T. Goodrich, and A. H. Kutscher. Philadelphia: Charles Press.

Gartner, A., and Riessman, F., eds. (1977). *Self-Help in the Human Services.* San Francisco: Jossey-Bass.

Gottlieb, B. H., ed. (1983). *Social Networks and Social Support.* Newbury Park, CA: Sage Publications.

Kasl, C. D. (1992). *Many Roads, One Journey: Moving Beyond the Twelve Steps.* New York: HarperCollins.

Katz, A. H. (1979). "Self-Help Health Groups: Some Clarifications." *Social Science and Medicine* 13A:491–494.

Katz, A. H. (1993). *Self-Help in America: A Social Movement Perspective.* New York: Twayne.

Katz, A. H.; Hedrick, H. L.; Isenberg, D. H.; Thompson, L. M.; Goodrich, T.; and Kutscher, A. H. (1992). *Self-Help: Concepts and Applications.* Philadelphia: Charles Press.

Mullan, F. (1992). "Rewriting the Social Contract in Health." In *Self-Help: Concepts and Applications,* ed. A. H. Katz, H. L. Hedrick, D. H. Isenberg, L. M. Thompson, T. Goodrich, and A. H. Kutscher. Philadelphia: Charles Press.

Parents Anonymous. (1993). *Hope for Our Future.* Los Angeles: Author.

Riessman, F. (1965). "The 'Helper' Therapy Principle." *Social Work* 10:27–32.

"Sharing Solutions: A Lighthouse Conference." (1992). *The Self-Help Reporter* (Summer):4.

Sidel, V. W., and Sidel, R. (1976). "Beyond Coping." *Social Policy* 7:67–69.

Silverman, P. R. (1992). "Critical Aspects of the Mutual Help Experience." In *Self-Help: Concepts and Applications,* ed. A. H. Katz, H. L. Hedrick, D. H. Isenberg, L. M. Thompson, T. Goodrich, and A. H. Kutscher. Philadelphia: Charles Press.

Stewart, M. J. (1990). "Professional Interface with Mutual-Aid Self-Help Groups: A Review." *Social Science and Medicine* 31:1143–1158.

KATE S. AHMADI

SEXUAL COERCION *See* RAPE

SEXUALITY

Sexual behavior is an integral part of the marital relationship. In fact, the right to engage in sexual activity is a defining characteristic of marriage in all cultures. Sexual behavior is behavior that produces sexual arousal and increases the chance of orgasm (Hyde 1994). This entry is concerned not only with sexual behavior but also with the beliefs and emotions that typically accompany sexual activity—that is, sexuality and its relationship to marriage. This discussion is focused on the United States but applies to many other societies as well.

Contemporary analyses of sexuality emphasize the social constructionist perspective. They maintain that sexuality is not merely a biological phenomenon whose character is the same across time and space; it is also a cultural construct. Who engages in sexual behavior with whom and under what circumstances reflect cultural norms and values; even the behaviors in which partners engage reflect social and cultural influence (Gagnon and Simon 1973). The meaning of sexuality in contemporary society is situated "in a dense network of interrelated categories, including the body, maleness and femaleness, reproduction, sensuality, health, selfhood and so on" (Seidman 1991, p. 3).

In the United States, there are several perspectives on sexuality. Michel Foucault (1978) refers to a way of thinking and talking about sex as a discourse. Each social institution, including religion, sexology, government, education, and medicine, has a discourse about sex. The meaning of sexuality for particular individuals reflects the discourses with which they have come in contact.

The understanding of contemporary discourses is enhanced by reviewing the changes that have occurred in views of sexuality, love, and marriage since the Victorian era. In the 1800s, sexuality, love, and marriage were seen as distinct experiences. During the period from 1880 to 1940, they came to be defined as integrated, with the emphasis on marriage.

Historical Context

Sexuality was severely repressed during the Victorian era. Both sexual behavior and public discussion of topics related to sexuality were suppressed. Women were thought to have no sexual desire. The only legitimate reason for engaging in sexual behavior was to reproduce, and the only acceptable behavior was heterosexual vaginal intercourse, since only that behavior can result in conception. Furthermore, reproduction was to be limited to married couples; the only acceptable partner was one's spouse. Thus, sexuality was tied to the family, a system of marriage, kinship, and inheritance. Nonprocreative sexual activity was prohibited (Foucault 1978).

One of the first empirical studies of sexuality was carried out between 1885 and 1915 by Clelia Mosher (Jacob 1981). Mosher (a woman) wrote a questionnaire and administered it to forty-seven women. The sample was nonrandom; 81 percent of the women had attended college. Contrary to the discourse of the time, most of the women reported that they experienced sexual desire and orgasm. Mosher's research shows that sexual behavior may deviate from social norms. Much information about sexuality in the past is from written documents, which tend to reflect norms and not necessarily behavior.

A new construction of love, the romantic love ideal, gained currency during the nineteenth century (Lantz, Keyes, and Schultz 1975). This ideal includes five beliefs: love at first sight, there is one "true love" for each person, love conquers all, the beloved is (nearly) perfect, and one should marry for love. The growth of this ideal can be seen in increases in the number of references to it in popular magazines from 1740 to 1865. This ideal encourages people to marry for love rather than any other possible considerations.

At the beginning of the twentieth century, another change in construction occurred, the "sexualization of love." Eroticism came to be seen as an appropriate basis for or component of love. People who were in love were expected to be sexually attracted to each other (and people who were sexually attracted to each other were expected to be in love). Sexual gratification became a goal of romantic relationships. "Mutual sexual fulfillment was intended to enhance intimate solidarity in a social context where other unifying forces (e.g., kinship, patriarchy, economic dependency) were losing their power" (Seidman 1991, p. 2).

These changes reshaped marriage. "Duty, moral character, personal sacrifice, and spiritual union were fast losing their appeal as the defining characteristics of . . . the conjugal relationship" (D'Emilio and Freedman 1988, p. 265). Instead, men and women sought happiness and mutual sexual gratification. Closely related was the gradual acceptance of sexual interest and motivation in women, at least within the marital relationship. The effect of these changes was to increase the expectations of and the demands made on marriage.

During the 1920s, numerous social changes occurred that both reflected and encouraged these new constructions of love and sexuality. The pursuit of love became a major theme in popular culture, especially magazines and films. Young people gained autonomy and financial independence, which they used to create their own culture. Erotic themes and expression in art, music, and film created a new, more open public discourse. A popular, if minority, view uncoupled sexual behavior from marriage. Sexual expression was seen as legitimate in its own right. This view led to the creation of new types of relationships and lifestyles. These changes were not universally accepted; there was continuing support for the old discourse that limited sexual behavior to marriage.

The institution of dating was established during the 1920s and 1930s, primarily by white, middle-class youths in cities (D'Emilio and Freedman 1988). Large numbers of these young people came together at work, in schools and colleges, and in leisure settings. With help from advice columns, they developed norms about various aspects of these interactions, especially the extent to which sexual intimacy was appropriate. Necking and petting were generally accepted and practiced. Some observers believe that up to 50 percent of young men and women engaged in intercourse (Smith 1973), although most women had intercourse only with the man they expected to marry (D'Emilio and Freedman 1988). Dating and sexual intimacy gradually diffused to high-school-age and lower-class youths in cities.

Literature giving advice regarding sexuality, much of it by physicians, has been available since the early 1800s. Although it has often phrased the advice in terms of achieving sexual health, it frequently has reflected the discourse or discourses of the time. In the 1920s, this literature extolled physical pleasure as the goal of marital sexual expression. It provided elaborate instruction in sexual technique (Seidman 1991). Male sexuality was portrayed as quickly aroused and physical in nature, whereas female sexuality was slowly aroused and diffuse. Since simultaneous orgasm was the goal, the male was instructed to exert self-control and engage in the elaborate foreplay necessary to arouse his wife. If a couple did not experience mutual fulfillment, this was attributed to poor technique, and at least implicitly was the man's responsibility. This demonstrates the effect of beliefs about gender on public discourse about sex within marriage.

These major changes in the construction of marriage, love, and sex in the United States from 1850 to 1940 increased the demands on the marital relationship; in addition to the traditional expectations, husbands and wives were now expected to love each other and to provide mutual sexual gratification. Men and women came to expect self-fulfillment from marital sex. Falling out of love or failing to experience sexual gratification were defined as problems. These "problems" became the bases for seeking help (from books, marriage counselors, or sex therapists) or for divorce.

Structural-functional theory, a major sociological perspective on the family, developed in the 1940s and is an alternative to the social constructionist view (Parsons and Bales 1955). This perspective adopted the discourse on the family prevailing at the time. Marriage was seen as playing several important functions, including procreation and socialization of offspring, sexual gratification, and companionship. The structure of marriage, and associated taboos such as those on incest and adultery, were explained as necessary for the achievement of these functions. Other forms of sexual expression were less desirable because they were not capable of serving or were incompatible with these functions.

Research and Discourses

Social constructions of sex, love, and marriage continued to evolve throughout the twentieth century, including views of female sexuality. The pioneering surveys of sexual behavior conducted by Alfred C. Kinsey and his colleagues (Kinsey et al. 1953; Kinsey, Pomeroy, and Martin 1948) found widespread premarital as well as extramarital sexual behavior among both men and women. This challenged the popular view that women were not interested in sex, or less interested in it than men. The work of William Masters and Virginia Johnson (1966) demonstrated that the processes of sexual arousal were very similar for men and women, in contrast to the earlier view that they were quite different. These findings led to what has been termed the "eroticization of female sexuality" (Seidman 1991), the view that men and women are equally erotic. However, there are some gender differences in sexual behavior. Surveys in the United States (Smith 1991), Britain (Johnson et al. 1994), and France (ACSF 1992) find that men report a larger number of sexual partners than women, both lifetime and in the recent past. Studies also find that men are more accepting of sexual activity in casual relationships than are women (Oliver and Hyde 1993).

A major change in the discourse about sex is the uncoupling of sex from marriage. As sexual gratification became accepted as an end in itself, people began to challenge the belief that intimate sexual activity should be limited to marriage. A liberal discourse emerged, which argued that sexual intimacy involving people who are not married nor planning to marry is acceptable. In the 1970s, some argued that extramarital sexual intimacy is acceptable if the spouse approves (O'Neill and O'Neill 1972). This discourse led to expansion of available sexual lifestyles, including nonmarital relationships, cohabitation, and "open marriage."

Since the mid-1960s, a minority discourse has developed that separates sex from love. According to this view, engaging in sexual intimacy for physical pleasure, or to express affection for one's partner, is legitimate. This discourse is the basis of a best-selling sexual advice book of the 1970s, *The Joy of Sex* (Comfort 1972), and its sequel, *The New Joy of Sex* (Comfort 1991). This discourse views male and female as essentially equal in sexual potential and in the right to sexual gratification. It challenges the "double standard" view that sexual intimacy outside marriage or a committed relationship is acceptable for men but not for women. This course is consistent with the view that sex need not be limited to heterosexual couples. Thus, it facilitated the movement toward greater diversity in sexual lifestyles, including casual heterosexual and homosexual contacts and living in committed gay and lesbian relationships.

Scientific knowledge about and research on sexuality have developed steadily since 1960. Data on the sexual behavior of various groups have been obtained via surveys, often using self-administered questionnaires to increase accuracy. Such data are valuable because they are a more direct approach to the study of sexuality than reviewing popular literature. However, the samples surveyed often do not represent the U.S. population as a whole and thus yield biased results. The bias is typically in the direction of inflated estimates of sexual behavior.

Data on the relationship status of adults in the United States document the availability of a variety of marital/sexual lifestyles. One survey of American adults (Leigh, Temple, and Trocki 1993) found that 58 percent of the respondents were married; 6 percent of this group reported that they had not had sexual intercourse in the past year. Five percent were cohabiting; again, some of these respondents had not had sex in the past year. Three percent were separated, and 8 percent were divorced; most of those in these two groups had been sexually active in the preceding year. Seven percent were widowed; two-thirds of this group had not had intercourse for at least one year. Finally, 20 percent had never been married; 23 percent of this group were virgins, and 9 percent had not had sexual intercourse in the prior year.

Sexual behavior within marriage became more diverse between 1940 and 1980. Compared to the data reported by Kinsey and his colleagues, subsequent surveys (Blumstein and Schwartz 1983; Johnson et al. 1994) have found that married persons are more likely to report that they engage in oral-genital activity and that they use positions other than man-above during intercourse. The incorporation of these practices into sexual expression reflects acceptance of the belief that sexual activity should be pleasurable for both men and women.

The most visible change in the United States since the mid-1970s is the increasing explicitness of public discourse about sexuality. Explicit sexual representations are found in newspapers, magazines, novels, and films. The individual's desire for sexual fulfillment is used to sell lipstick, colognes, beer, clothing, travel, and automobiles. Personal advertisements, singles magazines, and dating services cater to the desire to find the (nearly) perfect spouse or the perfect sexual partner. The sex industry provides lubricants, vibrators, erotic clothing, and explicit videos to people seeking sexual fulfillment. Thus, stimuli associated with arousal are almost everywhere, creating a culture in which the sexual is ever present. This sexualization of the culture undoubtedly contributes to the occurrence of sexual activity in places and among persons formerly prohibited.

Marital and Extramarital Sexuality

Those who study the family have long been interested in extramarital sexuality. Unfortunately, research has often focused narrowly on its incidence. Studies of representative samples (Billy et al. 1993; Smith 1991) indicate that less than 2 percent of married men and women engage in extramarital sexual activity in any given year. The traditional discourse about sex and marriage attributes extramarital sexuality to problems in the marital relationship or to an unsatisfactory sexual relationship. A large-scale study of couples reports data that support this view (Blumstein and Schwartz 1983). At the same time, most respondents who had had extramarital sex endorsed the ideal of monogamy. They did not engage in it because they subscribed to an alternative discourse.

A formal theory that provides an explanation for extramarital sexuality is equity theory, presented by Elaine Hatfield and her colleagues (Walster [Hatfield], Traupmann, and Walster 1978). According to this view, people assess intimate relationships by comparing their own outcomes (rewards minus inputs) with their partner's outcomes. If the individual perceives her outcomes as equal to her spouse's outcomes, she will be satisfied. Inequity, feeling that she is getting less than her spouse, is associated with distress. To relieve distress, individuals attempt to restore equity. One way that a married person can restore equity is to engage in extramarital sexuality.

Other research on adultery has approached it from a dialectical perspective, viewing it as a consequence of conflicting motives within the person. Annette Lawson (1988) argues that extramarital relationships occur when people discover that their marriage does not live up to their expectations and believe that their personal nurturance is more important than marital fidelity. This leads to an internal dialogue as they contemplate an extramarital liaison. If the person engages in adultery, the consequences may be supportive of the marriage, challenge the marriage, or serve as a transition out of it.

Although several alternative discourses have developed since the mid-1960s, the dominant discourse in the United States remains the view that fuses love, sex, and marriage. The contemporary family is the anchor for sexuality; its role is not to exclude or restrain sexual desire but to support it (Foucault 1978). Thus, the family is "a hotbed of constant sexual excitement" (Foucault 1978, p. 109). It is not surprising that there is an almost universal incest taboo; such a taboo is essential to counter sexual desire between parents and children or siblings.

Marital relationships also involve power, and power becomes intertwined with marital sexuality. Both men and women use sex to influence each other (Blumstein and Schwartz 1983). The distribution of power within the couple can be an important influence on the frequency and nature of sexual activity. The fusion of power and sexual desire is not limited to the marital relation. It occurs in many, perhaps all, relationships. Greater power is associated with being older, superior in position in a hierarchy, or male. Many of the contemporary problems involving sexuality reflect the use of power to coerce someone into sexual activity (Sprecher and McKinney 1993). Within the family these include spousal abuse and sexual abuse of siblings. Outside the family these include sexual harassment or assault of student by teacher, of worker by supervisor, of client by counselor or therapist. Acquaintance or date rape and gang rape are other forms of sexuality that involve coercion.

Conclusion

The connections observed between sexuality and marriage in any society reflect the discourses of social constructions of sexuality and of marriage found in that society. The experience of love, sexuality, and marriage reflects the coupling of these phenomena in the public discourse. This experience may result in sexual fulfillment or frustration, marital satisfaction or dissatisfaction, seeking counseling/treatment or engaging in adultery, or divorce. Therefore, the health of the institution of marriage reflects, in part, beliefs about sexuality.

(*See also:* Adolescent Sexuality; Exchange Theory; Extramarital Sex; Incest Taboo; Intimacy; Love; Marital Power; Marital Sex; Rape; Sexuality Education; Sexuality in the Life Cycle; Sexual Orientation; Sexual Problems)

BIBLIOGRAPHY

ACSF Investigators. (1992)."AIDS and Sexual Behavior in France." *Nature* 360:407–409.

Billy, J. O. G.; Tanfer, K.; Grady, W.; and Klepinger, D. (1993). "The Sexual Behavior of Men in the United States." *Family Planning Perspectives* 25:52–60.

Blumstein, P.; and Schwartz, P. (1983). *American Couples: Money, Work, Sex.* New York: William Morrow.

Comfort, A. (1972). *The Joy of Sex.* New York: Crown.

Comfort, A. (1991). *The New Joy of Sex: A Gourmet Guide to Lovemaking for the Nineties.* New York: Crown.

D'Emilio, J., and Freedman, E. (1988). *Intimate Matters: A History of Sexuality in America.* New York: Harper & Row.

Foucault, M. (1978). *The History of Sexuality:* Vol. 1, *An Introduction*, tr. R. Hurley. New York: Pantheon.

Gagnon, J., and Simon, W. (1973). *Sexual Conduct: The Social Origins of Human Sexuality.* Chicago: Aldine.

Hyde, J. (1994). *Understanding Human Sexuality*, 5th edition. New York: McGraw-Hill.

Jacob, K. A. (1981). "The Mosher Report." *American Heritage* (June/July): 56–64.

Johnson, A.; Wadsworth, J.; Wellings, K.; and Field, J. (1994). *Sexual Attitudes and Lifestyles.* Oxford, Eng.: Basil Blackwell.

Kinsey, A. C.; Pomeroy, W. B.; and Martin, C. E. (1948). *Sexual Behavior in the Human Male.* Philadelphia: Saunders.

Kinsey, A. C.; Pomeroy, W. B.; Martin, C. E.; and Gebhard, P. H. (1953). *Sexual Behavior in the Human Female.* Philadelphia: Saunders.

Lantz, H. R.; Keyes, J.; and Schultz, H. (1975). "The American Family in the Preindustrial Period: From Baselines in History to Change." *American Sociological Review* 40:21–36.

Lawson, A. (1988). *Adultery: An Analysis of Love and Betrayal.* New York: Basic Books.

Leigh, B.; Temple, M.; and Trocki, K. (1993). "The Sexual Behavior of U.S. Adults: Results from a National Sample." *American Journal of Public Health* 83:1400–1408.

Masters, W., and Johnson, V. (1966). *Human Sexual Response.* Boston: Little, Brown.

Oliver, M. B., and Hyde, J. (1993). "Gender Differences in Sexuality: A Meta-Analysis." *Psychological Bulletin* 114:29–51.

O'Neill, G., and O'Neill, N. (1972). *Open Marriage: A New Lifestyle for Couples.* New York: M. Evans.

Parsons, T., and Bales, R. (1955). *Family Socialization and Interaction Process.* New York: Free Press.

Seidman, S. (1991). *Romantic Longings: Love in America, 1830–1980.* New York: Routledge.

Smith, D. (1973). "The Dating of the American Sexual Revolution: Evidence and Interpretation." In *The American Family in Social-Historical Perspective*, ed. M. Gordon. New York: St. Martin's Press.

Smith, T. W. (1991). "Adult Sexual Behavior in 1989: Number of Partners, Frequency of Intercourse, and Risk of AIDS." *Family Planning Perspectives* 23:102–107.

Sprecher, S., and McKinney, K. (1993). *Sexuality.* Newbury Park, CA: Sage Publications.

Walster [Hatfield], E.; Traupmann, J.; and Walster, W. (1978). "Equity and Extramarital Sexuality." *Archives of Sexual Behavior* 7:127–141.

John DeLamater
Janet Shibley Hyde

SEXUALITY EDUCATION

There can be no doubt that "sex" and "sexuality" as words in the English language elicit great attention and sensitivity. Whether seen in print or heard in conversation, there is almost instant recognition. When writers refer to "sex education" or "sexuality education," it is not surprising that feelings become intense. Researchers and teachers in this area also use the terms "family life education," "human growth and development," and often "human sexuality" to describe instruction in human reproduction and sexuality (Roth 1993). The Sex Information and Education Council of the U.S. (SIECUS) recommends the term "sexuality education" (1992). This term refers to a comprehensive curriculum of instruction that covers not only sexual anatomy and physiology but also reproduction, contraception, sexually transmitted diseases, and related topics in sexuality. These programs commonly address issues of personality, values formation, decision making, peer and social pressures, communication strategies, and various sexual behaviors (Haffner and de Mauro 1991). Sexuality education often examines other areas of human sexuality as well. Despite differences in programs across the United States, each attempts to educate students in the domain of human sexuality.

Sexuality Education and Development Stages

Authors have suggested that human sexual development is best considered a subset of overall human development (Croft and Asmussen 1993). As human beings develop, there is a relatively slow yet constant progression through these developmental stages, in both physical and mental areas, with strong implications for understanding sexual differentiation and behavior. Understanding characteristics that define each stage is also crucial for designing educational interventions (Johnson 1989). Different sexual concerns and dilemmas will emerge during the childhood, preadolescent, adolescent, adulthood, and even the later adulthood stages (D'Augelli and D'Augelli 1994). Any educational intervention, especially if designed for sexuality education, is destined to fail if the development stage of the recipients is not part of program planning (Kirby 1984). Too often a sound program may fail to affect students' knowledge, attitude, or behavior favorably because of a failure by the program designers to match material and in-class exercises with developmental level.

Following is a brief overview of major characteristics governing the primary developmental stages. Such information provides a basic understanding of the role sexuality education plays across developmental periods. For clarity, the developmental stages are classified into four very broad categories: younger children (five to seven), intermediate children (eight to ten), older children (eleven to twelve), and teenagers. Education regarding sex for children one to four years of age is not specifically examined, since so little data on sexuality during these ages exist. It is crucial to note, however, that these children do receive "education" in the form of modeling from their caregivers. Caregivers may by their actions send very basic messages about sexual concepts to these children. These early models can exert influence on a child's later behavior.

Younger children (five to seven). Children who are five to seven years of age tend to be egocentric in their thinking toward the world around them. They lack complexity in how they think about events and people. Such children do not see the distinction between causes and their effects. Their thinking processes are centered around themselves, and they have considerable difficulty seeing the perspectives of others (Piaget 1930; Werner 1948).

From a sexual standpoint, young children at this stage generally have a clearer sense of the basic anatomical distinctions between the sexes. There is typically some sense of modesty regarding public exposure of their bodies. Not surprisingly, there is strong influence regarding issues such as nudity in the home from parents and other adults (Masters, Johnson, and Kolodny 1992). At the same time, there is children's natural and normal curiosity about exploring their bodies. This is usually seen in a parent catching the child in various "games" such as playing doctor or house with peers or siblings. Since the child considers the parent to be the main guide for appropriate behavior, it is critical that parents not overreact to such situations. In fact, many experts suggest that one thing adults can do in such a situation is to relax (Feitel 1990). If the child's behavior is blatantly inappropriate, however, such as public display of genitals, the parent must establish clear disciplinary boundaries, retaining control and making certain the child knows the behavior is not acceptable.

By the time the child enters first grade, the frequency of games usually decreases, and exchange of sex information emerges in the form of sexual jokes. Children here are fascinated with the new array of words that have sexual or forbidden connotations. Researchers have studied this phenomenon in children and have reported that when information is not provided by adults, sexual jokes become the primary source of such knowledge (Money 1980). It is readily apparent how even the very young child learns that "sex is dirty" after being scolded by panicked adults for telling "dirty jokes." If there is any hallmark of guidance on fostering sexuality education at this period of life, it is that children at this level of development see things in concrete, literal terms. If parents consistently model affection, patience, and tolerance in front of their children, they will learn that such behaviors and attitudes are positive and reinforcing. These children stand a better chance of exhibiting these characteristics when they reach adulthood. Conversely, parents who never publicly show affection or who regularly punish a child's natural sexual curiosity may be inadvertently educating their children to avoid these behaviors and attitudes later in life. Researchers have found that young children possess superb powers of observation (Duryea 1991). They see much more than adults give them credit for, and at these ages the children interpret actions and words with simplicity. Sexuality education at this level needs to emphasize the importance of knowing one's sexual self while avoiding any negative modeling. A sound educational foundation at this level will foster greater social and sexual maturity at later stages of development.

Intermediate children (eight to ten). Children at this level perceive and make distinctions that are not obvious to younger children (Werner 1948). During this period thinking is characterized by being able to differentiate between self and others, between internal and external bodily events, and by an ability to comprehend cause-and-effect relationships. Children at this stage develop thinking that is less simplistic and more relativistic. In contrast to the younger child, these children are able to understand, for instance, that a virus can invade the external self (skin) and cause sickness internally (body). Because these students have the cognitive ability to see cause-and-effect linkages, sexuality education for them can incorporate more complex information. At this stage children are no longer intrigued by sexual jokes and stories. They try to absorb as much new information as possible, becoming especially intrigued with reproductive mechanisms and anatomical function. The idea of hormones as crystal-like structures flowing through one's blood is not unbelievable or abstract at this developmental stage. Sexuality programs at this stage have a twofold purpose: (1) provision of relevant knowledge and (2) instruction that facilitates the child's ability to prevent problems.

The goal of preventive sexuality education is especially important in view of the AIDS/HIV epidemic in the United States. Various medical and scientific authorities agree that the most promising method for controlling this crisis is preventive education. The consistent recommendation from experts is that programs begin informing children about basic concepts in sexual function and behavior as soon as an understanding of causality is part of their cognitive repertoire. Programs in traditional "sex ed" have not always adhered to this suggestion.

Older children (eleven to twelve). In general, by age eleven or twelve children begin to move toward thinking that tries to integrate the distinctions they now can make. They now can see themselves as separate from but still in relation to others. During this time children can integrate internal and external phenomena into one system. For example, students at this level can readily see how media portray certain people (external) to motivate (internal) consumers to purchase specific products. The level of cognitive sophistication is also more intricate. At this stage young persons usually can explain multiple causes with multiple effects. The vast majority of students think interactively at about this time. Essentially they can describe conditions under which certain events are more or less likely to occur. They can easily see how one factor (lack of knowledge) may interact or combine with another factor (lack of self-esteem) to produce teenage pregnancies. Such interactive relationships are crucial in the sexuality education designed to foster preventive thinking among recipients. In sharp contrast to prior stages, however, the biological side of development now begins to play a major role. There is a strong sense of one's external appearance and how it may be perceived by significant others. Most children experience puberty at this age even though there exists no definite time for the onset. Pubertal changes signal the shift from biological immaturity to biological maturity (Masters, Johnson, and Kolodny 1992). Sex hormones begin to increase in activity and produce bone growth. This "growth spurt" typically occurs two years earlier for females than males (on average, age twelve versus fourteen). As a result, girls are normally taller than boys of the same age from about ages eleven to fourteen (Marshall 1975). Since the increase in growth occurs at different times for different parts of the body (foot growth begins about four months before the leg), some adolescents' feet may also look disproportionately large. These physical changes can cause some self-consciousness for boys as well as girls.

At about midadolescence (age fifteen), when bone growth in various body systems tends to even out, males "catch up" to the females. Students who feel inhibited or self-conscious about their developing, changing bodies should note that there exists no relationships between the early adolescent growth phase and final height as an adult.

Sexuality education is of great importance during this time for adolescents. For girls, there is a need to know about breast development (phelarche), appearance of pubic hair (pubarche), and the onset of menstrual cycles (menarche). There is also a need to know about vaginal secretion changes that may occur (transudation) and, probably most importantly, that these body changes are part of normal, healthy sexual development. In boys, there is a need for information on genital growth and ejaculation. While males do not have a direct counterpart to menarche in females, the first ejaculation of a young boy can cause the same sense of psychological and emotional concern. If the boy is prepared beforehand in a factual, relaxed manner, the chance of this sexual event causing mental anguish can be lessened. Just as the uninformed young girl may perceive her first menstrual flow as a sign of illness, the uninformed young boy may perceive his first nocturnal emission as a sign of injury or disease. Boys also need to know about the onset of pubic and facial hair. A condition known as gynecomastia or breast enlargement occurs in many pubertal males. Boys need to know that this condition is not life-threatening or cancerous; it typically disappears within a year or two without any harmful effects.

Physical changes are also part of sexual differentiation at this period of development. Young girls tend to be overly concerned with the shape of their bodies as estrogen causes fat to accumulate under the skin and give rise to the female figure. Boys, conversely, are more fixated on muscles and muscle mass as testosterone production begins to influence various muscles that eventually produce the male physique. Both of these obsessions result from normal social learning processes.

Because physical appearance is such a high priority for youth at this stage, sexuality education must address issues of self-esteem and self-image. Students need to know how normal and expected these dramatic changes are for all adolescents. However, the continued occurrence of eating disorders and steroid use seems to show that American media often have more influence on self-image and self-esteem than do parents and sexuality educators.

Teenagers. By the time young people reach fourteen or fifteen years of age, their biological development is well established. Most pubertal changes have occurred, and most of their physical attributes are set. Still, the teen years are considered by most authorities in development to be the most stressful. Personal appearance and social popularity grow to be overwhelming forces on the teens' daily life. In most cases, these influences cannot be ignored, and often teens become obsessed with gaining the acceptance and affirmation of a peer group. Such goals inevitably conflict with parental views on where the teenagers should be investing time and effort. Teenagers naturally make sexual behavior a part of attaining acceptance and affirmation. A teen may be asked, dared, or even belittled into proving solidarity with the peer group by performing sexual acts (Lewis and Lewis 1984). Such challenges signal to the individual that membership in a group is achievable if one conforms to specific demands. Numerous research studies have shown that teenagers consistently submit to these pressures *without* any request or inducement from peers (Duryea 1991; Saarni 1989). So strong is the pull toward peer group affiliation that even teenagers knowledgeable of the consequences of risky sexual behavior (e.g., not using condoms) will compromise their health.

Sexuality education designed for teens needs to present material, perceived as relevant and important to them, in a factual manner that strictly avoids the appearance of preaching. Teenagers at this developmental level possess a firm sense of autonomy; they easily detect in adults, especially their teachers, hidden strategies designed to alter their behavior or thinking. Material and exercises examining reproduction, contraception, and communication are among the more meaningful at this stage, but prevention of sexual assault and information on "sexual varieties" also generate interest among teenagers. At this age students require contemporary information and skills to form a thorough knowledge base from which to make inordinately complex health-related decisions. Some research evidence suggests, however, that while sexuality programs are providing the information and skills, they are not consistently decreasing risky sexual behavior (Kipke, Futterman, and Hein 1990).

Comprehensive sexuality education is developed and implemented sequentially over a span of development years. Where to begin and where to conclude such curricula is almost always a point of serious emotional contention among teachers, administrators, and parents (SIECUS Fact Sheet 1993).

Contexts and Types of Sexuality Education

According to Diane de Mauro (1990) of the Sex Information and Education Council of the United States (SIECUS), approximately half of the states now mandate school-based sexuality education. More than half mandate preventive AIDS/HIV education, and most prevention advocates recommend that the school curricula provide *comprehensive* sexuality education.

The most dominant trend in sexuality education since the mid-1980s has been peer-based programs. These curricula are partly designed and taught by older-age peers in collaboration with the teacher. The rationale for using peers to help conduct these programs is student desire for some ownership of such instruction. Peer participation helps achieve this goal. Such curricula are extremely helpful to "sex ed" teachers who are uncomfortable with much of the content. Popular students or team leaders recruited to help teach these programs often lessen this uneasiness and facilitate topical discussion. Results of such peer-based strategies have been favorable.

The teaching of sexuality in the family setting has been relatively ignored for many years. A number of studies indicate that only a minority of parents educate their children in sexuality (Cross 1991; Kallen, Stephenson, and Doughty 1983) Those parents who do invest time and effort in this important area of their children's lives are normally difficult to access for research purposes. Thus, little data or information exists on either the extent or effects of sexuality education in the family setting. Seventy-seven percent of American adults believe sexuality education should be taught in the schools, and only 5 percent of adults ban their children from attending (Alan Guttmacher Institute 1981; Gordon and Gordon 1983). Few American fathers play an active role in providing their children with age-appropriate sex information, but parents who fail to participate run the risk of allowing children to interpret what they see in the media as an accurate depiction of what sex constitutes. This neglect can and often does produce serious consequences. Even when there exists a progressive, comprehensive, and developmentally sound school curriculum, parental involvement at home is needed to reinforce and support the skills and viewpoints being explored at school. How to foster this parental reinforcement consistently remains a major dilemma for sexuality programs in schools.

There is a growing move to implement sexuality education within various medical settings (Mansfield et al. 1993). Such education is implemented in physicians' offices or hospitals during patient visits. Normally, a nurse conducts the education although health educators, or even a physician, can be employed. Carol Mansfield and her associates (1993) studied the effects of one such physician-delivered HIV education program on high-risk adolescents. After thorough counseling and preventive education in the medical office, sexual behaviors of these adolescents were not significantly changed. Other research teams (Rickert, Gottlieb, and Jay 1990) have had similar difficulty altering sexual behavior of female adolescents in clinic-based interventions. Many health maintenance organizations (HMOs) routinely employ health educators to implement sexuality and related health behavior programs with youths. These interventions employ interactive videos, reading material, and counseling to motivate youths to make responsible choices in health areas. How effective these education efforts are is still uncertain. While knowledge levels are favorably enhanced, the degree to which they prevent risky sexual *actions* remains inconsistent.

Since the mid-1980s, various religious organizations have instituted their own sexuality or "family life" education programs. Whereas schools and medical settings tend to emphasize personal responsibility in sexual behavior, religious programs are more likely to emphasize abstinence, a choice included in most major sexuality programs, including those outside religious settings.

The curricula offered in more conservative and/or religious areas usually have prohibitions against specific topics and language. Diane de Mauro's review in "Sexuality Education 1990" indicated that Utah, Idaho, Delaware, and Louisiana each contained significant limitations in their state curricula. Idaho's curriculum warns against having sex with anyone with swollen glands. The Delaware program omits major sexual anatomy of the female (clitoris) and fails to mention girls at all in certain sections.

The findings of this review and others suggest that students may be given information on abstinence at the expense of information on other available prevention options. In light of the AIDS/HIV epidemic, debates have been conducted about whether or not conservative and/or religious sexuality education advocates can provide information on nonabstinence options without sacrificing their values. This is but one of a number of difficult debates involving sexuality education.

Despite the wide range of contexts and types of sexuality education, they all revolve around the concept of providing relevant knowledge in the hope of preventing problems (Zabin and Hayward 1993).

Multicultural Sexuality Education

Effective sexuality education for individuals from different cultural or ethnic backgrounds takes place only when there is a firm knowledge of those individuals' beliefs, values, and behavioral heritages and traditions (Ward and Taylor 1992). The available data suggest an urgent need for culturally sensitive sexuality curricula in the school as well as in the community and family settings. Twenty percent of teenage African-American males have their first sexual encounter before age thirteen, and 35 percent prior to age fourteen (Sonenstein, Pleck, and Kul 1991). African-American and Hispanic teens are less likely then whites to use contraception during first sexual intercourse (Forrest and Singh 1990).

Traditionally, sexuality curricula were designed and implemented by white middle-class educators. Racial and ethnic minorities were not generally solicited for input on design, presentation, or content of these materials. Minority youths felt excluded in sexuality education, since the curricular perspective was unicultural.

Since the mid-1980s, however, there has been tremendous growth and progress in producing sexuality curricula that incorporate multicultural perspectives. Karen Pittman and her associates (1992) offer the following guidelines for making sexuality education programs more culturally relevant: Gain familiarity of the culture of the students who will receive the educational program; know the dynamics between the students' beliefs and values, and how these relate to sexual issues such as contraception, relationships, childbearing and family; collaborate with community groups and parents in the design and delivery of the program; and enlist the help of bilingual educators when possible language barriers may exist. As Pittman (1992) states, "The more sexuality educators learn about a particular group of adolescents, the better able they will be to meet youth *where they are*, rather than where adults *would like them to be.*"

Methods of Sexuality Intervention

Sexuality programs since the mid-1980s have been influenced strongly by learning theory, specifically the concept of plural approaches. In this logic, acquiring knowledge and motivation to act on that knowledge are best derived from exposure to an array of different methods. Learners are said to learn more efficiently when the material is presented from a variety of approaches. This principle appears to be a constant across developmental stages, cultures, program goals, and gender.

A brief summary of the more common methods used in sexuality interventions includes:

- Role play simulations where students act out certain situations involving sexual and social pressures.
- Adversary panels in which students formally debate a sexual issue of concern to them (date rape), but from the opposition's viewpoint.
- Interactive video exercises where students view a program on a topical area (teen pregnancy) and try to answer questions in the video.
- Stress reduction/assertiveness training exercises where students learn techniques to help them relax and calm themselves or assert their rights in adverse situations.
- Group discussions and fact-finding exercises to help students practice collaboration and make sure information they receive is accurate.
- Metaphor techniques with younger students to help them gain understanding of basic concepts; for instance, a hormone can be explained as a messenger that delivers a message (substance in the blood) to an office (body part) so that something happens (pubertal changes).
- Guest lectures by local experts, which often show students that there are knowledgeable persons in their community whom they can contact for further information or advice.
- Field trips to hospital maternity wings, Planned Parenthood offices, or universities, where they can learn about or participate in specific sexuality education programs, projects, or research activities.
- Choice dilemma vignettes, which have students, either in group or alone, read a short situation involving sexual risk; select one choice from among those available (each choice has a specific level of jeopardy associated with it); and defend to classmates the rationale for the choice.

Exemplary interventions, such as the McMaster Teen Program in Ontario, Canada, use tutors in small-group sex education exercises (Thomas et al. 1992). Such tutors or team leaders are trained to help their peers apply problem-solving strategies to manage their daily sexual lives. Most programs like McMaster employ tutors in conjunction with the methods previously mentioned. While this list does not include all methodologies currently in use, it does represent the philosophy of most effective curricula, which is that learning occurs more often when a variety of techniques and approaches are employed.

Controversies in U.S. Sexuality Education

Many debates rage over sexuality education in the United States. Some of these controversies come from different beliefs and values toward what should be taught and how. Such debates are a natural and expected part of the sociocultural diversity of the American landscape. While communities disagree across America on specific sexuality education issues, there is some consensus that young people need information and skills to survive their formative years.

However, the innovation of "school-based clinics" (SBCs) has generated some volatile debate. Such clinics normally operate along with ongoing sexuality curricula in schools. School nurses in conjunction with health educators dispense desired sexuality information, health services, and in many cases contraceptives. The philosophy of such clinics is that students should be provided access to contraceptives so that sexually transmitted disease and pregnancies can be prevented. Opponents of these programs contend that such access encourages youths to be more sexually active. There is also strong feeling that the school should not be using tax monies for health services that belong in medical-care settings (Nation's Health 1994).

Whichever viewpoint one adheres to, it is readily evident that school-based clinics have a favorable role to play in preventing not only pregnancy and disease but other problems as well. Joy Dryfoos (1988) reported that SBCs have been associated with decreases in truancy and lowering of dropout rates. Laurie Zabin and her associates (1986) found similar outcomes for SBCs in other studies, as well as decreases in pregnancy rates and drug use. The American School Health Association (1988) has presented testimony that 38 percent of students in one New York City school reported their attendance had improved as a result of the clinic. Marcella McCord and her associates at the University of North Carolina at Chapel Hill (1993) found these same results for attendance and graduation rates of African–American males.

The United States possesses a wealth of sexuality curricula and program interventions ongoing across the nation. There are educational interventions in the schools. There are reproductive health interventions in medical and social-service settings as well as in schools. There are also "life options" interventions (Polit 1989). These particular programs, intervening on high-risk populations, attempt to improve self-concept and raise the aspirations of individuals to pursue a more health-enhancing range of life opportunities. These programs also have reported success in lowering pregnancy rates, increasing employment, and improving social skills.

Despite the attraction of sexuality-related education in all forms throughout the country, teen pregnancy remains at an unacceptable level (Zabin and Hayward 1993). Teenage abortions and sexually transmitted disease still exist. Children continue to suffer from *preventable* conditions. How then does sexuality education in all its varied forms affect the American family and influence the institution of marriage in the United States?

The Family and Marriage

The American family has changed dramatically since the mid-1970s because of social, economic, technological, and medical influences. The government, for instance, has established national health objectives (Healthy Children 2000 1992). Many of these objectives relate to sexual behavior of adolescents, calling for reductions in teenage pregnancies and abortions and increases in the percentage of teens consistently using contraceptives. The U.S. Centers for Disease Control and Prevention have sponsored numerous projects to learn more about sexual behavior. The majority of school districts in the nation implement some form of sexuality education (SIECUS Fact Sheet 1993). Families across American now have children and adolescents with greater levels of sexual knowledge than ever before. It is impossible to know what changes in the American family are due solely to sexuality education. Noted sexologist David Kirby, however, suggested in a paper presented at the American Enterprise Institute that sexuality education was *not* encouraging teenagers toward risky sex (Associated Press 1994). At a time when teenage violence, pregnancy, abortion, and AIDS appear beyond control, preventive sexuality education is a widespread countermeasure to keep children healthy.

The effects of sexuality education on the institution of marriage are not fully documented. There is strong evidence that young, newly married couples who are able to plan their families (e.g., skill in contraception) experience greater success in avoiding divorce and economic hardship (Fielding and Williams 1990). Because couples who are skillful in negotiating the emotional stresses of early marriage will have a greater chance of remaining married, previous exposure to effective sexuality curricula or programs that help prepare youths for these challenges may foster a more successful marriage.

In 1987 alone, the cost of teenage childbearing in the United States was estimated at $19.27 *billion* (Center for Population Options 1988). This burden is shared by all Americans in different ways. Americans will always debate whether such "costs" are due to the breakdown of the family and the traditional American marriage. What seems readily evident to the majority of U.S. citizens, however, is that education, specifically education to prevent problems for youths, is to be pursued with excitement and debated in truth. The American family will continue to survive. The institution of marriage will also survive. The question that all Americans must consider is whether widespread sexuality education facilitates or impedes this survival.

(*See also:* Adolescent Sexuality; AIDS; Birth Control: Contraceptive Methods; Conception: Medical Aspects; Family Life Education; Family Planning; Family Values; Pregnancy and Birth; Sexually Transmitted Diseases; Teenage Parenting)

BIBLIOGRAPHY

Alan Guttmacher Institute. (1981). *Teenage Pregnancy: The Problem That Hasn't Gone Away.* New York: Author.

American School Health Association. (1988). *Testimony on the Year 2000 Objectives for the Nation: Recommendations for the School Health Program.* Dayton, OH: Author.

Associated Press. (1994). "Director Says Sex Ed Does Not Encourage Teens." (Speech given to the American Enterprise Institute.) Washington, DC.

Center for Population Options. (1988). *1987 Report: Estimates of Costs for Teenage Childbearing.* Washington, DC: Author.

Croft, C., and Asmussen, L. (1991). "A Developmental Approach to Sexuality Education: Implications for Medical Practice." *Journal of Adolescent Health* 14:109–114.

Cross, R. (1991). "Helping Adolescents Learn about Sexuality." *SIECUS Report* (April–May).

D'Augelli, A., and D'Augelli, J. (1994). "The Enhancement of Social Skills and Competence: Promoting Lifelong Sexual Unfolding." In *Handbook of Social Skills Training and Research,* ed. L. L. Abate. New York: Wiley.

de Mauro, D. (1990). "Sexuality Education 1990: A Review of State Sexuality and AIDS Education Curricula." *SIECUS Report* (December–January).

Dryfoos, J. (1988). "School-Based Health Clinics." *Family Planning Perspectives* 20:193–200.

Duryea, E. (1991). "Principles of Nonverbal Communication in Efforts to Reduce Peer and Social Pressure." *Journal of School Health* 61:5–10.

Elders, J. (1994). Cited in Forward to *The Comprehensive School Health Challenge: Promoting Health Through Education,* ed. P. Cortese and K. Middleton. Santa Cruz, CA: ETR Publishing.

Feitel, L. (1990). "My Body My Self." *Sesame Street Magazine Parent's Guide* (April):20–25.

Fielding, J., and Williams, C. (1990). "Unwanted Teenage Pregnancy: A U.S. Perspective." In *Preventing Disease: Beyond the Rhetoric: Frontiers of Primary Care,* ed. M. Lipkin. New York: Springer-Verlag.

Forrest, J., and Singh, S. (1990). "The Sexual and Reproductive Behavior of American Women, 1982–1988." *Family Planning Perspectives* 22:206–214.

Gordon, S., and Gordon, J., (1983). *Raising a Child Conservatively in a Sexually Permissive World.* New York: Simon & Schuster.

Haffner, D., and de Mauro, D. (1991). *Winning the Battle: Developing Support for Sexuality and HIV/AIDS Education.* New York: Sex Information and Education Council of the United States.

Healthy Children 2000. (1992). *National Health Promotion and Disease Prevention Objectives Related to Mothers, Infants, Children, Adolescents, and Youth.* Boston: Jones and Bartlett.

Johnson, R. (1989). "Adolescent Growth and Development." In *Adolescent Medicine,* ed. A. Hofmann and D. Greydanus. Norwalk, CT: Appleton and Lange.

Kallen, D.; Stephenson J.; and Doughty, A. (1983). "The Need to Know: Recalled Adolescent Sources of Sexual and Contraceptive Information and Sexual Behavior." *Journal of Sex Research* 19:137–159.

Kipke, D.; Futterman, J.; and Hein, J. (1990). "HIV Infection and AIDS During Adolescence." *Medical Clinics of North America* 74:1149–1167.

Kirby, D. (1984). *Sexuality Education.* Santa Cruz, CA: Network Publications.

Lewis, C., and Lewis, M. A. (1984). "Peer Pressure and Risk-Taking Behaviors in Children." *American Journal of Public Health* 74:580–584.

Mansfield, C.; Conroy, M. E.; Emans, J.; and Woods, E. (1993). "A Pilot Study of AIDS Education and Counseling of High-Risk Adolescents in an Office Setting." *Journal of Adolescent Health* 14:115–119.

Marshall, W.; A. (1975). "Growth and Sexual Maturation in Normal Puberty." *Clinics in Endocrinology and Metabolism* 4:3–25.

Masters, W.; Johnson, V.; and Kolodny, R. (1992). *Human Sexuality,* 4th edition. New York: HarperCollins.

McCord, M.; Kelin, J.; Foy, J.; and Fothergill, K. (1993). "School-Based Clinic Use and School Performance." *Journal of Adolescent Health* 14:91–98.

Money, J. (1980). *Love and Love Sickness.* Baltimore: Johns Hopkins University Press.

Nation's Health. (1994). "Court Strikes Down NYC School Condom Distribution Program." Washington, DC: American Public Health Association.

Piaget, J. (1930). *The Child's Conception of Physical Causality.* London: Kegan Paul.

Pittman, K.; Wilson, P.; Adams-Taylor, S.; and Randolph, S. (1992). "Making Sexuality Education and Prevention Programs Relevant for African-American Youth." *Journal of School Health* 62:339–342.

Polit, D. (1989). "Effects of a Comprehensive Program for Teenage Parents: Five Years After Project Redirection." *Family Planning Perspectives* 21:164–169.

Rickert, V.; Gottlieb, A.; and Jay, S. M. (1990). "A Comparison of Three Clinic-Based AIDS Education Programs on Female Adolescents' Knowledge, Attitudes, and Behavior." *Journal of Adolescent Health Care* 11:298–302.

Roth, B. (1993). "The School Nurse as Adolescent Health Educator." *Journal of School Nursing* (December Supplement):1–15.

Saarni, C. (1989). "Children's Understanding of Strategic Control of Emotional Expression in Social Transactions." In *Children's Understanding of Emotion,* ed. C. Saarni and P. Harris. Cambridge, Eng.: Cambridge University Press.

SIECUS Fact Sheet. (1992). "Comprehensive Sexuality Education." *SIECUS Report* (August–September).

SIECUS Fact Sheet. (1993). "Comprehensive Sexuality Education: Guidelines for Comprehensive Sexuality Education, Kindergarten–12th Grade." *SIECUS Report* (April–May).

Sonenstein, F.; Pleck, J.; and Kul, L. (1991). "Levels of Sexual Activity Among Adolescent Males in the United States." *Family Planning Perspectives* 23:162–167.

Thomas, H.; Mitchell, A.; Devlin, C.; Goldsmith, C.; Singer, J.; and Waters, D. (1992). "Small-Group Sex Education at School." In *Preventing Adolescent Pregnancy,* ed. B. Miller, J. Card, R. Paikoff, and J. Peterson. Newbury Park, CA: Sage Publications.

Ward, J., and Taylor, J. (1992). "Sexuality Education for Immigrant and Minority Students." In *Sexuality and the Curriculum: The Politics and Practices of Sexuality Education*, ed. J. Sears. New York: Teachers College Press.

Werner, H. (1948). *Comparative Psychology of Mental Development.* New York: Science Editions.

Zabin, L., and Hayward, S. (1993). "Adolescent Sexual Behavior and Childbearing." In *Developmental Clinical Psychology and Psychiatry*, ed. A. E. Kazdin. Newbury Park, CA: Sage Publications.

Zabin, L.; Hirsh, M.; Smith, E.; Streett, R.; and Hardy, J. (1986). "Evaluation of a Pregnancy Prevention Program for Urban Teenagers." *Family Planning Perspectives* 18:119–126.

Elias J. Duryea

SEXUALITY IN THE LIFE CYCLE

Sexuality is an integral part of being human, and its expression undergoes particular developmental changes. With regard to sexual development, there are some biological milestones that are typical for all humans, but to understand sexuality across the lifespan requires consideration of the sociocultural context. The environment surrounding the development and expression of sexuality includes one's larger culture as well as one's parents and family, a context particularly important when considering sexuality during childhood.

Sexual Development

There are three primary theoretical approaches to the explanation of sexual development: evolutionary, psychoanalytic, and learning. These approaches must be presented before considering the life cycle.

Evolutionary approaches. To an evolutionary theorist the development of sexuality consists of the unfolding of developmental mechanisms contained in the genetic makeup of each member of the species. That is, each person is born with the capacity to function sexually (e.g., by possessing a full set of reproductive organs) or contains the genetic information necessary for development of sexual capabilities at a later stage (e.g., at puberty the body begins producing greater levels of sex hormones, marking the beginning of fertility).

These capacities and developmental mechanisms, which comprise sexuality, are said to be the result of natural selection operating over millions of years. It is theorized that among humans' earliest ancestors those individuals who possessed particular characteristics were probably more reproductively successful than were their counterparts who did not possess these traits. If these characteristics led to more offspring or greater rates of survival of offspring and were at least partially heritable, then a greater proportion of each subsequent generation would possess these qualities. Over thousands of generations, these traits eventually would become typical for the species, and every member would possess them (Daly and Wilson 1983). Through this process of evolution by natural selection, humans have come to possess the sexual characteristics considered typical.

One can see how natural selection has shaped the development of bodily organs and physiological processes, but how do evolutionary theorists explain psychological aspects of human sexuality, such as attraction to particular potential mates (Buss 1994), sexual fantasy (Symons 1979), and sexual jealousy (Wiederman and Allgeier 1993)? The human brain is simply a highly evolved organ and, like all organs, was shaped through the process of natural selection. The ways in which individuals process sexual information from the environment, make judgments, exert sexual preferences, and learn from those around them are all capacities selected for in evolutionary history (Buss 1994). For example, from an evolutionary standpoint, it is no coincidence that around the world some physical characteristics (such as smooth, clear skin and good muscle tone) are considered more sexually attractive than others (wrinkled or blemished skin, rotted teeth), because earliest humans who preferred to mate with individuals who possessed those characteristics, indicative of good health, probably had more offspring who survived (Symons 1979). If the offspring of those parents were more likely to exhibit the same preferences when they chose mates, eventually all members of the species would possess the same basic set of preferences for certain physical qualities in mates (Buss 1994).

Evolutionary theorists note that the very ability to learn from family and larger culture are capacities of the human brain that were selected for through millions of years of evolution (Barkow, Cosmides, and Tooby 1992). Therefore, evolutionary approaches to understanding sexuality do not necessarily include notions of sexual behaviors being "hard-wired" in brains, with all humans then acting the same (like preprogrammed robots). It is a behavioral flexibility, made possible by evolution of the brain, which has allowed the human species to survive.

Psychoanalytic approaches. Sigmund Freud, the creator of psychoanalytic theory, transformed Western thought about sexuality, particularly with regard to childhood. At the heart of the psychoanalytic explanation of sexual development is the concept of life instinct, the drive to enhance and preserve the individual and the species. Freud theorized that the life instinct is accompanied by an intrapsychic energy source, libido, pushing for release or expression. Freud further posited that a person's drive for bonding and sex can be repressed by the individual or society, yet the libido remains. The ways in which the libido is subsequently channeled determine whether that energy will be used productively or result in psychological problems (Freud [1905] 1963).

Freud theorized that humans possess libido from birth and that each person progresses through a series of psychosexual developmental stages in which libido is channeled into different erogenous zones (Hall 1979). In the first year of life, the mouth is the primary erogenous zone, followed in the second or third year by the anal stage. By age four or five years, the youngster primarily experiences the genitals as the center of eroticism. Each stage of psychosexual development poses particular conflicts that must be resolved for healthy development. If the conflicts of a given stage are not resolved, the individual may experience fixation, in which some libido remains invested in that unresolved phase of development. Fixation is said to be reflected in adult behavior, so that smokers, for example, may be seen as partially fixated at the oral stage of psychosexual development.

Of particular importance in the psychoanalytic approach are the Oedipus and Electra complexes experienced by young boys and young girls, respectively. Freud maintained that youngsters go through a period of sexual attraction toward, and conflict with, their parents. Both boys and girls initially identify with their mothers; however, boys must somehow shift their identification to their fathers. During the Oedipal stage, at about ages three to five, the boy is said to develop sexual desire for his mother and wishes to usurp his father's spousal role. At the same time, the boy fears retaliation from his father, particularly in the form of castration, as the genitals are the erotic center for the child of this age. To resolve this castration fear the boy learns to repress his sexual feelings for his mother and begins to identify with his father. Freud believed that boys generally resolve the Oedipus complex by about age six.

The corresponding developmental conflict for girls, the Electra complex, involves a young girl's sexual desire for her father. Freud believed that penis envy drove the dynamics of the Electra complex. Realizing that she does not have a penis, the young girl assumes that she was castrated and blames her mother for the loss. In so doing, the girl shifts her identification to her father, but eventually learns that she cannot usurp her mother's role as her father's partner and thereby completely win her father's affections. The girl then returns to identifying with her mother and subsequently develops a feminine identity.

The psychoanalytic account of psychosexual development, particularly as elaborated by Freud, is masculine in focus, a bias that probably resulted from the culture and era in which Freud lived and wrote. Regardless of whether one agrees with the psychoanalytic explanation, the concepts proposed by Freud, and later elaborated by others, have deeply influenced thinking about childhood sexuality. A large part of this influence was simply through the recognition that eroticism is present well before adulthood.

Learning approaches. The assumption of learning theorists is that most human behavior, including sexual behavior, is strongly influenced by learning processes that can occur at a number of levels. In classical conditioning, certain responses become associated with (conditioned to) particular stimuli if the stimuli are presented with other cues that already elicit a response in the individual. How does this process of conditioning explain the acquistion of some sexual behaviors? In a classic experiment (Rachman 1966), three male students were shown a series of slides where the image alternated between nude women and black boots. After repeated pairings of the nudes and the boots, the students responded with sexual arousal when they were shown the boots alone. In this way it is theorized that humans learn to find particular cues or behaviors sexually stimulating.

In addition to learning through the simple association of one stimulus with another, humans also learn sexual behaviors as a function of the response they elicit. Through the process called operant conditioning, individuals acquire or reject particular behaviors based on whether they are rewarded, ignored, or punished. For example, the pleasurable sensations that result when a young boy plays with his penis are likely to result in an increase in the frequency of that behavior. However, if the boy is severely punished for masturbation, he may be more likely to associate those behaviors with negative consequences and may be less likely to masturbate in the future.

The focus of classical and operant conditioning is the individual, yet much learning about sexuality occurs in a social context. Social learning theorists posit that humans learn much sex-related behavior and attitudes without experiencing the behavior firsthand and without receiving direct reward or punishment (Bandura 1977). Instead, individuals notice other people and events in their environment and learn behaviors based on the consequences they observe. For example, if television programs contain depictions of extramarital sex and if most of these portrayals are highly positive (showing extramarital sex as enjoyable, exciting, etc.), social learning theorists would predict that viewers would be more likely to engage in extramarital sex themselves.

When considered in a larger context, most sexual behavior consists of complex combinations of feelings, thoughts, actions, setting, and usually another person. Those positing a social scripting perspective emphasize that such a complex sequence cannot result from classical or operant conditioning alone, but rather is learned through the process of growing up in a culture (socialization) (Gagnon and Simon 1973). The guidelines one uses to organize feelings, thoughts, and actions around any given area of one's life can be thought of as scripts. These scripts, which to some extent humans share as a culture and which individuals carry around in their heads, define what are appropriate feelings and behaviors with regard to each facet of sexuality (Reiss 1986). The cultural aspect of these scripts is demonstrated by the fact that although humans around the world are born with the same capacities for sexual pleasure, there is marked cultural variation as to the actual experience of sexual pleasure (Allgeier and Allgeier 1991). For example, among the So tribe of Uganda, genital touching is taboo, women do not enjoy sex but endure it to produce children, and orgasms are assumed to occur only in males (Laughlin and Allgeier 1979).

The evolutionary, psychoanalytic, and learning approaches are each useful for explaining some facets or levels of sexuality. None is "right" or "wrong," but rather the approaches vary in their explanatory usefulness depending on the portion of human sexuality one wishes to consider. Some combination of the perspectives, therefore, is probably the most useful for trying to understand the complex development of sexuality in the life cycle.

The Life Cycle

There are four approximate life stages that need to be considered in any discussion of sexuality in the life cycle. These stages are early childhood, adolescence, early and middle adulthood, and later adulthood. To understand sexual development and expression at each of these stages, it is important to study the familial and cultural influences as they change throughout the life cycle.

Early childhood. Understanding of childhood sexuality is severely limited due to cultural taboos about studying the topic. In Western cultures at least, childhood is seen as a period of innocence, and there is often strong opposition to the idea of researchers asking children questions about sexuality. This view of childhood sexuality as forbidden is also frequently expressed by parents or caretakers who actively prohibit sexual exploration and expression by children. One reason for adults' discomfort with expressions of sensuality/sexuality by children may be that the activities are being judged by adult standards. By the time individuals become adults, they have learned to differentiate sexual feelings from other sensations. Young children, however, do not appear to make such distinctions.

From before birth, male babies are capable of penile erection, and it is common during the first twenty-four hours after birth for female infants to experience clitoral erection and vaginal lubrication (Masters, Johnson, and Kolodny 1986). During the first year of life these erotic responses appear to be reflexive and may occur after incidental touching of the genitals or during nursing. Infants appear to enjoy playing with their genitals (Bakwin 1974), but it does not appear that genital stimulation is goal-directed at this stage of life. However, one report described observations of infants of less than one year of age masturbating (Kinsey et al. 1953). For infants and very young children, touching or rubbing their genital area is simply a pleasurable experience of bodily sensations, much like sucking their fingers. By age five, orgasm can be achieved through masturbation (Martinson 1981).

Although young children do not seem to differentiate their erotic sensations from other sensual experiences, parents in Western cultures often do. Most parents make a joyful fuss when their infant discovers his or her toes and will play along with the child around the new discovery. Those same parents are usually less thrilled when their son starts pulling on his penis or their daughter starts pulling on her labia. The typical parental reaction might be to ignore this discovery or actively move the child's hands away from the genitals. One can speculate as to what message these early parental responses send to the child regarding sexuality. Avoidance of childhood genital stimulation is not universal, and self-exploration and self-stimulation are accepted or promoted in some cultures. Mothers in Trinidad, for example, masturbate their babies to calm them and help them fall asleep (Allgeier and Allgeier 1991).

In the early and middle childhood years curiosity about sexual organs, both one's own and others', is prominent (Martinson 1981). Most children engage in some kinds of sexuality-related play, which serve as means for exploring sexuality (Kinsey, Pomeroy, and Martin 1948). Such sex play often involves members of the child's own gender, but these common experiences do not lead to a homosexual orientation (Hite 1982; Van Wyk and Geist 1984). What appears to have a greater impact on sexuality development is the reaction to sex play from adults in the child's life. Severe punishment or ridicule is likely to make a childhood experience of sexual exploration a traumatizing event and can lead to difficulties when the child reaches adolescence.

Adolescence. Puberty is a period lasting from one and one-half years to six years during which sexual maturation, or the ability to reproduce sexually, takes place. Although there is a wide band of variation, girls typically have their first menstrual period, menarche, at age twelve or thirteen (Masters, Johnson, and Kolodny 1986). By age thirteen most boys have experienced sperarche, the beginning of sperm emission (Hirsch et al. 1985). This is also a period during which boys begin to have nocturnal emissions ("wet dreams"). Up to this point in the life cycle, both boys and girls have relatively the same levels of circulating sex hormones. However, during puberty, testosterone secretion in boys increases to ten to twenty times the previous level, and circulating estrogen levels in girls increases eight- to tenfold (Allgeier and Allgeier 1991). This dramatic rise in hormone production accounts for many of the marked characteristics of adolescence such as acne, mood swings, a noticeable growth spurt, and increased sexual interest in others.

Whereas earlier experiences of sexuality were primarily self-focused, interest in potential partners becomes evident during adolescence. As continued from childhood, the majority of adolescents masturbate; however, there is now the frequent invasion of sexual fantasies. These mental rehearsals are probably an important developmental step in the adolescent's start toward relating sexually to others. During adolescence the first sexual interactions are likely to occur as the young individual begins developing a repertoire of sexual behaviors (DeLamater and MacCorquodale 1979). These sexual interactions during adolescence are likely to follow the scripts provided by the culture. In the United States, for example, first sexual contact with adolescent peers typically involves kissing and does not include genital stimulation. Next in the sequence, whether talking about a single sexual episode or the developmental experiences of the individual, is usually petting or fondling of breasts and/or genitals through clothing. In this stepwise fashion most adolescents expand their sexual repetoire by building on earlier experiences.

By age seventeen or eighteen, most young people in the United States have experienced sexual intercourse. In this culture at least, the first experience of coitus most often occurs during the summer season (Rodgers, Harris, and Vickers 1992). Although premarital intercourse in America appears to be more common and acceptable than it was in the 1940s and 1950s (Allgeier and Allgeier 1991), most adolescent sexuality still occurs in the context of the traditional social script. That is, most Americans describe their first sexual partner as someone toward whom they felt strong affection or love. Adolescents typically are involved in only one sexual relationship at a time, although such relationships may be relatively short-lived. These affectionate/sexual interactions with peers during adolescence are necessary steps toward learning how to achieve relationship with a primary partner as one moves into adulthood.

Early and middle adulthood. In early adulthood, the primary concern is often the negotiation of lasting sexual relationships. Since more than 90 percent of Americans marry at least once, dating and cohabitation are commonly means to securing a spouse. The sexual activities and the frequencies of sexual behaviors vary widely, both among individuals and during phases of adulthood as people's priorities and relationship status change. Although the large majority of Americans marry at some point, at any given time a significant portion of the population is single (Martin and Bumpass 1989), and the sexual experiences of married, divorced, and never-married individuals sometimes vary widely (Smith 1991). National statistics indicate that American adults participate in sexual intercourse about once or twice a week on average (Seidman and Rieder 1994), yet using such averages masks the tremendous variability among individuals. For example, among a nationally representative sample of American men aged twenty to thirty-nine (Billy et al. 1993), the median number of lifetime sex partners for married men was 5.3, compared with a median of 14.7 partners for divorced men. Although it is difficult to talk about what is "typical" sexuality during adulthood, some milestones are common.

Folklore says that if a couple, when they first become sexually involved, put a penny in a jar each time they have sex, and then, after a year of putting pennies in, begin to take a penny out each time they have sex, they will never get to the bottom of the jar. Although not as extreme as this illustration, research has shown that the frequency with which most couples have sex gradually decreases as the newness of the relationship wears off and other pursuits and responsibilities creep in (Blumstein and Schwartz 1983). There is still a great deal of variability among couples, however, when it comes to the frequency of sex (Greenblat 1983), and such frequency is liable to fluctuate due to life changes of each of the individuals as well as the couple. One such life change is the arrival of children, immediately after which the frequency of sexual intimacy often sharply declines (James 1981).

In the United States, there is a commonly held belief about men and women reaching their "sexual peaks" at widely different times of life, but this generalization is not true. As the myth goes, men reach their peak at about age eighteen, whereas women reach theirs fifteen to twenty-five years later. This belief is based on data collected in the 1940s by Alfred Kinsey and his colleagues (Kinsey et al. 1953; Kinsey, Pomeroy, and Martin 1948), who interviewed thousands of American men and women and computed the average number of "sexual outlets" experienced by each in a typical week. The average number of outlets was highest among young men and women in their thirties to forties, and hence the sexual peak myth was born. However, it is likely that this gender difference in Kinsey's data was a function of the era and culture in which he worked. From what can now be told, American women in the 1940s simply took about fifteen years longer than men to experience their sexuality fully, due to strong societal prohibitions; the prevailing value at the time was that sexual enjoyment was not proper for women. The myth of gender differences in sexual peaks does not correspond with more recent data or with what is known about cultures other than that in the United States. This is not to say that there are not physiological changes in adulthood that are related to sexuality.

One such change is the gradual cessation of ovulation and menstruation in women, which is referred to as the perimenopausal period. This seven-year transitional time culminates in menopause (the woman's last menstrual period), which usually occurs between ages forty-eight and fifty-two (Masters, Johnson, and Kolodny 1986). During this stage of a woman's life, estrogen secretion declines, which may cause such physical symptoms as hot flashes and fatigue. Also, decreased estrogen results in thinning of the vaginal walls and decreased vaginal lubrication. If these symptoms go untreated, sexual intercourse may become painful. Although there is still some disagreement about the effect of menopause on sexuality, the latest research does not support the notion that sexual interest necessarily declines during this period of a woman's life; for some women sexual interest appears to increase (Cutler, Garcia, and McCoy 1987). Men's androgen secretion declines slightly throughout middle and later adulthood, yet for the typical male there is no developmental stage analogous to the perimenopausal period experienced by women.

Later adulthood. Just as relatively little is known about childhood sexuality because of the cultural taboos about the topic, so sexuality during old age has not been extensively explored by researchers. The idea that elderly men and women engage in sexual activity is unacceptable to some people. However, surveys of older adults demonstrate that the large majority of those who have a spouse continue to engage in intercourse, and a substantial proportion of those who do not have a partner masturbate (Brecher 1984). It appears that the frequency of sexual expression gradually declines in later life (Botwinick 1978), but there is notable variation among elderly individuals in the extent to which sexuality remains a part of life (Brecher 1984; Weizman and Hart 1987). The extent to which individuals remain sexually active in their senior years appears to depend on some combination of personal preference, health status, availability of a partner, living arrangements, and cultural expectations (Winn and Newton 1982). Many adults in later life experience loss of their mate, health problems that make sexual activity less appealing or possible, and/or institutionalization in a care facility (where sexual expression is usually discouraged).

Apart from illness, certain physiological changes are typical during later adulthood. For women, the vagina, uterus, and cervix all shrink, and vaginal lubrication is at lower levels than in earlier stages of life (Masters, Johnson, and Kolodny 1986). Vaginal contractions during orgasm are also less intense and last for shorter periods of time. Among men, androgen secretion decreases only slightly until the seventh or eighth decades of life, and until then sperm production remains relatively unchanged as well (Nieschlag 1986). Sexual functioning, however, is markedly different from youth, as the elderly male needs more time and more stimulation to attain an erection, erections are not as firm, and ejaculation is not as forceful (Allgeier and Allgeier 1991). The refractory period (the length of time after ejaculation before another erection is physiologically possible) is longer during later adulthood and may be twelve to twenty-four hours after age sixty (Masters, Johnson, and Kolodny 1986). These physiological changes may explain why there is often less of an emphasis on sexual intercourse as an expression of sexuality during this stage of life. After age eighty, the three most common forms of sexual activity are, in order of frequency, caressing without intercourse, masturbation, and sexual intercourse (Bretschneider and McCoy 1988).

Conclusion

Sexuality is a vital part of being human and there are specific developmental stages that all people share. However, the experience of sexuality varies greatly from person to person and from culture to culture. Any review of this topic can only cover some experiences and statistics that are "typical" for members of a particular culture. Therefore, the extent to which a discussion of sexuality across the life cycle describes any particular individual is probably very limited. It is also possible that different cultures will ascribe entirely different meanings to each stage. This variability among individuals and cultures in the experience of sexuality makes the topic a complex and difficult one to study. On the other hand, the variability allows for a sense of adventure for individuals as they discover their own sexuality.

(*See also:* Adolescent Sexuality; Elders; Extramarital Sex; Marital Sex; Menopause; Middle Age; Personality Development; Sexuality; Sexuality Education; Sexual Orientation; Sexual Problems; Widowhood)

BIBLIOGRAPHY

Allgeier, E. R., and Allgeier, A. R. (1991). *Sexual Interactions*, 3rd edition. Lexington, MA: D. C. Heath.

Bakwin, H. (1974). "Erotic Feelings in Infants and Young Children." *Medical Aspects of Human Sexuality* 8:200–215.

Bandura, A. (1977). *Social Learning Theory*. Englewood Cliffs, NJ: Prentice Hall.

Barkow, J.; Cosmides, L.; and Tooby, J., eds. (1992). *The Adapted Mind: Evolutionary Psychology and the Generation of Culture*. New York: Oxford University Press.

Billy, J. O. G.; Tanfer, K.; Grady, W. R.; and Klepinger, D. H. (1993). "The Sexual Behavior of Men in the United States." *Family Planning Perspectives* 25:52–60.

Blumstein, P. W., and Schwartz, P. (1983). *American Couples*. New York: William Morrow.

Botwinick, J. (1978). "Sexuality and Sexual Relations." In *Aging and Behavior*, ed. J. Botwinick. New York: Springer-Verlag.

Brecher, E. M. (1984). *Love, Sex, and Aging*. Boston: Little, Brown.

Bretschneider, J. G., and McCoy, N. L. (1988). "Sexual Interest and Behavior in 80- to 102-Year Olds." *Archives of Sexual Behavior* 17:109–129.

Buss, D. M. (1994). *The Evolution of Desire: Strategies of Human Mating*. New York: Basic Books.

Cutler, W. B.; Garcia, C. R.; and McCoy, N. L. (1987). "Perimenopausal Sexuality." *Archives of Sexual Behavior* 16:225–234.

Daly, M., and Wilson, M. (1983). *Evolution and Behavior*, 2nd edition. Boston: Willard Grant Press.

DeLamater, J. D., and MacCorquodale, P. (1979). *Premarital Sexuality: Attitudes, Relationships, Behavior*. Madison: University of Wisconsin Press.

Freud, S. ([1905] 1963). *Three Essays on the Theory of Sexuality*, ed. and tr. U. Strachey. New York: Basic Books.

Gagnon, J. H., and Simon, W. (1973). *Sexual Conduct: The Social Sources of Human Sexuality*. Chicago: Aldine.

Greenblat, C. S. (1983). "The Salience of Sexuality in the Early Years of Marriage." *Journal of Marriage and the Family* 45:289–299.

Hall, C. S. (1979). *A Primer of Freudian Psychology*. New York: New American Library.

Hirsch, M.; Zunenfield, B.; Modan, M.; Ovadia, J.; and Shemesh, J. (1985). "Spermarche: The Age of Onset of Sperm Emission." *Journal of Adolescent Health Care* 6:35–39.

Hite, S. (1982). *The Hite Report on Male Sexuality*. New York: Ballantine.

James, W. H. (1981). "The Honeymoon Effect on Marital Coitus." *The Journal of Sex Research* 17:114–123.

Kinsey, A. C.; Pomeroy, W.; and Martin, C. (1948). *Sexual Behavior in the Human Male*. Philadelphia: Saunders.

Kinsey, A. C.; Pomeroy, W.; Martin, C.; and Gebhard, P. (1953). *Sexual Behavior in the Human Female*. Philadelphia: Saunders.

Laughlin, C. D., and Allgeier, E. R. (1979). *Ethnography of the So of Northeastern Uganda*. New Haven, CT: Human Relations Area Files.

Martin, T. C., and Bumpass, L. L. (1989). "Recent Trends in Marital Disruption." *Demography* 26:37–51.

Martinson, F. M. (1981). "Eroticism in Infancy and Childhood." In *Children and Sex: New Findings, New Perspectives*, ed. L. L. Constantine and F. M. Martinson. Boston: Little, Brown.

Masters, W. H.; Johnson, V. E.; and Kolodny, R. C. (1986). *Masters and Johnson on Sex and Human Loving*. Boston: Little, Brown.

Nieschlag, E. (1986). "Testicular Function in Senescence." In *Male Reproductive Dysfunction*, ed. R. J. Stanten and R. S. Swerdloff. New York: Marcel Dekker.

Rachman, S. (1966). "Sexual Fetishism: An Experimental Analogue." *Psychological Record* 16:293–295.

Reiss, I. L. (1986). *Journey into Sexuality: An Exploratory Voyage*. Englewood Cliffs, NJ: Prentice Hall.

Rodgers, J. L.; Harris, D. F.; and Vickers, K. B. (1992). "Seasonality of Coitus in the United States." *Social Biology* 39:1–14.

Seidman, S. N., and Rieder, R. O. (1994). "A Review of Sexual Behavior in the United States." *American Journal of Psychiatry* 151:330–341.

Smith, T. W. (1991). "Adult Sexual Behavior in 1989: Number of Partners, Frequency of Intercourse, and Risk of AIDS." *Family Planning Perspectives* 23:102–107.

Symons, D. (1979). *Evolution of Human Sexuality.* New York: Oxford University Press.

Van Wyk, P. H., and Geist, C. S. (1984). "Psychosocial Development of Heterosexual, Bisexual, and Homosexual Behavior." *Archives of Sexual Behavior* 13:505–544.

Weizman, R., and Hart, J. (1987). "Sexual Behavior in Healthy Married Elderly Men." *Archives of Sexual Behavior* 16:39–44.

Wiederman, M. W., and Allgeier, E. R. (1993). "Gender Differences in Sexual Jealousy: Adaptionist or Social Learning Explanation?" *Ethology and Sociobiology* 14:115–140.

Winn, R. L., and Newton, N. (1982). "Sexuality in Aging: A Study of 106 Cultures." *Archives of Sexual Behavior* 11:283–298.

Michael W. Wiederman

SEXUALLY TRANSMITTED DISEASES

Sexually transmitted diseases (STDs), once known as venereal diseases, have menaced humankind since the dawn of recorded history. There are references to STDs in Egyptian papyri dating to 1550 B.C., and according to biblical scholars, there are similar references in the Old Testament (Holmes et al. 1990). STDs operate at the intersection of individual human behaviors, collective sociodemographic trends, and specific disease pathogens. They are infectious diseases caused by both bacteria and viruses. In society and within the lives of families and individuals, STDs continue to inflict considerable suffering, trauma, serious medical conditions, and medical expense. They still can stigmatize the infectee; they also can cause death.

The three most common and threatening sequelae (i.e., aftereffects) of STDs to infected individuals are impaired fertility for women, adverse pregnancy outcomes, and increased susceptibility to the human immunodeficiency virus (HIV), the virus that causes acquired immunodeficiency syndrome (AIDS). Since World War II, advances in epidemiology, disease surveillance, behavioral and social sciences, demography, and medical science have greatly contributed to a better understanding of how STDs occur, are sustained, and shift into new populations in society; how they interact with each other; how several STDs can be successfully treated and cured (although many still cannot); and how they and their most common sequelae can often be prevented. Despite these modern advances, STDs continue to menace society, families, and individuals.

Approximately 12 million infections from STDs occur annually in the United States; two-thirds occur among people less than twenty-five years of age (Noegel et al. 1993). Women and the poor suffer disproportionately, and it is estimated that one of every four Americans will have an STD in his or her lifetime. STDs are most commonly transmitted either from males to their female sex partners or from females to their male sex partners. Male to male transmission occurs often with some STDs, while female to female transmission occurs infrequently with nearly all STDs. Although there are more than thirty known pathogens that are classified as causing STDs in humans, only the most important will be addressed here.

Bacterial STDs

Though readily curable, these STDs account for considerable morbidity in the United States, ranking among the most frequently reported communicable diseases. Chlamydia and gonorrhea pose threats to the reproductive health of women and are readily transmitted between sex partners. These and many other bacterial STDs influence adverse pregnancy outcomes, either during fetal development or during birth. No effective vaccines exist for these diseases.

Chlamydia. This disease is thought to be the most common of all STDs in the United States (see Table 1). Between 20 percent and 40 percent of sexually active women have been exposed; they have chlamydial antibodies. Since the 1970s, the pathogenesis of chlamydia and its threats to reproductive health have become better understood; it has emerged as an STD with major consequences. It has been estimated that more than $2 billion is spent each year in the United States on treatment of chlamydia and its complications (Noegel et al. 1993). Reported cases of chlamydia in the United States number more than 1 million per year; an estimated 4 million annual cases are thought to occur (Centers for Disease Control and Prevention 1994). The most common clinical manifestations of chlamydial infections in women are salpingitis and mucopurulent cervicitis, with the endocervix being the most common site of infection. Chlamydia is a particularly insidious STD because women with active infections usually have minimal or no symptoms. Most women are unlikely to be treated unless they undergo a screening test (a rapid, inexpensive diagnostic test is unfortunately still not available) that specifically cultures the pathogen or their male sex partner develops a symptomatic infection and the

Table 1 Estimated Incidence and Prevalence of Selected STDs in the United States

STD	*Incidence*	*Prevalence*
Gonorrhea (GC)	1,100,000	–
Syphilis	120,000	–
Congenital syphilis	3,500	–
Chlamydia (CT)	4,000,000	–
Human papillomavirus	500,000–1,000,000	≥24,000,000
Genital herpes	200,000–500,000	≥31,000,000
Trichomoniasis	3,000,000	–
Hepatitis B	100,000–200,000	–
Urethritis (non-GC, non-CT)	1,200,000	–
Mucopurulent cervicitis (non-GC, non-CT)	1,000,000	–
Reported AIDS cases*	45,472	140,000–168,000†
HIV infection	–	1,000,000

* Based on cases reported through September 1992.

† Number of persons diagnosed with AIDS who were still alive at some time during 1992.

SOURCE Centers for Disease Control and Prevention 1994.

woman is informed. Seven-day oral antibiotic regimens of either doxycycline or azithromycin are effective treatment of chlamydia in men and woman. A single-dose azithromycin regimen is equally effective and, although more expensive, is now available.

Gonorrhea. This disease is the second most commonly reported STD in the United States; the number of cases reported per year is about 600,000 (c. 200 cases per 100,000 U.S. population for both men and women; c. 1.1 million cases are thought to occur annually). The highest age-specific rates are for women ages fifteen to nineteen and for men ages twenty to twenty-four (Centers for Disease Control and Prevention 1993b). For women, gonococcal infection occurs primarily in the cervix, although the pharynx, rectum, and urethra can also be infected. Approximately 40 percent to 60 percent of women with gonorrhea have symptoms, sometimes painful. Gonorrhea, which is less "silent" than chlamydia, can cause a purulent vaginal discharge, dysuria, and frequent urination. Cervical gonococcal infection is usually diagnosed via an endocervical culture. Most infected men have painful symptoms, usually pain and discharge upon urination, that cause them to seek treatment. Several antibiotic regimens (e.g., a single oral dose of cefixime) are safe and effective for most cases (Centers for Disease Control and Prevention 1993a). Ominously, about one-third of all gonococcal isolates now manifest some degree of resistance to this conventional therapy, thus causing reliance on more expensive antibiotics.

Comparison of chlamydia and gonorrhea. About 25 percent to 40 percent of women with gonorrhea also have a concurrent chlamydial infection. Yet the percentage of women with gonorrhea who also have a concurrent chlamydial infection varies dramatically by subpopulation (Holmes et al. 1990). Since 1975, trends in reported U.S. gonorrhea rates have steadily declined. Chlamydia is thought to be more homogeneously distributed in the population, although focused in those who are younger, yet sexually active, whereas gonorrhea disproportionately affects minority populations. In 1992, the ratio of cases reported in African Americans to whites was 40 to 1; in Hispanics to whites, 3 to 1 (Centers for Disease Control and Prevention 1993b). However, these differences should be viewed cautiously. Research analyzing population-based survey data suggests that the real differences may be less striking (Anderson, McCormick, and Fichtner 1994). Case reporting from publicly funded medical facilities tends to be more complete than that from private facilities, and minority populations disproportionately use publicly funded facilities. Despite the existence of statutes in all states requiring the medical reporting of most STDs, inconsistent adherence as well as frequent self-treatment of STDs prevent more accurate estimates of the incidence of STDs in the United States and thereby inhibit a better understanding of their respective epidemiologies.

Pelvic inflammatory disease (PID). PID broadly defines a range of inflammatory conditions, the most common of which are endometritis and salpingitis, that affect the upper reproductive tract of women. Symptoms are often pain with concurrent fever. There are approximately 2.5 million symptomatic outpatient visits to medical facilities for PID annually. Nearly 300,000 women are hospitalized annually, and more than 100,000 associated surgical procedures need to be performed (Centers for Disease Control and Prevention 1994). Most cases of PID are caused, directly or indirectly, by gonococcal and chlamydial infections. PID is frequently episodic, with initial acute episodes being directly caused by untreated or repeat infections of gonorrhea or chlamydia. Subsequent episodes can be caused by nonsexually transmitted pathogens or intrauterine contraceptive devices. Infertility caused by occlusion of the fallopian tubes, chronic pelvic pain, and ectopic pregnancy is the most frequent and serious complication of repeat episodes of PID. Diagnosis of PID is often difficult because there is a wide range of signs and symptoms. Often there are only mild early symptoms, or there may be none at all. Women and health-care providers should be suspicious of symptoms, especially if there is a history of considerable sexual activity. A variety of antibiotic therapies (e.g., cefoxitin plus doxycycline) are available for PID; most require aggressive, extended regimens, usually up to fourteen days, for maximum effectiveness.

Syphilis. This disease has been central to the development of the practice of medicine. Epidemic and a scourge in Europe in the fifteenth century, its symptoms, natural history, and transmission dynamics have fascinated students of medicine for years; its malevolence has caused great personal suffering; and it continues to be a challenge. In the late 1980s, there was a surge in the reported incidence of syphilis in the United States, peaking at about 135,000 cases in 1990. Only about 50,000 of those cases in 1990 represented occurrences of syphilis in primary or secondary stages, when the disease is infectious (i.e., transmissible). In 1992, the number of reported cases of infectious syphilis had declined to approximately 35,000 (Centers for Disease Control and Prevention 1993b).

About one-third of persons sexually exposed to infectious syphilis acquire it. Within twenty-one days, primary, relatively painless lesions (ulcers or chancres) appear. Often these lesions disappear (after ten to ninety days) if the disease is untreated. The disease then reemerges in a secondary stage characterized by more disseminated symptoms, usually malaise, sore throat, and adenopathy (sore lymph glands). During this secondary stage, the classic rash of syphilis appears, often visible on the palms of the hands and soles of the feet. If the disease is still untreated in the secondary stage, a latent period of variable duration is entered by the patient. Subsequently, approximately 15 percent to 40 percent of the untreated patients develop tertiary syphilis, and small numbers of those (c. 5% to 20%) develop serious neurological and/or cardiovascular manifestations that can become life-threatening (Holmes et al. 1990). These late manifestations are now rarely seen in the United States.

The rise of syphilis in women in the early 1990s increased the concern for preventing cases of congenital syphilis. A peak in reported cases (c. 4,400) of congenital syphilis occurred in 1991 (Centers for Disease Control and Prevention 1993b). Untreated pregnant women who are infected with syphilis have a 50 percent chance of transmitting the disease to their newborns. About half of these women deliver a preterm baby or a stillbirth. This is the most serious direct outcome of syphilis.

Syphilis is readily diagnosed by serologic testing; screening tests are inexpensive and routinely performed in a variety of settings. Premarital screening is required by statute in nearly all states, a reminder of the history of the disease. One intramuscular injection of benzathine penicillin is the usual, effective treatment for syphilis during its early stages.

Viral STDs

These diseases are incurable, but during the 1980s, many improved tests were developed to provide better diagnostic tools, thus enabling a clearer understanding of the distribution of these diseases in society. For some of the viral STDs, therapies to minimize symptoms exist. Hepatitis B virus (HBV), which is often but not always sexually transmitted, is the only STD for which an effective vaccine has been developed and is readily available.

Herpes simplex virus (HSV) infection. There are two major types of HSV: HSV-1 and HSV-2. Genital herpes, the clinical condition, is most often caused by HSV-1, which is about four times more common than HSV-2. These viruses are widespread in society; approximately 70 percent of older women have antibodies to one or both HSV types. Several studies have linked HSV, especially the less common HSV-2, with genital cancers in women (Holmes et al. 1990). Of the approximately 150 million people with HSV antibodies, as many as 20 million have several symptomatic recurrences each year. Symptoms are usually in the form of genital lesions or rashes. Transmission usually occurs when sex occurs during periods of asymptomatic viral shedding. Unlike gonorrhea and syphilis, HSV seems to be distributed homogeneously in the sexually active population. Together with syphilis and chancroid, genital herpes forms a group of diseases called "genital ulcer disease" because of the dermatological eruptions they can cause. Patients with symptomatic genital herpes can be treated topically with acylovir to moderate severity and duration of symptoms. Most often, genital herpes is a fairly benign STD; however, it can be of urgent concern during pregnancy when there can be danger of transmission of the infection to the newborn. Neonatal herpes causes frequent morbidity and even mortality, but infants who are delivered by cesarean section avoid risk of transmission, as do infants born to women with no recent symptomatic outbreak.

Human papillomavirus infection (HPV). This disease, most often manifested as genital warts, is the most common viral STD. Although case surveillance of HPV is relatively poor, physicians report seeing increases in numbers of cases. The wart, or condyloma acuminata, that is seen in about 30 percent of all HPV patients is usually a small, pimply tumor, pigmented or nonpigmented, with fingerlike projections. In women with HPV, it is commonly seen in the lower genital tract; in men, it can appear at various sites in the genital region. The presence of HPV in the cervix and vulva is cause for concern. Certain HPV DNA types have been found in more than 90 percent of patients with certain forms of genital tract cancer, and it is therefore thought that the HPV infections caused by these HPV DNA types are precursors of later cancers in women. Although the clinical management of HPV varies greatly, several therapies, including physical agents (e.g., electrocautery) and immunotherapy, are available and widely used.

HIV and other STDs. HIV and AIDS disproportionately affected white homosexual and bisexual men in the early stages of the epidemic (early 1980s). Then the epidemic appeared in subpopulations of injecting drug users, most of whom were of racial or ethnic minorities. Since 1989, the group showing the greatest increase in reported HIV infection has been the group infected through heterosexual transmission, especially in subpopulations in which STDs are most prevalent (Wasserheit 1994). Persons with STDs, especially those infected with genital ulcer disease, appear to be at elevated risk for acquiring HIV from an infected sex partner. A person who is coinfected (HIV and an STD) is also more likely to transmit HIV to a sex partner. Thus, an important strategy for modulating the HIV epidemic is the successful prevention of STDs and the successful treatment of the curable STDs.

Factors Affecting STDs in Society

Increasingly, many STDs (e.g., gonorrhea, syphilis, HIV) have become concentrated among the urban poor and unemployed; among racial or ethnic minorities; and among persons living with fractured families. STDs also appear in neighborhoods and social networks where substance abuse (especially crack and injection drugs) is fueled by the street economies of sex for drugs and shelter; among adolescents who are on the street; and among women who are powerless in their relationships to insist that their sex partners use condoms to protect them from unintended pregnancies and many STDs. These diseases are also concentrated among persons who do not or cannot access medical care; among those who ignore or are ashamed of symptoms; among those uneducated about STDs, their symptoms, and their prevention; among men and women with multiple sex partners; and among newborns unable to protect themselves from STDs from their infected mothers (Heise 1994).

Conclusion

People are becoming sexually active at younger ages; having more sex partners earlier in life; getting married later in life; and, in general, exposing themselves more often to the risk of acquring STDs. Society, by means of better health care and expanded prevention programs, must address STD epidemics on multiple fronts. Despite society's responsibilities, however, individuals must also shoulder responsibilities themselves and be sexually cautious, decrease risks of acquiring STDs, and practice routine medical care to protect their own health and that of their partner and offspring.

(*See also:* Adolescent Sexuality; AIDS; Health and the Family; Sexuality; Sexuality Education)

BIBLIOGRAPHY

Alan Guttmacher Institute. (1994). *Sex and America's Teenagers.* New York: Author.

Anderson, J.; McCormick, L.; and Fichtner, R. (1994). "Factors Associated with Reported STDs: Data from a National Survey." *Sexually Transmitted Diseases* 21:303–308.

Cates, W., and Hinman, A. (1991). "Sexually Transmitted Diseases in the 1990s." *New England Journal of Medicine* 325:1368–1369.

Centers for Disease Control and Prevention. (1993a). "1993 Sexually Transmitted Diseases Treatment Guidelines." *Morbidity and Mortality Weekly Report* 42(RR-14).

Centers for Disease Control and Prevention. (1993b). *Sexually Transmitted Disease Surveillance 1992.* Washington, DC: U.S. Department of Health and Human Services.

Centers for Disease Control and Prevention. (1994). *Annual Report, Division of STD/HIV Prevention.* Washington, DC: U.S. Department of Health and Human Services.

Fichtner, R.; Aral, S.; Blount, J.; Zaidi, A.; Reynolds, G.; and Darrow, W. (1983). "Syphilis in the United States: 1967–1979." *Sexually Transmitted Diseases* 10:77–80.

Germain, A.; Holmes, K. K.; Piot, P.; and Wasserheit, J. N. (1992). *Reproductive Tract Infections.* New York: Plenum.

Heise, L. L. (1994). *Violence Against Women: The Hidden Health Burden.* Washington, DC: World Bank.

Holmes, K. K.; Mardh, P.-A.; Sparling, P. F.; and Wiesner, P. J. (1990). *Sexually Transmitted Diseases*, 2nd edition. New York: McGraw-Hill.

Noegel, R.; Kirby, J.; Schrader, M.; and Wasserheit, J. N. (1993). "Sexually Transmitted Disease Accelerated Prevention Campaigns." *Sexually Transmitted Diseases* 20:118–119.

Schmid, G. (1994). "Recent Developments in Chancroid and Syphilis." *Current Opinion in Infectious Diseases* 7:34–40.

Wasserheit, J. N. (1994). "Effect of Changes in Human Ecology and Behavior on Patterns of Sexually Transmitted Diseases, Including Human Immunodeficiency Virus Infection." *Proceedings of the National Academy of Science of the United States* 91:2430–2435.

Yankauer, A. (1994). "Sexually Transmitted Diseases: A Neglected Public Health Priority." *American Journal of Public Health* 84:1894–1896.

RONALD R. FICHTNER

SEXUAL ORIENTATION

Human sexuality encompasses a wide range of behaviors and practices that are selectively chosen and conditioned by societies. Each society encodes particular categories as acceptable; individuals growing up in different cultures will experience sexuality in different ways. The range of sexual practices and meanings cross-culturally provides insight into American understandings of sexuality and sexual orientation.

Sexual orientation refers to a person's sexual and affectional feelings; people who have sexual and affectional feelings for the other sex are said to be heterosexual, while people with such feelings for their same sex are called gay or lesbian. As used in this entry, the terms "heterosexual" and "homosexual" refer to types of sexual behavior. Although "heterosexual" may also be used to refer to a person whose personal identity is based on a heterosexual orientation, the use of the term "homosexual" to refer to people whose personal identity is based on a homosexual orientation is not appropriate because of its clinical connotations and its historic association with pathology (Herek 1991).

Although sexual orientation is commonly thought to be fixed, in fact a person's sexual and affectional feelings can change over the course of a lifetime. Many individuals have sexual experiences with either sex. Alfred C. Kinsey and his colleagues (1948, 1953) found that 37 percent of men and 13 percent of women had engaged in sex with members of the same sex at some point in their lives. In another study, 71 percent of gays and lesbians were found to have engaged in sex with members of the other sex (Bell and Weinberg 1978).

The variability in sexual behavior and the high percentage of bisexuality among Americans suggests that sexual orientation is not discrete or static, but a fluid and dynamic phenomenon with multiple components (Greene and Herek 1994). Some people engage in homosexual acts without considering themselves to be gay. For instance, individuals in prison may have sex with members of their own sex but still prefer heterosexual contacts outside prison. Others may consider themselves gay or lesbian and never have engaged in homosexual activity, such as some radical feminists of the 1970s and the "social" lesbians of the 1990s, who identify with lesbians but maintain heterosexual relationships. The term "sexual preference" implies a sexuality that is changeable, while "sexual orientation" refers to an enduring attraction to individuals of a particular sex.

The percentage of the American population that is gay or lesbian has been difficult to ascertain. Given the still prevalent negative stereotypes about gays and lesbians, many are reluctant to identify themselves as such even in anonymous surveys. Moreover, the number who self-identify as gay or lesbian is probably different from the number who engage primarily or frequently in homosexual activity. Estimates have ranged from as low as 1 percent to as high as 20 percent, but the actual figure is somewhere in between. A 1989 national poll found that 6.2 percent of national respondents and 10 percent of San Francisco Bay Area respondents identified themselves as lesbian, gay, or bisexual; a 1970 study found that 3 percent to 6.2 percent of American men engaged in homosexual behavior fairly often; and Kinsey's oft-cited studies found that 10 percent of men and 6 percent of women were more or less exclusively homosexual (Herek 1991).

"Origins" of Homosexuality

Despite commonly held stereotypes about lesbians and gay men, there are no distinguishing differences between them and the heterosexual population. Various theories put forth since the late nineteenth century to explain homosexuality have argued that homosexuality is inborn, immoral, or a disease to be cured. During the same period, heterosexuality was considered normal and natural, and no effort was made to understand why or how people become heterosexual other than to assert that people were simply made that way. Because heterosexuality was considered natural and inborn according to these theories, homosexuality could be a deviant expression of sexuality.

Early negative explanations for the "causes" of homosexuality were legitimized by legal sanctions against homosexuality. Most states had sodomy laws that made homosexual acts criminal (twenty-three states still had such laws on their books in 1994). The father of psychoanalysis, Sigmund Freud, was the first to assert that homosexual orientation should not be viewed as a form of pathology. He believed that all humans are innately bisexual, and that they become heterosexual or homosexual as a result of their experiences with parents and others. According to Freud, homosexuality was the result of arrested development of sexual functioning.

Later psychoanalysts rejected Freud's assumption of inherent human bisexuality and developed various theories elaborating the idea of arrested development. Some argued that homosexuality resulted from pathological family relationships during the critical Oedipal period, about four to five years of age. Psychoanalytic theories of homosexuality have had considerable influence in American society, forming, for example, the basis for military rejection or discharge of individuals who declared or were found to have homosexual preferences (Berube 1990). Despite their general acceptance, these theories have never been subjected to rigorous scientific tests. Yet even without substantial evidence connecting homosexuality to mental illness, psychologists and psychiatrists routinely treated homosexual patients as sick, forlorn misfits in need of a cure.

Kinsey's studies of the late 1940s and early 1950s were the first to cast doubt on the idea that homosexuality was associated with social deviance, revealing as it did a significant number of individuals who had engaged in homosexual activity after age sixteen (Kinsey, Pomeroy, and Martin 1948; Kinsey et al. 1953). It was not until Evelyn Hooker's famous study in the 1950s that clear scientific evidence was obtained that refuted the association of homosexuality with mental illness. Hooker gave standard psychological tests to a group of thirty heterosexual and thirty homosexual men. The results were evaluated by experts who were unaware of each subject's sexual orientation. When asked to identify which men were homosexual on the basis of the tests, the experts were unable to classify the men accurately according to their sexual orientation. Hooker concluded from this experiment that homosexuality is not inherently associated with pathology (Hooker 1957).

Numerous studies since that time have supported Hooker's conclusions. Due to this evidence and the efforts of gay and lesbian psychologists and activists, the American Psychiatric Association (APA) in 1973 concurred that homosexuality was not a mental illness and removed it as a diagnostic category. A more restrictive diagnosis of "ego-dystonic homosexuality" (or sexual orientation disorder) was retained to be used for individuals who are unhappy with or are seeking to change their sexual orientation. In 1986, that category was also removed (Bayer 1987). The APA now defines homosexuality as a non-pathological variant of human sexuality. A few religiously-oriented psychologists and psychiatrists continue to regard homosexuality as a disease and to encourage use of conversion therapies for gays and lesbians, but scientific evidence does not support their views or their claims that such therapies are successful.

Development of Sexual Orientation

The relationships and sexual practices that gays, lesbians, and heterosexuals engage in cover a wide range. Their relationships may be monogamous coupling with one partner, or serial monogamy, in which a person moves from one long-term relationship to another after divorce or breakup. Other practices include long-term relationships with occasional outside partners or one-night stands, anonymous sex, sex for hire, multiple partners, and multiple forms of sexual acts. There is no one type of personality that can be equated with either a heterosexual or a homosexual orientation. The variety of experiences within each category has led some scholars to refer to each as homosexualities and heterosexualities (Bell and Weinberg 1978).

Many Americans believe that a person's gender identity is closely related to his or her sex and sexual orientation. A person's sex refers to his or her physiological characteristics—that is, physical possession of male or female genitalia. Gender refers to attributes of masculinity or femininity, that is, patterns of behavior based on social norms and expectations for each sex. A person's gender identity may have little connection to his or her sex or sexual orientation. A man can be masculine and have a homosexual orientation, while a woman may be "butch," acting in a way that is considered to be more properly masculine (aggressive, independent, a tomboy), and be heterosexual. People's misconceptions regarding gender are related to the way American society defines gender and the belief that homosexuality is always connected with gender variance. A person's physiological sex may also be at variance with his or her gender identity. For example, transgender individuals in American society belong to the gender other than the one assigned to them on the basis of their physiological sex. Such individuals frequently seek surgical remedies to bring their bodies into congruence with their gender.

Sexual orientation develops as a result of the interaction of biological, social, and psychological influences. No direct link has been found between biology and sexual orientation, and scientists continue to debate to what extent either nature or nurture conditions sexual orientation. Some argue that sexual orientations are inborn, hard-wired into the genes, and thus not the result of experience or learning. Advocates of this theory point to genetic endowment, prenatal hormonal factors, or brain differentiation as the possible biological mechanisms that steer individual desire or behavior toward either men or women. According to its critics, this point of view ignores the fact that most human brain development occurs after birth and that genes are unspecified potentialities whose effects are manifested only in some environmental contexts (DeCecco and Elia 1993).

Others argue that environmental conditions are more critical, from unconscious mental processes related to early childhood events to bonding experiences with same-sex or other-sex peer groups at the onset of sex drive in adolescence. Still others—social constructionists—argue that it is the meanings that culture attaches to sexuality and gender that shape sexual orientation. According to this view, sexuality is the product of human action, culture, and history, which provide the social circumstances and ideas that foster particular forms of sexuality (*Homosexuality* 1989). If the sexual urge is biologically derived, it is still culture that conditions sexual expression and practice. As cross-cultural data show, what is sexually appealing or proper in one culture, or even in one class or ethnic group, may be quite undesirable or unimagined in another. To say that sexual orientation is socially constructed, however, does not mean it is a voluntary choice. To the extent that sexual identities are embedded in social roles, institutions, and ways of life, they cannot be abolished by an arbitrary act of the will (Greenberg 1988).

Although individuals throughout history and across cultures have engaged in homosexual acts or formed homosexual partnerships, the meanings of those acts are as different as the historical periods and cultures in which they took place. Prior to the nineteenth century, "homosexual" did not exist as a category of persons. That identity resulted from medical discourse that defined homosexual acts as persons and then separated them from a heterosexual population. The gay or lesbian person of the late twentieth century possesses an identity that in its cultural and social dimensions is unique.

No single theory concerning the origin of sexual orientation has solid empirical support. Given the lack of knowledge concerning the development of a heterosexual or homosexual orientation, most social and behavioral scientists share the view that sexuality is not preordained but the result of complex processes (Money 1987). Understanding sexual orientation requires an analysis of a person's self-identity, the cultural influences on sexual and gender behavior, along with biological factors (DeCecco and Elia 1993).

Formation of Sexual Identity

Although sexuality can be fluid and changing, Americans tend to form stable sexual identities. Americans believe that sexual orientation is a core aspect of a person's identity. Any possibility of change in that orientation would represent a serious threat to most people's experience of social reality and the way they view themselves (Hart and Richardson 1981), particularly because social interactions support and encourage maintenance of a particular identity.

Sexual orientation may be formed rather early and is likely established by adolescence, before sexual activity begins. It is usually preceded by a subjective awareness of attraction to one sex or the other. In the case of homosexual orientation, the actual point at which a person will become sexually active with members of his or her own sex may be delayed for years because of the social stigma and legal and religious sanctions against homosexuality in the United States. In fact, social conditioning toward heterosexuality may actively prevent youths and adults from exploring or recognizing their attractions to or feelings for the same sex. Individuals who are heterosexual, the dominant sexual orientation in American society, tend not to question their sexual orientation and may consider it quite fixed and natural (Greene and Herek 1994).

Adolescents who are attracted to members of their own sex find themselves in a difficult situation. Their feelings seem to contradict all social norms and cues they have learned about sexuality, causing them to feel confused and anxious about their attraction. The pressure to become heterosexual and the belief that heterosexuality is superior and more natural may cause many gay or lesbian youths to deny their feelings and engage in heterosexual behavior despite the fact that they do not find it satisfactory or emotionally fulfilling. Disapproval expressed by teachers, peers, and counselors toward homosexuality has resulted in a high suicide rate for gay and lesbian teens who feel they are alone and despised and have no hope for the future (*Report* 1989). For others, it is the beginning of coming to terms with a sexuality they were taught to despise.

Once a person begins to realize that she or he is a lesbian or a gay man, she or he begins to construct a sense of self, or identity, that is congruent with sexual experience and interest. Gays and lesbians refer to this process as "coming out," that is, accepting that they are lesbian or gay and feeling comfortable enough to begin to disclose their orientation to their friends and relatives. This process varies according to an individual's socialization, ethnicity, and class.

Because gays and lesbians have learned negative stereotypes and attitudes toward homosexuality as they were growing up, and have seen negative portrayals of gays and lesbians in the media, the recognition that they are lesbian or gay can be frightening and distressing. Many are reluctant to take on an identity they have been taught to despise, and they may continue to conceal their sexual orientation in many situations. This process of concealment is referred to as being "closeted" because one's sexual orientation is hidden from view.

Because gay people are not readily identifiable, they are often assumed to be or may even "pass" as heterosexual. Passing is a tool used by minority groups to avoid or escape harm and to gain access to goods or services, jobs, and housing that might be inaccessible if the stigmatized identity were known. In the case of gays and lesbians, being closeted (or passing as heterosexual) has negative psychological affects, such as the loss of spontaneity, self-hate, and constant dread of exposure, that build high levels of stress in everyday life. Being closeted is often accompanied with a subconscious feeling of inferiority, which results from an inner acceptance of society's negative stereotypes or "internalized homophobia" (Greene and Herek 1994).

As a result of a radicalized gay liberation movement that in 1969 took to the streets in New York City in what is now called the Stonewall riots, many lesbians and gay men began to see that their sexual orientation was a normal expression of their feelings and experiences. The new movement prompted lesbians and gay men to come out and identify themselves publicly in an effort to alter the stereotypes Americans held about them. For lesbians and gay men, coming out is not just a question of when and where to reveal their sexual orientation, it is also an individual process of learning to accept their sexual orientation as a healthy part of themselves. It is an ongoing process in which each new situation raises the question of whether to come out or to be closeted.

Coming out to others often produces painful results, especially from families of origin, whose reactions may range from tolerance to outright rejection of the gay or lesbian relative. For gays and lesbians of color, this process is complicated by the need to maintain the support of one's family and community against the racism of American society; the risk of rejection by the family and community may be intolerable. In any family, a son's or daughter's disclosure of his or her sexual orientation may cause upset and even disruption of family functioning. Eventually, most families begin a long process of reevaluation of their previously accepted attitudes toward lesbians and gays, which may lead to greater understanding of the gay offspring (Greene and Herek 1994).

The development of a stable sexual identity is not just a process of personal growth but the result of strong social and community support. A large number of institutions and social norms support a heterosexual identity. Heterosexuals are encouraged to form and maintain stable sexual relations with a partner in marriage. Much effort is expended by the state, as well as family and friends, to keep a heterosexual couple together, particularly once they have produced children. These efforts include bridal and baby showers, legal benefits and tax exemptions for married couples, joint property and inheritance rights, and the resultant difficulty of breaking up the marital unit through divorce. For most heterosexual couples, their relationship embeds them in particular kin, social, and religious networks; the threat of dissolution of their relationship leads to much anxiety and stress not only for the couple but for their peers and relatives as well. In America, similar forms of community support and social validation work to secure and support the gay or lesbian identity, particularly in urban areas. Lesbians and gay men have created a large number of social institutions such as churches, social centers, professional associations, theater companies, and sports leagues that are identified as gay and lesbian and that provide a supportive environment.

The urban lesbian and gay community contains a wide diversity of individuals from different cultural, racial, economic, and social backgrounds (Greene and Herek 1994). Although it reflects many of the problems of the larger society, such as racism, sexism, and intolerance, it provides a point of reference, a shared experience of identity, and for some, a home. Within this community, there is an uneasy alliance with bisexuals, persons attracted to either sex, who are often inaccurately viewed by gays and lesbians as fence-sitters. Despite the fact that bisexuals are also rejected by heterosexual society, many lesbians and gays are reluctant to expand the boundaries of an identity they have gained through years of struggle and pain.

A great majority of lesbians and gay men maintain long-term relationships; gay men have outside liaisons to a somewhat greater degree than lesbians (Bell and Weinberg 1978; Peplau 1991). Both lesbians and gay men find they have few role models on which to base their relationships. Lesbian feminists reject the heterosexual model of hierarchical relationships and have sought to develop egalitarian relationships that avoid the dominance of one partner by the other. In the egalitarian model, both partners are responsible for household chores and share equally in decision making. Despite gender similarities, the personal differences partners bring to a relationship give rise to problems and conflicts that reflect some of the inequalities of the larger society.

Lesbian and gay couples lack the kind of support that heterosexual couples take for granted. If lesbian and gay couples are not "out" to their relatives, their relationship will be given no recognition or status. Even if they are out to their families, their biological families may make demands that ignore the responsibilities a lesbian or gay man has to her or his partner. Holidays and visits from relatives can be particularly stressful times for a lesbian or gay couple as they try to negotiate family expectations against their own needs and desires as a couple. In times of critical need—whether illness, change of job, relocation, or breakup—couples generally do not receive the attention or support from biological families that they need to help them through the crisis.

Often because of this lack of support, gay and lesbian couples look to their own partners, friends, and ex-lovers to build a supportive family network. Most gay families are characterized by fluid boundaries and eclectic composition. In choosing their own families and choosing to have children, lesbians and gay men claim and construct their own kinship ties. These families pose a radical critique of heterosexual norms and assumptions about parenting, procreation, hierarchy, and householding. But even in their difference they share a common ground with heterosexuals in the recognition of the importance of kinship and family (Weston 1991).

In the 1990s, the drive for legitimation and social recognition of lesbian and gay relationships led to efforts to pass legislation granting same-sex couples the same status as a husband and a wife. Those seeking to establish same-sex marriage argue that homosexual relationships should be given the same state-sanctioned benefits and rights, and hence the same value, as heterosexual relationships. Gay marriage is recognized in several European countries; Denmark was the first in 1989, although it excludes the right of adoption and church weddings (Bech 1992). As of 1995, the United States had not recognized gay marriage, although several states, Hawaii in particular, faced challenges to their marriage laws. Domestic partnerships, which provide only a few of the rights granted male/female couples, have been recognized by some cities, businesses, and universities.

The issue of gay marriage has also caused much debate among lesbians and gay men. Some argue that granting gay relationships the same rights as heterosexual marriage may in fact limit gay families to the heterosexual model, at least legally. The quest for marriage rights, according to this view, privileges the heterosexual model as the desired model, with all its faults, including isolation of the nuclear family and inequalities in economics and power between spouses (Weston 1991). Others argue that recognition of same-sex marriage will bring gay life completely into the open, where it will be part of the dominant culture and no longer separate from it. Critics view it as assimilationist, while proponents see it as liberation.

Cross-Cultural Sexual Diversity

The evidence from cross-cultural data shows that sexuality changes its form and meaning in different cultural contexts. Humans are capable of a wide range of sexual behaviors, but most societies recognize and institutionalize only two or three variations of the many possible expressions of sexuality. In addition to heterosexual behavior, which is institutionalized and supported through marriage, inheritance, and property laws, many societies recognize transgenerational, ritual, and bond relationships between individuals of the same sex.

Cross-cultural data on homosexuality show that there are many non-Western societies in which forms of homosexuality are part of the repertoire of sexual practices. This fact refutes the commonly held belief that homosexuality is aberrant or antisocial behavior. An early survey found that 64 percent of societies sampled considered homosexual behavior to be normal and socially acceptable (Ford and Beach 1951). More recent anthropological studies show that homosexual practices and relationships constitute part of the social or religious domain of particular societies. The diversity of homosexual behaviors historically and culturally can be understood best within the cultural contexts in which they are found.

Terms such as "lesbian" and "gay" are problematic when used in cross-cultural studies. These terms refer to a particular European-American type of homosexuality that may be quite different from any expression of homosexuality in another society. Consequently, the terms "female homosexuality" and "male homosexuality" will be used when discussing non-Western cultures, although it should not be assumed that such terms refer to a single entity.

Female and male homosexuality are not necessarily similar entities even within the same society, because of the different constraints placed on men and women. (Blackwood 1986). For example, the ritual homosexuality of New Guinea men is a result of the belief that boys do not develop strength or masculinity naturally and need to be inseminated by older males. No ritual homosexuality is practiced between women and girls, however, because girls are believed to possess the female essence from birth (Herdt 1984). Thus, female homosexuality may take forms different from male homosexuality.

The expressions of homosexuality cross-culturally range from formal to informal relations. Examples of informal relations include adolescent sex play and affairs among women in, for instance, harems or households in which the husband has several wives. A formal lesbian relation is one that is recognized as part of the social structure and includes bond friendship, such as that among Azande women or cowives in Sudan, who formalized their relationship ritually; Chinese sisterhoods in the silk province of Kwangtung—groups of women who took vows not to marry and lived together cooperatively, even supporting each other in old age; age-graded relations, such as those in black South Africa and the Caribbean between older married women and younger, often unmarried women; and woman-marriage, a type of marriage in certain parts of Africa in which a childless woman could marry another woman to bear her heir (Evans-Pritchard 1970; Gay 1986; Herskovits 1967; Sankar 1986; Smith 1962). In societies where women have control over their productive activities, both formal and informal relations may occur. Where women lack control over their lives, particularly in male-dominant class societies, they maintain only informal lesbian ties, unrecognized by the larger society, or build institutions separate from the dominant culture.

A type of homosexuality that is common to both males and females occurs between individuals who occupy different genders but have the same physical sex. Two-spirit people are present among many native North American groups. (During and following the colonial period, they were inappropriately and derogatorily labelled "berdache.") They are usually spiritually directed individuals who express both masculine and feminine attributes and traditionally were good at tasks and duties assigned to the other sex. Many two-spirit people cohabited with or had sexual relations with individuals of the same physiological sex but different gender. Contemporary two-spirit people embody the traditional values and alternative sex and gender identities of Native-American cultures while they incorporate and contest European-American gay and lesbian identity (Blackwood 1984; Roscoe 1988, 1991; Williams 1986).

Instances of male homosexuality cross-culturally include various types of transgenerational relations, in which the partners are of different ages, such as that in previously mentioned New Guinea. In certain African groups in the past, soldiers were given younger boys to provide sexual and domestic services for them, and in ancient Greece, adult men mentored young boys socially and sexually. Egalitarian homosexuality, where the partners are socially similar, include bond friendship (South Africa) and sexual play among initiates or members of men's houses (Greenberg 1988).

Conclusion

The study of homosexuality and sexual orientation provides important clues to understanding human sexuality. Based on a biological urge, sexuality is embedded in and takes its meaning from culture. In male-dominant societies, sexuality is usually considered the prerogative of the man and penetration is defined as the "true" sexual act. However, evidence from other societies reveals that a wide range of human sexual practices is possible and culturally accepted.

In American society, sexual orientation is seen as an enduring attraction or desire that, among heterosexuals, lesbians, and gay men, forms the basis for an identity and community that integrates the various aspects of people's lives into a coherent sense of self.

(*See also:* Gay and Lesbian Parents; Gender; Gender Identity; Sexuality; Sexuality Education; Sexuality in the Life Cycle)

BIBLIOGRAPHY

Bayer, R. (1987). *Homosexuality and American Psychiatry: The Politics of Diagnosis*, 2nd edition. New York: Basic Books.

Bech, H. (1992). "Report from a Rotten State: 'Marriage' and 'Homosexuality' in 'Denmark.' " In *Modern Homosexualities: Fragments of Lesbian and Gay Experience*, ed. K. Plummer. London: Routledge.

Bell, A., and Weinberg, M., eds. (1978). *Homosexualities: A Study of Diversity Among Men and Women.* New York: Simon & Schuster.

Berube, A. (1990). *Coming Out Under Fire: The History of Gay Men and Women in World War Two.* New York: Free Press.

Blackwood, E. (1984). "Sexuality and Gender in Certain Native American Tribes: The Case of Cross-Gender Females." *Signs* 10:27–42.

Blackwood, E. (1986). "Breaking the Mirror: The Construction of Lesbianism and the Anthropological Discourse on Homosexuality." In *The Many Faces of Homosexuality: Anthropological Approaches to Homosexual Behavior*, ed. E. Blackwood. New York: Harrington Park Press.

DeCecco, J., and Elia, J. (1993). "Critique and Synthesis of Biological Essentialism and Social Constructionist Views of Sexuality and Gender." *Journal of Homosexuality* 24:1–26.

Evans-Pritchard, E. E. (1970). "Sexual Inversion Among the Azande." *American Anthropologist* 72:1428–1434.

Ford, C., and Beach, F. (1951). *Patterns of Sexual Behavior.* New York: Harper & Brothers.

Freud, S. (1953). *The Standard Edition of the Complete Psychological Works of Sigmund Freud*, ed. J. Strachey. London: Hogarth.

Gay, J. (1986). " 'Mummies and Babies' and Friends and Lovers in Lesotho." In *The Many Faces of Homosexuality: Anthropological Approaches to Homosexual Behavior*, ed. E. Blackwood. New York: Harrington Park Press.

Greenberg, D. F. (1988). *The Construction of Homosexuality.* Chicago: University of Chicago Press.

Greene, B., and Herek, G. M., eds. (1994). *Lesbian and Gay Psychology: Theory, Research, and Clinical Applications.* Newbury Park, CA: Sage Publications.

Hart, J., and Richardson, D. (1981). *The Theory and Practice of Homosexuality.* London: Routledge & Kegan Paul.

Herdt, G. (1984). *Ritualized Homosexuality in Melanesia.* Berkeley: University of California Press.

Herek, G. M. (1991). "Myths About Sexual Orientation: A Lawyer's Guide to Social Science Research." In *Law and Sexuality: A Review of Lesbian and Gay Legal Issues*, Vol. 1. New Orleans: Tulane University School of Law.

Herskovits, M. J. (1967). *Dahomey: An Ancient West African Kingdom.* Evanston, IL: Northwest University Press.

Homosexuality, Which Homosexuality? International Conference on Lesbian and Gay Studies. (1989). London: GMP Publishers.

Hooker, E. (1957). "The Adjustment of the Male Overt Homosexual." *Journal of Projective Techniques* 21:18–31.

Kinsey, A. C.; Pomeroy, W. B.; and Martin, C. E. (1948). *Sexual Behavior in the Human Male.* Philadelphia: Saunders.

Kinsey, A. C.; Pomeroy, W. B.; Martin, C. E.; and Gebhard, P. H. (1953). *Sexual Behavior in the Human Female.* Philadelphia: Saunders.

Money, J. (1987). "Sin, Sickness, or Status? Homosexual Gender Identity and Psychoneuroendocrinology." *American Psychologist* 42:384–399.

Peplau, L. (1991). "Lesbian and Gay Relationships." In *Homosexuality: Research Implications for Public Policy*, ed. J. Gonsoriek and J. Weinrich. Newbury Park, CA: Sage Publications.

Report of the Secretary's Task Force on Youth Suicide. (1989). Rockville, MD: U.S. Department of Health and Human Services.

Roscoe, W., ed. (1988). *Living the Spirit: A Gay American Indian Anthology.* New York: St. Martin's Press.

Roscoe, W. (1991). *The Zuni Man–Woman.* Albuquerque: University of New Mexico Press.

Sankar, A. (1986). "Sisters and Brothers, Lovers and Enemies: Marriage Resistance in Southern Kwangtung." In *The Many Faces of Homosexuality: Anthropological Approaches to Homosexual Behavior*, ed. E. Blackwood. New York: Harrington Park Press.

Smith, M. G. (1962). *Kinship and Community in Carriacou.* New Haven, CT: Yale University Press.

Weston, K. (1991). *Families We Choose: Lesbian, Gays, Kinship.* New York: Columbia University Press.

Williams, W. L. (1986). *The Spirit and the Flesh: Sexual Diversity in American Indian Culture.* Boston: Beacon Press.

Evelyn Blackwood

SEXUAL PROBLEMS

Sexual problems encompass a wide range of social and behavioral phenomena. They can include rape and the paraphilias (the love of the unusual, including atypical sexual patterns such as voyeurism, pedophilia, and fetishes). However, this entry will concentrate on those factors that disrupt normal sexual functioning, as well as the treatment and prevention of sexual dysfunction.

There is ongoing debate over the definition and classification of the various sexual dysfunctions. The first two editions of the American Psychiatric Association's *Diagnostic and Statistical Manual* (DSM), a handbook used by almost all mental health professionals, omitted sexual dysfunctions in its list of sexual problems. Sexual problems were limited to those that society disapproved of at the time (e.g., homosexuality) and those involving coercion or violation of other's freedom (e.g., pedophilia). Psychosexual disorders (the terms dysfunction and disorder are used interchangeably in the clinical literature) were listed for the first time in 1980, in the third edition of the manual, known as DSM-III, and its subsequent revision in 1994, known as DSM-IV.

Normal sexual functioning is presented as a sequential unfolding, beginning with sexual desire and proceeding through sexual arousal and orgasm. Interruption of any stage of this process is seen as dysfunctional. The approach is basically mechanical, with little weight given to the context in which sexual behavior occurs.

Many individuals do not fit neatly into any single diagnostic category. In one study, almost half the patients seeking treatment had a sexual problem in more than one area. Thus, in many cases problems with desire, arousal, and orgasm can overlap (Segraves and Segraves 1991).

Sexual Desire Disorders

Deciding whether a particular response should be considered a problem is particularly difficult in the case of desire disorders, where the variable is the amount of sexual interest. What is a "normal" level of sexual desire? In American culture, men are expected to want sex more frequently than are women. Thus, gender-role expectations are related to beliefs about what constitutes normal levels of sexual desire.

Desire disorders are divided into two categories: hypoactive sexual desire disorders and sexual aversion disorders. The first of these, hypoactive sexual desire disorder, is diagnosed when a person has recurrently deficient or absent sexual fantasies and desire for sexual activity. The judgment of deficiency or absence is made by a clinician taking into account factors that affect sexual functioning such as age, sex, and the context of the person's life. The deficiency may be selective; the person may experience erection, lubrication, or orgasm but derive little pleasure from the physical sensations. In other cases, the individual's desire is so deficient that he or she has no interest in self-stimulation or in participating in sexual interaction that might lead to arousal. A person may avoid a romantic relationship or marriage because he or she feels that a lack of sexual desire serves as a deterrent to forming such attachments. Such individuals can be described as asexual—that is, they do not experience desire for any kind of sexual activity. This would not be considered a dysfunction if the individual is satisfied with not engaging in sexual activity.

Sexual aversion disorder is diagnosed when a person experiences recurrent aversion to and avoidance of all or almost all genital sexual contact with a partner. Whereas individuals with hypoactive sexual desire are often indifferent about sexual interaction, sexual aversion reflects fear, disgust, or anxiety about sexual contact with a partner. Individuals with sexual aversion disorder may still engage in autosexual behavior such as masturbation and fantasy while avoiding interpersonal sexual behavior.

The sources of sexual desire disorders have not been well clarified. In fact, until the 1979 publication of H. J. Kaplan's model, most investigators did not distinguish between desire and excitement disorders. Most knowledge of the causes of low sexual desire is based on clients seen in therapy and thus must be viewed with caution until more objective research using nonclinical samples has been conducted. With that caveat in mind, low sexual desire has been associated with such factors as anxiety, religious orthodoxy, depression, habituation to a sexual partner, fear of loss of control over sexual urges, sexual assault, medication side effects, marital conflict, and fear of closeness (Letourneau and O'Donohue 1993; LoPiccolo and Friedman 1988). A comparison of married women experiencing inhibited sexual desire with married women expressing normal sexual desire revealed no differences in psychological adjustment or hormonal levels (Stuart, Hammond, and Pett 1987). In this study, however, women with inhibited sexual desire did report significantly greater dissatisfaction with their marital relationships than did the control group. Depression may play a crucial role in hypoactive sexual desire; women with inhibited sexual desire report twice as many depressive episodes as women with normal sexual desire (Schreiner-Engel and Schiavi 1986). The initial episode of the depressive disorder almost always coincided with or preceded the onset of lack of sexual desire.

Reports from a number of clinics that treat sexual dysfunction indicate that problems with desire are among the most common complaints that clients describe when they seek therapy (LoPiccolo and Friedman 1988; Spector and Carey 1990). In the early 1980s, the number of couples seeking help for desire disorders reached 55 percent in clinical samples, with more men than women presenting this complaint.

Excessive sexual desire, which has also been called hyperactive desire, sexual compulsion, or sexual addiction, has received considerable publicity in the popular media. Despite this attention, clinicians and therapists seldom encounter individuals with excessive sexual desire (Leiblum and Rosen 1988). Although people with enormous sexual appetites are fairly common in erotic literature and films, nymphomania in women and satyriasis in men appear to be rarities in real life. Donald Symons (1979, p. 92) suggested that the "sexually insatiable woman is to be found primarily, if not exclusively, in the ideology of feminism, the hopes of boys, and the fears of men."

Sexual Arousal Disorders

Some individuals feel sexual desire but experience little or no physical response (erection or vaginal lubrication and swelling) to sexual stimulation. Sexual arousal disorders are diagnosed when there is recurrent (1) failure by a woman to attain or maintain a lubrication and swelling response or absence in a man of erection during sexual activity or (2) lack of a subjective sense of sexual excitement and pleasure in sexual activity.

It is important to realize that occasional nonresponsiveness during sexual interaction is common. Many individuals have experienced sexual arousal and the desire for sexual activity when they have had too much to drink, only to find that although the mind was willing, the genitals were unresponsive. Similarly, fatigue, stress, and minor irritations with one's partner can temporarily interfere with sexual response. Such occasional nonresponsiveness can become problematic if people fear that they may not be able to respond sexually in the future. This fear of failure can create anxiety about sexual performance, which can lead, in turn, to future problems in responding.

Women's reactions to an inability to respond to erotic stimulation show a much greater variation than do men's. Most men react to erectile dysfunction as if it were a disaster, whereas women's responses range from anxiety or distress to casual acceptance of the dysfunction. To some extent, cultural expectations are responsible for these differences. In most cultures, men are expected to be sexually active and to perform satisfactorily. Women are not generally subjected to the same performance pressures and in some cultures are not expected to be sexually responsive. In addition, differences in anatomy and physiology make it more difficult for men to cover up and compensate for dysfunction. A limp penis is difficult to hide and to use in sexual interaction, whereas a dry vagina is more easily hidden, and with the aid of a lubricant, can even accommodate sexual intercourse.

The inability to attain or maintain an erection—erectile dysfunction—is generally the most common complaint among men who seek sex therapy. Community-based research, however, indicates that fewer than 10 percent of all men experience erectile dysfunction (Spector and Carey 1990).

Most men who experience problems with erection after a period of normal responsiveness respond well to treatment. The prognosis is not so good for men who have never been able to attain or maintain an erection with a partner (Hawton 1992).

Nonclinical studies suggest that arousal phase disorder occurs in 11 percent to 48 percent of the general population of women (Spector and Carey 1990). Often the problem stems from the combination of widespread ignorance regarding women's sexual anatomy and the socialization of women to attend more to others' needs than to their own.

Orgasm Disorders

People vary enormously in the amount of stimulation they enjoy before having an orgasm. The fact that one person responds quickly and his or her partner responds more slowly does not necessarily imply that either is dysfunctional. Orgasm need not and generally does not occur simultaneously for a couple. In fact, using simultaneousness as a standard can lead to an inappropriate exchange of labels. (A woman whose partner achieves orgasm before she does may be labeled as frigid or as afflicted with orgasmic dysfunction; the partner, in turn, may be branded a premature ejaculator. A man whose partner climaxes before he does may be described as a retarded ejaculator.) This does not imply that there are no such things as an orgasmic dysfunction or an ejaculation problem. Rather, the point is that differences between two people are not necessarily problematic or indicative of sexual dysfunction.

Premature ejaculation. The variety of ways in which experts have defined premature ejaculation should instill a healthy skepticism regarding the diagnostic process. Among the vague criteria that have been used to determine and define premature ejaculation are (1) time between penetration and ejaculation, (2) whether the man ejaculates before his partner has orgasm at least half the time, and (3) the number of penetrations before ejaculation.

Perhaps the most useful conception of premature ejaculation is that found in DSM-IV: recurrent ejaculation with minimal sexual stimulation before the person wishes it. Speed of ejaculation is associated with such factors as age (older men have fewer problems with ejaculatory control than do younger men, particularly adolescents), experience with intercourse, and novelty of the sexual partner.

Roughly one-third of men report that they ejaculate more rapidly than they would like (Frank, Anderson, and Rubinstein 1978). Premature ejaculation is a presenting complaint in sexual dysfunction clinics for 15 percent to 46 percent of those men treated (Spector and Carey 1990). Cultural factors play an important role in determining whether rapid ejaculation is perceived as a problem. In a society where sexual pleasure for woman is not valued, rapid ejaculation may be desirable because it shortens the time spent on an activity that women do not enjoy. In contrast, within cultures that value sexual interaction for its role in strengthening emotional intimacy, the expression of loving feelings, and the sharing of intense pleasure, rapid ejaculation is less desirable (Bixler 1986).

Inhibited male orgasm. In clinical studies, inhibited male orgasm (also known as retarded ejaculation or ejaculatory incompetence) accounts for about 3 percent to 8 percent of men seeking treatment. This form of sexual dysfunction has been found to occur in about 1 percent to 10 percent of community samples (Spector and Carey 1990). It is defined as the recurrent inhibition of orgasm and may involve delayed ejaculation or total inability to ejaculate despite adequate periods of sexual excitement. Interestingly, many men diagnosed as having inhibited ejaculation sustain erections for extended periods of time during coitus, and their wives are often multiorgasmic (Apfelbaum 1989). Many of these men say that they prefer masturbation over intercourse even though they continue to produce an erect penis for coitus with their partner. Clinicians have identified various factors that may contribute to inhibited orgasm. Religious orthodoxy, fear of creating a pregnancy, negative feelings toward the sexual partner, hostility, aggression, fears of abandonment, and tendencies toward holding back have been implicated in the development of this condition (Dekker 1993).

Inhibited female orgasm. Difficulty with orgasm is one of the most common sexual complaints among women who seek treatment at sex therapy clinics. Community-based research indicates that 5 percent to 10 percent of women experience orgasmic difficulty (Spector and Carey 1990). Women with this dysfunction may look forward to sex and may experience high levels of sexual excitement with vaginal swelling and lubrication, but they are unable to have orgasm. Sexual arousal causes congestion of the pelvic blood vessels and, without orgasm, the congested blood remains for a while (analogous to the congestion of the testes associated with the absence of orgasmic release in highly aroused men). Consistent arousal in women without orgasmic release can result in cramps, backache, irritation, and chafing. It is debatable whether a dysfunction exists when a woman does not have orgasm during coitus but does climax during other kinds of stimulation—oral or manual stimulation, for example. Calling this pattern a sexual dysfunction and assuming that it requires sex therapy would dictate treatment for a large number of women, given that fewer than 50 percent of women consistently have orgasm during coitus. In one study of professional nurses, it was found that the major factors they believed inhibited them from having orgasm during coitus were lack of foreplay, fatigue, preoccupation with nonsexual thoughts, ejaculation (by their partner) too soon after intromission, and conflicts with partners unrelated to intromission (Darling, Davidson, and Cox 1991).

Sexual Pain Disorders

DSM-IV lists two conditions under the category of sexual pain disorders: dyspareunia, which can be experienced by males and females, and vaginismus, which is exclusively a female experience. Dyspareunia is the technical term for recurrent and persistent genital pain in either a male or a female before, during, or after sexual intercourse. In women, repeated dyspareunia is likely to result in vaginismus. The pain may be experienced as repeated intense discomfort, momentary sharp sensations of varying intensity, or intermittent twinges and/or aching sensations. Dyspareunia rates in community-based research range from 8 percent to 23 percent (Spector and Carey 1990). Dyspareunia in men appears to be much less common and painful compared to women's experiences (Quevillon 1993). Men may experience pain in the testes and/or glans after ejaculation.

Vaginismus refers to the involuntary spasm of the pelvic musculature surrounding the outer third of the vagina. Women who experience these spasms of the pubococcygeus (PC) and related muscles cannot have intercourse but may be quite capable of becoming sexually aroused, lubricated, and experiencing orgasms (Beck 1993). The partner of a woman with this dysfunction who tries to have intercourse with her may have the sensation that his penis is hitting a rigid wall about an inch inside the vagina. Vaginismus rates have ranged from 12 percent to 17 percent of the women treated in clinics (Spector and Carey 1990).

The vaginismus spasm can be triggered by anticipated penetration of the vagina. Vaginismus can be a source of dyspareunia, just as recurrent dyspareunia can precede vaginismus. One study of eighty women who were diagnosed as having vaginismus indicated that half of these women developed the condition after a history of dyspareunia. A third of the women had never been able to have intercourse (married women in this category are technically virgin wives), and 14 percent developed vaginismus after a period of pleasurable intercourse (Lamont 1977).

Among the events triggering vaginismus are rape, abortion, painful gynecological exams, pelvic inflammatory disease, and accidents producing vaginal injury. Other factors in women's history related to vaginismus include vaginal surgery, problems stemming from episiotomies (surgical incision of the vagina in preparation for childbirth), vaginal infections, constipation, and pelvic congestion (Beck 1993). Imagined rapes and general fears about men and vaginal penetration can also be related to vaginismus.

Regardless of the source of the difficulty, the contractions of vaginismus cannot be controlled by the woman. Attempts at vaginal penetration produce pain and anxiety, and the woman may then try to avoid the possibility of such pain by avoiding sexual encounters. Treatment ranges from the medical correction of physical problems to the use of psychotherapy, although it is sometimes difficult to determine the precise source or sources of vaginismus. Treatment appears to be highly effective in eliminating this dysfunction (Hawton 1992). Relaxation training and gradual insertion of successively bigger dilators into the vagina appear to be very effective in curing vaginismus. It is very important, however, that the woman (rather than a therapist or a partner) control the pace of treatment and the size of the dilator (LoPiccolo and Stock 1986).

Sex Therapy

Until the 1960s, the predominant approach to the treatment of sexual dysfunction was psychoanalysis. Sexual problems were viewed as symptoms of emotional conflict originating in childhood. The sexual difficulties or symptoms would persist, the analysts claimed, unless the conflict could be resolved and the personality of the individual restructured. The trouble with this approach is that the sexual difficulties may persist even after the client understands or gains insight into the origins of the problem.

Behavioral psychologists have long taken issue with the psychoanalytic approach. They believe that a person may be emotionally healthy and still have sexual difficulties. Maladaptive sexual functioning is learned, they believe, and can be unlearned without probing extensively into a client's past. Behavioral approaches deal directly with sexual dysfunction by using techniques designed to overcome anxiety and to lessen sensitivity to anxiety-provoking stimuli. Behavioral therapies were first applied to sexual problems in the 1950s. Joseph Wolpe (1958) was one of the first to employ anxiety-relieving techniques to treat sexual difficulties. The behavioral approach was later popularized by William H. Masters and Virginia E. Johnson (1970). Although they did not use learning theory in a formal way, the various tasks they assigned a client were similar to techniques that Wolpe employed. Although sexual dysfunctions have also been treated by a wide array of psychotherapies, including cognitive, behavioral, object-relations, and family systems, the most commonly encountered therapies usually employ some variation of the program developed by Masters and Johnson.

The treatment program developed by Masters and Johnson was a two-week process. It was conducted by two therapists, a man and a woman, one of whom was a physician. Each partner in the couple seeking treatment is given a thorough medical examination and is interviewed by the therapist of the same gender. This interview is followed by a meeting with the other therapist. All four people (the couple and the two therapists) then discuss treatment goals. Masters and Johnson recommended the use of both the male and female therapist to provide a "friend in court" for the client of the same gender. They stressed the treatment of specific symptoms rather than extensive psychotherapy aimed at determining potential underlying unconscious sources of difficulty.

One of the most impressive aspects of the Masters and Johnson therapeutic approach was that they were successful in treating more than 80 percent of their clients who experienced various types of sexual dysfunctions (Kolodny 1981). Of the successful clients who could be found five years later (313 couples), only 5 percent reported recurrence of the dysfunctions for which they had obtained treatment. The therapeutic community was quite impressed with the success of Masters and Johnson's approach, and for years other therapists used modified versions of many of their methods.

Gradually, however, outcome statistics reported from clinical practice revealed overall improvement in only about two-thirds of the cases. The improvements obtained from controlled treatment studies have all been more modest than the proportions reported by Masters and Johnson (Hawton 1992). Other studies reveal relapse rates as high as 54 percent (Zilbergeld and Evans 1980). These differences between the failure rates reported by Masters and Johnson and those reported by other sex therapists and researchers are probably due to a combination of factors other than Masters and Johnson's skill as therapists.

One factor in Masters and Johnson's reported success rates may have been that 90 percent of their clients traveled to St. Louis from other parts of the country. Having left behind the routines and cares of their daily lives and making the commitment of time and money to improve their relationships, these couples were likely candidates for rekindling sexual interest and changing sexual attitudes and behavior.

Another factor may have been cultural attitudes toward information about sexuality. Many of the problems experienced by Masters and Johnson's clients stemmed from misinformation and ignorance; people in the 1950s and 1960s did not have the easy access to information about sexuality that is available today. Clients who simply lack information today may be "curing" themselves instead of seeking professional treatment.

Thanks to the increased availability of information about sexuality, the number of people seeking help with relatively simple problems based on sexual ignorance has fallen. The caseloads of today's sex therapist may include a greater proportion of clients with sexual difficulties resulting from deeply rooted emotional problems or from conflicts within their relationships. These kinds of sexual problems are often difficult to treat. This factor would, of course, result in lower success rates and higher relapse rates.

Another question that must be addressed in evaluating the effects of sex therapy is whether the treatment yields sustained change over the years. There is very little available research on this subject. Summarizing what is known, K. Hawton (1992) reported that the successful short-term results of sex therapy for erectile dysfunction were maintained in the long term (one to six years), whereas those for premature ejaculation were less permanent. Men with low sexual desire had fairly poor response to treatment in the short and the long term. Sex therapy for vaginismus is highly effective in the short and the long term, whereas the long-term results of treatment for low sexual desire in women are fairly poor. Interestingly, there was improvement in the way clients felt about their sexuality, despite the fact that some had returned to pretreatment dysfunctions in sexual behavior. If these clients had received occasional clinical "booster" sessions over the years, their posttreatment improvement would perhaps have been maintained through relapse prevention (McCarthy 1993).

Prevalence

Although there is little systematic survey information on the frequency of sexual dysfunction in the United States or in any other country, most experts believe that sexual distress is common (Spector and Carey 1990). One study of 100 couples, most of whom were well educated, middle-class, and white, offers some support for this idea (Frank, Anderson, and Rubinstein 1978). No couples in this study were in sex therapy, and 80 percent claimed to find their sexual relations satisfying. However, 40 percent of the men had experienced problems with erection and ejaculation, and 63 percent of the women had encountered difficulty in becoming sexually aroused or reaching orgasm. One conclusion that can be drawn from this study is that, at the least, occasional difficulties with sexual functioning may be widespread but do not strongly affect individuals' ratings of satisfaction.

Experiences with the body and with sexuality begin in infancy. Deprivation of physical contact and love can blunt emotional growth and potential for sexual expression (Hatfield 1994). Although most early experiences take place within a family, the nature and qualities of those experiences can depend on the larger social context that encompasses the family. For example, some cultures are extremely restrictive about eroticism; others are relatively permissive. The restrictiveness of a culture is linked to the prevalence of erectile difficulties. An examination of thirty preindustrial and industrializing countries found that the more restrictive a society was regarding such behaviors as premarital, marital, and extramarital sex, the greater number of reported problems with erectile functioning (Welch and Kartub 1978).

Sexual Problems and Marriage

A study of 160 societies indicated that infidelity, particularly by the wife, was the most common reason given for divorce (Betzig 1989). Infertility was the next most commonly mentioned reason. Cruelty, especially by the husband, ranked third among worldwide reasons for divorce. All these reasons are closely related to sex and reproduction. Divorce by contemporary Americans seems to be less tied to sex and reproductive reasons. Individuals' accounts of their own divorces implicate such factors as substance abuse, infidelity, personal incompatibility, sexual incompatibility, physical and emotional abuse, financial problems, and gender role disagreements (White 1991). A review of the available studies indicates that troubled marriages lead to sexual dysfunctions more frequently than sexual dysfunctions lead to troubled marriages (Allgeier and Allgeier 1995). Many of the therapies for sexual dysfunctions now take a relationship approach, emphasizing improved communication skills and resolving nonsexual problems.

Prevention

Many sexual problems originate in myths and misinformation that individuals are exposed to at a fairly young age. These mistaken ideas can lead to misguided or ineffective attempts at sexual interaction that leave the individual feeling depressed and incompetent. Several botched sexual experiences can result in the avoidance of future sexual contact.

Differences between backgrounds of people with healthy sexual responses and those of people with sexual dysfunctions do not lead to the conclusion that being brought up in a sexually restrictive environment is sufficient, by itself, to cause sexual dysfunction. Many people with adequate sexual functioning have family and cultural backgrounds similar to those of people who experience sexual dysfunction (Heiman et al. 1986).

The abundance of sexual misinformation can also contribute to sexual problems. Men may succumb to the myth that they should always be ready to engage in genital sex with regularity and efficiency, regardless of their mood and situation. When they experience temporary fluctuations in desire or when their sexual response is diminished by fatigue, they may react with alarm and subsequently become obsessed with "failing" again. Women may succumb to the myth that they should be interested in sex only when their partners are, or that they should reach orgasms only through stimulation of the vagina in intercourse, and then wonder why they experience orgasm problems.

Sexual dysfunctions are often related to nonsexual problems that are not discussed openly in a relationship. Money worries, conflicts involving dominance, decision-making controversies, and problems in the expression of affection are a few of the difficulties that can manifest themselves as sexual problems. For example, women who feel that their partners are not affectionate except when making love may express their resentment by not becoming aroused or orgasmic. Their partners then cannot have the satisfaction of bringing them sexual pleasure.

From a sexological perspective, John Money (1980) has described U.S. society as a sex-negative culture dominated by an "intrusive sense of shame and guilt that historically and culturally permeates and contaminates our sexual philosophies" (p. 43). Rather than integrating sexuality into the flow of daily living, Americans tend to view the erotic as a titillating and out-of-the-ordinary experience, as reflected in the media. Until American society is able to integrate the expression of sexuality into the fabric of daily life, it will continue to create large numbers of individuals with sexual problems.

(*See also:* Extramarital Sex; Family Therapy; Marital Sex; Marriage Counseling; Rape; Sexuality; Sexuality in the Life Cycle)

BIBLIOGRAPHY

Allgeier, A. R., and Allgeier, E. R. (1995). *Sexual Interactions*, 4th edition. Lexington, MA: D. C. Heath.

American Psychiatric Association. (1994). *Diagnostic and Statistical Manual of Mental Disorders*, 4th edition. Washington, DC: American Psychiatric Press.

Apfelbaum, B. (1989). "Retarded Ejaculation: A Much-Misunderstood Syndrome." In *Principles and Practices of Sex Therapy*, ed. S. R. Leiblum and R. C. Rosen. New York: Guilford.

Beck, J. G. (1993). "Vaginismus." In *Handbook of Sexual Dysfunctions: Assessment and Treatment*, ed. W. O'Donohue and J. H. Geer. Boston: Allyn & Bacon.

Betzig, L. (1989). "Causes of Conjugal Dissolution: A Cross-Cultural Study." *Current Anthropology* 30:654–676.

Bixler, R. H. (1986). "Of Apes and Men (Including Females)." *The Journal of Sex Research* 22:255–267.

Darling, C. A.; Davidson, J. K., Sr.; and Cox, R. R. (1991). "Female Sexual Response and the Timing of Orgasm." *Archives of Sexual Behavior* 17:3–20.

Dekker, J. (1993). "Inhibited Male Orgasm." In *Handbook of Sexual Dysfunctions: Assessment and Treatment*, ed. W. O'Donohue and J. H. Geer. Boston: Allyn & Bacon.

Frank, E.; Anderson, C.; and Rubinstein, D. (1978). "Frequency of Sexual Dysfunction in 'Normal Couples.'" *The New England Journal of Medicine* 299:111–115.

Hatfield, R. (1994). "Touch and Sexuality." In *Human Sexuality: An Encyclopedia*, ed. V. L. Bullough and B. Bullough. New York: Garland.

Hawton, K. (1992). "Sex Therapy: Has It Withered on the Vine?" In *Annual Review of Sex Research*, ed. J. Bancroft, C. M. Davis, and H. J. Ruppel, Jr. Lake Mills, IA: Society for the Scientific Study of Sex.

Heiman, J. R.; Gladue, B. A.; Roberts, C. W.; and LoPiccolo, J. (1986). "Historical and Current Factors Discriminating Sexually Functional from Sexually Dysfunctional Married Couples." *Journal of Marital and Family Therapy* 12:163–174.

Kaplan, H. J. (1979). *Disorders of Sexual Desire.* New York: Brunner/Mazel.

Kolodny, R. C. (1981). "Evaluating Sex Therapy: Process and Outcome at the Masters and Johnson Institute." *The Journal of Sex Research* 17:301–318.

Lamont, J. (1977). "Vaginismus." In *Progress in Sexology*, ed. R. Gemme and C. Wheeler. New York: Plenum.

Leiblum, S. R., and Rosen, R. C. (1988). "Introduction: Changing Perspectives on Sexual Desire." In *Sexual Desire Disorders*, ed. S. R. Leiblum and R. C. Rosen. New York: Guilford.

Letourneau, E., and O'Donohue, W. (1993). "Sexual Desire Disorders." In *Handbook of Sexual Dysfunctions: Assessment and Treatment*, ed. W. O'Donohue and J. H. Geer. Boston: Allyn & Bacon.

LoPiccolo, J., and Friedman, J. M. (1988). "Broad Spectrum Treatment of Low Sexual Desire: Integration of Cognitive, Behavioral, and Systemic Therapy." In *Sexual Desire Disorders*, ed. S. R. Leiblum and R. C. Rosen. New York: Guilford.

LoPiccolo, J., and Stock, W. E. (1986). "Treatment of Sexual Dysfunction." *Journal of Consulting and Clinical Psychology* 54:158–167.

Masters, W. H., and Johnson, V. E. (1966). *Human Sexual Response.* Boston: Little, Brown.

Masters, W. H., and Johnson, V. E. (1970). *Human Sexual Inadequacy.* Boston: Little, Brown.

McCarthy, B. W. (1993). "Relapse Prevention Strategies and Techniques in Sex Therapy." *Journal of Sex and Marital Therapy* 19:142–146.

Money, J. (1980). *Love and Lovesickness.* Baltimore: Johns Hopkins University Press.

Quevillon, R. P. (1993). "Dyspareunia." In *Handbook of Sexual Dysfunctions: Assessment and Treatment*, ed. W. O'Donohue and J. H. Geer. Boston: Allyn & Bacon.

Schreiner-Engel, P., and Schiavi, R. C. (1986). "Lifetime Psychopathology in Individuals with Low Sexual Desire." *The Journal of Nervous and Mental Disease* 174:646–651.

Segraves, K. B., and Segraves, R. T. (1991). "Multiple Phase Sexual Dysfunction." *Journal of Sex Education and Therapy* 17:153–156.

Spector, I. P., and Carey, M. P. (1990). "Incidence and Prevalence of Sexual Dysfunction." *Archives of Sexual Behavior* 19:389–408.

Stuart, F. M.; Hammond, D. C.; and Pett, M. A. (1987). "Psychological Characteristics of Women with Inhibited Sexual Desire." *Journal of Sex and Marital Therapy* 12:108–115.

Symons, D. (1979). *The Evolution of Human Sexuality.* New York: Oxford University Press.

Welch, M. R., and Kartub, P. (1978). "Sociocultural Correlates of Impotence: A Cross-Cultural Study." *The Journal of Sex Research* 14:218–230.

White, L. K. (1991). "Determinants of Divorce: A Review of Research in the Eighties." In *Contemporary Families: Looking Forward, Looking Back*, ed. A. Booth. Minneapolis, MN: National Council on Family Relations.

Wolpe, J. (1958). *Psychotherapy by Reciprocal Inhibition.* Stanford, CA: Stanford University Press.

Zilbergeld, B., and Evans, M. (1980). "The Inadequacy of Masters and Johnson." *Psychology Today* 14:29–43.

A. R. Allgeier

SHYNESS

Shyness is defined as excessive self-focus and exaggerated emotional arousal (e.g., anxiety) in the presence of other people. It is often associated with inadequate social and communication skills, as well as with passivity and self-consciousness. The importance of shyness in the everyday experience of people and from the perspective of psychological research primarily derives from the emotional distress experienced by the shy person as well as the tendency of chronically shy persons to fail to exercise and take advantage of their social and interpersonal opportunities. Moreover, overt manifestations of shyness frequently result in negative interpersonal evaluations; that is, the shy person is seen not only as reticent, but also as unfriendly, arrogant, or even hostile.

State Versus Trait Shyness

The immediate emotional experience of shyness—arousal and excessive self-focus in response to socially threatening situations—defines what is known as state or situational shyness. This type of shyness may be experienced by virtually everyone from time to time, especially in certain social situations such as those involving formality, evaluations, strangers, or high-status others. State shyness is distinguished from trait shyness, which refers to the propensity to experience state shyness more frequently or the predisposition to experience state shyness at lower levels of social threat (Buss 1980). Trait or dispositional shyness is considered more serious than state shyness because the latter is presumed to dissipate when the individual leaves the situation, whereas the former characteristic continues over time and, to some extent, across situations (Russell, Cutrona, and Jones 1986). Finally, trait and state shyness differ in that the former is conceptualized as a dimension of personality, whereas the latter is seen as a transitory experience or feeling.

The Experience of State Shyness

Shyness as a state is more likely to occur when an individual perceives that he or she is being evaluated, especially by a high-status person; in novel situations in which the person must interact with strangers; in social situations calling for assertiveness; and in social interactions where he or she is the center of attention. Whereas trait shy persons identify themselves as shy across most situations, their specific level of state shyness may vary from situation to situation. For example, one may be less shy when interacting with family members or close friends and more shy in situations involving social threats or when the "appropriate" social behavior is less than obvious.

Shyness is related to other social emotions such as guilt, shame, audience anxiety, and embarrassment. All involve some degree of social withdrawal, but the differences between shyness and these other emotions are more noteworthy (Izard 1972). For example, guilt results from violation of a personal standard and has as its consequence the responsibility for harm to someone else, whereas shyness simply increases avoidant behavior without regard to the welfare of others. The emotional profile of a guilty conscious includes feelings of fear and sadness. By contrast, shyness elicits interest and fear (Izard 1972).

Shame experiences are usually elicited by self-disclosure, generally focus on past behavior, and induce helpless self-awareness and emotional anguish. Shyness, on the other hand, prohibits self-disclosure, is future-oriented (individuals desire to present a favorable image but question their ability to do so), and thus involves anxiety about being evaluated (Buss 1980). Shame has been described as a more negative experience than shyness; in fact, shyness is reported to be one of the more favorable of the negative emotions (Bartlett and Izard 1972).

The Development of Trait Shyness

Because dispositional or trait shyness is seen as a relatively stable personality characteristic, central questions here include how it develops and how it is expressed at various points in the life cycle. Trait shyness is generally believed to develop in either of two ways (Buss 1984). First, shyness often reflects genetic predispositions. Several studies have found a strong relationship between shyness scores of identical twins (as measured by self-reports, parental ratings, and ratings by independent observers) and little or no relationship between that of fraternal twins (Plomin and Rowe 1979). Genetic factors have also been discovered in ostensibly environmental relationships. For example, it appears that heredity mediates the relationship between a child's shyness and certain aspects of the family environment. Specifically, an inverse relationship has been found between shyness and personal growth (e.g., cultural, recreational, and expressive aspects of the home) that is stronger in biological families than in adoptive families (Plomin and Daniels 1986). Alternatively, in some instances, shyness appears to emerge in conjunction with problems in development, especially the establishment of a personal identity in adolescence (e.g., Asendorpf 1989).

These alternative pathways to the emergence of behaviors and feelings labelled as shyness may crystallize in the phenomenon of social inhibition. Social inhibition has been found to be one of the few tempermental qualities that is stable over the first five years of life and beyond (Kagan et al. 1984). Inhibition in an infant may be described as stranger anxiety and is common at about nine months of age. Not all infants are equally afraid of strangers, and even those who exhibit stranger anxiety usually become much less apprehensive during the second year. For a minority, however, such trepidation continues and is characterized by avoidant and reticent behavior similar to that of shy adults. Children with a chronically inhibited social interaction style beyond age three are usually labeled as shy (Kagan and Moss 1983). Thus, the idea that some children are born with the proclivity to be shy is further supported by research showing that social inhibition is fairly consistent across situations and is also related to a specific pattern of physiological responses: Shy-inhibited children tend to have higher and less variable heart rates and larger pupil dilation associated with cognitive tasks than uninhibited children (Garcia-Coll, Kagan, and Reznick 1984; Kagan et al. 1984).

It is also possible that such children may be further conditioned for inhibition by their parents, other adults in their lives, or their peers (Asendorpf 1989). Being intimidated, harassed, or rejected by adults and peers can result in a chronic dread of unfamiliar people and a motivation to avoid interactions for fear of being hurt. Also, some evidence suggests that shyness as an emotional experience is exacerbated by parent–child interactions. Mothers' and babies' emotional expressions are remarkably similar, and parents also reinforce some facial expressions more than others (Malatesta and Haviland 1982). Thus, early childhood presents an excellent environment for learning interactive styles that could encourage shyness—perhaps by parents modeling shyness or reinforcing shy expressions and behavior. Although children may be born with a greater or lesser degree of readiness for physiological arousal, this inclination may only actualize through stressful experience such as parental conflict or withdrawal.

Being shy during childhood does not automatically mean that an individual will remain shy throughout his or her lifetime, however. An individual's level of shyness may vary during childhood and is not an especially good indicator of future shyness. In fact, there is only a modest relationship between an individual's shyness at age seven and at age twelve (MacFarlane, Allen, and Honzik 1954). On the other hand, shyness appears to stabilize by approximately eighth or ninth grade (shyness at age eleven is strongly predictive of shyness at age fourteen, and adolescent shyness predicts adult shyness twenty-five years later). Thus, adolescent shyness often proves to be a persistent personality trait (Morris, Soroker, and Burruss 1954).

During adolescence, shyness is likely to be intensified by the physical impact of puberty as well as changes in social context in the adolescent's life (e.g., going from elementary school to junior high school), which may contribute to disturbances in self-image. For example, researchers have found that only 22 percent of twelve-year-olds still in elementary school are highly self-conscious, whereas 41 percent of twelve-year-olds who are in junior high school are highly self-conscious. Further, 54 percent of junior high school students classified themselves as shy, compared to only 40 percent of elementary school students (Simmons, Rosenberg, and Rosenberg 1973). The emergence of gender role stereotypes may also play a role in adolescent shyness. In terms of social stereotypes, both shyness and passivity are considered to be feminine traits. Therefore, it is not surprising that girls report more self-conscious shyness after age eleven than boys do (Simmons and Rosenberg 1975). Stereotypes make it more appropriate for girls to be shy, and not surprisingly, girls are more often perceived by their teachers as being shy students (Lazarus 1982). On the other hand, shyness appears to represent more serious problems for boys because they are expected to take on a more assertive social role and initiate interactions (Porteus 1979).

Shyness among adults is evidenced by inhibited social behavior, impeding the development of friendships, romantic relationships, and work relationships. Shy people will often completely avoid social encounters, preferring to work alone and dating infrequently (Jones and Russell 1982; Phillips and Metzger 1973). Further, they are less likely to be perceived as knowledgeable by others because of their relative lack of strong opinions; in fact, shy individuals tend to temper their attitudes presumably so they will not have the "wrong" one (Cialdini and Mirels 1978). In work-related situations, chronically shy persons are more likely to lack high occupational status. Among unemployed adults, shyness can become a considerable problem, preventing effective and necessary job search strategies (e.g., employment interviews) and leading to negative work attitudes. Thus, shy individuals perceive and experience more obstacles to gaining employment (Hansson et al. 1984).

Research indicates that shyness and sociability are inversely related, but they do not necessarily represent opposite ends of a continuum (Cheek and Buss 1981; Jones, Briggs, and Smith 1986). Individuals can be high in both shyness and sociability; persons with this personality type are rated by their peers as tense, inhibited, and unfriendly (Cheek and Buss 1981). Further, shyness shares features with both introversion (e.g., social inhibition) and anxiety (e.g., social agitation and lack of self-efficacy) (Briggs 1988). Unfortunately, it is not yet clear at what point shyness ceases to be an everyday problem common to many people and becomes a "social phobia" of clinical significance.

For elderly adults, shyness is associated with greater life disruption as a result of retirement, widowhood, and other changes toward the end of the life cycle (Hansson 1986). It is also related to a more intense fear of being victimized by crime, perhaps because of a scarcity of social support. As shy people grow older, they report seeing fewer people each day, further resulting in negative attitudes toward aging. However, because the social roles of the elderly have fewer effects on other people and the evaluations of others are not as important to the elderly, social interactions begin to have less evaluative power (Hansson 1986). Therefore shyness presumably loses some of its ability to interfere with interpersonal behavior as a person grows older.

(*See also:* Attachment; Conflict; Intimacy; Loneliness; Personality Development; Personal Relationships; Self-Disclosure; Self-Esteem; Social Networks; Trust)

BIBLIOGRAPHY

Asendorpf, J. B. (1989). "Shyness as a Final Common Pathway for Two Different Kinds of Inhibition." *Journal of Personality and Social Psychology* 57:481–492.

Bartlett, C. S., and Izard, C. E. (1972). "A Dimensional and Discrete Emotions Investigation of the Subjective Experience of Emotion." In *Patterns of Emotions: A New Analysis of Anxiety and Depression*, ed. C. E. Izard. New York: Academic Press.

Briggs, S. R. (1988). "Shyness: Introversion or Neuroticism?" *Journal of Research in Personality* 22:290–307.

Buss, A. H. (1980). *Self-Consciousness and Social Anxiety.* San Francisco: Freeman.

Buss, A. H. (1984). "Two Kinds of Shyness." In *Self-Related Cognitions in Anxiety and Motivation,* ed. R. Schwarzer. Hillsdale, NJ: Lawrence Erlbaum.

Cheek, J. M., and Busch, C. M. (1981). "The Influence of Shyness and Loneliness in a New Situation." *Personality and Social Psychology Bulletin* 7:572–577.

Cheek, J. M., and Buss, A. H. (1981). "Shyness and Sociability." *Journal of Personality and Social Psychology* 41:330–339.

Cialdini, R. B., and Mirels, H. L. (1978). "Sense of Personal Control and Attributions About Yielding and Resisting Persuasion Targets." *Journal of Personality and Social Psychology* 33:395–402.

Garcia-Coll, C.; Kagan, J.; and Reznick, J. S. (1984). "Behavioral Inhibition in Young Children." *Child Development* 55:1005–1019.

Hansson, R. O. (1986). "Shyness and the Elderly." In *Shyness: Perspectives in Research and Treatment,* ed. W. H. Jones, J. M. Cheek, and S. R. Briggs. New York: Plenum.

Hansson, R. O.; Rule, B.; Briggs, S. R.; and Thompson, C. (1984). *Shyness and Coping Among Older Unemployed Adults.* Paper presented at the meeting of the American Psychological Association, Toronto, Ont., Canada.

Izard, C. E., ed. (1972). *Patterns of Emotions: A New Analysis of Anxiety and Depression.* New York: Academic Press.

Jones, W. H., and Briggs, S. R. (1984). "The Self–Other Discrepancy in Social Shyness." In *The Self in Anxiety, Stress, and Depression,* ed. R. Schwarzer. Amsterdam: North Holland.

Jones, W. H.; Briggs, S. R.; and Smith, T. G. (1986). "Shyness: Conceptualization and Measurement." *Journal of Personality and Social Psychology* 51:629–639.

Jones, W. H.; Cheek, J. M.; and Briggs, S. R., eds. (1986). *Shyness: Perspectives on Research and Treatment.* New York: Plenum.

Jones, W. H., and Russell, D. (1982). "The Social Reticence Scale: An Objective Instrument to Measure Shyness." *Journal of Personality Assessment* 46:629–631.

Kagan, J., and Moss, H. A. (1983). *Birth to Maturity.* New Haven, CT: Yale University Press.

Kagan, J.; Reznick, J. S.; Clarke, C.; Snidman, N.; and Garcia-Coll, C. (1984). "Behavioral Inhibition to the Unfamiliar." *Child Development* 55:2212–2225.

Lazarus, P. J. (1982). "Incidence of Shyness in Elementary School Age Children." *Psychological Reports* 51:904–906.

MacFarlane, J. W.; Allen, L.; and Honzik, M. D. (1954). "A Developmental Study of the Behavior Problems of Normal Children Between 21 Months and 14 Years." *University of California Studies in Child Development* 2:1–221.

Malatesta, C. Z., and Haviland, J. M. (1982). "Learning Display Rules: The Socialization of Emotion Expression in Infancy." *Child Development* 53:991–1003.

Morris, D.; Soroker, M.; and Burruss, A. (1954). "Follow-Up Studies of Shy Withdrawn Children: 1. Evaluation of Later Adjustment." *American Journal of Orthopsychiatry* 24:743–754.

Phillips, G. M., and Metzger, N. J. (1973). "The Reticence Syndrome: Some Theoretical Considerations About Etiology and Treatment." *Speech Monographs* 40:15–24.

Plomin, R., and Rowe, D. C. (1979). "Genetic and Environmental Etiology of Social Behavior in Infancy." *Developmental Psychology* 15:62–72.

Porteus, M. A. (1979). "Survey of the Problems of Normal 15-Year-Olds." *Journal of Adolescence* 2:307–323.

Russell, D.; Cutrona, C. E.; and Jones, W. H. (1986). "A Trait–Situational Analysis of Shyness." In *Shyness: Perspectives on Research and Treatment,* ed. W. H. Jones, J. M. Cheek, and S. R. Briggs. New York: Plenum.

Simmons, R., and Rosenberg, R. (1975). "Sex, Sex Roles, and Self-Image." *Journal of Youth and Adolescence* 4:229–258.

Simmons, R.; Rosenberg, R.; and Rosenberg, M. (1973). "Disturbance in the Self-Image at Adolescence." *American Sociological Review* 38:553–568.

KRISTINE M. KELLY
WARREN H. JONES

SIBLING RELATIONSHIPS

Siblings hold the unique status of being both family members and peers. The sibling relationship is (usually) the most enduring, and individuals are likely to live into old age with only brothers and/or sisters as surviving kin (Cicirelli 1991). Sibling relationships are dynamic and vary depending on the stage in the life cycle; they are no less important during old age than when children are toddlers or adolescents. However, what one expects from and what one gives to a sibling in old age are different from expectations and exchanges at earlier ages.

Research on Infant and Preschool Siblings

There is growing recognition that siblings play a potentially important role in socializing each other's social, emotional, and cognitive development. One example of the effects of this socialization role is the finding that older siblings are not as accommodating to young children as adults are and thus encourage the development of pragmatic skills in their younger siblings. That is, older siblings will make younger children perform such tasks as tying their own shoes and getting their own bowl of ice cream.

Psychologists studying the interaction patterns of preschool children and their infant siblings report that the arrival of a newborn in the family has immediate consequences for older siblings' adjustment and behavior. Bed-wetting, withdrawal, aggressiveness, dependency, and anxiety are among the most problematic behaviors reported in these studies (Dunn and Kendrick 1982). Positive roles for older siblings include the opportunity to learn caretaking skills and serving as models for appropriate social and cultural behaviors. Numerous studies find that young siblings benefit from observing and imitating their older brothers and sisters. This happens because older siblings "engage in activities during interaction that are within the scope of actions that the younger child is capable of reproducing immediately or slightly after observation" (Zukow 1989, p. 85). That is, a two-year-old cannot drive a car after riding in the front seat beside his or her parent but can negotiate a ride down a slide at the playground after watching an older sibling do it a time or two.

Sometime between their third and fourth year, older siblings begin to take a more active interest in younger siblings, and brothers and sisters become both more effective companions and antagonists at this age. One study revealed that older siblings demonstrated a clear understanding of how to provoke and annoy a younger child as early as age two (Dunn and Kendrick 1982). Countering this negative tendency is an increasing interest in alleviating the distress of others during the second year (Yarrow, Zahn-Waxler, and Chapman 1983). There is some evidence that the way mothers talk to an older sibling about a newborn child is associated with the quality of the behavior between the children over time (Dunn and Kendrick 1982). Children become increasingly more involved with their older siblings during the preschool years.

Sibling Relationships in Middle Childhood

Children become more egalitarian during the middle childhood years. When fifth- and sixth-grade children were asked about the relationship with their siblings, the quality noted most was companionship. This was followed by antagonism, admiration of sibling, and quarreling (Furman et al. 1989). These positive and negative qualities of the relationship were independent of one another, illustrating the ambivalence and complexity of sibling interaction. Younger siblings report feeling more affection, closeness, and respect for older siblings than the reverse.

Brothers and sisters tend to influence each other's gender role development. Boys with sisters score higher on expressiveness than boys with brothers, and girls with brothers score higher on instrumentality (Brim 1958). Boys with only brothers are reported as being more violent than boys with sisters (Straus, Gelles, and Steinmetz 1980). Kevin J. Gully and his colleagues (1981) found that interaction with siblings was the most important family interaction variable associated with individuals' tendencies to engage in violent behavior, in particular when perpetrating such behavior.

A study looking at the relation between parental behaviors and sibling behaviors found that negative parental care (hostile/detached behavior) was associated with sibling quarreling/antagonism among children in middle childhood. Differential treatment by mothers is associated with more conflicted and hostile sibling relationships (Boer, Goedhart, and Treffers 1992).

Dimensions of the sibling relationship. Sibling relationships can be analyzed according to a number of factors, including position within the sibling system, roles assumed by different siblings, family norms for children's expected behavior, the extent of coalition formation within the sibling system, and the functions siblings perform for each other. Expected behaviors for siblings may depend on where the child is in the sibling hierarchy (oldest, middle, or youngest child) and whether the child is male or female. At all ages, sisters are reported to be, and report themselves to be, closer to one another than are brothers or cross-sex sibling pairs. Position and sex may dictate role behavior (e.g., who assumes outside versus inside chores or acts as caretaker for younger siblings). Coalitions foster sibling solidarity, counter the power of parents or other sibling subgroups, and develop to strengthen siblings' position in times of conflict. Siblings serve many functions for one another. Some of these include serving as a "testing" ground for one another when experimenting with new behaviors or ideas before exposing them to parents or peers; serving as teachers; practicing negotiation skills; and learning the consequences of cooperation and conflict and the benefits of commitment and loyalty. Older siblings may serve a protective function, "translate" parental and peer meanings for younger brothers and sisters, and act as pathbreakers when new ideas or behaviors are introduced into the family. For example, a younger son may have little difficulty with parents when he decides to get his ear pierced because an older brother already weakened parental resistance (Schvaneveldt and Ihinger 1979). Lastly, it is within the sibling group that children first experience feelings of fairness and justice. Siblings compete for resources within the family, and if resources (such as affection, time, attention from parents, space, or material goods) are scarce, children watch closely to ensure that they are getting their fair share (Ihinger 1975).

Sibling similarities and differences. Despite commonalities of shared factors such as social class; physical and mental health of family members; the parental relationship; the emotional climate of the family; and the child-rearing skills, values, and attitudes of parents, siblings are a good deal different from one another. Only about 50 percent of siblings' genetic background is shared. In terms of weight and height, they are about 50 percent similar. Siblings resemble each other even less when examining the degree to which they are likely to be affected by diseases (e.g., the percentage of sibling pairs in which both siblings develop breast cancer is 10%; for diabetes it is 8%). The correlation between siblings and their IQ scores is only .47 for siblings as children; it is .31 when they reach adulthood. Severe mental retardation occurs for more than one sibling only 10 percent of the time. When one elderly sibling shows signs of Alzheimer's disease, 90 percent of the time his or her sibling does not show these symptoms. There also are pronounced differences in social and psychological adjustment and personality traits between siblings in the same family (Dunn and Plomin 1990).

By comparing the shared and nonshared family experiences of siblings, it can be seen that differential treatment and expressions of affection and interest by parents and other kin, perceptions of this differential treatment by siblings, and the effects of peer groups and school experiences coalesce to create a separate "life" for each child growing up in the same family. Helen Koch (1960) interviewed young siblings aged five and six and found that two-thirds of them felt that their mother favored either their sibling or themselves. Only a third perceived equal treatment. However, most of the siblings did not agree as to the recipient of the parental partiality. Perceptions of fathers' favoritism were particularly discrepant. In another study, about half of the adolescent and early adult siblings who were interviewed felt that their parents treated them and their siblings differently. When mothers were asked about the quality of their relationships with their children, only a third reported that they gave similar attention to all siblings; only a third reported feeling a similar extent of affection and level of intensity for all children. Most mothers reported favoring the youngest child with more affection and attention (Dunn and Plomin 1990). The consequences for children who perceived that they were differentially treated, receiving less attention and affection, were feelings of anxiety, worry, and depression. Differential treatment by the mother also was associated with disobedience, teasing, and argumentative and hyperactive behavior. These effects could not be accounted for by differences in siblings' personalities. Thus, Judy Dunn and Robert Plomin (1990, pp. 42, 59) concluded: "Environmental influences that affect development operate on an individual-by-individual basis, not on a family-by-family basis. . . . The salient environmental features of development are those that are experienced differently by children growing up in the same family."

Adult Sibling Relationships

Most adult Americans have at least one living brother or sister. Because of their shared past, and because they are typically close in age, siblings are potential sources of financial, physical, emotional, and psychological support and assistance in their old age. Some of the topics related to elderly siblings that have been investigated include the frequency of contact, felt closeness, feelings of solidarity, types of assistance exchanged, and whether siblings contribute to the morale of the elderly.

A curvilinear relationship exists between age and feelings of closeness between siblings. Relations are very close during early and middle childhood, decrease slightly during adolescence and middle age, and increase as an individual nears the end of the life cycle. Victor Cicirelli (1980, 1982, 1991) found that 68 percent of adults aged thirty to sixty described their relationship with siblings as close or very close; only 5 percent reported that they were not close at all. Seventy-eight percent felt they got along with their siblings well or very well; 4 percent reported they got along poorly. Forty-one percent said they felt free to discuss personal or intimate matters with a sibling; 36 percent said they rarely or never did. Seventy-three percent rarely or never discussed important decisions with a sibling. Similar findings were reported by Jean P. Scott and Karen A. Roberto (1981), who interviewed adults aged sixty-five to ninety. The men and women in this study reported high regard for their brothers and/or sisters, but sociability consisted of brief visits and telephone conversations several times a year. Mutual assistance was rarely offered or received. Graham Allan (1977) found that the range of activities siblings enjoy together rarely includes more than visits to each other's home. These visits usually involve no more than sitting and discussing matters of mutual interest and having ordinary (as opposed to exciting) conversations. This interaction is all that is necessary to maintain contact. Bert Adams (1968) suggests that such mundane contacts are sufficient to meet the general obligation adult siblings have to maintain their relationship.

Some life crises affect sibling closeness, improve relations, or increase frequency of contact among adult siblings. Ingrid Connidis (1992) found that sibling ties were heightened when divorce, widowhood, or health problems occurred. However, life experiences such as marriage or having children seldom influenced the sibling relationship. Crisis does not always produce increased interaction. Helena Lopata (1978) found that only 46 percent of widows with siblings mentioned a brother or sister as a source of any support. Gary Lee and Marilyn Ihinger-Tallman (1980) found no increase in sibling interaction among those in poor health. In this latter study, when controls for marital status, parental status, affection for siblings, and health were applied, the researchers found no circumstance under which the morale of the elderly was positively related to frequency of interaction with siblings. However, despite a lack of association between sibling interaction and the morale of the elderly, during old age siblings do act as companions, provide emotional support for one another, share reminiscences, validate each other's sense of self, and more than a few provide aid and services for one another.

Stepsiblings and Half Siblings

Since about 60 percent of those who remarry and 40 percent of those who cohabit have children (Bumpass and Sweet 1991), being a stepsibling or a half sibling is a condition of family life that an increasing number of children will experience.

Stepsiblings. When children from different family backgrounds are brought together to live in the same household, the new situation contains more ambiguities and fewer guidelines than exist for full brothers and sisters who live in an intact family. In an early study of remarriage (Duberman 1975), 24 percent of the parents reported poor relationships between the stepsiblings in their families; in 38 percent of the families, stepsibling relations were reported to be good; and in another 38 percent they were considered excellent. In a more recent study of remarried families in which both spouses had children living in the household, 38 percent of the adults reported normal sibling rivalry among the stepsiblings, 33 percent reported jealousy, and 4 percent reported competitiveness that was problematic. Twelve percent of the adults perceived that stepsiblings had nothing in common (Ganong and Coleman 1994b). Although stepsibling relationships tend to be less close than full sibling relationships (White and Reidmann 1992), they are generally characterized by positive feelings, and stepsiblings are likely to stay in contact (by visiting, telephoning, and letter writing) after childhood.

Based on clinical practice, Elinor B. Rosenberg and Fady Hajal (1985) identified several features that uniquely characterize the stepsibling relationship. First, children whose parents remarry usually have not had the luxury of getting to know and adjust to one another before living together. Second, remarriage brings with it household living arrangements that have fluid boundaries where shifts in membership are common. Children come and go, visiting their other parent or perhaps moving to his or her residence for some period of time. Third, stepsiblings lack a shared family history, where "styles, habits, customs, and modes of discipline that were part of the old family (particularly in the single-parent stage) do not necessarily work in the new remarried family" (Rosenberg and Hajal 1985, p. 289). Fourth, children bring to the new family a common experience of loss of the old family. Lastly, stepsiblings may face conflicting loyalties, a change in family size with accompanying shifts in sibling position and roles, and an incongruence between individual developmental tasks and family life-cycle expectations. For example, a newly remarried couple may be committed to bringing family members closer together to establish trust, cohesion, and affection, but an adolescent child may be seeking to implement his or her own developmental need to disengage from the family and establish a separate identity.

Another consequence of remarriage is the creation of sexual tensions that stem from bringing unrelated adolescent stepsiblings of the opposite sex together in an intimate living arrangement. This is a situation where the normative sexual boundaries do not pertain as they do with children who are raised in an intact first-marriage family.

Half siblings. Data collected in 1980 estimated that about half of all children under age five at their parent's remarriage have a half sibling from the new marriage; 16 percent of those aged ten to thirteen have a half sibling (Bumpass 1984). According to Lawrence Ganong and Marilyn Coleman (1994a), half siblings who live together rarely use that term, preferring to refer to themselves as brother or sister. Only when children have little to do with one another (i.e., do not share vacations or other time together) do they tend to use the term "half sibling." Anne Bernstein (1989) proposed several factors that improve half-sibling relationships. These include a parental remarriage that is well established, an age gap between half siblings, a shared residence, and children who have similar temperaments.

Very little theory has been developed that applies to stepsibling or half-sibling relationships. Ihinger-Tallman (1987) made a contribution toward building such a theory by specifying the conditions under which stepsiblings develop positive feeling for one another. These conditions include frequent contact; shared experiences; family conditions fostering intimacy and interdependency; similarities in age, sex, values, and family culture; mutual benefit from association; perceived equality or equity regarding the costs of the children's changed circumstances and new living arrangements; and a minimum of competition over scarce resources.

Cross-Cultural Differences

Cicirelli (1994) noted that across societies sibling relationships differ according to how siblings are defined or identified (i.e., biological, legal, and fictive); the norms that define their role relationships and behaviors (e.g., caretaking and socialization responsibilities); the importance of the sibling structure for defining roles and relationships within the family (considering structural factors such as number of siblings, age spacing between siblings, and gender); and whether sibling relationships are voluntary or obligatory. The biggest difference occurs between industrial and nonindustrial societies.

When studying cross-cultural differences, Thomas S. Weisner (1982) noted that siblings in most of the world strongly influence much of the life course of their brothers and sisters by their behavior. "They share life crisis and rite of passage ceremonies essential to their cultural and social identity; they take on ritual and ceremonial responsibilities for each other essential to community spiritual ideas" (Weisner 1982, p. 305). In non-Western societies, siblings perform essential tasks for each other and for the family, such as cooperative child rearing, protection and warfare roles, and household tasks essential to the subsistence of the family. As adults they may help arrange marriages and provide marriage payments for each other. Weisner (1982, p. 307) observes that in many non-Western societies "children spend most of their time after infancy cared for by their older brothers and sisters, not primarily their mothers." Child care is usually a shared activity that takes place in the context of other activities such as doing chores, participating in games or play, or just lounging. Sibling caretaking serves several major functions for a family and community. It provides support for parents who must spend their time in vital subsistence tasks, it is a training ground for parenting, it provides exposure to important superordinant and subordinant role behaviors that will have to be carried out later in adulthood (e.g., male and female roles), and it stresses interdependence—an important characteristic of the group in which these children will live. According to Weisner (1982, p. 311), sibling care "provides analogues to patterns of adult life."

Conclusion

Sibling relationships are dynamic and vary depending on the stage in the life cycle. While the majority of individuals in the United States report feeling close to their siblings, only a minority depend on these kin for intimate companionship or for financial, emotional, or physical assistance when they are adults. However, certain life experiences (e.g., never marrying, having no children, becoming widowed, or experiencing divorce) can produce closer contact and greater feelings of closeness among siblings.

Throughout the course of the life cycle, siblings are significant socializing agents for each other. They use each other as a measuring rod and the interaction that takes place between them is influenced by perceptions of equitable or unfair treatment by parents or other significant persons. For a few, the relationship is contentious, competitive, and characterized by negative affect. However, for the majority of people, interactions with siblings are positive and lead to the development of an affectionate life-long bond.

(*See also:* CHILDHOOD; DIVORCE: EFFECTS ON CHILDREN; ELDERS; FAMILY GENDER ROLES; MIDDLE AGE; ONLY CHILD; REMARRIAGE AND CHILDREN; STEPPARENTING)

BIBLIOGRAPHY

Adams, B. N. (1968). *Kinship in an Urban Setting.* Chicago: Markham.

Allan, G. (1977). "Sibling Solidarity." *Journal of Marriage and the Family* 39:177–183.

Bernstein, A. (1989). *Yours, Mine, and Ours.* New York: Scribner.

Boer, F., and Dunn, J. (1992). *Children's Sibling Relationships: Developmental and Clinical Issues.* Hillsdale, NJ: Lawrence Erlbaum.

Boer, F.; Goedhart, A. W.; and Treffers, P. D. A. (1992). "Siblings and Their Parents." In *Children's Sibling Relationships: Developmental and Clinical Issues*, ed. F. Boer and J. Dunn. Hillsdale, NJ: Lawrence Erlbaum.

Brim, O. G. (1958). "Family Structure and Sex-Role Learning by Children: A Further Analysis of Helen Koch's Data." *Sociometry* 21:1–16.

Bumpass, L. (1984). "Some Characteristics of Children's Second Families." *American Journal of Sociology* 90:608–623.

Bumpass, L., and Sweet, J. A. (1991). "The Role of Cohabitation in Declining Rates of Marriage." *Journal of Marriage and the Family* 53:913–927.

Cicirelli, V. (1980). "Sibling Relationships in Adulthood: A Lifespan Perspective." In *Aging in the 1980s*, ed. L. Poon. Washington, DC: American Psychological Association.

Cicirelli, V. (1982). "Sibling Influence Throughout the Lifespan." In *Sibling Relationships: Their Nature and Significance Across the Lifespan*, ed. M. E. Lamb and B. Sutton-Smith. Hillsdale, NJ: Lawrence Erlbaum.

Cicirelli, V. (1991). "Sibling Relationships in Adulthood: A Lifespan Perspective." *Marriage and Family Review* 16:291–310.

Cicirelli, V. (1994). "Sibling Relationships in Cross-Cultural Perspective." *Journal of Marriage and the Family* 56:7–20.

Connidis, I. A. (1992). "Life Transitions and the Adult Tie: A Qualitative Study." *Journal of Marriage and the Family* 54:972–982.

Duberman, L. (1975). *The Reconstituted Family: A Study of Remarried Couples and Their Children.* Chicago: Nelson-Hall.

Dunn, J., and Kendrick, C. (1982). *Siblings: Love, Envy, and Understanding.* Cambridge, MA: Harvard University Press.

Dunn, J., and Plomin, R. (1990). *Separate Lives: Why Siblings Are So Different.* New York: Basic Books.

Furman, W.; Jones, L.; Buhrmester, D.; and Adler, T. (1989). "Children's, Parents', and Observers' Perspectives on Sibling Relationship." In *Sibling Interaction Across Cultures: Theoretical and Methodological Issues*, ed. P. G. Zukow. New York: Springer-Verlag.

Ganong, L., and Coleman, M. (1994a). "Adolescent Stepchild–Stepparent Relationships: Changes over Time." In *Stepparenting: Issues in Theory, Research, and Practice*, ed. K. Pasley and M. Ihinger-Tallman. Westport, CT: Greenwood Press.

Ganong, L., and Coleman, M. (1994b). *Remarried Family Relationships.* Newbury Park, CA: Sage Publications.

Gully, K. J.; Dengerink, H. A.; Pepping, M.; and Bergstrom, D. (1981). "Research Note: Sibling Contribution to Violent Behavior." *Journal of Marriage and the Family* 43:333–337.

Ihinger, M. (1975). "The Referee Role and Norms of Equity: A Contribution Toward a Theory of Sibling Conflict." *Journal of Marriage and the Family* 37:515–524.

Ihinger-Tallman, M. (1987). "Sibling and Stepsibling Bonding in Stepfamilies." In *Remarriage and Stepparenting: Current Research and Theory*, ed. K. Pasley and M. Ihinger-Tallman. New York: Guilford.

Ihinger-Tallman, M., and Pasley, K. (1987). *Remarriage.* Newbury Park, CA: Sage Publications.

Koch, H. L. (1960). "The Relation of Certain Formal Attributes of Siblings to Attitudes Held Toward Each Other and Toward Their Parents." Monographs of the Society for Research in Child Development 25 (Serial no. 4), Lafayette, IN.

Lee, G. R., and Ihinger-Tallman, M. (1980). "Sibling Interaction and Morale: The Effects of Family Relations on Older People." *Research on Aging* 2:367–391.

Lopata, H. Z. (1978). "Contributions of Extended Families to the Support System of Metropolitan Area Widows." *Journal of Marriage and the Family* 40:355–364.

Rosenberg, E. B., and Hajal, F. (1985). "Sibling Relationships in Remarried Families." *Social Casework* 66:287–292.

Schvaneveldt, J. D., and Ihinger, M. (1979). "Sibling Relationships in the Family." In *Contemporary Theories About the Family*, ed. W. R. Burr, R. Hill, F. I. Nye, and I. L. Reiss. New York: Free Press.

Scott, J. P., and Roberto, K. A. (1981). "Sibling Relationships in Later Life." Paper presented at the annual meeting of the National Council on Family Relations, Milwaukee, WI.

Straus, M.; Gelles, R. J.; and Steinmetz, S. (1980). *Behind Closed Doors: Violence in the American Family.* New York: Doubleday.

Weisner, T. S. (1982). "Sibling Interdependence and Child Caretaking: A Cross-Cultural View." In *Sibling Relationships: Their Nature and Significance Across the Lifespan*, ed. M. E. Lamb and B. Sutton-Smith. Hillsdale, NJ: Lawrence Erlbaum.

White, L. K., and Reidmann, A. (1992). "When the Brady Bunch Grows Up: Step-, Half-, and Full Sibling Relationships in Adulthood." *Journal of Marriage and the Family* 54:197–208.

Yarrow, M.; Zahn-Waxler, C.; and Chapman, M. (1983). "Children's Prosocial Dispositions and Behavior." In *Handbook of Child Psychology*, ed. P. H. Musen. New York: Wiley.

Zukow, P. G. (1989). "Siblings as Effective Socializing Agents: Evidence from Central Mexico." In *Sibling Interaction Across Cultures: Theoretical and Methodological Issues*, ed. P. G. Zukow. New York: Springer-Verlag.

MARILYN IHINGER-TALLMAN

SINGLE PARENTS

The single-parent family has become a significant family form since the early 1960s. The rapid and drastic increase in the number of single-parent families has been used by some to argue that the breakdown of the family as an institution is occurring (Popenoe 1988). Others suggest that single-parent families have been present in all societies over time and should not be evaluated as deviant or problematic but rather as an alternative family form (Gongla 1982). Regardless of how the change in family form is viewed, the increase in and prevalence of families headed by one parent have a major influence on the social, economic, and political context of family life (McLanahan and Booth 1989).

Demographic Trends

In 1990, 15.9 million children under age eighteen lived in one-parent households, representing one-fourth of all families (Baca-Zinn and Eitzen 1993). By comparison, only 9 percent of all families were headed by a single parent in 1960 (Lamanna and Riedmann 1994). Forty-four percent of African-American families, 23 percent of Hispanic families, and 13 percent of European-American families were headed by single women in 1990 (Anderson 1993). Estimates suggest that 60 percent of all children will spend at least part of their childhood in a single-parent family, with African-American children more likely to continue to live in a single-parent household throughout childhood (Lamanna and Riedmann 1994).

Ninety percent of single-parent families are headed by women and are formed largely as a consequence of divorce or separation, births to never-married mothers, or the tendency for unmarried mothers to establish independent households (Baca-Zinn and Eitzen 1993). The factors most commonly related to the change in family structure are changing social and cultural trends, increased employment opportunities for women, decreased employment opportunities for men (especially African-American men), and the availability of welfare benefits that enable women to set up their own households (Garfinkel and McLanahan 1986; Wilson 1987). In cases of divorce, mothers are most often awarded custody, either by mutual consent or by default. The custodial arrangement is seen as an exchange involving financial responsibility by fathers, while the physical, day-to-day care is assigned to mothers. The role of fathers in the family is changing, and this is reflected in an increase in fathers gaining custody following separation and divorce. However, fathers with sole custody comprise only 3 percent of all households, with little variation by race (Lamanna and Riedmann 1994).

The rate of never-married mothers has doubled since 1980. More than 25 percent of all births in 1988 were to unwed mothers, the majority concentrated among African Americans and teenagers. More than half of African-American women heading families have never been married, compared to one in seven among European-American mothers (Burns and Scott 1994). The increase in births to unwed mothers is the consequence of unplanned, accidental pregnancy coupled with the decision not to marry. Also, women are delaying marriage while pursuing educational and career opportunities, resulting in an increased probability of pregnancy outside of marriage.

Early childbearing is of concern, with the overall rate of teen births remaining relatively high; in 1987, teens accounted for 10 percent of European-American births, 23 percent of African-American births, and 17 percent of Hispanic births (Anderson 1993). Since 1990, births have declined among African-American teens and risen among European-American teens. The factors contributing to teen pregnancy and childbirth include lack of close contact with adult role models; peer pressure; family poverty; the perception among many teens that few opportunities for success are available; and inadequate sex education, especially about contraception and family planning (Baca-Zinn and Eitzen 1993).

Another form of parenthood outside of marriage involves single women choosing to bear or adopt and raise children alone. Technological developments allowing insemination without intercourse contribute to women's choices in this regard. Women choosing to conceive children alone include lesbian women, who may raise their children as a single parent or with a same-sex partner; and heterosexual women who are in their thirties, single, and want children before they are past childbearing age (Burns and Scott 1994).

Family Typology

Single-parent families can be generally categorized by the sex of the family head. Father-only families are often formed as a result of widowhood, desertion by the mother, or wives refusing custody. Despite the lack of choice, single fathers report that they feel competent as primary parents and, in taking responsibility for the activities of caregiving usually assigned to mothers, are able to develop intimate and affectionate relationships with their children (Risman 1986). Fathers seeking custody at the time of divorce adapt well to the role of single parent. Other factors supporting their transition into primary parenthood include financial security, prior involvement in housework and child care during the marriage, satisfaction with child-care arrangements, and a shared sense of responsibility for the marital breakup (Greif 1985).

Mother-only families have been categorized as widows, who are a declining group of single mothers

(7%); divorced and separated women, constituting the largest category of single mothers (42%); never-married mothers (29%), who tend to be younger, less educated, have younger children, have less work experience, and to be poorer than other groups of single mothers; and teenage mothers, who have problems beyond marital status, including physical and emotional immaturity and limited capacity to care for dependent children emotionally and financially (Kamerman and Kahn 1988).

Another type of single-parent family is headed by lesbian or gay parents; there are 6 million to 14 million gay fathers and lesbian mothers in the United States (Lamanna and Riedmann 1994). These families present a challenge in examining single-parent family life, since the role of a same-sex partner as coparent is often invisible, and the experience of the biological or adoptive parent approximates that of a single parent in the larger community. Gay fathers tend to value paternal nurturance over economic provision as the principal role of father and to be more expressive than instrumental in their parenting. Lesbian mothers are more alike than different from heterosexual mothers, both in terms of gender role behavior and ideals and in holding their identity as mother as primary (Green and Bozett 1991). However, lesbian mothers are fearful of losing custody of their children and of their children encountering discrimination. These women see the intersection of motherhood and sexual identity as political work in that it challenges existing structures that limit the ways in which women can create and sustain family life (Ainslie and Feltey 1991).

Regardless of gender or sexuality, the term "single-parent family" (be it mother-only or father-only) implies that there is only one person responsible for the children and family life, which may or may not be the case. Therefore, a typology that distinguishes among parenting styles used in single-parent families is helpful (Mendes 1988).

A single parent may be a sole executive and as such the only parental figure actively involved in the lives of the children. This parent risks overload trying to meet excessive psychological, physical, and social demands and may qualify as a "tyrannized" single parent, never recovering from the absence of the other parent and feeling broken or incomplete as a single parent. A more positive version of the sole executive model is the coordinator role, in which the parent works within a social support system to allocate family functions.

The auxiliary parent shares responsibility for the children and family with the other parent through a joint custody or shared parenting arrangement. Parents with higher incomes and education are more likely to share custody, with both parents taking equal responsibility for important decisions regarding the children. The children either reside full-time with one parent or move periodically (usually weekly, biweekly, or monthly) to alternate residence between parents (Lamanna and Riedmann 1994).

An unrelated substitute can be a live-in housekeeper or unmarried cohabiting partner who shares parental and household responsibilities. The related substitute may be a blood or legal relative who assumes a parental role, including grandparents and siblings. This can contribute to unique problems with role configuration in that the parent can become peer to her or his own children—for example, by moving back into the neighborhood or home of the grandparents (Glenwick and Mowrey 1986). This problem emerges in shelters for homeless single-parent families as well. The shelter staff becomes the parental authority, responsible for managing family life, with homeless mothers feeling that they share the dependent status of their children (Feltey 1990).

The titular parent physically lives with his or her children but has abdicated parental responsibilities, often through alcoholism, drug addiction, or psychological or emotional illness. The level of dysfunction in this family necessitates intervention by public agencies, often resulting in the breakup of the family.

The advantages of a model based on parenting styles is that it encompasses the complexity of single-parent life and the ways in which relationships are constructed to make family life possible. Moving beyond structure, the focus becomes process in families, with attention to the various forms that single-parent families can manifest. Further, the limitations of comparing between single-parent versus couple-parent families or among types of single-parent families are overcome by exploring questions related to the ways in which a family is construed and reconstrued in the event of divorce or single parenting (Gongla 1982).

Effects on Parents and Children

Living in a single-parent family has effects on both parents and children. The most profound effect is economic deprivation for families headed by mother alone; following a divorce, fathers retain about 90 percent of their predivorce income, while mothers experience a decrease in household income of 40 percent to 67 percent (Weitzman 1985). The typical pattern for both middle-class and working-class newly divorced mothers is to move into inadequate apartments in undesirable neighborhoods due to the scarcity of affordable housing that will accommodate children (Wekerle 1985). The result is that they often leave their social networks and sources of support at the same time that they are forced to enter the labor force or increase their working hours.

Child support, money paid by the noncustodial parent to the custodial parent toward the support of the children, does not offset the economic deprivation experienced by single-parent families. Since mothers retain custody in the majority of cases, fathers are typically ordered to pay child support. However, award levels have consistently accounted for less than half of the expense of supporting a child, representing about 10 percent of the noncustodial father's income (Lamanna and Riedmann 1994). According to one study, a father's child support payments average less than his car payments (Pearce 1990). Less than half of all mothers who are awarded child support receive the full amount. When the situation is reversed and custody is granted to the father, the percentage of noncustodial mothers who pay child support is less than the percentage of noncustodial fathers who pay child support in the original situation. This, in part, is due to the lower earnings of women. Compared to noncustodial mothers not paying support, mothers who pay support earn a higher income, have more regular visitation with their children, are consulted more by the fathers, and have more positive feelings about their arrangement (Greif 1986).

In addition to a decreased standard of living, there are stressors specific to maintaining a household and managing family life alone. Coping with child rearing for single parents becomes more difficult because of responsibility overload, in which one parent makes all the decisions and provides for all of the family needs; task overload, in which the demands for work, housework, and parenting can be overwhelming for one person; and emotional overload, in which the single parent must always be available to meet the emotional needs of both the children and the self (Baca-Zinn and Eitzen 1993).

Support from friends and relatives can offset the effects of overload, with friends offering a buffer against loneliness and with relatives giving more practical help (Gladow and Ray 1986). One problem is the difficulty of asking for help in a society that views the successful family as one that takes care of its own (Anderson 1990). However, few women can successfully parent totally alone, despite the social expectation that noncustodial parents should provide only supplemental financial support and that single mothers should heroically take on both parental and economic roles (Goldscheider and Waite 1991).

Another source of support essential to the ability of single parents to manage the demands of work and home is child care. A disruption in child-care arrangements can be stressful for any family in which both parents work; for the single-parent family, it can create an immediate crisis. Single mothers report that child care is one of the most difficult obstacles in their efforts to provide for their families through paid employment (Kamerman and Kahn 1988).

On the more positive side, separation or divorce in conflict-filled and stressful situations can be a relief. Women who were dependent may gain self-esteem and develop a more positive family environment. In fact, there are relatively few long-term negative effects of parental divorce on the development and adjustment of children, and the relationships in most one-parent families are close and mutually supportive (Amato 1988).

The effects of single-parent family life on children fall into two categories: (1) those attributed to the lower socioeconomic status of single parents and (2) the short-term consequences of divorce that moderate over time. Four factors are predictive of children's adjustment to the divorce of their parents: the passage of time, the quality of the children's relationship with their residential parent, the level of conflict between parents, and the economic standing of the children's residential family (Brehm 1992). Children of divorce, when compared to those of intact families, have higher rates of emotional and behavioral problems, higher rates of delinquency for boys, and higher levels of anxiety and depression among preschool children (Reiss and Lee 1988). However, decreased socioeconomic status and resources associated with divorce appear to be the conditions associated with long-term behavioral and emotional problems in children (Weitzman 1985).

In mother-only families, children tend to experience short- and long-term economic and psychological disadvantages; higher absentee rates at school, lower levels of education, and higher dropout rates (with boys more negatively affected than girls); and more delinquent activity, including alcohol and drug addiction. Adolescents, on the other hand, are more negatively affected by parental discord prior to divorce than by living in single-parent families and actually gain in responsibility as a result of altered family routines (Demo and Acock 1991). Later, as children from single-parent families become adults, they are more likely to marry early, have children early, and divorce. Girls are at greater risk of becoming single mothers as a result of nonmarital childbearing or divorce (McLanahan and Booth 1989).

A common explanation for the problems found among the children of single parents has been the absence of a male adult in the family (Gongla 1982). The loss of a father in the family, especially in cases where the father becomes disinterested and detached, can have implications beyond childhood (Wallerstein and Blakeslee 1989). However, the lack of a male presence may not be as critical as the lack of a male income to the family (Cherlin 1981). The economic deprivation of single-parent family life, in combination with other sources of strain and stress, is a major source of the problems experienced by both parents and children.

Economics of Single-Parent Families

The most pronounced effect of divorce for women with children is a decrease in socioeconomic status and resources. Similarly, teenage pregnancy is related to economic adversity, as it interrupts the education of the mother and, as she moves into adulthood, she often remains unskilled, unemployed, and unemployable (Sidel 1986). The outcome is that single-parent families are disproportionately represented among the poor; in 1990, more than one-third of single-mother families, compared to 10 percent of married-parent families, were living below the poverty line. Overall, women with dependent children comprise two-thirds of the poor population, a phenomenon referred to as the "feminization of poverty." This is especially pronounced for African-American and Hispanic women who head families, with 48 percent of each group living below poverty in 1990, compared to 27 percent of European-American mothers who head families (Anderson 1993).

The poverty of families headed by women can be attributed to the fact that women provide the majority of support for their children, and these women are disadvantaged in the labor market (Pearce 1990). In addition to a relatively low earning potential, child support from the noncustodial parent remains low and transfer payments, with the exception of support for widows, maintain families well below the poverty level (Garfinkel and McLanahan 1986; McLanahan and Booth 1989).

Even full-time employment does not guarantee financial security, given the structure of the labor force, the lower wages paid in female-dominated occupations, and the lower human capital investment of single mothers (education, training, and work experience). The average woman employed full-time still earns about 66 percent of what the average male earns, regardless of education; in 1988, the average woman college graduate earned less than the average male high school graduate, even working full-time throughout the year (Pearce 1990). However, only 40 percent of women heading families work full-time year-round, with 30 percent to 40 percent reporting no earnings at all in a given year.

Gender differences in earnings are exacerbated by race; in 1990, the median income for full-time year-round work was $20,840 for European-American women, $18,518 for African-American women, and $16,186 for Hispanic women. When part-time and seasonal workers are taken into account, the median income of European-American women decreases to $10,317, African-American women to $8,328, and Hispanic women to $7,532. Of all workers, only European-American men earn an income above the federal poverty line for a family of four ($13,359) (Anderson 1993).

The income of mothers heading families is used to provide for all family members, in addition to meeting costs of employment such as child care and transportation. These expenses are usually shared in two-parent families, while the single mother earns less than the highest earner in a two-parent family and carries the costs alone. Child support, designed to supplement the income of single parents in meeting the costs of home and family maintenance, is inadequate, with an average amount of $3,129 received annually by European-American mothers and $1,698 by African-American mothers (Garfinkel and McLanahan 1986). Child support and alimony combined account for about 10 percent of the total income of European-American mothers and for about 3.5 percent of the income of African-American mothers. However, alimony or spousal support is awarded in less than 15 percent of all divorce cases, is received in less than 7 percent, and has been virtually eliminated in marriages ending in fewer than five years (Weitzman 1985).

An alternative to paid employment for mothers heading families is public assistance in the form of Aid to Families with Dependent Children (AFDC). This means-tested program, established in 1935 as part of the Social Security Act, was designed financially to support mothers and children who had lost a male earner in the family. Historically, welfare policy was based on a distinction between worthy women who were dependent through no fault of their own (widows) and undeserving mothers who were divorced or never married. Program regulations were developed in ways that reflected this distinction, along with racist assumptions about the role of immigrant and African-American women within both the family and the paid labor force (Amott 1990; Kemp 1994).

In addition to AFDC, there are supplemental in-kind transfer programs such as food stamps and medical benefits available to dependent families. About one-third of all female-headed families receive benefits from AFDC, 38 percent have Medicaid coverage, 50 percent have children receiving free or reduced-price school meals, 39 percent receive food stamps, and 18 percent live in public or subsidized housing. However, public assistance, including noncash transfers, maintains families well below the poverty line. In thirty states, AFDC benefits are less than 50 percent of the poverty level, with the median state's maximum monthly payment set at $360 for a family of three (Rodgers 1986).

Despite the poverty-level support provided by AFDC, when supplemented by food stamps and other in-kind transfers, public assistance can provide a higher level of income than a single mother can earn working at a full-time, year-round, minimum-wage job. Half of the women on welfare could not earn as much in the labor market as they receive in transfer payments, and only one-fourth could increase their income by as much as $1,000 a year by working full time (Sawhill 1976).

Overall, the single parent is in a situation of working for wages that for most will not keep the family out of poverty or relying on welfare as the family's source of support. The working single mother faces the challenge of balancing work and family demands. However, most of the services designed to meet the new needs created by women's increased labor force participation are too expensive for single mothers. Welfare mothers, on the other hand, are labeled and stigmatized, with serious effects in terms of self-esteem and lower efficacy. There is also concern that welfare entitlements have actually contributed to the increase in single-parent families, by making it possible for women to form their own households outside of marriage (Garfinkel and McLanahan 1986).

Single parents, regardless of the source, are working with inadequate economic resources in providing a home and support for dependent children. While families in general can benefit from the type of community and region of the country in which they reside, female-headed families do not benefit from increased labor force opportunities or from a favorable industrial mix in local communities (Feltey 1991). Moreover, local communities are not designed to meet the special needs of single-parent families. Single parents are challenged to locate affordable housing in safe neighborhoods with decent school systems and opportunities for recreation. This is complicated by the various transportation needs of individual family members and a dependency on public transit to meet at least some of those needs. Single parents are making choices about their private lives in the context of public institutions, and this is the arena where policy decisions about family are made.

Race, Class, Gender, and Family Politics

The politics of single-parent family life are based on gender (the vast majority of single parents are women), class (single mothers are disproportionately poor), and race (a large number of single mothers are African-American or Hispanic). Strategies for developing policy around family life have focused on economics, attitudes, and changing gender roles. The economic approach includes modifying and reforming the welfare system and developing employment policies (training and educational opportunities in particular) to make it possible for low-income women to obtain jobs and decent salaries. Efforts to change attitudes and behaviors that lead to the formation of single-parent families take the form of educational programs designed to reach adolescents. Changing gender roles influence perceptions about the desirability of women's paid labor force involvement, even when there are young children at home (Kamerman 1986). The trend is to discourage early childbearing, promote opportunities for paid labor force involvement, and normalize the double day of paid and domestic work for women (Glazer 1980).

More specifically, a combination of private and public solutions is recommended to address the problems of single-parent families. Proposals for policy changes include the following elements (Feltey 1990; Kamerman 1986; McLanahan and Booth 1989):

1. a family or child allowance to all parents, regardless of income, as a universal child benefit,
2. child support for all children from noncustodial parents, with standardized amounts, improved collections, and a guaranteed minimum benefit,
3. housing allowances for low-income families, with an emphasis on "scattered site" housing rather than concentrated populations of poor families in "projects,"
4. health-care insurance for employed single mothers and their children who do not have benefits,
5. improved maternity and parenting policy for all families, and

6. improved subsidies for child care, increased availability of high-quality child care, and increased wage levels in the child-care profession.

Private solutions of child support from noncustodial parents, and programs to enhance the employability of mothers have received the most attention. However, the public debate over health care and welfare reform reflects an increased level of awareness that problems within the family as a public institution cannot be addressed solely through private means.

(*See also:* Alimony and Spousal Support; Child Care; Child Custody; Child Support; Demography; Divorce: Economic Aspects; Divorce: Effects on Children; Dysfunctional Family; Entitlements; Family Gender Roles; Family Policy; Family Values; Fathers; Gay and Lesbian Parents; Loneliness; Mothers; Nonmarital Pregnancy; Poverty; Remarriage; Singles; Social Networks; Substitute Caregivers; Teenage Pregnancy; Work and Family)

BIBLIOGRAPHY

Ainslie, J., and Feltey, K. M. (1991). "Definitions and Dynamics of Motherhood and Family in Lesbian Communities." *Marriage and Family Review* 17:63–85.

Amato, P. R. (1988). "Parental Divorce and Attitudes Toward Marriage and Family Life." *Journal of Marriage and the Family* 50:453–461.

Amott, T. L. (1990). "Black Women and AFDC: Making Entitlement out of Necessity." In *Women, the State, and Welfare*, ed. L. Gordon. Madison: University of Wisconsin Press.

Anderson, J. (1990). *The Single Mother's Book: A Practical Guide to Managing Your Children, Career, Home, Finances, and Everything Else.* Atlanta: Peachtree.

Anderson, M. L. (1993). *Thinking About Women.* New York: Macmillan.

Baca-Zinn, M., and Eitzen, D. S. (1993). *Diversity in Families.* New York: HarperCollins.

Brehm, S. S. (1992). *Intimate Relationships.* New York: McGraw-Hill.

Burns, A., and Scott, C. (1994). *Mother-Headed Families and Why They Have Increased.* Hillsdale, NJ: Lawrence Erlbaum.

Cherlin, A. (1981). *Marriage, Divorce, Remarriage.* Cambridge, MA: Harvard University Press.

Demo, D. H., and Acock, A. C. (1991). "The Impact of Divorce on Children." In *Contemporary Families: Looking Forward, Looking Back*, ed. A. Booth. Minneapolis, MN: National Council on Family Relations.

Feltey, K. M. (1990). *Women and Children in Crisis: Homelessness in Northeast Ohio.* Akron, OH: University of Akron Press.

Feltey, K. M. (1991). "Female-Headed Family Poverty." *Sociological Focus* 24:329–341.

Garfinkel, I., and McLanahan, S. S. (1986). *Single Mothers and Their Children: A New American Dilemma.* Washington, DC: The Urban Institute Press.

Gladow, N. W., and Ray, M. P. (1986). "The Impact of Informal Support Systems on the Well-Being of Low-Income Single Parents." *Family Relations* 35:113–123.

Glazer, N. (1980). "Everyone Needs Three Hands: Doing Unpaid and Paid Work." In *Women and Household Labor*, ed. S. Berk. Newbury Park, CA: Sage Publications.

Glenwick, D. S., and Mowrey, J. D. (1986). "When Parent Becomes Peer: Loss of Intergenerational Boundaries in Single-Parent Families." *Family Relations* 35:57–62.

Goldscheider, F. K., and Waite, L. J. (1991). *New Families, No Families?* Berkeley: University of California Press.

Gongla, P. A. (1982). "Single-Parent Families: A Look at Families of Mothers and Children." *Marriage and Family Review* 5:5–27.

Green, G. D., and Bozett, F. W. (1991). "Lesbian Mothers and Gay Fathers." In *Homosexuality: Research Implications for Public Policy*, ed. J. C. Gonsiorek and J. D. Weinrich. Newbury Park, CA: Sage Publications.

Greif, G. L. (1985). *Single Fathers.* Lexington, MA: D.C. Heath.

Greif, G. L. (1986). "Mothers Without Custody and Child Support." *Family Relations* 35:87–93.

Kamerman, S. B. (1986). "Women, Children, and Poverty: Public Policies and Female-Headed Families in Industrialized Countries." In *Women and Poverty*, ed. B. C. Gelpi, N. C. M. Hartsock, C. C. Novak, and M. H. Strober. Chicago: University of Chicago Press.

Kamerman, S. B., and Kahn, A. J. (1988). *Mothers Alone: Strategies for a Time of Change.* Dover, MA: Auburn House.

Kemp, A. A. (1994). *Women's Work: Degraded and Devalued.* Englewood Cliffs, NJ: Prentice Hall.

Lamanna, M. A., and Riedmann, A. (1994). *Marriages and Families: Making Choices and Facing Change.* Belmont, CA: Wadsworth.

McLanahan, S., and Booth, K. (1989). "Mother-Only Families: Problems, Prospects, and Politics." *Journal of Marriage and the Family* 5:557–580.

Mendes, H. A. (1988). "Single-Parent Families: A Typology of Lifestyles." In *Current Issues in Marriage and the Family*, ed. J. G. Wells. New York: Macmillan.

Pearce, D. M. (1990). "Welfare Is Not for Women: Why the War on Poverty Cannot Conquer the Feminization of Poverty." In *Women, the State, and Welfare*, ed. L. Gordon. Madison: University of Wisconsin Press.

Popenoe, D. (1988). *Disturbing the Nest: Family Change and Decline in Modern Societies.* New York: Aldine.

Reiss, I. I., and Lee, G. R. (1988). *Family Systems in America.* New York: Holt, Rinehart and Winston.

Risman, B. J. (1986). "Can Men 'Mother'? Life as a Single Father." *Family Relations* 35:95–102.

Rodgers, H. R., Jr. (1986). *Poor Women, Poor Families: The Economic Plight of America's Female-Headed Families.* New York: M. E. Sharp.

Sawhill, I. (1976). "Discrimination and Poverty Among Women Who Head Families." *Signs* 1:201–211.

Sidel, R. (1986). *Women and Children Last: The Plight of Poor Women in Affluent America.* New York: Viking.

Wallerstein, J., and Blakeslee, S. (1989). *Second Chances: Men, Women, and Children a Decade After Divorce.* New York: Ticknor & Fields.

Weiss, R. S. (1979). *Going It Alone: The Family Life and Social Situation of the Single Parent.* New York: Basic Books.

Weitzman, L. J. (1985). *The Divorce Revolution: The Unexpected Social and Economic Consequences for Women and Children in America.* New York: Free Press.

Wekerle, G. (1985). "From Refuge to Service Center: Neighborhoods That Support Women." *Sociological Focus* 18:79–96.

Wilson, W. J. (1987). *The Truly Disadvantaged: The Inner City, the Underclass, and Public Policy.* Chicago: University of Chicago Press.

Zimmerman, S. L. (1994). "Family Trends: What Implications for Family Policy?" In *Race and Gender in the American Economy,* ed. S. F. Feiner. Englewood Cliffs, NJ: Prentice Hall.

KATHRYN M. FELTEY

SINGLES

Until the 1970s, singles were considered merely a residual category—that is, to be single was to be unmarried. Except in the case of those who chose to be priests or nuns, singleness was seen as perhaps not-quite-deviant but certainly as nonnormative for persons aged eighteen and older. For much of American history, the normative lifestyle has been and still is marriage—at least once.

During the 1970s, however, when a number of social factors converged to create a new interest in singleness as a meaningful lifestyle, scholars pointed out that to be single was to belong to an extremely diverse category of persons. Subsequent scholarship about singles is greatly indebted to the pioneering writers who first examined singleness in its own right and described its multidimensional nature. Among these scholars were Margaret Adams (1978), Marie Edwards and Eleanor Hoover (1974), and, perhaps best known, Peter J. Stein (1975, 1976, 1981a–c).

Serious interest in singles was stimulated by a rise in the number of young adults postponing marriage, causing a noticeable upward shift in the age at first marriage. This has been true in the developing world as well as in developed countries (Robey, Rustein, and Morris 1993). The social developments that led to these changes, according to Stein (1981a), include increasing numbers of women in higher education, expanding job and career opportunities for women, and a shift in attitudes about the desirability of marriage among both college and noncollege youths. The first two factors are, in part, a result of the impact of the women's movement that began in the mid-1960s and has flourished since. They are also a result of the increased availability and acceptability of birth-control methods such as "the pill" (also since the mid-1960s). The third factor is partly a result of the increasing divorce rate, which has led to a questioning of the appeal of marriage and family life.

Traditionally, marriage was seen as an economic partnership in which spouses depended on each other for skills and capabilities that each did not have individually. However, another legacy of the women's movement has been the trend toward equalitarian marriages (i.e., shared decision making and shared tasks replacing the older patriarchal pattern of separate spheres of activities for the husband and wife, with the husband "in charge"). This modern view of marriage is of a partnership based on the mutual provision of emotional support and intimacy. Equalitarian ideals also include the belief that each individual's potential and personal growth should be maximized in marriage. However, high divorce rates have led singles of both sexes to question whether these ideals actually can be implemented in marriage which, in the law and as practiced by many couples, is still more patriarchal than equalitarian.

As women have moved toward (and often have achieved) financial independence, the question of whether marriage would enhance or diminish their lives has become more salient. Most married women have a full-time job outside the home for wages and also a full-time job in the home—cleaning, cooking, and child rearing among other tasks. Age at marriage in 1992—just over twenty-six years for men and twenty-four years for women—was higher for women than at any previous time in American history (U.S. Bureau of the Census 1992). These high ages at marriage create a large pool of younger adults, and these are the persons who are stereotypically thought of when the term "singles" is used. (Proportionately, however, the 26.1% of men and 19.3% of women who are unmarried are not as large as, for example, in the year 1910, when 33.3% of men and 23.3% of women were single, according to the Census Bureau.)

However, the stereotype is far from the whole picture. These never-married young adults include some who want and expect to marry (the majority), as well as others who have no such hopes or plans—for instance, those who disapprove of marriage, see it as unnecessary, or remain permanently unmarried because of a religious vocation. However, even among those who might seem to be permanently single by choice—priests and nuns—there are some who will eventually marry. Also, many unmarried young adults are persons whose physical and/or psychological impairments make it unlikely that they will ever marry, whether they want to or not. This category of persons, then, like most of those with a religious impediment to marriage, will continue to be single well beyond young adulthood.

In the past, stereotypes of older single persons included the "confirmed bachelor" and the "spinster" or "old maid"—terms that implied that something was wrong with such individuals. Research indicates, however, that later-life singles are very often successful (Cargan and Melko 1982), that some "confirmed bachelors" do eventually marry (Darling 1981), and that so-called old maids may be women at the top of their professions for whom there are very few eligible men of comparable status (Doudna and McBryde 1981). Barbara L. Simon's (1987) study of older single women indicates that most of them had declined marriage proposals and that the typical reason was their fear of becoming subordinate to their husbands. Other studies (Gubrium 1975; Scott 1979) report that levels of life satisfaction for elderly singles are similar to those of elderly married persons. As Eleanor Macklin (1987, p. 319) has pointed out, "In the balancing of life's costs and benefits, elder never-marrieds find lack of intimacy to have been offset by . . . opportunity for personal achievement and independence." This trade-off may be more true for older women than older men. As long as society values the conjunction of good looks and youth in women more than in men, older single women may have some difficulty in leading happy lives. For older single men, whose appearance is often thought to be enhanced by age and who may have achieved a high level of financial security, there is an ever-enlarging pool of younger women with whom relationships are possible. Yet, even for older women, the support of the women's movement and of friends both single and married are positive factors. In general, the higher the income, the greater the sense of well-being for *either* sex. Moreover, research shows the majority of elder singles to be socially active (Stull and Scarisbrick-Hauser 1989) and, beyond socializing with friends, neighbors, and relatives, many date and have sexual relationships (Bulcroft and O'Conner-Roden 1986).

Some singles, whether older or younger, see an alternative to marriage in one or more cohabiting relationships. Research indicates that most of these are of fairly short duration, but others may be of considerable length. Under the law in some states, these may eventually become what are called common-law marriages (Koff 1989). However, living with someone prior to marriage may not guarantee positive results (see Bennett, Blanc, and Bloom 1988; DeMaris and Rao 1992; Tomson and Colella 1992; Popenoe 1987; Schoen 1992). The general conclusion that most scholars have reached is that those who choose to cohabit before marriage are less committed to their relationships than those who do not cohabit. Cohabiting individuals may also have certain characteristics (e.g., unconventionality and irresponsibility) that predict both subsequent marriages of lower quality and a higher likelihood of marital dissolution. Single heterosexuals who cohabit may think their arrangement is like a marriage, but most scholars see it as an aspect of courtship. Further, in terms of household chores, research indicates that, for women, cohabiting is more like living alone than like living with a husband (Shelton and John 1993).

Unmarried cohabitation with another adult may include an affectional and/or sexual relationship or it may be platonic, may be more or less (or not at all) committed, and may include one or more children of either partner. Cohabitation is usually thought of in terms of two unmarried adults who are involved with each other, but a single person may cohabit with one or more children, with some other relative(s), with a friend, or with a number of unrelated persons (e.g., in a commune). Unmarried persons also include homosexual men and women, in one or another of the living arrangements just described, or who live alone.

In addition to variation by sexual/affectional orientation, age, and living arrangements, singles are as varied as married persons by social-class background, education, occupation, and income level. All of these factors affect their life chances which, as Stein (1981a, p. 3) puts it, are "the opportunities individuals have to meet their goals through the use of their resources—chiefly money." Whether goals are constrained or attainable affects the lifestyles that men and women engage in.

Thus, the unmarried could be clustered into the following subtypes: once-or-more previously married versus never-married, cohabiting versus not cohabiting, heterosexual versus homosexual. All other subtypes would derive from these (e.g., cohabiting with an intended marital partner versus cohabiting as a temporary, casual, merely convenient arrangement).

Questions that interest scholars about singles are usually treated under subcategorical headings. For instance, in researching homosexual men and women, there might be an interest in studying the "coming out" process versus remaining "closeted." Researcher Joseph Harry (1993) has shown that, for men, being out is related to "income, type of occupation, where one lives, and the nature of one's friends" rather than to a number of other possible factors (p. 38). Others might study the community life of lesbian women, as Deborah Wolf (1980) has done.

Another example of the utility of studying separate subcategories of singles comes from research on religiosity. It has been found that "when marriage ends in widowhood, ties to religion intensify. When marriage ends in separation or divorce, however, religious involvement decreases, often sharply" (Gallup and Castelli 1989, p. 51). Never-married singles show less interest in religion than married and widowed persons do and about the same level of interest as divorced and separated persons; this is also true for regularity of church attendance as well as other measures of religiosity.

Stein (1981a) identified four groups of unmarried persons: the voluntarily temporarily single, the voluntarily stable single, the involuntarily temporarily single, and the involuntarily stable single. There are also cross-cutting dimensions, as Stein explains. For instance, in terms of sexual activity, singles may be active (with one or more partners) or abstinent (i.e., celibate). Among single young adults, William H. Masters, Virginia E. Johnson, and Robert C. Kolodny (1988) identified common sexual behavior patterns. In the minority are the "experimenters," who seek a variety of partners and sexual behaviors; there are also the "seekers," who are looking for an ideal partner; and there are "traditionalists," who believe in serious relationships as the only appropriate place for sexual behavior and who are likely to have only one partner at a time.

Beyond sexual considerations, singles may have social relationships with members of both sexes, or mostly with their own or with the other sex. Moreover, lifestyles are not static. They change across the lifespan as other factors change—such as increased education or altered circumstances of various kinds (e.g., the arrival or departure of children or changes in health)—or with age itself.

Among the 95 percent of young adult singles who expect to marry, what factors motivate them to do so and what factors push or pull them toward the single life? Stein (1975) studied this question in a small sample of relatively young, unmarried adults, and that study was later expanded (Laner, Laner, and Palmer 1978) with considerably larger samples. Among both men and women, love, desire for a family, the "romantic" aspects of marriage, and the desire for economic security were the most often cited attractions to marriage. However, large majorities of these same men and women wanted the unrestricted career opportunities and the freedom to change and experiment that are associated with singleness. In addition, men were attracted by the "exciting" lifestyle that singleness can provide and felt "pushed away" from marriage by its restrictive nature. Women, in contrast, wanted to be self-sufficient and felt "pushed away" from marriage by the possibility of poor communication with a future husband. Should these men and women eventually marry, it seems likely that (if their motives remain stable) their marriages will be both individualistic and equalitarian. This is what Pepper Schwartz (1994) has called "peer marriage."

A great deal of attention has been paid in both the popular and the scholarly press to the problems of single parents and especially to the effects of poverty among single women and their children (McLanahan and Booth 1989). Increasing proportions of younger singles of both sexes are in the paid labor force (U.S. Bureau of the Census 1992), but more young adults are living with their parents rather than independently (Glick and Lin 1986)—a phenomenon attributed to such factors as marriage postponement and college enrollment, in addition to hardships such as difficulty finding work, divorce, and unwed motherhood. A possible negative outcome of such living arrangements is a clash between the independent ideas of these young adults and the more conventional lifestyles of their parents.

Adding to the list of reasons for the growth of singles, Macklin (1987) has pointed out the ease with which singles can enjoy active social and sexual lives, the growing acceptance of nonmarital cohabitation, and the fact that there are more women than men of marriageable age. This last concern is particularly acute among African Americans (Peters and McAdoo 1983; Porter 1979; Staples 1981).

As Arthur B. Shostak (1987) has observed, the majority of surveys on the well-being of the unmarried find that their primary concerns focus on employment uncertainty (especially among men) and on vulnerability to crime (especially if they live alone). Marcia Bedard (1992) has argued that the happiness of single people is related to meeting their economic needs, not to the issue of being single. Most unmarried persons report well-being in terms of friendships, general health, physical condition, and finances. Only 4 percent find life dull, in contrast to the majority, who find it "exciting." The likelihood is growing that individuals may be single more than once during their lives—before marriage, following divorce or widowhood, and following remarriage. This once-denigrated segment of the population is no longer either a mere residual category nor one that compares unfavorably to the married majority.

(*See also:* Cohabitation; Divorce: Emotional and Social Aspects; Friendship; Intimacy; Loneliness; Love; Religion; Remarriage; Sexuality; Single Parents; Social Networks; Widowhood)

BIBLIOGRAPHY

Adams, M. (1978). *Single Blessedness.* New York: Penguin Books.

Bedard, M. (1992). *Breaking with Tradition: Diversity, Conflict and Change in Contemporary American Families.* Dix Hills, NY: General Hall.

Bennett, N. G.; Blanc, A. K.; and Bloom, D. E. (1988). "Commitment and the Modern Union: Assessing the Link Between Premarital Cohabitation and Subsequent Marital Stability." *American Sociological Review* 53:127–138.

Bulcroft, K., and O'Conner-Roden, M. (1986). "Never Too Late." *Psychology Today* (June):66–69.

Cargan, L., and Melko, M. (1982). *Singles: Myths and Realities.* Newbury Park, CA: Sage Publications.

Cockrum, J., and White, P. (1985). "Influences on the Life Satisfaction of Never-Married Men and Women." *Family Relations* 34:551–556.

Darling, J. (1981). "Late-Marrying Bachelors." In *Single Life: Unmarried Adults in Social Context,* ed. P. J. Stein. New York: St. Martin's Press.

DeMaris, A., and Rao, K. V. (1992). "Premarital Cohabitation and Subsequent Marital Stability in the United States: A Reassessment." *Journal of Marriage and the Family* 54:178–190.

Doudna, C., and McBryde, F. (1981). "Where Are the Men for the Women at the Top?" In *Single Life: Unmarried Adults in Social Context,* ed. P. J. Stein. New York: St. Martin's Press.

Edwards, M., and Hoover, E. (1974). *The Challenge of Being Single.* New York: Signet Books.

Gallup, G., Jr., and Castelli, J. (1989). *The People's Religion: American Faith in the '90s.* New York: Macmillan.

Glick, P. C., and Lin, S. L. (1986). "More Young Adults Are Living with Their Parents: Who Are They?" *Journal of Marriage and the Family* 48:107–112.

Gubrium, J. F. (1975). "Being Single in Old Age." *International Journal of Aging and Human Development* 6:29–41.

Harry, J. (1993). "Being Out: A General Model." *Journal of Homosexuality* 26:25–39.

Kain, E. L. (1990). *The Myth of Family Decline.* New York: Lexington Books.

Koff, G. J. (1989). *Love and the Law.* New York: Simon & Schuster.

Laner, M. R.; Laner, R. H.; and Palmer, C. E. (1978). "Motivated to Marry or Satisfied with Singlehood? Stein's 'Pushes' and 'Pulls' Revisited." *Cornell Journal of Social Relations* 14:59–74.

Macklin, E. D. (1987). "Nontraditional Family Forms." In *Handbook of Marriage and the Family,* ed. M. B. Sussman and S. K. Steinmetz. New York: Plenum.

McLanahan, S., and Booth, K. (1989). "Mother-Only Families: Problems, Prospects, and Politics." *Journal of Marriage and the Family* 51:557–580.

Masters, W. H.; Johnson, V. E.; and Kolodny, R. C. (1988). *Human Sexuality,* 3rd edition. Glenview, IL: Scott, Foresman.

Peters, M. F., and McAdoo, H. P. (1983). "The Present and Future of Alternative Lifestyles in Ethnic American Cultures." In *Contemporary Families and Alternative Lifestyles: Handbook on Research and Theory,* ed. E. D. Macklin and R. Rubin. Newbury Park, CA: Sage Publications.

Popenoe, D. (1987). "Beyond the Nuclear Family: A Statistical Portrait of the Changing Family in Sweden." *Journal of Marriage and the Family* 49:173–183.

Porter, J. R. (1979). *Dating Habits of Young Black Americans: And Almost Everybody Else's Too.* Dubuque, IA: Kendall-Hunt.

Robey, B.; Rustein, S. O.; and Morris, L. (1993). "The Fertility Decline in Developing Countries." *Scientific American* (December):60–67.

Schoen, R. (1992). "First Unions and the Stability of First Marriages." *Journal of Marriage and the Family* 54:281–284.

Schwartz, P. (1994). *Peer Marriage.* New York: Free Press.

Scott, J. P. (1979). "Single Rural Elders: A Comparison of Dimensions of Life Satisfaction." *Alternative Lifestyles* 2:358–379.

Shelton, B. A., and John, D. (1993). "Does Marital Status Make a Difference? Housework Among Married and Cohabiting Men and Women." *Journal of Family Issues* 14:401–420.

Shostak, A. B. (1987). "Singlehood." In *Handbook of Marriage and the Family,* ed. M. B. Sussman and S. K. Steinmetz. New York: Plenum.

Simon, B. L. (1987). *Never-Married Women.* Philadelphia: Temple University Press.

Staples, R. (1981). *The World of Black Singles.* Westport, CT: Greenwood Press.

Stein, P. J. (1975). "Singlehood: An Alternative to Marriage." *Family Coordinator* 24:489–503.

Stein, P. J. (1976). *Single.* Englewood Cliffs, NJ: Prentice Hall.

Stein, P. J. (1981a) "Introduction." In *Single Life: Unmarried Adults in Social Context,* ed. P. J. Stein. New York: St. Martin's Press.

Stein, P. J. (1981b). "The Never-Marrieds." In *Single Life: Unmarried Adults in Social Context*, ed. P. J. Stein. New York: St. Martin's Press.

Stein, P. J. (1981c). "Understanding Single Adulthood." In *Single Life: Unmarried Adults in Social Context*, ed. P. J. Stein. New York: St. Martin's Press.

Stull, D. E., and Scarisbrick-Hauser, A. (1989) "Never-Married Elderly: A Reassessment with Implications for Long-Term Care Policy." *Research on Aging* 11:124–139.

Thomson, E., and Colella, U. (1992). "Cohabitation and Marital Stability: Quality or Commitment?" *Journal of Marriage and the Family* 54:259–267.

U. S. Bureau of the Census. (1992). *Statistical Abstract of the United States*, 112th edition. Washington, DC: U.S. Government Printing Office.

Wolf, D. G. (1980). *The Lesbian Community*. Berkeley: University of California Press.

MARY RIEGE LANER

SOCIALIZATION *See* PARENT EDUCATION

SOCIAL NETWORKS

Married couples do not exist in isolation, but are embedded in a network of social relationships. Even prior to marriage, relations with family, friends, and others can influence dating activities and romantic relationships. When couples marry, they must deal with the demands of both their own social ties and those of their spouses. Couples must negotiate the degree to which they will maintain separate friendships, balance their own and their partner's family relationships, and engage in social activities as a couple. It is increasingly clear that couples' social relationships help shape the nature of married life.

Researchers have used social network analysis to help them study the social context of marriage. This involves study of the network methods used to enumerate the characteristics of couples' social worlds and the ways in which social network forces are thought to influence dating, courtship, and marriage.

Defining Social Networks

Although some researchers have used the term "social network" as a metaphor for the various kinds of social and community connections that individuals may have (Brown, Bhrolchain, and Harris 1975; Lin et al. 1979), social network analysis is a formal approach to the study of complex social relations (Wellman 1981). In network analysis, personal social networks are typically defined as "a collection of individuals who know and interact with a particular target individual or couple" (Milardo 1988). Researchers can assess the structural characteristics of an individual's network such as network size, role composition (amount of family, friends, work associates, etc., in the network), or network density (interconnectedness among members). Content characteristics of networks describe the nature of linkages between the individual and network members such as relationship satisfaction or reciprocity. Functional characteristics of networks describe linkages in which a given person serves some function for the focal individual, such as providing social support or informal help (Laireiter and Baumann 1992; Stein and Rappaport 1986).

Robert M. Milardo (1988) summarizes the three major ways in which researchers assess network ties. In an exchange network delineation, respondents are asked to list people with whom they interact in specified social settings (e.g., at work or in their personal household) and on whom respondents rely for emotional or tangible exchanges (e.g., child care, financial aid, or personal assistance). To identify members of an interactive network, respondents are asked to keep track of their social activity mainly through use of logs or diaries and to list those people with whom they interacted for a specified period of time (daily, weekly, monthly). However, a majority of researchers have asked respondents to list those people whom respondents feel "close to" or consider "important" in studying personal social networks. This network of close associates delineation typically has respondents limit the maximum number of network members they can list, with the upper range consisting of five to twenty network members. The ease of administration and "cost-effectiveness" of this type of network delineation strategy may help to explain its overwhelming popularity among researchers.

Methodological studies find that these different network delineation strategies generally yield different types of social network data from respondents (see Milardo 1992). This has led some researchers to conclude that individuals live in "multiple social worlds" (Hammer 1984) and that researchers must take particular care to select network delineation methods that are most appropriate to the type of research question they are asking (Rapkin and Stein 1989). The issue of which "social network" is appropriate to study becomes even more complex when attempting to assess the social context of married couples, since network relationships of two people must somehow be considered.

Researchers have investigated the social networks of couples in three major ways. Using an individual perspective, researchers have defined a couple's social ties in terms of the separate personal networks maintained by each partner. At the dyadic level, a couple's network has been viewed as those network members jointly shared by the couple. A configural approach conceptualizes a couple's network as a composite of the shared and separate ties contributed by both partners. Individual, dyadic, and configural perspectives differ in their assumptions about the role of network structure for couples, and each perspective has certain advantages and limitations (Stein et al. 1992).

This overview of social network methods suggests the importance of distinguishing among the structure, content, and function of social network relationships in examining the social context of marriage. Moreover, research suggests that there is no one "correct" definition of a social network, but rather that different network delineation strategies yield different data about social relationships. Researchers who study married couples must further decide if they are interested in the separate networks of marital partners, the degree of overlap between the partners' social ties, or some composite picture of the couple's network relations.

Social Network Opportunities and Constraints

Social networks are thought to provide opportunities and constraints for the development and maintenance of personal relationships. Friends and family can introduce an individual to others who may have the potential for friendship or romantic involvement. Existing network ties can also limit opportunities to form new relationships, given that a person has only a finite amount of time and energy to engage in social relationships. Researchers typically acknowledge the reciprocal influence of married couples and their social networks—namely, that network ties influence the development and maintenance of a couple's relationships and that being "a married couple" affects the nature of their social network ties.

Research suggests that social networks have an influence in the mate selection and courtship process that leads to marriage. Studies of heterosexual dating relationships have examined the degree to which individuals withdraw from their networks as they become romantically involved and the likelihood that interference from network members will hamper the development of a romantic relationship.

A review of the research on social withdrawal suggests that some network withdrawal occurs during the development of dating relationships but that it is likely not a universal network phenomenon. Instead, different types of networks (e.g., interactive versus close associates) and different network sectors (e.g., family, close friends, peripheral friends) undergo various changes as partners become more involved in a dating relationship (Johnson and Leslie 1982). For example, in order to assess the interactive networks of college-age dating couples, Milardo, Michael P. Johnson, and Ted L. Huston (1983) had respondents keep daily logs for two ten-day periods separated by a ninety-five-day span. Results of cross-sectional analyses found that respondents in later stages of couple involvement reported that they interacted with fewer total network members than respondents in earlier stages of involvement. However, longitudinal data results found no significant differences in total network size between respondents whose dating relationships had become more involved and respondents whose dating relationships had deteriorated. In fact, there was an increase in the number of family members and of intermediate friends in the network of dating couples who increased in romantic involvement.

Early studies of network interference found support for a "Romeo and Juliet" effect where opposition from parents about a dating relationship was positively related to romantic love in a college-age sample (Driscoll, David, and Lipetz 1972). However, further work has found that the amount of support provided by parents about a child's dating relationship was not related to further development of that relationship (Leslie, Huston, and Johnson 1986). Johnson and Milardo (1984) investigated interference from other network members as well as parents in a sample of college-age respondents at different stages of relationship involvement. Findings indicate that network interference occurred differently across different stages of dating involvement, with the most interference experienced by respondents in the middle stages of involvement.

Networks of family and friends are also thought to shape the nature of the marital relationship itself. In her now classic study of twenty married couples, Elizabeth Bott (1957) examined associations between structural patterns in the social networks of married couples and different aspects of the marital relationship. Bott concluded that the degree to which conjugal roles were segregated between husbands and wives (i.e., specific household tasks and duties were performed by one spouse most or all of the time) was a result of the personal social networks of husbands and wives. Specifically, she stated that partners who had more tightly knit, interconnected individual networks would be more likely to have marriages with a segregated division of labor between husbands and wives. Bott believed that close-knit networks provided the support needed for an individual, who consequently would not need to turn to a spouse for support, resulting in greater segregation of their conjugal roles.

Although attempts to replicate Bott's work have produced mixed results (Aldous and Strauss 1966; Rogler and Procidano 1986), Bott's study was pioneering in its focus on the possible structural influence of the larger social context on marital relationships. However, Bott's research and studies that followed (see Lee 1979) treated the networks of individual partners separately and examined associations between personal social network structure and properties of the marital dyad. This approach makes it difficult to examine the mutual influence of network ties on the marital relationship, since each partner's network is considered independently.

There is evidence that as couples become increasingly interdependent in their personal lives, they develop increasingly interdependent social networks (Milardo 1982). In general, studies indicate that married couples maintain both separate and mutual family and friend relationships (Babchuck and Bates 1963; Shulman 1975; Veiel et al. 1991). Studies investigating couples' networks at the dyadic level have assessed the degree of overlap between network members listed by both husbands and wives. Shared networks of family were found to be a particularly valuable source of support for a sample of middle-aged married couples experiencing chronic stress in the form of a critically ill child (Veiel et al. 1991). Of the emotional support and tangible assistance received by husbands in the study, more than 50 percent came from kin members shared with their wives, while women received slightly less than 50 percent of their emotional support and tangible assistance from shared kin. Yet, husbands and wives in the study rarely shared the same network member as their closest confidant. These findings suggest the importance of both individual and shared network ties as supportive resources for married couples.

A number of authors have conceptualized couples' networks in configural terms, emphasizing the importance of different patterns of mutual and separate network relationships that characterize the couples' social worlds (Milardo 1986; Stein et al. 1992). For example, Catherine A. Surra (1988) proposed six hypothetical types of network structures that vary in the amount of interconnectedness of partners' individual networks and degree of overlap of shared network ties. She then made predictions about how these different types of networks are likely to be associated with a couple's degree of marital interdependence. Similarly, in studying how married couples adapt to a geographic move, Wendy L. Jones (1980) grouped twenty-four couples into three network types according to the degree to which they had developed shared and separate clusters of interconnected ties over the course of one year. She identified different social advantages and costs associated with relocation of partners in each types of couples network.

Catherine H. Stein and her colleagues (1992) empirically grouped a random sample of forty-nine non-distressed married couples according to the amount of shared family members and shared and separate friendships they reported. The authors found that four different types of couples' networks characterized the sample and that couples with different types of networks reported significantly different levels of marital satisfaction and individual well-being. For example, couples whose conjoint networks featured a relatively large number of friends for both husbands and wives also reported significantly higher levels of marital satisfaction than couples in some of the other network types. Yet, husbands in this type of network reported significantly higher levels of depression than wives in this type of network. Postulating a direct relationship between separate friendships and individual well-being would suggest that female friends may help wives with feelings of depression in a way that men's separate friendships do not. Such findings suggest that conjoint network structure may have different implications for the marital relationship and the psychological well-being of individual partners.

Gender Differences in Social Networks

Developing and maintaining network ties requires a set of interpersonal skills and a desire and opportunity to use those skills. There is evidence that men and women often differ in the nature of their interpersonal exchanges and in their opportunities for social interaction (Dykstra 1990).

Research indicates that men and women structure their personal networks differently and that networks may serve different functions for husbands and wives. For example, wives generally report larger networks of kin and greater network interconnectedness than husbands (Antonucci and Akiyama 1987; Bott 1957).

Some research suggests that age and lifestyle stage account for network differences, with young married men having larger networks than their wives, and the reverse being true for older married couples (Fischer and Oliker 1983). Studies of middle-aged and older adults indicate that married men are more likely to report their wives as their primary confidants and sources of support, while women are more likely to report confidants other than their husbands and to rely on friends and children as sources of support (Antonucci and Akiyama 1987; Lowenthal and Haven 1968). Women are more likely than men to request assistance from network members in general (Butler, Giodano, and Neren 1985), and social support is found to have different associations with well-being for men and women (Sarason et al. 1983). Such findings suggest that gender may be a critical variable in understanding the importance of network ties in married life.

Relationship Processes in Social Networks

Although most studies have focused mainly on structural aspects of network ties for individual partners or couples, authors have also speculated about the processes by which social networks influence marriage. Researchers suggest that network ties can provide support and resources for couples or individual partners, as well as a standard for social comparison for couples to judge their relationships.

There is ample research to demonstrate that the nuclear family is not isolated but has regular and often frequent contact with relatives and friends (Shulman 1975). Studies indicate that network members provide couples and individual partners with both emotional support and a variety of different kinds of tangible assistance (Stein and Rappaport 1986). Yet, research suggests some possible negative outcomes when couples use their networks to help them deal with marital distress.

Danielle Julien and Howard J. Markman (1991) examined associations among spouses' problems, the support partners sought within and outside of marriage, and levels of individual and marital adjustment in a sample of eighty-seven distressed and nondistressed married couples. Findings suggest that within marriage, husbands' support was a particularly relevant component of wives' marital satisfaction, and marital distress was associated with less mobilization of spouses' support. Mobilization of support from network members was associated with greater marital distress. Discussing marital problems with outsiders was associated with low marital adjustment. The authors speculate that network members may provide alternative resources, reducing spouses' motivation to address each other to solve personal problems. Talking to a large number of people about marital problems decreases the chances that the problems will remain in confidence and increases the chances that others unknown to or disliked by the partners will share the information.

Other authors have highlighted the importance of close network ties in making social comparisons about marriage (Surra and Milardo 1991). People can use information and observations of other married couples or individual spouses to evaluate their own feelings, behaviors, and marital expectations. Social comparisons can provide information about the equity of one's relationship relative to others, validate the correctness of one's attributions or expectations, or reduce uncertainty.

In an exploratory study, Sandra L. Titus (1980) found that more than half of the thirty married couples in her sample reported explicitly comparing their own marriage with friends' marriages during interactions with friends or their spouses. Social comparisons were more common in younger couples with children less than five years of age and more common among wives than husbands. Social comparisons seemed to establish a frame of reference for marital expectations, helped couples identify issues to discuss in thier own marriages, and helped couples to evaluate or affirm the quality of their marriages. Surra and Milardo (1991) hypothesize that the frequency and influence of social comparisons increase as the network interdependence of the couple increases. The authors contend that a couple's standard of comparison may not always be an individual or even a specific couple; the standard may also be *groups* of married couples with whom the couple associates.

Conclusion

Social network analysis has helped researchers to more systematically describe different kinds of social relationships that exist and develop within the context of marriage. Yet, researchers are only beginning to examine the complex, reciprocal influence of network forces on marital ties. Much more methodological and conceptual work is needed to understand the network conditions that best help to nurture and support marriage and family life.

(*See also:* Friendship; Marital Quality; Mate Selection; Peer Pressure; Personal Relationship)

BIBLIOGRAPHY

Aldous, J., and Straus, M. A. (1966). "Social Networks and Conjugal Roles: A Test of Bott's Hypothesis." *Social Forces* 43:471–482.

Antonucci, T. C., and Akiyama, H. (1987). "An Examination of Sex Differences in Social Support Among Older Men and Women." *Sex Roles* 17:737–749.

Babchuck, N., and Bates, P. (1963). "The Primary Relations of Middle-Class Couples: A Study in Male Dominance." *American Sociological Review* 28:377–384.

Bott, E. (1957). *Family and Social Networks.* New York: Free Press.

Brown, G. W.; Bhrolchain, M. N.; and Harris, T. O. (1975). "Social Class and Psychiatric Disturbance Among Women in an Urban Population." *Sociology* 9:225–254.

Butler, T.; Giodano, S.; and Neren, S. (1985). "Gender and Sex-Role Attributions as Predictors of Utilization of Natural Support Systems During Personal Stress Events." *Sex Roles* 13:515–524.

Driscoll, R.; Davis, K.; and Lipetz, M. (1972). "Parental Interference and Romantic Love: The Romeo and Juliet Effect." *Journal of Personality and Social Psychology* 24:1–10.

Dykstra, P. A. (1990). "Disentangling Direct and Indirect Gender Effects on the Supportive Network." In *Social Network Research,* ed. C. P. Kees, M. Knipscheer, and T. C. Antonucci. Amsterdam: Swets and Zeitlinger.

Fischer, C. S., and Oliker, S. J. (1983). "A Research Note of Friendship, Gender, and the Life Cycle." *Social Forces* 62:124–133.

Hammer, M. (1984). "Explorations into the Meaning of Social Network Interview Data." *Social Networks* 6:341–371.

Johnson, M. P., and Leslie, L. (1982). "Couple Involvement and Network Structure: A Test of the Dyadic Withdrawal Hypothesis." *Social Psychology Quarterly* 45:34–43.

Johnson, M. P., and Milardo, R. M. (1984). "Network Interference in Pair Relationship: A Social Psychological Recasting of Slater's Theory of Social Regression." *Journal of Marriage and the Family* 46:893–899.

Jones, W. L. (1980). "Couple Network Patterns of Newcomers in an Australian City." *Social Networks* 2:357–370.

Julien, D., and Markman, H. J. (1991). "Social Support and Social Networks as Determinants of Individual and Marital Outcomes." *Journal of Social and Personal Relationships* 8:549–568.

Laireiter, A., and Baumann, U. (1992). "Network Structures and Support Functions: Theoretical and Empirical Analyses." In *The Meaning and Measurement of Social Support,* ed. H. Veiel and U. Baumann, New York: Hemisphere.

Lee, G. R. (1979). "Effects of Social Networks on the Family." In *Contemporary Theories About the Family,* ed. W. R. Burr, R. Hill, F. I. Nye, and I. L. Reiss. New York: Free Press.

Leslie, L. A.; and Huston, T. L.; and Johnson, M. P. (1986). "Parental Reactions to Dating Relationships: Do They Make a Difference?" *Journal of Marriage and the Family* 48:57–66.

Lin, N.; Simeone, R.; Ensel, W.; and Kuo, W. (1979). "Social Support, Stressful Life Events, and Illness: A Model and an Empirical Test." *Journal of Health and Social Behavior* 20:108–119.

Lowenthal, M. F., and Haven, C. (1968). "Interaction and Adaptation: Intimacy as a Critical Variable." *American Sociological Review* 33:20–30.

Milardo, R. M. (1982). "Friendship Networks in Developing Relationships: Converging and Diverging Social Environments." *Social Psychology Quarterly* 45:162–172.

Milardo, R. M. (1986). "Personal Choice and Social Constraint in Close Relationships: Applications of Network Analysis." In *Friendship and Social Interaction,* ed. V. J. Derlega and B. A. Winstead. Homewood, IL: Dorsey Press.

Milardo, R. M. (1988). "Families and Social Networks: An Overview of Theory and Methodology." In *Families and Social Networks,* ed. R. M. Milardo. Newbury Park, CA: Sage Publications.

Milardo, R. M. (1992). "Comparative Methods for Delineating Social Networks." *Journal of Social and Personal Relationships* 9:447–461.

Milardo, R. M.; Johnson, M. P.; and Huston, T. L. (1983). "Developing Close Relationships: Changing Patterns of Interaction Between Pair Members and Social Networks." *Journal of Personality and Social Psychology* 44:964–976.

Rapkin, B. D., and Stein, C. H. (1989). "Defining Personal Networks: The Effect of Delineation Instructions on Network Structure and Stability." *American Journal of Community Psychology* 17:259–267.

Rogler, L. H., and Procidano, M. E. (1986). "The Effect of Social Networks on Marital Roles: A Test of the Bott Hypothesis in an Intergenerational Context." *Journal of Marriage and the Family* 37:693–701.

Sarason, I. G.; Levine, H. M.; Basham, R. B.; and Sarason, B. R. (1983). "Assessing Social Support: The Social Support Questionnaire." *Journal of Personality and Social Psychology* 44:127–139.

Shulman, N. (1975). "Life-Cycle Variations in Patterns of Close Relationships." *Journal of Marriage and the Family* 37:813–821.

Stein, C. H.; Bush, E. G.; Ross, R. R.; and Ward, M. (1992). "Mine, Yours, and Ours: A Configural Analysis of the Networks of Married Couples in Relation to Marital Satisfaction and Individual Well-Being." *Journal of Social and Personal Relationships* 9:365–383.

Stein, C. H., and Rappaport, J. (1986). "Social Network Interviews as Sources of Etic and Emic Data: A Study of Young Married Women." In *Stress, Social Support, and Women,* ed. Steven E. Hobfoll. New York: Hemisphere.

Surra, C. A. (1988). "The Influence of Interactive Networks on Developing Relationships." In *Families and Social Networks,* ed. R. M. Milardo. Newbury Park, CA: Sage Publications.

Surra, C. A., and Milardo, R. M. (1991). "The Social Psychological Context of Developing Relationships." In *Advances in Personal Relationships*, ed. W. H. Jones and D. Perlman. London: Kingsley.

Titus, S. L. (1980). "A Function of Friendship: Social Comparisons as a Frame of Reference for Marriage." *Human Relations* 33:409–431.

Veiel, H. O. F.; Crisland, M.; Strosreck-Somschor, H.; and Herrie, J. (1991). "Social Support Networks of Chronically Strained Couples: Similarity and Overlap." *Journal of Social and Personal Relationships* 8:279–292.

Wellman, B. (1981). "Applying Network Analysis to the Study of Support." In *Social Networks and Social Support*, ed. B. Gottlieb. Newbury Park, CA: Sage Publications.

CATHERINE H. STEIN
WILLIAM E. RUSSNER

SPOUSAL SUPPORT *See* ALIMONY AND SPOUSAL SUPPORT; DIVORCE: ECONOMIC ASPECTS

SPOUSE ABUSE AND NEGLECT

Although most people consider marriage and family life as the source of warmth, comfort, and protection from the stresses and dangers of the outside world, the family is one of society's most violent social institutions. Individuals are more likely to be physically and sexually assaulted, injured, or killed in their homes by family members than anywhere else, or by anyone else. The high risk of assault, injury, and even death is especially true for women.

Although spouse abuse receives considerably more attention today, it has been a part of the family throughout history, not only in American families, but in England, Western Europe, and many other countries and societies around the world.

Terms and Definitions

Various terms have been used in the study of violence and abuse between marital partners, including "spouse abuse and neglect," "domestic violence," and "family violence." "Spouse abuse," although a term widely used, is considered a controversial and even inappropriate term. The inappropriateness lies in the fact that the term is neutral when it comes to gender, giving the impression that men are as, or nearly as, likely as women to be victimized by their partners. Feminist scholars in particular criticize the gender-neutral term and use terms such as "violence toward women," "woman abuse," or "violence against wives" (Dobash and Dobash 1979; Wardell, Gillespie, and Leffler 1983; Yllo 1993). It is important to recognize that women are by far the most likely victims of all forms of violence, abuse, and neglect in marital relations.

The initial definitions of spouse abuse focused on acts of damaging physical violence directed toward women by their spouses or partners (Gelles 1974; Martin 1976). Further research broadened the definition to include sexual abuse, marital rape, and acts of emotional or psychological violence. Feminist scholars conceptualize the problem as one of coercive control of women by their partners (Yllo 1993). The coercion can be physical, emotional, or sexual.

Prevalence

Because violence between husbands and wives was traditionally hidden in the home, there has been a general lack of awareness of the seriousness and extent of the problem. Whereas mandatory reporting laws for child abuse and neglect were enacted in every state in the late 1960s and early 1970s, very few states have mandatory reporting laws for spouse violence. Some hospitals record the number of women treated for spousal violence, and most police departments keep a rough record of domestic disturbance calls. Even without official records on spouse abuse, a variety of data sources suggest that spousal violence is far more extensive than commonly realized.

One other source of information on the extent and patterns of domestic violence is the National Crime Victims Survey, conducted by the U.S. Department of Justice. This survey estimates the amount of crime committed both against persons aged twelve and older and against households. Two reports on intimate violence based on data collected for the National Crime Survey have been published (U.S. Department of Justice 1980, 1984). There were two major findings from these interviews: (1) There were about 3.8 million incidents of violence among intimates in the four-year period of the survey, with nearly a third committed by offenders related to the victims, and (2) an analysis of single-offender incidents revealed 1,055,000 incidents between relatives, with 616,000 (58%) of these occurring between spouses or ex-spouses. The 1984 report states that the yearly incidence of domestic violence among those twelve years of age or older was 1.5 per thousand people in the population.

There have also been two National Family Violence Surveys that examined violence between husbands and wives by interviewing a national sample of families (Gelles and Straus 1988; Straus and Gelles 1986; Straus, Gelles, and Steinmetz 1980). In 16 percent of the homes surveyed, some kind of violence between spouses had occurred in the year prior to the survey. More than one in four (28%) of the couples reported marital violence at some point in their marriages. The milder forms of violence were the most common. More than 3 in 100 women were victims of abusive violence during the twelve-month period prior to the interview in 1985. Projecting this rate to the total number of married women suggests that approximately 2 million women are victims of wife abuse each year. Wife beating is a pattern, not a single event, in most violent households. On average, a woman who is a victim of wife abuse is abused three times each year.

While the survey data probably underestimate the extent of the problem, homicide is the one aspect of spousal violence on which reliable official data are available. Researchers generally report that intrafamilial homicides account for between 20 percent and 40 percent of all murders (Curtis 1974). About 700 husbands and boyfriends are killed by their wives and girlfriends each year, while more than 1,400 wives and girlfriends are slain by their husbands or boyfriends (U.S. Department of Justice 1993).

Emotional abuse, or what some call psychological abuse or verbal aggression, are nonphysical acts, either verbal or nonverbal, that are intended to cause psychological pain to another person. Murray A. Straus and Stephen Sweet (1992) analyzed the data from the Second National Family Violence Survey and found that 74 percent of the men and 75 percent of the women surveyed reported engaging in one or more acts of psychological aggression in the previous year. The averages were 10.0 incidents per year for man-to-woman verbal aggression and 10.3 incidents per year for woman-to-man acts.

Marital rape is one of the most common forms of sexual assault adult women experience. David Finkelhor and Kersti Yllo (1985) report that 10 percent of a sample of 323 women said they had been forced to have sex with their husbands. Of the 644 married women interviewed by Diana Russell (1984), 14 percent reported one or more incidents of marital rape. The Second National Family Violence Survey found that 1.2 percent of the 2,934 married women interviewed said they were victims of attempted or completed forced sexual intercourse with their husbands.

There has been quite a controversy in the field of family violence regarding the extent of male victimization. Data from the earliest studies of spousal violence detected violence by women toward their husbands (Gelles 1974). The two National Family Violence Surveys (Straus and Gelles 1986; Straus, Gelles, and Steinmetz 1980) also found a higher-than-expected incidence of violence toward men—the rate of violence was the same or even higher than that reported for male-to-female violence. However, the researchers qualified their findings by noting that much of the female violence appeared to be in self-defense and that females, because of their size and strength, appeared to inflict less injury than male attackers. Using only the most conservative indicator of battering, the rate of injury-producing assaults by women, and projecting to only the 52 million married couples in the United States in 1990, would still suggest there are 104,000 men who are injured by their wives each year (Gelles 1993).

Explanations

Six theoretical models have been developed to explain spouse abuse and neglect: social learning theory, social situational/stress and coping theory, general systems theory, resource theory, exchange/social control theory, and patriarchy.

Social learning theory proposes that individuals who experienced violence are more likely to use violence in the home than those who have experienced little or no violence. Children who either experience violence themselves or who witness violence between their parents are more likely to use violence when they grow up. This finding has been interpreted to support the idea that family violence is learned. The family is the institution and social group where people learn the roles of husband and wife, parent and child. The home is the primary place in which people learn how to deal with various stresses, crises, and frustrations. In many instances, the home is also where a person first experiences violence. Not only do people learn violent behavior, but they learn how to justify being violent. For example, hearing a father say, "This will hurt me more than it will hurt you," or a mother say, "You have been bad, so you deserve to be spanked," contributes to how children learn to justify violent behavior.

Social situation/stress and coping theory explains why violence is used in some situations and not others. The theory proposes that abuse and violence occur because of two main factors. The first is structural stress and the lack of coping resources in a family. For instance, the association between low income and family violence indicates that an important factor in violence is inadequate financial resources. The second factor is the cultural norm concerning the use of force and violence. In contemporary American society, as well as many other societies, violence is normative (Straus, Gelles, and Steinmetz 1980). Thus, individuals learn to use violence both expressively and instrumentally as a way to cope with a pileup of stressor events.

General systems theory, a social system approach, was developed and applied by Straus (1973) and Jean Giles-Sims (1983) to explain family violence. Here, violence is viewed as a system product rather than the result of individual pathology. The family system operations can maintain, escalate, or reduce levels of violence in families. General systems theory describes the processes that characterize the use of violence in family interactions and explains the way in which violence is managed and stabilized. Straus (1973) argues that a general systems theory of family violence must include at least three basic elements: (1) alternative courses of action or causal flow, (2) the feedback mechanisms that enable the system to make adjustments, and (3) system goals.

The resource theory of family violence assumes that all social systems (including the family) rest to some degree on force or the threat of force. The more resources—social, personal, and economic—a person can command, the more force that individual can muster. However, according to William Goode (1971), the more resources a person actually has, the less that person will actually use force in an open manner. Thus, a husband who wants to be the dominant person in the family, but has little education, has a job low in prestige and income, and lacks interpersonal skills, may choose to use violence to maintain the dominant position.

Exchange/social control theory was developed by Richard J. Gelles (1983) on the basic propositions of an exchange theory of aggression. The exchange/social control model of family violence proposes that wife abuse is governed by the principle of costs and rewards. Drawing from exchange theory, Gelles (1983) notes that violence and abuse are used when the rewards are higher than the costs. Drawing from social control theories of delinquency, he proposes that the private nature of the family, the reluctance of social institutions and agencies to intervene, and the low risk of other interventions reduce the costs of abuse and violence. The cultural approval of violence as both expressive and instrumental behavior raises the potential rewards for violence.

The patriarchy theory's central thesis is that economic and social processes operate directly and indirectly to support a patriarchal (male-dominated) social order and family structure. The central theoretical argument is that patriarchy leads to the subordination and oppression of women and causes the historical pattern of systematic violence directed against wives (Dobash and Dobash 1979; Pagelow 1984; Yllo 1983, 1993). The patriarchy theory finds the source of family violence in society at large and how it is organized, as opposed to within individual families or communities.

Prevention and Control

There are a number of options available to women who want to either escape violence or to force their husbands to stop hitting them. One choice is to call the police. The best-known assessment of intervention into marital violence is the Minneapolis Police Experiment (Sherman and Berk 1984). Those households receiving the arrest intervention had the lowest rate of recidivism (10%), and those who were separated had the highest (24%).

Replications of the Minneapolis study, however, found that arrest had no more effect in deterring future arrests or complaints of violence than did separation or counseling (Berk et al. 1992; Dunford, Huizinga, and Elliott 1990; Pate and Hamilton 1992; Sherman and Smith 1992). The replications did find that men who were employed at the time of the arrest were less likely to be violent after they were arrested, compared to employed men who were not arrested. However, men who were unemployed at the time of the arrest were actually more likely to be violent after they were arrested, compared to unemployed men who were not arrested.

Abused wives also have the option of going to a shelter or safe house. There were only six such shelters in the United States in 1976, but there were more than 1,000 by 1994. Researchers find that the effects of shelters seem to depend on the attributes of the victims. When a victim is actively engaged in taking control of her life, a shelter stay can dramatically reduce the likelihood of new violence. For some victims, a shelter stay may have no effect, while for others it may actually lead to an escalation of violence when they return home (Berk, Newton, and Berk 1986).

Lee H. Bowker (1983) talked to women who had been beaten and who managed to get their husbands to stop being violent. Among the things these women did were to talk to friends and relatives, threaten their husbands, aggressively defend themselves from their husbands, go to shelters, call social service agencies, and call the police. No one action worked best. Bowker (1983) concluded that ultimately, the crucial factor was the woman taking a stand and showing her determination that the violence had to stop.

Researchers have also evaluated group programs developed for violent men. Donald G. Dutton (1986) reports that fifty men enrolled in a court-mandated program and followed for up to three years had recidivism rates as low as 4 percent. Edward W. Gondolf (1987) reports that men who complete voluntary programs show nonviolent rates of two-thirds to three-quarters. Results of assessments of men's groups must be read cautiously because such groups tend to have low recruitment rates and high attrition rates (Pirog-Good and Stets 1986). The more optimistic findings typically apply to only those men who complete counseling programs.

Steps that can prevent spousal abuse and neglect before it occurs include eliminating the norms that legitimize and glorify violence in the society and the family, reducing violence-provoking stress created by society, integrating families into a network of kin and community, changing the sexist character of society, and breaking the cycle of violence in the family.

(*See also:* Child Abuse and Neglect: Sociological Aspects; Exchange Theory; Family Gender Roles; Family Systems Theory; Family Violence; Marital Power; Rape)

BIBLIOGRAPHY

Berk, R. A.; Campbell, A.; Klap, R.; and Western, B. (1992). "The Deterrent Effect of Arrest Incidents on Domestic Violence: A Bayesian Analysis of Four Field Experiments." *American Sociological Review* 57:698–708.

Berk, R. A.; Newton, P.; and Berk, S. F. (1986). "What a Difference a Day Makes: An Empirical Study of the Impact of Shelters for Battered Women." *Journal of Marriage and the Family* 48:481–490.

Bowker, L. H. (1983). *Beating Wife Beating.* Lexington, MA: Lexington Books.

Curtis, L. (1974). *Criminal Violence: National Patterns and Behavior.* Lexington, MA: Lexington Books.

Dobash, R. E., and Dobash, R. (1979). *Violence Against Wives.* New York: Free Press.

Dunford, F. W.; Huizinga, D.; and Elliott, D. S. (1990). "The Role of Arrest in Domestic Assault: The Omaha Police Experiment." *Criminology* 28:183–206.

Dutton, D. G. (1986). "The Outcome of Court-Mandated Treatment for Wife Assault: A Quasi-Experimental Evaluation." *Violence and Victims* 1:163–176.

Finkelhor, D., and Yllo, K. (1985). *License to Rape: Sexual Abuse of Wives.* New York: Holt, Rinehart and Winston.

Gelles, R. J. (1974). *The Violent Home.* Newbury Park, CA: Sage Publications.

Gelles, R. J. (1983). "An Exchange/Social Control Theory." In *The Dark Side of Families: Current Family Violence Research*, ed. D. Finkelhor, R. Gelles, M. Straus, and G. Hotaling. Newbury Park, CA: Sage Publications.

Gelles, R. J. (1993). "Violence Toward Men: Fact or Fiction?" Paper prepared for the Council on Scientific Affairs, American Medical Association, Chicago.

Gelles, R. J., and Straus, M. A. (1988). *Intimate Violence.* New York: Simon & Schuster.

Giles-Sims, J. (1983). *Wife-Beating: A Systems Theory Approach.* New York: Guilford.

Gondolf, E. W. (1987). "Evaluating Progress for Men Who Batter: Problems and Prospects." *Journal of Family Violence* 2:95–108.

Goode, W. (1971). "Force and Violence in the Family." *Journal of Marriage and the Family* 33:624–636.

Martin, D. (1976). *Battered Wives.* San Francisco: Glide.

Pagelow, M. (1984). *Family Violence.* New York: Praeger.

Pate, A. M., and Hamilton, E. E. (1992). "Formal and Informal Social Deterrents to Domestic Violence." *American Sociological Review* 57:691–697.

Pirog-Good, M. A., and Stets, J. (1986). "Programs for Abusers: Who Drops Out and What Can Be Done." *Response* 9:17–19.

Russell, D. E. H. (1984). *Sexual Exploitation: Rape, Child Sexual Abuse, and Workplace Harassment.* Newbury Park, CA: Sage Publications.

Sherman, L. W., and Berk, R. A. (1984). "The Specific Deterrent Effects of Arrest for Domestic Assault." *American Sociological Review* 49:261–272.

Sherman, L. W., and Smith, D. A. (1992). "Crime, Punishment, and Stake in Conformity: Legal and Informal Control of Domestic Violence." *American Sociological Review* 57:680–690.

Straus, M. A. (1973). "A General Systems Theory Approach to a Theory of Violence Between Family Members." *Social Science Information* 12:105–125.

Straus, M. A., and Gelles, R. J. (1986). "Societal Change and Change in Family Violence from 1975 to 1985 as Revealed in Two National Surveys." *Journal of Marriage and the Family* 48:465–479.

Straus, M. A.; Gelles, R. J.; and Steinmetz, S. K. (1980). *Behind Closed Doors: Violence in the American Family.* New York: Doubleday/Anchor.

Straus, M. A., and Sweet, S. (1992). "Verbal/Symbolic Aggression in Couples: Incidence Rates and Relationships to Personal Characteristics." *Journal of Marriage and the Family* 54:346–357.

U.S. Department of Justice. (1980). *Intimate Victims: A Study of Violence Among Friends and Relatives.* Washington, DC: U.S. Government Printing Office.

U.S. Department of Justice. (1984). *Family Violence.* Washington, DC: Bureau of Justice Statistics.

U.S. Department of Justice. (1993). *Uniform Crime Reports for the United States, 1992.* Washington, DC: Federal Bureau of Investigation.

Wardell, L.; Gillespie, D. L.; and Leffler, A. (1983). "Science and Violence Against Women." In *The Dark Side of Fam-*

ilies: Current Family Violence Research, ed. D. Finkelhor, R. Gelles, M. Straus, and G. Hotaling. Newbury Park, CA: Sage Publications.

Yllo, K. (1983). "Using a Feminist Approach in Quantitative Research." In *The Dark Side of Families: Current Family Violence Research*, ed. D. Finkelhor, R. Gelles, M. Straus, and G. Hotaling. Newbury Park, CA: Sage Publications.

Yllo, K. (1993). "Through a Feminist Lens: Gender, Power, and Violence." In *Current Controversies on Family Violence*, ed. R. Gelles and D. Loseke. Newbury Park, CA: Sage Publications.

RICHARD J. GELLES

STEPFAMILIES AND THE LAW

See ALIMONY AND SPOUSAL SUPPORT; CHILD CUSTODY; CHILDREN'S RIGHTS; CHILD SUPPORT

STEPPARENTING

Stepfamilies consist of at least one minor child who is living with a biological parent and that parent's spouse—a stepparent—who is not the child's other biological parent. Paul Glick (1989) estimated that, in the United States, 17.4 percent of all married-couple families with children were stepfamilies, that 19.1 percent of all children under the age of eighteen live in stepfamilies, and that 12.7 percent of all children are stepchildren.

The large number of parents and children who live in stepfamilies has prompted researchers to study how well family members adjust to living in a stepfamily. Much of this research has focused on the parenting role of the stepparent.

Parenting Roles

What are parenting roles? According to Roy H. Rodgers and James M. White (1993, p. 234), a social role is defined as "all the norms attached to a given social position." Social norms are beliefs that prescribe (i.e., allow or encourage) certain behaviors that are considered to be desirable (e.g., helping others) and proscribe (i.e., do not allow or discourage) others that are not considered to be desirable (e.g., harming others) (Burr, Day, and Bahr 1993). Because a parenting role is one type of social role, a parenting role can be defined as a set of beliefs pertaining to how parents should behave.

The beliefs included in a parent's notion of a parenting role are reflected in how a parent behaves toward the children. Two types of parenting behaviors that are a part of the parenting role—control and warmth—have been identified as being particularly important for child development (Maccoby and Martin 1983). Control refers to the degree to which parents set and enforce limits and monitor their children's activities. Warmth refers to the extent to which parents communicate with, show caring toward, and support their children. Empirical evidence has consistently shown that the more parents exhibit both control and warmth, the more positive is children's (Steinberg, Elmen, and Mounts 1989).

Before discussing the stepparent role, an important distinction needs to be drawn between the content of a parenting role and the clarity of that role. These two aspects of a parenting role are independent. For example, one parent may be very clear that he should spend considerable time with and act friendly toward his child, whereas another parent may be clear that she should maintain her distance from the child to be an effective disciplinarian. In this instance, both parents are clear about their parenting role (i.e., they have little role ambiguity), but the content of their perceived role differs (supportive friend versus detached disciplinarian).

As another example, consider two parents who both believe that they should quickly and firmly discipline the child for each and every misbehavior. Although these two parents may have the same perceptions of their parenting role, one may be very clear and confident that the parenting role is the one that should be assumed, whereas the other parent may not be so sure (i.e., is somewhat ambiguous). In this instance, the content of the parenting role is similar for both parents, but the extent of role ambiguity differs.

Content of the Stepparent Role

Research that has addressed the content of the stepparent role has suggested that the stepparent role, according to the beliefs, reported behaviors, and observed behaviors of stepparents, is a less active one than is the role of the biological parent. Mark Fine and Lawrence Kurdek (1994) found that stepparents believe that they are less active and should be less active as parents than are biological parents. These differences were present on both the warmth and control aspects of the parenting role, although they were strongest on the warmth dimension.

A study by Andrew Schwebel, Fine, and Maureena Renner (1991) also supported that the stepparent role is less active than the biological parent role. In response to hypothetical case scenarios that call for some type of parenting behavior, college students were asked to rate how likely it was that a parent or a stepparent would engage in a parenting behavior and to what extent the parent or stepparent should engage in the behavior. The students reported that stepparents, relative to biological parents, would be less likely to engage in parenting behavior and had less of an obligation to do so.

Furthermore, when stepparents are asked how they actually behave, not just what their beliefs are, they report being less active as parents than do biological parents. In a sample of stepfamilies included in the National Survey of Families and Households (Fine, Voydanoff, and Donnelly 1993), parents and stepparents were asked how often they engage in positive behaviors (e.g., spending time with the child), negative behaviors (e.g., yelling at the child), and control behaviors. Stepfathers reported behaving less positively and less negatively toward their stepchildren than did fathers, indicating that they refrain from becoming involved with their stepchildren. However, stepmothers reported responding as positively to their stepchildren as did biological mothers in stepfamilies, although they responded less negatively. This suggests that stepfathers may be less active in demonstrating warmth to children than are fathers, but that stepmothers show as much warmth to children as biological mothers. Moreover, these findings indicate that stepmothers may be more active in parenting than stepfathers. No differences in control parenting behaviors were found between stepparents and biological parents.

Finally, some studies have had observers rate the parenting behaviors of stepparents and biological parents. It should be noted that the majority of these behavioral observation studies have assessed stepfathers and not stepmothers. As is consistent with the previously discussed studies, these investigations indicate that stepfathers are less active as parents than are biological fathers. It was found that stepfathers' parenting style was characterized by disengagement, meaning that stepfathers, compared with biological fathers, were less involved with, showed less awareness of, and exerted less discipline over their stepchildren (Hetherington and Clingempeel 1992; Hetherington 1993). When stepfathers in newly formed stepfamilies tried to establish a positive relationship with the stepchild by talking and sharing activities, these efforts were often met with resistance, particularly when the stepchild was an adolescent. Despite this resistance, many stepfathers continued to try to remain involved in the lives of their stepchildren. Over time, however, because of continued resistance or distancing behaviors on the part of the stepchild, most of these stepfathers stopped trying to establish close stepfather–stepchild relationships.

Ambiguity of the Stepparent Role

There is considerable evidence that the parenting role of the stepparent is ambiguous (Crosbie-Burnett 1989; Giles-Sims 1984). Andrew Cherlin (1978) suggested that this ambiguity stemmed from a lack of social consensus regarding how stepfamily members, especially stepparents, should behave in their families. He labeled this lack of societal guidance the "incomplete institutionalization" of remarriage.

The ambiguity of the stepparent role is reflected in the notion that there are several plausible ways that the role of the stepparent can be filled. The following are some, but not all, of these possible ways to fill the stepparent role: to act "just like" a parent to the stepchild; to act like a supportive friend to the stepchild, meaning that the stepparent is warm and friendly to the child without actively engaging in discipline; to support the disciplinary policies of the biological parent without independently establishing and enforcing rules of one's own; and to be detached from the child, meaning that the stepparent does not become involved in the stepchild's life. In the absence of clear social norms, stepparents may not know which of these ways, or others, is the most desirable way for them to fill the stepparent role. There is some limited empirical evidence to support the notion that the role of the stepparent is ambiguous (Fine and Kurdek 1994; Fine, Kurdek, and Hennigen 1992; Marsiglio 1991; Schwebel, Fine, and Renner 1991).

The gender of the stepparent seems to be related to the extent to which the stepparent role is ambiguous. A number of scholars have suggested that the role of stepmother is more ambiguous than is that of the stepfather. There are several reasons why this may be the case. First, there are many more stepfathers than stepmothers (Coleman and Ganong 1990), which could mean that stepmothers have even fewer institutionalized guidelines than do stepfathers to help them determine how to behave as parents.

Second, stepmothers must cope with stronger negative stereotypes than do stepfathers (Ganong, Coleman, and Mapes 1990). These negative stereotypes are reflected in the "wicked stepmother" theme that is sometimes found in children's literature.

A third reason that the stepmother role may be more ambiguous than the stepfather role is based on the notion that children have difficulty being loyal to two "mothers." Mothers who do not live with their children following divorce remain in closer contact with their biological children than do fathers who do not live with their children following divorce (Seltzer and Bianchi 1988). This contact may hamper the development of stepmother–stepchild relationships because stepchildren feel that they are being disloyal to their mothers if they become close to their stepmothers.

Fourth, stepmother families may begin differently than stepfather families. Frank Furstenberg and Christine Nord (1985) suggest that children living with their fathers following divorce may have experienced a difficult custody negotiation, may have a history of troubled family relations, and/or may have mothers who cannot effectively manage single-parent status. Consequently, because these children have had particularly stressful histories before becoming part of a stepfamily, they may have more problematic relations with their stepmothers.

Finally, women are traditionally expected to assume responsibility for child care and other household tasks (Thompson and Walker 1989). Because of these expectations, stepmothers may face more pressure to provide care, maintenance, and nurturance of their stepchildren than do stepfathers (Visher and Visher 1988). Because these pressures to be active as parents may conflict with the less active parenting role expected of stepparents, role ambiguity may be magnified.

There are several other factors that may influence the ambiguity of the stepparent role, including the following three factors. First, the role of the stepparent may be more ambiguous in "complex" stepfamilies (i.e., both spouses have children from a previous marriage) than in "simple" stepfamilies (i.e., only one spouse has a child from a previous marriage) (Visher and Visher 1988). Role ambiguity is thought to be accentuated in complex stepfamilies because each spouse is simultaneously both a parent and a stepparent.

Second, the role of the stepparent is likely to be more ambiguous when the nonresidential parent is highly involved with the child, particularly when the nonresidential parent is the mother. When there is an active nonresidential parent, the stepparent, residential biological parent, and the child may feel that there is little need for the stepparent to assume an active parenting role. Without a perceived need for the stepparent to be active, stepfamily members may be unclear about how the stepparent should relate to the stepchild.

Finally, the extent of role ambiguity may vary with the length of time since the stepfamily was formed. As noted by Patricia Papernow (1993), for those stepfamilies that remain together, roles generally become clearer over the lifespan of the stepfamily, and, consequently, one would expect that the stepparent's role would become less ambiguous over time.

Stepparent Role and Adjustment

There is evidence that both the content of the stepparent role and the extent to which the role is ambiguous are related to the adjustment of members of stepfamilies. In terms of the content of the stepparent role, children's adjustment is facilitated when stepparents, at least initially, do not take an active role in discipline. E. Mavis Hetherington (1993) and James H. Bray and Sandra H. Burger (1993) found that stepparent–stepchild relations and child adjustment were most positive when stepfathers did not actively discipline their stepchildren, but rather supported the disciplinary practices of the child's biological parent. In addition, Fine and Kurdek (1992) found that the adjustment of young adolescents in stepfamilies was more positive to the extent that they characterized their families as providing high levels of supervision, warmth, and order and low levels of conflict. Interestingly, these findings were strongest for girls living with stepmothers.

With respect to ambiguity regarding the stepparent role, there is evidence that greater stepparent role ambiguity is associated with some dimensions of adjustment. For example, Kurdek and Fine (1991) found that high levels of stepparent role ambiguity were related to mothers' reports of low family/marital/personal life satisfaction and stepfathers' reports of low parenting satisfaction. This may indicate that parenting is a more vulnerable and less comfortable area than personal life satisfaction for stepfathers, and the reverse may be true for mothers. Similarly, Fine, Kurdek, and Lorraine Hennigen (1992) found that adolescents who tended to see the role of their stepmother as ambiguous also tended to see themselves as low in self-competence.

Conclusion

Stepparents seem to be less involved with their stepchildren than biological parents are with their children, and the role of the stepparent seems to be more ambiguous than is the role of the biological parent. Although few supportive empirical studies exist, there are conceptual reasons to believe that the role of the stepmother is more stressful than is the role of the stepfather. Furthermore, there is limited evidence that the adjustment of stepfamily members is related to both the content of the stepparent role and the extent to which the stepparent role is ambiguous. However, further research is needed concerning the roles that stepparents play and how these roles affect the well-being of stepfamily members.

(*See also:* Child Custody; Family Gender Roles; Fathers; Gay and Lesbian Parents; Mothers; Remarriage; Remarriage and Children)

BIBLIOGRAPHY

Bray, J. H., and Berger, S. H. (1993). "Developmental Issues in Stepfamilies Research Project: Family Relationships and Parent–Child Interactions." *Journal of Family Psychology* 7:76–90.

Burr, W. R.; Day, R. D.; and Bahr, K. S. (1993). *Family Science.* Pacific Grove, CA: Brooks/Cole.

Cherlin, A. (1978). "Remarriage as an Incomplete Institution." *American Journal of Sociology* 84:634–650.

Coleman, M., and Ganong, L. H. (1990). "Remarriage and Stepfamily Research in the 1980s: Increased Interest in an Old Family Form." *Journal of Marriage and the Family* 52:925–940.

Crosbie-Burnett, M. (1989). "Application of Family Stress Theory to Remarriage: A Model for Assessing and Helping Stepfamilies." *Family Relations* 38:323–331.

Fine, M. A., and Kurdek, L. A. (1992). "The Adjustment of Adolescents in Stepfather and Stepmother Families." *Journal of Marriage and the Family* 54:725–736.

Fine, M. A., and Kurdek, L. A. (1994). "Parenting Cognitions in Stepfamilies: Differences Between Parents and Stepparents and Relations to Parenting Satisfaction." *Journal of Social and Personal Relationships* 11:95–112.

Fine, M. A.; Kurdek, L. A.; and Hennigen, L. (1992). "Perceived Self-Competence and Its Relations to Stepfamily Myths and (Step)Parent Role Ambiguity in Adolescents from Stepfather and Stepmother Families." *Journal of Family Psychology* 6:69–76.

Fine, M. A.; Voydanoff, P.; and Donnelly, B. W. (1993). "Relations Between Parental Control and Warmth and Child Well-Being in Stepfamilies." *Journal of Family Psychology* 7:222–232.

Furstenberg, F. F., Jr., and Nord, C. W. (1985). "Parenting Apart: Patterns of Child Rearing After Marital Disruption." *Journal of Marriage and the Family* 47:893–904.

Ganong, L.; Coleman, M.; and Mapes, D. (1990). "A Meta-Analytic Review of Family Structure Stereotypes." *Journal of Marriage and the Family* 52:287–297.

Giles-Sims, J. (1984). "The Stepparent Role: Expectations, Behavior, and Sanctions." *Journal of Family Issues* 5:116–130.

Glick, P. C. (1989). "Remarried Families, Stepfamilies, and Stepchildren: A Brief Demographic Profile." *Family Relations* 38:24–27.

Hetherington, E. M. (1993). "An Overview of the Virginia Longitudinal Study of Divorce and Remarriage with a Focus on Early Adolescence." *Journal of Family Psychology* 7:39–56.

Hetherington, E. M., and Clingempeel, W. G. (1992). "Coping with Marital Transitions: A Family Systems Perspective." *Monographs of the Society for Research in Child Development* 57 (2–3, Serial no. 227).

Kurdek, L. A., and Fine, M. A. (1991). "Cognitive Correlates of Adjustment for Mothers and Stepfathers in Stepfather Families." *Journal of Marriage and the Family* 53:565–572.

Maccoby, E. M., and Martin, J. (1983). "Socialization in the Context of the Family: Parent–Child Interaction." In *Handbook of Child Psychology:* Vol. 4, *Socialization, Personality, and Social Development*, ed. E. M. Hetherington. New York: Wiley.

Marsiglio, W. (1991). "Paternal Engagement Activities with Minor Children." *Journal of Marriage and the Family* 53:973–986.

Papernow, P. L. (1993). *Becoming a Stepfamily: Patterns of Development in Remarried Families.* San Francisco: Jossey-Bass.

Rodgers, R. H., and White, J. M. (1993). "Family Development Theory." In *Sourcebook of Family Theories and Methods: A Conceptual Approach*, ed. P. G. Boss, W. J. Doherty, R. LaRossa, W. R. Schumm, and S. K. Steinmetz. New York: Plenum.

Schwebel, A. I.; Fine, M. A.; and Renner, M. A. (1991). "An Empirical Investigation of Perceptions of the Stepparent Role." *Journal of Family Issues* 12:43–57.

Seltzer, J., and Bianchi, S. (1988). "Children's Contact with Absent Parents." *Journal of Marriage and the Family* 50:663–677.

Steinberg, L.; Elmen, J. D.; and Mounts, N. S. (1989). "Authoritative Parenting, Psychological Maturity, and Academic Success Among Adolescents." *Child Development* 60:1424–1436.

Thompson, L., and Walker, A. J. (1989). "Women and Men in Marriage, Work, and Parenthood." *Journal of Marriage and the Family* 51:845–871.

Visher, E. B., and Visher, J. S. (1988). *Old Loyalties, New Ties: Therapeutic Interventions with Stepfamilies.* New York: Brunner/ Mazel.

Mark A. Fine

STRESS

The study of stress in families has focused on three major issues: the typical effects of stress on families, resistance/vulnerability to stress, and social sources of exposure to stress.

The concept of stress is extremely popular, despite continuing ambiguity and disagreement about what is meant by this term. Some scholars use the word to refer to causative factors—events or conditions that may arouse specific responses or may cause distress. Other scholars use the same term to refer to effects or outcomes—the response that has been evoked or the distress that has been aroused by those events or conditions. Both stressful agents and stress outcomes are linked in what Leonard Pearlin, a noted social-stress theorist and researcher, has labeled "the stress process" (Pearlin et al. 1981). This process includes other variables as well: social factors that influence exposure to stressful conditions and events and individual and group resources that shape responses to stress. For this entry, agents of causative factors are labeled "stressors" and responses or effects are labeled "stress outcomes."

Early Research

Early stress research focused first on unpleasant physical stressors such as electric shock or exposure to cold (see Selye 1982). These stressors had a clear onset and ending, and their occurrence was beyond the control of the research subject. Later work concentrated on the amount of change associated with specific events that could happen to an individual; Thomas A. Holmes and Richard H. Rahe (1967) developed a checklist of stressful life events that many other researchers adopted. These checklist approaches to the measurement of stress are notable for two assumptions. First, they assumed that one could calculate a standard estimate of the amount of change demanded by a specific event such as divorce or the birth of a child, which would be generally applicable to all who experienced that event. Second, they assumed that one could capture the effects of the accumulation of several events in a short period of time by summing the amount of change implied by each. These life-event checklist measures also differed from earlier assessments of stressors because they included events that were neither random occurrences nor events whose occurrence was controlled by an investigator. In including events that were at least partially under the control of the individual, such as being fired from a job or getting a promotion, this line of research opened up questions about how much control individuals had in avoiding or precipitating adverse life events.

Neither of these early definitions of stressors took into account how well different individuals deal with the same specific changes or circumstances. Over time, however, the concept of stress has expanded to include attention to both environmental demands and individual capacities or resources; stress occurs when there is a discrepancy between individual capacities and environmental demands. This discrepancy could be in either direction; demands could be greater than a person's capacities or demands could be far below individual capacities. According to this expanded view, therefore, restricted opportunities can be at least as stressful as high demands, and individual differences are explicitly recognized as intimately connected to stressful experience.

Just as important, the concept of environmental demands/stressors began to expand beyond the notion of a discrete life event with a specific date of onset to include chronic or persisting circumstances. Since such circumstances are likely to be linked to social status—as indicated by one's race, gender, marital status, family composition, employment status, and economic position—this expanded definition of stress brought stress research closer to traditional sociological topics such as social stratification and race and gender discrimination. Therefore, it offered a new way of thinking about the way that normatively structured family and occupational social roles shape individual opportunities, individual distress, and family well-being. Social stress researchers have begun to give greater attention to what Carol Aneshensel (1992) calls "the stressful consequences of social organization," while still continuing to study individual variations in response to stressors.

Family Stress Research

Ironically, while studies of individual stressors and individual stress have gradually moved toward greater attention to the links between societal factors and experienced stressors, in some ways family stress research has shown some movement in the opposite direction. Family stress theory began with study of stressors linked to social organization and societal crises—widespread unemployment, extended separations brought on by World War II, and so on. However, much of the subsequent work has emphasized normative family stressors—changes or transitions that are built into the expectable sequences of family life as children are born, begin school, become adolescent, and establish their own residences and families. This increasing focus on everyday events and on normatively and biologically expectable changes that happen to most families led to reduced attention to variations in social stressors and a greater concern for which families handled these transitions more and less well. Rather than studying how to avoid such stressors, researchers focused on learning how, despite presumably ubiquitous stressors, individuals and families could respond in adaptive ways to preserve positive family relationships. Paralleling the emphasis on cumulative life-change scores that was occurring in research on individual stress, family stress researchers have also examined a family's "pile-up" of life events, reasoning that events might be benign if occurring singly may overwhelm family resources if they occur in close succession. For example, the combination of both an unexpected pregnancy and job loss may have effects that exceed the separate effects of each event.

Resistance/vulnerability to stress. Following Reuben Hill's (1949) ABCX model, family stress researchers have conceptualized stressful outcomes (which Hill labeled X) as a function of three major factors: A (the stressor), B (family resources), and C (appraisal or interpretation). Extending this model, Hamilton I. McCubbin and his colleagues emphasized potential changes over time in each of these factors, using the double ABCX model label for their own extension to highlight the nonstatic nature of the stress process (see Lavee, McCubbin, and Olson 1987; Lavee, McCubbin, and Patterson 1985; McCubbin and Patterson 1983). Researchers have continued to emphasize the role of family resources or strengths (factor B) and the meaning or interpretation that members of the family give to an event or stressor (factor C) in shaping outcomes.

These same factors are also central to studies of stress at the individual level. Richard Lazarus and Susan Folkman (1984) put a heavy emphasis on the importance of individual appraisal processes in determining both how threatening a life change seems to be and how an individual will attempt to adapt to the situation. Pearlin and his colleagues (1981) stress how material, social, and psychosocial resources help to account for variations in the individual distress aroused by stressful circumstances in normative adult roles such as marriage, employment, and parenting. In both literatures, economic resources, social supports from others, and individual levels of self-esteem and mastery are viewed as critical resources. Therefore, both at the individual level and in the study of families, resources and interpretations are viewed as central variables conditioning the impact of stressors.

Life events and stressful conditions. Much of the family stress literature has emphasized the stressful potential of changes in life circumstances. However, it is increasingly clear that the impact of transitions and eventful changes depends in part on the circumstances prevailing prior to a specific life event. A notable example is marital termination; while the end of a marriage is generally viewed as a stressful event, termination of a conflict-filled or unsatisfying relationship may actually improve well-being. Blair Wheaton (1990) has shown that for a range of life events, role exits including retirement, widowhood, divorce, and a child's move away from home have more positive effects on mental health the more stressful were prior conditions in that role. Thus, effects of life events depend in part on prior circumstances. They also depend in part on the subsequent level of chronic problems. It is largely because major life events typically result in an enduring alteration in social circumstances, thereby increasing chronic problems, that they affect individual and family outcomes; when these secondary results can be avoided, life events per se may have little discernible impact (Lavee et al. 1985; Pearlin et al. 1981).

Social Sources of Exposure to Stress

In considering the relationship between stressful circumstances on the one hand and family members' individual well-being and overall family functioning on the other, research has tended to focus on two main questions: (1) how can variations in exposure to stressors (or amount of life change) explain variations in individual and family outcomes and (2) how, in a group of individuals or families exposed to the same stressor, may variations in individual and family capacities, resources, and coping efforts explain variations in outcomes. An example of the former is the investigation conducted by Pearlin and his colleagues (1981) into the effect of occupational disruptions on emotional distress. They compared those who had faced recent disruptions with respondents who had not, with statistical controls for other variables known to affect emotional distress, and traced the effects of disruption through diminished self-esteem and compromised sense of mastery to increased distress. An example of the latter question is Glen Elder's (1974) study of families who faced serious economic decline during the Great Depression. Elder investigated whether couples with more cohesive marital bonds at a prior point were better able to respond to the economic difficulties they faced and found that prior marital cohesion was a significant buffer against negative effects.

Each of these questions is very important in better understanding the processes by which stressors affect families, but these questions also tend to treat exposure to stress as a random process. Because exposure to difficult life events or constraining social circumstances is *not* a random process (exposure is intimately linked to social characteristics and social location), it is important to try to understand the sources of the stressors affecting the families, to view variations in exposure to stressors as a phenomenon that needs to be explained, and to seek the social sources of stressors. Family stress research is now focusing more on these issues and asking how does the larger social context shape families' exposure to stressors and influence family outcomes. In particular, researchers are examining how economic and occupational conditions in one's community, region, and nation enhance or limit families and how the opportunities and barriers linked to race, gender, and age affect exposure to stressors and family outcomes.

Race. Two useful discussions of how membership in a racial minority affects exposure to stressors are provided by Marie Peters and Grace C. Massey (1983) and Vonnie McLoyd (1990). Research has shown that when economic problems become pervasive in a community, each family loses a sense of security and becomes less able to rely on community supports, and overall community levels of family violence and child abuse rise as economic indicators decline. This pattern has implications for racial and ethnic differences in stress exposure and stress effects. To the extent that discriminatory labor-market practices compromise minority members' access to income, job security, and occupational quality, racially segregated communities will lack the resources families need to resist stress.

Gender. Attention to gender differences in stress exposure and stress outcomes has also highlighted differences *within* families; individual family members do not always encounter the same stressors or experience the same outcomes. Family roles are themselves socially stratified, and some family members may be exposed to more stressors than are others. While many families provide critical positive support for their members, other families inflict severe violence and patterns of physical and emotional abuse that wreak havoc on individual life chances and on subsequent generations. Thus, the study of stress in families must encompass both individual and family stressors and both individual and family outcomes, without assuming that stressors affect all family members equally.

Employment and earnings. Family stress research is increasingly focusing on the socially structured stressors that are built into the rhythms of daily employment and family interaction. In part, this reflects the massive changes in occupational and family structures, in assumptions about gender-differentiated family roles, and in family economic well-being that occurred in the twentieth century. In the early 1990s, nearly 25 percent of American children were living in families with incomes below the official poverty level; after an improvement in the 1960s and 1970s, the proportions of children who are poor have returned to the high levels of the 1940s and 1950s. The poverty rates of children in female-headed households are especially high, varying between 51 percent and 56 percent since 1970, but poverty rates have climbed among married-couple families as well (Coontz 1992).

Two kinds of changes—in parents' employment and earnings and in family composition—are implicated in these overall changes in total family income. To sketch these trends very broadly, young men have seen a decline in their earning power and an increase in their vulnerability to layoff and job loss. This decline in American men's earnings largely reflects changes in the national structure of employment opportunities. Agricultural jobs have been mechanized, reducing the need for workers; many corporations have closed factories that provided secure, unionized, high-paying employment and moved those manufacturing jobs to other countries; jobs in the service sector of the economy have increased, but they provide lower wages than many of the jobs that were lost. Young men with limited educations have been particularly hard hit; the number of jobs that require only physical strength and hard work have decreased and jobs that require technical skills and advanced training have increased.

Conversely, young women have experienced some improvements in their earning power, and their presence in the labor force has been growing. In the past, married women with children under the age of three were not likely to work, but women now return fairly rapidly to the labor force after childbirth. It is estimated that the majority of mothers of school-aged children are employed at least part-time. However, men and women still differ sharply in the average conditions they encounter at work, since occupations, and jobs within occupations, remain segregated by sex; much of women's employment still tends to be in "female ghetto" occupational areas (i.e., secretarial and clerical, retail sales, beauty/cosmetics, and young children's education). Employment in such "women's jobs" carries lower average wages than in occupations that have been typically male.

In two-parent families, mothers' employment has helped to avoid or at least reduce the economic shortfalls that would otherwise have resulted as men's earning power declined. Maternal employment increases family economic resources, but at the cost of available maternal time with children. It has also generated widespread societal debate about women's economic dependence, about whether children suffer when mothers are employed, and about whether men are doing their fair share of household work and child rearing.

In one-parent families, mothers' earnings are still more critical to avoid economic stressors, but many unmarried mothers find that the amount of money they can earn is relatively little, given the gender gap in earnings; even when single mothers are employed full-time year-round, they earn significantly less than single-father families, and their families have much lower incomes than dual-earner married-couple families. In addition, single mothers' employment also creates time pressures that are hard to manage when mothers are the sole adults in their households, and quality child-care arrangements are often difficult to arrange and to afford.

Household composition. Accompanying these changes in gender roles and employment have been pervasive changes in family and household composition during the twentieth century. Nonfamily households—people living alone or with people to whom they are not linked by kinship, marital, or adoptive ties—constitute an increasing proportion of all households; the majority of these are single adults living alone. Family households are further distinguished by whether or not they contain children under age eighteen, and by the number of adults and their relationships to one another. The proportion of family households with children that are headed by married couples has been decreasing, and mother–stepfather and father–stepmother families comprise a growing share of the family households that do have two parents. These latter families face the difficult challenge of negotiating satisfying family bonds with little cultural guidance regarding the appropriate relations between stepparents and stepchildren. The proportion of children living with never-married and formerly married parents, particularly mothers, has also been increasing over time.

Effects of Stress on the Family

The economic changes and the changes in family formation and stability are linked. As men's ability to support children has declined, their initial commitment to marriage has waned. Marriages stressed by economic uncertainties have also been more likely to disrupt. As Scott South and Kim Lloyd (1992) have documented, higher rates of male nonemployment have been shown to be associated with reduced marriage rates and increased rates of births to unmarried women for both African–American and white population groups; South and Glenna Spitze (1986) also show that among married couples, husbands' nonemployment increases the likelihood of marital disruption. This occurs in part because men react to employment loss and associated economic hardship with anger, irritability, and withdrawal from interaction (Conger et al. 1990). Donald Hernandez (1993) has also found that married-couple families below the poverty level are more likely to disrupt their marriages than are couples who have greater economic resources.

Therefore, declining economic conditions make marital formation less likely and marital disruption more common. Within marriage, such economic pressures make wives' employment more necessary. As wives' greater employment and earnings prompt them to question undiluted female responsibility for housework and child care, new sources of conflict are created in marriages. As the financial pressures rise, husbands and wives treat each other more negatively, quarrel more, and feel increasingly distant; thoughts of divorce become more common, and couples struggling to survive on poverty-level incomes are at higher risk of divorce than are other couples. When economic stressors increase—for example, through heightened insecurity about job stability, increases in required overtime work, disruption in child-care arrangements, or deterioration in occupational conditions—parent–child relations also suffer, as parents become more preoccupied by encroaching problems and less responsive to children.

As a result of these economic and social stressors, increasing numbers of children are experiencing the breakup of their parents' marriage and in most cases the departure of their fathers from their households. Such changes are occurring more rapidly for nonwhite ethnic groups, but they are occurring for virtually all groups in society. And in the absence of marriage or after its end, American fathers have been relatively unlikely to share income or time with their biological children. These trends have implications for women, who may maintain enduring links to children but not to the men who have fathered them; for men, who may lose touch with biological children but take on stepfathering responsibilities of other men's children; and for children, who may have a lifelong relationship with their mothers and their mothers' kin but interact with a series of father figures, often in relationships of uncertain duration.

Conclusion

The connection between social contexts and stress outcomes involves three key links. First, societal stressors affect individual emotional well-being. Second, each individual's emotional well-being in turn affects family interaction; individuals struggling with emotional turmoil or depression are less available for satisfying interaction and more prone either to withdraw from interaction or to become aggressive and argumentative. Third, distressing patterns of interaction constitute an additional stressor further undermining individuals' emotional equilibrium. Precisely because individual family members find it difficult to discern the social and economic roots of problematic interaction, they can be bewildered by interpersonal difficulties and prone to attribute problems to personality flaws or moral failings. Because economic and occupational stressors affect adults' emotional well-being, which in turn affects spousal and parent–child interaction patterns, they forge an important link in the intergenerational transmission of emotional disadvantage. As family stress researchers study the resourceful ways in which individuals and families resist stressors, they are also becoming increasingly aware of the social constraints on those efforts.

(*See also:* Conflict; Death and Mourning; Divorce: Emotional and Social Aspects; Ethnicity; Family Gender Roles; Family Violence; Marital Power; Marital Quality; Marriage Counseling; Poverty; Remarriage; Suicide; Unemployment; Widowhood)

BIBLIOGRAPHY

Aneshensel, C. (1992). "Social Stress: Theory and Research." *Annual Review of Sociology* 18:15–38.

Boss, P. (1987). "Family Stress: Perceptions and Context." In *Handbook of Marriage and the Family,* ed. M. B. Sussman and S. K. Steinmetz. New York: Plenum.

Conger, R. D.; Elder, G. H., Jr.; Lorenz, F. O.; Conger, K. J.; Simons, R. L.; Whitbeck, L. B.; Huck, S.; and Melby, J. N. (1990). "Linking Economic Hardship to Marital Quality and Instability." *Journal of Marriage and the Family* 52:643–656.

Coontz, S. (1992). *The Way We Never Were: American Families and the Nostalgia Trap.* New York: Basic Books.

Dohrenwend, B. S., and Dohrenwend, B. P. (1981). *Stressful Life Events and Their Contexts.* New Brunswick, NJ: Rutgers University Press.

Elder, G. H., Jr. (1974). *Children of the Great Depression.* Chicago: University of Chicago Press.

Elder, G. H., Jr.; Nguyen, T. V.; and Caspi, A. (1985). "Linking Family Hardship to Children's Lives." *Child Development* 56:361–375.

Furstenberg, F. F., and Cherlin, A. J. (1991). *Divided Families.* Cambridge, MA: Harvard University Press.

Hansen, D., and Hill, R. (1964). "Families Under Stress." In *Handbook of Marriage and the Family,* ed. H. T. Christensen. Chicago: Rand McNally.

Hernandez, D. (1993). *America's Children: Resources from Family, Government, and the Economy.* New York: Russell Sage Foundation.

Hill, R. (1949). *Families Under Stress.* New York: Harper & Row.

Holmes, T. A., and Rahe, R. H. (1967). "The Social Readjustment Rating Scale." *Journal of Psychosomatic Research* 11:213–218.

Lavee, Y.; McCubbin, H. I.; and Olson, D. H. (1987). "The Effects of Stressful Life Events and Transitions on Family Functioning and Well-Being." *Journal of Marriage and the Family* 49:857–873.

Lavee, Y.; McCubbin, H. I.; and Patterson, J. M. (1985). "The Double ABCX of Family Stress and Adaptation: An Empirical Test by Analysis of Structural Equations with Latent Variables." *Journal of Marriage and the Family* 47:811–825.

Lazarus, R. S., and Folkman, S. (1984). *Stress, Appraisal, and Coping.* New York: Springer-Verlag.

McCubbin, H. I., and Patterson, J. M. (1983). "Family Stress and Adaptation to Crisis: A Double ABCX Model of Family Behavior." In *Advances in Family Stress Theory and Research,* ed. H. McCubbin, M. Sussman, and J. Patterson. New York: Haworth Press.

McLoyd, V. C. (1989). "Socialization and Development in a Changing Economy." *American Psychologist* 44:293–302.

McLoyd, V. C. (1990). "The Impact of Economic Hardship on Black Families and Children: Psychological Distress, Parenting, and Socioemotional Development." *Child Development* 61:311–346.

Mederer, H., and Hill, R. (1983). "Critical Transitions over the Family Lifespan: Theory and Research." *Marriage and Family Review* 6:39–60.

Menaghan, E. G. (1989). "Role Changes and Psychological Well-Being: Variations in Effects by Gender and Role Repertoire." *Social Forces* 66:693–714.

Menaghan, E. G. (1990). "Social Stress and Individual Distress." In *Research in Community and Mental Health:* Vol. 6, *Mental Disorder in Social Context,* ed. J. R. Greenley. Greenwich, CT: JAI Press.

Menaghan, E. G. (1991). "Work Experiences and Family Interaction Processes: The Long Reach of the Job?" *Annual Review of Sociology* 17:419–444.

Mirowsky, J., and Ross, C. E. (1986). "Social Patterns of Distress." *Annual Review of Sociology* 12:23–45.

Moen, P., and Wethington, E. (1992). "The Concept of Family Adaptive Strategies." *Annual Review of Sociology* 18:233–251.

Pearlin, L. I. (1989). "The Sociological Study of Stress." *Journal of Health and Social Behavior* 30:241–256.

Pearlin, L. I.; Lieberman, M. A.; Menaghan, E. G.; and Mullan, J. T. (1981). "The Stress Process." *Journal of Health and Social Behavior* 22:337–356.

Peters, M., and Massey, G. C. (1983). "Mundane Extreme Environmental Stress in Family Stress Theories: The Case of Black Families in White America." *Marriage and Family Review* 6:193–218.

Selye, H. (1982). "History and Present Status of the Stress Concept." In *Handbook of Stress*, ed. L. Goldberger and S. Breznitz. New York: Free Press.

South, S. J., and Lloyd, K. M. (1992). "Marriage Opportunities and Family Formation: Further Implications of Imbalanced Sex Ratios." *Journal of Marriage and the Family* 54:440–451.

South, S. J., and Spitze, G. (1986). "Determinants of Divorce over the Marital Life Course." *American Sociological Review* 51:583–590.

Wheaton, B. (1990). "Life Transitions, Role Histories, and Mental Health." *American Sociological Review* 55:209–223.

Elizabeth G. Menaghan

SUBSTANCE ABUSE

Substance abuse has a profound impact on the American people, of all ethnic groups, from birth to death. In 1992, household survey results estimated that about 103 million people had used alcohol and 13 million people had used illicit drugs during the previous month (National Institute on Drug Abuse 1993). Total economic costs associated with substance abuse were about $165 billion and included expenditures for treatment, medical care for associated illnesses, costs incurred by the law enforcement and correctional systems, and lost work productivity from premature death (Institute for Health Policy 1993). Physiological, psychological, and social effects of substance abuse extend well beyond any person and have especially adverse effects on the basic building block of any society: the family.

Drug Effects

This entry focuses mainly on alcohol, marijuana, cocaine, and heroin, but all abused drugs, including hallucinogens (e.g., LSD) and inhalants (e.g., aerosols) have both physical and behavioral effects. Specific effects are responses to the size of dose, rates of increase of concentration in blood plasma, the extent of previous exposure to the drug or a similar compound, and any possible medical or psychological disorders (Schuckit 1994). After repeated exposures to a drug, the body adjusts, or develops tolerance. Adjustments include metabolic tolerance, or increased degradation in the liver; cellular tolerance, which results from altered flow of ions in nerve cells; and behavioral tolerance, whereby actions are modified to compensate for drug-related deficits. As exposure continues, tolerance persists. Prolonged exposure in tolerant individuals leads to dependence, a condition in which continued doses of a drug become necessary simply to maintain usual physical and behavioral functioning. This more technical term, "dependence," is the body state implied by the popular term "addiction." The physical and behavioral alterations in functioning that occur when a dependent person ceases drug administration are termed signs of "withdrawal" or "abstinence." The profile of responses to a drug reflects characteristics of that drug, so that there are marked differences among withdrawal symptoms for various classes of drugs.

Alcohol. Alcoholic beverages are the most commonly abused substances. Alcoholic drinks can be fermented from almost any plant product, and the degree of fermentation or distillation affects the content of "absolute alcohol," or ethanol. Typically, 12 ounces of 5 percent beer, 4 ounces of 12 percent wine, and 1.5 ounces of an 80-proof (40%) distilled beverage contain equivalent amounts of ethanol. Alcoholic beverages also contain congeners, which include compounds such as tannin or phenols, or elements such as iron, lead, and cobalt. Congeners may confer a distinctive color (as in whiskies or red wine) or are added to produce a desirable effect, as in a "foamy head" on beer, but sometimes have undesirable effects, including "hangovers." Small amounts of ethanol are absorbed through the mouth, moderate amounts through the stomach and large bowel, and the most from the small intestine. Because ethanol is water-soluble, it can enter almost every water-permeable body cell, and it can affect almost every body organ. About 90 percent to 98 percent is metabolized through the action of enzymes or oxidation in the liver. The primary effect of ethanol is to decrease the rate at which neurons fire, thus depressing the central nervous system (CNS). Accordingly, alcohol and related drugs (barbiturates, benzodiazepines) are termed CNS depressants.

Typical reasons that people offer for alcohol use include relaxation, sociability, and relief from anxiety. However, impairment in cognition or behavior can occur after as few as one or two drinks (Moskowitz, Burns, and Williams 1985). At larger doses, speech is slurred, gait impaired, and complex activities such as operating a vehicle or machinery become dangerous. "Blackouts," or memory loss for events that occurred during intoxication, commonly result when large doses are consumed rapidly. Mood states are not necessarily pleasant. Laboratory studies show that chronic heavy drinkers or alcohol-dependent persons become more agitated, anxious, and depressed as drinking progresses (Tamerin, Weiner, and Mendelson 1970). Even moderate alcohol consumption (one or two drinks per occasion) has been shown to increase women's feelings of anger and depression while sober (Birnbaum, Taylor, and Parker 1983). Alcohol-related tension and dysphoria may prompt an alcohol abuser to seek medical help, but physicians who lack information about alcoholism may prescribe mood-altering drugs (such as tranquilizers or sedatives), which can produce drug dependence in patients who are already alcohol dependent.

Accumulating evidence indicates that women become tolerant, dependent, and develop serious alcohol problems at a faster rate than men, but at lower doses. This phenomenon is known as "telescoping," whereby development of cardiovascular, gastrointestinal, and liver disease are accelerated. Liver cirrhosis is more prevalent in women than in men, and occurs following lower absolute alcohol intake (Zetterman 1992). It has been suggested that higher blood alcohol levels (BALs) in women can be attributed to less "first-pass," or initial, metabolism and oxidation by gastric tissue (Frezza et al. 1990). Other studies have shown that threshold levels for hazardous drinking by women should be established at about 4.5 drinks per episode (Whitehead and Layne 1987; Wilsnack and Wilsnack 1991).

Marijuana. Marijuana is the most commonly used illicit drug (Mendelson and Mello 1994). Major subjective effects include euphoria, relaxation, and an altered time sense (feeling "high" or "stoned"). The source is *Cannabis sativa*, a tall plant that grows readily in temperate and tropical areas. In recent years, clandestine domestic marijuana cultivation has become the primary source for users in the United States, replacing plant material of lesser potency that was previously imported from Central and South America or the Middle East. Marijuana products are most frequently introduced into the body through the lungs by smoking the dried leaves and flowers in a pipe or as rolled cigarettes. Water pipes can humidify the smoke, and this route of administration permits deeper inhalation. Hashish, derived from concentrated plant resin, and hashish oil, made by distillation in organic solvents, are more potent products, and both are smoked in pipes. There are more than four hundred organic compounds in *Cannabis sativa.* The major active compound, Δ^9-THC, is converted in the liver to its major metabolite, 11-hydroxy-THC. Major sites of action are the lungs, heart, and brain. Its pharmacological action constricts the blood vessels and increases the heart rate. About half of smoked Δ^9-THC actually enters the lungs and then the bloodstream, with the peak effect on heart rate occurring about twenty to thirty minutes after smoking. Subjective effects such as altered time sense and euphoria, as well as paranoia, are sustained for two or three hours after smoking because THC is highly soluble in fatty tissue, where it is stored and then released. After a single dose, THC can be detected in urine for about two days. For persons who engage in chronic use—that is, who smoke one to five marijuana cigarettes per day—THC can be detected for about two weeks (Mendelson and Mello 1994). Chronic use diminishes euphoric response. Mood effects associated with chronic use also include increased tension, fatigue, and irritability. Heavy use of marijuana appears highly correlated with heavy alcohol intake. Marijuana has been called a "gateway drug," since in some age groups its use precedes use of opiates or cocaine (Kandel 1984).

Cocaine. Cocaine is the second most commonly used illicit drug (Weiss, Mirin, and Bartel 1994). Cocaine is a stimulant that potentiates the sympathetic nervous system. Its physiological action constricts blood vessels rapidly, increasing heart rate and raising blood pressure. It can be introduced into the body intranasally by inhalation ("snorting"), by intravenous use, or through the lungs by smoking. The source is leaves of coca plants, *Erythroxylon coca*, a shrub that grows mainly in the Andes Mountains of South America. Leaves can be readily harvested several times a year. Although various programs have attempted to persuade Andean farmers to substitute other crops, coca is easily grown and yields the most money. Each leaf contains about 0.5 percent to 1 percent of cocaine; 100 to 200 kilograms of leaves yield about 1 kilogram of coca paste. Initial processing using kerosene, water, sodium carbonate, and sulfuric acid occurs in simple village processing plants. Purity ranges from about 40 percent to 90 percent, and coca paste is conveniently transported for further processing. About 2.5 kilograms of coca paste are transformed into cocaine hydrochloride, a white powder, by the addition of chemicals such as hydrochloric acid, potassium permanganate, acetone, ether, ammonia, calcium carbonate, sulfuric acid, and additional kerosene. "Crack" cocaine, an easily smoked form, is manufactured by heating a mixture of cocaine hydrochloride and sodium bicarbonate (baking soda). As this product cools, crystals form as small pieces ("rocks"). At each stage of the distribution process, from major traffickers to "street" sellers, adulterants are added and the price is inflated. Some have estimated that there is a 15,000 percent inflation from the price of leaves to the price on the street. Acute cocaine action is brief, and reinforcing properties include transient mood enhancement and actual or expected increase in libido. Pharmacological effects alter transport of the neurotransmitter dopamine, and within an hour the user may experience a dysphoric cocaine "crash" that is possibly associated with dopamine depletion. Chronic users quickly develop tolerance and may inject or smoke several times in an hour to regain the acute "high" associated with initial use. Cocaine overdose may cause hallucinations, hyperactivity, and stereotypic behavior. Other drug dependence may develop concurrently, since chronic users often attempt to palliate cocaine withdrawal with alcohol, marijuana, or tranquilizers (Carroll, Rounsaville, and Bryant 1993). Some users combine cocaine with heroin for an intravenous "speedball." Accordingly, use of cocaine frequently signals abuse of other drugs.

Opioids. Opiates, including opium, morphine, heroin, and codeine, are derived from the sap of the opium poppy plant *Papaver somniferum* (Schuckit and Segal 1994). These plant derivatives, and molecularly similar synthetic opioids, bind and act at special nerve cell sites, called "receptors," that usually are the targets of endogenous (naturally occurring) peptides with similar molecular structures. Distribution of receptors is best understood in CNS regions that modulate pain and in the smooth muscle of the intestines. For centuries, opioid drugs, whether derived from poppies or developed in laboratories, have been used to relieve pain, induce sleep, and stop diarrhea. Euphoria (action on the hypothalamus) is a major appealing side effect, but tolerance and dependence occur at therapeutic dosages, and "overdose" can result in respiratory depression, since receptors also are found in the medulla. Routes of administration include eating (opium), oral tablets (codeine, Percodan, Darvon), smoking (opium and heroin), injection (heroin, morphine, synthetics such as Demerol), or oral liquid (methadone). All of these peptides are designated as "agonists"—that is, they bind to receptors and produce opiatelike effects. Opioid drugs that bind at these sites but *block or reverse* these effects are designated "antagonists." Considerable research has been expended to identify "nonaddicting" opioid drugs with limited euphorigenic properties, so that some "mixed agonist-antagonists" such as pentazocine (Talwin) are now used to relieve pain. Antagonist opioid drugs also have important therapeutic uses in the treatment of opioid addiction. Naloxone is used in emergencies to "reverse" overdoses of agonists, and about 50 milliliters of naltrexone will block receptor sites from heroin for about seventy-two hours. Another type of chemotherapy for opioid dependence is methadone, a longer-acting agonist prescribed for use by mouth. Intravenous use delivers these drugs most rapidly, followed by smoking, and oral ingestion. Major metabolism occurs in the liver. Since intravenous users may share needles that have not been cleaned, transmission of hepatitis B and C also can occur and damage the liver. Other serious health complications include damage to the heart. Further, heroin users may find their supply interrupted and substitute alcohol or tranquilizers to ease withdrawal.

Scope of alcohol and drug problems. A household survey of alcohol and drug use conducted during 1992 reported consumption patterns (National Institute on Drug Abuse 1993). The vast majority (83.0%) of all Americans over age twelve had used alcohol at least once during their lifetime, about two-thirds (64.7%) during the previous year, and about half (47.8%) during the previous month. Overall, slightly more than one-third (36.2%) of the persons said that they had ever used an illicit drug (31.7% of the women and 41.0% of the men). Access to marijuana was relatively common. Of persons who reported ever using any "illicit drug," less than 4 percent had *not* tried marijuana. Close to one-third (32.8%) of all persons surveyed stated that they had tried marijuana at least once in their lifetime; the overall rate for men (38.0%) was 10 percent greater than that for women (28.0%). About one-tenth (11.0%) of the 1992 sample had tried cocaine.

Costs of treatment, medical care, and deaths from drug abuse largely involve younger persons, and total economic costs were approximately $67 billion in 1990. Alcohol problems more frequently involve older persons, and total economic costs were approximately $99 billion in 1990 (Institute for Health Policy 1993). According to a survey of drug and alcohol treatment facilities in the United States, 213,681 female and 562,388 male clients received services in 1991 (Office of Applied Studies 1993). The profile of diagnoses differed dramatically between women and men. More women (36.4%) than men (26.7%) were diagnosed with drug problems, 25.4 percent of women *and* men were diagnosed with both drug and alcohol problems, while 38.2 percent of women and 47.9 percent of men were diagnosed as alcoholic. Consequently, when women seek substance abuse treatment, at least one-fourth will be concurrently abusing alcohol with other drugs, proportionately more women than men will require drug treatment, and there remains a strong need for alcohol treatment for men.

Adverse Social Consequences of Drug Use

Social indicators show the adverse impact of substance abuse on the family, and accumulating evidence indicates a trend toward earlier use of alcohol and other drugs as well as an increase in the rates of family history of alcoholism. Adverse consequences with a direct impact on family life include deleterious effects on children and involvement in the criminal justice system.

Involvement in the justice system. Illicit drug use and crime are increasingly associated for women. In 1986, 12 percent of female prisoners served a sentence for a drug offense, but by 1991, the proportion was 33 percent. Of all female inmates in state prisons in 1991, 36 percent said they were under the influence of a drug at the time of their offense, 54 percent had used drugs in the month before committing the offense, about 50 percent had committed the offense to obtain drugs, and 65 percent had used drugs daily during their lifetime—with 36 percent reporting crack cocaine use and 34 percent reporting intravenous drug use. Roughly two-thirds of drug users had received some type of treatment, and 12 percent were in drug treatment at the time of their offense (Snell and Morton 1994).

About 80 percent of female inmates had children, and two-thirds had children under age eighteen (rates for men were about 10% lower). About half of these minor children resided with grandparents, one-fourth with fathers, and 20 percent with other relatives, but only about 10 percent of women's children were placed in foster homes or institutions. The vast majority of women (90%) maintained contact with their minor children (versus 80% of men). About one-third of female inmates, in contrast to 27 percent of men, had family histories of alcohol or drug abuse (Snell and Morton 1994).

Child neglect and abuse. Most illicit drug use occurs in the childbearing years, eighteen to thirty-five (National Institute on Drug Abuse 1993). About 10 million children reside in households with substance abusers (Blau et al. 1994), and a minimum of 675,000 children per year are neglected or abused by drug- or alcohol-dependent caretakers (Bays 1990). Foster care placements increased by 30 percent between 1986 and 1989 (Kelley 1992). Estimates point to more than 30,000 to 100,000 infants born to women who use crack cocaine, 10,000 born to women who use heroin, and 10 million children living with drug- or alcohol-dependent parents.

Many of these children are born drug-dependent, and they must be detoxified (Finnegan and Kandall 1992). Some physical defects can be treated, some cases are fatal, but other anomalies in growth and development require complicated medical and behavioral management. As children grow, substance abuse and child abuse may co-occur under similar family conditions and dynamics, or substance abuse can lead to child abuse (Kelley 1992). Certainly, mediating factors such as social support and education, income, alternative sources of nurturing, and parents' own histories of familial substance abuse and histories of neglect and abuse are important. However, it is likely that when mothers who use drugs or alcohol are primary caregivers, they will be unable to fulfill some aspect of their children's emotional or physical needs (Tracy and Farkas 1994).

Both the mother and her partner may be substance users. The major vector of drug use, both licit and illicit, has been from men to women via dating or intimate contact (Ferrence and Whitehead 1980). However, licit drugs (alcohol, tobacco cigarettes) are easy to obtain and relatively low in cost and thus are available directly to women (Lex 1985). Cocaine use through snorting or injection is both relatively expensive and related to sexual activity. But crack cocaine is inexpensive, rendering it readily accessible to women, and crack produces dependence rapidly. Some women exchange sexual favors or engage in prostitution to obtain it. In the early 1990s, the cost of a cocaine "rock" in New York City fell to about $2, and fees for sex acts decreased concomitantly, in some instances from $10 or more to $2 or $3 per episode. Low-cost crack has contributed strongly to the epidemic of infants exposed to cocaine *in utero*. In a study of babies delivered in 1985 and 1986 at Harlem Hospital, 355 cocaine-exposed newborns were compared with a randomly selected sample of 199 newborns not exposed to cocaine (Phibbs, Bateman, and Schwartz 1991). Cocaine-exposed infants were more likely to be born to African-American mothers who were older, who had more previous pregnancies, and who had not received prenatal care. Infants exposed to cocaine had significantly lower birthweight; 31.3 percent weighed less than 2,500 grams, and 3.7 percent weighed less than 1,500 grams. Mothers of cocaine-exposed infants also are more likely to smoke tobacco cigarettes, to use alcohol, and to have erratic patterns of drug use. Multiple drug use is a typical prenatal pattern that precludes attributing causality to any single drug. For babies exposed to multiple drugs, hospital costs were $8,450, versus $1,283 for babies exposed to cocaine alone, a sixfold increase, with lengths of stay averaging 10 days versus 2.7 days. At birth, cocaine-exposed infants also were an average of one less week in gestational age (38.1 weeks versus 39.2 weeks), and almost 20 percent had a gestational age less than 37 weeks. Fully one-fourth (24.6%) of the babies were admitted to a neonatal intensive care unit. Estimating that 158,400 cocaine-exposed infants were born during 1990 in the United States, and assuming an average hospital cost of $3,182 per infant, the overall cost for 1990 was $504 million.

Infants exposed to drugs *in utero* can present problems to caretakers, such as consequences of prematurity, low birthweight, retarded intrauterine growth, and developmental delays (Scherling 1994). Cocaine-exposed infants can be irritable, easily overstimulated, exhibit increased muscle tone, and resist attempts at soothing (Kelley 1992), but there also is a large literature on alcohol effects *in utero*, which may affect at least 2.6 million infants annually (see Finnegan and Kandall 1992). For drug-dependent mothers, these babies present sometimes overwhelming challenges that are often interpreted as "personal" rejection. Mothers' emotions can include guilt about exposure of their child to drugs, as well as anger that their efforts at parenting hyperactive babies with feeding difficulties and abnormal sleep patterns seem unsuccessful and generate only more stress. Attachment may be disrupted as mothers experience their infants as highly demanding and ignore and withdraw from them, or continue to use drugs. Child neglect includes failure to secure necessary immunizations or to keep routine clinic appointments and can stem from several factors, including homelessness.

Of foster placements, 40 percent in one study were with grandmothers (Kelley 1992), and a review noted that 12 percent to 50 percent of African-American children reside with their grandmothers (Minkler, Roe, and Robertson-Beckley 1994). Responsibilities for young children so late in the life cycle tend to diminish support from social network members; to increase role strains on teenage children still residing at home; and to decrease marital satisfaction, especially if male partners fail to share household tasks evenly. As a consequence, the inability or unsuitability of drug-addicted mothers to care for children can have a widely disruptive effect on their extended family.

Factors That Contribute to Substance Abuse

While the adverse consequences of substance abuse are relatively easy to identify, the exact factors that contribute to an individual's substance abuse are much more elusive. However, researchers have been able to identify some general trends.

Family history of substance abuse. It is a truism in the substance abuse field that "alcoholism runs in families." Son and daughters of alcoholics may be less sensitive or reactive to subjective, physiological, or behavioral effects of moderate doses of alcohol, and thus increased exposure to alcohol may accelerate alcohol tolerance and promote alcohol dependence (Schuckit 1987). Adoption and cross-fostering studies that used registry data from Denmark and Sweden provided early findings about genetic factors in transmission of alcoholism. A study of Danish male adoptees compared control adoptees with men separated from alcoholic biological parents soon after birth and raised by nonrelatives. Of the boys separated from alcoholic biological parents, 18 percent had alcoholism treatment as adults or met clinical criteria for alcoholism, in contrast to only 5 percent of the control adoptees. Thus, nearly four times the rate of alcoholism was found for men separated from alcoholic biological parents (Goodwin et al. 1973).

Assessments of substance abuse problems are appropriate for both women and men. Although most earlier studies focused on the men, alcoholism in women now appears strongly and consistently correlated with a family history of alcohol problems (Glenn and Parsons 1989; Hill and Smith 1991), especially in fathers (Pollock et al. 1987). As in men, early onset of alcoholism and severity of alcoholism appear associated with positive family history in women. National survey data has reported that 26.5 percent of women and 20.5 percent of men claimed to have an alcoholic first-degree relative (Harford 1992), and a study of wives of alcoholic men in treatment found that 50 percent, while not alcoholic themselves, had a family history of alcoholism (Casey, Griffin, and Googins 1993). Gender and relative age of an individual's alcoholic siblings and maternal relatives are risk factors for alcoholism (Turner et al. 1993).

A study of twins (McGue, Pickins, and Svikis 1992) showed an apparent strong effect of alcoholism in a male cross-sex twin on the likelihood of his female cross-sex twin developing alcoholism. One study (Haver 1987) examined patterns of alcoholism among the parents of forty-four alcoholic women. Sixty-four percent reported having at least one alcoholic first-degree relative, 50 percent reported alcoholism in their father, and 14 percent reported alcoholism in their mother. The ratio of female to male alcoholics in the mother's family was approximately 1:2.0, while the ratio in the father's family was 1:3.5. A family history of alcoholism was correlated with younger age at onset of drinking, and alcoholism in first-degree relatives was associated with early antisocial behavior, while alcoholism in the mother and her family was associated with borderline personality disorder. Anecdotally, several women in this study reported a high tolerance for alcohol when they began drinking. In a sample of women receiving treatment as mandated by civil commitment, 75 percent had a family history of alcoholism, and polydrug users had a mean of one more alcoholic male relative than alcohol-dependent women (Lex et al. 1990). Older male alcoholics in families of alcohol- or drug-abusing women may indicate family environments in which excessive drinking and intoxicated behavior have been accepted, facilitated, condoned, excused, modeled, or else ignored. Women with a family history of alcoholism who lack external social support, such as from friends, report greater concern about developing substance abuse problems (Ohannessian and Hesselbrock 1993).

Theodore Reich and his colleagues (1988) studied sixty female and 240 male alcoholics, their fathers, mothers, brothers, sisters, offspring, and spouses. The alcoholism rates for sons and daughters of these 300 patients were higher than the rates for their fathers and mothers. Male and female alcoholics had similar numbers of first-degree alcoholic relatives. Lifetime occurrence of alcoholism for persons born since 1955 was calculated at about 22 percent for males, and 10 percent for females, while occurrence of alcoholism for persons born before 1940 was calculated at about 12.3 percent for males and 4 percent for females. Thus, rates for females have more than doubled, while rates for males have almost doubled.

Substance abuse and family life. The family plays an important role in factors involved in the development, maintenance, and treatment of substance abuse. The fundamental significance of families as dynamic systems has been recognized and studied (Wolin et al. 1980), to the extent that now few treatment plans for substance abusers would be considered adequate if family members or significant others were omitted. The disorganizing impact of alcoholism on families is perhaps best known, but information about the impact of other drug use is increasing (Bernardi, Jones, and Tennant 1989; Kosten, Rounsaville, and Kleber 1985). Further, disrupted family dynamics occur irrespective of socioeconomic status and ethnic group membership. Research involving a large cross-sectional sample found that offspring of substance abusers were more likely to experience marital instability and psychiatric symptoms, especially if they had experienced physical and sexual abuse (Greenfield et al. 1993), and alcohol abuse often co-occurs with domestic violence (Dinwiddie 1992; Fagan, Barnett, and Patton 1988). Background factors significant for women include childhood violence experiences, violence from a cohabiting partner, and presence of concurrent antisocial and/or borderline personality disorders (Haver 1987). The importance of family organization and relationships is reflected clinically in inclusion of items that assess the quality of family and marital interactions in the most commonly used problem severity rating scales (e.g., McLellan et al. 1980; Selzer 1971) and in the construction of family trees, or genograms, as clinical tools to depict the degree to which abuse of various substances has had effects on several generations in a family, the extent that support is available from family members, and the emotional "valence" of kinship relationships (Lex 1990).

One typical factor in family lives of substance abusers is the "absent father," usually affected in some way by substance abuse, whose familial role has had to be reallocated among other relatives (Bekir et al. 1993). This pattern often has been transmitted from the grandparental generation to the parental generation. Involuntarily or out of necessity, the "missing" role is frequently assigned to a child, who has to assume responsibilities inappropriate to age and generation (i.e., to act as a spouse or parent). Some children recall having to "raise" themselves, since parents neglected to nurture, or abused, scapegoated, or controlled activities excessively. Childhood responses can be acting out through anger, antisocial behavior, and estrangement or compliance and assumption of domestic tasks, including housekeeping and care for siblings. In adulthood, resentment from burdens of childhood "role reversals" can affect relationships with offspring, and onset of substance abuse in some cases occurs at the age or life-cycle stage when a parent may have begun substance abuse. In some instances, substance abusers appear to expect parental "unconditional love" from spouses, including unquestioned acceptance of substance abuse and irresponsible behavior (Bekir et al. 1993). Unstated expectations and other communication difficulties occur when moods and behaviors of substance abusers are closely tied to those of family members (McKay et al. 1993). However, emotionally dependent ("low autonomy") substance abusers appear to respond well to treatment if family members provide more nurture and support. Conversely, male substance abusers whose attitudes and actions are independent and detached from family concerns seem to exhibit a pernicious individualism associated with poor outcome.

Male to female transmission. Addiction careers were examined for 546 male and female clients in methadone maintenance programs in Southern California (Hser, Anglin, and Booth 1987; Hser, Anglin, and McGlothlin 1987). At admission, women were younger, approximately twenty-six years of age versus twenty-nine for men, but women and men averaged about 10.5 years of education. Roughly 90 percent of men and women had been arrested, with first arrests at approximately 16.5 and 18.5 years, respectively. About 85 percent had lived with a partner in consensual union, and about 80 percent of men and women had been married, with an average number of 2.5 children. Approximately 60 percent used marijuana, and 40 percent drank daily. More men than women reported having been a gang member and having had school problems. Male addicts were also more frequently incarcerated for more than thirty days and were more likely to be on probation.

No men, but about 15 percent of women reported initiation into heroin use by their spouse or common-law partner. Women reported more often than men that they were initiated by a daily user. In contrast, men were more likely to initiate drug use in a group context, and no man reported living with an addicted woman prior to his initial heroin use. Women took less time to develop heroin dependence (fourteen months for women versus twenty-one months for men), and many women became dependent within one month. During the interval between initiation of use to physiological dependence, women also sharply curtailed nonopiate drug use and slightly decreased alcohol use. Women may have replaced use of other drugs with heroin, while men continued to experiment simultaneously with many drugs. Women and men seemed to follow similar opiate use patterns, but for women, addiction careers seemed "compressed" into a shorter cycle (Hser, Anglin, and Booth 1987). This pattern of differential time to dependence for women is consistent with findings from other studies of opiate use (Kosten, Rounsaville, and Kleber 1986) and is reminiscent of "telescoping" of alcohol dependence. Compared to men opioid users, women in the California sample reported shorter durations of consistent daily use (twenty-three months versus thirty-two months). About one-third of men and women reported that they had abstained after becoming dependent, but women were abstinent for shorter intervals (approximately three and a half months) than men (approximately eight months), in part because men were incarcerated more frequently. Female opiate users entered treatment after significantly less time, averaging about five years from first drug use to admission to a methadone maintenance program, versus an average of eight years for men.

Women were most likely to attribute their opiate use to social reasons, especially use by a partner (approximately 36%), but about 10 percent of men and women reported social use by friends as a major social reason for using opiates. For about 50 percent of men and 30 percent of women, "liking the high" and developing tolerance perpetuated use. Men also cited ready availability or cheaply priced heroin, but women were less likely to obtain their own heroin (Hser, Anglin, and McGlothlin 1987). Influence of an opiate-using partner is a strong factor in opiate use by women (Kosten, Rounsaville, and Kleber 1985), perhaps because opiate use becomes an adjunct to sexual activity (Lex 1990). Involvement or cohabitation with a drug-dependent partner may contribute to the more rapid development of cocaine addiction in some women (Griffin et al. 1989).

Assortative mating. In addition to a family history of substance abuse problems, women may be more likely to have spouses or mates who are substance abusers. One study (Bromet and Moos 1976) found that 51 percent of currently married women and 18 percent of currently married men had alcoholic spouses. However, another report (Jacob and Bremer 1986) reasoned that assortative mating rates for male and female alcoholics are similar when adjusted for the sex differential in alcoholism rates, but suggested that exposure to a heavy-drinking mate might serve as an environmental vector for transmission of heavy drinking. In a study of women in treatment for alcohol problems (Vaglum and Vaglum 1987), more than half attributed their drinking problems to characteristics of conjugal partners. However, the effects of a heavy drinking partner were bimodal. Escalated alcohol consumption was used by one-third of the sample as a strategy to maintain a relationship with an alcoholic partner, while about one-fifth attributed onset of alcohol problems to escalated drinking that resulted after abandonment by an alcoholic partner. In the first instance, women were attached to alcoholic partners and over time escalated their drinking to join the partner in attempts to sustain a deteriorating relationship. Case material from the second group indicated that loss of a partner prompted a catastrophic, self-destructive reaction in which women engaged in heavy alcohol consumption while withdrawing from friends, work, and social contacts.

Stressful life events. Substance abuse may be both cause and result of stressful life experiences, marital problems, employment problems, physical illness, or depression. Further, the effects of substance use may be age- or gender-specific, circumscribed by events, delayed, or accumulate through time. Certain life stages, such as young adulthood, are generally associated with drug experimentation and excessive alcohol intake. Women are believed to be more likely to react to unusual or stressful experiences by increasing alcohol intake or trying additional drugs. Alcoholic men may respond to events that mark their inability to fulfill their occupational roles and function as "breadwinners," while women generally focus on events that compromise their role as "homemakers." Each gender may tend to inflate the importance of their usual family roles.

One study (Remy, Soukup-Stepan, and Tatossian 1987) examined the impact of life events on eighty-six male and thirty-five female alcoholics ages twenty to sixty years. It was expected that gender would affect the type of events considered important. Subjects were internal medicine, gastroenterology, or psychiatric patients, with a control group of sixty moderate alcohol users matched by age and sex drawn from an occupational health center. On a scale of one to six, each subject indicated which of forty-eight events on a checklist had occurred during his or her lifetime. Events mentioned more than five times and by at least four subjects identified twenty-nine for men and twenty for women, and their co-occurrence was intercorrelated.

For male alcoholics, twenty of a possible 144 pairs of events were significantly associated, in contrast to only four associations for control men. Among alcoholic women, seventeen of 125 possible pairs of events were significantly correlated, but no events were significantly correlated for control women. Data for alcoholic men indicated strong intercorrelations among conjunctions of three events: marriage, sexual difficulties, and arguments with spouse. Alcoholic men additionally cited work-related events. For alcoholic women, two main sequences of events emerged. The first focused on changes in working conditions, social activities, marital relations, and lifestyle, while the second focused on family losses, including changes in family stability, sexual difficulties, stillbirth or abortion, death of a close relative, or ending a job.

Patterns were evaluated according to the extent of impact. Men had three clusters of events. The first included events with social connotations, such as those resulting from unemployment, change in physical appearance, change in family get-togethers, and change in social activities. The second cluster identified events with direct impact on the family, such as change in working conditions or hours, increase in arguments with spouse, birth of a child, or minor illness. A third cluster included events with more personal meaning, such as a change in religious activities, sexual difficulties, or ending a job as a result of an accident or hospitalization.

Men gave greater importance to work events and judged the impact of other events on work performance, but relationships among events were more complicated for women. Women reported events that affect private life, including changes in residence, sexual difficulties, divorce, marriage, financial problems, birth of a child, and serious illness or accident, injury, or hospitalization.

A comprehensive national survey studied characteristics of 917 women (Wilsnack, Wilsnack, and Klassen 1984; Wilsnack, Klassen, and Wilsnack 1986). Early onset of heavy drinking and adverse consequences were more common for younger women and may reflect an acceleration of drinking experience and alcohol abuse among young women. Median age for initiating drinking was eighteen, and 87 percent of the nonabstainers had begun regular drinking by age twenty-one. Regular marijuana use occurred about age eighteen, while depressive episodes occurred at an average age of twenty-seven, and regular tranquilizer use occurred at about age thirty-seven. Alcohol problems and symptoms of tolerance or dependence were typically recognized early in adult life. It is commonly believed that stress from reproductive problems promotes alcohol abuse. Of women who ever were pregnant, 28 percent had a miscarriage or stillbirth, and premature deliveries, birth defects, and infertility lasting for at least one year occurred during women's midtwenties. However, the majority of women who reported drinking in association with these reproductive events stated that drinking increased after the event.

One study of 300 female alcoholics in treatment examined social consequences of heavy drinking and alcoholism on social isolation (Gomberg and Schilit 1985). Women with alcohol problems were criticized and rejected by family and friends. Social responses included serious family quarrels, decreased communication with parents or other relatives, and anger from family or friends. Women perceived criticism from friends, diminished their contacts, avoided nondrinkers, engaged in solitary activities and solitary drinking, and experienced increased loneliness. Younger women reported more rejection by family and friends. Women in their twenties were more likely to maintain contact with heavy drinkers and felt suspicious and distrustful.

Some believe that women attribute heavy drinking to causes that elicit sympathy as opposed to censure, especially because of stigmatized attitudes toward heavy-drinking females. A general population sample of 230 women was interviewed about their alcohol consumption and recent life events (Allan and Cooke 1986). Middle-aged women, once considered at high risk, consumed about three drinks per week, in contrast to middle-aged men, who consumed about thirty-six drinks per week.

Alcohol and drug abuse are often denied for many years and may distort perceptions. Attribution of drinking or drug use to life problems can discourage individuals from seeking substance abuse treatment and may promote use of prescription drugs to ameliorate dysphoria or other emotional distress. Apparent links between stressful life events and increased consumption may simply reflect activities of a subgroup of people who behave impulsively and aggressively and are thus likely to experience both excessive drinking and adverse consequences.

Dual diagnoses. Comorbidity with other psychological disorders, including schizophrenia, anxiety disorders, affective disorders, personality disorders, and attention deficit hyperactivity disorder should be anticipated in persons with substance abuse problems (Gastfriend 1993). Diagnosis of different disorders that can result in alcohol or other drug dependence is especially important because management and treatment of disorders such as depression or anxiety require different strategies (Woody and Cacciola 1992), and appropriate treatment matching may improve outcome. Possible confounding in diagnosis can result from lack of differentiation between primary and secondary alcoholism (Turnbull 1988), especially since about one-third of all women with alcohol problems may have a primary diagnosis of depression. Women also have higher rates of anxiety, bulimia, and psychosexual disorders (Ross, Glaser, and Stiasny 1988).

Individuals with drug dependence are more likely to have intercurrent psychiatric disorders (Kosten, Rounsaville, and Kleber 1986). When 522 treated opiate addicts, including 126 women (24%), were rated on the Addiction Severity Index (McLellan et al. 1980), women had a severity rating of 4.0 for intercurrent psychological problems, whereas men averaged 3.3. Intercurrent psychiatric diagnoses differed by gender, and women were twice as likely to have received their first psychiatric treatment by age fifteen (10%). Women had more depression and anxiety disorders (64% versus 49%), and more men had antisocial personality disorder (30% versus 17%). Women in treatment for cocaine-related problems appear more likely to have depression, while men are more likely to have antisocial personality disorder (Griffin et al. 1989). However, there is limited evidence to support the "self-medication" hypothesis, one among numerous theories that have attempted to explain the etiology of substance abuse. Many alcohol- and drug-dependent patients claim that they began to use a particular drug to relieve symptoms of distress, but few studies have supporting data.

Treatment Modalities

Several basic principles govern substance abuse treatment. Similarity of practice now generally outweighs differences driven by beliefs about the etiology and maintenance of substance abuse. Knowledge of the basic neurobiology of substance abuse has spread among clinicians, along with increased awareness that substance abuse affects all aspects of life. Accordingly, multimodality approaches deliver the best care, because both medical treatments and behavioral treatments are necessary and important (Mendelson and Mello 1994; Schuckit 1994; Schuckit and Segal 1994).

Detoxification. Because chronic substance abuse has many adverse and potentially life-threatening health consequences, detoxification should be the first stage of treatment (Alling 1992). A substance abuse history should be obtained immediately, especially since polydrug use complicates withdrawal. A thorough physical and neurological examination is always needed (Geller 1991) and should include laboratory tests to indicate liver function, glucose or electrolyte imbalance, gastrointestinal bleeding, or cardiac arrhythmia. A thorough assessment also addresses nutritional status; infectious diseases (including HIV and hepatitis B and C); and chronic disorders including cardiovasculuar disease, pulmonary disease, comorbidity with other psychological disorders, and derangements of reproductive systems in both women and men.

Withdrawal symptoms are relieved by appropriate medications, which are given in decreasing doses. Psychopharmacology is both a science and an art, involving general treatment protocols and individualized treatment plans. For alcohol dependence, the benzodiazepines are considered the safest for detoxification. Persons detoxified from opioids may be given a slower-acting opioid such as methadone, or clonidine, a nonopiate drug that decreases activity of the sympathetic nervous system. There is no specific drug to be used for alleviation of cocaine dependence, but feelings of depression and guilt, sleep disturbance, and lack of appetite often can be successfully treated with tricyclic antidepressants or newer antidepressant drugs. Withdrawal from high doses of marijuana may include irritability, gastrointestinal distress, and sleep disturbance, but no specific pharmacological agents are recommended or commonly used. However, severe depression and anxiety may follow discontinuation of marijuana use and also result when polydrug users become drug-free. Accordingly, a psychiatric evaluation is strongly recommended to determine treatment needs, including psychopharmacological medications, for any concurrent depression, manic-depressive illness, phobias, anxiety disorders, or schizophrenia.

Since there may be cognitive impairment associated with some substances, especially alcohol, cocaine, and marijuana, neuropsychological evaluation should be obtained, but not before detoxification is completed. Two weeks are usually adequate, although protracted withdrawal symptoms may continue for six or more months (Geller 1991; Roehrich and Goldman 1993). Similarly, meetings with family members or other significant others are best scheduled when the patient can be an active participant—after treatment of withdrawal symptoms, an opportunity for rest, and adjustment to the idea that treatment is needed.

Treatment and rehabilitation. Substance abuse constitutes a chronic, relapsing disease. It is inappropriate to anticipate a "cure," and there is no single "recipe" for rehabilitation. No one, especially the patient, should expect steady improvement, rapid return to pre-drug use levels of functioning, or swift establishment of a new drug-free life. Cycles of remission and relapse may last years instead of months. Effective treatment will incorporate urinalysis to monitor substance abuse; involvement of significant others and, if possible, employers; and frequent evaluation of treatment plans (Najavits and Weiss 1994). All patients and their significant others benefit from drug and alcohol education (through informational pamphlets or in group sessions) about effects of alcohol and other drugs; the possibility that relapse will be "triggered" by environmental or internal cues that stimulate "craving" (Daley and Marlatt 1992); and the long-term physical, legal, and social consequences of continued use.

Psychopharmacology can play a key role by stabilizing patients so that gains can be made in psychosocial areas. For alcohol dependence, disulfuram (Antabuse) is a useful adjunct that can be taken at home. This drug produces an unpleasant response to alcohol, including nausea, vomiting, diarrhea, and anxiety (Jaffee, Kranzler, and Ciraulo 1992). Choices for managing opioid dependence include maintenance on methadone, an oral, long-acting opioid that blocks the "high" from heroin and usually requires clinic attendance for administration, or administration of naltrexone, an opiate-blocking tablet form that has no euphoric properties, few side effects, and is discontinued easily (Lowinson et al. 1992). Although cannabinoid receptors exist in the brain and antagonists are known, there are no approved long-term psychopharmacological agents to reverse the actions of marijuana. There also are no long-term psychopharmacological agents that directly block cocaine action or generate aversive consequences in the presence of cocaine.

Almost all types of individual therapies have been used in group formats (Rounsaville and Carroll 1992; Washton 1992), and most substance abuse treatment programs use groups for didactic and therapeutic purposes. For inpatient or outpatient programs, groups offer both economy of scale and "safety in numbers." Substance abusers who participate in groups can effectively and rapidly reduce stigma, share experiences, confront denial, and enhance life skills. Self-help groups such as Alcoholics Anonymous, Al-Anon, and Narcotics Anonymous are inexpensive and effective community resources that express beliefs and values that encourage and facilitate responsible, insightful behavior without use of drugs (Vaillant 1983). Under the larger rubric of each group, meetings can be found in many localities and facilities, and there are meetings for subpopulations, such as for gay and lesbian individuals, adult children of alcoholics, or "graduates" of specific inpatient programs. Most "drug-free" residential programs, including therapeutic communities and halfway houses, typically have adopted twelve-step principles and are especially helpful because their ready availability means that the detoxified drug user does not have to return to an environment in which substance use is permitted or facilitated (Emrick 1987; Miller 1991). Coping with problems without resort to drugs is modeled continuously by peers who are farther along in rehabilitation. If complete abstinence is the primary treatment goal, then the effectiveness of Alcoholics Anonymous,

Narcotics Anonymous, or related twelve-step programs appears helpful for both women and men.

As noted, substance abuse treatment proceeds more effectively with management of concurrent psychological disorders. One major caveat is that for patients taking medication for comorbid disorders (e.g., tricyclic antidepressants or lithium carbonate), a "drug-free" philosophy may be extended naively to include pharmacology for intercurrent major depression, panic disorder, or bipolar disorder. Consequently, this issue should be discussed with patients with dual diagnosis. They should be encouraged to find a "home" twelve-step group that accepts medical management (Nace 1992).

Many substance abusers, male or female, need habilitation rather than rehabilitation. It is of particular concern that initiation of onset of drug abuse now occurs much earlier in the life cycle, before social roles crystallize. Normal adolescent development is disrupted so early that minimal occupational, interpersonal, and child-rearing skills, together with limited education, constitute serious disadvantages, if not barriers, to recovery (Harrison 1989). Persons from minority backgrounds may have multiple problems that complicate treatment (Kearney, Murphy, and Rosenbaum 1994; Mondanaro 1989; Weiner, Wallen, and Zankowski 1990), are likely to have experienced abuse during childhood (Boyd 1993; Yama et al. 1993), and are likely to have alcohol or other drug use in their family of origin. Women may have economic and emotional dependency on men who have introduced them to drug use. Disadvantaged families are likely to depend on public assistance, but public assistance programs are poorly equipped to contend with substance abuse problems (Schmidt 1990). However, "parenting groups" impart especially useful information and skills. Typical difficulties include maintaining generational differences and responsibilities, using consistent discipline, lack of knowledge about appropriate parental behavior, impediments to overcoming guilt about substance abuse, conflicts between generations, accusations by their children, and contending with maturing adolescents (Greif and Drechsler 1993).

Denial of substance abuse problems. Denial is a primary barrier to effective treatment. For example, women have typically sought help for marital problems, family problems, physical illness, or emotional problems but have not necessarily considered their problems to be related to substance abuse (Duckert 1987). Drinking problems were studied among 112 men and women enrolled in a community-based volunteer treatment program over a six-month period (Allan and Phil 1987). Only men (11% of original referrals) attended the clinic for six or more months; all the women dropped out. Individuals who had been referred by agencies remained in treatment longer, with 14 percent of agency-referred clients remaining in treatment six months, versus only 1.8 percent of self-referrals. Referrals from shelters, employers, or courts had an average of 6.1 appointments over 9.1 weeks, while self-referrals attended 3.4 sessions over 3.7 weeks. Only one-half of the clients referred from coercive sources spontaneously left treatment, in contrast to 80 percent of those who were self-referred, but only two women were referred by coercive sources. Since the vast majority of women were self-referrals or were referred by noncoercive sources, their attrition rate may reflect low motivation rather than greater pathology. Because most clients were seen only once, initial interviews should include a thorough evaluation resulting in a highly specific treatment plan.

A comprehensive study (Thom 1986) disclosed barriers to help-seeking in twenty-five men and twenty-five women who were new referrals to an alcohol clinic. Both women and men were in their midforties and did not differ significantly in marital status, living situation, employment status, or education level. However, many women felt that heavy alcohol consumption was a legitimate response to personal problems and did not see that alcohol use could further complicate these problems. Women believed that drinking for the sake of drinking was the major reason that people should be engaged in alcohol treatment, thus denying that the clinic was an appropriate place for them. The major obstacle for men, however, was their concern about having a problem that could not be solved without assistance. Men believed that they should be able to control their drinking and found it difficult to ask for help. Some men reported that coworkers would think them lacking in masculinity if it were known that they attended an alcohol clinic. While women objected to being labeled as in need of alcohol treatment, men were worried that they would be labeled in need of psychiatric care. Both men and women were afraid of the hospital context, and fears included shame and embarrassment about discussing personal problems, fear and lack of knowledge about treatment requirements, fear of being told never to drink again, and fear of physicians as authority figures. Child care was not a salient issue. Instead, women felt awkward about obtaining time off from work. The majority of women were referred from an emergency clinic, suggesting that women may delay treatment until health problems become urgent.

Intriguingly, two men and three women reported that an encouraging life event prompted them to feel worthy and to have hope for the future, and influence of significant others also provided encouragement. Most men were encouraged by their wives, but only women reported that other relatives or their coworkers encouraged them to seek treatment.

Gender and treatment. Gender issues in treatment philosophies have received considerable attention. Marsha Vannicelli (1984) has identified three barriers to efficacious alcoholism treatment for women. Barriers included expectations that women do not profit from treatment because they are more depressed, experience mood swings, and are self-centered. Next, women's potential for change was believed limited by stereotyped sex role expectancies. Last, lack of basic information about prognosis for alcoholic women had led to the assumption that their treatment is ineffective. In addition, there also may be bias by treatment providers. Case vignettes amply illustrate the extent to which female alcoholics are infantilized, which undercuts their progress. In addition, it has been suggested that women are less likely to use conventional substance abuse treatment facilities but more likely to seek help from private physicians (Duckert 1987). Some also argue that women's substance abuse can remain more covert than that of men or that women are actively dissuaded by partners—often themselves heavy users—from seeking treatment. Finally, it is frequently alleged that available treatment facilities fail to accommodate problems unique to women, including sexual issues (Wilsnack and Wilsnack 1991). Whether women need to be treated separately or in mixed groups and the effectiveness of female or male therapists are other issues that have been debated.

The greater societal stigma attached to women with alcohol problems may manifest itself in lower self-esteem, which continues to affect women as they recover (Underhill 1986). For this reason, confrontational treatment techniques are counterproductive. The concepts of "learned helplessness," assertiveness, and recognition of anger are valuable in women's treatment programs. Other relevant issues include sexual abuse, including incest, physical abuse, and sexual assault. It has been estimated that the prevalence of these events in the histories of women seeking treatment for substance abuse dependence may range from 40 percent to 74 percent.

Some have suggested that residential treatment in therapeutic communities or halfway houses is most appropriate for treating women from highly disadvantaged backgrounds (De Leon and Jainchill 1991; Huselid, Self, and Gutierres 1991). In these contexts, women who minimized the importance of drug use effects across several dimensions of their lives and believed that they could control drug use were less likely to remain in treatment and achieve treatment goals.

Engagement in treatment. In some instances, substance abusers appear to expect parental "unconditional love" from spouses, including unquestioned acceptance of substance abuse and irresponsible behavior (Bekir et al. 1993). Such unstated expectations and other communication difficulties appear to occur when the moods and behaviors of substance abusers are closely tied to those of family members (McKay et al. 1993). However, these emotionally dependent ("low autonomy") substance abusers appear to respond well to treatment when family members provide more nurture and support. In contrast, male substance abusers whose behaviors are independent and detached from those of family members appear to suffer from a pernicious individualism associated with poor treatment outcome.

A number of investigators have compared different treatment experiences of women. Beckman and coworkers investigated the effects of three types of characteristics that might differentiate experiences of men and women in treatment settings (Beckman and Amaro 1986). Sociodemographic, personal, and social characteristics were all associated with gender differences. Women's typically lower levels of disposable income and paucity of other economic resources were major potential obstacles to obtaining treatment. Women were more likely than men to acknowledge problems with family and friends and financial problems. Roughly one-half (48%) of women reported having had one or more types of treatment-related problems, in contrast to 20 percent of men. Men and women had similar concerns about health and expectations of medical care and were similar in their scores for locus of control. While both men and women received limited encouragement from sources other than family and friends, more than 20 percent of women reported opposition from family and friends during the months prior to treatment. Finally, women were in greater need of educational counseling.

Treatment outcome. Concerns about social conditions peculiar to women have promoted a demand for all-female treatment programs. A number of programs provide child care or are targeted toward pregnant women. Treatment outcomes for programs specifically targeted to women were reviewed by Fanny Duckert (1987). Results indicated improvement rates from 20 percent to close to 60 percent. A follow-up study (Haver 1987) of women treated for alcohol problems was conducted, with interviews occurring about 6.5 years after first admission. Among the abstainers, all had relapsed one or more times after treatment, and all women had used alcohol during the year prior to the interview. Six women were long-term abstainers who changed their identities to nondrinkers by informing drinking partners that they chose to abstain, avoiding social situations in which other people drank, attending self-help groups, or through religious participation. However, even long-term abstainers relapsed into heavy drinking following life crises. Typical crises were divorce or removal of children from the household, but these factors could be consequences of relapse and not predictors. Thirty-seven women were short-term abstainers who attempted to remain abstinent over time but could not maintain sobriety over the entire follow-up interval. These women responded to responsibilities such as holding a job or caring for children by reducing their frequency of drinking. A shift by social drinking was reported by seventeen women, but a check of registry records indicated that only eight gave accurate information. However, life situations improved, with some women separating from former partners and living with their children, with a new partner, or by themselves. Average consumption by social drinkers ranged from one to two glasses of an alcoholic beverage to four to six glasses per occasion. Among eight long-term heavy drinkers, four maintained heavy drinking following treatment, while two retained jobs and two had unstable employment.

Changes in treatment approaches. It has been argued that the common experience of substance abuse can be effectively handled in groups including men and women. Others assert that treatment is most effective in same-sex groups. Because men are more expressive about emotional problems in mixed groups, they may receive nurturing support from women, with the net result that men improve while women do not. The evidence favors special groups for women and for men, according to their experiences and circumstances.

Women may need to discuss issues and express feelings, especially those involving victimization by men, that are difficult to address objectively in mixed groups. Improved functioning in family, work, and social adjustment are major treatment goals, irrespective of gender. One promising strategy is case management. This approach addresses multiple needs through referrals to a "menu" of appropriate community resources. Case managers assess needs, develop pertinent plans, identify services, monitor positive changes, remain involved with patients, and evaluate efficacy of interventions. Thus, the individualized needs of many substance abusers—whether for securing housing, enhancement of self-esteem, development of job skills, or training for parenthood—ideally can be met by case management (Sullivan, Wolk, and Hartmann 1992). The concept and its practice are highly flexible, and sustained interaction between manager and client can provide rapid responses as changes occur in social roles or drug use status. Cause-and-effect sequences are readily identified so that evaluation of outcomes can be easily integrated into the case management process. Adaptability of case management to focus on problematic life domains appears well suited for integration with "reality" or "cognitive" therapies.

Conclusion

Substance abusers exhibit complex problems. Since the early 1970s, multiple substance use has become common. General perspectives see substance abuse as a lifelong disorder—a "chronic relapsing disease." Thus, substance abuse burdens seem almost insufferable. At the same time, there are reasons for optimism. Prognosis has improved. Most clinicians no longer view substance abuse as intractable. Instead, substance abuse may be an important "window" that discloses fundamental processes in human behavior. Basic science research and medications development targeted to uncover brain mechanisms involved in substance use contribute new knowledge to biology and biochemistry. Treatment modalities have increased in number and type, with cross-fertilization among many social service and treatment approaches that have emerged to aid human problems. Thus, alcohol and drug abuse and dependence may persist, but their prevalence may diminish as knowledge increases. That knowledge can contribute to winning the numerous small battles against human difficulties that occur within the context of the family.

(*See also:* Child Abuse and Neglect: Emotional and Psychological Aspects; Codependency; Dysfunctional Family; Gangs; Health and the Family; Juvenile Delinquency; Psychiatric Disorders; Self-Esteem; Self-Help Groups)

BIBLIOGRAPHY

Allan, C. A., and Cooke, D. (1986). "Women, Life Events, and Drinking Problems." *British Journal of Psychiatry* 48:462.

Allan, C. A., and Phil, M. (1987). "Seeking Help for Drinking Problems from a Community-Based Voluntary Agency.

Patterns of Compliance Amongst Men and Women." *British Journal of Addiction* 82:1143–1147.

Alling, F. A. (1992). "Detoxification and Treatment of Acute Sequelae." In *Substance Abuse: A Comprehensive Textbook*, 2nd edition, ed. J. H. Lowinson, P. Ruiz, R. B. Millman, and J. G. Langrod. Baltimore: Williams & Wilkins.

Bays, J. (1990). "Substance Abuse and Child Abuse." *Pediatric Clinics of North America* 37:881–904.

Beckman, L. J., and Amaro, H. (1986). "Personal and Social Difficulties Faced by Women and Men Entering Alcoholism Treatment." *Journal of Studies on Alcohol* 47:135–145.

Bekir, P.; McLellan, T.; Childress, A. R.; and Gariti, P. (1993). "Role Reversals in Families of Substance Misusers: A Transgenerational Phenomenon." *The International Journal of the Addictions* 28:613–630.

Bernardi, E.; Jones, M.; and Tennant, C. (1989). "Quality of Parenting in Alcoholics and Narcotic Addicts." *British Journal of Psychiatry* 154:677–682.

Birnbaum, I. M.; Taylor, T. H.; and Parker, E. S. (1983). "Alcohol and Sober Mood State in Female Social Drinkers." *Alcoholism: Clinical and Experimental Research* 7:362–368.

Blau, G. M.; Whewell, M. C.; Gullotta, T. P.; and Bloom, M. (1994). "The Prevention and Treatment of Child Abuse in Households of Substance Abusers: A Research Demonstration Progress Report." *Child Welfare* 73:83–94.

Boyd, C. J. (1993). "The Antecedents of Women's Crack Cocaine Abuse: Family Substance Abuse, Sexual Abuse, Depression, and Illicit Drug Use." *Journal of Substance Abuse Treatment* 10:433–438.

Bromet, E., and Moos, R. (1976). "Sex and Marital Status in Relation to the Characteristics of Alcoholics." *Journal of Studies on Alcohol* 37:1302–1312.

Carroll, K.; Rounsaville, B.; and Bryant, K. (1993). "Alcoholism in Treatment-Seeking Cocaine Abusers: Clinical and Prognostic Significance." *Journal of Studies on Alcohol* 54:199–208.

Casey, J. C.; Griffin, M. L.; and Googins, B. K. (1993). "The Role of Work for Wives of Alcoholics." *American Journal of Drug and Alcohol Abuse* 19:119–131.

Daley, D. C., and Marlatt, G. A. (1992). "Relapse Prevention: Cognitive and Behavioral Interventions." In *Substance Abuse: A Comprehensive Textbook*, 2nd edition, ed. J. H. Lowinson, P. Ruiz, R. B. Millman, and J. G. Langrod. Baltimore: Williams & Wilkins.

De Leon, G., and Jainchill, N. (1991). "Residential Therapeutic Communities for Female Substance Abusers." *Bulletin of the New York Academy of Medicine* 67:277–290.

Dinwiddie, S. H. (1992). "Psychiatric Disorders Among Wife Batterers." *Comprehensive Psychiatry* 33:411–416.

Duckert, F. (1987). "Recruitment into Treatment and Effects of Treatment for Female Problem Drinkers." *Addictive Behaviors* 12:137–150.

Emrick, C. D. (1987). "Alcoholics Anonymous: Affiliation Processes and Effectiveness as Treatment." *Alcoholism Clinical and Experimental Research* 11:416–423.

Fagan, R.; Barnett, O.; and Patton, J. (1988). "Reasons for Alcohol Use in Maritally Violent Men." *American Journal of Drug and Alcohol Abuse* 14:371–392.

Ferrence, R. G., and Whitehead, P. C. (1980). "Sex Differences in Psychoactive Drug Use: Recent Epidemiology." In *Research Advances in Alcohol and Drug Problems:* Vol. 5, *Alcohol and Drug Problems in Women*, ed. O. J. Kalant. New York: Plenum.

Finnegan, L. P., and Kandall, S. R. (1992). "Maternal and Neonatal Effects of Alcohol and Drugs." In *Substance Abuse: A Comprehensive Textbook*, 2nd edition, ed. J. H. Lowinson, P. Ruiz, R. B. Millman, and J. G. Langrod. Baltimore: Williams & Wilkins.

Frezza, M.; di Padova, C.; Pozzato, G.; Terpin, N.; Baraona, E.; and Lieber, C. (1990). "High Blood Alcohol Levels in Women: The Role of Decreased Gastric Alcohol Dehydrogenase Activity and First-Pass Metabolism." *New England Journal of Medicine* 322:95–99.

Gastfriend, D. (1993). "Pharmacotherapy of Psychiatric Syndromes with Comorbid Chemical Dependence." *Journal of Addictive Diseases* 12:155–170.

Geller, A. (1991). "Neurological Effects of Drug and Alcohol Addiction." In *Comprehensive Handbook of Drug and Alcohol Addiction*, ed. N. S. Miller. New York: Marcel Dekker.

Glenn, S. W., and Parsons, O. A. (1989). "Alcohol Abuse and Familial Alcoholism: Psychosocial Correlates in Men and Women." *Journal of Studies on Alcohol* 50:116–127.

Gomberg, E. S. L., and Schilit, R. (1985). "Social Isolation and Passivity of Women Alcoholics." *Alcohol and Alcoholism* 20:313–314.

Goodwin, D.; Schulsinger, F.; Hermansen, L.; Guze, S. B.; and Winokur, G. (1973). "Alcohol Problems in Adoptees Raised Apart from Alcoholic Biological Parents." *Archives of General Psychiatry* 28:238–243.

Greenfield, S. F.; Swartz, M. S.; Landerman, L. R.; and George, L. K. (1993). "Long-Term Psychosocial Effects of Childhood Exposure to Parental Problem Drinking." *American Journal of Psychiatry* 150:608–613.

Greif, G. L., and Drechsler, M. (1993). "Common Issues for Parents in a Methadone Maintenance Group." *Journal of Substance Abuse Treatment* 10:339–343.

Griffin, M. L.; Weiss, R. D.; Mirin, S. M.; and Lange, U. (1989). "A Comparison of Male and Female Cocaine Abusers." *Archives of General Psychiatry* 46:122–126.

Harford, T. C. (1992). "Family History of Alcoholism in the United States: Prevalence and Demographic Characteristics." *British Journal of Addiction* 87:931–935.

Harrison, P. A. (1989). "Women in Treatment: Changing Over Time." *International Journal of the Addictions* 24:655–673.

Haver, B. (1987). "Female Alcoholics: The Relationship Between Family History of Alcoholism and Outcome 3–10 Years After Treatment." *Acta Psychiatrica Scandinavica* 76:21–27.

Hesselbrock, M. N.; Meyer, R. E.; and Keener, J. J. (1985). "Psychopathology in Hospitalized Alcoholics." *Archives of General Psychiatry* 42:1050–1055.

Hill, S. Y., and Smith, T. R. (1991). "Evidence for Genetic Mediation of Alcoholism in Women." *Journal of Substance Abuse* 3:159–174.

Hser, Y. I.; Anglin, M. D.; and Booth, M. W. (1987). "Sex Differences in Addict Careers: 3. Addiction." *American Journal of Drug and Alcohol Abuse* 13:231–251.

Hser, Y. I.; Anglin, M. D.; and McGlothlin, W. (1987). "Sex Differences in Addict Careers: 1. Initiation of Use." *American Journal of Drug and Alcohol Abuse* 13:33–57.

Huselid, R. F.; Self, E. A.; and Gutierres, S. E. (1991). "Predictors of Successful Completion of a Halfway House Program for Chemically Dependent Women." *American Journal of Drug and Alcohol Abuse* 17:89–101.

Institute for Health Policy. (1993). *Substance Abuse, the Nation's Number One Health Problem: Key Indicators for Policy.* Waltham, MA: Brandeis University Press.

Jacob, T., and Bremer, D. A. (1986). "Assortative Mating Among Men and Women Alcoholics." *Journal of Studies on Alcohol* 47:219–222.

Jaffe, J. H.; Kranzler, H. R.; and Ciraulo, D. A. (1992). "Drugs Used in the Treatment of Alcoholism." In *Medical Diagnosis and the Treatment of Alcoholism*, ed. J. H. Mendelson and N. K. Mello. New York: McGraw-Hill.

Kandel, D. B. (1984). "Marijuana Users in Young Adulthood." *Archives of General Psychiatry* 41:200–209.

Kearney, M. H.; Murphy, S.; and Rosenbaum, M. (1994). "Mothering on Crack Cocaine: A Grounded Theory Analysis." *Social Science and Medicine* 38:351–361.

Kelley, S. J. (1992). "Parenting Stress and Child Maltreatment in Drug-Exposed Children." *Child Abuse and Neglect* 16:317–328.

Kosten, T. R.; Rounsaville, B. J.; and Kleber, H. D. (1985). "Parental Alcoholism in Opioid Addicts." *Journal of Nervous and Mental Diseases* 173:461–469.

Kosten, T. R.; Rounsaville, B. J.; and Kleber, H. D. (1986). "Ethnic and Gender Differences Among Opiate Addicts." *International Journal of the Addictions* 20:1143–1162.

Lex, B. W. (1985). "Alcohol Problems in Special Populations." In *The Dignosis and Treatment of Alcoholism*, 2nd edition, ed. J. H. Mendelson and N. K. Mello. New York: McGraw-Hill.

Lex, B. W. (1990). "Male Heroin Addicts and Their Female Mates: Impact on Disorder and Recovery." *Journal of Substance Abuse* 2:147–175.

Lex, B. W. (1994). "Women and Substance Abuse: A General Review." In *Addictive Behaviors in Women*, ed. R. Watson. Clifton, NJ: Humana Press.

Lex, B. W.; Teoh, S. K.; Lagomasino, I.; Mello, N. K.; and Mendelson, J. H. (1990). "Characteristics of Women Receiving Mandated Treatment for Alcohol or Polysubstance Dependence in Massachusetts." *Drug and Alcohol Dependence* 25:13–20.

Lowinson, J. H.; Marion, I. J.; Joseph, H.; and Dole, V. P. (1992). "Methadone Maintenance." In *Substance Abuse: A Comprehensive Textbook*, 2nd edition, ed. J. H. Lowinson, P. Ruiz, R. B. Millman, and J. G. Langrod. Baltimore: Williams & Wilkins.

McGue, M.; Pickins, R. W.; and Svikis, D. S. (1992). "Sex and Age Effects on the Inheritance of Alcohol Problems: A Twin Study." *Journal of Abnormal Psychology* 101:3–17.

McKay, J. R.; Longabaugh, R.; Beattie, M. C.; Maisto, S. A.; and Noel, N. E. (1993). "Changes in Family Functioning During Treatment and Drinking Outcomes for High and Low Autonomy Alcoholics." *Addictive Behaviors* 18:355–363.

McLellan, A. T.; Luborsky, L.; Woody, G. E.; and O'Brien, C. P. (1980). "An Improved Diagnostic Evaluation Instrument for Substance Abuse Patients: The Addiction Severity Index." *Journal of Nervous and Mental Disease* 168:26–33.

Mendelson, J. H.; and Mello, N. K. (1994). "Cocaine and Other Commonly Abused Drugs." In *Harrison's Principles of Internal Medicine*, ed. K. J. Isselbacher, E. Braunwald, J. D. Wilson, J. B. Martin, A. S. Fauci, and D. L. Kasper. New York: McGraw-Hill.

Miller, C. E. (1991). "Women in a Drug Treatment Therapeutic Community." In *Preventions and Treatments of Alcohol and Drug Abuse: A Socio-Epidemiological Sourcebook*, ed. B. Forster and J. C. Salloway. Lewiston, NY: Edwin Mellen Press.

Minkler, M.; Roe, K. M.; and Robertson-Beckley, R. J. (1994). "Raising Grandchildren from Crack Cocaine Households: Effects on Family and Friendship Ties of African-American Women." *American Journal of Orthopsychiatry* 64:20–29.

Mondanaro, J. (1989). *Chemically Dependent Women: Assessment and Treatment.* Lexington, MA: D. C. Heath.

Moskowitz, H.; Burns, M. M.; and Williams, A. F. (1985). "Skills Performance at Low Blood Alcohol Levels." *Journal of Studies on Alcohol* 46:482–485.

Nace, E. P. (1992). "Alcoholics Anonymous." In *Substance Abuse: A Comprehensive Textbook*, 2nd edition, ed. J. H. Lowinson, P. Ruiz, R. B. Millman, and J. G. Langrod. Baltimore: Williams & Wilkins.

Najavitz, L. M., and Weiss, R. E. (1994). "The Role of Psychotherapy in the Treatment of Substance-Use Disorders." *Harvard Review of Psychiatry* 2:84–96.

National Institute on Drug Abuse. (1993). *National Household Survey on Drug Abuse: Population Estimates 1992.* Washington, DC: U.S. Government Printing Office.

Office of Applied Studies. (1993). *National Drug and Alcoholism Treatment Unit Survey (NDATUS): 1991 Main Findings Report.* Rockville, MD: Substance Abuse and Mental Health Services Administration.

Ohannessian, C., and Hesselbrock, V. M. (1993). "The Influence of Perceived Social Support on the Relationship Between Family History of Alcoholism and Drinking Behaviors." *Addiction* 88:1651–1658.

Phibbs, C. S.; Bateman, D. A.; and Schwartz, R. M. (1991). "The Neonatal Costs of Maternal Cocaine Use." *Journal of the American Medical Association* 266:1521–1526.

Pollock, V. E.; Schneider, L. S.; Gabrielli, W. F.; and Goodwin, D. W. (1987). "Sex of Parent and Offspring in the Transmission of Alcoholism: A Meta-Analysis." *Journal of Nervous and Mental Disease* 175:668–673.

Reich, T.; Cloninger, C. R.; Van Eerdewegh, P.; Rice, J. P.; and Mullaney, J. (1988). "Secular Trends in the Familial Transmission of Alcoholism." *Alcoholism Clinical and Experimental Research* 12:458–464.

Remy, M.; Soukup-Stepan, S.; and Tatossian, A. (1987). "For a New Use of Life Event Questionnaires: Study of the Life Events World of a Population of Male and Female Alcoholics." *Social Psychiatry* 22:49–57.

Roehrich, L., and Goldman, M. S. (1993). "Experience-Dependent Neuropsychological Recovery and the Treatment of Alcoholism." *Journal of Consulting and Clinical Psychology* 61:812–821.

Ross, H. E.; Glaser, F. B.; and Stiasny, S. (1988). "Sex Differences in the Prevalence of Psychiatric Disorders in Patients with Alcohol and Drug Problems." *British Journal of Addiction* 83:1179–1192.

Rounsaville, B. J., and Carroll, K. M. (1992). "Individual Psychotherapy for Drug Abusers." In *Substance Abuse: A Comprehensive Textbook*, 2nd edition, ed. J. H. Lowinson, P. Ruiz, R. B. Millman, and J. G. Langrod. Baltimore: Williams & Wilkins.

Scherling, D. (1994). "Prenatal Cocaine Exposure and Childhood Psychopathology: A Developmental Analysis." *American Journal of Orthopsychiatry* 64:9–19.

Schmidt, L. A. (1990). "Problem Drinkers and the Welfare Bureaucracy." *Social Service Review* 37:390–406.

Schuckit, M. A. (1987). "Biological Vulnerability to Alcoholism." *Journal of Consulting and Clinical Psychology* 55:301–309.

Schuckit, M. A. (1992). "Treatment of Alcoholism in Office and Outpatient Settings." In *Medical Diagnosis and the Treatment of Alcoholism*, 2nd edition, ed. J. H. Mendelson and N. K. Mello. New York: McGraw-Hill.

Schuckit, M. A. (1994). "Alcohol and Alcoholism." In *Harrison's Principles of Internal Medicine*, ed. K. J. Isselbacher, E. Braunwald, J. D. Wilson, J. B. Martin, A. S. Fauci, and D. L. Kasper. New York: McGraw-Hill.

Schuckit, M. A., and Segal, D. S. (1994). "Opioid Drug Use." In *Harrison's Principles of Internal Medicine*, ed. K. J. Isselbacher, E. Braunwald, J. D. Wilson, J. B. Martin, A. S. Fauci, and D. L. Kasper. New York: McGraw-Hill.

Selzer, M. L. (1971). "The Michigan Alcoholism Screening Test: The Quest for a New Diagnostic Instrument." *American Journal of Psychiatry* 127:1653–1658.

Snell, T., and Morton, D. C. (1994). "Women in Prison." *Bureau of Justice Statistics Special Report* (March). Washington, DC.

Sullivan, P. S.; Wolk, J. L.; and Hartmann, D. J. (1992). "Case Management in Alcohol and Drug Treatment: Improving Client Outcomes." *Journal of Contemporary Human Services* 73:195–203.

Tamerin, J. S.; Weiner, S.; and Mendelson, J. H. (1970). "Alcoholics' Expectancies and Recall of Experiences During Intoxication." *American Journal of Psychiatry* 126:1679–1704.

Thom, B. (1986). "Sex Differences in Help-Seeking for Alcohol Problems: 1. The Barriers to Help-Seeking." *British Journal of Addiction* 81:777–786.

Tracy, E. M., and Farkas, K. J. (1994). "Preparing Practitioners for Child Welfare Practice with Substance-Abusing Families." *Child Welfare* 73:57–68.

Turnbull, J. E. (1988). "Primary and Secondary Alcoholic Women." *Social Casework* 69:290–297.

Turner, W. M.; Cutter, H. S. G.; Worobec, T. G.; O'Farrell, T. J.; Bayog, R. D.; and Tsuang, M. T. (1993). "Family History Models of Alcoholism: Age of Onset, Consequences, and Dependence." *Journal of Studies on Alcohol* 54:164–171.

Underhill, B. L. (1986). "Issues Relevant to Aftercare Programs for Women." *Social Casework* 11:46–48.

Vaglum, S., and Vaglum, P. (1987). "Partner Relations and the Development of Alcoholism in Female Psychiatric Patients." *Acta Psychiatrica Scandinavica* 76:499–506.

Vaillant, G. (1983). *The Natural History of Alcoholism: Course, Patterns, and Paths to Recovery.* Cambridge, MA: Harvard University Press.

Vannicelli, M. (1984). "Barriers to Treatment of Alcoholic Women." *Substance and Alcohol Actions/Misuses* 5: 29–37.

Washton, A. M. (1992). "Structured Outpatient Group Therapy with Alcohol and Substance Abusers." In *Substance Abuse: A Comprehensive Textbook*, 2nd edition, ed. J. H. Lowinson, P. Ruiz, R. B. Millman, and J. G. Langrod. Baltimore: Williams & Wilkins.

Weiner, H. D.; Wallen, M. C.; and Zankowski, G. L. (1990). "Culture and Social Class as Intervening Variables in Relapse Prevention with Chemically Dependent Women." *Journal of Psychoactive Drugs* 22:239–248.

Weiss, R. D.; Mirin, S. M.; and Bartel, R. L. (1994). *Cocaine*, 2nd edition. Washington, DC: American Psychiatric Press.

Whitehead, P. C., and Layne, N. (1987). "Young Female Canadian Drinkers: Employment, Marital Status, and Heavy Drinking." *British Journal of Addiction* 82:169–174.

Wilsnack, R. W.; Klassen, A. D.; and Wilsnack, S. C. (1986). "Retrospective Analysis of Lifetime Changes in Women's Drinking Behavior." *Advances in Alcohol and Substance Abuse* 5:9–28.

Wilsnack, S. C., and Wilsnack, R. W. (1991). "Epidemiology of Women's Drinking." *Journal of Substance Abuse* 3:133–157.

Wilsnack, S. C.; Wilsnack, R. W.; and Klassen, A. D. (1984). "Drinking and Drinking Problems Among Women in a U.S. National Survey." *Alcohol Health and Research World* 9:3–13.

Wolin, S. J.; Bennett, L. A.; Noonan, D. L.; and Teitelbaum, M. A. (1980). "Disrupted Family Rituals: A Factor in the Intergenerational Transmission of Alcoholism." *Journal of Studies on Alcohol* 41:199–214.

Woody, G. E., and Cacciola, J. (1992). "Diagnosis and Classification: DSM-III-R and ICD-10." In *Substance Abuse: A Comprehensive Textbook*, 2nd edition, ed. J. H. Lowinson, P. Ruiz, R. B. Millman, and J. G. Langrod. Baltimore: Williams & Wilkins.

Yama, M. F.; Fogas, B. S.; Teegarden, L. A.; and Hastings, B. (1993). "Childhood Sexual Abuse and Parental Alcoholism: Interactive Effects in Adult Women." *American Journal of Orthopsychiatry* 63:300–305.

Zetterman, R. K. (1992). "Cirrhosis of the Liver." In *Diseases of the Liver and Biliary Tract*, ed. G. Gitnick, D. R. LaBrecque, and F. G. Moody. St. Louis, MO: Mosby-Year Book.

Barbara W. Lex

SUBSTITUTE CAREGIVERS

Recent increases in the employment of mothers of young children have focused attention on the issue of substitute care (sometimes called nonmaternal care) of young children. The percentage of mothers of preschool-age children in the labor force has doubled since the early 1970s, and more than half of all children under the age of five years have mothers who work outside the home.

Types of Substitute Caregivers

Who cares for these children while their mothers are at work? Substitute caregivers can be broadly grouped into two categories: familial and nonfamilial. Familial caregivers are related to the child. They include fathers (who care for one in six children of employed mothers), grandparents, older siblings, aunts and uncles, and other relatives. Combined, almost half of all children of working mothers are cared for by some family member while their mother works.

Nonfamilial caregivers are those not related to the child and include group arrangements (preschool, nurseries, day-care centers), in-home care (nannies or babysitters), and family day homes. Family day home providers are persons who care for a small number of children (usually fewer than six) in the provider's home. The family day home provider is not necessarily related to the child; the term "family day home" comes from the assumption that care provided in a small-group arrangement in a private home more nearly approximates the type of care the child would receive in his or her own home. Family day homes are often not licensed or regulated by government agencies. Such arrangements account for about one-fifth of all caregiver arrangements.

Although most concern about substitute care has been focused on group arrangements, only about 30 percent of children of employed mothers are cared for in group centers, preschools, and nurseries. Group centers are generally licensed by government agencies, which set regulations concerning safety, sanitation, caregiver/child ratios, and other matters. Such centers vary greatly in quality, caregiver training, physical facilities, and use of developmental and educational programs.

Effects of Substitute Care

Many researchers have studied the possible effects of substitute forms of child care during the first year of life (Belsky 1990; Clarke-Stewart 1989; Scarr, Phillips, and McCartney 1989; Thompson 1991). It has been suggested that substitute care—particularly when it is of low quality (Howes 1990; Phillips et al. 1987)—may be responsible for impairing social development or creating undesirable behavior such as aggression and noncompliance.

Research by social scientists in this area has centered on effects on emotional insecurity and on sociability and aggression. The emotional insecurity of children cared for in nonmaternal settings has been the focus of a hotly contested debate. Some researchers have found that infants of full-time employed mothers are more likely to be classified as insecurely attached than are infants of nonemployed mothers or mothers employed part-time. Jay Belsky (1988, p. 235), for example, has argued that "some nonmaternal care arrangements in the first year for more than 20 hours per week may be a risk factor in the emergence of developmental difficulties."

Many clinical studies suggest that children who had extensive nonmaternal care experiences as infants tend to be less compliant with their parents and more aggressive with their peers (Haskins 1985; Vaughn, Deane, and Waters 1985). However, K. Alison Clarke-Stewart (1989) suggests that these findings may simply reflect the fact that children in substitute-care arrangements

> think for themselves and that they want their own way. They are not willing to comply with adults' arbitrary rules. . . . Children who have spent time in day care, then, may be more demanding and independent, more disobedient and more aggressive, more bossy and bratty than children who stay at home because they want their own way and do not have the skills to achieve it smoothly, rather than because they are maladjusted [p. 269].

There have been four large-scale studies of the effects of maternal employment during early childhood and substitute-care experiences on child emotional and cognitive outcomes using data from the National

Longitudinal Survey of Youth. Summarizing his analyses of one- to four-year-olds, Frank L. Mott (1991, p. 147) concluded that "extensive use of infant nonmaternal care did not either substantially enhance or negatively influence subsequent scores" on the Memory for Location and Motor and Social Development instruments. His analyses of effects on the Peabody Picture Vocabulary Test, however, suggest that use of group-care arrangements during infancy may enhance cognitive abilities, especially among healthy female infants. Male infants, on the other hand, do not exhibit effects of care arrangement on this cognitive dimension.

Nazli Baydar and Jeanne Brooks-Gunn (1991) studied cognitive and behavioral outcomes for children who were three to four years of age. Some of their analyses show a small but significant negative effect of maternal employment during infancy and suggest that different types of substitute care may affect boys differently from the way they affect girls.

The study by Belsky and David Eggebeen (1991) of two- to six-year-olds suggests that children whose mothers were employed during infancy may be less compliant than other children, while Theodore N. Greenstein (1993, p. 349) found in his study of 1,657 children that "early and extensive maternal employment does not seem to have generally adverse effects on the behavior of [four- and five-year-old children]."

In general, it appears that nonmaternal or substitute care in early childhood does not have a large effect on child development. In those studies in which differences between children cared for at home by their mothers and children with extensive nonmaternal care experiences are observed, the differences tend to be small. The determining factor most likely is the *quality* of the care received by the child; children who receive high-quality care and high levels of emotional support are likely to be well-adjusted, regardless of who the caregiver is. Conversely, children who are neglected or receive little emotional support will probably exhibit emotional adjustment problems.

(*See also:* Attachment; Child Care; Personality Development; Work and Family)

BIBLIOGRAPHY

Baydar, N., and Brooks-Gunn, J. (1991). "Effects of Maternal Employment and Child-Care Arrangements on Preschoolers' Cognitive and Behavioral Outcomes: Evidence from the Children of the National Longitudinal Survey of Youth." *Developmental Psychology* 27:932–945.

Belsky, J. (1988). "The 'Effects' of Infant Day Care Reconsidered." *Early Childhood Research Quarterly* 3:235–272.

Belsky, J. (1990). "Developmental Risks Associated with Infant Day Care: Attachment Insecurity, Noncompliance, and Aggression?" In *Psychosocial Issues in Day Care*, ed. S. S. Chehrazi. Washington, DC: American Psychiatric Press.

Belsky, J., and Eggebeen, D. (1991). "Early and Extensive Maternal Employment and Young Children's Socioemotional Development: Children of the National Longitudinal Survey of Youth." *Journal of Marriage and the Family* 53:1083–1110.

Clarke-Stewart, K. A. (1989). "Infant Day Care: Maligned or Malignant?" *American Psychologist* 44:266–273.

Greenstein, T. N. (1993). "Maternal Employment and Child Behavioral Outcomes: A Household Economics Analysis." *Journal of Family Issues* 14:323–354.

Haskins, R. (1985). "Public School Aggression Among Children with Varying Day-Care Experience." *Child Development* 56:689–703.

Howes, C. (1990). "Can the Age of Entry and the Quality of Infant Child Care Predict Behaviors in Kindergarten?" *Developmental Psychology* 26:292–303.

Mott, F. L. (1991). "Developmental Effects of Infant Care: The Mediating Role of Gender and Health." *Journal of Social Issues* 47:139–158.

Phillips, D.; McCartney, K.; Scarr, S.; and Howes, C. (1987). "Selective Review of Infant Day-Care Research: A Cause for Concern!" *Zero to Three* 7:18–21.

Scarr, S.; Phillips, S. D.; and McCartney, K. (1989). "Working Mothers and Their Families." *American Psychologist* 44:1402–1409.

Thompson, R. A. (1991). "Infant Day Care: Concerns, Controversies, Choices." In *Employed Mothers and Their Children*, ed. J. V. Lerner and N. L. Galambos. New York: Garland.

Vaughn, B.; Deane, K.; and Waters, E. (1985). "The Impact of Out-of-home Care on Child–Mother Attachment Quality." *Monographs of the Society for Research in Child Development* 50 (1–2, Serial no. 209).

Theodore N. Greenstein

SUICIDE

Suicide is the act or instance of taking one's own life, voluntarily and intentionally. In general, there are three different, but overlapping, groups of "suicidal" people: those who are troubled with suicidal thoughts and feelings (ideators), those who have attempted to commit suicide (attempters), and those who have succeeded in killing themselves (completers). The popular press often make no distinctions among these groups. While there are similarities, there are also important differences. Demographically, for example, attempters tend to be young white females, whereas completers tend to be older white males (Linehan 1986; Maris 1981).

The suidical phenomenon is very complex, and many subgroups are created by the overlapping of the three basic groups. These subgroups include those who had for some time thought about suicide and later made an unsuccessful attempt, those who finally killed themselves following at least one previous attempt, and those who thought of committing suicide for some time and then were successful on their first attempt.

One of the consistent findings across a number of studies is that, contrary to what many people think, having thoughts of killing oneself is not very unusual; even some young children think of suicide (Shafii 1989). A number of community surveys report that it is during adolescence when many individuals begin to think of suicide (Bolger 1989). About half of the population reports that they had thought of suicide by age fifteen. By the age of twenty about seventy percent of the population had given thought to committing suicide. Disturbing as this may be, a great many of these people never attempt suicide. Although contemplating suicide reflects distress, pain, or despair, having suicidal thoughts is fairly common, especially among adolescents.

A good deal of what appears in the suicide literature is about attempters. Numerous surveys reveal that thousands of adolescents in the United States make suicide attempts each year (Berman and Jobes 1991). The group with the highest rate of attempts consists of young white females, who usually attempt suicide by taking an overdose of medication or drugs (rarely lethal) in what professionals consider a "cry for help." In general, it is estimated that 10 percent of all attempters become completers (Maris 1981).

Suicide Rates in the United States

"Official" suicide is operationally defined as a death that a medical examiner or some other state authority has ruled a suicide. There are more than 30,000 such suicides a year in the United States. Experts agree that for a number of reasons there is some degree of underreporting of suicide. Survivors, for example, often do not want to believe that a member of their family committed suicide, or they may not want it made public. Committing suicide is often thought to be "bad" or something shameful. For centuries, families of those who committed suicide were subjected to all sorts of repercussions, including loss of property, refusal to have the deceased buried in hallowed cemeteries, and even the indignities of having the deceased's body subjected to all manner of public cruelty. While reactions are no longer as harsh, attempts are still made to deny the reality of the suicide or at least to keep it from public scrutiny because there is often shame and stigma attached to suicide and because it is so traumatic an event psychologically (Colt 1987; Perlin 1975). In addition, medical examiners, physicians, and others may not even consider the possibility that deaths resulting from single car crashes or overdoses by elderly people might in fact have been suicides.

While virtually all experts agree that there is some underreporting of suicide, there is less agreement on the *extent* of that underreporting. While some authors estimate that the official rate may underreport the actual rate by 50 percent, a more reasonable estimate is between 10 percent and 15 percent. Some evidence also exists that the extent of underreporting may be decreasing as the stigma of suicide has decreased and as public health officials have learned more about suicide (Hoberman and Garfinkel 1989).

Taking these reporting errors into consideration, the suicide completion rates for females are still considerably lower than those for males, and the suicide completion rates are higher for whites than for African Americans. One significant change that has taken place since the 1950s is that the rates of suicide in the younger population have increased while the rates of suicide in the older population have generally decreased.

Suicide and Causality

Despite the fact that newspaper and research articles may often conclude that X causes suicide, one of the most important things to realize is that "suicide is caused by a complex web of factors" (O'Carroll 1993, p. 27). Many factors have been demonstrated to be *associated* with suicide, for example problems with alcohol, drugs, family, work, school, and so on. This is not the same as saying that a person's depression, drinking, or divorce *caused* the suicide.

To further complicate things with regard to the family, one's relationship with family may be alternately described as a protective factor, a stressor, a predisposing factor, or a precipitating factor. In fact, it may be thought of as all these things.

Being a family member ideally involves a sense of belonging, a feeling of being loved, and having value to others. Being a family member provides a sense of purpose, structure, and order to life. Deliberately taking one's life often results from a feeling that life is meaningless, that one has no value to others, and that one is unloved or unworthy of love. Suicide is a dramatic leave-taking of all family involvement.

One of the early contributors to the study of suicide was Emile Durkheim, a French sociologist. Prior to his work, suicide had been thought of as either an evil act or a pathologic act. In either case, it was considered an individual act. Durkheim studied rates of suicide in different countries in Europe over a long period of time and discovered predictable patterns. Some countries had relatively high rates of suicide, for instance, and others had relatively low rates. Whatever was going on with those individuals who chose to kill themselves, Durkheim had uncovered a social cause. He posited a number of different social reasons to explain the different rates of suicide.

Durkheim ([1897] 1951) argued that, with some unusual exceptions, the more socially integrated people were, the more connected and involved, the less likely they were to commit suicide. In this regard, he compared rates of suicide among people who were married and those who were not and discovered that those who were married were less likely to commit suicide. This has proven to be an enduring feature of the demographics of suicide. Among adults, being married is a highly protective status. If one is divorced or widowed, this protection is ended, and the possibility of suicide is increased, especially with men.

It appears that, as people endure life's disappointments and difficulties, having a loving partner can ward off suicidal despair. Unfortunately, losing that very important person in one's life can lead at times to suicidal despair. Those adults who are widowed have the highest rates of suicide, followed by those who are divorced, then those who never married, and last those who are married. Thus, the protective quality of marital status leads to a certain vulnerability, particularly with men, who have the more difficult time when their wives die or divorce them. This is especially the case with elderly men. Building on Durkheim's work, more recent research by Ronald Maris (1981) emphasizes the role of social conflict:

> *Contra* Emile Durkheim and many other writers, *negative interaction is more of a factor in nonfatal suicide attempts and suicide completions than social isolation is.* Suicide prevention workers need to concentrate on the *quality* of social interaction among suicides and their significant others rather than assume that suicides tend to have no significant others. Suicides are not so much isolated and alone as they are involved in self-destructive interpersonal relationships that may ultimately lead them to cut themselves off from life itself or to use non-lethal suicide attempts to try to change the quality of their interpersonal relations [emphasis in original, pp. 335–336].

Family Roles and the Aftermath of Suicide

The death of a family member is one of the greatest stressors in life (Holmes and Rahe 1967). However, there is a typical process of bereavement that follows the death. This bereavement consists of "two components: grief and mourning. *Grief* specifically refers to the feelings and emotional responses related to bereavement. *Mourning* refers to the social customs and rituals which help the bereaved person grieve, that is, to express thoughts, feelings, and memories related to the loss of the deceased" (emphasis in original, Hauser 1987, p. 58).

Marilyn J. Hauser (1987) considers the following seven factors that contribute to difficulties with the grieving process in suicide deaths, some of which are shared by other types of deaths:

1. Suicide death is usually sudden and unexpected.
2. Death by suicide is often violent.
3. Suicide engenders guilt in the survivors.
4. Suicide often occurs in systems already experiencing stress.
5. Death by suicide can compromise usual mourning rituals.
6. Suicide may lead to harmful expressions of unconscious anger and ultimately to distorted communication patterns.
7. Following a suicide, some of the usual social supports may be withdrawn.

In addition to considering how the bereavement process may be different or troublesome in the case of a suicide, it is useful to consider the role of the deceased in the family.

The death of any child puts enormous strain on the family (Rando 1986). Parents of a child who commits suicide are left feeling guilty, feeling responsible for the suicide, and feeling that they have failed in the most egregious way (McIntosh 1987). This may be compounded by the critical reaction of the community to the parents, even when there is evidence that the child had difficulties not necessarily related to the parents, for example, problems with school performance (Calhoun, Selby, and Faulstich 1982).

Survivors often find it hard to discuss the suicide. This includes difficulty talking with friends about the suicide, but it also includes difficulty with communication between parents of a child who has committed suicide. Not knowing what to say, sometimes friends will spend time with the parents and act as though nothing has happened. Sometimes there is little discussion between spouses or between the surviving couple and their friends because one of the parents refuses to accept that the death was in fact a suicide (McIntosh 1987). For example, difficulty may be encountered in helping a school come to grips with a suicide if the parents insist that what appears to be an obvious suicide was in fact not and forbid the school to refer to the death in that way, despite the fact that the students believe it to be a suicide.

Whatever the cause of difficulty in discussing a child's suicide, it leads to a disturbed bereavement process. In particular, it limits parents' ability to correct distortions in their sense of themselves as parents since avoidance and lack of communication can lead to isolation, reinforcing feelings of failure.

Children are also survivors of parental death by suicide. The impact of the death of a parent by suicide, as with the death of a parent from any cause, is related to the age of the child. The most prominent findings in the research of children whose parent(s) committed suicide are threefold: (1) There tends to be no information given about the suicide or information is distorted, (2) there is often guilt associated with the suicide, and (3) there is often an identification with the parent. It is difficult for some children to come to grips with the suicide of a parent because there is reluctance to talk about it; this has been referred to as a "conspiracy of silence" (Cain and Fast 1972, p. 149). According to Cynthia Pfeffer (1981), these disturbed ways of dealing with the death of a parent can interfere with a healthy mourning process and cause problems in the child's development.

In the survivor literature, less has been written about sibling survivors than other relationships. Some of the issues reported have to do with siblings sometimes trying to help parents deal with the death, worrying that they too might kill themselves, postponing satisfaction of their own needs, and having to grow up too fast. How the parents deal with the suicide of a child is a major determinant of how the surviving siblings handle it (McIntosh 1987).

Most of the time, the death of a spouse by suicide deals with the suicide of the husband. There is some evidence that most of the difficulties faced by widows whose husbands have committed suicide are the same as those all widows experience, no matter the cause of death. The differences involved in surviving the suicide of a spouse are associated with the stigma attached to suicide and the cultural problems with regard to mourning.

Breaking the Silence

Prior to 1959, there was little in the way of help for what is now called the "survivors" of suicide. Indeed, the term "survivor" was not used. That year, however, the Los Angeles Suicide Prevention Center began to study suicide by contacting relatives and others who had known the person who committed suicide.

> They found widespread resistance, suppression of evidence and mental trauma among suicide survivors. But they found something else as well. Although they had been apprehensive about approaching distraught relatives, they quickly discovered that survivors had a great need to talk—about their grief, their guilt, their anger, and often their own suicidal feelings. It was usually the first time the survivors had been given the opportunity to talk about the suicide, and they frequently found the interviews to be therapeutic [Colt 1987, p. 14].

Survivors of Suicide (Cain 1972) was the first book to be published about suicide survivors, and since that time, a number of celebrities have come out publicly to discuss suicides in their family. What was once a problem for which there was little help and little understanding has become one for which there are services, research, and, perhaps most important, a network of self-help groups. In virtually every state there are now services available. However, even with the development of suicide prevention centers across the country, there is no evidence that the overall rate of suicide has been reduced. This makes it all the more critical that help be made available for those families that are touched with the tragedy of suicide.

(*See also:* Adolescence; Attachment; Communication; Death and Mourning; Family Therapy; Widowhood)

BIBLIOGRAPHY

Berman, A., and Jobes, D. (1991). *Adolescent Suicide Assessment and Intervention.* Washington, DC: American Psychological Association.

Bolger, N.; Downey, G.; Walker, E.; and Steininger, P. (1989). "The Onset of Suicidal Ideation of Childhood and Adolescence." *Journal of Youth and Adolescence* 18:175–190.

Bolton, I. (1983). *My Son . . . My Son: A Guide to Healing After Death, Loss, or Suicide.* Atlanta: Bolton Press.

Cain, A. C., ed. (1972). *Survivors of Suicide.* Springfield, IL: Charles C Thomas.

Cain, A. C., and Fast, I. (1972). "The Legacy of Suicide: Observations on the Pathogenic Impact of Suicide upon Marital Partners." In *Survivors of Suicide*, ed. A. C. Cain. Springfield, IL: Charles C Thomas.

Calhoun, L. G.; Selby, J. W.; and Faulstich, M. E. (1982). "The Aftermath of Childhood Suicide: Influences on the Perception of the Parent." *Journal of Community Psychology* 10:250–254.

Colt, G. H. (1987). "The History of the Suicide Survivor." In *Suicide and Its Aftermath*, ed. E. J. Dunne, J. L. McIntosh, and K. Dunne-Maxim. New York: W. W. Norton.

Durkheim, E. ([1897] 1951). *Suicide*. New York: Free Press.

Hauser, M. J. (1987). "Special Aspects of Grief After Suicide." In *Suicide and Its Aftermath*, ed. E. J. Dunne, J. L. McIntosh, and K. Dunne-Maxim. New York: W. W. Norton.

Hoberman, H. M., and Garfinkel, B. D. (1989). "Completed Suicide in Youth." In *Suicide Among Youth: Perspectives on Risk and Prevention*, ed. C. Pfeffer. Washington, DC: American Psychiatric Press.

Holmes, T. H., and Rahe, R. H. (1967). "The Social Readjustment Rating Scale." *Journal of Psychosomatic Research* 11:213–218.

Linehan, M. (1986). "Suicidal People: One Population or Two?" *Annals of the New York Academy of Sciences* 487:16–33.

McIntosh, J. L. (1987). "Survivor Family Relationships: Literature Review." In *Suicide and Its Aftermath*, ed. E. J. Dunne, J. L. McIntosh, and K. Dunne-Maxim. New York: W. W. Norton.

Maris, R. (1981). *Pathways to Suicide*. Baltimore: Johns Hopkins University Press.

O'Carroll, P. (1993). "Suicide Causation: Pies, Paths, and Pointless Polemics." *Suicide and Life-Threatening Behavior* 23:27–36.

Perlin, S. (1975). *A Handbook for the Study of Suicide*. New York: Oxford University Press.

Pfeffer, C. (1981). "Parental Suicide: An Organizing Event in the Development of Latency Age Children." *Suicide and Life-Threatening Behavior* 11:43–50.

Rando, T. A., ed. (1986). *Parental Loss of a Child*. Champaign, IL: Research Press.

Shafii, M. (1989). "Completed Suicide in Children and Adolescents: Methods of Psychological Autopsy." In *Suicide Among Youth*, ed. C. Pfeffer. Washington, DC: American Psychiatric Press.

PATRICK HYNES

SYMBOLIC INTERACTIONISM

Symbolic interactionism is a sociological perspective on self and society based on the ideas of George H. Mead (1934), Charles H. Cooley (1902), W. I. Thomas (1931), and other pragmatists associated, primarily, with the University of Chicago in the early twentieth century. The central theme and guiding principle of symbolic interactionism is that human life is lived in the symbolic domain. Symbols are culturally derived social objects having shared meanings that are created and maintained in social interaction. It is by means of symbols, via language and communication, that human realities are constructed. Therefore, reality is primarily a social product. For symbolic interactionists, all that is humanly consequential—self, mind, society, culture—emerges from and is dependent on symbolic interactions for its existence. Even the physical environment is relevant to human conduct *only* as it is interpreted or filtered through symbolic systems.

Importance of Meanings

The label "symbolic interactionism" was actually coined by Herbert Blumer (1969), one of Mead's students. Blumer, who did much to shape the nature and content of this perspective, specified three basic premises central to symbolic interactionism: (1) Humans act toward things on the basis of the meanings that things have for them; (2) the meanings of things derive from social interaction; and (3) these meanings are dependent on, and modified by, an interpretive process of the interactants; The focus here is on meaning, which is defined in terms of action and its consequences (reflecting the influence of pragmatism). That is, the meaning of a thing resides in the action that it elicits. For example, the meaning of "grass" is food to a cow, shelter to a fox, and so on. In the case of symbols, meanings also depend on a certain degree of consensual or congruent responses of two or more interactants. The meaning of the word "husband," for example, depends on the consensual responses of those who use the term. If there is high consensus, the meaning of a symbol is clear; if there is low consensus, the meaning is ambiguous and communication is problematic. Within a culture, there is a degree of general consensus on the meanings associated with various words or symbols. However, in practice, the meanings of things are highly variable and depend on processes of interpretation and negotiation of the interactants.

The interpretive process entails what Blumer refers to as role-taking, the cognitive ability to take the perspective or attitude of another. It is a critical process in communication, since it enables actors to interpret one anothers' responses, thereby facilitating greater consensus on the meanings of the symbols used. The determination of meanings in interaction also depends on negotiation, that is, on mutual adjustments and accommodations of the interactants. In short, meaning is emergent, problematic, and dependent on processes of role-taking and negotiation in social interaction. Most of the other concepts of symbolic interactionism are in some way related to the concept of meaning.

Nature of Definitions

The importance of meanings is clearly reflected in Thomas's (1931) famous dictum: If situations are defined as real, they are real in their consequences. The definition of the situation stresses that people act in situations not on the basis of how things are, but on the basis of how they are defined. Furthermore, definitions (even when they are quite false or at variance with any "objective" reality) have real consequences for people's actions and for the course of events. Whether a situation is defined as dangerous or benign, altruistic or exploitative, romantic or economic will affect people's actions.

An important element in the definitional process is the determination of the relevant identities and attributes of the interactants. If, for example, a teacher defines a student in her class as a "slow learner" (based on inaccurate information), her subsequent, discriminatory behavior (e.g., less attention and encouragement, and lower expectations) may have a negative effect on the student's intellectual development, resulting in a "self-fulfilling prophecy." This process, in combination with interactionist ideas about self-concept formation, is the basis of the "labeling theory" of deviance. Labeling theory proposes that a key factor in the development of deviants is the negative label of identity imposed on the person (e.g., "criminal," "pervert," "psycho") who engages in deviant behavior (Becker 1963).

Defining a situation is not a static process. An initial definition, based on past experiences or cultural expectations, may be modified or revised in the course of interaction. Much of the negotiation that takes place within social situations is an attempt to present the self in a favorable light or to defend a valued identity when it is challenged. Erving Goffman's (1959) insightful analyses of impression management and the use of deference and demeanor, as well as Marvin E. Scott and Stanford M. Lyman's (1968) examination of the use of excuses, justifications, and accounts, speak to the intricacies involved in situational definitions. It should be noted that when there are power or status disparities between the interactants in a situation, the dominant person's definition of the situation is more likely to prevail.

Self-Concept Formation

Along with symbols, meaning, and interaction, the "self" is a foundational concept in symbolic interactionism. The essential feature of the self is that it is a reflexive phenomenon. Reflexivity enables humans to act toward themselves as objects, that is, to reflect on themselves, argue with themselves, evaluate themselves, and so forth. It is considered a uniquely human attribute, based on the social character of human language and the ability to role-take, that enables individuals to see themselves from the perspective of another and thereby to form a conception of themselves, a self-concept.

Two types of "others" are critical in the development of the self. The significant other refers to specific persons who are important to an individual, whose opinions matter. The generalized other refers to a conception of the community, group, or any organized system of roles (e.g., a baseball team) that are used as a point of reference from which to view the self.

The importance of others in the formation of self-concepts is captured in Cooley's (1902) influential concept, "the looking-glass self." Cooley proposed that to some extent individuals come to see themselves as they think others see them. Self-conceptions and self-feelings (e.g., pride or shame) are a consequence of how people imagine others perceive and evaluate them. Within contemporary symbolic interactionism, this process is called "reflected appraisals" and is the main process emphasized in the development of the self.

The self is considered a social product in other ways as well. The content of self-concepts reflects the content and organization of society, or at least that part of society that an individual experiences. This is most evident with regard to the roles that are internalized as role identities (e.g., "father," "student," "mediator"). Roles, as behavioral expectations associated with a status within a set of relationships, constitute a major link between social organization and personal organization. Sheldon Stryker (1980) proposes that differential commitment to various role identities provides much of the structure and organization of self-concepts. To the extent that individuals are committed to a particular role identity, they are motivated to act in accordance with their conception of the identity and to maintain and protect it, since their role performance will have implications for their self-esteem. Much of socialization, particularly during childhood, involves the learning of social roles and some of the values, attitudes, and beliefs associated with them. Initially this takes place in the context of family relations, and eventually in larger arenas (e.g., peer groups, school, work settings) as the individual's social world expands. The role identities formed early in life, such as gender and filial identities, typically remain some of the most important throughout one's life. Since socialization is a lifelong process, individuals come to assume various role identities throughout their life course.

Socialization, for interactionists, is not a passive process of role learning and conformity to the expectations of others. On the contrary, the self is highly active and selective in this process, having a major influence on its environment and on itself. For many of the roles people play, role making is as evident as role learning. In role making, individuals actively construct, interpret, and uniquely express their roles. When they perceive an incongruity between a role imposed on them and some valued aspect of their self-conception, they may engage in role distance, the disassociation of self from role. A pervasive theme in much of this literature is that the self actively engages in the process of its own development, a process that may be quite unpredictable with frequent unanticipated consequences.

Divisions Within Symbolic Interactionism

Symbolic interactionism is not a homogeneous theoretical perspective. Although all interactionists share the view that humans rely on shared symbols to construct their realities in a process of social interaction and the methodological requirement of "getting inside" the reality of the actor in order to understand behavior, there are substantial divisions within this perspective. The main division is between those who emphasize process and those who emphasize structure in studying human realities. The former, associated with Blumer (1969) and the "Chicago School," advocates the use of qualitative methods in studying the process of reality construction within natural social settings. The latter, associated with Manford Kuhn (1964) and the "Iowa School," advocates the use of quantitative methods in studying the products of social interaction, especially self-concepts. The differences between these two "schools" of symbolic interactionism reflect the fundamental division in the social sciences between humanistic/interpretive orientations, which align with history and the humanities, and positivistic/nomothetic orientations, which align with the physical sciences (see Meltzer, Petras, and Reynolds 1975). Both of these major orientations to symbolic interactionism are evident in studies of marriage and the family, although the structural orientation predominates in contemporary research.

Symbolic Interactionism and Family Studies

Symbolic interactionism has been an important theoretical perspective in family studies since its early development in the 1920s and 1930s (LaRossa and Reitzes 1993). Thomas and Florian Znaniecki's (1918–1920) monumental study, *The Polish Peasant in Europe and America*, was an early application of some of the main themes and concepts of the perspective. This study focused on the adjustments and transformations in personality and family patterns in the Polish peasant community in the course of immigration to America during the early 1900s. Processes of socialization, adaptation, definition formation, role-making, and self-concept development were major themes in their analysis.

It is Earnest W. Burgess, however, who is credited with being the first to call for the systematic application of symbolic interactionism to family studies. He proposed that the family can best be viewed as "a unity of interacting personalities" (Burgess 1926), a little universe of communication and interaction in which roles and selves are shaped and each personality affects every other personality. Unfortunately, few heeded Burgess's call to study whole families in their dynamic interactions (for an exception, see Hess and Handel 1959). It is simply too difficult and impractical for most family researchers to study the dynamics of whole families over time. Even Burgess did not do this kind of research. Most of his own empirical studies used conventional survey methods and measurement techniques in studying marital adjustment (see Burgess and Cottrell 1939). So, while Burgess's conceptual approach to the family advocated "processual interactionism," his empirical work reflects a more "structural interactionist" orientation.

Another pioneer in the symbolic interactionist approach to family research was Willard Waller (1937, 1938). Waller used qualitative methods (e.g., case studies and novels) to study family dynamics, particularly processes of interpersonal conflict, bargaining, and exploitation. His "principle of least interest" suggests that the person least interested or committed to the marital or dating relationship has the most power in that relationship and frequently uses it to exploit the other. The theme of conflict and exploitation was prominent in his analysis of college dating patterns in the 1930s. Waller argued the college men and women defined dating as an exchange relationship, with men seeking sexual gratification and women seeking to enhance their social status or obtain financial benefits. These mixed motives in premarital relations, Waller argued, often carried over into marriage, setting the stage for subsequent marital problems. Waller's highly perceptive analyses offered a darker view of dating and family relations than was characteristic of family scholars, especially of symbolic interactionists. Interestingly, Reuben Hill, who helped shape much of the contemporary research on the family, reworked Waller's treatise on the family by shifting the focus from a conflict and process orientation to a relatively structured developmental perspective emphasizing family roles and a more harmonious view of family life (Waller and Hill 1951).

Much contemporary family research from a symbolic interactionist perspective deals with some type of role analysis, such as how the roles of "husband" and "wife" are defined as various stages of family life; how conceptions of gender roles affect the definitions of spousal roles; how the arrival of children and the transition to new roles (e.g., mother, father) change the role constellations and interaction patterns in the family; how external events (e.g., parental employment or unemployment, natural disasters, migration) and internal events (e.g., births, deaths, divorces) affect role definitions, performance, stress, or conflict; and how these role-specific variables affect the attitudes, dispositions, and self-conceptions of family members (see Hutter 1985; Stryker 1964). It should be noted that the concept of role is not unique to symbolic interactionism. It is an important concept for most of the major sociological perspectives (e.g., structural functionalism, social exchange theory, and even conflict theory). The symbolic interactionist perspective on the concept of role is to emphasize the processes of role making, role definition, role negotiation, and role identity within the family (see Hochschild 1989).

Another large area of the symbolic interactionist research deals with socialization—the processes through which personalities and self-concepts are formed, values and attitudes are transmitted, and the culture of one generation is passed on to the next. Since the socialization of children is one of the few remaining functions (and the most critical function) of the family in modern societies, it has received considerable attention from researchers. A symbolic interactionist perspective on child socialization is potentially quite broad, encompassing the multitude of processes and outcomes involved in integrating the newborn into its family's system of meanings, behaviors, and personalities. In practice, most of the socialization research has focused on the development of some aspect of the self (e.g., self-esteem, gender and filial identities). In general, the research indicates that positive reflected appraisals from parents along with parental support and use of inductive control have positive socialization outcomes for the children's self-concept (see Gecas and Schwalbe 1986; Peterson and Rollins 1987). It should be emphasized that this process is highly reciprocal; not only do parents affect their children's self-concepts, but children affect their parents' self-concepts. The high levels of reciprocity characteristic of family socialization processes (and a hallmark of symbolic interactionism) are still rarely reflected in family research, although family researchers are increasingly sensitive to this problem.

Conclusion

There are many other areas of family research that reflect symbolic interactionist ideas, often in diffuse and diluted form. For instance, in much of the research on marital satisfaction, marital quality, patterns of dating and mating, and various family-relevant attitudes (e.g., premarital sex, abortion), symbolic interactionist ideas are more likely to be implicit rather than explicitly stated and tested. On the one hand, this hinders the development and refinement of symbolic interactionism. On the other hand, it can be viewed as an indication of the success of this theoretical perspective—that many of its concepts and ideas have become a part of the common wisdom of family studies.

(*See also:* Communication; Exchange Theory; Family Development Theory; Family Systems Theory; Family Theory; Gender; Gender Identity; Personality Development; Self-Esteem)

BIBLIOGRAPHY

Becker, H. S. (1963). *Outsiders: Studies in the Sociology of Deviance.* New York: Free Press.

Blumer, H. (1969). *Symbolic Interactionism: Perspective and Method.* Englewood Cliffs, NJ: Prentice Hall.

Burgess, E. W. (1926). "The Family as a Unity of Interacting Personalities." *Family* 7:3–9.

Burgess, E. W., and Cottrell, L. S., Jr. (1939). *Predicting Success or Failure in Marriage.* New York: Prentice Hall.

Charon, J. (1989). *Symbolic Interactionism,* 3rd edition. Englewood Cliffs, NJ: Prentice Hall.

Cooley, C. H. (1902). *Human Nature and the Social Order.* New York: Scribner.

Gecas, V., and Schwalbe, M. L. (1986). "Parental Behavior and Adolescent Self-Esteem." *Journal of Marriage and the Family* 48:37–46.

Goffman, E. (1959). *The Presentations of Self in Everyday Life.* New York: Doubleday.

Hess, R. D., and Handel, G. (1959). *Family Worlds.* Chicago: University of Chicago Press.

Hochschild, A. R. (1989). *The Second Shift: Working Parents and the Revolution at Home.* New York: Viking.

Hutter, M. (1985). "Symbolic Interaction and the Study of the Family." In *Foundations of Interpretive Sociology: Studies in Symbolic Interaction*, ed. H. A. Farberman and R. S. Perinbanayagam. Greenwich, CT: JAI Press.

Kuhn, M. H. (1964). "Major Trends In Symbolic Interaction Theory in the Past Twenty-Five Years." *Sociological Quarterly* 5:61–84.

LaRossa, R., and Reitzes, D. C. (1993). "Symbolic Interactionism and Family Studies." In *Sourcebook of Family Theories and Methods*, ed. P. G. Boss, W. J. Doherty, R. LaRossa, W. R. Schumm, and S. K. Steinmetz. New York: Plenum.

Mead, G. H. (1934). *Mind, Self, and Society.* Chicago: University of Chicago Press.

Meltzer, B. N.; Petras, J. W.; and Reynolds, L. T. (1975). *Symbolic Interactionism: Genesis, Varieties, and Criticism.* Boston: Routledge & Kegan Paul.

Peterson, G. W., and Rollins, B. C. (1987). "Parent–Child Socialization." In *Handbook of Marriage and the Family*, ed. M. B. Sussman and S. K. Steinmetz. New York: Plenum.

Scott, M. E., and Lyman, S. M. (1968). "Accounts." *American Sociological Review* 33:46–62.

Stryker, S. (1964). "The Interactional and Situational Approaches." In *Handbook of Marriage and the Family*, ed. H. T. Christensen. Chicago: Rand McNally.

Stryker, S. (1980). *Symbolic Interactionism.* Menlo Park, CA: Benjamin/Cummings.

Thomas, W. I. (1931). *The Unadjusted Girl.* Boston: Little, Brown.

Thomas, W. I., and Znaniecki, F. (1918–1920). *The Polish Peasant in Europe and America*, 5 vols. Boston: Badger.

Waller, W. (1937). "The Rating-Dating Complex." *American Sociological Review* 2:727–734.

Waller, W. (1938). *The Family: A Dynamic Interpretation.* New York: Dryden.

Waller, W., and Hill, R. (1951). *The Family: A Dynamic Interpretation*, revised edition. New York: Dryden.

Viktor Gecas

T

TEENAGE PARENTING

Teenage parenting refers primarily to women and men nineteen years or younger who give birth to and elect to parent the child. Estimates suggest that nearly 44 percent of sexually active adolescent females become pregnant (Furstenberg, Brooks-Gunn, and Chase-Landsdale 1989). While the majority of teenage pregnancies are unintended, an increasing number of pregnant adolescents are choosing to continue the pregnancy and become parents.

At any age, pregnancy and first parenthood produce changes that necessitate adaptation. For the adolescent, three transitions occur simultaneously. They must adjust to changes in their family-of-origin relationships during adolescence, changes in their physical and cognitive abilities, and changes in their social reality. Add to this the changes caused by premature parenthood and the potential for stress increases. Typically teenage parents experience stress from five sources: relationships with the self, relationships with partners, parent–child relations, intergenerational relations, and relations with nonfamily institutions. Thus, the adolescent parent faces a series of competing developmental tasks that increase the likelihood of stress (Pasley, Langfield, and Kreutzer 1993).

Trends

Compared to other industrialized countries, the United States has the highest premarital pregnancy rate and correspondingly one of the highest rates of births to young, unmarried women. Until the mid-1980s, there was a decrease in the childbearing rate of females fifteen to nineteen years of age. More recently, the childbearing rate for this age group has increased. Much of the concern over teenage parenting stems from the dramatic increase in its occurrence to young, unmarried women, an increase that is especially pronounced for white women (National Center for Education Statistics 1993). For example, in 1950, there were 12.6 births to unmarried women per 1,000 unmarried women aged fifteen to nineteen. By 1990, this figure had increased to 42.5 births. For white women, the change was from 5.1 births in 1950 to 30.6 births in 1990. For African-American women, the same figures were 68.5 births in 1950 compared to 88.3 births in 1990.

Since 1972, the increase in pregnancy and birth rates to adolescent women represents a larger increase for those eighteen to nineteen years of age than for younger adolescents. In 1991, the birthrate among women aged fifteen to seventeen rose 3 percent, to 39 per 1,000 women. The birthrate rose by 7 percent among those aged eighteen to nineteen, to 94 per 1,000, representing the highest rate for older teenagers since 1972 (National Center for Health Statistics 1993).

However, the fathers of the babies born to adolescent mothers are less likely to be adolescents themselves. Only about 29 percent of births to teen mothers involved a father nineteen years of age or younger; 52 percent of fathers were twenty to twenty-four years of age; and 15 percent were older than twenty-five years of age (Males 1992).

African-American women are more than twice as likely as whites to have had a teenage birth: 42 percent versus 19 percent (Kahan and Anderson 1992). African Americans also are more likely to have low self-esteem, low educational aspirations, poorer attitudes toward school (Plotnick 1992), and to have a mother who was a teenage parent (Furstenberg, Brooks-Gunn, and Chase-Landsdale 1989). While daughters of white teenage mothers were 75 percent more likely to have a teenage birth than were daughters of older mothers, daughters of African-American teenage mothers were only 34 percent more likely to have a teenage birth.

Other factors predict teenage parenting for whites, including religious affiliation, urban residence, and generational cohort. These factors do not predict teenage parenthood as consistently for African-American adolescents (Kahan and Anderson 1992).

Fewer pregnant adolescents relinquish babies for adoption today, and some differences exist between those who relinquish babies and those who do not. Adolescents who relinquish are characterized as being in school at the time, older, white, and having mothers who had some college education. Adolescent females who do not relinquish their babies and become teenage mothers are more likely to have lived in a single-parent family at age fourteen, were working at the time of pregnancy, and gave birth to male children (Bachrach, Stolley, and London 1992).

Cost of Teenage Parenting

Much of the literature suggests that teenage childbearing has large educational and economic costs (Hoffman, Foster, and Furstenberg 1993). Women who gave birth in their twenties and thirties are more likely to have graduated from high school and to have attended college than those who gave birth as teenagers. Older mothers also have more income and are less likely to live in poverty than are teenage mothers. Estimated probabilities of educational attainment suggest that 54 percent of teenage mothers graduate from high school; had these same women delayed parenthood until at least age twenty, the proportion graduating from school would have been 86 percent. Teenage parents who remain in school do as well academically as those who delay childbearing.

Racial differences are found in school attainment. African Americans are more likely than white or Hispanic teens to complete school after the birth of a child. Whereas African Americans are more likely to assume the parental role as an adolescent, they are less likely than whites and Hispanics to become a spouse. White adolescents are more likely to marry, and being married hinders their school completion. Hispanic adolescents are more likely than either African Americans or whites to assume both the parental and spousal roles. Hispanics have the highest dropout rates of all racial groups regardless of whether they are adolescent parents. Both adolescent parenthood and adolescent marriage contribute to the higher probability of dropout by Hispanic females, with teenage parenthood being the most significant predictor of the two (Forste and Tienda 1992).

Economic costs of adolescent parenting are noted. Adolescent parents are more likely to receive Aid to Families with Dependent Children (AFDC) four years after the birth of a first child than are older parents. Teenage mothers are most likely to have the longest careers on welfare. Of all families earning less than $10,000 in 1991, almost half were headed by a lone mother with children under eighteen years residing in the home. Poverty is especially pronounced by race, with African-American families (regardless of family structure) to be among those in poverty.

Single and Married Teenage Parents

Two-thirds of all adolescent births and 90 percent of all African-American adolescent births in the United States are out of wedlock. White women are more than twice as likely as African-American women to marry as teenagers: 35 percent and 17 percent, respectively (Kahan and Anderson 1992). In fact, African Americans experience higher rates of teenage births and much lower rates of teenage marriage than whites or Hispanics. Hispanics experience the highest teen marriage rates of all groups (Forste and Tienda 1992). The majority of births to white teenagers occur within marriage, whereas the majority of births to African-American teenagers occur outside of marriage. Teenage mothers with more egalitarian attitudes are less likely to marry than teenage mothers with more traditional views (Plotnick 1992).

In general, studies have found that early marriage both truncates the education of young women and leads to future economic hardship. Because pregnancy and childbirth are associated with adolescent marriage, teenage pregnancy and marriage may have an additive effect on one's life chances. Some research has shown that males who married as adolescents did not do as well educationally, financially, or occupationally as their same-aged, same-race peers who married as adults, even after an extended period of time. Other research found that when both marriage and childbirth occurred during adolescence, teenagers were at a greater socioeconomic disadvantage than when either occurred alone (Teti and Lamb 1989). These disadvantages may result from the fact that adolescents who become parents are likely to come from environments where support for educational achievement and educational/career goals are lacking compared with those who postpone childbirth and marriage.

Adolescent marriages are noted to be less stable and more prone to divorce than are marriages of persons older than twenty years. The risk of dissolution of subsequent marriages also is higher when the first marriage occurrs during adolescence. When children are present, teenage marriages are more stable than when marriage occurs without children (Teti and Lamb 1989), although adolescent marriages have a much higher dissolution rate than other marriages.

Effects of Teenage Parenthood on Children

About 12 percent of infants in the United States are born to adolescent mothers. Much of the research suggests that being born to an adolescent mother is a risk factor for young children. Overall, children of teenage parents are developmentally disadvantaged compared to children born to older mothers. Although they are small, consistent differences in cognitive functioning are reported for preschool-age children that continue into middle childhood. Preschool children of adolescent mothers seem to be more active, aggressive, and undercontrolled than children of older mothers, a finding especially pronounced for boys. Psychosocial problems also are more common, with children of adolescent parents being rated as more active and aggressive, and possessing less self-control. Children of mothers who have higher levels of education and who do not live in poverty are more likely to do well academically. The school achievement of adolescent children of teenage parents is lower than that of children of older parents. In adolescence, more problems begin to show up, such as grade failure, delinquent acts, and early sexual activity. However, many of these effects are believed to result from the broader environment in which children of adolescent parents grow and develop (Chase-Landsdale, Brooks-Gunn, and Paikoff 1991).

Research finds that the health of infants is affected more by family background characteristics (e.g., race, residence in two-parent home, mother's education) and mother's health-related behavior (e.g., smoking, drinking, prenatal care) than by mother's age (Geronimus and Korenman 1993). In part, providing good care for a child is influenced by knowledge of child development and beliefs about appropriate parenting. Teenage mothers sixteen years of age or younger are less knowledgeable about child development, hold more punitive attitudes toward child rearing, and are more depressed than mothers seventeen to twenty-five years of age (Reis 1990). Therefore, they are less likely to provide adequate care for their children.

The effect of teenage parenting on child outcome is not direct. Instead, the effects of age of mother at birth affect child outcome primarily as a result of family factors such as level of education of the teen's own mother and responsiveness and stimulation provided to the child. Support provided by grandmothers and husbands or boyfriends can enhance or hinder the outcomes for children. Also, disadvantaged social and economic situations of early parenthood are probable causes of the poorer performance of children of teenage parents (Brooks-Gunn and Chase-Landsdale 1991). Changes in welfare status and entrance to stable marriages are found to buffer many of the negative effects of early parenthood on children (Furstenberg, Brooks-Gunn, and Chase-Landsdale 1989).

Teenage Mothers

Stress in adolescent mothers has been studied by several scholars. High levels of stress are believed to affect the quality of parenting adversely. Unmarried, nonwhite teen mothers reported high levels of stress stemming from unwanted, unsolicited advice; criticism; gratuitous negative comments; and conflict with families and husbands or boyfriends (Garcia-Coll, Hoffman, and Oh 1987). Some research finds that adolescent women who are pregnant experience different stress from adolescent women who are currently parenting their child and that the correlates of stress for these two groups are unique also. For example, the satisfaction of adolescent mothers with the level of social support they received predicts stress in general and stress stemming from issues of autonomy specifically; this finding does not hold for pregnant adolescents (Pasley, Langfield, and Kreutzer 1993). Other research shows that social support buffers some but not all of the negative effects of stress for teenage mothers.

Teenage Fathers

Adolescent fathers (those who are nineteen years of age or younger) are more likely than men who become fathers between ages twenty and twenty-three to have experienced academic difficulties for as long as ten years prior to becoming a father (Dearden, Hale, and Alvarez 1992). For teen fathers, much of their stress involves vocational-educational issues, interpersonal relationships, health, and concern over future parenting competence.

Like adolescent mothers, teenage fathers are more likely to have had a parent or sibling who was a teenage parent. African-American teenage fathers are more likely than either whites or Hispanics to enter parenthood early, are less likely to marry at the time of birth, and are more likely to be absent after birth. The relationship with the mother of the child is often unstable and becomes a source of stress rather than support (Elster 1991).

Also, like teenage mothers, teenage fathers tend to be younger at first marriage and are more likely to divorce than nonfathers. They also are more likely to have several marriages and to father more children than their same-age peers. Teenage fathers have poorer academic records than their peers and more often drop out of school or obtain GEDs. They also are involved in more problem behaviors (delinquency and substance use). Over time, differences between teenage fathers and other fathers diminish in terms of employment rates and income. Adolescent fathers also hold more traditional views of family life, are more realistic regarding the time they will spend with the child, and view the provider role as more important than the child-care role. In terms of interaction with their children, they are similar to adult fathers (Elster 1991).

Teenage fathers are more involved with their children and the mothers than might be expected; about half are married to or have regular contact with the mother one year after birth. However, contact with the child typically diminishes over time. The lack of contact is related to economic status such that those fathers with more resources (e.g., education and income) are more involved. Financial support follows a similar pattern, although when support is provided, it is often modest (Neville and Parke 1991); only about 14 percent of unwed mothers collected any child support in 1989. The lack of vocational skills of teenage fathers is related to providing little financial support for their children.

Grandparenting

Findings suggest that the presence of a grandmother in the home appears to be both beneficial and harmful to the teenage parent and her child. Grandmothers often assist their teenage children with child-care responsibilities and provide additional financial resources. The presence of a grandmother in the home is beneficial for the health and development of low-birthweight infants born to young mothers (Pope 1993). Grandmother support for older teenage mothers also is associated with the mother completing her education, especially if the grandmother provides child care. This care adds to the overall cognitive stimulation in the home. However, residence with the grandmother may not foster optimal child-rearing environments in that the teenage mother may assume less responsibility for the care of her child, leaving an already overburdened grandmother in charge. As the grandmother's stress increases, the quality of the care she provides may diminish.

Policy Related to Teenage Parenting

There are several policy concerns around the economic and social/psychological burdens of teenage parenting for individuals and the broader society. Many adolescent parenting programs attempt to address these concerns by providing services to teenagers with the goal of decreasing the likelihood of second births, increasing self-sufficiency through vocational training, and enhancing parenting skills through parent education. Additional policy concerns focus on the provision of child support. Shirley L. Zimmerman (1992) argues that teenage parenting must be examined in the larger context in which it occurs, because the states where there are higher poverty rates, higher unemployment rates, higher divorce rates, and low rates of school completion report higher rates of births to teens. Zimmerman suggests that policy must address the forces that "give rise to high birthrates among the young, cultural norms, family instability, academic failure, and individual motivation within the context of persistent inequality and growing social isolation of the poor" (p. 428). As such, specific policy recommendations might address how to simplify the process of establishing paternity and how to provide for the care of children so parents can gain the necessary skills for economic independence (e.g., child-care subsidies for low-income mothers, or a refundable child-care tax credit).

(*See also:* Adolescence; Adolescent Sexuality; Family Values; Fathers; Grandparenthood; Mothers; Nonmarital Pregnancy; Poverty; Single Parents)

BIBLIOGRAPHY

Bachrach, C. A.; Stolley, K. S.; and London, K. A. (1992). "Relinquishment of Premarital Births: Evidence from National Survey Data." *Family Planning Perspectives* 24:27–32, 48.

Brooks-Gunn, J., and Chase-Landsdale, P. L. (1991). "Teenage Childbearing: Effects on Children." In *Encyclopedia of Adolescence*, ed. R. M. Lerner, A. C. Peterson, and J. Brooks-Gunn. New York: Garland.

Chase-Landsdale, L.; Brooks-Gunn, J.; and Paikoff, R. F. (1991). "Research and Programs for Adolescent Mothers: Missing Links and Future Promises." *Family Relations* 40:396–403.

Dearden, K.; Hale, C.; and Alvarez, J. (1992). "The Educational Antecedents of Teen Fatherhood." *British Journal of Educational Psychology* 62:139–147.

Elster, A. B. (1991). "Fathers, Teenage." In *Encyclopedia of Adolescence,* ed. R. M. Lerner, A. C. Peterson, and J. Brooks-Gunn. New York: Garland.

Forste, R., and Tienda, M. (1992). "Race and Ethnic Variation in the Schooling Consequences of Female Adolescent Sexual Activity." *Social Science Quarterly* 73:12–30.

Furstenberg, F. F., Jr.; Brooks-Gunn, J.; and Chase-Landsdale, L. (1989). "Teenaged Pregnancy and Childbearing." *American Psychologist* 44:452–469.

Garcia-Coll, C. T.; Hoffman, J.; and Oh, W. (1987). "The Social Ecology of Early Parenting of Caucasian Adolescent Mothers." *Child Development* 58:955–963.

Geronimus, A. T., and Korenman, S. (1993). "Maternal Youth or Family Background: On the Health Disadvantages of Infants with Teenage Mothers." *American Journal of Epidemiology* 137:213–225.

Hoffman, F. D.; Foster, E. M.; and Furstenberg, F. F., Jr. (1993). "Reevaluating the Costs of Teenage Childbearing." *Demography* 30:1–14.

Kahan, J. R., and Anderson, K. E. (1992). "Intergenerational Patterns of Teenage Fertility." *Demography* 29:39.

Males, M. (1992). "Adult Liaison in the 'Epidemic' of 'Teenage' Birth, Pregnancy, and Venereal Disease." *Journal of Sex Research* 29:525–545.

National Center for Education Statistics. (1993). *Youth Indicators 1993: Trends in the Well-Being of American Youth.* Washington, DC: U.S. Government Printing Office.

National Center for Health Statistics. (1993). "Advanced Report of Final Natality Statistics, 1991." *Monthly Vital Statistics Report,* Vol. 42, no. 3, suppl. Hyattsville, MD: U.S. Public Health Service.

Neville, B., and Parke, R. D. (1991). "Fathers, Adolescent." In *Encyclopedia of Adolescence,* ed. R. M. Lerner, A. C. Peterson, and J. Brooks-Gunn. New York: Garland.

Pasley, K.; Langfield, P. A.; and Kreutzer, J. A. (1993). "Predictors of Stress in Adolescents." *Journal of Adolescent Research* 8:326–347.

Plotnick, R. D. (1992). "The Effects of Attitudes on Teenage Premarital Pregnancy and Its Resolution." *American Sociological Review* 57:800–811.

Pope, S. K. (1993). "Low-Birth-Weight Infants Born to Adolescent Mothers: Effects of Coresidency with Grandmother on Child Development." *Journal of the American Medical Association* 269:1396–1400.

Reis, J. (1990). "A Comparison of Young Teenage, Older Teenage, and Adult Mothers on Determinants of Parents." *Journal of Psychology* 123:141–151.

Teti, D. M., and Lamb, M. E. (1989). "Socioeconomic and Marital Outcomes of Adolescent Marriage, Adolescent Childbirth, and Their Co-occurrence." *Journal of Marriage and the Family* 51:203–212.

Zimmerman, S. L. (1992). "Family Trends: What Implications for Family Policy?" *Family Relations* 41:423–429.

KAY PASLEY

THERAPY

See FAMILY THERAPY

TRUANCY

For students to be successful in school (as preparation for success in their adult life), they must attend school and do so on a regular and consistent basis. However, excessive absence from public schools is a serious problem in both urban and suburban school districts. Estimates of unexcused school absences range from 8 percent to 30 percent daily, with fluctuations related to specific days of the week or to specific scheduled events such as tests or field trips. In general, absences that are unexcused may be considered truancy.

There are three types of unexcused school absences: absence with parental consent in violation of school policy (e.g., to go on vacation with parents); absence with parental support based on school phobia or school avoidance behaviors, generally the result of a high anxiety level associated with some aspect of the school or the child's unconscious reaction to disturbance within the family; absence without parental knowledge or support, willful and voluntary behavior by the child. For the purpose of this entry, the third type of unexcused absence is defined as truancy.

Compulsory Attendance

Truancy is a violation of law in all fifty states. Required attendance under these laws varies from state to state, with mandated age of entry to school ranging from five to eight years of age. The permissive age of discontinuing school attendance ranges from sixteen to eighteen.

Compulsory-education laws were developed in the last half of the nineteenth century in response to America's emergence as a world power. Advocates of compulsory education focused on a social and moral rationale for their passage: Democratic society requires a well-educated citizen population to assure the continuation of democracy; children of recently arrived immigrants need to be taught the values of American society; and an industrial society will require a well-educated work force to assure its continued growth and development

As of the mid-1990s, advocates of maintaining or expanding the compulsory attendance laws (longer school day, year-round schooling) presented similar reasons for their advocacy: Children from minority ethnic groups or disadvantaged homes might not receive an adequate education; international competition requires a well-educated work force; and children must be kept out of the labor force until they are sufficiently mature and capable of contributing without being exploited.

Penalties

Almost every state provides a penalty for violation of compulsory education laws. As with entry and exit ages, there are wide differences. The possible penalties range from a minimal monetary fine to a jail term for parents. In some instances children may be removed from the family and placed in a specialized residential treatment facility at which personal counseling and school attendance are required.

In most instances when a child is referred to legal authorities for nonattendance, the child is ordered to resume attendance, with limited sanctions imposed. Juvenile court caseloads are such that compulsory-attendance violations are often not treated seriously.

Impact of Truancy

The impact of truancy can be significant for individual children, their families, and society as a whole. Inconsistent school attendance interferes with learning and the orderly acquisition of academic and social skills. It can result in a failure to acquire adequate pre-employment skills. Poor school attendance reduces the likelihood of the student pursuing vocational education or training and/or continuing on to any form of postsecondary education. Access to meaningful employment in a technology-oriented society without adequate education becomes extremely limited.

Truancy can often be the beginning of a pattern whereby poor attendance leads to poor grades, which leads to increased negative attitudes toward school, which ultimately leads to dropping out of school.

From a broader and less personal perspective, truancy may reduce the funds available for the education of other students. In many states, a substantial portion of financial support for schools is based on average daily attendance figures. In some large school districts, each percentage point of absence may cost the district more than $1 million in funding.

Characteristics

Who are the pupils who are truants? What are they like? Before remedies for the problem of truancy can be developed, the defining characteristics of the truants and their families must be examined.

Pupils who are chronically truant often have a general dislike for school, often beginning in elementary school, which becomes more pronounced as the student enters the more "impersonal" secondary school level and at the same time becomes more autonomous as a result of advanced chronological age. They have a tendency to be older than their classmates due to retention in grade. Truants often exhibit behaviors that are associated with depression and anger, and they usually have no positive role model that they admire and want to emulate. Social competence is often limited to a circle of friends who support truancy and who often join the truant in unexcused absences and delinquent behaviors, including frequent use of alcohol and/or drugs. There is generally an unwillingness to participate in school sponsored activities, a tendency to challenge teacher (adult) authority, and resentment at the impersonal response such challenges may generate. These individuals tend to be placed in the vocational, business, or general programs.

Families of pupils found to be chronically truant often lack structure within the home setting; pupils do not get parent support or supervision in developing appropriate daily routines for such things as going to bed, awakening on time for school, leaving home on time for school, and completing homework. Parent–child relationships are distant and/or negative; these families do not eat meals together, do not go on vacations together, and do not routinely participate in school functions. Families of truants are subject to multiple significant stressors, including separation, divorce, unemployment, underemployment, general discord, financial problems, frequent moves, serious illness, and substance abuse. In these families, more than one child is usually truant.

School-Based Factors

A review of individual and family characteristics associated with truancy could easily lead one to focus on the family unit and the many variables related to its functioning as a unit as the singular source of truant behaviors. This would be a simplistic and misleading approach, omitting another major causative variable: schools themselves.

School-based factors associated with, or perhaps leading to, truancy include lowered expectations for pupils based on stereotypic or biased beliefs related to ethnic group, gender, or social class, which lead to "educational tracking" of students into inappropriate or intellectually demeaning programs. There is often an overemphasis on fixed dates for school entry and school completion. The major focus is on raising standards and expectations for academic achievement without developing understanding of and support for the reforms with the students and families most in need. The approach to education becomes even less personal as students exit elementary school.

The schools usually have policies that require retention in grade without requiring extensive review and analysis of individual pupil need. There is a tendency to see truant or "at risk" pupils as a reminder of personal or institutional inadequacies. There is also a desire to find fault or place blame outside of school. Budget constraints reduce or eliminate essential instructional support staff (school psychologists, social workers, guidance counselors). There is also an unwillingness or an inability to get personally involved with students, to support them in their efforts even though they do not always conform, and to work closely with families who do not meet the school's "accepted" standards.

Conclusion

Improving pupil attendance is an important societal goal. The reduction or elimination of truancy will pay substantial dividends to society in the form of lower unemployment (or underemployment), a lowered adolescent crime rate, a higher level of literacy and academic achievement, and better ability to compete economically.

Most programmatic efforts to reduce truancy tend to be individually focused. Typical school efforts include daily contact with parents or absentees; in-school or out-of-school suspension when truancy is proven, with a mandated parent meeting prior to reentry; loss of academic credit for missing a percentage of classes; individual contracts with pupils; and contingency reinforcers for improved attendance, including food, T-shirts, and early dismissal from school.

Programs such as these often show positive short-term results, but because few if any changes are made in the community, they have little long-term carryover. The truancy problem is potentially renewed each year as a new kindergarten class is enrolled.

If school-based efforts are to succeed, a more comprehensive and longer-term series of interventions is required. These interventions must lead to significant change in the behaviors of pupils, their families, and school staff.

Suggestions for intervention include training for school staff that will lead to improved ability (and willingness) to work with a diverse pupil population; teacher-based initiatives to assist pupils to complete class requirements both in and out of school; and early identification of pupil and family characteristics related to truancy.

Truancy can also be reduced by a thorough assessment of the truant's or potential truant's total environment, including home, school, and peer group, with resources available to provide direct personal and family counseling when needed; education and training for families in a nonstigmatizing manner that will help support family efforts to comply with school and societal mores; and a systematic effort that will allow families to join the school community and to participate in school activities regularly.

(*See also:* Adolescence; Home Schooling; Juvenile Delinquency; Runaway Children; School)

BIBLIOGRAPHY

American Association of School Administrators. (1989). *Critical Issues Report: Students at Risk, Problems and Solutions.* Arlington, VA: Author.

Beckham, J. (1985). "Getting a Grasp on Compulsory Education Issues." *School Board Policies* 16:1–3.

Bonikowske, D. (1987). *Truancy: A Prelude to Dropping Out.* Bloomington, IN: National Educational Service.

Hamby, J. V. (1989). "How to Get an A on Your Dropout Prevention Report Card." *Educational Leadership* 46:21–27.

Hess, A. M.; Rosenberg, M. S.; and Levy, G. K. (1990). "Reducing Truancy in Students with Mild Handicaps." *Remedial and Special Education* 11:14–28.

Lines, P. (1985). *Compulsory Education Laws and Their Impact on Public and Private Education.* Denver, CO: Education Commission of the States.

Nidsen, A., and Gerber, D. (1979). "Personal Aspects of Truancy of Early Adolescence." *Adolescence* 14:313–326.

Schultz, R. M. (1987). "Truancy: Issues and Interventions." *Behavioral Disorders* 12:117–130.

Gerald Feldman

TRUST

Trust in an intimate partner or family member is central to most people's idea of a rewarding and successful relationship. In fact, trust is commonly perceived as one of the most important components of a loving relationship (Fehr 1988). Surprisingly, however, theoretical and empirical research on the concept of trust in close relationships has occurred primarily since

1980. Prior to that time, scholars such as Julian B. Rotter (1967) examined the concept of trust as a belief people held about others in general. As such, the focus was typically restricted to trust in nonintimate relationships.

Defining Trust

Trust is a fundamental component of virtually all social relationships. Trust in a close relationship refers to the level of confidence one has that another person will act in ways that will fulfill expectations. It grows out of the basic human capacity to develop goals and make plans for the future. Since humans are social beings, other people play an integral part in fulfilling an individual's vision of the future. In fact, many cherished hopes and dreams require the active presence and participation of important people in an individual's life. However, while some control does exist over events necessary to make dreams a reality, the actions and responses of others are frequently uncontrollable. Sometimes it can confidently be assumed that people will come through as hoped—other times, it is not so certain.

Although this definition specifies the process of trust, it leaves the question of how to characterize the multitude of goals, plans, and expectations. Trust researchers have offered various systems for organizing these expectations, and despite the differences in these organizational schemes, they tend to have one theme in common. In virtually all cases, researchers have related trust to what they consider to be the most important interpersonal goal in a close relationship—the belief that one's partner is motivated by feelings of love and caring. Robert E. Larzelere and Ted L. Huston (1980) suggested that the most important expectations involve confidence in another person's benevolence and honesty. These authors define benevolence as the extent to which an individual is genuinely interested in a partner's welfare and motivated to maximize the positive outcomes for both of them. Honesty refers to the extent to which the other person's future intentions are believable.

In an experimental study, Cynthia Johnson-George and Walter C. Swap (1982) identified a similar theme. These researchers developed a scale that measured two different components of trust. The first, a measure of a partner's reliableness, was more important for interactions among strangers, whereas a measure of the partner's emotional trust was seen more as a special characteristic of intimate relationships. The measures of emotional trust tapped into expectations of a partner's openness, honesty, and concern for the other's welfare. Thus, once again the most important set of expectations revolves around confidence in a partner's expressions of caring and concern.

This same theme also occurs in the work of John G. Holmes and John K. Rempel and their colleagues. For example, Rempel, Holmes, and Mark P. Zanna (1985) organized expectations along a dimension from specific concrete behaviors to abstract interpersonal motives. The most concrete set of expectations is labeled "predictability," which refers to expectations for specific behaviors such as a morning kiss. As expectations move to the next level, labeled "dependability," they are based more on qualities and characteristics such as honesty and reliability that identify the partner as a trustworthy person. Finally, the most general and abstract level of expectations is labeled "faith." It reflects an emotional security on the part of individuals that enables them to go beyond the available evidence and feel, with assurance, that their partner will be responsive and caring whatever the future may hold. An emphasis on a partner's motives of love and caring as the central component of trust in a close relationship occurs consistently in other works by these authors (e.g., Holmes 1991; Holmes and Rempel 1989; Rempel and Holmes 1986).

Therefore, however goals and expectations are organized, the most significant aspect of trust in an intimate relationship appears to involve expectations that individuals will be caring and will act in ways that will take the needs and desires of their partner into account, even at personal cost. Confidence in this central belief includes a variety of more specific goals and expectations.

Development of Trust

To trust another person means to give that individual some control over events, with the confidence that rejection or betrayal will not occur. How does such confidence develop?

As with many things in life, there is evidence that the foundation for trust is established in the earliest relationships with parents. In his influential theory of psychosocial development, Erik Erikson (1963) theorizes that the critical developmental task or crisis that must be confronted during the first year of life is trust versus mistrust. Trust in infancy sets the stage for a lifelong expectation that the world will be a good and pleasant place to live.

This idea is echoed in the foundational thinking and research of attachment theorists John Bowlby (1973) and Mary Ainsworth and her colleagues (1978). These theorists hypothesize that human infants share a biological drive to form an attachment with a caregiver in order to achieve a feeling of security. However, the quality of the attachment depends on the nature of the interactions the infants have with their primary caregivers during the first year of life. According to Bowlby (1973), infants develop "working models" of themselves and others based on the sensitivity and responsiveness of the caregiver to the infant's needs. These working models are believed to set the stage for the infant's later social interactions.

If caregivers are sensitive and responsive to their infants' needs, the infants develop a secure attachment. The infants learn that the world is a secure place where others can be relied on and they come to believe that they are worthy of being cared for and having their needs met. In other words, the infants learn to trust the most important people in their lives. If caregivers respond inconsistently or are not responsive to the needs of their infants at all, these infants develop an insecure attachment. They learn that the world is an unpredictable or hostile place where they cannot rely on others to meet their needs. These infants also come to feel that they are not worthy of love and care.

From this evidence that earliest relationships establish a foundation for trust, it may be speculated that people may develop different capacities to trust others. Some, because of their past experiences, may be ready to trust others fully if features of the relationship warrant it, whereas some individuals may be much more hesitant to rely on others, even if they have no objective reasons to be fearful. There is no reason to believe, however, that this "ceiling" on the ability to trust is completely fixed and immovable. Certainly there is anecdotal evidence to suggest that, with time, even individuals who have been hurt badly by their past experiences can learn to put their faith in people who prove themselves to be consistently caring and trustworthy. More important, even if individuals carry with them their own unique capacity to trust, the features of their specific relationships with other individuals will ultimately determine how much confidence they are willing to place in the motives of others.

How does trust develop in a specific relationship? There are no definitive answers to this question. However, scholars generally agree that trust is demonstrated most clearly in situations where there is risk and vulnerability. As paradoxical as it may sound, people can only learn about how much a partner genuinely cares for them when the situation makes it possible for that partner not to care. For feelings of trust to grow, it must be possible for the partner to leave the other's expectations unfulfilled. Only in this way will people be able to confidently interpret the behaviors they expect from their partner as voluntary and motivated by love. The growth of trust depends on each person's willingness to demonstrate caring by taking risks and responding to the partner's needs at some personal cost.

Although risk-taking fuels the development of trust, the strength and patterning of interactions involving risk will change as the relationship progresses. The earliest expressions of confidence in a romantic partner may be "blind trust" in an idealized image of the partner constructed from carefully selected fragments of information. Indeed, strong feelings of trust appear to be present even among casually dating couples who have had few opportunities to base their feelings of trust on diagnostic experiences involving risk and vulnerability (Larzelere and Huston 1980). However, as intimacy grows, images of the partner based on an idealized representation will be increasingly challenged by evidence from actual behaviors, and the opportunities for disagreement will be expanded. Additionally, as the relationship progresses and the lives of both partners become increasingly intertwined, the possibilities for conflict are further intensified. These points of conflict present opportunities for each partner to demonstrate concern for the relationship and a willingness to take the other's needs into account. At the same time, they represent, for each partner, the risk that this issue could result in rejection and the loss of the relationship. If the issue is successfully resolved, not only is trust strengthened, but each partner develops greater confidence in the couple's ability to solve future problems.

In a similar way, relationships progress as each partner discloses more personal information to the other. Early in a relationship, as each partner evaluates the possibility of deeper involvement, disclosures will be reciprocated in a way that maintains an equality of vulnerability and risk. However, if the relationship continues, the disclosures move to deeper, more personal topics where the risks of rejection and betrayal become increasingly costly. To the extent that each partner reacts to the other's disclosure in a supportive and concerned manner, trust in the relationship will be enhanced. By sharing intimate information, each can also learn if the other keeps confidences, honors promises, and demonstrates a willingness to take risks.

Thus, trust develops as people take risks and indicate that they are willing to sacrifice their own interests as they take their partner's concerns into account. With each successful experience of disclosure or conflict resolution, there is further evidence of the partner's commitment to the relationship and greater confidence that the relationship will be fulfilling.

Effect of Trust in Established Relationships

Trust is a dynamic process. Even after a solid foundation of trust has been established, feelings of confidence continue to respond to any changes and transitions in the relationship. Just as trust has been built up, it can also wear down. Although much still remains to be learned about the effect that different levels of trust have on the nature of a close relationship, it is clear that the relationships of people with higher levels of trust are categorically different from relationships where trust levels are lower.

The beliefs of high-trust people are anchored both by positive conclusions about their partner's motives drawn from past evidence and by faith in what the future holds. They expect their partner to act in ways that are motivated by a desire to improve the relationship. These positive expectations form a "filter" through which new events and experiences are interpreted. Even when faced with events that could potentially challenge their convictions, such as a conflict or disagreement, people in high-trust relationships are unlikely to call their partner's motives into question. Rather, as much as possible, negative events are seen as less significant when compared against the large accumulation of positive experiences. Negative incidents are likely to be explained in less harmful ways, treated as isolated events, or understood to reflect an unfortunate but less significant component of the relationship. This is not to say that trusting people are unaware of or naively ignore the negative events that occur in their relationship. However, unless the incident truly merits suspicion, they tend to place some limits on the negative implications the event could have for their relationship. Therefore, a high-trust relationship is one in which partners share openly with each other and give each other the benefit of the doubt.

For many couples, a trusting relationship remains elusive. For some, past experiences with parents or former partners have left them unable to set their doubts aside completely and relinquish control to an intimate partner confidently. Others, who started out with high levels of trust, may have run out of convincing charitable explanations for their partner's negative behaviors. Worn down from the growing accumulation of negative evidence, they increasingly entertain doubts and concerns about their partner's caring motives.

Whatever the cause, people in medium-trust relationships are uncertain about their partner's intentions. They have been hurt before and now look for signs that indicate further risk. They still have hope for their relationship and want to achieve the sense of security that seems to be missing. Yet, ironically, despite a desire for positive conclusions, people in medium-trust relationships appear to perceive negative events as the clearest source of evidence about their relationship. Negative events represent the most direct test of the hypothesis that the partner no longer cares as much as in the past. In addition, negative events are likely to trigger feelings of insecurity and vulnerability that are connected to earlier experiences of disappointment. These feelings can serve to make medium-trust individuals cautious about ignoring warning signs that could signal further disappointment. To avoid drawing unwarranted positive conclusions and having their hopes dashed once again, people in medium-trust relationships also appear to establish more stringent criteria for accepting a positive event as evidence that the relationship is improving. If such risk-avoidant strategy is adopted, medium-trust couples may, paradoxically, pay particular attention to events that fuel their fears, while underestimating the importance of events that could advance their hopes.

As feelings of confidence continue to diminish, people arrive at the point where they no longer expect the events in their relationship to reflect motives of concern and caring. They are more likely to expect indifference, if not open hostility. Low-trust people cannot, with any confidence, embrace residual hopes that their partner is concerned about them or the relationship. Consequently, they are likely to confront positive incidents with skepticism, discounting the encouraging implications such events might have for the future of their relationship. Negative events, on the other hand, offer evidence to confirm the conviction that confidence in the partner is not warranted and are likely to support the conclusion that the partner no longer cares. To protect themselves from the risk of drawing unwarranted positive conclusions and to remove themselves from the pain of involvement with an unconcerned partner, low-trust people may attempt to reduce their emotional investment in their relationship. Lurking close to the surface of most low-trust relationships is a history of broken promises, unmet expectations, and emotional disappointments. The reluctance of low-trust individuals is understandable—they have taken risks and lost. The sad irony is that, once trust has been betrayed, it may be doubly difficult to restore. Even if the offending partner "turns over a new leaf" and begins to work at the relationship, it is all too easy for the betrayed partner to explain these positive events away. The possibility of further deception and disappointment is simply too painful and frightening to confront. Thus, couples enter a downward spiral in which rebuilding a trusting relationship represents a daunting prospect.

The scenario is not hopeless, of course, but it is certainly difficult to rebuild trust once it has been betrayed. For trust to grow after it has been violated, the injured party must resist the natural reaction to jump to harsh conclusions about the partner's motives and character in new situations. Furthermore, the partner must be allowed the necessary room to make mistakes. The offending partner, in turn, must make a profound effort to live up to promises of change in ways that clearly signal to the offended partner that these risks are worth taking. To be able to trust, people must take the risk of trusting. By giving their partner a second chance to renew trust in the relationship, people risk being wrong, but if they do not try they can never be right.

(*See also:* ATTACHMENT; FRIENDSHIP; INTIMACY; JEALOUSY; LOVE; MARITAL QUALITY; PERSONALITY DEVELOPMENT; PERSONAL RELATIONSHIPS; SELF-DISCLOSURE; SELF-ESTEEM)

BIBLIOGRAPHY

Ainsworth, M. D. S.; Blehar, M. C.; Waters, E.; and Wall, S. (1978). *Patterns of Attachment.* Hillsdale, NJ: Lawrence Erlbaum.

Bowlby, J. (1973). *Attachment and Loss:* Vol. 2, *Separation.* New York: Basic Books.

Erikson, E. H. (1963). *Childhood and Society.* New York: W. W. Norton.

Fehr, B. (1988). "Prototype Analysis of the Concepts of Love and Commitment." *Journal of Personality and Social Psychology* 55:557–579.

Holmes, J. G. (1991). "Trust and the Appraisal Process in Close Relationships." In *Advances in Personal Relationships,* Vol. 2, ed. W. H. Jones and D. Perlman. London: Kingsley.

Holmes, J. G., and Rempel, J. K. (1989). "Trust in Close Relationships." In *Review of Personality and Social Psychology,* Vol. 10, ed. C. Hendrick. Newbury Park, CA: Sage Publications.

Johnson-George, C., and Swap, W. (1982). "Measurement of Specific Interpersonal Trust: Construction and Validation of a Scale to Assess Trust in a Specific Order." *Journal of Personality and Social Psychology* 43:1306–1317.

Larzelere, R. E., and Huston, T. L. (1980). "The Dyadic Trust Scale: Toward Understanding Interpersonal Trust in Close Relationships." *Journal of Marriage and the Family* 42:595–604.

Rempel, J. K., and Holmes, J. G. (1986). "How Do I Trust Thee?" *Psychology Today* 20:28–34.

Rempel, J. K.; Holmes, J. G.; and Zanna, M. P. (1985). "Trust in Close Relationships." *Journal of Personality and Social Psychology* 49:95–112.

Rotter, J. B. (1967). "A New Scale for the Measurement of Interpersonal Trust." *Journal of Personality* 35:651–665.

JOHN K. REMPEL

TYPOLOGIES

See MARITAL TYPOLOGIES

U–V

UNEMPLOYMENT

Perhaps no stressful experience has a more significant effect on family life than the inability to meet basic material needs for food, shelter, and adequate clothing. During the 1980s, when the automobile industry, the farm economy, and a host of other commercial enterprises entered a deep economic recession, television news stories repeatedly featured interviews with unemployed, homeless workers living in cars with their families as a result of their recent loss of income. Similarly, television commentators frequently talked with farm operators who related heartbreaking stories regarding the loss of land that often had been handed from one family generation to the next for a century or more. These individual stories convey the real meaning of unemployment, which, as defined here, involves the involuntary loss of work for those wanting a job.

In addition to losing financial resources, the unemployed worker frequently loses much of the structure, meaning, and sense of self that are important to daily living. Work typically provides an important dimension of one's identity within a framework of continuing social relationships. The loss of a job, therefore, often involves both a decline in income as well as the need to adjust to whole new patterns of living and feelings about oneself (Jahoda 1988). Because of its pervasive influence on so many aspects of individual and family functioning, the experience of being unemployed continues to be a focus of study by social and economic scholars (Dooley and Catalano 1988).

Who Becomes Unemployed?

The rate of unemployment varies among major subgroups in the total U.S. population. The subgroups most vulnerable to unemployment tend to be those that are more financially disadvantaged even before job loss occurs. The following discussion considers three of the more salient social subdivisions that identify important differences in risk for job loss: social class, race and ethnicity, and gender.

Social class. The several markers of social class standing include years of education, occupational status, and income. These indicators of class are highly intercorrelated—that is, those who have more education tend to have higher incomes and more prestigious occupations. In addition, individuals with higher-status professions (e.g., doctors and lawyers) also have higher incomes. Individuals with the least education, the lowest previous incomes, and the least prestigious occupations experience the greatest vulnerability to job loss.

In 1980, 5 percent of adults wanting a job were unemployed, similar to the unemployment rate of 4.4 percent in 1990. More than 8 percent of workers with less than a college education were unemployed in 1980 and 1990, however, compared to an unemployment rate of about 2 percent for those with four or more years of college. Thus the least educated members of the work force have a risk for unemployment that is four times greater than those with a college education (U.S. Bureau of the Census 1993).

Occupational status reflects similar social class differences in vulnerability to involuntary job loss. For example, only 3.1 percent of workers in the professions (e.g., doctors, educators, managers) experienced an episode of unemployment in 1992, compared with 11 percent of those who were laborers or assembly line workers, again suggesting an approximately fourfold increase of risk for unemployment for lower social class workers (U.S. Bureau of the Census 1993).

Education and occupation directly relate to the third marker of social class, income. In 1991, for example, average household income for workers with less than a ninth-grade education was only $13,221 compared to $52,270 for those who had completed four or more years of college. For the same year, managers and other professionals earned an average of $53,812 compared to $30,249 for laborers and assembly line workers (U.S. Bureau of the Census 1993). Taken together, the evidence clearly shows that those with the fewest resources in terms of education, occupational standing, and prior income are most vulnerable to experiencing a period of unemployment.

Race and ethnicity. Although the United States includes several ethnic minorities, this section considers the two largest ethnic subgroups: Americans with an African or a Hispanic heritage. As shown earlier, social class characteristics predict who is most vulnerable to unemployment. Ethnic or racial background predicts who is most likely to enjoy higher social class standing and thus lower risk for involuntary job loss. In 1991, 14.6 percent of white Americans had received a bachelor's degree compared to 8.3 percent of African Americans and 6.3 percent of Hispanic Americans. These differences in educational attainment were reflected in the median household incomes for 1991: white Americans ($31,569), African Americans ($18,807), and Hispanic Americans ($22,691) (U.S. Bureau of the Census 1993).

As expected, these differences in class standing relate directly to vulnerability to involuntary job loss. In 1992, the unemployment rate for African Americans (13%) and for Hispanic Americans (11.3%) was about twice that for white Americans (6%). These ethnic differences in unemployment characterize the trends since the early 1980s and before (U.S. Bureau of the Census 1993). Clearly, a history of ethnically related discrimination places these minority groups at high risk for unemployment and reduces the likelihood of their securing the social class advantages that reduce the probability of job loss. Income differentials among these groups also suggest that minority households face periods of unemployment with fewer material resources, such as accumulated savings, to reduce the financial impact of job loss.

Gender. Historically, women, compared to men, have been more vulnerable to unemployment. Men in the United States had unemployment rates of 5.4 percent, 4.4 percent, and 6.9 percent in 1960, 1970, and 1980, respectively, compared to rates of 5.9 percent, 5.9 percent, and 7.4 percent for women during the same time periods. In 1990, however, the unemployment rate for women was 5.4 percent, slightly less than the rate of 5.6 percent for men. This trend continued in 1992, with a rate of 7.8 percent for men and 6.9 percent for women (U.S. Bureau of the Census 1993). This shift in gender-related risk for unemployment likely reflects the changing nature of the U.S. economy, which has experienced significant reductions in male-dominated manufacturing enterprises and a significant increase in service occupations more likely to employ women.

The unemployment data for women, however, provide an incomplete picture of their economic standing in contemporary American society. For example, women are less likely than men to occupy higher-status occupations, and even when they have similar professions, they average only 70 percent of the earnings of men. To illustrate this differential, women in professional roles in 1991 had a median income of $30,487 compared to $42,358 for men in similar positions. Moreover, women twenty-five years or older who were full-time workers in 1991 had an average income of $23,778, compared to $35,850 for men. Finally, 46 percent of single mothers lived below the poverty line in 1991, compared to only 7 percent of families with a male worker present (U.S. Bureau of the Census 1993). These data indicate that when women do become unemployed, they are much less likely than men to have accumulated financial resources to help buffer the impact of job loss. Moreover, they are much less likely to acquire a new job with a salary sufficient to speed economic recovery from a period of unemployment.

The Unemployed Worker

How does the unemployed worker respond to the involuntary loss of a job? Although research from the Great Depression years of the 1930s suggested that men were more likely than women to become psychologically distressed by job loss, more recent studies show that contemporary women are just as likely to experience emotional problems when they are unemployed but want work (Menaghan 1991). In fact, research findings document that the involuntary loss of a job by either a man or a woman has a range of negative influences, including increased psychological distress (e.g., depression, anxiety, and hostile feelings); loss of self-esteem and a sense of mastery; greater risk for substance abuse; and increases in physical illness, somatic complaints, and physiological markers of life stress (Barling 1990; Brenner and Starrin 1988; Catalano et al. 1993; Hamilton et al. 1990; Iverson and Sabroe 1988; Kessler, Turner, and House 1988; Liem and Liem 1990; Menaghan 1991; McLoyd et al. 1994; Warr, Jackson, and Banks 1988). Unemployed workers are also more vulnerable to negative health consequences associated with other stressful events or conditions in their lives (Kessler, Turner, and House 1988).

For many years scholars suggested that the health problems associated with unemployment might actually produce job loss (the social selection argument). That is, many investigators proposed that depressed, anxious, unhappy workers might be most vulnerable to job loss rather than unemployment being the cause of these and other health difficulties. Now the evidence seems clear that, even if some psychologically impaired individuals have problems holding a job, involuntary job loss also leads to health problems in community populations (the social causation argument). First, prospective longitudinal studies that control for emotional or behavioral problems prior to job loss, and that include continuously employed control groups, show an increase in physical and emotional health problems as a result of unemployment (Brenner and Starrin 1988; Catalano et al. 1993). Second, comparisons of workers from plants that close (i.e., job loss is not related to characteristics of individual workers) with workers who remain continuously employed show the negative health effects of unemployment (Hamilton et al. 1990; Iverson and Sabroe 1988). Finally, reemployment reverses the adverse health consequences of job loss, indicating that work itself affects individual well-being (Kessler, Turner, and House 1989; Liem and Liem 1990).

With the association between unemployment (when it involves the involuntary loss of a desired job, see Wheaton 1990) and emotional and physical health problems clearly established, research has turned to identification of the processes that might account for this correlation. Researchers have proposed two principal pathways through which job loss might affect the unemployed worker's health. Marie Jahoda (1988) and Elizabeth G. Menaghan (1991) have both suggested that unemployment poses a threat to one's identity, self-esteem, and feelings of competence. These attacks on one's sense of self, in turn, are expected to produce emotional and behavioral difficulties. Rand D. Conger and his colleagues (Conger et al. 1994), on the other hand, have proposed that job loss and other dimensions of work instability primarily influence one's health through the economic strains and pressures they produce. A growing body of research evidence demonstrates the important role that financial strains play in linking unemployment to emotional and physical health problems (Broman, Hamilton, and Hoffman 1990; Kessler, Turner, and House 1988).

It is likely that both of these processes help to account for the association between unemployment and individual well-being. Indeed, Menaghan (1991) proposes that threats to identity may produce pervasive negative emotional arousal or distress consistent with the model developed by Conger and his colleagues (Conger et al. 1994). The combination of this adult emotional distress and the economic difficulties associated with unemployment has been linked directly to problems in family functioning.

Unemployment and Family Functioning

Julian Barling (1990) has reviewed evidence showing that unemployment is related to a number of family problems, including marital instability, increased family conflict and violence, and reduced closeness and cohesion in family relationships. The major question concerns the means by which the health and financial hardship dimensions of unemployment relate to these several dimensions of family functioning.

As reviewed earlier and as illustrated in Figure 1, research findings indicate that unemployment involving the involuntary loss of a job leads to emotional distress for the unemployed worker. It also leads to financial strain or economic pressure (i.e., the inability to pay bills or to afford the most basic material needs), which, in turn, also leads to emotional distress for both the unemployed worker and his or her spouse (Conger et al. 1994). Indeed, the unemployed worker's distress appears to "spill over" such that it exacerbates emotional problems for a spouse (Dew, Bromet, and Schulberg 1987; Liem and Liem 1990).

A growing research literature indicates that emotionally troubled family members tend to be both more irritable and more withdrawn in their interactions with spouses and children. In addition, economic pressures intensify conflicts in marriage, especially conflicts related to money (Conger, Ge, and Lorenz 1994; Liker and Elder 1983). Therefore, as shown in Figure 1, both the psychological problems and the economic difficulties associated with job loss have been found to increase the risk of marital conflict, which in many instances leads to separation or divorce (Liem and Liem 1990). In addition, parents' emotional distress, as well as the conflicts between them, tend to disrupt effective parenting practices by distracting parents from caregiving and by increasing their irritable, hostile, and sometimes violent interchanges with their children (Brody et al. 1994; Conger and Elder 1994; Dodge, Pettit, and Bates 1994).

As shown in Figure 1, children and adolescents living in homes characterized by economic pressures,

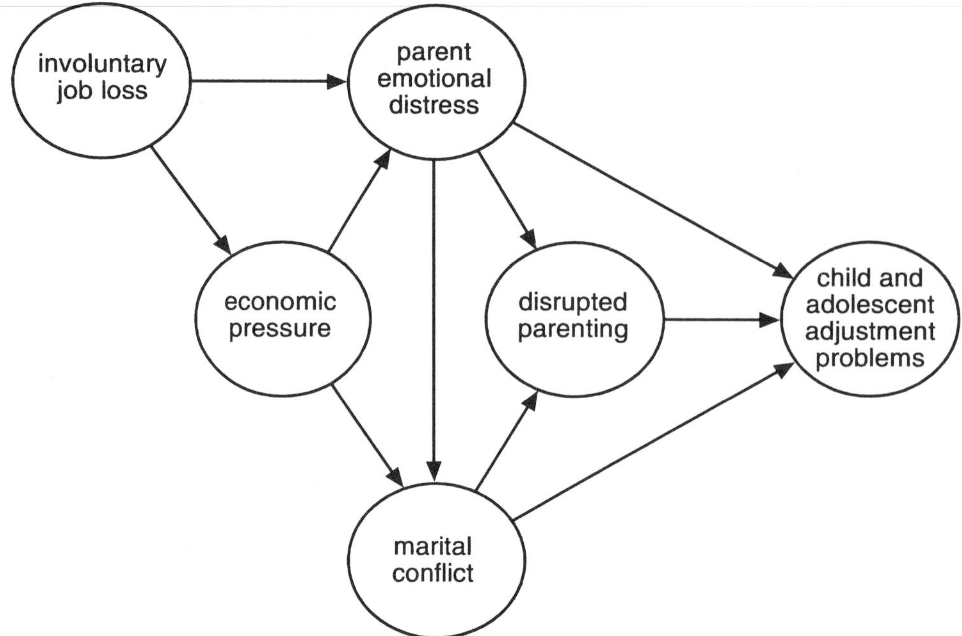

Figure 1 Linking unemployment to family functioning.

marital conflicts, emotionally distressed parents, and disrupted parenting practices are at increased risk for a number of behavioral and emotional problems (Broman, Hamilton, and Hoffman 1990; Conger and Elder 1994). They are more likely to demonstrate symptoms of depression, anxiety, or aggressive behavior. In addition, they experience less success in their academic work and social relations and feel less competent and self-confident (Conger et al. 1992, 1993, 1994). Thus, the children of the unemployed tend to experience the negative consequences of job loss through the troubles of their parents.

Conclusion

Unemployment does not affect everyone equally. An important question for future research involves the identification of processes or mechanisms that reduce the adverse consequences of job loss. Some research, for example, has shown that the maintenance of close marital relations protects against the negative health consequences of unemployment (Liem and Liem 1990). Programs that facilitate an effective job search also ameliorate the stress of displacement from work (Price, Van Ryn, and Vinokur 1992). Because economic cycles appear to generate periods of unemployment in different industries at different times, future research that identifies types of support and coping that can improve individual response to job loss should be of especially high priority. One dimension of such support, of course, involves economic relief that can reduce the level of economic pressure that is so destructive for displaced workers and their families.

(*See also:* Entitlements; Ethnicity; Family Policy; Homeless Families; Poverty; Work and Family)

BIBLIOGRAPHY

Barling, J. (1990). *Employment, Stress, and Family Functioning.* New York: Wiley.

Brenner, S.O., and Starrin, B. (1988). "Unemployment and Health in Sweden: Public Issues and Private Troubles." *Journal of Social Issues* 44:125–140.

Brody, G. H.; Stoneman, Z.; Flor, D.; McCrary, C.; Hastings, L.; and Conyers, O. (1994). "Financial Resources, Parent Psychological Functioning, Parent Co-Caregiving, and Early Adolescent Competence in Rural Two-Parent African-American Families." *Child Development* 65:590–605.

Broman, C. L.; Hamilton, V. L.; and Hoffman, W. S. (1990). "Unemployment and Its Effects on Families: Evidence from a Plant Closing Study." *American Journal of Community Psychology* 18:643–659.

Catalano, R.; Dooley, D.; Wilson, G.; and Hough, R. (1993). "Job Loss and Alcohol Abuse: A Test Using Data from the Epidemiologic Catchment Area Project." *Journal of Health and Social Behavior* 34:215–225.

Conger, R. D.; Conger, K. J.; Elder, G. H., Jr.; Lorenz, F. O.; Simons, R. L.; and Whitbeck, L. B. (1992). "A Family

Process Model of Economic Hardship and Adjustment of Early Adolescent Boys." *Child Development* 63:526–541.

Conger, R. D.; Conger, K. J.; Elder, G. H., Jr.; Lorenz, F. O.; Simons, R. L.; and Whitbeck, L. B. (1993). "Family Economic Stress and Adjustment of Early Adolescent Girls." *Developmental Psychology* 29:206–219.

Conger, R. D., and Elder, G. H., Jr., eds. (1994). *Families in Troubled Times: Adapting to Change in Rural America.* New York: Aldine.

Conger, R. D.; Ge, X.; Elder, G. H., Jr.; Lorenz, F. O.; and Simons, R. L. (1994). "Economic Stress, Coercive Family Process, and Developmental Problems of Adolescents." *Child Development* 65:541–561.

Conger, R. D.; Ge, X.; and Lorenz, F. O. (1994). "Economic Stress and Marital Relations." In *Families in Troubled Times: Adapting to Change in Rural America*, ed. R. D. Conger and G. H. Elder, Jr. New York: Aldine.

Dew, M. A.; Bromet, E. J.; and Schulberg, H. C. (1987). "A Comparative Analysis of Two Community Stressors' Long-Term Mental Health Effects." *American Journal of Community Psychology* 15:167–184.

Dodge, K. A.; Pettit, G. S.; and Bates, J. E. (1994). "Socialization Mediators of the Relation Between Socioeconomic Status and Child Conduct Problems." *Child Development* 65:649–665.

Dooley, D., and Catalano, R. (1988). "Recent Research on the Psychological Effects of Unemployment." *Journal of Social Issues* 44:1–12.

Elder, G. H., Jr., and Caspi, A. (1988). "Economic Stress in Lives: Developmental Perspectives." *Journal of Social Issues* 44:25–45.

Hamilton, V. L.; Broman, C. L.; Hoffman, W. S.; and Renner, D. S. (1990). "Hard Times and Vulnerable People: Initial Effects of Plant Closing on Autoworkers' Mental Health." *Journal of Health and Social Behavior* 31:123–140.

Iverson, L., and Sabroe, S. (1988). "Psychological Well-Being Among Unemployed and Employed People After a Company Closedown: A Longitudinal Study." *Journal of Social Issues* 44:141–152.

Jahoda, M. (1988). "Economic Recession and Mental Health: Some Conceptual Issues." *Journal of Social Issues* 44:13–23.

Kessler, R. C.; Turner, J. B.; and House, J. S. (1988). "Effects of Unemployment on Health in a Community Survey: Main, Modifying, and Mediating Effects." *Journal of Social Issues* 44:69–85.

Kessler, R. C.; Turner, J. B.; and House, J. S. (1989). "Unemployment, Reemployment, and Emotional Functioning in a Community Sample." *American Sociological Review* 54:648–657.

Liem, J. H., and Liem, G. R. (1990). "Understanding the Individual and Family Effects of Unemployment." In *Stress Between Work and Family*, ed. J. Eckenrode and S. Gore. New York: Plenum.

Liker, J. K., and Elder, G. H., Jr. (1983). "Economic Hardship and Marital Relations." *American Sociological Review* 48:343–359.

McLoyd, V. C.; Jayaratne, T. E.; Ceballo, R.; and Borquez, J. (1994). "Unemployment and Work Interruption Among African-American Single Mothers: Effects on Parenting and Adolescent Socioemotional Functioning." *Child Development* 65:562–589.

Menaghan, E. G. (1991). "Work Experiences and Family Interaction Processes: The Long Reach of the Job?" *Annual Review of Sociology* 17:419–444.

Price, R. H.; Van Ryn, M.; and Vinokur, A. D. (1992). "Impact of a Preventive Job Search Intervention on the Likelihood of Depression Among the Unemployed." *Journal of Health and Social Behavior* 33:158–167.

U.S. Bureau of the Census. (1993). *Statistical Abstract of the United States*, 113th edition. Washington, DC: U.S. Department of Commerce.

Warr, P.; Jackson, P.; and Banks, M. (1988). "Unemployment and Mental Health: Some British Studies." *Journal of Social Issues* 44:47–68.

Wheaton, B. (1990). "Life Transitions, Role Histories, and Mental Health." *American Sociological Review* 55:209–223.

RAND D. CONGER

UTOPIAN COMMUNITIES

In Greek, *utopia* can mean either "nowhere" or "a good place." In 1516, amid the decline of medievalism in Western Europe, Thomas More, a British humanist, wrote a book titled *Utopia*, in which he attacked the economic and social conditions as well as other evils affecting the society of his time. He was particularly critical of the ruling elite in the government and the church officials who were abusing their powers at the expense of the commoners. The essence of early utopian thought was that human beings had the potential for goodness and that they could attain that goodness if they lived in the proper kind of society. More designed an imaginary society based on a shared life and called this society a utopia. His book, which is a critique of the Elizabethan social order and status quo, has become one of the most read and cited works in literature. More's *Utopia* inspired hundreds of other thinkers throughout the centuries to share their visions of an ideal society.

Varieties of Utopias

What is the proper type of society? How should society be structured so humans can aspire to goodness? What are the components of an ideal or perfect society? These are questions that have troubled people and nations for centuries. Pre–French Revolutionary utopians espoused equality, moderation, and the establishment of a tranquil environment. Another variety of utopians supported a hierarchical model of society that utilized science to provide an unequal but just system of rewards. Others established utopias that supported evolutionary and universalistic thinking that encouraged an increasing self-awareness in people. Utopians were and are considered to be social experimenters.

The word "utopian," according to William McCord (1989), is frequently used in a pejorative sense and is understood to refer to a society that is too idealized for human attainment, one that is free from faults. McCord views this position with disdain and suggests that striving for better societies is a worthwhile venture even though one might never attain the objective of a perfect society. True utopians are not just concerned with one aspect of life, they aim to improve all aspects of life—economic, social, religious, cultural, and political. Utopians search for a better way of life. "They seek to create institutions that embrace and inform and improve the whole person" (McCord 1989, p. 21).

Benjamin Zablocki (1980) identifies three varieties of utopias: exhorted, imposed, and communitarian. Exhorted utopias such as those discussed in Plato's *Republic*, Augustine's *City of God*, More's *Utopia*, and B. F. Skinner's *Walden Two*, are fictional places. These utopias have been created with no practical plans for implementation. Imposed utopias are actual attempts sovereign powers have made to provide citizens with a better-functioning communal structure. Examples of imposed utopias include Calvin's City of Geneva, the Jesuit order of seventeenth-century Paraguay, and the New Town movement in England and America. The Chinese communes are probably the most ambitious of these types of utopias. In 1949, after the defeat of Chiang Kai-shek and the ascendancy of Mao Tse-tung, 80 percent of the Chinese were peasants. Mao organized 500 million peasants into 24,000 communes. His goal was to create a socialist utopia through collective agricultural communes. In 1977, Deng Xiaoping came to power in China and revealed that Mao's experiment with communes had failed (McCord 1989). Communitarian utopias are those that develop from the combined interests and intentions of their participants.

The majority of utopian experiments have been communitarian utopias. This entry will concentrate primarily on explanations for the development and growth of communitarian utopias, and a brief discussion of a variety of historical utopian communities will be provided.

Ron E. Roberts (1971) considers communes a subclass of utopias. He believes that modern communes differ from other communitarian utopias in three important ways: Communes generally reject the notion of hierarchy and gradations of social status; communes attempt to remain small; and communes are antibureaucratic in organization. Whether all modern communes aspire to and attain these characteristics is debatable; the point is that traditional utopian communities were generally not characterized by these qualities. Scholars tend to use the terms "communes," "utopias," "communal groups," "communitarian utopias," "alternative communities," and other derivations interchangeably. That practice will be followed in this entry.

Development and Growth of Utopias

Traditional utopian communities, according to Rosabeth Moss Kanter (1972), shared the following core values: perfectibility, order, brotherhood, unity of body and mind, experimentation, and coherence as a group. These were idealizations, not necessarily truths. Utopians attempted to mold these values together to produce a synergistic outcome, one producing an overall sense of harmony.

Kanter (1972) also summarizes the origins of American utopias and communes. She believes that the formation of American utopias and communes can be traced to one of three major themes: a rejection of the established order and a desire to follow religious and spiritual values; a willingness to reform society from corruption, injustice, inhumanity, and evil, especially within the realms of economics and politics; and a rejection of the alienation and isolation of society by promoting the psychosocial growth of the individual within community. These three themes compare quite favorably with the three historical waves of development and growth among communitarian utopias. The first wave of communitarianism began in the early years of the development of the United States and lasted until approximately 1845. Religious themes were popular during this time. The second wave began in 1820, peaked in the 1840s, but continued until 1930. It emphasized economic and political issues. The third wave, or the psychosocial period, emerged following World War II and peaked in the late 1960s.

Yaavoc Oved (1993) agrees with Kanter's summary of the emergence and growth of communitarian utopias and also identifies three slightly different periods or waves of development. In this conceptualization, the first period began in the seventeenth century and ended with the appearance of the Shakers (1787).

Oved argues that the majority of communitarian development during this time was begun by those who had recently arrived from Europe. The second period encompasses the years between 1780 and 1880. The majority of communalists were still arriving from Europe, but there were some communes of American origin. The third period, which still continues, began in the late 1880s, when communes were formed primarily by Americans inspired by utopian ideas that emerged in the United States.

Oved suggests that five factors aided the growth of utopian movements in the United States: the wide-open frontier settlement; a tradition of independent communities; aspiring to an ideal society; liberty and religious tolerance; and immigration and an immigrant society. These five factors along with initial settlement in the United States by radical dissenting European Protestants coalesced to nurture the establishment and development of utopian groups in the United States.

William G. McLoughlin (1978) identifies five great awakenings that fostered the growth of utopias and reshaped culture: the Puritan Awakening; the period preceding the Revolutionary War; the period after the writing of the Constitution; the period after the Civil War; and the most recent period, beginning in 1960. These were periods of fundamental ideological transformation brought on by social, political, ecological, psychological, and economic changes.

Michael Barkun (1984) reports that the United States experienced four periods of communitarian utopianism (1842–1848, 1894–1900, the 1930s, and the 1960s), and he believes that history strongly suggests the presence of a utopian cycle in the United States. Barkun hypothesizes that utopian development occurs in approximately fifty- to fifty-five-year waves that follow Kondratiev waves (accelerations and deceleration of prices—i.e., deflationary depressions). Utopian waves, especially the first wave (1842–1848), tend to coincide with periods of millennial expectation—Christ's Second Coming (the advent) and the end of the world. Brian J. L. Berry (1992) identifies a distinctive difference among millenarians. Apocalyptic or premillenarians believe that the advent is ahead, while progressive or postmillenarians believe that advent has already occurred. A few apocalyptic millenarians did develop utopian communities, but the progressive millenarians developed the majority of the early utopias in the United States.

Berry adds significantly to the work of Kanter and Oved in providing possible explanations for the origins of utopian movements. Berry links relationships among religion, politics, and economics to explain the development of utopian communities. His central hypothesis states that

> utopian surges, embedded within upwellings of millenarian excitation, have been triggered by the long-wave crises (economic fluctuations) that periodically have affected American economic development. A corollary is that the utopias that have been built have been critical reactions to the moving target of capitalism; as capitalism has been transformed, so have the utopian alternatives [1992, p. xv].

Berry (1992) agrees with Barkun's (1984) assessment of utopian cycles but carries the argument one step further. Berry argues that the lesser utopian surges of the 1790s, 1820s, and 1870s (which occurred during minor depressions), along with the first major wave of utopian development (which followed a major depression in the 1840s), and the second wave of utopian development (which followed another major depression in the 1890s), are correlated with long-wave crises. He believes that long-wave crises trigger millenarian responses. Long waves bring capitalist crises at regular intervals and stimulate progressive millenarians to start utopian settlements.

Utopian Communities in the United States

The United Society of Believers in Christ's Second Appearing, more commonly known as the Shakers, began during the depression and millenarian upsurge following the American Revolutionary War. The Shakers built twenty-four communities, and scholars estimate that overall membership was about 17,000 persons. The Shakers were founded by Ann Lee, a charismatic woman who made celibacy a central tenet of Shakerism. They were known for their religious dances and business acumen (Horgan 1987).

The German Pietist groups found the United States very appealing, at first because of religious freedom. The Community of True Inspiration, or Amana, rejected Lutheranism and believed in biblical prophecy. The Community of True Inspiration was founded by Christian Metz, who settled near Iowa City, Iowa, and created seven villages. Communal living was eventually eliminated, and members separated economic functions from religious functions and formed a joint-stock company in 1932. The religious dimension of Amana life continues, with seven active congregations (Shambaugh 1988).

John Humphrey Noyes founded the Oneida Community in Oneida, New York, and preached a theology of perfectionism. Noyes was a charismatic leader who introduced his community to mutual criticism, complex marriage, and male continence. Noyes's ideas and practices eventually forced him into hiding, and the community eventually disbanded into a joint-stock company similar to Amana. One of the Oneida Community's many successful business ventures was the manufacture of Oneida Silverware (Carden 1971).

Conclusion

The Shakers, the Oneidans, and the Amanas are three of the more well-known utopian communities. However, even though the Shakers are a celibate group and are one of the most long-lived and successful utopian groups, other groups (such as the Hutterites and the Israeli *kibbutzim*) show that nuclear families can be successfully integrated into a communal setting. Only a minority of utopian communities abolished the nuclear family, and in most utopian communities the family was maintained.

Most religious utopian communities began with the leadership of a charismatic individual (e.g., the Shakers, the Oneidans, and the Hutterites). Authoritarian leadership was typical for religious utopians, although there were exceptions. Authoritarian leadership in socialist communes was unusual because it went against the ideology of these groups (Oved 1993).

Most traditional utopian communities had criteria for membership and would be categorized as closed or selective communities. Only a very few practiced the open-door policy that was characteristic of some of the communes of the 1960s and 1970s. Open-door policies generally proved fatal for these latter groups because noncommitted people freeloaded and caused turmoil.

(*See also:* Communes)

BIBLIOGRAPHY

Barkun, M. (1984). "Communal Societies as Cyclical Phenomena." *Communal Societies* 4:35–48.

Berry, B. J. L. (1992). *America's Utopian Experiments: Communal Havens from Long-Wave Crises.* Hanover, NH: University Press of New England.

Carden, M. L. (1971). *Oneida: Utopian Community to Modern Corporation.* New York: Harper Torchbooks.

Dare, P. N. (1990). *American Communes to 1860: A Bibliography.* New York: Garland.

Fogarty, R. S. (1980). *Dictionary of American Communal and Utopian History.* Westport, CT: Greenwood Press.

Fogarty, R. S. (1990). *All Things New: American Communes and Utopian Movements, 1860–1914.* Chicago: University of Chicago Press.

Horgan, E. R. (1987). *The Shaker Holy Land: A Community Portrait.* Boston: Harvard Common Press.

Kanter, R. M. (1972). *Commitment and Community: Communes and Utopias in Sociological Perspective.* Cambridge, MA: Harvard University Press.

McCord, W. (1989). *Voyages to Utopia: From Monastery to Commune, the Search for the Perfect Society.* New York: W. W. Norton.

McLoughlin, W. G. (1978). *Revivals, Awakenings, and Reform: An Essay on Religion and Social Change in America, 1607–1977.* Chicago: University of Chicago Press.

Miller, T. (1990). *American Communes, 1860–1960: A Bibliography.* New York: Garland.

More, T. ([1516] 1965). *Utopia,* tr. P. Marshall. New York: Washington Square Press.

Oved, Y. (1993). *Two Hundred Years of American Communes.* New Brunswick, NJ: Transaction.

Roberts, R. E. (1971). *The New Communes: Coming Together in America.* Englewood Cliffs, NJ: Prentice Hall.

Shambaugh, B. (1988). *Amana: The Community of True Inspiration.* Iowa City, IA: Penfield Press.

Skinner, B. F. (1976). *Walden Two.* New York: Macmillan.

Zablocki, B. (1980). *Alienation and Charisma: A Study of Contemporary American Communes.* New York: Free Press.

William L. Smith

VENEREAL DISEASE

See Sexually Transmitted Diseases

VIOLENCE AND THE FAMILY

See Child Abuse and Neglect: Sociological Aspects; Family Violence; Spouse Abuse and Neglect

WEDDINGS *See* Marriage Ceremonies; Marriage Definition

WELFARE *See* Child Support; Entitlements; Poverty; Unemployment

WIDOWHOOD

Losing one's mate is clearly among the most stressful of all life events and presents one of the most painful adaptational challenges to confront spouses and families. It dramatically marks the transition to widowhood status—a transition that affects an increasing proportion of the diverse aging population. (For purposes of this entry, the term "widowhood" will be used to refer to both male and female bereavement, although male bereavement is more commonly referred to by the term "widowerhood.") The varied adaptations to widowhood reflect, in part, societal expectations; gender, racial, and class differences; ethnic norms; and differing circumstances surrounding the period of transition.

Demography of the Widowed

At the end of the 1980s, there were more than 13.5 million currently widowed persons in the United States, not counting many others who had previously lost spouses and subsequently remarried. The large majority, about 85 percent, of the widowed are women. In fact, for the past several decades female survivors have been outdistancing their male counterparts by a continually widening margin. Thus, in 1940 there were twice as many widows as widowers. During following decades, this disparity steadily increased, so that by 1990 the ratio of widows to widowers had climbed to more than 5 to 1. This difference is expected to increase to 10 to 1 by 2020 (F. Berardo 1992).

Several factors help account for this imbalanced sex ratio among the widowed (F. Berardo 1968, 1970). First, women experience greater longevity than males. That is to say, their death rate is lower than it is for men and, therefore, larger numbers of them survive into advanced years. Second, wives are generally younger than their husbands. Even without the sex differences in death rates, they have a greater probability of surviving their spouses. Hence, women are four times more likely to outlive their marital partners than are men. Moreover, wives are likely to be widowed at earlier ages than husbands and to remain widowed for many more years. Three of four wives will eventually become widows (U.S. Bureau of the Census 1990). Third, among the widowed, remarriage rates are significantly lower for women than men. Therefore, while many men leave widower status by wedding again, many women do not, thereby adding to the surplus of female survivors.

Advances in medical technology, widespread sanitation and health programs, and improved living conditions have extended life expectancy. In the process, the probability of dying prior to midlife has greatly diminished. Consequently, widowhood has for the most part now been postponed to the later stages of the life cycle. At the turn of the twentieth century, about one in twenty-five persons was sixty-five years of age or older, as compared to one in nine at the end of the twentieth century. The gains in longevity have been more rapid for women than for men; hence, the growing proportion of elderly women in the population accents their more striking overall rates of widowhood. It has been estimated that about one-fourth of all married women in America will be widowed by age sixty-five, and that one-half of the remaining women will have lost their husbands by age seventy-five (F. Berardo 1992). Since there is little chance that the mortality differences between the sexes will be reversed anytime soon, the excess of women at the upper ages will continue to increase, and the older population will be comprised of a larger proportion of widows. Aware of these trends, researchers have focused their attention primarily on the conditions surrounding female survivors. Consequently, comparative knowledge about the experiences and needs of males who have lost their wives remains insufficient (Blieszner 1993).

Bereavement and Adaptation

The death of a spouse presents a life condition for which most people are inadequately prepared. Much of the stress of bereavement derives from the disorganization effected by the loss of a husband or wife from the social support system of the family. From a sociological perspective, the difficult transition to widowhood can be viewed as necessitating a reintegration of roles suitable to a new status. If children are present, parental death precipitates a reorganization of the family as a social system. Roles and status positions must be shifted, values and goals reoriented, and personal and family time restructured. The potential for role strains and interpersonal conflicts becomes evident as relationships are lost, added, or redefined (Pitcher and Larson 1989). Loneliness emerges as a major problem. In the case of older bereaved spouses, in particular, loneliness and difficulties associated with the tasks of daily living are among the most common and trying adjustments encountered (Lund 1989). In many modern societies, this adaptive process typically proceeds with few or no guidelines, or even ambiguous signals from the culture as to how to act. In this regard, it has been suggested that the role of the widowed person tends to be a "roleless" role, inasmuch as it lacks clearly specified norms or prescriptions for appropriate behavior (Hiltz 1979).

While survivors face some common problems both within and outside the immediate family, it is difficult to specify a normative course of adjustment. This is partly because widows and widowers are a diverse group characterized by wide differences in social and psychological characteristics. It is also due to the fact that spousal loss evokes a wide spectrum of emotional and behavioral responses from the bereaved, depending on such factors as the nature of the marital relationship, and the timing and the circumstances under which death occurred. For example, a wife whose husband was killed on the battlefield, in an automobile accident, or in a robbery will respond differently than if he had committed suicide or suffered a long terminal illness. Many other types of such antecedent conditions, such as the quality of the marital relationship or the age of the deceased, affect bereavement reactions and coping strategies of survivors. In American society, for instance, a young wife whose life is suddenly taken is mourned differently from a much older woman, married fifty years, who succumbs after a lengthy illness. As a result of such factors, responses to bereavement often show substantial variation.

Studies of whether anticipatory grief, or forewarning of the pending death of a spouse, contributes to bereavement adjustment have yielded conflicting results (Roach and Kitson 1989). Some suggest that such anticipation is important because it allows the survivor to begin the process of role redefinition prior to the death, whereas unanticipated death produces more severe grief reactions. Those who experienced unexpected deaths of their marital partners report more somatic problems and longer adjustment periods than those who anticipated the loss. Anticipatory role rehearsal does not consistently produce smoother or more positive adjustment among the bereaved. Again, the effects of such preparation vary with the age of the person, whether death occurs as an on-time versus off-time event, and other factors. In sum, the coping strategies of survivors vary with the timing and mode of death, which in turn influence the bereavement outcome.

In making the transition to widowed status, the bereaved are often confronted with a variety of personal and familial problems. They are not always successful in adapting to these circumstances. This is reflected in the findings that, when compared to married persons, the widowed rather consistently show higher rates of mortality, mental disorders, and suicide (Balkwell 1981). While it is generally agreed that the bereavement process is stressful, studies of its effect on physical health have not yielded consistent results. The evidence does show that people who have lost their mates generally experience poorer health than those who are still married, but the reasons for this remain unclear.

Bereavement and Developmental Stages

The degree of adjustment encountered by widowed people in the transition to their new status varies by developmental stages. The death of a marital partner in young marriages is relatively uncommon; nevertheless, when it does occur it is apt to make bereavement and the survivor role much more difficult to accommodate than in later life "because of unfulfilled hopes and dreams, the lack of fit with other couples at the same life phase, and the lack of models of the same cohort" undergoing this experience (Walsh and McGoldrick 1991, p. 18). Typically there has been little or no emotional preparation for the shock and isolation of early widowhood (Parkes and Weiss 1983). Being suddenly left alone to rear young children, for example, can be extremely trying, and at the same time impedes the progress of personal and familial recovery. The immediate and growing financial and caretaking obligations of single parenthood can interfere with the tasks of mourning. Adult friends and relatives can and often do provide assistance with everyday chores, such as cooking and housecleaning. Bereaved husbands, generally speaking, are more apt to receive these kinds of practical supports than bereaved wives. On the other hand, the wives are more likely to have a more extensive range of intimate family and friendship relationships that help to facilitate their emotional grief work (Walsh and McGoldrick 1991).

Older people adapt more readily to widowhood because losing a spouse at advanced ages is more the norm and often anticipated, thus making acceptance of the loss somewhat easier. However, grief over the death of a husband or wife at older ages can be exacerbated if additional significant others also die, requiring multiple or simultaneous grieving. This can cause bereavement overload, which makes it difficult for the survivor to complete the grief work and bring closure to the bereavement process (D. Berardo 1988). There is general consensus that the distress associated with conjugal bereavement diminishes over time. Grief becomes less intense as years pass, but this is not a simple, linear process. The emotional and psychological traumas of grief and mourning may sporadically reappear long after the spouse has died.

Gender Differences

Widows and widowers represent diverse populations whose responses to bereavement and recovery may exhibit wide variations due to interacting influences of gender, class, and race/ethnicity (Blieszner 1993). The issue of gender differences in adaptation to widowhood has long been debated. The evidence does suggest a somewhat greater vulnerability for widowers (Stroebe and Stroebe 1983). Men are less likely to have same-sex widowed friends, more likely to be older and less healthy, have fewer family and social ties, and experience greater difficulty in becoming proficient in domestic roles (F. Berardo 1970; Hyman 1983). Higher mortality and suicide rates also suggest somewhat greater distress among widowers. It is important to stress, however, that widows and widowers share many similar bereavement experiences and adjustments. There is much empirical support for the conclusion that while they do experience some aspects of grief differently, men and women have a good deal in common with respect to loss-related feelings, mental and physical health, and social life (Lund 1989).

Continuous widowhood has been associated with loss of income and increased risk of poverty. Studies have shown that the death of husbands results in lowered financial status for wives, many of whom become impoverished following bereavement. Two-fifths of widows fall into poverty at some time during the five years following the death of their husbands. Widowers also suffer a decline in economic well-being, albeit to a lesser degree than their female counterparts (Zick and Smith 1988). People often fail to plan for the economic consequences of spousal loss. Elderly persons frequently have below-average incomes prior to the death of their marital partner. Once bereaved, their circumstances may worsen, especially if they have been stay-at-home wives who were highly dependent on their husband's income. They may be unwilling or unable to seek or find employment, and they are likely to face discrimination in the labor market (Morgan 1989). Given their age, they may lack the education or skills required to compete for jobs. The younger widowed are more likely to have lost a spouse suddenly and may thus be unprepared to cope with lowered financial subsistence. Poor adjustment to being widowed, therefore, can often be attributed to socioeconomic deprivation. This is especially apt to be the case among members of disadvantaged racial/ethnic groups, whose recovery may be impeded by discrimination and inequitable social policies that affect their health and financial circumstances (D. Berardo 1994; Blieszner 1993).

Widowhood often leads to changes in living arrangements. Reduced income may force surviving spouses to seek more affordable housing. They may also choose to relocate for other reasons such as future financial and health concerns, a desire to divest of possessions, or to be near kin or friends (Hartwigsen 1987). Most often, the people living alone are women—usually elderly widows. Isolation and lack of social support can lead to deterioration in physical and mental well-being. Compared to elderly married couples, widows and widowers are much more apt to live in poverty and are less likely to receive medical care when needed (Kasper 1988).

The probability for remarriage is significantly less for widows than widowers, especially at older ages. They may feel they are committing psychological bigamy and therefore reject remarriage as an option (DiGiulio 1989). There is also a tendency to idealize the former partner, a process known as "sanctification" (Lopata 1979). This makes it difficult to find a new partner who can favorably compare with the idealized image of the deceased (D. Berardo 1982). There are other barriers to remarriages for the widowed. Dependent children may limit the opportunities of their widowed parents to meet potential mates or to develop relationships with them. Older children may oppose remarriage out of concern for their inheritance. Widowed persons who cared for a dependent spouse through a lengthy, terminal illness may be unwilling to risk this burden again. As noted earlier, widowers remarry much more frequently than widows. This is due to the lack of eligible men and cultural norms that degrade the sexuality of older women and discourage them from selecting younger mates. Many women manage to develop and value a new and independent identity beyond widowhood, leading them to be less interested in reentering the marriage market.

Social Support and Reintegration

While social support is presumed to play an important role in bereavement outcomes and act as a buffer for stressful life events, the research is inconclusive. Nevertheless, there is evidence that the extent to which members of the social network provide various types of assistance to the bereaved is important to the *pattern* of recovery and adaptation. Available confidants and access to self-help groups to assist with emotional management can help counter loneliness and promote the survivor's reintegration into society. The social resources of finances and education have been found to be particularly influential in countering the stresses associated with the death of a spouse.

Community programs that provide education, counseling, and financial services can facilitate the efforts of the widowed and their families to restructure their lives. To be most effective, services and intervention programs must be actively introduced early in the bereavement process, since the early months tend to be the most difficult and can affect later recovery outcomes. Moreover, such services should remain available over long periods of time (Lund 1989). Much of the variability in bereavement response can be attributed to intrapersonal resources that make coping easier. For example, it has been found that a sense of optimism and meaning in life is integral to how well the widowed adapted to their bereavement (Caserta and Lund 1993). Some other major factors that strongly influence the degree of difficulty experienced by widowed individuals include self-confidence, that is, the belief that one will be able to manage the situation; a sense of optimism and self-efficacy, derived from having coped with previous life transitions; and perhaps most important, strong self-esteem (Parkes 1988).

Widows and widowers show considerable variation in concluding their grief work, some essentially completing the process in months, others sometimes taking years to adapt to life without their mate. A small minority never do get over the trauma wrought by the loss (Lund 1989). With help, however, the majority of the widowed are capable of eventually adapting to their new circumstances, managing their everyday affairs and maintaining a sense of purpose and a life of personal satisfaction.

(*See also:* Death and Mourning; Elders; Inheritance; Later-Life Families; Loneliness; Stress; Retirement)

BIBLIOGRAPHY

Balkwell, C. (1981). "Transition to Widowhood: A Review of the Literature." *Family Relations* 30:117–127.

Berardo, D. H. (1982). "Divorce and Remarriage at Middle-Age and Beyond." *The Annals of the American Academy of Political and Social Science* 464:132–139.

Berardo, D. H. (1988). "Bereavement and Mourning." In *Dying: Facing the Facts*, 2nd edition, ed. H. Wass, F. M. Berardo, and R. A. Neimeyer. New York: Hemisphere.

Berardo, D. H. (1994). "Social and Psychological Issues of Aging and Health." In *Therapeutics in the Elderly*, 2nd edition, ed. J. C. Delafuente and R. B. Stewart. Cincinnati: Harvey Whitney Books.

Berardo, F. M. (1968). "Widowhood Status in the United States: A Neglected Aspect of the Family Life Cycle." *The Family Coordinator* 17:191–203.

Berardo, F. M. (1970). "Survivorship and Social Isolation: The Case of the Aged Widower." *The Family Coordinator* 19:11–25.

Berardo, F. M. (1992). "Widowhood." In *Encyclopedia of Sociology*, ed. E. F. Borgatta and M. L. Borgatta. New York: Macmillan.

Blieszner, R. (1993). "A Socialist-Feminist Perspective on Widowhood." *Journal of Aging Studies* 7:171–182.

Caserta, M., and Lund, D. A. (1993). "Intrapersonal Resources and the Effectiveness of Self-Help Groups for Bereaved Older Adults." *The Gerontologist* 33:616–629.

Clark, P. G.; Siviski, R. W.; and Weiner, R. (1986). "Coping Strategies of Widowers in the First Year." *Family Relations* 35:425–430.

DiGiulio, R. C. (1989). *Beyond Widowhood.* New York: Free Press.

Dimond, M.; Lund, D. A.; and Caserta, M. S. (1987). "The Role of Social Support in the First Two Years of Bereavement in an Elderly Sample." *The Gerontologist* 27:599–604.

Hartwigsen, G. (1987). "Older Widows and the Transference of Home." *International Journal of Aging and Human Development* 25:195–207.

Hiltz, S. R. (1979). "Widowhood: A Roleless Role." In *Marriage and Family,* ed. M. B. Sussman. Collected Essay Series. New York: Haworth Press.

Hyman, H. H. (1983). *Of Time and Widowhood.* Durham, NC: Duke University Press.

Kasper, J. D. (1988). *Aging Alone: Profiles and Projections.* Baltimore: Commonwealth Fund.

Lopata, H. Z. (1973). *Widowhood in an American City.* Cambridge, MA: Schenkman.

Lopata, H. Z. (1979). *Women as Widows.* New York: Elsevier.

Lund, D. A. (1989). "Conclusions About Bereavement in Later Life and Implications for Interventions and Future Research." In *Older Bereaved Spouses,* ed. D. A. Lund. New York: Hemisphere.

Morgan, L. (1989). "Economic Well-Being Following Marital Termination." *Journal of Family Issues* 10:86–101.

Parkes, C. M. (1988). "Bereavement as a Psychological Transition." *Journal of Social Issues* 44:53–65.

Parkes, C. M., and Weiss, R. (1983). *Recovery from Bereavement.* New York: Basic Books.

Pitcher, B. L., and Larson, D. C. (1989). "Elderly Widowhood." In *Aging and the Family,* ed. S. J. Bahr and E. T. Peterson. Lexington, MA: D. C. Heath.

Roach, M. J., and Kitson, G. T. (1989). "Impact of Forewarning and Adjustment to Widowhood and Divorce." In *Older Bereaved Spouses,* ed. D. A. Lund. New York: Hemisphere.

Stroebe, M. S., and Stroebe, W. (1983). "Who Suffers More: Sex Differences in Health Risks of the Widowed." *Psychological Bulletin* 93:279–299.

U.S. Bureau of the Census. (1990). *Statistical Abstract of the United States: 1988.* Washington, DC: U.S. Government Printing Office.

Walsh, F., and McGoldrick, M. (1991). "Loss and the Family: A Systemic Perspective." In *Living Beyond Loss: Death in the Family,* ed. F. Walsh and M. McGoldrick. New York: W. W. Norton.

Zick, C. D., and Smith, K. R. (1988). "Recent Widowhood, Remarriage, and Changes in Economic Well-Being." *Journal of Marriage and the Family* 50:233–244.

Felix M. Berardo

WORK AND FAMILY

In her 1977 monograph on work and family in the United States, Rosabeth Moss Kanter observed: "If any one statement can be said to define the most prevalent sociological position on work and family, it is the 'myth' of separate worlds." Kanter goes on to identify the elements of this myth, the most important being the idea that work and family "constitute two separate and nonoverlapping worlds, with their own functions, territories, and behavioral rules" (Kanter 1977b, p. 8). Although the myth of separate worlds continues to hold sway in some areas of American life, sociologists have become increasingly critical of this concept of work–family relations. Instead, sociologists have begun to explore the interconnections between work and family, and the consequences of these links for individuals, families, employers, and society.

Sociologists' rejection of the myth of separate worlds can be understood both as a response to societal changes that have transformed relations between families and work and as a reflection of new conceptual approaches that have forced a rethinking of how social institutions are understood.

Relation Between Work and Family

How should the relations between work and family be characterized? What are the differences between conceptions that emphasize objective characteristics of work and family and those emphasizing subjective reactions to those characteristics? How do relations between work and family vary by gender, social class, race or ethnicity, age, sexual orientation, or other demographic, job, or family characteristics? These questions have inspired numerous attempts to theorize about and concretely model work–family relations. Efforts to put forward a single, dominant conception of work–family relations have been abandoned in favor of attempts to explore the conditions under which particular conceptions may be valid (Lambert 1990). Hence, understanding sources of vulnerability in work–family relations has become important.

At the most general level, work–family relations can be arrayed on a continuum ranging from segmentation to integration. Segmentation represents a view of work and family as two mutually exclusive spheres separated in time and space, while integration implies that these realms overlap in significant ways. The segmentation view is consistent with the "myth of separate worlds" position described by Kanter (1977b). As Chaya Piotrkowski (1978, p. 31) states, this view implies that "people simply take on different roles in different settings and move easily between them." From this perspective, the subject of relations *between* work and family is irrelevant, since it is assumed that these are two separate and independent realms.

The segmentation–integration distinction represents a very general way to characterize work–family relations and therefore is applicable to a range of concerns. This formulation can refer to both objective and subjective aspects of work and family, and it can characterize institutions as well as individuals. For instance, work and family are physically segmented for the commuter, while these realms are physically integrated for those who "telecommute" from their homes. Alternatively, some may subjectively "segment" work and family life by maintaining mental boundaries between these realms, while others may subjectively "integrate" realms by mental processes that stress continuity and overlap. The distinction between integration and segmentation can also be used to characterize broad historical trends in work–family relations. These relations more closely resembled integration in pre- and early-industrial United States, whereas segmentation has been more characteristic of industrial society (Kanter 1977b).

Although the segmentation–integration distinction is useful, many seek more nuanced ways to capture work–family relations. In particular, researchers are interested in understanding *how* and *why* work and family patterns assume particular forms, and want to identify the consequences of these patterns. Conflict models of work–family relations, which assume that the demands, responsibilities, and requirements for participation in one sphere conflict with those associated with another, have received perhaps the most attention from researchers (Greenhaus and Beutell 1985). For example, Max Weber (1947) and, in a more general way, Sigmund Freud ([1930] 1962) viewed the affective and highly particularistic ties of family life as incompatible with the discipline and rationality required in the workplace. Talcott Parsons and Robert Bales (1955) echoed these sentiments in their claim that industrial society required a gender division of labor in the family whereby men were responsible for the "instrumental" tasks associated with work, while women performed the "expressive" tasks associated with family life. Parsons (1964) believed that this division of labor between husbands and wives was "functional" for workplaces and households because it ensured that the incompatible demands and requirements of these two spheres would never directly confront one another. This view thus assumes that segmentation between work and family reflects underlying irreconcilable conflicts between these two realms. Because a conflict view of work–family relations implies that work–family integration is difficult, if not impossible, this perspective has been advanced as an explanation for segmentation between work and family.

There is a vast empirical literature exploring people's experiences of particular work–family conflicts (Greenhaus and Beutell 1985). These conflicts may result from incompatibilities between the structural characteristics of work and family life or the psychological dimensions of these realms (Voydanoff 1987). For example, spending long hours on the job necessarily reduces the amount of time available for family life. Hence, it is not surprising that those who work long hours are more likely than others to report that work and family interfere with one another (Voydanoff 1987). Along these lines, some argue that women are more likely than men to work part-time because women retain primary responsibility for housework and child care in the family. In other words, the time commitment required by their family responsibilities interferes with women's ability to be full-time workers (Emmons et al. 1990).

The psychological dimensions of work and family may also conflict. One potential source of work–family conflict that has become the focus of research concerns the "emotional" demands associated with work and family. Work–family conflict, as well as individual psychological distress, may result when jobs require workers to exhibit different kinds of emotions than those expected of family members (Wharton and Erickson 1993). A former professional football player interviewed about his reasons for leaving the game expressed this form of work–family conflict: "'Football's so aggressive. Things get done by force. And then you come home, you're supposed to turn it off? "Oh, here's your lovin' daddy." It's not that easy.'" (Berkow 1993). While research has identified many structural and psychological sources of work–family conflict, it must be remembered that not all aspects of work and family life are necessarily experienced as incompatible with one another.

In contrast to those who view segmentation between work and family as the inevitable result of fundamental work–family conflicts, many researchers believe that other types of work–family relations are possible. These views rest on the assumption that complete segmentation between work and family is, as Kanter (1977b) claims, a "myth" and that some overlap between spheres is inevitable. In addition, researchers argue that segmentation is only one response to work–family conflicts. These conceptions of work–family relations thus aim to identify the different forms of work–family integration and their consequences. Rhona Rapoport and Robert Rapoport (1965) distinguish between two forms of work–family integration: Work and family are "isomorphic" when they reinforce one another, while they are "complementary" (or "heteromorphic") when one compensates for the other (see also Piotrkowski 1978). In simpler language, these two patterns represent "spillover" and "compensation."

Spillover, which refers to either positive or negative carryover between work and family, has been a useful concept for work–family researchers (Burke and Bradshaw 1981; Voydanoff 1987; Eckenrode and Gore 1990). Positive spillover results when the carryover from work to family (or vice versa) disseminates the positive aspects of one realm to another, while negative spillover spreads negative aspects of one setting to another. Patricia Voydanoff's (1982) study of male professionals and managers reveals one form of positive spillover between work and family. She found that high levels of job satisfaction were related to high levels of marital and family satisfaction among this group of male workers. Positive correlations between job and life satisfactions have also been found by other researchers (Burke and Bradshaw 1981). Interest in negative spillover is reflected in studies examining the degree to which the experience of stress or problems in one sphere carries over to another. Evelyn Bromet, Mary Amanda Dew, and David Parkinson (1990) found extensive evidence of this kind of spillover in their study of blue-collar wives. In addition, and perhaps more important, they found that women who experienced spillover were at greater risk of poor mental health than those reporting no spillover between work and family.

> Compared to women who reported no spillover, blue-collar working wives who acknowledged the occurrence of spillover . . . report more job and marital strain, perceive less coworker support, are three times more likely to have been depressed or anxious in the year preceding the interview, have higher current levels of depression, anxiety, and somatic symptoms, consume more alcohol, and are more likely to be heavier smokers [Bromet, Dew, and Parkinson 1990, p. 146].

As these examples reveal, work–family spillover is not confined to one gender. Moreover, spillover may occur from either work to family or family to work. Some researchers have suggested job-to-family spillover should be more common for men, while family-to-job spillover should be more common for women. According to Joseph Pleck (1977), this pattern stems from gender differences in the permeability of the boundaries between work and family. Because wives retain primary responsibility for family caregiving, family-to-work spillover is more common and more acceptable for them than their male partners. Conversely, Pleck argues that because husbands are assumed to be their family's primary breadwinner, they are more likely to experience work-to-family spillover than their wives. However, while work–family relations are shaped by gender, Pleck's argument is not fully supported by the data (Bolger et al. 1990).

Relations between work and family may also take the form of compensation. In this view, when workers are unable to achieve gratification from their work roles, they achieve alternative gratification in roles outside of work (Piotrkowski 1978). This implies that people compensate for unsatisfying conditions in one sphere by finding greater satisfaction in another. This argument has often been used to explain the connections between work and leisure, especially as these are experienced by male manual workers, who are assumed to use their leisure time as compensation for unsatisfying and undesirable jobs (Andrew 1981). The compensation hypothesis has been similarly applied to work–family relations, where it has been used to describe men who view their families as "havens" from work. As Piotrkowski (1978, p. 275) shows, however, people's desire to treat their families as havens does not necessarily imply that they have the means or resources to accomplish this: "It may be that the very conditions of occupational life that require workers to find havens in their families make it difficult for families to serve this function." Both structural and psychological aspects of jobs may thus interfere with workers' capacities to treat their families as compensation for work.

Segmentation, conflict, spillover, and compensation represent alternative ways to conceive of the relations between work and family. However, researchers diverge not only with respect to which of these relations they emphasize, but also with respect to the aspects of work and family they view as most central. Some researchers are most concerned with unraveling the relations between "objective" (structural) aspects of work and family (e.g., the relations between work schedules and time spent with family members). Alternatively, others explore the relations between subjective (psychological) aspects of these two spheres (e.g., the relations between job satisfaction and marital satisfaction), while still others examine the effects of structural characteristics on psychological reactions (e.g., the relations between job conditions and marital satisfaction).

Other lines of divergence within the work–family literature concern the types of workplaces and families that are the focus of study. As Jeylan Mortimer and Jane London (1984) note, work and family can be linked by either one wage-earner or two. In relatively recent years, the number of single-provider families has fallen, while the number of dual-earner families has been on the rise. Within both of these categories are further distinctions, such as those related to social class, race, or ethnicity. These variations in individual, work, and family characteristics must also be taken into consideration in studies of work–family relations.

Historical Trends

Historical circumstances shape relations between work and family. The political, social, and economic contexts within which work and family activities are located make possible certain types of relations, while closing off other possibilities. Kanter (1977b) argues that the modern conception of work and family as separate is a fairly recent development in the United States, having its roots in changes that took place around the beginning of the twentieth century. Moreover, she suggests that this conception was more applicable historically to the situations of the middle class than other social groups.

Prior to industrialization, when the United States was a primarily agricultural economy, work and family were closely intertwined and the distinction between home and workplace was nonexistent. Homes were workplaces and vice versa. As Randy Hodson and Teresa Sullivan (1990) note, the word "housework" was not introduced into the written English language until 1841, suggesting that the distinction between work performed at home and work performed elsewhere did not exist in previous eras. The situations of native-born families in preindustrial United States have received much attention from historians and historical sociologists (Demos 1970; Cowan 1983; Hareven 1990). These accounts describe the functioning of family economies within which wives, husbands, and children contributed their labor to the household and produced goods for sale in the market. Although tasks were divided on the basis of gender and age, neither women nor men experienced a separation between the worlds of family and work.

Industrialization profoundly altered these arrangements. According to Tamara Hareven (1990), families not only responded to changes brought about by industrialization, but also helped make these changes possible. The most significant change taking place during this time was the geographical separation of work and family life. This shift severed the interdependence of work and family that characterized preindustrial America. It did not eliminate the connections between these realms, however, but instead altered the nature of work–family linkages. Industrialization and its related implications for work–family relations did not emerge overnight, but instead developed over an extended period that has been extensively studied by sociologists.

With the creation of factories, goods production moved out of the home, and families began sending one or more of their members to work in these industrial settings (Clawson 1980). In some New England villages, for instance, entire families went to work in local textile mills. This "family employment system," which often involved fathers paying wives, children, and other relatives out of their own wages, represented one way that work organization in the industrial era began to reflect familial influences. The New England "mill girls" offer yet another example of the newly emerging links between work and family. The "mill girls" were young women from rural backgrounds sent by their families to work in factories for a few years before getting married (Hareven 1990). These women, whose labor was viewed as less necessary to the family farm than the labor of sons, contributed to their family's economic well-being by sending their wages home. Gradually, the "mill girls" were replaced by newly arriving European immigrants. Immigrant workers, who could be employed more cheaply than the "mill girls," were often recruited as families.

The experiences of African Americans under slavery diverged from this pattern. As Jacqueline Jones (1987) shows, the institution of American slavery undermined slaves' ability to maintain family life. In Jones's words, "If work is any activity that leads either directly or indirectly to the production of marketable goods, then slave women did nothing *but* work" (p. 85, emphasis in original). Within the confines of a brutal slave system, however, African Americans did attempt to carve out a private life where familial obligations and sentiments could be expressed. In fact, "under slavery, blacks' attempts to maintain the integrity of family life amounted to a political act of protest" (Jones 1987, p. 84). Slavery thus represents perhaps the clearest example of a system of work organized to eliminate family life altogether.

As industrialization unfolded, it was associated with other important changes in American society, such as urbanization. These developments, in turn, shaped and were shaped by work–family relations. Not all groups within the population were affected the same way, however. For the growing middle class of managers and professionals, work and family continued to grow apart, both geographically and symbolically. As Kanter (1977b, p. 13) explains, "Those who could afford to remove their residences to 'pastoral' surroundings far from places of employment often did so, also removing, in the process, points of contact between the rest of the family and the organization." This separation was facilitated by zoning laws and various architectural arrangements that created clearly defined boundaries between industrial and residential areas. These physical boundaries between work and family were further reinforced by a gender division of labor. Among the middle class, the workplace became men's domain, while families were seen as populated by women and children.

Although such arrangements seemed to confirm "the myth of separate worlds," important—if unobtrusive—connections between family and work remained. Though not an official employee herself, the wife of a male executive made important contributions to her husband's career, as homemakers married to executives continue to do (Kanter 1977a). Because wives cooked, cleaned, raised children, provided emotional support, entertained, and sacrificed their own ambitions for their husbands' careers, it was as if married men brought two people to work, rather than one. Accordingly, despite the geographical separation of work and family, middle-class marriages and family lives were shaped by the demands of middle-class work.

Industrialization had a different effect on the working class. These workers, employed in blue-collar, clerical, and service jobs, could not afford to relocate to the suburbs and hence lived much closer to the workplace than their middle-class counterparts. The cities therefore became home to workers, who lived in densely populated areas not far from their workplaces. Unlike the middle class, where most women worked exclusively at home caring for their families, many working-class women combined their family responsibilities with a wage-earning job. Working-class men were employed in factories, while their wives worked in clerical or service positions. These gender-segregated work environments spilled over into the social lives and activities of the working class, which some have characterized as more gender-segregated than those of the middle class.

Many members of the working class are racial minorities. Because racial minorities of both genders have historically received lower wages than whites, two wage-earners rather than one has been a typical pattern among minority families. While the work and family configurations of these families are themselves diverse, minority men have generally been employed in factories or in agriculture. Minority women have found employment in these settings as well. During the early stages of industrialization, many minority women were also employed as domestic servants in middle-class homes. As Evelyn Nakano Glenn (1992, p. 7) observes, "White middle-class women were thereby freed for supervisory tasks and for cultural, leisure, and volunteer activity or, more rarely during this period, for a career."

These descriptions of work and family illustrate the complex evolution of these arrangements over time, and they reveal the susceptibility of these relations to the influences of social class and race. The physical separation of work and family that accompanied industrialization had significant effects in the middle class, where work and family came to be seen as distinct domains inhabited by different genders. Middle-class men's roles were organized around the statuses of "worker" and "breadwinner," while the roles of "mother" and "homemaker" were assigned to middle-class women. Industrialization had different consequences for working-class families, who could often not afford a full-time homemaker and thus sent both women and men out to seek wage work. Ironically, minority women often found such work as domestic servants in middle-class homes.

Industrialization's impact on work–family relations was intrinsically connected to its role in reshaping gender roles. Despite the fact that many working-class and minority women were employed for pay, the experiences of the middle class became the basis for cultural norms and employer practices that defined the workplace and workers as "male." As Barbara Reskin and Irene Padavic (1994, p. 23) observe,

> [T]he sexual division of labor that assigned men to the labor force and women to the home encouraged employers to structure jobs on the assumptions that all permanent workers were men and that all men had stay-at-home wives. These assumptions freed workers (that is, male workers) from domestic responsibilities so they could work 12- to 14-hour days. These assumptions also bolstered the belief that domestic work was women's responsibility, even for women who were employed outside the home.

Changing Patterns

The latter half of the twentieth century witnessed profound changes in the organization and meaning of "work" and "family." Some trace these changes to economic and cultural shifts that transformed the United States from an "industrial" to a "postindustrial" society. How this transformation has reshaped work–family relations is a topic of considerable debate, requiring attention both to changes in the workplace and to changes in family life.

Manufacturing industries, such as automobile and steel production, formed the economic backbone of industrial society. These goods-producing industries expanded their share of employment until the 1950s, but have declined with every decade since that time (Urquhart 1984). The percentage of the population employed in agriculture has also been declining steadily; this sector now employs only about 2 percent of the entire labor force. By contrast, service-producing industries, such as finance, insurance, and real estate, have been increasing their share of employment over time. These employment trends document that the United States has become a "service" economy, or, in Daniel Bell's (1973) words, a "postindustrial society."

In contrast to the kinds of products generated by a goods-producing economy, such as cars or machinery, the products of a postindustrial economy are services. Services, such as depositing money in one's bank account or consuming a meal in a restaurant, are intangible products, because they are produced and consumed simultaneously (Hochschild 1983). Social interaction between the customer and the service provider is also a key aspect of service work. As Bell (1973, p. 163) observed, workers in a postindustrial economy "now talk to other individuals rather than interact with a machine."

American society's shift to a service economy is associated with two related social changes that have together begun to alter work–family relations. Most important has been the sharp increase in women's labor-force participation, which occurred in the decades following World War II, with most women filling predominantly "female" jobs in service industries. As Michael Urquhart (1984, p. 21) notes, "The primary source of new employees in the services sector was the employment of women who had previously not held jobs." This increase in women's labor-force participation was not confined to single women or women without children. By 1992, 58 percent of all women worked for pay, including a majority of married women and women with children. Women constitute approximately 47 percent of all workers (Reskin and Padavic 1994).

While the expansion of the service sector has increased employment opportunities for women, this sector offers lower wages than have historically been available to workers in manufacturing. Hence, women's employment opportunities have grown at the same time as the standard of living for American workers and their families has declined. In Bennett Harrison and Barry Bluestone's (1988, p. 3) words, "For every affluent 'yuppie' in an expensive big-city condominium, working as a white-collar professional for a high-flying high-technology concern or a multibillion dollar insurance company, there are many more people whose wages have been falling and whose families are finding it more and more difficult to make ends meet." Although some service-sector jobs pay high wages, many are low-paying (Smith 1984). Increasing inequality has therefore been another consequence of a service economy.

Changes in the family can be seen as both cause and consequence of these trends (i.e., the expansion of the service sector, the increasing employment of women, and growing economic inequality). For example, many service jobs involve tasks that have been performed historically by women in the home. As jobs such as food preparation, child care, and care for the elderly have been transformed from unpaid to paid work, women have also moved from the status of homemaker to worker. The increasing availability of services, in turn, makes families less dependent on women's unpaid work in the home, making it possible for women with families to seek paid employment. Families with two wage-earners have thus become the norm, rather than the exception. Women's employment has other consequences for family life, however, as it has also been associated with higher rates of divorce (Booth et al. 1984). Further, when marriages break up, mothers are more likely than fathers to retain custody of children. Because women are likely to be employed in low-paying, service-sector jobs, single parenthood for women has been associated with high rates of poverty (Smith 1984).

These societal-level patterns begin to illustrate the connections between work and family in postindustrial society. Exploring the implications of these patterns for individual women and men, for families, and for employers has become a priority for research. Researchers have devoted particular attention to dual-earner families, who confront different work–family problems and opportunities than families with a single breadwinner and a full-time homemaker.

The "second shift" is a concept used to describe women's lives in dual-earner households (Hochschild 1989). This concept refers to the time women spend performing unpaid household work, in addition to their time working in the paid labor force. In her study of dual-earner families, Arlie Hochschild (1989) quotes from a woman interviewed about the second shift: "'You're on duty at work. You come home, you're on duty. Then you go back to work and you're on duty'" (p. 7). As Hochschild notes, women perceived the second shift as "their issue" and "seemed to be far more deeply torn between the demands of work and family than were their husbands" (p. 7).

The second shift captures an important work–family issue for women in dual-earner households. Women's large-scale entrance into the paid labor force has not been accompanied by any significant corresponding change in husbands' participation in family work. Thus, balancing the demands of work-and family falls heavily on women, rather than men. One primary consequence of this disparity in workload is that women have less time for themselves than men. A recognition of the potential problems associated with balancing the demands of paid work, husband, and children leads some professional women to postpone or forgo marriage and childbearing. In addition, men's reluctance to assume their share of the second shift is an ongoing source of marital tension in some households (Hochschild 1989).

At the same time, it should be noted that women's participation in paid employment has important benefits for women and their families. For instance, among married couples who both work full-time, wives contribute approximately 40 percent of total household income (Crispell 1993). This contribution may mean the difference between poverty and an adequate standard of living for the family. In addition, employment can have psychological benefits for women, even when paid work is combined with other roles, such as wife or mother (Reskin and Coverman 1985). Research suggests that "parallel" marriages, where wives and husbands both work for pay and share household tasks, can be psychologically beneficial for both women and their spouses.

Although balancing the demands of work and family may be a more familiar activity to wives than husbands, men's work and family lives are also increasingly intertwined. Whereas masculinity in previous eras was defined primarily by men's role as "good providers," this role has been redefined. As Jesse Bernard (1981) shows, men face mounting pressure from spouses and the larger society to become more involved in family life and child care. Men's responsibilities to their families are thus starting to be defined more broadly than simply those associated with earning a living. Along these lines, researchers have begun to identify the circumstances that influence men's participation in household work, and the conditions under which they share this work equally with their employed wives. These analyses suggest that a man's role in the household division of labor is shaped by numerous factors, including his education, income, racial and ethnic background, and relations with his own father.

Implications

Understanding the relations between work and family has become an important topic. Many studies of work–family relations assume that achieving work–family balance is desirable and not impossible, but is sometimes difficult. Identifying ways to reduce or eliminate these difficulties is a critical agendum for work–family researchers.

Given these considerations, what kinds of issues require attention? First, a greater understanding is needed of the roles employers play in shaping work–family relations. Some research has already begun to address how employer policies, such as flexible schedules and family leave, affect families' ability to manage work and family concerns. In addition, more studies of nontraditional families are needed. Although dual-earner families have received most of researchers' attention, more families are headed by single parents than ever before. The work–family concerns of this group require consideration, as do the concerns of other nontraditional families, such as those of gays and lesbians.

Women's entry into the paid labor force in greater numbers has been accompanied by a recognition that work and family are not separate domains, but rather spheres intersecting in complex ways. As relations between women and men continue to change, those between work and family are likely to be redefined as well. Work and family are therefore not static, unchanging institutions, but reflect and adapt to developments in the wider society.

(*See also:* Dual-Earner Families; Entitlements; Family Gender Roles; History of the Family; Poverty; Resource Management; Retirement; Unemployment)

BIBLIOGRAPHY

Andrew, E. (1981). *Closing the Iron Cage.* Montreal: Black Rose Books.

Bell, D. (1973). *The Coming of Post-Industrial Society.* New York: Basic Books.

Berkow, I. (1993). "Rosenbach Now Out of Harm's Way." *The Spokesman-Review,* Oct. 6, p. C1.

Bernard, J. (1981). "The Good-Provider Role: Its Rise and Fall." *The American Psychologist* 36:1–12.

Bolger, N.; DeLongis, A.; Kessler, R. C.; and Wethington, E. (1990). "The Microstructure of Daily Role-Related Stress in Married Couples." In *Stress Between Work and Family,* ed. J. Eckenrode and S. Gore. New York: Plenum.

Booth, A.; Johnson, D. R.; White, L.; and Edwards, J. N. (1984). "Women, Outside Employment, and Marital Instability." *American Journal of Sociology* 90:567–583.

Bromet, E. J.; Dew, M. A.; and Parkinson, D. K. (1990). "Spillover Between Work and Family: A Study of Blue-Collar Working Wives." In *Stress Between Work and Family,* ed. J. Eckenrode and S. Gore. New York: Plenum.

Burke, R. J., and Bradshaw, P. (1981). "Occupational Life Stress and the Family." *Small Group Behavior* 12:329–375.

Clawson, D. (1980). *Bureaucracy and the Labor Process.* New York: Monthly Review Press.

Cowan, R. S. (1983). *More Work for Mother.* New York: Basic Books.

Crispell, D. (1993). "Odds and Ends." *Wall Street Journal,* Sept. 13, p. B1.

Demos, J. (1970). *A Little Commonwealth: Family Life in Plymouth Colony.* New York: Oxford University Press.

Eckenrode, J., and Gore, S., eds. (1990). *Stress Between Work and Family.* New York: Plenum.

Emmons, C.-A.; Biernat, M.; Tiedje, L. B.; Lang, E. L.; and Wortman, C. B. (1990). "Stress, Support, and Coping Among Women Professionals with Preschool Children." In *Stress Between Work and Family,* ed. J. Eckenrode and S. Gore. New York: Plenum.

Freud, S. ([1930] 1962). *Civilization and Its Discontents.* New York: W. W. Norton.

Glenn, E. N. (1992). "From Servitude to Service Work: Historical Continuities in the Racial Division of Paid Reproductive Labor." *Signs* 18:1–43.

Greenhaus, J. H., and Beutell, N. J. (1985). "Sources of Conflict Between Work and Family Roles." *Academy of Management Review* 10:76–88.

Hareven, T. K. (1990). "A Complex Relationship: Family Strategies and the Processes of Economic and Social Change." In *Beyond the Marketplace,* ed. R. Friedland and A. F. Robertson. New York: Aldine.

Harrison, B., and Bluestone, B. (1988). *The Great U-Turn: Corporate Restructuring and the Polarizing of America.* New York: Basic Books.

Hochschild, A. (1983). *The Managed Heart.* Berkeley: University of California Press.

Hochschild, A. (1989). *The Second Shift: Working Parents and the Revolution at Home.* New York: Viking Penguin.

Hodson, R., and Sullivan, T. A. (1990). *The Social Organization of Work.* Belmont, CA: Wadsworth.

Jones, J. (1987). "Black Women, Work, and the Family Under Slavery." In *Families and Work,* ed. N. Gerstel and H. E. Gross. Philadelphia: Temple University Press.

Kanter, R. M. (1977a). *Men and Women of the Corporation.* New York: Basic Books.

Kanter, R. M. (1977b). *Work and Family in the United States: A Critical Review and Agenda for Research and Policy.* New York: Russell Sage Foundation.

Lambert, S. J. (1990). "Processes Linking Work and Family: A Critical Review and Research Agenda." *Human Relations* 3:239–257.

Mortimer, J. T., and London, J. (1984). "The Varying Linkages Between Work and Family." In *Work and Family,* ed. P. Voydanoff. Palo Alto, CA: Mayfield.

Parsons, T. (1964). *Essays in Sociological Theory.* New York: Free Press.

Parsons, T., and Bales, R. F. (1955). *Family Socialization and Interaction Process.* New York: Free Press.

Piotrkowski, C. S. (1978). *Work and the Family System.* New York: Free Press.

Pleck, J. (1977). "The Work-Family Role System." *Social Problems* 24:417–427.

Rapoport, R., and Rapoport, R. (1965). "Work and Family in Contemporary Society." *American Sociological Review* 30:381–394.

Reskin, B., and Coverman, S. (1985). "Sex and Race Interactions in the Determinants of Psychological Distress: A Reappraisal of the Sex-Role Hypothesis." *Social Forces* 63:1038–1059.

Reskin, B., and Padavic, I. (1994). *Women and Men at Work.* Thousand Oaks, CA: Pine Forge Press.

Smith, J. (1984). "The Paradox of Women's Poverty: Wage-Earning Women and Economic Transformation." *Signs* 10:291–310.

Urquhart, M. (1984). "The Employment Shift to Services: Where Did It Come From?" *Monthly Labor Review* 73: 15–22.

Voydanoff, P. (1982). "Work Roles and Quality of Family Life Among Professionals and Managers." In *Families and Work,* ed. B. M. Hirschlein and W. J. Braun. Stillwater: Oklahoma State University Press.

Voydanoff, P. (1987). *Work and Family Life.* Newbury Park, CA: Sage Publications.

Weber, M. (1947). *The Theory of Social and Economic Organization.* New York: Oxford University Press.

Wharton, A. S., and Erickson, R. J. (1993). "Managing Emotions on the Job and at Home: Understanding the Consequences of Multiple Emotional Roles." *Academy of Management Review* 18:457–486.

AMY S. WHARTON

YOUTH *See* ADOLESCENCE; ADOLESCENT SEXUALITY; CHILDHOOD; GANGS; JUVENILE DELINQUENCY; PEER PRESSURE; PERSONALITY DEVELOPMENT; PLAY; RUNAWAY CHILDREN; SCHOOL; TRUANCY

ZERO POPULATION GROWTH *See* FAMILY PLANNING

Index

Page numbers in **boldface** refer to the main entry on the subject.
Page numbers in *italics* refer to tables or charts.

D